THE COMPLETE WORKS OF
JOHN LYLY

My duety humbly remembred.
My fortunes are come to this issue, ye Q:s mercy, & mr
Attrbutes care, yor St: good word probably may worke
a conclusion of all my cares.
Mr Attorney delivered my petition to ye Q: who accepted it graciously,
& as I desyred, referred it to Mr Grevill, for I durst
not presume to name yor honnor.
Ye Copye I have sent inclosed, not to troble yor Hon: but
onely to yorself, a veiw of ye p'ticulers, are wooven
in oure, is but to have somethyng to find prayng for
yor Hon: Long Life, wth mhany of happynes, I humbly
end / Feb: 4. 1602

                              yor ff: in all duety.

                                   Jhon Lyly

To ye right Ho: Syr Robt:
Cecill knight Principall
Secretary thie these

THE COMPLETE WORKS

OF

JOHN LYLY

NOW FOR THE FIRST TIME COLLECTED
AND EDITED FROM THE EARLIEST QUARTOS
WITH LIFE, BIBLIOGRAPHY, ESSAYS
NOTES, AND INDEX

BY

R. WARWICK BOND, M.A.

Sad patience that waiteth at the doore.—*The Bee.*

Ceux qui ont été les prédécesseurs des grands esprits, et qui ont contribué en quelque façon à leur éducation, leur doivent d'être sauvés de l'oubli. Dante fait vivre Brunetto Latini, Milton du Bartas; Shakespeare fait vivre Lyly.—MÉZIÈRES.

VOL. III

THE PLAYS (CONTINUED). ANTI-MARTINIST

WORK. POEMS. GLOSSARY AND

GENERAL INDEX

OXFORD
AT THE CLARENDON PRESS

Oxford University Press, Ely House, London W.1
GLASGOW NEW YORK TORONTO MELBOURNE WELLINGTON
CAPE TOWN SALISBURY IBADAN NAIROBI LUSAKA ADDIS ABABA
BOMBAY CALCUTTA MADRAS KARACHI LAHORE DACCA
KUALA LUMPUR HONG KONG TOKYO

PR
2300
.A2
1967
v.3

FIRST PUBLISHED 1902

REPRINTED LITHOGRAPHICALLY IN GREAT BRITAIN
AT THE UNIVERSITY PRESS, OXFORD
BY VIVIAN RIDLER
PRINTER TO THE UNIVERSITY
1967 (twice)

CONTENTS

VOLUME I

	PAGE
GATE OF THE REVELS OFFICE	*Frontispiece*
LIFE OF JOHN LYLY	1
EUPHUES:	
DISCUSSION OF THE TEXT AND BIBLIOGRAPHY	83
LIST OF EDITIONS	100
TITLES, &c.	106
ESSAY ON EUPHUES AND EUPHUISM	119
EUPHUES—THE ANATOMY OF WYT (Text)	177
" " " " " (Notes)	327
BIOGRAPHICAL APPENDIX	377
ENTERTAINMENTS (Introduction)	404
" (Text)	410
A FUNERAL ORATION	509
NOTES:	
ENTERTAINMENTS	517
A FUNERAL ORATION	538
NOTE ON SENTENCE-STRUCTURE IN EUPHUES	539
ERRATA AND ADDENDA TO THE THREE VOLUMES	542

VOLUME II

TITLE-PAGE OF EUPHUES, PT. I	*Frontispiece*
EUPHUES AND HIS ENGLAND (Text)	1
THE PLAYS:	
CHRONOLOGICAL TABLE	230
ESSAY ON LYLY AS A PLAYWRIGHT	231
CAMPASPE (Introduction)	302
" (Text)	313
SAPHO AND PHAO (Introduction)	362
" " (Text)	369
GALLATHEA (Introduction)	418
" (Text)	429
NOTE ON ITALIAN INFLUENCE	473
NOTES:	
EUPHUES AND HIS ENGLAND	486
CAMPASPE	540
SAPHO AND PHAO	554
GALLATHEA	564

CONTENTS

VOLUME III

AUTOGRAPH LETTER OF LYLY (Feb. 4, 1602–3) . . *Frontispiece*	
THE PLAYS (CONTINUED):	PAGE
INTRODUCTORY MATTER OF BLOUNT'S EDITION . .	1
ENDIMION (INTRODUCTION)	6
„ (TEXT)	17
„ ESSAY ON THE ALLEGORY IN . . .	81
MIDAS (INTRODUCTION)	106
„ (TEXT)	113
MOTHER BOMBIE (INTRODUCTION)	164
„ „ (TEXT)	171
THE WOMAN IN THE MOONE (INTRODUCTION) . .	229
„ „ „ (TEXT)	239
LOVES METAMORPHOSIS (INTRODUCTION) . . .	289
„ „ (TEXT)	299
THE MAYDES METAMORPHOSIS (DOUBTFUL)—	
(INTRODUCTION)	333
(TEXT)	341
ANTI-MARTINIST WORK, &c.:	
PAPPE WITH AN HATCHET (INTRODUCTION) . .	388
„ „ „ „ (TEXT)	393
A WHIP FOR AN APE (INTRODUCTION) . . .	415
„ „ „ (TEXT)	417
MAR-MARTINE (PART OF)	423
THE TRIUMPHS OF TROPHES	427
POEMS (DOUBTFUL):	
LIST OF SOURCES	433
INTRODUCTION	434
TEXT	448
NOTES:	
ENDIMION	503
MIDAS	519
MOTHER BOMBIE	537
THE WOMAN IN THE MOONE	554
LOVES METAMORPHOSIS	563
THE MAYDES METAMORPHOSIS	569
PAPPE WITH AN HATCHET	573
A WHIP FOR AN APE, &c.	589
INDEX OF FIRST LINES OF SONGS OR POEMS . . .	592
GLOSSARY TO THE THREE VOLUMES	596
GENERAL INDEX TO THE THREE VOLUMES . . .	605

SINCE the sheets of my book have been printed off and bound, the following of the pieces which in Vol. III I have, under the title Doubtful, printed as being possibly (see pp. 438, 440, 442) or probably written by Lyly, have been found by Professor H. Littledale or myself to be the work of other hands, viz. :—

No. 1 forms ll. 112–53 of an eclogue in *Arcadia*, Bk. i, ad fin., added in 1593 fol.,—not in 1590 4º, and perhaps not certainly Sidney's. No. 63 (p. 498) is from *Arcadia* (1590 4º), Bk. ii, f. 176v. Nos. 2, 3 (p. 449) are by W. Baldwine; No. 4 (p. 450) by John Higgins: No. 5 (p. 450), No. 22 (p. 452), and No. 54 by Robert Southwell: No. 57 is an extract from Spenser's *Mother Hubberd's Tale*: and the English lines in No. 68 form the closing couplets of stt. 120, 144, 145, 179, 213 of *The Rape of Lucrece*. I must have included both these last by some lapse of memory for which I cannot now account; *The Mirror for Magistrates*, which contains Nos. 2, 3, 4, and Southwell's Poems, from which 5, 22 and 54 are taken, I had not searched, being misled by Harl. MS. 6910, which gave these books as the sources of other of its extracts. The key to the authorship of No. 64 is bound up, I think, with that to the cast of *The Returne from Pernassus*.

INTRODUCTORY MATTER OF BLOUNT'S EDITION

TITLE.

SIXE COVRT Comedies.

Often Presented and Acted *before Queene* ELIZABETH, by the Children of her Maiesties Chappell, and the Children of Paules.

W⟨r⟩itten
By the onely Rare Poet of that Time, The Witie, Comicall, *Facetiously-Quicke and* vnparalelld :
IOHN LILLY, Master *of Arts.*
Decies Repetita placebunt.

LONDON
Printed by *William Stansby* for *Edward Blount.* 1 6 3 2.

[The six plays, given in this order of enumeration, are 1. *Endimion* (for which play alone there appears no separate title-page in the half-dozen copies known to me). 2. *Campaspe* (with running-title

'A tragicall Comedie of | Alexander and Campaspe'). 3. *Sapho and Phao*. 4. *Gallathea*. 5. *Mydas*. 6. *Mother Bombie*. Blount's edition first prints the words of the numerous Songs, though some of those mentioned in the dialogue or in stage-directions are still missing. It prints, however, from the later and more corrupt quartos, correcting but a very few of their errors and adding an immense number of its own, the majority of which have been reproduced in Fairholt's edition. Blount, moreover, misplaces several pages in the fifth Act of *Sapho and Phao*.]

The Epistle Dedicatorie

To the Right Honovrable Richard Lvmley, Viscount Lvmley of Waterford.

My noble Lord:

It can be no dishonor, to listen to this Poets Musike, whose Tunes alighted in the Eares of a great and euer-famous Queene: his Inuention, was so curiously strung, that *Elizaes* Court held his notes in Admiration. Light Ayres are now in fashion; And these being not sad, fit the season, though perchance not sute so well with your more serious Contemplations.

The spring is at hand, and therefore I present you a Lilly, growing in a Groue of Lawrels. For this Poet, sat at the *Sunnes* Table: *Apollo* gaue him a wreath of his owne *Bayes*; without snatching. The *Lyre* he played on, had no borrowed strings.

I am (my Lord) no executor, yet I presume to distribute the Goods of the Dead: Their value beeing no way answerable to those Debts of dutie and affection, in which I stand obliged to your Lordship. The greatest treasure our Poet left behind him, are these six ingots of refined inuention: richer than Gold. Were they Diamonds they are now yours. Accept them (Noble Lord) in part; and Mee

Your Lordships euer Obliged and Deuoted

Ed. Blount.

To the Reader.

Reader, I haue (for the loue I beare to Posteritie) dig'd vp the Graue of a Rare and Excellent Poet, whom Queene Elizabeth then heard, Graced, and Rewarded. These Papers of his, lay like dead Lawrels in a Churchyard; But I haue gathered the scattered branches vp, and by a Charme (gotten from *Apollo*) made them greene againe, and set them vp as Epitaphes to his Memory.

A sinne it were to suffer these Rare Monuments of wit, to lye couered in Dust, and a shame, such conceipted Comedies, should be Acted by none but wormes. *Obliuion* shall not so trample on a sonne of the *Muses*; And such a sonne, as they called their Darling. Our Nation are in his debt for a new English which hee taught them. *E⟨u⟩phues* and his England began first that language: All our Ladies were then his Schollers; And that Beautie in Court, which could not Parley, *Euphueisme*, was as litle regarded; as shee which now there, speakes not French.

These his playes Crown'd him with applause, and the Spectators with pleasure. Thou canst not repent the Reading of them ouer: when Old *Iohn Lilly*, is merry with thee in thy Chamber, Thou shalt say, Few (or None) of our Poets now are such witty Companions: And thanke mee, that brings him to thy Acquaintance.

Thine. ED. BLOVNT.

[The book has no colophon.]

NOTE ON THE TREATMENT ADOPTED IN THE TEXT OF THE PLAYS

The text followed in the Plays is that of the earliest quarto, in every case except that of *Campaspe*, where only the second (though of the same year) was accessible. In later quartos corruption outweighs correction; and Blount's ed. 1632, which Fairholt unfortunately followed, is the worst offender. Obvious errors are corrected from the earliest edition where the correction is found, and the reading of the *editio princeps* given in the footnotes, where also all variants are reported. Each footnote implies a collation of all editions.

All modern insertions are enclosed in angular brackets ⟨ ⟩, all those due to preceding editors being assigned to them in footnotes.

The numbering of Acts *and Scenes* is that of the quartos; the numbering of lines in a scene, and the arrangement of them in the verse of *The Woman*, my own. I have localized the scenes, and noted at the same time any case of abrupt transfer.

Old stage-directions appear here, though not invariably in the old editions, un-bracketed and in italics, the original spelling being always retained. Many, even for entry and exit, were omitted in the old editions; some carelessly, some as inferable from the dialogue. In inserted stage-directions names are spelt as in the modern list of Dramatis Personae, to which the prefixes to speeches are also conformed, any mistakes of the quartos being noted.

In speeches the general rule of the quartos, to print names of persons in italics and geographical or national names in romans, has been uniformly followed.

As to punctuation, I have inserted, omitted, or transposed stops with less scruple than in the *Euphues*, retaining the old irregularity wherever possible without injury to effect, and reporting every change that could affect sense.

The Bibliography, Sources, Date, and other matters appertaining to each Play are discussed in their several Introductions; for general criticism of each, or of all, the reader is referred to the essay on Lyly as a Playwright, pp. 231–89 of the second volume.

In the footnotes italics are reserved for the editor's comment.

Q, QQ = Quarto, Quartos: the small distinguishing numbers referring to the list of 'Editions' prefixed to each play.

Bl. = Blount's *Sixe Covrt Comedies* (1632).

Dil. = C. W. Dilke's *Old Plays*, vol. i or ii (1814).

F. = F. W. Fairholt's edition of Lyly's Plays (*Library of Old Authors*, 2 vols. 1858).

Bak. = G. P. Baker's *Lyly's Endymion* (New York, 1894).

s. D. = Stage-direction.

'Rest' after a symbol implies the agreement of all subsequent editions.

'Before' and 'after,' always of some addition, not of mere substitution or transposition.

'Only,' of words entirely unrepresented in other editions.

If a word cited from a line in the text occurs more than once in that line, it has a small distinguishing number affixed to it in the footnote; thus, his²].

ENDIMION

EDITIONS

'4to Octobris 1591 mystres Broome Wydowe Late Wyfe of William Broome Entred for her copies vnder the hand of the Bishop of London: Three Comedies plaied before her maiestie by the Children of Paules th one Called. Endimion. Th other. Galathea and th other, Midas . . . xviij^d.' *Sta. Reg.* ii. p. 596 (ed. Arb.).

Q.   *Endimion,* | *The Man in the* | *Moone.* | *Playd before the Queenes Ma-*|*iestie at Greenewich on Candlemas day* | *at night, by the Chyldren of* | *Paules.* | *At London,* | *Printed by I. Charlewood, for* | *the widdowe Broome.* | 1591. | 4to. A, A 2, B–K 3 in fours. No col. (Br. Mus.)

On Aug. 23, 1601 the play is transferred together with *Campaspe, Sapho and Phao, Gallathea,* and *Midas* from 'mystres Brome Lately Deceased' to George Potter (*Sta. Reg.* iii. 191, ed. Arb.); and on Jan. 9, 1628 is entered to Blount as one of the *Sixe Covrt Comedies* (*Sta. Reg.* iv. 192).

Second ed. (Blount's).   In the *Sixe Covrt Comedies, Endimion* is printed first, but follows the Preface without any separate title-page. The Prologue occupies sig. A 6 verso, the play itself the sixty leaves of sigs. B–F in twelves, and the Epilogue G recto, the verso being left blank.

Also given with Introduction and Notes in Dilke's *Old English Plays*, 1814, vol. ii; in Fairholt's edition of the plays, 1858, vol. i; and separately with Biographical Introduction and Notes by G. P. Baker (New York, 1894, 8vo).

ENDIMION

Argument. — Tellus, whom Endimion has abandoned to follow a hopeless passion for Cynthia, disregards the dissuasions of her confidante Floscula, and plots with the witch Dipsas to bring him into trouble. Cynthia grows cold to him (ii. 3. 2–3, iv. 3. 80–3), and he himself lying in despair upon a lunary-bank is charmed by Dipsas to a slumber of forty years. Cynthia, relenting, dispatches his friend Eumenides and others to seek aid; and punishes some malicious words of Tellus by close imprisonment under Corsites. The latter, in love with his captive, allows himself to be engaged in a hopeless attempt to remove Endimion from his position; but is himself attacked by fairies, pinched black and blue, and made a laughing-stock to Cynthia visiting the spot with her Court. The philosophers she has summoned cannot break the spell: but Eumenides, by double virtue of his truth as a lover and a friend, has learned from a magic fountain that the sleeper can be awakened by the kiss of Cynthia; and the remedy, coyly applied, proves successful. Bagoa, Dipsas' maid, now betrays her mistress' wicked arts, and Tellus confesses her revenge taken upon Endimion, who thereupon acknowledges his passion for Cynthia. Her gracious allowance of a love she will not openly return restores him to youth. Tellus is pardoned and united to Corsites; Semele, condemned to a year's silence for spiteful speech, breaks the prohibition to protest against her forced bestowal on Eumenides; but is won by her lover's offer of his own tongue to ransom hers: Geron, exiled to the fountain for fifty years by his wife Dipsas' intrigues, is reunited with her: and Bagoa, changed by her to an aspen-tree, recovers her true shape and finds a husband in the foolish braggart Sir Tophas. The latter's intercourse with three chaffing pages supplies a somewhat tedious comic element, connected, however, with the main-plot by his ridiculous passion for the crone Dipsas, which is probably intended as the parody of Endimion's for Cynthia.

Text and Bibliography. — The text here followed is that of the first and only known quarto, that of 1591. From the absence of Lyly's name on the title-page, and from the Printer's statement to the Reader that the play came into his hands by chance after the Paul's boys were silenced, we may perhaps infer that Lyly was not personally concerned in its publication. Its errors are comparatively few, twenty-five in all; of which four (i. 3. 33, iii. 3. 31, iv. 3. 18, 27) are of punctuation affecting the sense, four others (i. 3. 43–4, 54, iii. 3. 29, v. 1. 119) may be called serious, and the rest are merely orthographical and easily corrigible by the reader.

Blount's edition (*Sixe Covrt Comedies*, 1632) corrects eleven of these minor errors, and adds the words of the Songs, and the Dumb Show before Act iii. It also makes thirteen corruptions, six of them important (i. 3. 31, ii. 2. 37, Dumb Show p. 39 'readeth,' iii. 3. 39, iv. 1. 35, iv. 3. 148), four of which persist until the present edition.

Dilke (*Old Eng. Plays*, vol. ii. 1814) corrects the text in fifteen places, including six of the eight important errors of the quarto, adds some needed stage-directions, and supplies a brief critical notice and a few notes: but he modernizes not merely the spelling, but also the idiom, in twenty-two places; makes a large number of quite otiose if slight changes, such as the substitution of the singular for plural of a substantive, the omission or insertion of 'a' and 'the,' &c., and is further guilty of twelve bad corruptions, e. g. i. 3. 9, ii. 3. 13, iii. 4. 118, iv. 2. 71, iv. 3. 130, v. 2. 87, v. 3. 240, &c.

Fairholt, in his collected edition of the plays, follows the text of Blount, making but one correction (i. 3. 54) and corrupting the text in twenty-nine places, of which i. 3. 1, ii. 2. 141, iii. 1. 17, 32, iii. 4. 19, 105, iv. 1. 50, iv. 3. 28, v. 1. 47, 70, may be called serious. His notes, however, and his restoration of the mistake, iii. 3. 32, 'pari' for 'Pari,' which Blount had corrected, show that he had the quarto before him.

Baker (*Lyly's Endymion*, New York, 1894) emends the text in six places (i. 1. 72, ii. 1. 32, iii. 1. 50, iv. 2. 36, 43, v. 3. 92); supplies about a score of stage-directions; makes eight other changes in the text, of which six are needless, and two (iv. 2. 14, iv. 3. 83) injurious; and, moreover, reproduces some of the corruptions introduced by Fairholt's edition. But Mr. Baker's *Endymion*, with its careful notes and full biographical introduction, is, in spite of its modernization, its want of access to the quarto, and its unsound hypotheses in the biography, a valuable and scholarly piece of work, which I have found useful in writing my own Life.

INTRODUCTION 9

Authorship. — Lyly is not named in the entry in the *Stationers' Register*, nor on the title-page of the quarto: but the performance of the play by the Paul's boys, its inclusion in the *Sixe Covrt Comedies*, its euphuistic style, and about a dozen marked reminiscences of *Euphues* which it exhibits, leave us in no doubt about the authorship.

Source: the Allegory in the Play. — In Lucian's short dialogue (*Deorum Dial.* 11) Selene draws for Venus a pretty picture of Endymion lying asleep on his cloak, after hunting, upon the mountain of Latmos, his darts slipping from his left hand while his right is thrown back round his head, and of herself advancing on tiptoe so as not to awake him, and—'but you know the rest,' she breaks off, 'and I needn't tell you more, except that I am terribly in love with him.' Brief allusions are also found in Pausanias v. 1, §§ 2–4; Hyginus *Fab.* 271; Ovid *Art. Am.* iii. 83, &c. But it is obvious that the materials afforded by the classical myth, the perpetual sleep and the kiss of Cynthia were insufficient for a play; and what Lyly has done is to weave around this beautiful picture an allegorical drama of Court-life whose action has no place nor counterpart at all in the myth. The Moon-Goddess becomes a queen surrounded by her Court; the Greek shepherd, her favourite courtier. As the double subject of this Court-allegory Lyly takes the two most salient features in the domestic history of the reign (1) the rivalry between Elizabeth (Cynthia) and Mary of Scotland (Tellus); (2) the Queen's perennial affection for, and temporary displeasure (in 1579) with, Robert Dudley, Earl of Leicester (Endimion); a sufficient warrant for the dramatic connexion of the two being supplied in the match actually contemplated between Mary and Leicester in 1563–1565. This double subject is supplemented by two subordinate and connected subjects (1) the quarrel between the Earl and Countess of Shrewsbury (Geron and Dipsas); (2) the relations of Sir Philip Sidney (Eumenides) with his uncle Leicester and his love Penelope Rich, née Devereux (Semele); while several other personages more or less prominent are introduced. With this Court-allegory Lyly attempts, without much success, to combine a physical allegory of the Moon and the Earth as heavenly bodies.

The proper development of this view, suggested of course by Halpin's well-known essay *Oberon's Vision* (Shakespeare Society, 1843), from which, however, I have made wide departures, would occupy too much space in this Introduction; I have, therefore, relegated it to a separate essay (see pp. 81–103), and merely append here my key to the cast, side by side with that of Halpin.

	HALPIN	BOND
Endimion	Earl of Leicester	Earl of Leicester
Eumenides	Earl of Sussex	Sir Philip Sidney
Corsites	Sir Edward Stafford	⎧ Sir Amyas Paulet
Geron	Earl of Shrewsbury	⎩ Earl of Shrewsbury
Panelion ⎫ Zontes ⎭	(unidentified)	? ⎧ Lord Burleigh ⎩ Sir Francis Walsingham
Sir Tophas	Stephen Gosson	Gabriel Harvey
Cynthia	Queen Elizabeth	Queen Elizabeth
Tellus	Lady Sheffield (née Howard)	Mary Queen of Scots
Semele	Frances Sidney	Lady Rich (née Penelope Devereux)
Floscula	Lady Essex	Lady Essex, or Frances Howard
Bagoa	(unidentified)	? Countess of Lennox
Dipsas	Countess of Shrewsbury	Countess of Shrewsbury

For the rest—Dares, Samias, Epiton, Scintilla, Favilla; Pythagoras and Gyptes—I have no suggestions to offer, feeling it unnecessary to suppose that Lyly had an original in mind for every one of his minor characters, especially where they have absolutely no effect on the plot[1]. But Halpin professes himself 'convinced, from the importance of their names, contrasted with the nothing they have to do in the action, that the two latter, at least, were not introduced merely to fill up the theatrical pomp, without any more dignity or significance' (*Oberon's Vision*, p. 75).

Sir Tophas, it may be added, apart from his allegorical significance as Harvey or Gosson, is founded on the *Miles Gloriosus* of Plautus: while that part of Endimion's dream (Dumb Show and v. 1. 104 sqq.) which relates to an old man offering a book with three leaves, is obviously adapted from the fable of Tarquin and the Sibyl, related by Aulus Gellius (*Noct. Att.* i. 19).

Date.—It is obvious that the view taken of the Allegory must affect that taken of the date. My interpretation requires a date not earlier than September 14, 1584, when Shrewsbury (Geron) made his moving appeal to the Privy Council ('The other old man, what

---

[1] Hence the note of interrogation appended to the two lords in my cast.

a sad speech vsed he, that caused vs almost all to weepe,' v. i. 3), and not later than the first half of 1586, for Sidney (Eumenides) died at Zutphen in September of that year, and Mary's (Tellus) long period of grace ended with her condemnation at Fotheringay on October 25. The commencement of Sir Amyas Paulet's (Corsites) custody of her on April 17, 1585, and the departure of Sidney and Leicester for the Netherlands (November 16 and December 10), after which Lyly is hardly likely to have undertaken the composition, suggest yet narrower limits. The title-page announces it as played on 'Candlemas day at night.' I believe the Candlemas in question to be February 2, 1535–6[1], and consider the play to have been written between May and November of the preceding year.

This date may find independent support (1) from that of its appearance in print. Whereas *Campaspe* and *Sapho* are published in 1584; and 'Titirus and Galathea,' i.e. *Gallathea*, is entered in the Stationers' Register on April 1, 1585—it was not proceeded with because, as Mr. Baker shows, the inhibition on the Paul's boys' acting was probably removed near the end of the month—we hear nothing of *Endimion* till the entry of October 4, 1591. The natural inference is that, at the time of these earlier publications and contemplated publication, it was not yet composed. Its description by the Printer in 1591 as 'the first' of 'certaine Commedies come to my handes by chaunce,' the others being *Gallathea* and *Midas*, need mean no more than that it was the first that so came to his hands on the fresh inhibition of the boys in 1590 or 1591. If Blount in 1632 prints it first among his *Sixe Covrt Comedies*, he probably does so because it is the best representative of that title: in his original entry of the volume (*Sta. Reg.* January 9, 1627–8) the plays appear in the following order—'Campaste, Sapho, and Phao, Galathea: Endimion Midas and Mother Bomby'—which I believe was that of their production.

(2) Lyly's appointment as Vicemaster of the Paul's boys in 1585

---

[1] In Chalmers' lists of payments extracted from the Council Registers (Boswell's *Malone's Shakespeare*, iii. 423–5 and 442 note) those made between June 26, 1582, and Feb. 19, 1586, are reported as lost. A similar gap exists in the fragments of the Revels Accounts recovered by Cunningham, from the end of Oct. 1585 to the end of Oct. 1587. The absence of any record of a Court-performance by the Paul's boys need not, therefore, constrain us, as it constrains Mr. Fleay (*Biog. Chron.* ii. 41), to date the play as late as Feb. 2, 1588; nor do the Revels Accounts, p. 198, afford us anything more precise for that year than that the Queen was spending that Christmas at Greenwich, and that the Paul's boys played before her some time 'betwixte Christmas and Shrovetid.'

(see Life, vol. i. pp. 32 sqq.) would make *Endimion*, in which the flattery of Elizabeth is more elaborate and direct than in any other play, a natural offering on receipt of that appointment.

(3) The amount and character of the euphuism which it exhibits indicate a date about the middle of Lyly's dramatic career. Considerably longer as it is than any other of his plays (occupying 61 pp.), it exhibits only eleven distinct reminiscences of *Euphues*, while his earliest play, *Campaspe* (45 pp.), has thirty, and *Mother Bombie* (56 pp.), his latest prose play with the partial exception of *Loves Metamorphosis*, only one or two. Of cases of single alliteration used to mark balance Mr. C. G. Child[1] counts an equal number with that in *Campaspe*, seventy, while he gives *Mother Bombie* only nineteen: of transverse alliteration *Campaspe* affords twenty-six instances, *Endimion* twelve, *Mother Bombie* only one. And the general effect, which is hardly expressible in tabular form, is to my ear smoother, less constrained to a perpetual antithesis, than it is not only, as Mr. Child allows, in *Campaspe* and *Sapho*, but also in *Gallathea* and *Loves Metamorphosis*.

This last argument alone is fatal to so early a date as the autumn of 1579, assigned by Mr. Baker in his Introduction to the play, and accepted without misgiving by Professor Ward[2]. The assignment is bound up with Mr. Baker's belief in an early connexion between Lyly and Leicester; and he considers that the delay in the issue of the Second Part of *Euphues*, which he supposes finished by July 24, 1579, the date of its entry, was due to the contemporary disgrace of Leicester. *Endimion*, he maintains, was composed and acted during a brief return of Court favour—between the middle of September and some date before November 12, when a letter of Leicester to Burleigh shows him to be again in disgrace—as an attempt on the favourite's part to present a softened view and excuse of his recent marriage to Lady Essex; and was one of those 'devises to Receave the Freenche' whose preparation involved Tylney in so much 'botehyer' to and from Greenwich during that autumn[3]. But not only does it seem little likely that Leicester would consent to represent his wife, who is *ex hypothesi* represented by Tellus, as a poor jealous dupe, the mere cloak of his passion for the Queen; but it is vastly improbable that either Lyly or Leicester would dream of

---

[1] See his Table, quoted above, vol. ii. p. 289.
[2] *English Dramatic Literature* (ed. 1899), i. 289-92.
[3] Baker's *Endymion*, pp. xxxiii, lxxxiv, xci, clix, &c., and *Revels Accounts*, pp. 153, 159.

dramatizing this delicate matter before the whole Court, at a time when the wound to the Queen's feelings was still fresh. The whole idea of a connexion between Leicester and Lyly rests on the most shadowy foundations. If it existed, would not Leicester have been eulogized along with Burleigh in *Euphues' Glasse for Europe*? This eulogy, together with the dedication to Burleigh's son-in-law Oxford, as well as Lyly's letter of 1582, are enough to show that Lyly was not yet attached to the faction of Leicester, to whom Burleigh was generally in opposition. The delay in publishing *Euphues and his England* was due, not to any disgrace of Leicester, but simply to its unfinished state, as is clear from the allusion in the middle of the book (vol. ii. p. 99, l. 17) to Gosson's *Ephemerides of Phialo*, which was not entered in the *Stationers' Register* till November 7, 1579: nor, if *Endimion* had been then written, would the youthful Lyly be likely to ignore it as he does in his Dedication, vol. ii. p. 4, l. 11 'I haue brought into the worlde *two* children,' namely, the First and Second Parts of *Euphues*. Lastly, to suppose that an allegory so long and elaborate as that of *Endimion* could be planned and composed by an inexperienced dramatist of twenty-five, and then rehearsed and performed, all in the narrow space of two or three weeks between Leicester's partial restoration to favour in September and the close of Tylney's rehearsing-work early in October, is to suppose what is practically impossible[1].

I date the composition, then, May to November, 1585, and the first performance at Court February 2, 1586.

Imitations. — The relation and character of Sir Tophas and Epiton are closely followed by Shakespeare in those of Armado and Moth, and Sir Tophas pairing with Bagoa is paralleled by Armado's declension upon Jaquenetta. The pinching of Corsites by fairies is borrowed for the punishment of Falstaff in the *Merry Wives*, Act v.

---

[1] Far less thoughtful, though more fortunate, was Mr. Joel Spingarn's attempt, in a letter to the *Athenæum* of Aug. 4, 1894, to show that the play was written in 1586, because seven years' waiting is three times alluded to (ii. 1. 14, iii. 4. 54, iv. 2. 114), and, as Tylney had been appointed Master of the Revels in 1579, Lyly had been waiting for the post since that date. In my answer (*Athen.* Aug. 11) I pointed out that 'seven years' is probably merely a conventional expression for a long period, and that if Lyly was only 'entertained her Majesties seruant' in 1579 his 'despair' at Tylney's appointment in that year was unreasonable. It now appears, since the first petition speaking of ten years' service dates in 1595 (see Life, vol. i. p. 33), that he did not even receive the vague promise of the Mastership till 1585.

See also the Essay in vol. ii. pp. 297–8 : the allegory of Oberon's speech in *Midsummer Night's Dream* is largely suggested by our play : and Dogberry and his fellows are indebted to the Watch, iv. 2, pp. 57–8.

Place and Time. — I have marked the localities of the several scenes, though Mr. Baker justly remarks on the difficulty of doing so satisfactorily. Either no hint is given, or it is contradicted by something else : thus Corsites speaks in iv. 3 of removing Endimion 'from this Caban,' though he fell asleep in ii. 3 on the lunary-bank (but see note ad loc.); and later on (in iv. 3, line 54) Cynthia and her courtiers speak as if on their way to the lunary-bank, while a few lines later (l. 75) they are evidently beside it. Mr. Baker concludes that 'Lyly's audience was to follow in imagination where he led : if it was important to know the place he gave a hint of it; if it was not, no one bothered about it; he could shift his place at will, even in the same scene.' This is quite the correct account of the matter : such imaginary transfer in the middle of a scene is pretty frequent in the pre-Shakespearean drama, where there was seldom any definite scenery to localize the stage as one particular spot in the first instance. Lyly employs it at least four times in his earliest play *Campaspe*, though but rarely afterwards (see for fuller notice, and instances from other dramatists, the essay on 'Lyly as a Playwright,' vol. ii. p. 269). Other examples of an ideal treatment of Place in the present play are found in the fact that, though Tellus is imprisoned in 'the Castle in the Deserte,' p. 41, she can dispatch Corsites to the lunary-bank in the neighbourhood of the Court, and witness his unavailing efforts from her prison, p. 54; while in v. 3, p. 72, the lords who have just left Cynthia speak of bringing Tellus, who is apparently still at the castle, immediately before her, and do so bring her forty lines later. Again, though Eumenides has been absent from Court so long that Cynthia fears he is dead, p. 60, and Geron alludes to the tedious journey from the fountain back to Court, p. 52, yet Epiton, iv. 2. 67, speaks of it as 'hard by,' i.e. near the lunary-bank, whose guardians enter just afterwards.

A similar confusion hangs over his treatment of Time. In regard to Endimion's slumber, Dilke noted the inconsistency between the 'almost these twentie yeeres,' of iii. 4. 19, and the 'fortie yeeres,' of v. 1. 50. This lapse of twenty years during the journey back to Court is contradicted by the fact that Geron, banished as a young man, has in iii. 4. 5 been at the fountain 'these fiftie Winters,' while in v. 3. 21, Dipsas has practised the wicked arts that caused his exile, not seventy, but only 'almost these fiftie yeeres.' There is the further inconsistency that, while the actual lapse of a long period is marked by the growth of the twig supporting Endimion's head into a tree, v. 1. 51–2, none of the characters except Endimion have aged at all. Cynthia, of course, was secure of an immortality of youth and beauty; but the pages still possess their pagehood and impudence, Semele's charms are still the object of ardent passion, and Tellus has lived but 'few yeres,' v. 3. 57. Clearly we must recognize a treatment of Time, as of Place, quite arbitrary. Where it is necessary to indicate intervals for a special effect, Lyly does so; but otherwise the play proceeds on the general assumption that the events are compressed into a few days. When it suits his purpose, the characters are sent on journeys to places far distant; but other passages show that, for stage-purposes, these same places, the magic fountain and the castle in the desert, are conceived as lying in the immediate neighbourhood of the Court. In the present case these inconsistencies, more marked than in any other play, may be adopted as appropriate to his 'tale of the Man in the Moone,' which, as the Prologue confesses, may 'seeme ridiculous for the method': but his general practice exhibits something of the same inconsistency, arguing not, I think, an incomplete intelligence of the dramatic Unities, but an indecision as to whether they should or should not be observed. Taking them as his working basis, he contradicts them when he feels inclined, without care to make his contradiction complete; and so this play, and his work considered as a whole, occupies an intermediate position between classical rule supported by contemporary precedent and that absolute freedom exercised by the later Romanticists.

ENDIMION,

The Man in the Moone.

Playd before the Queenes Maiestie at Greenewich on Candlemas day at night, by the Chyldren of Paules.

AT LONDON,
Printed by I. Charlewood, for
the widdowe Broome.
1591.

The Printer to the *Reader.*

Since the Plaies in Paules were dissolued, there are certaine Commedies come to my handes by chaunce, which were presented before her Maiestie at seuerall times by the children of Paules. This is the first, and if in any place it shall dysplease, I will take more paines to perfect the next. I referre it to thy indifferent iudgement to peruse, whom I woulde willinglie please. And if this may passe with thy good lyking, I will then goe forwarde to publish the rest. In the meane time, let this haue thy good worde for my better encouragement.

Farewell.

1 This address is found in the Quarto only

⟨DRAMATIS PERSONÆ.

ENDIMION, *in love with Cynthia.*
EUMENIDES, *his friend, in love with Semele.*
CORSITES, *a Captain, in love with Tellus.*
PANELION, ⎫
ZONTES,   ⎭ *Lords of Cynthia's Court.*
PYTHAGORAS, *a Greek Philosopher.*
GYPTES, *an Egyptian Soothsayer.*
GERON, *an old man, husband to Dipsas.*
SIR TOPHAS, *a foolish braggart.*
DARES, *Page to Endimion.*
SAMIAS, *Page to Eumenides.*
EPITON, *Page to Sir Tophas.*
Master Constable.
1st and 2nd Watchmen.
CYNTHIA, *the queen.*
TELLUS, *in love with Endimion.*
FLOSCULA, *her attendant and confidante.*
SEMELE, *beloved by Eumenides.*
SCINTILLA, ⎫
FAVILLA,   ⎭ *Maids in waiting at the Court.*
DIPSAS, *an old Enchantress.*
BAGOA, *her Servant.*
Watchmen, Fairies, three Ladies and an old Man in the Dumb Show.

SCENE.—*Chiefly at Cynthia's Court.*⟩

DRAM. PERS.] *list first suppl.* Dil.   4 PANELION] PANTALION *Dil. F. and so in* Act iii. sc. 1, l. 50 *Bl. Dil. F.*: Pantlion *in* Q. *But later* (iv. 3; v. 1 *and* 3) *always* PANELION *all edd.*: *and so Baker here and* iii. 1   10–11 *I reverse the services of the two Pages, as given by Dil. F. Bak. See note*

THE PROLOGUE.

*M*Ost *high and happy Princesse, we must tell you a tale of the Man in the Moone, which if it seeme ridiculous for the method, or superfluous for the matter, or for the meanes incredible, for three faultes wee can make but one excuse. It is a tale of the Man in the Moone.*

It was forbidden in olde time to dispute of Chymera, because it 5 *was a fiction: we hope in our times none will apply pastimes, because they are fancies; for there liueth none vnder the Sunne, that knowes what to make of the Man in the Moone. Wee present neither Comedie, nor Tragedie, nor storie, nor anie thing, but that whosoeuer heareth* 10 *may say this, Why heere is a tale of the Man in the Moone.*

8 know *Bak.*

ENDIMION

ACTUS PRIMUS

SCÆNA PRIMA.—⟨*Gardens of* CYNTHIA'S *Palace.*⟩

⟨*Enter*⟩ ENDIMION. EUMENIDES.

End. I Finde *Eumenides* in all thinges both varietie to content, & satietie to glut, sauing onelie in my affections, which are so stayed, and withall so statelie, that I can neither satis-fie my hart with loue, nor mine eyes with wonder. My thoughts *Eumenides* 5 are stitched to the starres, which beeing as high as I can see, thou maist imagin how much higher they are then I can reach.

Eum. If you be enamored of any thing aboue the Moone, your thoughts are ridiculous, for that thinges immortall are not subiect to affections; if allured or enchaunted with these transitory things 10 vnder the Moone, you shew your selfe sencelesse, to attribute such lofty tytles, to such lowe trifles.

End. My loue is placed neither vnder the Moone nor aboue.

Eum. I hope you be not sotted vpon the man in the Moone.

End. No; but setled, eyther to die, or possesse the Moone 15 herselfe.

Eum. Is *Endimion* mad, or doe I mistake? doe you loue the Moone *Endimion*?

End. Eumenides, the Moone.

Eum. There was neuer any so peeuish to imagin the Moone 20 eyther capable of affection, or shape of a Mistris: for as impossible it is to make loue fit to her humor which no man knoweth, as a coate to her forme, which continueth not in one bignesse whilst she is measuring. Cease of *Endimion* to feed so much vpon fancies.

ACTUS PRIMUS ... Palace] *the division into Acts and Scenes is that of the oldest and all succeeding editions. The localities of the several scenes are first marked in this*   11 lowe] loue *all eds.*   21 sit *Bl. F. the latter giving the true reading in the notes*   22–3 continueth ... measuring, *and just below* melancholy ... purged, *are printed by Bl. in italics*   23 Cease of *Q Bl. F.*: Cease *Dil.*: Cease off *Bak.*

That melancholy blood must be purged, which draweth you to
a dotage no lesse miserable then monstrous.

End. My thoughts haue no vaines, and yet vnlesse they be let
blood, I shall perrish.

Eum. But they haue vanities, which beeing reformed, you may be
restored.

End. O fayre *Cynthia*, why doe others terme thee vnconstant,
whom I haue euer founde vnmoueable? Iniurious tyme, corrupt
manners, vnkind men, who finding a constancy not to be matched
in my sweete Mistris, haue christned her with the name of wauering,
waxing, and waning. Is shee inconstant that keepeth a setled
course, which since her first creation altereth not one minute in her
mouing? There is nothing thought more admirable or commend-
able in the sea, then the ebbing and flowing; and shall the Moone,
from whom the Sea taketh this vertue, be accounted fickle for
encreasing, & decreasing? Flowers in theyr buds are nothing worth
till they be blowne, nor blossomes accounted till they be ripe
fruite: and shal we then say they be changeable, for that they growe
from seedes to leaues, from leaues to buds, from buds to theyr
perfection? then, why be not twigs that become trees, children that
become men, and Mornings that grow to Euenings, termed wauering,
for that they continue not at one stay? I, but *Cynthia*, being in her
fulnes, decayeth, as not delighting in her greatest beautie, or withering
when she should be most honoured. When mallice cannot obiect
any thing, folly will, making that a vice, which is the greatest vertue.
What thing (my Mistris excepted) being in the pride of her beauty,
& latter minute of her age, that waxeth young againe? Tell mee
Eumenides, what is hee that hauing a Mistris of ripe yeeres, & infinite
vertues, great honors, and vnspeakeable beauty, but woulde wish
that shee might grow tender againe? getting youth by yeeres, and
neuer decaying beauty by time, whose fayre face, neyther the
Summers blase can scorch, nor Winters blast chappe, nor the
numbring of yeeres breede altering of colours. Such is my sweete
Cynthia, whom tyme cannot touch, because she is diuine, nor will
offend because she is delicate. O *Cynthia*, if thou shouldest alwaies
continue at thy fulnes, both Gods and men woulde conspire to
rauish thee. But thou to abate the pride of our affections, dost
detract from thy perfections, thinking it sufficient, if once in a month

31 immoueable *Dil. Bak.*   50 that *om. Dil.*   56 colour *Dil.*

we enioy a glymse of thy maiestie, and then, to encrease our greefes, thou doost decrease thy glemes, comming out of thy royall robes, wherewith thou dazelist our eyes, downe into thy swath clowtes,
65 beguiling our eyes. And then—

Eum. Stay there *Endimion*, thou that committest Idolatry, wilt straight blaspheme, if thou be suffered. Sleepe woulde doe thee more good then speech : the Moone heareth thee not, or if shee doe, regardeth thee not.

70 *End.* Vaine *Eumenides*, whose thoughts neuer grow higher thē the crowne of thy head. Why troublest thou me, hauing neither heade to conceiue the cause of my loue, or a hart to receiue the impressions? followe thou thine owne fortunes, which creepe on the earth, & suffer me to flye to mine, whose fall though it be desperate,
75 yet shall it come by daring. Farewell. ⟨*Exit.*⟩

Eum. Without doubt *Endimion* is bewitched, otherwise in a man of such rare vertues there could not harbor a minde of such extreame madnes. I wil follow him, least in this fancie of the Moone, he depriue himselfe of the sight of the Sunne. *Exit.*

Scæna Secunda.—⟨*The same.*⟩

⟨*Enter*⟩ Tellus. Floscula.

Tellus. Trecherous and most periurde *Endimion*, is *Cynthia* the sweetnes of thy life, and the bitternes of my death? What reuenge may be deuised so full of shame, as my thoughts are replenished with mallice? Tell me *Floscula* if falsenes in loue can possibly be
5 punished with extremitie of hate. As long as sworde, fire, or poison may be hyred, no traytor to my loue shall liue vnreuenged. Were thy oathes without number, thy kisses without measure, thy sighes without end, forged to deceiue a poore credulous virgin, whose simplicity had beene worth thy fauour and better fortune? If the
10 Gods sitte vnequall beholders of iniuries, or laughers at Louers deceipts, then let mischiefe be as well forgiuen in women, as periurie winked at in men.

Flosc. Madame, if you woulde compare the state of *Cynthia* with your owne, and the height of *Endimion* his thoughts, with the meane-

---

67-8 Sleepe . . . speech *italicized Bl.*   72 a *om. Dil. Bak. the latter reading* nor heart   73 impression *Dil.*   s. d. [Exit] *suppl. Dil.*   14 Endimion his] Endymion's *Bak.*

nesse of your fortune, you would rather yeeld then contende, being
betweene you and her no comparison, and rather wonder then rage
at the greatnes of his minde, beeing affected with a thing more then
mortall.

Tellus. No comparison *Floscula?* and why so? is not my beauty
diuine, whose body is decked with faire flowers, and vaines are
Vines, yeelding sweet liquor to the dullest spirits, whose eares are
Corne, to bring strength, and whose heares are grasse, to bring
abundance? Doth not Frankinsence & Myrrhe breath out of my
nostrils, and all the sacrifice of the Gods breede in my bowels?
Infinite are my creatures, without which neyther thou, nor *Endimion,*
nor any could loue, or liue.

Flosc. But know you not fayre Ladie, that *Cynthia* gouerneth all
things? Your grapes woulde be but drie huskes, your Corne but
chaffe, and all your vertues vaine, were it not *Cynthia* that preserueth
the one in the bud, and nourisheth the other in the blade, and by
her influence both comforteth all things, and by her authoritie commaundeth all creatures. Suffer then *Endimion* to followe his affections, though to obtaine her be impossible, and let him flatter himselfe
in his owne imaginations, because they are immortall.

Tellus. Loth I am *Endimion* thou shouldest die, because I loue
thee well; and that thou shouldest liue it greeueth mee, because
thou louest *Cynthia* too well. In these extremities what shall I
doe? *Floscula* no more words, I am resolued. He shall neyther
liue, nor die.

Flosc. A strange practise, if it be possible.

Tellus. Yes, I will entangle him in such a sweet nette, that he
shall neither find the meanes to come out, nor desire it. All allurements of pleasure will I cast before his eyes, insomuch that he shall
slake that loue which he now voweth to *Cynthia*, and burne in mine,
of which he seemeth carelesse. In thys languishing, betweene my
amorous deuises, and his owne loose desires, there shall such dissolute
thoughts take roote in his head, and ouer his hart grow so thicke
a skinne, that neither hope of preferment, nor feare of punishment,
nor counsel of the wisest, nor company of the worthiest, shall alter
his humor, nor make him once to thinke of his honor.

Flosc. A reuenge incredible, and if it may be, vnnaturall.

Tellus. Hee shall knowe the mallice of a woman, to haue neither

21 sprits *Q* he *Dil*.   36 thou *om. F. but not Bl. as F. supposes*   38 resolved

meane, nor ende; and of a woman deluded in loue, to haue neither rule, nor reason. I can doe it, I must, I will! All his vertues will
55 I shadow with vices; his person (ah sweet person) shall he decke with such rich Roabes, as he shall forget it is his owne person; his sharp wit (ah wit too sharpe, that hath cut off all my ioyes) shall hee vse, in flattering of my face, and deuising Sonnets in my fauour. The prime of his youth and pride of his time, shall be spent in
60 melancholy passions, carelesse behauiour, vntamed thoughts, and vnbridled affections.

Flosc. When thys is done what then? shall it continue tyll hys death, or shall he doate for euer in this delight?

Tellus. Ah *Floscula*, thou rendest my hart in sunder, in putting
65 me in remembrance of the end.

Flosc. Why if this be not the end, all the rest is to no ende.

Tellus. Yet suffer mee to imitate *Iuno*, who woulde turne *Iupiters* louers to beastes on the earth, though she knew afterwards they should be starres in heauen.

70 *Flosc.* Affection that is bred by enchauntment, is like a flower that is wrought in silke, in colour and forme most like, but nothing at all in substance or sauour.

Tellus. It shall suffice me if the world talke that I am fauoured of *Endimion*.

75 *Flosc.* Well, vse your owne wyll; but you shall finde that loue gotten with witch-craft is as vnpleasant, as fish taken with medicines vnwholsome.

Tellus. Floscula, they that be so poore that they haue neyther nette nor hooke, will rather poyson dowe then pyne with hunger:
80 and she that is so opprest with loue, that shee is neyther able with beauty nor wit to obtaine her freende, wyll rather vse vnlawfull meanes, then try vntollerable paines. I will doe it.

Exit.

Flosc. Then about it. Poore *Endimion*, what traps are layde for thee, because thou honourest one that all the world wondreth at.
85 And what plots are cast to make thee vnfortunate, that studiest of all men to be the faithfullest. *Exit.*

59–61 The ... affections *ital. Bl. except* shall be *and* melancholy passions
75–82 loue ... paines *ital. Bl.*   79 dowe] dough *Dil. Bak.*

SCÆNA TERTIA.—⟨*The same.*⟩

DARES, SAMIAS, SIR TOPHAS, EPITON.

⟨*Enter* DARES *and* SAMIAS.⟩

Dares. Now our Maisters are in loue vp to the eares, what haue wee to doe but to be in knauery vp to the crownes?

Samias. O that we had Sir *Tophas*, that braue Squire, in the midst of our myrth, *&* *ecce autem*, wyl you see the deuill?

Enter SIR TOPHAS ⟨*and* EPITON⟩.

Top. Epi! 5

Epi. Heere syr.

Top. I brooke not thys idle humor of loue, it tickleth not my lyuer, from whence the Loue-mongers in former age seemed to inferre they should proceede.

Epi. Loue, sir, may lye in your lunges, and I thinke it doth, 10 and that is the cause you blow, and are so pursie.

Top. Tush boy! I thinke it but some deuise of the Poet to get money.

Epi. A Poet? whats that?

Top. Doost thou not know what a Poet is? 15

Epi. No.

Top. Why foole, a Poet is as much as one shoulde say, a Poet. ⟨*Perceiving* DAR. *and* SAM.⟩ But soft, yonder be two Wrennes, shall I shoote at them?

Epi. They are two lads. 20

Top. Larkes or wrennes, I will kill them.

Epi. Larkes! are you blinde? they are two lyttle Boyes.

Top. Byrdes, or boyes, they are both but a pittance for my breakefast, therefore haue at them, for theyr braines must as it were imbroder my bolts. 25

Sam. Stay your courage valiant Knight, for your wisdome is so wearie that it stayeth it selfe.

Dar. Why Syr *Tophas* haue you forgotten your olde freendes?

Top. Freendes? *Nego argumentum.*

Sam. And why not freends? 30

Top. Because *Amicitia* (as in old Annuals we find) is *inter pares*:

---

1 our] are *F.*   S. D. [and EPITON] *supplied Dil.*   9 they] it *Dil. Bak.*
18 [Perceiving &c.] *supplied Bak.*   31 Annals *Bl. mods.*

now my pretty companions, you shall see how vnequall you be to
mee : but I will not cut you quite off, you shall be my halfe friendes;
for reaching to my middle, so farre as from the ground to the wast
35 I wil be your freend.
  Dar. Learnedly. But what shall become of the rest of your
bodie, from the wast to the crowne?
  Top. My children *quod supra vos nihil ad vos*, you must thinke
the rest immortall, because you cannot reach it.
40 *Epi.* Nay I tell ye my Maister is more then a man.
  Dar. And thou lesse then a mouse.
  Top. But what be you two?
  Sam. I am *Samias*, page to *Eumenides*.
  Dar. And I *Dares*, page to *Endimion*.
45 *Top.* Of what occupation are your Masters?
  Dar. Occupation, you clowne, why they are honourable, and
warriers.
  Top. Then are they my prentises.
  Dar. Thine, and why so?
50 *Top.* I was the first that euer deuised warre, and therefore by
Mars himselfe giuen me for my Armes a whole Armorie, and thus
I goe as you see, clothed with Artillary; it is not Silkes (milksops)
nor Tyssues, nor the fine wooll of Seres, but yron, steele, swords,
flame, shot, terror, clamor, blood, and ruine, that rocks a sleepe my
55 thoughts, which neuer had any other cradle but crueltie. Let me
see, doe you not bleede?
  Dar. Why so?
  Top. Commonly my words wound.
  Sam. What then doe your blowes?
60 *Top.* Not onely wound, but also confound.
  Sam. Howe darst thou come so neere thy Maister *Epi?* Syr
Tophas spare vs.
  Top. You shall liue. You *Samias* because you are little; you
Dares, because you are no bigger; and both of you, because you
65 are but two; for commonly I kil by the dosen, and haue for euerie
particular aduersarie, a peculiar weapon.

33-4 friendes; *F.* : *semicolon transferred to* middle *Dil. Bak. perhaps rightly* :
comma at both Q Bl. 36 But *om. Dil.*   43-4 Samias, page to Eumenides &c.]
all prev. eds. transpose the names Eumenides *and* Endimion. *See note on* Dram.
Pers.   51 was *before* given *Dil.* : had *before* given *F. Bak.*   53 nor[1]] not
Dil.   Seres] Ceres *all eds.*   54 rock *Dil. Bak.*   60 wound . . .
confound *F. Bak.* : confound . . . confound *Q Bl.* : confound . . . contund *Dil.*

Sam. May we know the vse for our better skyll in warre?

Top. You shall. Heere is a burbolt for the vglie beast the Black-bird.

Dar. A cruell sight.

Top. Heere is the Muskit, for the vntamed (or as the vulgar sort terme it) the wilde Mallard.

Sam. O desperate attempt!

Epi. Nay my Maister will match them.

Dar. I if he catch them.

Top. Heere is a speare and shielde, and both necessarie, the one to conquer, the other to subdue or ouercome the terrible Trowte, which although he be vnder the water, yet tying a string to the top of my speare and an engine of yron to the ende of my lyne, I ouerthrowe him; and then heerein I put him.

Sam. O wonderfull warre! ⟨*Aside.*⟩ *Dares*, didst thou euer heare such a dolt?

Dar. ⟨*aside*⟩. All the better, we shall haue good sport hereafter, if we can get leysure.

Sam. ⟨*aside*⟩. Leysure! I will rather loose my Maisters seruice then his companie! looke howe he stroutes!—But what is this, call you it your sword?

Top. No, it is my Simiter; which I by construction often studying to bee compendious, call my Smyter.

Dar. What, are you also learned, sir?

Top. Learned? I am all *Mars* and *Ars*.

Sam. Nay, you are all Masse and Asse.

Top. Mock you mee? You shall both suffer, yet with such weapons, as you shall make choise of the weapon wherewith you shall perrish. Am I all a masse or lumpe, is there no proportion in me? Am I all Asse? is there no wit in mee? *Epi*, prepare thē to the slaughter.

Sam. I pray sir heare vs speake! we call you Masse, which your learning doth well vnderstande is all Man, for *Mas maris* is a man. Then *As* (as you knowe) is a weight, and we for your vertues account you a weight.

Top. The Latine hath saued your lyues, the which a world of siluer could not haue ransomde. I vnderstand you, and pardon you.

68 bird-bolt *Bl. mods.*   s. d. [Aside] *the asides first marked in Bak.*   86 strowtes *Bl.* : struts *Dil. Bak.*   94 weapons *so all. See note*

105 *Dar.* Well Sir *Tophas* we bid you farewell, & at our next meeting we will be readie to doe you seruice.

Top. *Samias* I thanke you, *Dares* I thanke you, but especiallie I thanke you both.

Sam. ⟨*aside*⟩. Wiselie. Come, next time weele haue some prettie
110 Gentle-women with vs to walke, for without doubt with them he will be verie daintie.

Dar. Come let vs see what our Maisters doe, it is high time.

Exeunt.

Top. Now will I march into the fielde, where if I cannot encounter with my foule enemies, I will withdraw my selfe to the
115 Riuer, & there fortifie for fish: for there resteth no minute free from fight. *Exit.*

S⟨C⟩ÆNA QUARTA.—⟨*The same.*⟩

⟨*Enter, at one side,*⟩ TELLUS, FLOSCULA, ⟨*at the other*⟩ DIPSAS.

Tellus. Behold *Floscula*, we haue met with the Woman by chaunce that wee sought for by trauell; I will breake my minde to her without ceremonie or circumstance, least we loose that time in aduise that should be spent in execution.

5 *Flosc.* Vse your discretion; I will in this case neither give counsell nor consent, for there cannot bee a thing more monstrous then to force affection by sorcery, neither doe I imagin anie thing more impossible.

Tellus. Tush *Floscula*, in obtaining of loue what impossibilities
10 will I not try? and for the winning of *Endimion*, what impieties will I not practise? *Dipsas*, whom as many honour for age as wonder at for cunning, listen in few words to my tale, & answere in one word to the purpose, for that neither my burning desire can afforde long speech, nor the short time I haue to stay manie delayes. Is it
15 possible by hearbes, stones, spels, incantation, enchauntment, exorcismes, fire, mettals, plannets, or any practise, to plant affection where it is not, and to supplant it where it is?

Dipsas. Faire Ladie, you may imagin that these horie heares are not void of experience, nor the great name that goeth of my cunning
20 to bee without cause. I can darken the Sunne by my skil, and remooue the Moone out of her course; I can restore youth to the

s. D. [Enter &c.] *so first in Bal*.   2-3 I will ... circumstance *and* (*below*) I will ... nor consent *ital. Bl.* .   15 incantantation *Q*   15-6 exorcism, fire, metal, *Dil.*

aged, and make hils without bottoms ; there is nothing that I can
not doe, but that onely which you would haue me doe ; and therin
I differ from the Gods, that I am not able to rule harts ; for were it
in my power to place affection by appointment, I would make such 25
euill appetites, such inordinate lusts, such cursed desires, as all the
worlde should be filled both with supersticious heates, and extreame
loue.

Tellus. Vnhappie *Tellus,* whose desires are so desperate, that they
are neither to be conceiued of any creature, nor to be cured by any 30
arte.

Dipsas. This I can,—breede slacknes in loue, though neuer
roote it out. What is he whom you loue, & what she that he
honoureth?

Tellus. *Endimion,* sweet *Endimion* is he that hath my hart; and 35
Cynthia, too too faire *Cynthia,* the myracle of Nature, of tyme, of
Fortune, is the Ladie that hee delightes in, and dotes on euery day,
and dies for ten thousand times a day.

Dipsas. Would you haue his loue, eyther by absence or sicknes
aslaked? Would you that *Cynthia* should mistrust him, or be 40
iealous of him without colour?

Tellus. It is the onelie thing I craue, that seeing my loue to
Endimion vnspotted, cannot be accepted, hys truth to *Cynthia*
(though it be vnspeakeable) may bee suspected.

Dipsas. I will vndertake it, and ouertake him, that all his loue 45
shal be doubted of, and therefore become desperate: but this will
weare out with time, that treadeth all things downe but trueth.

Tellus. Let vs goe.

Dipsas. I follow. *Exeunt.*

ACTUS SECUNDUS

Scæna Prima.—⟨ *Gardens of the Palace, as before.* ⟩

Endimion. Tellus.

⟨ *Enter* Endimion. ⟩

End. O Fayre *Cynthia!* ô vnfortunate *Endimion!* Why was
not thy byrth as high as thy thoughts, or her beautie
lesse then heauenlie? or why are not thyne honors as rare as her

47 time, . . . but trueth *italics Bl. except* that

beautie? or thy fortunes as great as thy deserts? Sweet *Cynthia*,
how wouldst thou be pleased, how possessed? wil labours (patient
of all extremities) obtaine thy loue? There is no Mountain so
steepe that I will not climbe, no monster so cruell that I will not
tame, no action so desperate that I will not attempt. Desirest thou
the passions of loue, the sad and melancholie moodes of perplexed
mindes, the not to be expressed torments of racked thoughts?
Beholde my sad teares, my deepe sighes, my hollowe eyes, my broken
sleepes, my heauie countenaunce. Wouldst thou haue mee vowde
onelie to thy beautie? and consume euerie minute of time in thy
seruice? remember my solitarie life, almost these seauen yeeres:
whom haue I entertained but mine owne thoughts, and thy vertues?
What companie haue I vsed but contemplation? Whom haue
I wondred at but thee? Nay whom haue I not contemned, for
thee? Haue I not crept to those on whom I might haue troden,
onelie because thou didst shine vpon them? Haue not iniuries
beene sweet to mee, if thou vouchsafedst I should beare them?
Haue I not spent my golden yeeres in hopes, waxing old with
wishing, yet wishing nothing but thy loue. With *Tellus*, faire *Tellus*,
haue I dissembled, vsing her but as a cloake for mine affections, that
others seeing my mangled and disordered minde, might thinke it
were for one that loueth me, not for *Cynthia*, whose perfection
alloweth no companion, nor comparison.

In the midst of these distempred thoughts of myne thou art not
onelie iealous of my truth, but careles, suspicious, and secure:
which strange humor maketh my minde as desperate as thy conceits
are doubtfull. I am none of those Wolues, that barke most when
thou shynest brightest; but that fish (thy fish *Cynthia* in the floode
Araris) which at thy waxing is as white as the driuen snowe, and at
thy wayning, as blacke as deepest darknes. I am that *Endimion*
(sweet *Cynthia*) that haue carryed my thoughts in equall ballance
with my actions, being alwaies as free from imagining ill, as enter-
prysing; that *Endimion*, whose eyes neuer esteemed anie thing
faire but thy face, whose tongue termed nothing rare but thy vertues,
and whose hart imagined nothing miraculous but thy gouernment.
Yea, that *Endimion*, who diuorsing himselfe from the amiablenes of
all Ladies, the brauerie of all Courts, the companie of al men, hath

4 thy] her *Dil. perhaps rightly*   7 monseer *F.*   20 vouchsafedst *Dil. Bak.*:
vouchsafest *Q Bl. F.*   23 affection *Dil.*   31 brightest; but *Dil. Bak.*:
brightest. But *Q Bl. F.*   32 Araris *Bak.*: Aranis *all preceding eds.*

chosen in a solitarie Cell to liue, onely by feeding on thy fauour, accounting in the worlde (but thy selfe) nothing excellent, nothing immortall; thus maist thou see euerie vaine, sinew, muscle, and artery of my loue, in which there is no flatterie, nor deceipt, error, nor arte. But soft, here commeth *Tellus*, I must turne my other 45 face to her like *Ianus*, least she be as suspicious as *Juno*.

Enter TELLUS ⟨, FLOSCULA *and* DIPSAS *following*⟩.

Tellus. Yonder I espie *Endimion*, I will seeme to suspect nothing, but sooth him, that seeing I cannot obtaine the depth of his loue, I may learne the height of his dissembling. *Floscula* and *Dipsas*, with-drawe your selues out of our sight, yet be within the hearing 50 of our saluting.—How now *Endimion*, alwaies solitary? no companie but your owne thoughts? no freende but melancholie fancies?

End. You know (fayre *Tellus*) that the sweet remembrance of your loue, is the onely companion of my life, and thy presence, my paradise: so that I am not alone when no bodie is with mee, and 55 in heauen it selfe when thou art with me.

Tellus. Then you loue me *Endimion*.

End. Or els I liue not *Tellus*.

Tellus. Is it not possible for you *Endimion*, to dissemble?

End. Not, *Tellus*, vnlesse I could make me a woman. 60

Tellus. Why, is dissembling ioyned to theyr sex inseparable? as heate to fire, heauines to earth, moysture to water, thinnesse to ayre?

End. No, but founde in their sex, as common as spots vpon Doues, moles vpon faces, Caterpillers vpon sweet apples, cobwebs vpon faire windowes. 65

Tellus. Doe they all dissemble?

End. All but one.

Tellus. Who is that?

End. I dare not tell. For if I shoulde say you, then would you imagin my flattery to be extreame; if another, then woulde you thinke 70 my loue to be but indifferent.

Tellus. You will be sure I shall take no vantage of your words. But in sooth *Endimion*, without more ceremonies, is it not *Cynthia*?

S. D. [FLOSC. . . . *following*] *supplied Dil.* 48–9 obtaine . . . dissembling, *and, below,* How now . . . fancies, *and Tellus' next speech but one are italicized in Blount, as well as many others in this scene. Since these frequent italicizations seem merely due to underlinings by some reader in the Q copy from which the compositor was printing, I report no more* 61 inseparably *Dil.* 72 advantage *Dil.* 73 ceremony *Dil.*

75 *End.* You know *Tellus*, that of the Gods we are forbidden to dispute, because theyr dieties come not within the compasse of our reasons; and of *Cynthia* we are allowed not to talke but to wonder, because her vertues are not within the reach of our capacities.

Tellus. Why, she is but a woman.
80 *End.* No more was *Venus.*
Tellus. Shee is but a virgin.
End. No more was *Vesta.*
Tellus. Shee shall haue an ende.
End. So shall the world.
85 *Tellus.* Is not her beautie subiect to time?
End. No more then time is to standing still.
Tellus. Wilt thou make her immortall?
End. No, but incomparable.
Tellus. Take heede *Endimion*, lest like the Wrastler in Olimpia,
90 that striuing to lifte an impossible weight catcht an incurable straine, thou by fixing thy thoughts aboue thy reach, fal into a disease without al recure! But I see thou art now in loue with *Cynthia*.

End. No *Tellus*; thou knowest that the statelie Cedar, whose toppe reacheth vnto the clowdes, neuer boweth his head to the
95 shrubs that growe in the valley; nor Iuie that climeth vp by the Elme, can euer get hold of the beames of the Sunne: *Cynthia* I honour in all humilitie, whom none ought, or care aduenture to loue, whose affections are immortall, & vertues infinite. Suffer me therefore to gaze on the Moone, at whom, were it not for thy selfe,
100 I would die with wondering. *Exeunt.*

SCÆNA SECUNDA.—⟨*The same.*⟩

⟨*Enter*⟩ DARES, SAMIAS, SCINTILLA, FAUILLA.

Dar. Come, *Samias*, diddest thou euer heare such a sighing, the one for *Cynthia*, the other for *Semele*, & both for moone shine in the water?

Sam. Let them sigh, and let vs sing: how say you gentlewomen,
5 are not our Masters too farre in loue?

Scint. Their tongues happily are dipt to the roote in amorous words and sweete discourses, but I thinke their hearts are scarce tipt on the side with constant desires.

76 deities *Bl. rest*   6 haply *Bak.*

Dar. How say you *Fauilla*, is not loue a lurcher, that taketh mens stomacks away that they cannot eate, their spleene that they cannot laugh, their harts that they cannot fight, theyr eyes that they cannot sleepe, and leaueth nothing but lyuers to make nothing but Louers?

Favil. Away peeuish boy, a rodde were better vnder thy girdle, than loue in thy mouth: it will be a forward Cocke that croweth in the shell.

Dar. Alas! good olde gentlewoman, how it becommeth you to be graue.

Scint. Fauilla though she be but a sparke, yet is shee fyre.

Favil. And you *Scintilla* bee not much more then a sparke, though you would be esteemed a flame.

Sam. ⟨*aside to* DARES⟩. It were good sport to see the fight betweene two sparkes.

Dar. ⟨*aside to* SAM.⟩. Let them to it, and wee will warme vs by theyr words.

Scint. You are not angry *Fauilla*?

Favil. That is, *Scintilla*, as you list to take it.

Sam. ⟨*to* SCINTILLA⟩. That! that!

Scint. This it is to be matched with girles, who comming but yesterday from making of babies, would before tomorrowe be accounted Matrons.

Favil. I crye your Matronship mercy; because your Pantables bee higher with corke, therefore your feete must needs be higher in the insteppes: you will be mine elder, because you stande vppon a stoole, and I on the floore.

Sam. ⟨*aside*⟩. Good, good.

Dar. ⟨*to* SAM.⟩. Let them alone, and see with what countenance they will become friendes.

Scint. Nay, you thinke to bee the wyser, because you meane to haue the last worde.

Sam. Step betweene them least they scratch.—In faith gentlewomen, seeing wee came out to bee merry, let not your iarring marre our iestes: be friendes, how say you?

Scint. I am not angry, but it spited mee to see howe short she was.

Favil. I ment nothing, till she would needs crosse me.

22 Sam. [aside &c.] *the asides first marked by Baker*   32 Pantables *so all*   35 floore] flowre *Q*   37 alone] loue *Bl. mods.*

Dar. Then so let it rest.

Scint. I am agreede.

Favil. And I, yet I neuer tooke anything so vnkindly in my life.
⟨ *Weeps.* ⟩

50 *Scint.* Tys I haue the cause, that neuer offered the occasion.
⟨ *Weeps.* ⟩

Dar. Excellent, and right like a woman.

Sam. A strange sight to see water come out of fire.

Dar. It is their propertie to carrie, in their eyes, fire and water, teares and torches, and in their mouthes, honie and gall.

55 *Scint.* You will be a good one if you liue; but what is yonder formall fellowe?

Enter SIR TOPHAS ⟨, EPITON *following*⟩.

Dar. Sir *Tophas,* syr *Tophas* of whom we tolde you: if you bee good wenches make as though you loue him, and wonder at him.

Favil. Wee will doo our parts.

60 *Dar.* But first let vs stand aside, and let him vse his garbe, for all consisteth in his gracing. ⟨ *The four retire.* ⟩

Top. Epi!

Epi. At hand, syr.

Top. How likest thou this Martiall life, where nothing but bloud
65 besprinkleth our bosomes? Let me see, be our enemies fatte?

Epi. Passing fat: and I would not chaunge this life to be a Lord; and your selfe passeth all comparison, for other Captaines kill and beate, and there is nothing you kill, but you also eate.

Top. I will drawe out their guttes out of their bellies, and teare
70 the flesh with my teeth, so mortall is my hate, and so eger my vnstaunched stomacke.

Epi. ⟨*aside to the ladies*⟩. My master thinkes himselfe the valiantest man in the world if hee kill a wren: so warlike a thing he accompteth to take away life, though it be from a Larke.

75 *Top.* Epi, I finde my thoughtes to swell, and my spirite to take winges, in so much that I cannot continue within the compas of so slender combates.

Favil. This passeth!

Scint. Why, is he not madde? ⟩ ⟨ *Aside.* ⟩

80 *Sam.* No, but a little vaine glorious.

S. D. [Weeps] (*bis*) *supplied Bak. after Dilke's note*   S. D. [EPITON following] *supplied Dil.*   S. D. [The four retire] *supplied Bak.*   72 S. D. [Aside] *supplied Dil.*   74 it *after* accompteth *Dil.*   79 Why is *Q*

Top. *Epi!*
Epi. Syr.
Top. I will encounter that blacke and cruell enemie that beareth rough and vntewed lockes vpon his bodie, whose Syre throweth downe the strongest walles, whose legs are as many as both ours, on whose head are placed most horrible hornes by nature, as a defence from all harmes.
Epi. What meane you, Master, to be so desperate?
Top. Honour inciteth mee, and very hunger compelleth mee.
Epi. What is that monster?
Top. The Monster *Ouis.* I haue saide,—let thy wits worke.
Epi. I cannot imagin it; yet let me see,—a black enemie with rough lockes—it may be a sheep, and *Ouis* is a sheep: his Syre so strong—a Ram is a sheepes Sire, that beeing also an engine of war: hornes he hath, and foure legs,—so hath a sheepe: without doubt this monster is a blacke sheepe. Is it not a sheepe that you meane?
Top. Thou hast hit it, that Monster will I kill and sup with.
Sam. Come let vs take him off. ⟨*Advancing.*⟩ Syr *Tophas*, all haile.
Top. Welcome children, I seldome cast mine eyes so low as to the crownes of your heads, and therfore pardon me that I spake not all this while.
Dar. No harme done: here be faire Ladies come to wonder at your person, your valour, your witte, the report whereof hath made them careles of their owne honours, to glut their eyes and harts vpon yours.
Top. Report cannot but iniure mee, for that not knowing fully what I am, I feare shee hath beene a niggard in her praises.
Scint. No, gentle knight, Report hath beene prodigal; for shee hath left you no equall, nor her selfe credite; so much hath she tolde, yet no more than we now see.
Dar. ⟨*aside*⟩. A good wench.
Favil. If there remaine as much pittie toward women as there is in you courage against your enemies, thē shall we be happie, who hearing of your person, came to see it, and seeing it, are now in loue with it.
Top. Loue me, Ladies? I easily beleeue it, but my tough heart receiueth no impression with sweet words. *Mars* may pearce it, *Venus* shall not paint on it.

    84 vntewed *so all*   85 wall *Dil.*   113 woman *Dil.*

120 *Favil.* A cruell saying.
   Sam. ⟨*aside*⟩. Ther's a girle.
   Dar. Will you cast these Ladyes away, and all for a little loue? doo but speake kindly.
   Top. There cōmeth no soft syllable within my lips; custome hath
125 made my wordes bloudy, and my hart barbarous: that pelting word loue, how watrish it is in my mouth, it carrieth no sound; hate, horror, death, are speaches that nourish my spirits. I like hony, but I care not for the bees. I delight in musicke, but I loue not to play on the bagpipes: I can vouchsafe to heare the voice of women, but
130 to touch their bodies I disdaine it, as a thing childish, and fit for such men as can disgest nothing but milke.
   Scint. A hard heart! shall wee dye for your loue, and finde no remedy.
   Top. I haue already taken a surfet.
135 *Epi.* Good master, pittie them.
   Top. Pittie them, *Epi*? no I do not thinke that this breast shalbe pestred with such a foolish passion. What is that the gentlewoman carrieth in a chaine?
   Epi. Why it is a Squirrill.
140 *Top.* A Squirrill? O Gods what things are made for money.
   Dar. ⟨*to the ladies*⟩. Is not this gentleman ouerwise?
   Favil. I could stay all day with him, if I feared not to be shent.
   Scint. Is it not possible to meete againe?
145 *Dar.* Yes, at any time.
   Favil. Then let vs hasten home.
   Scint. Sir *Tophas*, the God of warre deale better with you, than you doe with the God of loue.
   Favil. Our loue we may dissemble, disgest we cannot; but
150 I doubt not but time will hamper you, and helpe vs.
   Top. I defie time, who hath no interest in my heart: come *Epi*, let me to the battaile with that hideous beast: loue is pappe and hath no relish in my taste, because it is not terrible.
⟨*Exeunt* Sir Tophas *and* Epiton.⟩
   Dar. Indeede a blacke sheepe is a perilous beast: but let vs in
155 till another time.
   Favil. I shall long for that time.   *Exeunt.*

---

124 syllables *Dil.*   126 it is *om. Bak.*   137 gentlewomen *F.*   141 gentlemen *F.*   otherwise *F.*   s. d. [Exeunt &c.] *supplied Bak.*

SCÆNA TERTIA.—⟨*A Grove.*⟩

⟨*Enter*⟩ ENDIMION: DIPSAS ⟨*and*⟩ BAGOA ⟨*in the background*⟩.

End. No rest *Endimion?* still vncertaine how to settle thy steps by day, or thy thoughts by night? thy trueth is measured by thy fortune, and thou art iudged vnfaithfull because thou art vnhappy. I will see if I can beguile my selfe with sleep, & if no slumber will take hold in my eyes, yet will I imbrace the golden thoughts in my 5 head, and wish to melt by musing: that as Ebone, which no fire can scorch, is yet cõsumed with sweet sauours; so my heart which cannot bee bent by the hardnes of fortune, may be brused by amorous desires. On yonder banke neuer grewe any thing but Lunary, and hereafter I will neuer haue any bed but that banke. 10 O *Endimion, Tellus* was faire, but what auaileth Beautie without wisedome? Nay, *Endimion,* she was wise, but what auaileth wisdome without honour? Shee was honourable *Endimion,* belie her not, I but howe obscure is honor without fortune? Was she not fortunate whome so many followed? Yes, yes, but base is fortune 15 without Maiestie: thy Maiestie *Cynthia* al the world knoweth and wondereth at, but not one in the world that can immitate it, or comprehend it. No more *Endimion!* sleepe or dye; nay die, for to sleepe, it is impossible; and yet I knowe not how it commeth to passe, I feele such a heauines both in mine eyes and hart, y^t I am 20 sodainly benummed, yea in euery ioint: it may be wearinesse, for when did I rest? it may bee deepe melancholy, for when did I not sigh? *Cynthia!* I so; I say *Cynthia!*   *He falles a sleepe.*

Dipsas ⟨*advancing*⟩. Little doost thou knowe *Endimion* when thou shalt wake, for hadst thou placed thy heart as lowe in loue, 25 as thy head lieth now in sleepe, thou mightest haue commanded *Tellus* whome nowe in stead of a Mistris, thou shalt finde a tombe. These eyes must I seale vp by Art, not Nature, which are to be opened neither by Art nor Nature. Thou that laist downe with golden lockes, shalt not awake vntill they bee turned to siluer haires; 30 and that chin, on which scarcely appeareth soft downe, shalbe filled with brissels as hard as broome: thou shalt sleep out thy youth and flowring time, and become dry hay before thou knowest thy selfe greene grasse, & ready by age to step into the graue whẽ thou

---

s. D. [Enter &c.] *old eds. Dil. F. simply* Endimion, Dipsas, Bagoa. *Baker brings in Dipsas and Bagoa after Endimion's speech*   13 believe *Dil.*   17 that *om. Dil.*   21 ioint] iont *Q*   29 liest *Bak.*   30 wake *Bak.*   33 knowest *Dil. Bak.*: knewest *Q Bl. F.*

35 wakest, that was youthfull in the Courte when thou laidst thee downe to sleepe. The malice of *Tellus* hath brought this to passe, which if shee could not haue intreated of mee by fayre meanes, shee would haue commaunded by menacing, for from her gather wee all our simples to maintaine our sorceries. Fanne with this hemlocke ouer
40 his face, and sing the inchantment for sleepe, whilst I goe in and finish those cerimonies that are required in our Art: take heede yee touch not his face, for the Fanne is so seasoned that who so it toucheth with a leafe shall presently dye, and ouer whom the wind of it breatheth, hee shall sleepe for euer. *Exit.*
45 *Bagoa.* Let me alone. I will bee carefull.—What happe hadst thou *Endimion* to come vnder the hands of *Dipsas!* O faire *Endimion!* how it grieueth me that that faire face must be turned to a withered skinne, & taste the paines of death before it feele the reward of loue. I feare *Tellus* will repent that which the heauens themselues
50 seemed to rewe. But I neare *Dipsas* comming; I dare not repine, least she make me pine, and rocke me into such a deepe sleepe, that I shall not awake to my marriage.

(*Re-*)*Enter* DIPSAS.

Dipsas. How now, haue you finished?

Bagoa. Yea.

55 *Dipsas.* Well then let vs in, and see that you doo not so much as whisper that I did this, for if you do, I will turne thy haires to Adders, and all thy teeth in thy heade to tongues: come away, come away.

Exeunt.

A DUMBE SHEW (*representing the dream of* ENDIMION).
Musique sounds.

Three Ladies enter; one with a Knife and a looking glasse, who by the procurement of one of the other two, offers to stab ENDIMION *as hee sleepes, but the third wrings her hands, lamenteth, offering still to preuent it, but dares not.*

At last, the first Lady looking in the glasse, casts downe the Knife.

Exeunt.

Enters an ancient man with bookes with three leaues, offers the same twice. ENDIMION *refuseth: hee rendeth two and offers the third, where hee stands a while, and then* ENDIMION *offers to take it.*

Exit ⟨*the Old Man*⟩.

---

35 wert *Dil.*: wast *Bak.*   S. D. *This Dumb Show first appears in Blount* rendeth *Dil. Bak.*: readeth *Bl. F. Cf.* v. 1, *p.* 66, *l.* 109   offers to take] takes *Dil.*   [the Old Man] added *Bak.*

ACTUS TERTIUS

SCÆNA PRIMA.—⟨*Gardens of the Palace, as before.*⟩

CYNTHIA, three Lordes, TELLUS.

⟨*Enter* CYNTHIA, TELLUS, SEMELE, EUMENIDES, CORSITES, ZONTES, PANELION.⟩

Cynthia. IS the report true, that *Endimion* is striken into such a dead sleep, that nothing can either wake him or mooue him?

Eum. Too true Madame, and as much to be pittied as wondered at.

Tellus. As good sleepe and doe no harme, as wake and doe no good.

Cynth. What maketh you *Tellus* to bee so short? the time was *Endimion* onely was.

Eum. It is an olde saying Madame, that a waking dog doth a farre off barke at a sleeping Lyon.

Sem. It were good *Eumenides* that you tooke a nappe with your friend, for your speech beginneth to be heauy.

Eum. Contrarie to your nature, *Semele*, which hath beene alwaies accounted light.

Cynth. What haue we heare, before my face, these vnseemely and malepart ouerthwarts? I will tame your tongues, and your thoughts, and make your speeches answerable to your dueties, and your conceits fitte for my dignitie, els will I banish you both my person and the worlde.

Eum. Pardon I humbly aske: but such is my vnspotted faith to *Endimion*, that whatsoeuer seemeth a needle to pricke his finger, is a dagger to wound my heart.

Cynth. If you bee so deere to him, howe happeneth it you neither go to see him, nor search for remedy for him?

Eum. I haue seene him to my griefe, and sought recure with despaire, for that I cannot imagine who should restore him that is the wounder to all men: your highnes on whose handes the

---

S. D. CYNTHIA, three Lordes, TELLUS *Q Bl. F. though* Sem. Eum. Cors. Zon. *appear in all three among the following prefixes, and* Pantlion *or* Pantalion *in the text. Dilke merely adds* SEMELE *to the imperfect enumeration of the old eds. Baker gives the list as here*   17 tame] take`*F*.   28 wounder *Q, i. e.* wonder *as Bl. mods.*   on] in *Dil.*

compasse of the earth is at cōmaund, (though not in possession)
may shewe your selfe both worthy your sex, your nature, and your
fauour, if you redeeme that honorable *Endimion*, whose ripe yeres
foretell rare vertues, and whose vnmellowed conceits promise rype
counsell.

Cynth. I haue had tryal of *Endimion*, & conceiue greater assurance of his age, then I coulde hope of hys youth.

Tellus. But timely, Madam, crookes that tree that wil be a
camock; and young it pricks that will be a thorne: and therefore
he that began without care to settle his life, it is a signe without
amendment he will end it.

Cynth. Presumptuous gyrle, I will make thy tongue an example
of vnrecouerable displeasure. *Corsites*, carry her to the Castle in
the Deserte, there to remaine and weaue.

Cors. Shall she worke stories or poetries?

Cynth. It skyleth not which—goe to! in both; for she shall find
examples infinite in eyther what punishment long tongues haue.
Eumenides, if eyther the Soothsayers in Egipt, or the Enchaunters in
Thessaly, or the Philosophers in Greece, or all the Sages of the
worlde, can find remedie, I will procure it; therefore dispatch with
al speede: you *Eumenides*, into Thessalie. You *Zontes* into Greece,
(because you are acquainted in Athens.) You *Panelion* to Egypt,
saying that *Cynthia* sendeth, and if you will, commaundeth.

Eum. On bowed knee I giue thanks, and with wings on my legs
I flye for remedie.

Zon. We are readie at your highnes commaund, & hope to returne
to your full content.

Cynth. It shall neuer be said that *Cynthia*, whose mercy and
goodnes filleth the heauens with ioyes, & the world with meruailes,
will suffer eyther *Endimion* or any to perrish, if he may be protected.

Eum. Your Maiesties wordes haue beene alwaies deedes, and
your deedes vertues.   *Exeunt.*

SCÆNA SECUNDA.—⟨*Before a Castle.*⟩

⟨*Enter*⟩ CORSITES, TELLUS.

Cors. Heere is the Castle (fayre *Tellus*) in which you must weaue,
till eyther time end your dayes, or *Cinthia* her displeasure. I am
sorrie so fayre a face shoulde bee subiect to so hard a fortune, and

32 whose] those *F.*   46 Soothsayers *Bl.*   50 Panelion *Bak.*: Pantlion
Q: Pantalion *Bl. Dil. F.*   57 meruailes] maruaile *Bl. F.*: marvel *Dil. Bak.*

that the flower of beautie, which is honoured in Courts, shoulde heere wither in pryson.

Tellus. *Corsites, Cynthia* may restraine the libertie of my bodie, of my thoughts she cannot, and therefore doe I esteeme my selfe most free, though I am in greatest bondage.

Cors. Can you then feede on fancie, and subdue the mallice of enuie by the sweetnes of imagination?

Tellus. Corsites, there is no sweeter musicke to the miserable then dispayre; and therefore the more bitternesse I feele, the more sweetnes I find; for so vaine were liberty, and so vnwelcome the following of higher fortune, that I chuse rather to pine in this Castle, then to be a Prince in any other Court.

Cors. A humor contrary to your yeeres, and nothing agreeable to your sex: the one commonly allured with delights, the other alwaies with soueraigntie.

Tellus. I meruaile *Corsites* that you being a Captain, who should sound nothing but terror, and suck nothing but blood, can finde in your hart to talke such smooth wordes, for that it agreeth not with your calling to vse words so soft as that of loue.

Cors. Ladie, it were vnfit of warres to discourse with womē, into whose minds nothing can sinck but smoothnes; besides, you must not thinke that Souldiours bee so rough hewne, or of such knottie mettle, that beautie cannot allure, and you beeing beyonde perfection enchaunt.

Tellus. Good *Corsites* talke not of loue, but let me to my labor: the little beautie I haue, shall be bestowed on my Loome, which I now meane to make my Louer.

Cors. Let vs in, and what fauour *Corsites* can shewe, *Tellus* shall commaund.

Tellus. The onely fauour I desire, is now and then to walke.

Exeunt.

SCÆNA TERTIA.—⟨*Gardens of the Palace, as before.*⟩

⟨*Enter*⟩ SYR TOPHAS *and* EPI⟨TON⟩.

Tophas. Epi.

Epi. Heere sir.

Tophas. Vnrigge mee. Hey ho!

Epi. Whats that?

Tophas. An interiection, whereof some are of mourning: as *eho, vah.*

7 I do *Dil.*

Epi. I vnderstand you not.
Tophas. Thou seest me.
Epi. I.
Tophas. Thou hearst me.
Epi. I.
Tophas. Thou feelest me.
Epi. I.
Tophas. And not vnderstand'st me?
Epi. No.
Tophas. Then am I but three quarters of a Nowne substantiue. But alas *Epi*, to tell thee the troth, I am a Nowne Adiectiue.
Epi. Why?
Tophas. Because I cannot stand without another.
Epi. Who is that?
Tophas. Dipsas.
Epi. Are you in loue?
Tophas. No: but loue hath as it were milkt my thoughts, and drained from my hart the very substance of my accustomed courage; it worketh in my heade like newe Wine, so as I must hoope my skonce with yron, least my head breake, and so I bewray my braines: but I pray thee first discouer me in all parts, that I may be like a Louer, and then will I sigh and die. Take my gunne and giue me a gowne: *Cedant arma togæ.*
Epi. Heere.
Tophas. Take my sworde and shielde, and giue mee beard-brush and Cyssers: *bella gerant alii, tu Pari semper ama.*
Epi. Will you be trimd sir?
Tophas. Not yet: for I feele a contention within me, whether I shall frame the bodkin beard or the bush. But take my pike and giue mee pen: *dicere quæ puduit, scribere iussit amor.*
Epi. I wyll furnish you sir.
Tophas. Nowe for my bowe and bolts giue me ynke and paper: for my Smiter a pen-knife: for *Scalpellum, calami, atramentum, charta, libelli, sint semper studiis arma parata meis.*
Epi. Sir, will you giue ouer warres, & play with that bable called loue?

---

10 hearest *Bl. mods.*   29 Cedant *Dil. Bak.*: Cædant *Q Bl. F.*   31 beard-brush *Dil. Bak.*: beard, brush *Q Bl. F.*   32 Pari *Bl. Dil. Bak.*: pari *Q F.*   36 a *before* pen *Dil.*   quæ] que *Q*   39 Smiter *Q*: Semiter *Bl. F.*: scimitar *Dil.*: simitar *Bak.*; *but cf.* i. 3. 89   41 bauble *Dil. Bak.*

Tophas. Giue ouer warres? no *Epi, Militat omnis amans, et habet sua castra Cupido.*

Epi. Loue hath made you very eloquent, but your face is nothing fayre.

Tophas. Non formosus erat, sed erat facundus Vlisses.

Epi. Nay, I must seeke a new Maister if you can speake nothing but verses.

Tophas. Quicquid conabar dicere versus erat. Epi, I feele all *Ouid de arte amandi* lie as heauie at my heart as a loade of logges. O what a fine thin hayre hath *Dipsas!* What a prettie low forehead! What a tall & statelie nose! What little hollowe eyes! What great and goodly lypes! Howe harmlesse shee is beeing toothlesse! her fingers fatte and short, adorned with long nayles like a Bytter! In howe sweete a proportion her cheekes hang downe to her brests like dugges, and her pappes to her waste like bagges! What a lowe stature shee is, and yet what a great foote shee carryeth! Howe thrifty must she be in whom there is no waste! Howe vertuous is shee like to be, ouer whom no man can be ielous!

Epi. Stay Maister, you forget your selfe.

Tophas. O *Epi,* euen as a dish melteth by the fire, so doth my wit increase by loue.

Epi. Pithily, and to the purpose. But what? beginne you to nodde?

Tophas. Good *Epi,* let me take a nappe: for as some man may better steale a horse, then another looke ouer the hedge: so diuers shall be sleepie when they woulde fainest take rest. *He sleepes.*

Epi. Who euer saw such a woodcock? loue *Dipsas!* without doubt all the world will nowe account him valiant, that ventureth on her, whom none durst vndertake. But heere commeth two wagges.

Enter DARES *and* SAMIAS.

Sam. Thy Maister hath slept his share.

Dar. I thinke he doth it because he would not paie me my boord wages.

Sam. It is a thing most strange, and I thinke mine will neuer returne, so that wee must both seeke newe Maisters, for we shall neuer liue by our manners.

Epi. If you want Maisters, ioyne with me, and serue Sir *Tophas,* who must needes keepe more men, because he is toward marriage.

44 castea *Q*   53 tall] tale *Q*   56 Bytter *Q, cf. l.* 96: Byttern *Bl. mods.*

Sam. What, *Epi!* wher's thy Maister?
Epi. Yonder, sleeping in loue.
Dar. Is it possible?
Epi. Hee hath taken his thoughts a hole lower, and sayth, seeing it is the fashion of the world, hee will vaile bonet to beautie.
Sam. How is he attyred?
Epi. Louelie.
Dar. Whom loueth this amorous knight?
Epi. Dipsas.
Sam. That vglie creature? Why shee is a foole, a scold, fat, without fashion, and quite without fauour.
Epi. Tush you be simple, my Ma. hath a good marriage.
Dar. Good? as how?
Epi. Why in marrying *Dipsas*, hee shall haue euerie day twelue dishes of meate to his dinner, though there be none but *Dipsas* with him. Foure of flesh, four of fish, foure of fruite.
Sam. As how *Epi*?
Epi. For flesh these; woodcock, goose, bitter, & rayle.
Dar. Indeed he shal not misse, if *Dipsas* be there.
Epi. For fish these; crab, carpe, lumpe, and powting.
Sam. Excellent! for of my word, she is both crabbish, lumpish, and carping.
Epi. For fruite these; fretters, medlers, hartichockes, and Lady longings. Thus you see hee shall fare like a King, though he be but a begger.
Dar. Well, *Epi*, dine thou with him, for I had rather fast then see her face. But see, thy Ma. is a sleepe: let vs haue a song to wake this Amorous knight.
Epi. Agreed.
Sam. Content.

THE FIRST SONG.

Epi.
    HEre snores *Tophas*,
      That Amorous Asse,
    Who loues *Dipsas*,
    With face so sweet,
    Nose and Chinne meet.

All three. { At sight of her each Fury skips
           { And flings into her lap their whips.

---

96 bitter *Q, cf. l.* 56: Byttern *Bl.* mods.   99 of *om. Dil.*   101 Fritters *Bl.* mods.   S. D. THE FIRST SONG so *Bl.* where it first appears; *Q* has merely Song, without giving it

Dar. Holla, Holla in his eare.
Sam. The Witch sure thrust her fingers there.
Epi. Crampe him, or wring the Foole by th' Nose.
Dar. Or clap some burning flax to his toes.
Sam. What Musique's best to wake him? 120
Epi. Baw wow, let Bandogs shake him
Dar. Let Adders hisse in's eare.
Sam. Else Eare-wigs wriggle there.
Epi. No, let him batten; when his tongue
Once goes, a Cat is not worse strung. 125
All three. { But if he ope nor mouth, nor eies,
He may in time sleepe himselfe wise.

Top. Sleepe is a bynding of the sences, loue a loosing.
Epi. ⟨*aside*⟩. Let vs heare him awhile.
Top. There appeared in my sleepe a goodly Owle, who sitting 130 vpon my shoulder, cryed twyt twyt, & before myne eyes presented her selfe the expresse image of *Dipsas*. I meruailed what the Owle said, til at the last, I perceiued twyt twyt, to it, to it: onely by contraction admonished by thys vision, to make account of my sweet *Venus*. 135

Sam. Sir *Tophas*, you haue ouer-slept your selfe.
Top. No youth, I haue but slept ouer my loue.
Dar. Loue? Why it is impossible, that into so noble and vnconquered a courage, loue should creepe; hauing first a head as hard to pearce as steele, then to passe to a hart arm'd with a shirt 140 of male.
Epi. I, but my Maister yawning one day in the Sun, loue crept into his mouth before he could close it, and there kept such a tumbling in his bodie, that he was glad to vntrusse the poynts of his hart, and entertaine Loue as a stranger. 145

Top. If there remaine any pittie in you, pleade for me to *Dipsas*.
Dar. Pleade? Nay, wee will presse her to it.—⟨*Aside to* SAM.⟩ Let vs goe with him to *Dipsas*, and there shall wee haue good sport.— But sir *Tophas* when shall we goe? for I finde my tongue voluble, 150 and my hart venturous, and all my selfe like my selfe.
Sam. ⟨*aside to* DAR.⟩. Come *Dares*, let vs not loose him till we

133-4 twyt ... admonished *so punctuated Q Bl.*: twit, twit, was to it, to it, only by contraction; admonished *Dil.*: 'Twit, twit,' 'To it, to it'—only, by contraction admonished *Bak.* S. D. [Aside &c.] *the asides here supplied by Bak.*

find our Maisters, for as long as he liueth, we shall lack neither mirth nor meate.

155 *Epi.* We will trauice. Will you goe sir?
Top. *I præ, sequar.* *Exeunt.*

SCÆNA QUARTA.—⟨*A desert place, with a fountain.*⟩
EUMENIDES, GERON.

⟨GERON *singing: to whom, at close of song, enter* EUMENIDES.⟩

Eum. Father, your sad musique beeing tuned on the same key that my harde fortune is, hath so melted my minde, that I wish to hang at your mouthes ende till my life end.

Ger. These tunes, Gentleman, haue I beene accusttomed with 5 these fiftie Winters, hauing no other house to shrowde my selfe but the broade heauens : and so familiar with mee hath vse made miserie, that I esteeme sorrowe my cheefest solace. And welcommest is that guest to mee, that can rehearse the saddest tale, or the bloodiest tragedie.

10 *Eum.* A strange humour, might I enquire the cause?

Ger. You must pardon me if I denie to tell it, for knowing that the reuealing of griefes is as it were a renewing of sorrow, I haue vowed therefore to conceale them, that I might not onely feele the depth of euerlasting discontentment, but dispaire of remedie. 15 But whence are you? What fortune hath thrust you to thys distresse?

Eum. I am going to Thessalie, to seeke remedie for *Endimion* my deerest freende, who hath beene cast into a dead sleepe, almost these twentie yeeres, waxing olde, and readie for the graue, beeing almost 20 but newlie come forth of the cradle.

Ger. You neede not for recure trauell farre, for who so can cleerely see the bottome of thys Fountaine shall haue remedie for any thing.

Eum. That mee thinketh is vnpossible : why, what vertue can 25 there be in water?

Ger. Yes, who soeuer can shedde the teares of a faythfull Louer shall obtaine any thing he would : reade these words engrauen about the brimme.

Eum. Haue you knowne this by experience, or is it placed heere 30 of purpose to delude men?

155 trauice] traverse *Bak.*   3 my *om. Bl. mods.*   19 and] am *F.*   29 knowe *F.*

Ger. I onely would haue experience of it, and then shoulde there bee an ende of my miserie. And then woulde I tell the strangest discourse that euer yet was heard.

Eum. ⟨aside⟩. Ah *Eumenides!*

Ger. What lacke you Gentleman, are you not wel? 35

Eum. Yes Father, but a qualme that often commeth ouer my hart doth nowe take hold of me. But did neuer any Louers come hether?

Ger. Lusters, but not Louers; for often haue I seene them weepe, but neuer could I heare they saw the bottome. 40

Eum. Came there women also?

Ger. Some.

Eum. What did they see?

Ger. They all wept that the Fountaine ouerflowed with teares, but so thicke became the water with theyr teares, that I could scarce 45 discerne the brimme, much lesse beholde the bottome.

Eum. Be faithfull Louers so skant?

Ger. It seemeth so, for yet heard I neuer of any.

Eum. Ah *Eumenides*, howe art thou perplexed! call to minde the beautie of thy sweet Mistris, and the depth of thy neuer dying 50 affections: howe oft hast thou honoured her, not onelie without spotte, but suspition of falsehoode! And howe hardly hath shee rewarded thee, without cause or colour of despight! Howe secrete hast thou beene these seauen yeeres, that hast not, nor once darest not, to name her, for discontenting her. Howe faythfull! that hast 55 offered to dye for her, to please her. Vnhappie *Eumenides!*

Ger. Why, Gentleman, did you once love?

Eum. Once? I Father, and euer shall.

Ger. Was she vnkind, and you faithfull?

Eum. Shee of all women the most froward, and I of all creatures 60 the most fond.

Ger. You doted then, not loued: for affection is grounded on vertue, and vertue is neuer peeuish: or on Beautie, and Beautie loueth to be praised.

Eum. I, but if all vertuous Ladies should yeelde to all that be 65 louing, or all amiable gentlewomen entertaine all that be amorous, theyr vertues would bee accounted vices, and their beauties deformities; for that loue can bee but betweene two, and that not proceeding of him that is most faithfull, but most fortunate.

<small>55 hath *F. Bak.*   67 their *om. Bl. mods.*</small>

    Ger. I would you were so faithfull, that your teares might make you fortunate.

    Eum. Yea father, if that my teares cleare not this fountaine, then may you sweare it is but a meere mockerie.

    Ger. So saith every one yet, that wept.

    Eum. Ah, I fainte, I dye! Ah sweete *Semele* let me alone, and dissolue, by weeping, into water.

    ⟨*He gazes into the fountain.*⟩

    Ger. This affection seemeth straunge: if hee see nothing, without doubt this dissembling passeth, for nothing shall drawe mee from the beleefe.

    Eum. Father, I plainlie see the bottome, and there in white marble engrauen these wordes, *Aske one for all, and but one thing at all.*

    Ger. O fortunate *Eumenides*, (for so haue I hearde thee call thy selfe) let me see. ⟨*Looks into the fountain.*⟩ I cannot discerne any such thing. I thinke thou dreamest.

    Eum. Ah Father, thou art not a faithfull louer, and therefore canst not beholde it.

    Ger. Then aske; that I may be satisfied by the euent, and thy selfe blessed.

    Eum. Aske? so I will: and what shall I doo but aske? and whome should I aske but *Semele*? the possessing of whose person is a pleasure that cannot come within the compasse of comparison; whose golden lockes seeme most curious, when they seeme most carelesse; whose sweete lookes seeme most alluring, when they are most chaste; and whose wordes the more vertuous they are, the more amorous they bee accounted. I pray thee, fortune, when I shall first meete with fayre *Semele*, dash my delight with some light disgrace, least imbracing sweetnesse beyond measure, I take a surfit without recure: let her practise her accustomed coynesse, that I may dyet my selfe vpon my desires: otherwise the fulnesse of my ioyes will diminish the sweetnesse, and I shall perrish by them before I possesse them.

    Why doe I trifle the time in words? The least minute, beeing spent in the getting of *Semele*, is more worth then the whole worlde: therefore let mee aske. What nowe *Eumenides*? Whether art thou

---

78 this *so all perhaps rightly*   81 one] once *Dil. perhaps rightly*   93 seeme²] are *Dil.*
104 of om. *Dil.*   105 aske.] aske, *F. spoiling sense*

drawn? Hast thou forgotten both friendship and duetie? Care of *Endimion*, and the commaundement of *Cynthia?* Shall hee dye in a leaden sleepe, because thou sleepest in a golden dreame? I, let him sleepe euer, so I slumber but one minute with *Semele*. Loue knoweth neither friendshippe nor kindred.   110

Shall I not hazard the losse of a friend, for the obtayning of her for whome I woulde often loose my selfe? Fonde *Eumenides*, shall the intycing beautie of a most disdainfull Ladie, bee of more force then the rare fidelitie of a tryed friend? The loue of men to women 115 is a thing common and of course: the friendshippe of man to man infinite and immortall. Tush, *Semele* dooth possesse my loue. I, but *Endimion* hath deserued it. I will helpe *Endimion*. I founde *Endimion* vnspotted in his trueth. I, but I shall finde *Semele* constant in her loue. I will haue *Semele*. What shall I doe? Father, thy gray haires are Embassadours of experience. Which shall I 120 aske?

Ger. *Eumenides*, release *Endimion*, for all thinges (friendship excepted) are subiect to fortune: Loue is but an eye-worme, which onely tickleth the heade with hopes and wishes: friendshippe the image of eternitie, in which there is nothing moueable, nothing 125 mischeeuous. As much difference as there is betweene Beautie and Vertue, bodies and shadowes, colours and life; so great oddes is there betweene loue and friendshippe.

Loue is a Camelion, which draweth nothing into the mouth but ayre, and nourisheth nothing in the bodie but lunges: beleeue mee 130 *Eumenides*, Desire dyes in the same moment that Beautie sickens, and Beautie fadeth in the same instant that it flourisheth. When aduersities flowe, then loue ebbes: but friendship standeth stifflie in stormes. Time draweth wrinckles in a fayre face, but addeth fresh colours to a fast friende, which neither heate, nor cold, nor 135 miserie, nor place, nor destiny, can alter or diminish. O friendship! of all things the most rare, and therefore most rare because most excellent, whose comforts in misery is alwaies sweet, and whose counsels in prosperitie are euer fortunate. Vaine loue, that onely comming neere to friendship in name, woulde seeme to be the same, 140 or better, in nature.

Eum. Father, I allowe your reasons, and will therefore conquer mine owne. Vertue shall subdue affections, wisdome lust, friendship

118 shall finde] found *Dil.*   129 chameleon *Bak.*   132 flourishes *Dil.*
133 friendships standeth *Dil.*   138 is] are *Dil.*

beautie. Mistresses are in euery place, and as common as Hares
in Atho, Bees in Hybla, foules in the ayre: but friends to be founde,
are like the Phœnix in Arabia, but one, or the Philadelphi in Arays,
neuer aboue two. I will haue *Endimion*: ⟨*again looking into the
fountain*⟩ sacred Fountaine! in whose bowels are hidden diuine
secrets, I haue encreased your waters with the teares of vnspotted
thoughts and therefore let mee receiue the reward you promise:
Endimion, the truest friende to mee, and faithfullest louer to
Cynthia, is in such a dead sleepe, that nothing can wake or
mooue him.

Ger. Doost thou see any thing?

Eum. I see, in the same Piller, these wordes: *When shee whose
figure of all is the perfectest, and neuer to bee measured—alwaies one,
yet neuer the same—still inconstant, yet neuer wauering—shall come
and kisse* Endimion *in his sleepe, hee shall then rise; els neuer.* This
is straunge.

Ger. What see you els?

Eum. There commeth ouer mine eyes either a darke mist, or
vppon the fountaine a deepe thicknesse: for I can perceiue nothing.
But howe am I deluded? or what difficult (nay impossible) thing
is this?

Ger. Me thinketh it easie.

Eum. Good father and howe?

Ger. Is not a circle of all Figures the perfectest?

Eum. Yes.

Ger. And is not *Cynthia* of all cyrcles the most absolute!

Eum. Yes.

Ger. Is it not impossible to measure her, who still worketh by
her influence, neuer standing at one stay?

Eum. Yes.

Ger. Is shee not alwaies *Cynthia*, yet seldome in the same
bignesse; alwaies wauering in her waxing or wayning, that our
bodies might the better bee gouerned, our seasons the daylier giue
their increase; yet neuer to bee remooued from her course, as long
as the heauens continue theirs?

Eum. Yes.

Ger. Then who can it bee but *Cynthia*, whose vertues beeing all
diuine, must needes bring things to passe that bee myraculous?
Goe, humble thy selfe to *Cynthia*, tell her the successe, of which

145 on Athos *Bak.* 146 Phænix *Q Bl. F.* Arays *so all* 176 be the better *Dil.*

my selfe shall bee a witnesse. And this assure thy selfe, that shee that sent to finde meanes for his safetie, will now worke her cunning. 185

Eum. How fortunate am I, if *Cynthia* be she that may doo it.

Ger. Howe fonde art thou, if thou doo not beleeue it?

Eum. I will hasten thither, that I may intreat on my knees for succour, and imbrace in mine armes my friend.

Ger. I will goe with thee, for vnto *Cynthia* must I discouer all my sorrowes, who also must worke in mee a contentment. 190

Eum. May I nowe knowe the cause?

Ger. That shall bee as wee walke, and I doubt not but the straungnesse of my tale will take away the tediousnesse of our iourney. 195

Eum. Let vs goe.

Ger. I followe. *Exeunt.*

ACTUS QUARTUS

Scæna Prima.—⟨*Before Corsites' Castle.*⟩

Tellus, Corsites.

⟨*Enter* Tellus.⟩

Tellus. I Maruell *Corsites* giueth me so much libertie: all the worlde knowing his charge to bee so high, and his nature to bee most straunge; who hath so ill intreated Ladies of great honour, that he hath not suffered them to looke out of windowes, much lesse to walke abroade: it may bee hee is in loue with mee, for (*Endimion*, hard-harted *Endimion*, excepted) what is he that is not enamourd of my beautie? But what respectest thou the loue of all the world? *Endimion* hates thee. Alas poore *Endimion*, my malyce hath exceeded my loue: and thy faith to *Cynthia* quenched my affections. Quenched *Tellus?* nay kindled them a fresh; in so much that I finde scorching flames for dead embers, and cruell encounters of warre in my thoughtes, in steede of sweete parlees. Ah that I might once againe see *Endimion*! accursed girle, what hope hast thou to see *Endimion*? on whose head already are growne gray haires, and whose life must yeelde to Nature, before *Cynthia* ende her displeasure. Wicked *Dipsas*, and most deuilish 5 10 15

187 fonde] silly *F.*   16 most] more *F. Bak.*

Tellus, the one for cunning too exquisit, the other for hate too intollerable. Thou wast commanded to weaue the stories & Poetries wherein were shewed both examples & punishments of tatling tongues, and thou hast only imbrodered the sweet face of *Endimion*, deuises of loue, melancholy imaginations, and what not, out of thy worke, that thou shouldst studie to picke out of thy mind. But here cometh *Corsites*, I must seeme yeelding and stoute, ful of mildnesse, yet tempered with a Maiestie : for if I be too flexible, I shall giue him more hope then I meane; if too froward, enioy lesse liberty then I would; loue him. I cannot, & therfore will practise that which is most customarie to our sex, to dissemble.

Enter CORSITES.

Cor. Faire *Tellus*, I perceiue you rise with the Larke, and to your selfe sing with the Nightingale.

Tellus. My Lord I haue no play-fellow but fancy : being barred of all companie I must question with my selfe, and make my thoughts my frindes.

Cor. I would you would account my thoughtes also your friends, for they be such as are only busied in wondering at your beautie & wisdome : & some, such as haue esteemed your fortune too hard ; and diuers of that kind that offer to set you free, if you will set them free.

Tellus. There are no colours so contrarie as white and blacke, nor Elements so disagreeing as fire and water, nor any thing so opposite as mens thoughts & their words.

Cor. He that gaue *Cassandra* the gift of prophecying, with the curse that, spake shee neuer so true, shee should neuer be beleeued, hath I think poysoned the fortune of men, that vttering the extremities of their inward passions, are always suspected of outward periuries.

Tellus. Well *Corsites* I will flatter my selfe, and beleeue you. What would you doe to enioy my loue ?

Cor. Sette all the Ladies of the Castle free, and make you the pleasure of my life : more I cannot doe, lesse I will not.

Tellus. These be great wordes, and fit your calling : for Captaines must promise things impossible. But wil you doe one thing for all ?

22 worke,] *Dil. om. comma*   27 customarie] contrarie *all prev. eds.*   sex.] *Bl. om. comma*   32 frindes Q: friends *Bl. rest*   35 wisdome :] *Bl. om. colon*
38 black and white *Dil.*   50 for *before* your *F. Bak.*

Cor. Any thing sweet *Tellus*, that am ready for all.

Tellus. You knowe that on the Lunary bancke sleepeth *Endimion*.

Cor. I knowe it.

Tellus. If you will remoue him from that place by force, and conuey him into some obscure caue by pollicie, I giue you here the faith of an vnspotted virgine, that you onelie shall possesse me as a louer, and in spight of malice haue mee for a wife.

Cor. Remooue him *Tellus*? Yes *Tellus*, hee shall bee remooued, and that so soone, as thou shalt as much commend my dilligence as my force. I goe.

Tellus. Stay, will your selfe attempt it?

Cor. I *Tellus*: as I would haue none partaker of my sweete loue, so shall none be partners of my labours: but I pray thee goe at your best leysure, for *Cynthia* beginneth to rise, and if she discouer our loue we both perish, for nothing pleaseth her but the fairenesse of virginitie. All things must bee not onely without lust, but without suspicion of lightnes.

Tellus. I will depart, and goe you to *Endimion*.

Cor. I flye *Tellus*, beeing of all men the most fortunate.

Exit.

Tellus. Simple *Corsites*, I haue set thee about a taske being but a man, y^t the gods thēselues cannot performe: for little doost thou knowe howe heauie his head lies, howe hard his fortune: but such shiftes must women haue to deceiue men, and vnder colour of things easie, intreat that which is impossible: otherwise we should be cūbred with importunities, oathes, sighes, letters, and all implements of loue, which to one resolued to the contrary, are most lothsome. I will in, and laugh with the other Ladies at *Corsites* sweating.

Exit.

SCÆNA SECUNDA.—⟨*Gardens of the Palace, as before.*⟩

SAMIAS *and* DARES, EPITON.

⟨*Enter* SAMIAS *and* DARES.⟩

Sam. Will thy master neuer awake?

Dar. No, I thinke hee sleepes for a wager: but how shall wee spende the time? Sir *Tophas* is so farre in loue that he pineth in his bedde, and commeth not abroade.

Sam. But here commeth *Epi*, in a pelting chafe.

73 y^t *om. Bl. mods.*   S. D. SAMIAS and DARES, EPITON *Q*: Samias, Dares and Epiton *Bl. Dil. F.*

⟨*Enter* EPITON.⟩

Epi. A poxe of all false Prouerbes, and were a Prouerbe a Page, I would haue him by the eares.

Sam. Why art thou angry?

Epi. Why? you knowe it is sayd, the tyde tarieth no man.

Sam. True.

Epi. A monstrous lye; for I was tide two houres, and tarried for one to vnlose mee.

Dar. Alas poore *Epi.*

Epi. Poore? No, no, you base⟨-⟩conceited slaues, I am a most complyt Gentleman, although I bee in disgrace with sir *Tophas*.

Dar. Art thou out with him?

Epi. I, because I cannot gette him a lodging with *Endimion*: hee would faine take a nappe for fortie or fifty yeeres.

Dar. A short sleepe, considering our long life.

Sam. Is he still in loue?

Epi. In loue? why he doth nothing but make Sonets.

Sam. Canst thou remember any one of his Poems?

Epi. I, this is one.

    The beggar Loue that knows not where to lodge:
        At last within my hart when I slept,
            He crept,
    I wakt, and so my fancies began to fodge.

Sam. That's a verie long verse.

Epi. Why the other was shorte, the first is called from the thombe to the little finger, the second from the little finger to the elbowe, and some hee hath made to reach to the crowne of his head, and downe again to the sole of his foote: it is sette to the tune of the blacke Saunce, *ratio est*, because *Dipsas* is a black Saint.

Dar. Very wisely: but pray thee, *Epi*, how art thou complet? and beeing from thy Maister what occupation wilt thou take?

Epi. Know my harts, I am an absolute Microcosmus, a pettie worlde of my selfe, my library is my heade, for I haue no other bookes but my braines: my wardrope on my backe, for I haue no more apparrell then is on my body; my armorie at my fingers ends,

---

S. D. [Enter EPITON] *inserted here by Bak.*   14 base-conceited] base, conceited *Bak. wrongly*   24–7 The beggar Loue ... fodge] *so arranged F. Bak.*: *first as verse Dil.*   31 hath *om. F. Bak.*   32 sole] soule *Q*   33 Saunce *so all*   36 Know *Bch.*: No *all other eds.*   39 finger ends *Bl. F.*: fingers' end *Bak.*

for I vse no other Artillarie then my nailes; my treasure in my purse. *Sic omnia mea mecum porto.*

Dar. Good!

Epi. Know, syrs, my Pallace is pau'd with grasse, and tyled with starres: for *cælo tegitur qui non habet vrnam*, he that hath no house, must lie in the yard.

Sam. A braue resolution. But how wilt thou spend thy time?

Epi. Not in any Melancholie sort: for mine exercise I will walke horses.

Dar. Too bad.

Epi. Why is it not saide: It is good walking when one hath his horse in his hand?

Sam. Worse, and worse! but how wilt thou liue?

Epi. By angling: O tis a stately occupation to stande foure houres in a colde Morning, and to haue his nose bytten with frost, before hys baite be mumbled with a Fish.

Dar. A rare attempt, but wilt thou neuer trauell?

Epi. Yes in a Westerne barge, when with a good winde and lustie pugges one may goe ten miles in two daies.

Sam. Thou art excellent at thy choyse, but what pastime wilt thou vse, none?

Epi. Yes the quickest of all.

Sam. What! dyce?

Epi. No, when I am in hast, xxj games at Chesse, to passe a fewe minutes.

Dar. A life for a little Lord, and full of quicknesse.

Epi. Tush, let mee alone! but I must needes see if I can finde where *Endimion* lieth: and then goe to a certaine fountaine hard by, where they say faithfull Louers shall haue althings they will aske. If I can finde out any of these, *ego et Magister meus erimus in tuto*, I and my Maister shall be freendes. He is resolued to weep some three or foure payle-fuls, to auoyde the rume of loue that wambleth in his stomacke.

Enter the Watch.

Sam. Shall we neuer see thy Maister, *Dares?*

Dar. Yes, let vs goe nowe, for to morrowe *Cynthia* will be there.

43 Know *Bak.*: Now *preceding eds.*   44 celo *Q*   48 horses, Dares. *F. Bak. misled by Bl.* (*sig.* D 12 *recto*) *where the following prefix appears as a catchword in the same line with* horses   53 foure] *all* : *query?* for   63 one and twentie *Bl. mods.*   71 pales full *Dil.*: pailfuls *Bak.*   rheume *Bl. F. Bak.* : theme *Dil.*

Epi. I will goe with you. But howe shall wee see for the Watch?

Sam. Tush, let me alone! Ile begin to them. Maisters God speede you.

80 *1 Watch.* Sir boy, we are all sped alreadie.

Epi. ⟨*aside*⟩. So me thinks, for they smell all of drinke, like a beggers beard.

Dar. But I pray sirs, may we see *Endimion* ?

2 Watch. No, we are commanded in *Cynthias* name that no man 85 shall see him.

Sam. No man ? Why we are but boyes.

1 Watch. Masse, neighbours, hee sayes true ; for if I sweare I will neuer drinke my liquor by the quart, and yet call for two pints, I thinke with a safe conscience I may carouse both.

90 *Dar.* Pithily, and to the purpose.

2 Watch. Tush, tush, neighbors, take me with you.

Sam. This will grow hote.

Dar. Let them alone.

2 Watch. If I saie to my wife, wife I will haue no Reysons in my 95 pudding, she puts in Corance, smal Reysons are Reysons, and boyes are men. Euen as my wife shoulde haue put no Reysons in my pudding, so shall there no boyes see *Endimion*.

Dar. Learnedly.

Epi. Let Maister Constable speake : I thinke hee is the wisest 100 among you.

Ma. Const. You know neighbors tis an old said saw, 'children and fooles speake true.'

All say. True.

Ma. Const. Well, there you see the men bee the fooles, because 105 it is prouided from the children.

Dar. Good.

Ma. Const. Then say I neighbors, that children must not see *Endimion*, because children & fooles speak true.

Epi. O wicked application !

110 *Sam.* Scuruily brought about !

1 Watch. Nay he sais true, & therfore till *Cynthia* haue beene heere he shall not be vnccuered. Therefore away !

s. D. [aside] *supplied Dil.* 95 Corance] currants *Dil. Bak.* 101 an] an an *Q* 101-2 *no inv. commas Q Bl. Dil.* : *ital. F.* 103 All say *Q Bl. F.* : All *Dil. Bak.* : *cf. note*

Dar. ⟨*aside to* Sam. *and* Epi.⟩. A watch, quoth you? a man may watch 7. yeres for a wise worde, & yet goe without it. Their wits are all as rustie as their bils.—But come on Ma. Const. shall we haue a song before we goe?

Const. With all my hart.

The second Song.

Watch.	STand: who goes there?
	We charge you, appeare
	Fore our Constable here.
	(In the name of the Man in the Moone)
	To vs Bilmen relate,
	Why you stagger so late,
	And how you come drunke so soone.
Pages.	What are yee (scabs?)
Watch.	The Watch:
	This the Constable.
Pages.	A Patch.
Const.	Knock'em downe vnlesse they all stand.
	If any run away,
	Tis the old Watchmans play,
	To reach him a Bill of his hand.
Pages.	O Gentlemen hold,
	Your gownes freeze with cold,
	And your rotten teeth dance in your head;
Epi.	Wine, nothing shall cost yee.
Sam.	Nor huge fires to roast yee.
Dares.	Then soberly let vs be led.
Const.	Come my browne Bils wee'l roare,
	Bownce loud at Tauerne dore,
Omnes.	And i'th' Morning steale all to bed.

Exeunt.

Scæna Tertia.—⟨*The Grove, with* Endimion *sleeping on the lunary-bank* (*with double transfer, to* Gardens l. 44, *back to* Grove l. 75).⟩

Corsites *solus.*

Corsites. I am come in sight of the Lunary bank: without doubt *Tellus* doteth vpon me, and cunningly that I might not perceiue her loue, shee hath sette mee to a taske that is done before it is begunne.

---

114 7. Q: seuen *Bl. rest*   s.d. The second Song *so Blount, from whom it is here given.* Q Song *without giving it*   124 came *Dil.*   130 him] them *Dil.*   s. d. Exeunt *printed in Bl. F. before song*: om. *Dil.*

Endimion, you must change your pillowe; and if you be not wearie of sleepe, I will carrie you where at ease you shall sleepe your fill. It were good that without more ceremonies I tooke him, least, beeing espyed, I be intrapt, and so incurre the displeasure of *Cynthia*, who commonly setteth watch that *Endimion* haue no wrong.

He lifts.

What nowe, is your Maistership so heauie? or are you nayld to the ground? Not styrre one whit? then vse all thy force though he feele it and wake. What! stone still? turnd, I thinke, to earth, with lying so long on the earth. Didst not thou, *Corsites*, before *Cynthia* pul vp a tree, that fortie yeeres was fastned with rootes and wrethed in knots to the grounde? Didst not thou with maine force pull open the yron Gates, which no Ram or Engine could moue? Haue my weak thoughts made braunfallen my strong armes? or is it the nature of loue or the Quintessence of the mind to breede numnesse, or lythernesse, or I knowe not what languishing in my ioynts and sinewes, beeing but the base strings of my bodie? Or dooth the remembraunce of *Tellus* so refine my spirits into a matter so subtill and diuine, that the other fleshie parts cannot worke whilst they muse? Rest thy selfe, rest thy selfe: nay, rent thy selfe in peeces *Corsites*, and striue in spight of loue, fortune, and nature, to lift vppe this culled bodie, heauier then deade, and more sencelesse then death.

Enter Fayries.

But what are these so fayre fiendes that cause my hayres to stand vpright, and spirits to fall downe? Hags—out alas! Nymphes!— I craue pardon. Aye me out! what doe I heere?

The Fayries *daunce, and with a song pinch him, and hee falleth a sleepe: they kisse* ENDIMION, *and depart.*

THE THIRD SONG BY FAIRIES.

Omnes.   Pinch him, pinch him, blacke and blue,

Sawcie mortalls must not view
What the Queene of Stars is doing,
Nor pry into our Fairy woing.

S. D. He lifts. *Q Bl.*: He tries to lift Endymion *Dil. F. Bak.*   12 thou not *F. Bak.*   18 numnesse *Q Bl.*   mumnesse *F.*: numbness *Dil. Bak.*   what] what, *Q Bl.*   20 so *om. Dil.*   22 rent] rend *Dil. Bak.*   27–8 Hags ... I¹] hags, out alas, Nymphes I *Q Bl. F.*: Hags, out!—Alas! nymphs, I *Dil. Bak.*   28 Aye] Ah *Dil.*   out! what *Dil.*: out what *Q Bl.*: but what *F. Bak.*   heere? *Q Bl. F. i.e.* hear *as Dil. Bak.*   S. D. The Fayries daunce &c.] *Q Bl. Dil. F.*: *but Q has no further direction for the song, nor the song itself, which is given from Bl. announced as in the text*   they] thy *Q*

1 *Fairy.*	Pinch him blue.
2 *Fairy.*	And pinch him blacke.
3 *Fairy.*	Let him not lacke 35
	Sharpe nailes to pinch him blue and red,
	Till sleepe has rock'd his addle head.
4 *Fairy.*	For the trespasse hee hath done,
	Spots ore all his flesh shall runne.
	Kisse Endimion, kisse his eyes, 40
	Then to our Midnight Heidegyes.

Exeunt ⟨leaving ENDIMION *and* CORSITES *sleeping⟩.*

⟨*Enter*⟩ CYNTHIA, FLOSCULA, SEMELE, PANELION, ZONTES,
PYTHAGORAS, GYPTES.

Cynth. You see *Pythagoras* what ridiculous opinions you hold, and I doubt not but you are nowe of another minde.

Pythag. Madam, I plainlie perceiue that the perfection of your brightnesse hath pearced through the thicknesse that couered my 45 minde; in so much that I am no lesse gladde to be reformed, then ashamed to remember my grosenes.

Gyptes. They are thrise fortunate that liue in your Pallace, where Trueth is not in colours, but life, vertues not in imagination, but execution. 50

Cynth. I have alwaies studied to haue rather liuing vertues then painted Gods; the bodie of Trueth, then the tombe. But let vs walke to *Endimion,* it may bee it lyeth in your Artes to deliuer him: as for *Eumenides,* I feare he is dead.

Pythag. I haue alledged all the naturall reasons I can for such 55 a long sleepe.

Gyptes. I can doe nothing till I see him.

Cynth. Come *Floscula,* I am sure you are glad that you shall behold *Endimion.*

Flosc. I were blessed if I might haue him recouered. 60

Cynth. Are you in loue with his person?

Flosc. No, but with his vertue.

Cynth. What say you, *Semele?*

Sem. Madame, I dare say nothing for feare I offende.

Cynth. Belike you cannot speake except you bee spightfull. 65 But as good be silent as saucie. *Panelion,* what punishment were

---

S. D. [leaving . . . CORSITES &c.] *Q Bl. F. add* Corsites *to the succeeding list of entries*: Corsites sleeping *Dil. Bak.*   S. D. ZONTE *Bl. Dil. F.*

fitte for *Semele*, in whose speech and thoughts is onely contempt and sowrenesse?

Panel. I loue not Madam to giue any iudgement. Yet sith your highnesse commaundeth, I thinke, to commit her tongue close prisoner to her mouth.

Cynth. Agreed; *Semele*, if thou speake thys twelue-month, thou shalt forfet thy tongue.—Behold *Endimion!* alas, poore Gentleman, hast thou spent thy youth in sleepe, that once vowed all to my seruice? Hollow eyes? gray haires? wrinckled cheekes? and decayed limmes? Is it destinie, or deceite that hath brought this to passe? If the first, who could preuent thy wretched starres? If the latter, I would I might knowe thy cruell enemie. I fauoured thee *Endimion* for thy honor, thy vertues, thy affections: but to bring thy thoughts within the compasse of thy fortunes, I haue seemed strange, that I might haue thee staied; and nowe are thy dayes ended before my fauour beginne? But whom haue we heere? is it not *Corsites?*

Zon. It is; but more like a Leopard then a man.

Cynth. Awake him. ⟨ZONTES *wakens* CORSITES.⟩ Howe nowe, *Corsites*, what make you heere? How came you deformed? Looke on thy hands, and then thou seest the picture of thy face.

Cors. Myserable wretch, and accursed. How am I deluded? Madame, I aske pardon for my offence, and you see my fortune deserueth pittie.

Cynth. Speake on, thy offence cannot deserue greater punishment: but see thou rehearse the trueth, else shalt thou not find me as thou wishest me.

Cors. Madam, as it is no offence to be in loue beeing a man mortall, so I hope can it be no shame to tell with whom, my Ladie beeing heauenlie. Your Maiestie committed to my charge fayre *Tellus*, whose beautie in the same moment tooke my hart captiue, that I vndertooke to carry her bodie prisoner. Since that time haue I found such combats in my thoughts betweene loue and dutie, reuerence and affection, that I coulde neyther endure the conflict, nor hope for the conquest.

Cynth. In loue? A thing farre vnfitting the name of a Captaine, and (as I thought) the tough and vnsmoothed nature of *Corsites*. But forth.

69 any] my *Dil.* 79 but] but, *Bak. wrongly* S. D. [ZONTES &c.]
supplied Bak. 96 the *before* faire *F. Bak.*

Cors. Feeling this continuall warre, I thought rather by parlee to yeeld, then by certaine danger to perrish. I vnfolded to *Tellus* the depth of my affections, and framed my tongue to vtter a sweet tale of loue, that was wont to sound nothing but threats of warre. Shee too fayre to be true, and too false for one so fayre, after a nice deniall, practised a notable deceyt; commaunding mee to remooue *Endimion* from this Caban, and carrie him to some darke Caue; which I seeking to accomplish, found impossible; and so by Fayries or fiendes haue beene thus handled.

Cynth. Howe say you, my Lordes, is not *Tellus* alwaies practising of some deceites? In sooth *Corsites*, thy face is nowe too foule for a Louer, and thine hart too fonde for a Souldiour. You may see, when Warriors become wantons, howe theyr manners alter with theyr faces. Is it not a shame *Corsites*, that hauing liued so long in *Mars* his Campe thou shouldest now bee rockt in *Venus* Cradle? Doost thou weare *Cupids* Quiuer at thy gyrdle, and make Launces of lookes? Well *Corsites*, rouse thy selfe, and be as thou hast beene; and let *Tellus* who is made all of loue, melt herselfe in her owne loosenes.

Cors. Madam, I doubt not but to recouer my former state; for *Tellus* beautie neuer wrought such loue in my minde, as now her deceite hath dispight; and yet to be reuenged of a woman, were a thing then loue it selfe more womanish.

Gyptes. These spots Gentleman are to be worne out, if you rubbe them ouer with this Lunarie; so that in place where you receiued this maime, you shall finde a medicine.

Cors. I thanke you for that. The Gods blesse mee frō loue & these prettie Ladies that haunt this greene.

Flosc. *Corsites*, I would *Tellus* saw your amiable face.

Zont. How spightfully *Semele* laugheth, that dare not speake.

Cynth. Coulde you not stirre *Endimion* with that doubled strength of yours?

Cors. Not so much as his finger with all my force.

Cynth. *Pythagoras* and *Gyptes*, what thinke you of *Endimion*? what reason is to be giuen, what remedie?

Pyth. Madame it is impossible to yeeld reason for things that happen not in compasse of nature. It is most certaine, that some strange enchauntment hath bound all his sences.

---

107 depths *Dil.* 119 Mars his] Mars' *Dil.* : Mars's *Bak.* 126 hath] and *Dil.* 128 gentlemen *F.* 129 the *before* place *Dil. Bak.* 130 maine *Q*

Cynth. What say you, *Gyptes*?

Gyptes. With *Pythagoras*, that it is enchauntment, and that so
strange that no Arte can vndoe it, for that heauines argueth a mallice
vnremooueable in the Enchauntresse ; and that no power can ende
it, till shee die that did it, or the heauens shew some meanes more
then miraculous.

Flosc. O *Endimion,* could spight it self deuise a mischiefe so
monstrous as to make thee dead with life, and lyuing beeing altogether
dead? Where others number their yeeres, their houres, their
minutes, and steppe to age by staires, thou onely hast thy yeeres
and times in a cluster, being olde before thou remembrest thou wast
younge.

Cynth. No more *Floscula,* pittie dooth him no good : I would
any thing els might, and I vowe by the vnspotted honour of a Ladie
he should not misse it : but is this all *Giptes,* that is to be done?

Gyptes. All as yet. It may be that either the Enchauntresse shall
dye, or els be discouered : if either happen, I will then practise the
vtmost of my arte. In the meane season, about this Groue would
I haue a watch, and the first liuing thing that toucheth *Endimion,*
to be taken.

Cynth. Corsites what say you, will you vndertake this?

Cors. Good Madame, pardon mee ! I was ouertaken too late.
I should rather breake into the middest of a maine battaile, than
againe fall into the handes of those fayre babies.

Cynth. Well, I will prouide others. *Pithagoras* and *Giptes,* you
shall yet remaine in my Courte, till I heare what may be done in this
matter.

Pyth. Wee attende.

Cynth. Let vs goe in. *Exeunt.*

ACTUS QUINTUS

SCÆNA PRIMA.—⟨ *The Grove, with* ENDIMION *sleeping as before.*⟩

⟨*Enter*⟩ SAMIAS, DARES.

Sam. ℰ *Vmenides* hath tolde such strange tales as I may well wonder
at them, but neuer beleeue them.

Dar. The other old man, what a sad speech vsed he, that
caused vs almost all to weepe. *Cynthia* is so desirous to knowe the

148 then Q *only*   165 would *Dil.*   166 in *Dil.*

experiment of her owne vertue, and so willing to ease *Endimions* 5
harde fortune, that she no sooner heard the discourse, but shee
made her selfe in a readines to trye the euent.

Sam. Wee will also see the euent; but whist! heere commeth
Cynthia, with all her traine! Let vs sneake in amongst them.

Enter CYNTHIA, FLOSCULA, SEMELE, EUMENIDES, PANELION, &c.

Cynth. *Eumenides*, it cannot sinke into my heade that I should 10
bee signified by that sàcred Fountaine, for many thinges are there in
the worlde to which those words may be applyed.

Eum. Good Madame vouchsafe but to trye, els shall I thinke my
selfe most vnhappie, that I asked not my sweete Mistris.

Cynth. Will you not yet tell me her name? 15

Eum. Pardon mee good Madame, for if *Endimion* awake, hee
shall: my selfe haue sworne neuer to reueale it.

Cynth. Well, let vs to *Endimion*. I will not be so statelie (good
Endimion) not to stoope to doe thee good: and if thy libertie consist
in a kisse from mee, thou shalt haue it. And although my mouth 20
hath beene heere tofore as vntouched as my thoughts, yet now to
recouer thy life, (though to restore thy youth it be impossible) I will
do that to *Endimion* which yet neuer mortall man coulde bost of
heretofore, nor shall euer hope for heereafter.

Shee kisseth him.

Eum. Madame, hee beginneth to stirre. 25

Cynth. Soft *Eumenides*, stand still.

Eum. Ah, I see his eyes almost open.

Cynth. I commaund thee once againe, stirre not: I wil stand
behinde him.

Pan. What doe I see, *Endimion* almost awake? 30

Eum. *Endimion!* *Endimion!* art thou deafe or dumbe? or hath
this long sleepe taken away thy memorie? Ah my sweet *Endimion*,
seest thou not *Eumenides*? thy faithfull friende, thy faythfull *Eumenides*,
who for thy saftie hath beene carelesse of his owne content. Speake
Endimion! *Endimion!* *Endimion!* 35

End. *Endimion?* I call to minde such a name.

Eum. Hast thou forgotten thy selfe, *Endimion?* then do I not
maruell thou remembrest not thy friend. I tell thee thou art

---

7 a *om. Dil.*   8 willl *Q*   S. D. EUMENIDES, PANELION, &c.] *Bak. first
inserts the needed* EUMENIDES, *and needlessly substitutes for* '&c.' ZONTES,
PYTHAGORAS, *and* GYPTES

Endimion, and I *Eumenides* : beholde also *Cynthia*, by whose fauour thou art awaked, and by whose vertue thou shalt continue thy naturall course.

Cynth. *Endimion*, speake sweete *Endimion*, knowest thou not *Cynthia* ?

End. O heauens, whom doe I beholde ? faire *Cynthia*, diuine *Cynthia* ?

Cynth. I am *Cynthia*, and thou *Endimion*.

End. *Endimion* ? What do I heere ? What, a gray beard ? hollow eyes ? withered bodie ? decayed lymbes ? and all in one night ?

Eum. One night ? thou hast heere slept fortie yeeres, by what Enchauntresse as yet it is not knowne : and behold, the twig to which thou laiedst thy head, is now become a tree. Callest thou not *Eumenides* to remembrance ?

End. Thy name I doo remember by the sounde, but thy fauour I doe not yet call to minde : onely diuine *Cynthia*, to whom time, fortune, destinie, & death, are subiect, I see and remember, and in all humilitie I regard and reuerence.

Cynth. You haue good cause to remember *Eumenides*, who hath for thy safetie forsaken his owne solace.

End. Am I that *Endimion* who was wont in Court to leade my life, and in Iustes, turneys, and armes to exercise my youth ? am I that *Endimion* ?

Eum. Thou art that *Endimion*, and I *Eumenides*, wilt thou not yet call me to remembrance ?

End. Ah sweete *Eumenides*, I now perceiue thou art hee, and that my selfe haue the name of *Endimion* ; but that this should bee my bodie I doubt : for howe coulde my curled lockes bee turned to gray haires, and my stronge bodie to a dying weaknesse, hauing waxed olde and not knowing it.

Cynth. Well *Endimion* arise, a while sit downe, for that thy limmes are stiffe, and not able to stay thee, and tell what hast thou seene in thy sleepe all this while ? What dreames, visions, thoughts, and fortunes ? For it is impossible, but in so long time, thou shouldest see things straunge.

End. Fayre *Cynthia*, I will rehearse what I haue seene, humblie desiring that when I exceede in length you giue me warning, that

47 heere *Q Bl. F.*: hear *Dil. Bak. with doubtful propriety*   What, *O Bl.* What! *Dil.*: *F. om. comma*   68 a *om. F.*   70, 71 thy limmes] my limbes *F.*

I may ende: for to vtter all I haue to speake would bee troublesome, although happilie the straungenesse may somewhat abate the tediousnesse.

Cynth. Well *Endimion* begin.

End. Me thought I sawe a Ladie passing faire, but verie mischeeuous; who in the one hande carryed a knife with which shee offered to cut my throte, and in the other a looking-glasse, wherein seeing how ill anger became Ladies, shee refrained from intended violence. She was accompanied with other Damsels, one of which with a sterne countenance, & as it were with a setled malice engrauen in her eyes, prouoked her to execute mischeefe: an other with visage sad and constant onelie in sorrow, with her armes crossed, and watery eyes, seemed to lament my fortune, but durst not offer to preuent the force. I started in my sleepe, feeling my verie veines to swell, and my sinewes to stretch with feare, and such a colde sweate bedewed all my bodie, that death it selfe could not be so terrible as the vision.

Cynth. A straunge sight. *Giptes* at our better leysure shall expound it.

End. After long debating with her selfe, mercie ouercame anger; and there appeared in her heauenly face such a diuine Maiestie, mingled with a sweete mildenes, that I was rauished with the sight aboue measure, and wished that I might haue enioied the sight without end; and so she departed with the other Ladyes, of which the one retained still an vnmoueable crueltie, the other a constant pittie.

Cynth. Poore *Endimion*, how wast thou affrighted? What els?

End. After her immediatly appeared an aged man with a beard as white as snow, carying in his hand a book with three leaues, & speaking as I remēber these words. *Endimion*, receiue this booke with three leaues, in which are contained counsels, policies, and pictures: and with that he offered mee the booke, which I reiected: wherwith, moued with a disdainefull pittie, hee rent the first leafe in a thousand shiuers; the second time hee offered it, which I refused also; at which bending his browes, and pitching his eyes fast to the ground, as though they were fixed to the earth, and not againe to be remoued—then sodainlie casting them vp to the heauens, he tore in a rage the second leafe, and offered the booke only with one leafe. I know not whether feare to offende, or desire to knowe

92 a]l *om. Dill.* 101 'an *om. Dil.* 105 and *before* carrying *Dil.*

some strange thing, moued mee: I tooke the booke, and so the olde
man vanished.

Cynth. What diddest thou imagine was in the last leafe?

End. There portraid to life, with a colde quaking in euery ioynt,
I behelde many wolues barking at thee *Cynthia*, who hauing ground
their teeth to bite, did with striuing bleede themselues to death.
There might I see ingratitude with an hundred eyes, gazing for
benefites, and with a thousand teeth, gnawing on the bowelles wherein shee was bred. Trecherie stoode all cloathed in white, with
a smyling countenance, but both her handes bathed in blood.
Enuye with a pale and megar face (whose bodie was so leane, that
one might tell all her bones, and whose garment was so totterd, that
it was easie to number every thred) stood shooting at starres, whose
dartes fell downe againe on her owne face. There might I beholde
Drones, or Beetles, I knowe not howe to terme them, creeping vnder
the winges of a princely Eagle, who being carried into her neast,
sought there to sucke that veine, that woulde haue killed the Eagle.
I mused that thinges so base, shoulde attempt a facte so barbarous,
or durst imagine a thing so bloody. And manie other thinges
Madame, the repeticion whereof may at your better leysure seeme
more pleasing: for Bees surfette sometimes with honnie, and the
Gods are glutted with harmony, and your highnesse may be dulled
with delight.

Cynth. I am content to bee dieted, therefore lette vs in. *Eumenides*, see that *Endimion* bee well tended, least eyther eating
immoderatlie, or sleeping againe too long, hee fall into a deadly
surfette, or into his former sleepe.

See this also bee proclaimed, that whosoeuer will discouer this
practise, shall haue of *Cynthia* infinite thankes, and no small rewardes. *Exit.*

Flosc. Ah *Endimion*, none so ioyfull as *Floscula* of thy restoring.

Eum. Yes, *Floscula*, let *Eumenides* be somewhat gladder, and doe
not that wrong to the setled friendship of a man, as to compare it
with the light affection of a woman. Ah my deere friend *Endimion*,
suffer mee to dye with gazing at thee.

End. Eumenides, thy friendshippe is immortall, and not to be
conceiued ; and thy good will, *Floscula*, better then I haue deserued.
But let vs all wayte on *Cynthia*: I maruell *Semele* speaketh not
a word.

119 I *before* portraid *Q Bl.*   ioynt. *Q*   127 all *om. Dil.*   tattered *Dil. Bak.*

Eum. Because if shee doe, shee loseth her tongue.
End. But how prospereth your loue?
Eum. I neuer yet spake worde since your sleepe.
End. I doubt not but your affection is olde, and your appetite colde.
Eum. No *Endimion*, thine hath made it stronger, and nowe are my sparkes growne to flames, and my fancies almost to frenzies: but let vs followe, and within wee will debate all this matter at large.

Exeunt.

SCÆNA SECUNDA.—⟨*Gardens of the Palace.*⟩

SIR TOPHAS, EPITON.

Top. *Epi*, loue hath iustled my libertie from the wall, and taken the vpper hand of my reason.

Epi. Let mee then trippe vp the heeles of your affection, and thrust your goodwill into the gutter.

Top. No *Epi*, Loue is a Lorde of misrule, and keepeth Christmas in my corps.

Epi. No doubt there is good cheere: what dishes of delight doth his Lordshippe feast you withal?

Top. First, with a great platter of plum-porrige of pleasure, wherein is stued the mutton of mistrust.

Epi. Excellent loue lappe.

Top. Then commeth a Pye of patience, a Henne of honnie, a Goose of gall, a Capon of care, and many other Viandes, some sweete and some sowre; which proueth loue to bee, as it was saide of in olde yeeres, *Dulce venenum*.

Epi. A braue banquet.

Top. But *Epi*, I praye thee feele on my chinne, some thing prycketh mee. What doost thou feele or see.

Epi. There are three or foure little haires.

Top. I pray thee call it my bearde. Howe shall I bee troubled when this younge springe shall growe to a great wood!

Epi. O, sir, your chinne is but a quyller yet, you will be most maiesticall when it is full fledge. But I maruell that you loue *Dipsas*, that old Crone.

---

160 thine] time *Dil.*   161 frenzy *Dil.*   8 with *bef.* withall *Bl. mods.*
9 plumb *Dil.*   11 loue lappe] love-pap *Bak. who thinks the* 1 *a printer's error*   14 and *om. Dil.*   14–5 as was said of it *Bak.*   23 fledged *Dil. Bak.*

Top. *Agnosco veteris vestigia flammæ*, I loue the smoke of an olde fyre.

Epi. Why shee is so colde, that no fyre can thawe her thoughts.

Top. It is an olde goose, *Epi*, that will eate no oates; olde Kine will kicke, olde Rats gnawe cheese, and olde sackes will haue much patching: I preferre an old Cony before a Rabbet sucker, and an ancient henne before a younge chicken peeper.

Epi. ⟨*aside*⟩. *Argumentum ab antiquitate*, My master loueth anticke worke.

Top. Giue mee a pippin that is withered like an olde wife.

Epi. Good, sir.

Top. Then, *a contrario sequitur argumentum*. Giue me a wife that lookes like an olde pippin.

Epi. ⟨*aside*⟩. Nothing hath made my master a foole, but flat Schollership.

Top. Knowest thou not that olde wine is best?

Epi. Yes.

Top. And thou knowest that like will be like?

Epi. I.

Top. And thou knowest that *Venus* loued the best Wine.

Epi. So.

Top. Then I conclude, that *Venus* was an olde woman in an olde cuppe of wine. For, *est Venus in vinis, ignis in igne fuit*.

Epi. O *lepidum caput*, O mad cap master! You were worthy to winne *Dipsas*, were shee as olde againe, for in your loue you haue worne the nappe of your witte quite off, and made it thredbare. But soft, who comes heere?

⟨*Enter* SAMIAS *and* DARES.⟩

Top. My solicitors.

Sam. All haile sir *Tophas*, how feele you your selfe?

Top. Statelie in euery ioynt, which the common people terme stifnes. Doth *Dipsas* stoope? wyll shee yeeld? will she bende?

Dar. O sir as much as you would wish, for her chin almost toucheth her knees.

Epi. Maister, she is bent I warrant you.

Top. What conditions doth she aske?

Sam. Shee hath vowed shee will neuer loue anie that hath not a tooth in his head lesse then she.

s. d. [aside] *asides of this scene first marked Dil.* s. d. [Enter &c.] *supplied Dil.*

Top. How manie hath shee?

Dar. One.

Epi. That goeth harde Maister, for then you must haue none.

Top. A small request, and agreeable to the grauitie of her yeeres. What shoulde a wise man doe with his mouth full of bones like a Charnell house? The Turtle true hath nere a tooth.

Sam. ⟨*to* EPI.⟩. Thy Maister is in a notable vaine, that will loose his teeth to be like a Turtle.

Epi. ⟨*aside to* SAM.⟩. Let him loose his tongue to, I care not.

Dar. Nay, you must also haue no nayles, for shee long since hath cast hers.

Top. That I yeelde to: what a quiet life shal *Dipsas* and I leade, when wee can neither byte nor scratch! You may see, youthes, how age prouides for peace.

Sam. ⟨*aside to* EPI.⟩. How shal we doe to make him leaue his loue, for we neuer spake to her?

Dar. Let me alone.—⟨*To* SIR TOPHAS.⟩ Shee is a notable Witch, and hath turnde her maide *Bagoa* to an Aspen tree, for bewraying her secretes.

Top. I honor her for her cunning; for now when I am wearie of walking on two legges, what a pleasure may she doe mee to turne me to some goodly Asse, and help mee to foure.

Dar. Nay, then I must tell you the truth: her husband *Geron* is come home, who this fifty yeeres hath had her to wife.

Top. What doe I heare? Hath she an husbande? Goe to the Sexton, and tell him desire is deade, and will him to digge his graue. O heauens, an husbande? What death is agreeable to my fortune?

Sam. Be not desperate, and we will helpe you to find a young Ladie.

Top. I loue no grissels; they are so brittle, they will cracke like glasse, or so dainty, that if they bee touched they are straight of the fashion of waxe: *Animus maioribus instat.* I desire olde Matrons. What a sight would it be to embrace one whose hayre were as orient as the pearle! whose teeth shal be so pure a watchet, that they shall staine the truest Turkis! whose nose shall throwe more beames from it then the fierie Carbuncle! whose eyes shall be enuirond about with

---

67 channel house *Q*   68 lose *Dil. Bak.*   70 lose *Dil. Bak.*   too *Bl. rest*   S. D. [To SIR TOPHAS] *supplied Bak.*   84 is] has *Dil.*   87 Sexteene *Q*   wills *Dil.*   89 fortunes *Dil.*   95 it would be *Dil.* were] was *Dil.*   96 the *om. Dil.*

rednesse exceeding the deepest Corall! And whose lippes might compare with siluer for the palenesse! Such a one if you can help me to, I will by peece-meale curtoll my affections towardes *Dipsas*, and walke my swelling thoughts till they be cold.

Epi. Wisely prouided. How say you, my freendes, will you angle for my Maisters cause?

Sam. Most willingly.

Dar. If wee speede him not shortly, I will burne my cappe: we will serue him of the spades, and digge an old wife out of the graue that shall be answerable to his grauitie.

Top. Youthes, adiew: hee that bringeth mee first newes, shall possesse mine inheritance. ⟨*Exit* SIR TOPHAS.⟩

Dar. What, is thy Maister landed?

Epi. Know you not that my Maister is *Liber tenens*?

Sam. What's that?

Epi. A Free-holder. But I will after him.

Sam. And wee to heare what newes of *Endimion* for the conclusion. *Exeunt.*

SCÆNA TERTIA.—⟨*The same.*⟩

⟨*Enter*⟩ PANELION, ZONTES.

Pan. Who would haue thought that *Tellus* beeing so fayre by nature, so honourable by byrth, so wise by education, woulde haue entred into a mischiefe to the Gods so odious, to men so detestable, and to her freend so malicious.

Zon. If *Bagoa* had not bewraied it, howe then shoulde it haue come to light? But wee see that Golde and fayre words are of force to corrupt the strongest men; And therefore able to worke sillie women like waxe.

Pan. I maruell what *Cynthia* will determine in this cause.

Zon. I feare, as in all causes, heare of it in iustice, and then iudge of it in mercy: for howe can it be that shee that is vnwilling to punish her deadliest foes with dysgrace, will reuenge iniuries of her trayne with death.

Pan. That olde witch *Dipsas*, in a rage, hauing vnderstoode her practise to bee discouered, turned poore *Bagoa* to an Aspen tree.

---

101 curtall *Bl. F.*: curtail *Dil.*: curtal *Bak.*   S. D. [Exit SIR TOPHAS]
supplied *Bak.*   4 friends *Dil.*

But let vs make hast and bring *Tellus* before *Cynthia*, for she was comming out after vs.

Zon. Let vs goe. *Exeunt.*

⟨*Enter*⟩ CYNTHIA, SEMELE, FLOSCULA, DIPSAS, ENDIMION, EUMENIDES, ⟨GERON, PYTHAGORAS, GYPTES, *and* SIR TOPHAS⟩.

Cynth. Dipsas, thy yeeres are not so manie as thy vices; yet more in number then commonly nature dooth affoorde, or iustice shoulde permit. Hast thou almost these fiftie yeeres practised that detested wickednes of witchcraft? Wast thou so simple, as for to know the nature of Simples, of all creatures to be most sinfull?

Thou hast threatned to turne my course awry, and alter by thy damnable Arte the gouernment that I now possesse by the eternall Gods. But knowe thou *Dipsas*, and let all the Enchaunters knowe, that *Cynthia*, beeing placed for light on earth, is also protected by the powers of heauen. Breath out thou mayst wordes, gather thou mayst hearbes, finde out thou maist stones agreeable to thine Arte, yet of no force to appall my heart, in which courage is so rooted, and constant perswasion of the mercie of the Gods so grounded, that all thy witch-craft I esteeme as weake, as the world dooth thy case wretched.

Thys noble Gentleman *Geron*, once thy husband, but nowe thy mortall hate, didst thou procure to lyue in a Deserte, almost desperate. *Endimion*, the flowre of my Courte, and the hope of succeeding time, hast thou bewitched by Arte, before thou wouldest suffer him to florish by nature.

Dipsas. Madam, thinges past may be repented, not recalled: there is nothing so wicked that I haue not doone, nor any thing so wished for as death. Yet among al the things that I committed, there is nothing so much tormenteth my rented and ransackt thoughts, as that in the prime of my husbands youth I diuorced him by my deuillish Arte; for which, if to die might be amendes, I would not liue till to morrowe. If to liue and still be more miserable would better content him, I would wish of all creatures to be oldest and vgliest.

Geron. Dipsas, Thou hast made this difference betweene me and

S. D. [GERON ... SIR TOPHAS] *supplied Bak.* 22-3 Wast thou ... most sinfull? *so punctuated Q Bl. F.*: *Bak. om. comma at* simple: *Dil. punctuates* ... simple, ... simples? ... sinful! 25 that *om. Dil.* 27 a *bef.* light *Dil.* 47 the *before* oldest *Dil.*

Endimion, that being both young, thou hast caused mee to wake in melancholie, loosing the ioyes of my youth, and hym to sleepe, not remembring youth.

Cynth. Stay, heere commeth *Tellus*: we shall nowe knowe all.

⟨*Re-enter* PANELION *and* ZONTES *with* CORSITES *and* TELLUS.⟩

Cors. I woulde to *Cynthia* thou couldest make as good an excuse in truth, as to me thou hast done by wit.

Tellus. Truth shall be mine answere, and therefore I will not studie for an excuse.

Cynth. Is it possible *Tellus*, that so few yeres should harbor so many mischiefes? Thy swelling pride haue I borne, because it is a thing that beautie maketh blamelesse, which the more it exceedeth fairenes in measure, the more it stretcheth it selfe in disdaine. Thy deuises against *Corsites* I smyle at; for that wits, the sharper they are, the shrewder they are. But this vnacquainted and most vnnaturall practise with a vile Enchauntresse against so noble a Gentleman as *Endimion*, I abhorre as a thing most malicious, and will reuenge as a deede most monstrous.

And as for you, *Dipsas*, I will send you into the Deserte amongst wilde beastes, and try whether you can cast Lyons, Tygars, Bores, and Beares, into as deade a sleepe as you did *Endimion*; or turne them to trees, as you haue doone *Bagoa*. But tell me *Tellus*, what was the cause of this cruel part, farre vnfitting thy sexe, in which nothing should be but simplenes: and much disagreeing from thy face, in which nothing seemed to bee but softnes.

Tellus. Diuine *Cynthia*, by whom I receiue my life, and am content to ende it, I can neyther excuse my faulte without lying, nor confesse it without shame; Yet were it possible that in so heauenlie thoughts as yours, there coulde fall such earthly motions as mine, I would then hope, if not to bee pardoned without extreame punishment, yet to be heard without great maruell.

Cynth. Say on, *Tellus*: I cannot imagine anie thing that can colour such a crueltie.

Tellus. Endimion, that *Endimion* in the prime of his youth, so rauisht my hart with loue, that to obtaine my desires, I coulde not finde meanes, nor to resi⟨s⟩te them, reason.

s. d. [Re-enter &c.] *so first Bak.*: Enter CORSITES, TELLUS, PANELION, &c. *preceding eds.*   72 bee] me *Dil.*   80 a *om. Dil.*   83 resiste] resite *Q*: recite *Bl. mods.*

What was shee that fauoured not *Endimion*, being young, wise, honorable, and vertuous; besides, what mettall was shee made of (be shee mortall) that is not affected with the spice, nay, infected with the poyson of that (not to be expressed, yet alwaies to be felt) Loue? which breaketh the braines, and neuer brooseth the browe: consumeth the hart, and neuer toucheth the skinne: and maketh a deepe wounde to be felt, before any skarre at all be seene. My hart too tender to withstande such a diuine furie, yeelded to Loue —Madame I not without blushing confesse, yeelded to Loue.

Cynth. A strange effect of loue, to worke such an extreame hate. How say you *Endimion*, all this was for loue?

End. I say, Madam, then the Gods sende mee a womans hate.

Cynth. That were as bad, for then by contrarie you shoulde neuer sleepe. But on *Tellus*, let vs heare the ende.

Tellus. Feeling a continuall burning in all my bowels, and a bursting almost in euerie vaine, I could not smoother the inwarde fyre, but it must needes bee perceiued by the outwarde smoke; and by the flying abroade of diuers sparkes, diuers iudged of my scalding flames. *Endimion* as full of arte as witte, marking mine eyes, (in which hee might see almost his owne,) my sighes, by which he might euer heare his name sounded, aymed at my hart, in which he was assured his person was imprinted; and by questions wrunge out that, which was readie to burst out. When he sawe the depth of my affections, he sware, that mine in respect of his were as fumes to Aetna, vallies to Alpes, Ants to Eagles, and nothing could be compared to my beautie but his loue, and eternitie. Thus drawing a smooth shoe vppon a crooked foote, hee made mee beleeue, that (which all of our sexe willinglie acknowledge) I was beautifull. And to wonder (which indeede is a thing miraculous) that any of his sexe should be faithfull.

Cynth. Endimion, how will you cleere your selfe?

End. Madam, by mine owne accuser.

Cynth. Well, *Tellus*, proceede, but breeflie; least taking delight in vttering thy loue, thou offende vs with the length of it.

Tellus. I will, Madame, quickly make an ende of my loue & my

---

88 bruseth *Bl. F.*: bruiseth *Dil. Bak.* 90 wounde ... be seene] *on Mr. P. A. Daniel's suggestion I transpose* skarre ... seene, ... wounde ... felt *of all previous eds.* 91–2 Loue. Madame. ... to Loue. *Q Bl. F., F. placing an additional comma at* I: love, madam; I, not without blushing, confess, yielded to love. *Dil.*: love. Madam, I, not without blushing, confess I yielded to love. *Bak.* 104 euer] even *Dil.* he *om. F.*

tale. Finding continuall increase of my tormenting thoughts, and
that the enioying of my loue made deeper woundes then the entering
into it, I could finde no meanes to ease my griefe but to followe
Endimion, and continually to haue him in the obiect of mine eyes,
who had me slaue and subiect to his loue.

But in the moment that I feared his falsehoode, and fryed my
selfe most in myne affections, I founde, (ah griefe! euen then I lost
my selfe!) I founde him in most melancholie and desperate termes,
cursing hys starres, his state, the earth, the heauens, the world, and
all for the loue of—

Cynth. Of whom? *Tellus* speake boldly.

Tellus. Madame, I dare not vtter for feare to offende.

Cynth. Speake, I say; who dare take offence, if thou be commaunded by *Cynthia?*

Tellus. For the loue of *Cynthia.*

Cynth. For my loue *Tellus*, that were strange. *Endimion*, is it
true?

End. In all things, Madame, *Tellus* doth not speak false.

Cynth. What will this breede to in the ende? Well *Endimion,*
wee shall heare all.

Tellus. I seeing my hopes turnde to mishaps, and a setled dissembling towards me, and an vnmooueable desire to *Cynthia*, for-
getting both my selfe and my sexe, fell vnto this vnnaturall hate;
for knowing your vertues, *Cynthia*, to be immortall, I coulde not
haue an imagination to withdraw him. And finding mine owne
affections vnquenchable, I coulde not carrie the minde that any els
should possesse what I had pursued. For though in maiestie,
beautie, vertue, and dignitie, I alwaies humbled and yeelded my
selfe to *Cynthia*, yet in affections, I esteemed my selfe equall with
the Goddesses; & all other creatures, according to theyr states, with
my selfe. For stars to theyr bignes haue theyr lights, and the sunne
hath no more. And little pytchers when they can holde no more,
are as full as great vessels that runne ouer. Thus Madam, in all
trueth, haue I vttered the vnhappinesse of my loue, and the cause of
my hate; yeelding wholy to that diuine iudgement which neuer erred
for want of wisedom, or enuied for too much partiality.

Cynth. How say you, my Lords, to this matter? But what say
you, *Endimion*, hath *Tellus* tolde troth?

---

129 Of whom, Tellus? *Dil.*   136 Madame, Tellus *so punctuated Dil. Bak.*:
Madame. Tellus *Q Bl. F.*   141 into *Dil. Bak.*

End. Madame in all things, but in that shee saide I loued her, and swore to honour her.

Cynth. Was there such a time when as for my loue thou didst vowe thy selfe to death, and in respect of it loth'd thy life? speake *Endimion*, I will not reuenge it with hate.

End. The time was Madam, and is, and euer shall be, that I honoured your highnesse aboue all the world; but to stretch it so far as to call it loue, I neuer durst. There hath none pleased mine eye but *Cynthia*, none delighted mine eares but *Cynthia*, none possessed my hart but *Cynthia*. I haue forsaken all other fortunes to followe *Cynthia*, and heere I stande ready to die if it please *Cynthia*. Such a difference hath the Gods sette between our states, that all must be dutie, loyaltie, and reuerence; nothing (without it vouchsafe your highnes) be termed loue. My vnspotted thoughts, my languishing bodie, my discontented life, let them obtaine by princelie fauour that, which to challenge they must not presume, onelie wishing of impossibilities: with imagination of which, I will spende my spirits, and to my selfe that no creature may heare, softlie call it loue. And if any vrge to vtter what I whisper, then will I name it honor. From this sweet contēplation if I be not driuen, I shall liue of al men the most content, taking more pleasure in mine aged thoughts, then euer I did in my youthful actions.

Cynth. Endimion, this honorable respect of thine, shalbe christned loue in thee, & my reward for it fauor. Perseuer *Endimion* in louing me, & I account more strength in a true hart, then in a walled Cittie. I haue laboured to win all, and studie to keepe such as I haue wonne; but those that neither my fauour can mooue to continue constant, nor my offered benefits gette to bee faithfull, the Gods shal eyther reduce to trueth, or reuenge their trecheries with iustice. *Endimion* continue as thou hast begun, and thou shalt finde that *Cynthia* shyneth not on thee in vaine.

⟨*At this point* ENDIMION *finds means to part with his white beard and other signs of age.*⟩

End. Your Highnesse hath blessed mee, and your wordes haue againe restored my youth: mee thinkes I feele my ioyntes stronge, and these mouldy haires to molt, & all by your vertue *Cynthia*, into whose hands the Ballance that weigheth time & fortune are committed.

159 as *om. Dil.*   169-70 (without Your Highness vouchsafe it) *Bak.*   S. D. [At this point &c.] *inserted on suggestion of Dilke's note*   191 weigtheth *F.* are *so all, cf. Mid.* i. 1. 50, 92.

Cynth. What younge againe? then it is pittie to punish *Tellus*.

Tellus. Ah *Endimion*, now I know thee and aske pardon of thee: suffer mee still to wish thee well.

195 *End.* *Tellus*, *Cynthia* must commaund what she will.

Flosc. *Endimion*, I reioyce to see thee in thy former estate.

End. Good *Floscula*, to thee also am I in my former affections.

Eum. *Endimion*, the comfort of my life, howe am I rauished with a ioy matchlesse, sauing onelie the enioying of my mistrisse.

200 *Cynth.* *Endimion*, you must nowe tell who *Eumenides* shrineth for his Saint.

End. *Semele*, Madame.

Cynth. *Semele*, *Eumenides?* is it *Semele?* the very waspe of all women, whose tongue stingeth as much as an Adders tooth?

205 *Eum.* It is *Semele*, *Cynthia*: the possessing of whose loue, must onelie prolong my life.

Cynth. Nay sith *Endimion* is restored, wee will haue all parties pleased. *Semele*, are you content after so long triall of his faith, such rare secresie, such vnspotted loue, to take *Eumenides?* Why speake 210 you not? Not a word?

End. Silence, Madame, consents: that is most true.

Cynth. It is true *Endimion*. *Eumenides*, take *Semele*. Take her I say.

Eum. Humble thanks, Madame: now onely doe I begin to liue.

215 *Sem.* A harde choyce, Madame, either to be married if I say nothing, or to lose my tongue if I speake a word. Yet doe I rather choose to haue my tongue cut out, then my heart distempered: I will not haue him.

Cynth. Speakes the Parrat? shee shall nod heereafter with signes: 220 cut off her tongue, nay, her heade, that hauing a seruant of honourable birth, honest manners, and true loue, will not be perswaded.

Sem. He is no faithfull Louer, Madame, for then would he haue asked his Mistris.

Ger. Had he not beene faithfull, he had neuer seene into the 225 fountaine, and so lost his friend and Mistrisse.

Eum. Thine own thoughts, sweet *Semele*, witnesse against thy wordes, for what hast thou founde in my life but loue? and as yet, what haue I founde in my loue but bitternesse? Madame, pardon *Semele*, and let my tongue ransome hers.

203 Semele, Eumenides?] Semele? Eumenides *Dil.*

Cynth. Thy tongue, *Eumenides*? what! shouldst thou liue wanting a tongue to blaze the beautie of *Semele*? Well *Semele*, I will not commaund loue, for it cannot bee enforced: let me entreat it.

Sem. I am content your Highnesse shall command, for now only do I thinke *Eumenides* faithfull, that is willing to lose his tongue for my sake: yet loth, because it should doe me better seruice. Madame, I accept of *Eumenides*.

Cynth. I thanke you, *Semele*.

Eum. Ah, happie *Eumenides*, that hast a friend so faithfull, and a mistris so faire: with what sodaine mischiefe wil the Gods daunt this excesse of ioye? Sweet *Semele*, I liue or dye as thou wilt.

Cynth. What shall become of *Tellus*? *Tellus*, you know *Endimion* is vowed to a seruice, from which death cannot remooue him. *Corsites* casteth still a louely looke towards you: how say you, will you haue your *Corsites*, and so receiue pardon for all that is past?

Tellus. Madame, most willingly.

Cynth. But I cannot tel whether *Corsites* be agreed.

Cors. I, Madame! more happie to enioy *Tellus* then the Monarchie of the world.

Eum. Why she caused you to be pincht with Fairies.

Cors. I, but her fairenesse hath pinched my hart more deepelie.

Cynth. Well, enioy thy loue. But what haue you wrought in the Castle, *Tellus*?

Tellus. Onely the picture of *Endimion*.

Cynth. Then so much of *Endimion* as his picture commeth to, possesse and play withall.

Cors. Ah my sweete *Tellus*, my loue shal be as thy beautie is, matchlesse.

Cynth. Now it resteth, *Dipsas*, that if thou wilt forsweare that vile Arte of Enchaunting, *Geron* hath promised againe to receiue thee; otherwise, if thou be wedded to that wickednes, I must and will see it punished to the vttermost.

Dipsas. Madam, I renounce both substance and shadow of that most horrible and hatefull trade; vowing to the Gods continuall penaunce, and to your highnes obedience.

Cynth. Howe say you, *Geron*, will you admit her to your Wife?

Ger. I, with more ioy then I did the first day: for nothing could

---

230 what!] *no stop in old eds.*   238 and *om. Dil.*   240 this] their *Dil.*
243 looke] lookes *Q*   you:...you, will] you,...you? Will *Bl. F.*   *Q's only stop is comma at first* you   you³ *om. Q*

happen to make me happy, but onely her forsaking that leude and detestable course. *Dipsas*, I imbrace thee.

Dipsas. And I thee, *Geron*, to whom I will heereafter recite the cause of these my first follies.

Cynth. Well, *Endimion*, nothing resteth nowe but that we depart. Thou hast my fauour, *Tellus* her friend, *Eumenides* in Paradice with his *Semele*, *Geron* contented with *Dipsas*.

Top. Nay soft, I cannot handsomly goe to bed without *Bagoa*.

Cynth. Well *Syr Tophas*, it may bee there are more vertues in mee then my selfe knoweth of; for *Endimion* I awaked, and at my words he waxed young; I will trie whether I can turne this tree againe to thy true loue.

Top. Turne her to a true loue or false, so shee be a wench I care not.

Cynth. *Bagoa*, *Cynthia* putteth an end to thy harde fortunes; for being turnd to a tree for reuealing a truth, I will recouer thee againe, if in my power be the effect of truth.

⟨BAGOA *recovers human shape.*⟩

Top. *Bagoa?* a bots vpon thee!

Cynth. Come my Lordes let vs in. You, *Gyptes* and *Pythagoras*, if you can content your selues in our Court, to fall from vaine follies of Phylosophers to such vertues as are here practised, you shall be entertained according to your deserts; for *Cynthia* is no stepmother to strangers.

Pythag. I had rather in *Cynthias* Court spende tenne yeeres, then in Greece one houre.

Gyptes. And I chuse rather to liue by the sight of *Cynthia*, then by the possessing of all Egipt.

Cynth. Then follow.

Eum. We all attend.   *Exeunt.*

FINIS.

---

276 I awaked Endimion *B¹. mods.*   S. D. [BAGOA &c.] *Bak. supplied*
[BAGOA becomes herself again]   286 can] cannot *all previous eds.*

The Epilogue.

A Man walking abroade, the wind and Sunne stroue for soueraignty, the one with his blast, the other with his beames. The wind blew hard, the man wrapped his garmēt about him harder: it blustred more strongly, he then girt it fast to him: I cannot preuaile, sayd the wind. The Sunne casting her Christall beames, began 5 to warme the man: he vnlosed his gowne. Yet it shined brighter: he then put it off. I yeelde, sayd the winde, for if thou continue shining, he will also put off his cote.

Dread Soueraigne, the malicious that seeke to ouerthrowe vs with threats, do but stiffen our thoughts, and make them sturdier in 10 stormes: but if your Highnes vouchsafe with your fauorable beames to glaunce vpon vs, we shall not onlie stoope, but with all humilitie, lay both our handes and heartes at your Maiesties feete.

ON THE ALLEGORY IN ENDIMION

NEARLY sixty years ago the Rev. N. J. Halpin laid before the world of Shakespearean scholars a most ingenious essay, in the course of which Lyly's play of *Endimion* was interpreted for the first time as an elaborate transcript of certain events in contemporary Court history, centreing round the passion entertained by Queen Elizabeth for Robert Dudley, Earl of Leicester[1]. Mr. Halpin's theory, advanced with much modesty and supported by a close reference to historical documents, has won a wide though not a universal acceptance. Attention has recently been called to special defects in it, and an attempt made, which I cannot regard as successful, to amend it in some particulars[2]. A closer consideration of the essay reveals, indeed, inconsistencies so glaring between the conduct and situation of the characters in the play and those of the people with whom it is sought to identify them, as make it impossible to accept Halpin's view as more than partially and approximately correct; the fact being that his desire to find support in *Endimion* for his interpretation of Oberon's speech has largely disqualified him as the interpreter of the former. In the following pages I shall endeavour to point out the inconsistencies alluded to, and to suggest a general emendation of the theory. Some of my objections were anticipated, though but inadequately met, by Mr. Halpin himself: and if I am obliged to reject the majority of his identifications, and to alter considerably the general scope of the play, it must always be remembered that to his clever initiative belongs the credit of first opening this line of inquiry and of pointing us to authorities by whom it might be verified or corrected.

In the first place it is necessary to observe that the allegory in *Endimion* is twofold. The classical myth afforded Lyly the bare suggestion of Endymion's slumber and the kiss of Cynthia; but it is obvious that these were insufficient materials for a play. He has, therefore, woven round this beautiful picture a drama of Court life, which has no place nor counterpart at all in the classical myth; and has, further, combined with this a physical allegory, accepted even by those who refuse to recognize the political one—an allegory, namely, under the names of Tellus and

---

[1] *Oberon's Vision in the Midsummer's Night's Dream. Illustrated by a comparison with Lylie's Endymion.* By the Rev. N. J. Halpin ... London, 1843. 8º (*Shakespeare Society*).
[2] *Endymion ... edited by George P. Baker, New York,* 1894. The allegory is dealt with in Mr. Baker's full biographical Introduction, pp. xli–lxxiv.

The physical allegory.

Cynthia, of the Earth and the Moon as heavenly bodies. This latter, a link between Lyly's work and the still-surviving Moral-Plays, and an idea which finds other development in the treatment of the Seven Planets in *The Woman in The Moone*[1], may be briefly illustrated and dismissed. It appears most prominently in the first Act, where Lyly is breaking his ground, and the desire of Endimion to mislead Eumenides as to the real object of his passion harmonizes with some timidity on the author's part in introducing his real subject. Endimion's defence of Cynthia from the charge of inconstancy on account of her waxing and waning (pp. 22–3), is followed in the second scene (ll. 19-26) by the following protest of Tellus—

'Is not my beauty diuine, whose body is decked with faire flowers, and vaines are Vines, yeelding sweet liquor to the dullest spirits, whose eares are Corne, to bring strength, and whose heares are grasse, to bring abundance? Doth not Frankinsence and Myrrhe breath out of my nostrils, and all the sacrifice of the Gods breede in my bowels? Infinite are my creatures, without which neyther thou, nor Endimion, nor any could loue, or liue.'

To which Floscula, one of the 'faire flowers' who perhaps help to ' deck ' Tellus, rejoins

'Your grapes woulde be but drie huskes, your Corne but chaffe, and all your vertues vaine, were it not Cynthia that preserueth the one in the bud, and nourisheth the other in the blade, and by her influence both comforteth all things, and by her authoritie commaundeth all creatures.'

But, attention once won for Cynthia and Tellus as women, their planetary significance emerges only occasionally, with fainter and rarer recurrence, to the end of the piece: e.g. p. 31 'thy fish Cynthia in the floode Araris, which at thy waxing is as white as the driuen snowe, and at thy wayning, as blacke as deepest darknes'; p. 33 'Suffer me therefore to gaze on the Moone, at whom, were it not for thyselfe, I would die with wondering'; p. 38 'On yonder banke neuer grewe any thing but Lunary, and hereafter I will neuer haue any bed but that banke'; ib. l. 26 (Dipsas charming End.) 'thou mightest haue commanded Tellus, whome nowe in stead of a Mistris, thou shalt finde a tombe'; and lower, l. 38, she is obliged to gratify Tellus, 'for from her gather wee all our simples to maintaine our sorceries'; iii. 1. 28 'your highnes, on whose handes the compasse of the earth is at comaund, though not in possession'; p. 51 the inscription on the pillar; iv. 1. 66 'Cynthia beginneth to rise'; v. 3. 24 'Thou hast threatned to turne my course awry' &c.; ib. l. 75 (Tellus to Cynthia) 'were it possible that in so heauenlie thoughts as yours there coulde fall such earthly motions as mine' &c., and ib. l. 145 'though in maiestie, beautie, vertue, and dignitie, I alwaies humbled and yeelded my selfe to Cynthia, yet in affections I esteemed my selfe equall

---

[1] Steinhäuser, *John Lyly als Dramatiker*, p. 19.

with the Goddesses; & all other creatures, according to theyr states, with my selfe. For stars to theyr bignes haue theyr lights, and the sunne hath no more'; ib. l. 185 'Endimion, continue as thou hast begun, and thou shalt finde that Cynthia shyneth not on thee in vaine.'

The existence of a Court allegory has, we have said, not been universally allowed; chiefly, perhaps, because the story told about Cynthia and her courtiers may quite well be regarded by itself as a pretty imaginative effort, perfectly intelligible without any reference to actual facts. It is so regarded by, among others, Professor Morley, who says à propos of the Court allegory suggested—'This way of hobbling Pegasus with logs of prose has friends enough. I am not of their company.... There is here, and in many another play, a surface reference to Queen Elizabeth, which comes of readily identifying the queen's grace and wisdom with the wisdom from above. But throughout there is also set forth clearly an impersonal allegory that touches the relation of the mind of man to Earth and Heaven[1].' Imitating Professor Morley's liberality we may cheerfully admit that there is here a surface reference to these serener matters, especially perceptible to those who readily identify the Queen's grace and wisdom from above; and suggestion of such impersonal allegory is prominent in the first two scenes, in the contrast between the 'sweet nette,' the 'allurements of pleasure,' in which Tellus (i. 2. 41 sqq.) tries to entangle the hero, and the vague aspirations he acknowledges towards a beauty far above him. It also appears in the pinching of Tellus' lover, Corsites, by fairies; the punishment allotted in folklore to sensual affection. But it is my decided belief that such a mystical interpretation of the main purport of the play, though quite in harmony with the spirit of Spenser's non-dramatic work a few years later, and not out of harmony even with the temper of the earlier Moralities, is considerably removed from the temper at which the contemporary drama in the natural course of its development had arrived, and is quite foreign to the spirit which dominates the other writings of John Lyly. It is abundantly clear that Lyly had thoroughly learned the lesson of realism taught by the progress of the drama up to his time. The sure process of evolution, the gradual sifting of the stock of dramatic pieces in the competition for popular favour, was steadily eliminating abstract allegory such as Professor Morley here imagines. Lyly's allegory is, I believe, almost invariably a personal allegory, a representation, more or less veiled, modified, and partial, of contemporary men and women; and even if Nature, with her handmaids Concord and Discord, in *The Woman in the Moone*, constitute a momentary exception, yet the Seven Planets in that play are not so much representations of abstract virtues and vices, as Steinhäuser asserts[2], as of definite personalities in classical mythology with which Lyly chose to combine the mediaeval notions of astrological influence.

The Court allegory— arguments for such.

---

[1] *English Writers*, ix. 204, 208.   [2] *John Lyly als Dramatiker*, p. 19.

Lyly had, in fact, grasped the necessity of presenting the concrete: and if he is unwilling wholly to discard the allegory out of which the drama of his day had grown, and which still possessed a certain hold, especially on educated minds, yet he brings it into line with the advance of dramatic usage and adroitly makes it the engine of a yet closer realism. And it by no means follows, because the Court allegory can be easily detached and leave the play still interesting and complete, that no such allegory was intended. It is equally possible, and more probable, that the author had grasped the notion that—while allegory of any kind is hardly a fit *métier* for the drama, which moves and has its being in action and leaves the spectator little time for pondering recondite meanings, and no opportunity of turning back to verify a new suggestion by reference to an earlier scene—yet, if it be admitted on the stage at all, that allegory will be the best which lies in the play juxtaposed rather than inextricably intertwined, parallel yet apart, perceptible to the reader and to the acuter spectator, but not essential to the intelligence and enjoyment of the piece. The perception of this principle by writers for the stage had no doubt been quickened by the royal proclamation of May 16, 1559, declaring 'that no dramatic production should be licensed, which touched matters of religion or governance of the estate of the commonweal[1].' If such matter, then, were to be handled at all, the play must at least seem innocent of the intention; which it could hardly seem if the underlying matter or meaning were necessary to its comprehension, if it had no proper vitality apart from such. And so we need not conclude that there is no allegory, merely because the piece can stand without it. While the author would recognize it as his business to make his play independent of such aid, he was perfectly conscious how much its interest would be enhanced by this addition to its significance. And in *Endimion* at any rate, the idea of the presence of something more than meets the eye is quite irresistible. One asks, if the presentation and embroidery of the classical myth were the sole intention, what could have induced the author to drag so lovely a glimpse of ideality down to the vulgar level of Court intrigue? Whereas, if the presentation of the latter is the main intention, the introduction of the myth idealizes and purifies it. And would a free imagination have gone out of its way to construct the absolutely unessential Corsites, with his futile effort, his pinchings and slumberings, effecting nothing, leading to nothing, but readily intelligible if introduced as part of a dramatized series of real events, which so often bear this incoherent and purposeless character? The same question may be asked in regard to the ineffectual Floscula. The language, too, used by Endimion under Cynthia's dis-

---

[1] Collier's *Hist. of Dram. Poetry*, i. 174. The earliest Act of Parliament for the control and regulation of the stage, on which later statutes and proclamations like that of 1559 were based, was that of 1543, 34 and 35 Henry VIII, c. 1. (Id. i. 127.)

pleasure is far more appropriate to the Earl of Leicester, suddenly deprived of a favour long enjoyed, than to the shepherd of Latmos[1]: Cynthia's bearing towards Semele and Tellus admirably reflects the domineering temper of Henry VIII's daughter: and the dream of Endimion, described in the fifth Act (pp. 66-7), would be altogether pointless and impertinent unless addressed *avec intention* to an actual Cynthia seated as spectator of the piece. Admit the dream as allegorical, and the rest must become wholly or partly so: moreover, the words in the Prologue about 'applying pastimes' are obviously the excuse which is its own accuser, an attitude exchanged in the Epilogue for one of frank acknowledgement and deprecation of a possible displeasure on the Queen's part[2]. Besides all this, we have already seen reason to suspect allegorical intention in *Sapho and Phao*, and at least a personification of Elizabeth in *Gallathea* and *Loves Metamorphosis* (supposing the latter to precede *Endimion*): it would be natural now to find him launching out on a more elaborate effort in the same direction, one that might serve at once as his acknowledgement for his recent appointment as Court dramatist, and as the best vindication of his claims to it.

But granting, as we must, the presence of a Court allegory, there are one or two things to be premised concerning it, one or two limitations to the precision we might expect to find. In the first place, Lyly's own opportunities for ascertaining the facts, if they equalled, would not exactly tally with those of the ingenious critic of to-day, with the stores of information from the most private sources which the research and editing of the nineteenth century have placed at his disposal. Lyly was simply a clever young man in a subordinate position about the Court, whose wit, address, and literary achievement would make him a natural recipient for such facts or gossip as were current, and whose special connexion with Oxford or Burleigh, or perhaps Leicester himself, would

Limitations to the closeness of the allegory.

---

[1] There is a noticeable resemblance between the soliloquy Act ii. sc. I, p. 31 and the language of a letter written by Leicester to Burleigh, about the Queen's displeasure, under date Nov. 12, 1579—a coincidence probably, though it is by no means impossible that Lyly, in his capacity as secretary to Burleigh's son-in-law Oxford, had actually read, or heard read, this letter, and in any case it only repeated the complaints with which Leicester had already filled the Court. It is quoted by Mr. Baker (*Endymion*, p. xlvii) from Wright's *Queen Elizabeth and Her Times*, ii. 103. E. g. *Endim*. 'Haue I not crept to those on whom I might haue troden, onelie because thou didst shine vpon them? Haue not iniuries beene sweet to mee, if thou vouchsafedst I should beare them? Haue I not spent my golden yeeres in hopes, waxing old with wishing, yet wishing nothing but thy loue?'—*Leic*. 'I must confess it greveth me not a lyttle, having so faythfully, carefully, and chargeably served her Majesty this twenty yeres, as I have done ... I wyll be found faythfull and just to her Majesty, no wrongs, dishonors, or other indygnites offered me, shall alter my dewtyfull affection towards her ... So may I say, I have lost both youth, liberty, and all my fortune reposed in her; and, my Lord, by that tyme I have made an even reckoning with the world, your Lordship wyll not give me much for the remainder of my twenty yeres' service,' &c.

[2] Baker's *Endymion*, pp. xlii, xliii.

afford him some special opportunities. In the second place, his allegory was conditioned by the form in which it was presented. The events of real life are rarely either so symmetrical or so ideal in their character as to be capable of presentation by art without selection or change of some sort; and the necessities of the stage may have compelled Lyly to falsify even the limited knowledge that he possessed. Another motive for such falsification would lie in the danger of being too direct: while indicating clearly his general intent, he must leave himself, and his originals, loopholes of escape from too close an identification. And, fourthly, seeing that the matters dealt with extended over a large portion of the reign, he could hardly treat them dramatically without some compression and recombination; so that while certain features of his story seem to point to one date, certain others are perhaps rather indicative of another, and the whole work cannot safely be regarded as other than a loose rendering of general facts with more detailed reference here and there. Dramatic necessity or the State censorship may compel him to alter times and places, to marry people who were not really married, or not to those whom they are represented as marrying, and even to combine in one character features of two persons holding successively the same position.

Nevertheless, if the claim of any particular interpretation is to be supported at all, there must be a general correspondence shown between the main facts of the drama and the main facts of the history, a general consonance between the characters and situations of the personages with those of their models. My complaint against many of Mr. Halpin's identifications is that they fail to satisfy this essential of a general correspondence. He divides the identified characters according to three degrees of probability; while for the nine minor parts not here enumerated he suggests no originals, though he considers that there probably were such for Pythagoras and Gyptes. None of these nine minor characters, however, at all affect the plot, and so may safely be ignored without damage to the general theory upheld about the rest. His cast is as follows:

Halpin's interpretation.

Highly Probable.

Endymion (in love with Cynthia, and beloved by Tellus and Floscula)	the Earl of Leicester.
Cynthia	Queen Elizabeth.
Tellus (in love with Endymion's 'person')	Lady Douglas Howard, Countess of Sheffield. iv. 3. p. 60.
Floscula (in love with Endymion's 'virtues')	Lady Lettice Knollys, Countess of Essex.
Corsites (married to Tellus) .	Sir Edward Stafford.
Eumenides (in love with Semele)	the Earl of Sussex.

Probable.

Semele	Lady Frances Sidney.
Dipsas (an old mischief-making crone) }	the Countess of Shrewsbury.
Geron (her husband) . . .	the Earl of Shrewsbury.

Not Improbable.

Sir Tophas (a pedantic 'militarist') }	Stephen Gosson, author of 'The Schoole of Abuse.'

In Halpin's view the subject of the play is the general relations of Elizabeth with her favourite Leicester, and particularly that temporary disgrace of Leicester brought about by the revelation by M. Simier, envoy of the Duke of Anjou, in late July or August, 1579, of Leicester's marriage with Essex's widow in the previous year; a revelation which led Leicester's previous (his second) wife, Lady Sheffield (Tellus), to claim her own marital rights in him, and caused Elizabeth to order him to confine himself to the palace at Greenwich (the lunary-bank), and even to think of committing him to the Tower (the 'darke Caue' of iv. 3. 111); a course from which she was, however, dissuaded by the generous remonstrance of Leicester's great enemy, the Earl of Sussex (Eumenides): while Corsites, Tellus' gaoler, whom she finally marries, represents Sir Edward Stafford, on whom Leicester finally persuaded Lady Sheffield to bestow her hand[1].

Against this view of Halpin, Mr. Baker has urged (1) that it errs in attempting to identify too many of the characters. There is no necessity to suppose that every character in the piece had a definite original (p. xliv); (2) that it confuses Leicester's two marriages, that with Lady Sheffield in 1573, and that with Lettice Countess of Essex in 1578. If Leicester's imprisonment in 1579 was caused by the revelation of his marriage to Lady Essex, surely she, and not Lady Sheffield, is the proper original for Tellus, Cynthia's rival (p. xlix). Accordingly Mr. Baker substitutes Lettice as Tellus for Lady Sheffield, regarding Endimion's statement that Tellus has been but a cloak for his affection for Cynthia[2], as Leicester's palliating version to the Queen of his recent marriage (p. l), and Tellus' 'allurements of pleasure' and employment of Dipsas as Leicester's way of saying that he was 'bewitched by Lettice's charms' (p. lii); while Elizabeth's subsequent displeasure with Leicester's new wife, who was for years forbidden to appear at Court, is represented by Tellus' exile to the castle in the desert (p. lvi). Further, Mr. Baker regards Endimion's treatment by Dipsas as a loose rendering of Simier's

Baker's changes.

---

[1] Camden's *Annals of Elizabeth*, 1579 (*Hist. of England*, 3 vols. fol. 1706, ii. p. 471).
[2] Act ii. sc. 1. 22-5.

information to the Queen (p. liv), his sleep on the lunary-bank (like Halpin) as meaning generally the royal disfavour, and, specifically, Leicester's confinement (p. lv), and Cynthia's concern for Endimion's fate as the allegorical way of expressing the paroxysm of anger with which Elizabeth received Simier's news, 'though naturally, in the allegory, gratitude for faithful service, not jealousy, is the cause of the concern' (p. lvi)[1]. Lastly, he accepts Halpin's highly improbable identification of Sussex with Eumenides (p. lvii), and notes (p. lxviii) that the references to Corsites' strength seem to point to some well-known figure; but for the rest of the characters, for Geron, Dipsas, Bagoa, Floscula, Semele, and Sir Tophas, he attempts no identification at all.

While Mr. Baker's stricture on Halpin's confusion of the incidents of the two marriages is a fairly just one [2], the reader will scarcely feel that the interpretation he substitutes is either very different or at all more plausible; and Professor Ward's easy acceptance of it fills one with surprise [3]. Mr. Baker's theory is bound up with a belief in a connexion between Leicester and Lyly, and a date for the play, as early as 1579, between the issue of the First and Second Parts of *Euphues*; an opinion for which we cannot find that he has any but the most illusory grounds, though he supports it with considerable ingenuity and a wide research. The question of date has already been discussed in the Prolegomena to the play. It depends largely, of course, on the view taken of the allegory. Confining ourselves here to the latter, we would point out that the numerous inconsistencies into which Mr. Halpin has fallen are probably due to too narrow a view taken at the outset of the general subject of the play, a view imposed on him no doubt by the special theory of Oberon's speech which he was advocating. In interpreting the allegory of *Endimion* it is surely best to proceed inductively. To attach ourselves at an early stage to a particular theory and to deduce our identifications from that, is far less safe a method than that of keeping the question of subject open till the task of identification is far advanced. And in the latter we should form no hasty conclusion from a single point of resemblance, but, keeping carefully before us all the conditions of a part, should cast about for that historical personage who fulfils the most, or

---

[1] Mr. Baker at this point refers us back to his p. xxxiv, where he quotes La Ferrière's description (*Les Projets de Mariage de la Reine Elisabeth*, pp. 220-1), 'À cette révélation inattendue, entrant dans une de ses colères de lionne, elle se roula par terre, injuriant tous ceux qui l'approchèrent, et refusant de manger.' Comparing this burst of mad rage with the dignified investigation by Cynthia in Act iii. sc. 1, we must confess that, if Mr. Baker's interpretation is correct, Lyly has little to learn in the art of discreet translation of his facts.

[2] It is just only as regards the difficulty caused in selecting a single original for the part of Tellus. In the facts connected with Simier's revelation of 1579, as related by Halpin, both women were intimately concerned; Lady Sheffield taking the more active part, while Lady Essex was perhaps, though passively, the more important.

[3] *English Dramatic Literature* (ed. 1899), i. ch. 3, pp. 289-92.

fulfils them best. Proceeding on this method, let us defer for the present any statement of subject, and let us ascertain the leading facts about the chief characters in the play, and see how far Halpin's choice of representatives corresponds with these.

To begin with, there can hardly be a doubt of the correctness of his identification of Endimion and Cynthia, an admission which is tantamount to an acknowledgement that he is at least partly right in supposing the play to be a complimentary version of the relations of Leicester with the Queen. A certainty almost as great attaches, in our judgement, to his choice of originals for Geron and Dipsas in the Earl and Countess of Shrewsbury, though he himself attaches to these only a secondary degree of probability. It is in the other parts, those of Tellus, Corsites, and Eumenides, that his selections, which he marks as 'highly probable,' seem so singularly unsatisfying; while we cannot feel that there is very much to recommend his representatives for the only other three for which he suggests any, for Floscula, Semele, and Sir Tophas. Let us examine them in turn.

Far the most important of the six, and technically at least the protagonist of the plot[1], is Tellus. The leading features about her are that she is the object of general admiration and courtship[2]; that she is placed in elaborate general opposition to Cynthia[3]; that she has been compelled by Endimion's desertion to *abandon* her hope of marrying him; that she plots revenge against him, a revenge associated (in the dream of Endimion) with dark threatenings of Cynthia herself[4]; that she is imprisoned by Cynthia's order, but still carries on her intrigues[5]; that on the discovery of her designs she is treated with great leniency, and finally married to her gaoler. Now not one of these features can

Tellus.

[1] Steinhäuser's *John Lyly als Dramatiker*, p. 33: 'Wie in "Sapho," so ist auch in "Endimion" der Titelheld nicht der eigentliche Träger der Handlung, sondern Tellus, die von Endimion verschmähte Geliebte ... Das Bewusstsein, in ihren heiligsten Gefühlen gekränkt zu sein, treibt Tellus zu einer verhängnissvollen That ... Der Höhepunkt der Handlung ist damit erreicht. Die Gegenspieler treten in Gestalt von Cynthia und Eumenides in die Handlung ein.'

[2] In ii. 3, p. 38, Endimion admits that she is 'faire,' 'wise,' and 'honourable,' and adds, 'Was she not fortunate whome so many followed?': while in iv. 1, p. 52, Tellus says, 'Endimion excepted, what is he that is not enamourd of my beautie?' and on p. 54 she defends women's shifts to ward off lovers, 'otherwise we should be cumbred with importunities, oathes, sighes, letters, and all implements of loue.'

[3] P. 24 she indignantly compares herself with Cynthia, while Floscula gently urges her inferiority. P. 30 'Endimion is he that hath my heart; and Cynthia, too too faire Cynthia ... is the Ladie that hee delights in.' P. 38 Endimion elaborately contrasts them. P. 75 Tellus, in Cynthia's presence, again institutes a comparison between herself and Cynthia, though here she is more inclined to admit the latter's superiority.

[4] See v. 1, pp. 66–7, and compare with the Dumb Show between the Second and Third Acts.

[5] Cynthia (pp. 40–1) specially notes her spiteful and presumptuous speeches, and in iv. 3. 115 remarks 'Howe say you, my Lordes, is not Tellus *alwaies* practising of some deceites?'

be claimed for either Lady Sheffield or Lady Essex: or, if Tellus' plot against Endimion might by straining be made to correspond to Lady Sheffield's claim of her marital rights, yet she was certainly not imprisoned; and if Tellus' exile to the castle might represent the disfavour shown to Lady Essex (after her *marriage*), yet the quiescent part played by Lettice is very ill represented by this turbulent and intriguing character; and neither lady could for a moment claim to stand in the position of marked opposition to and competition with the Queen which Tellus occupies[1]. It is the more remarkable that Halpin, with Warburton's interpretation of Oberon's speech before him, did not realize that there is one personage, and only one, to whom the features of Tellus' part, as detailed above, are really applicable. That personage is Mary Queen of Scots. Mary's personal beauty and the romantic passions she inspired need no illustration. Throughout the reign, until her condemnation on October 25, 1586, she figures as Elizabeth's great rival and opponent; and the Queen's throne and even life were continually in danger from the Catholic plots of which she was the centre. With these machinations Tellus is connected in the play through the dream of Endimion[2]. A project of marriage between the Queen of Scots and Leicester actually occupied the attention of Elizabeth and her government during the years 1563-5, a plan entertained by Mary at first with reluctance, and pressed by Elizabeth with diminishing warmth as Mary's willingness increased[3]. The serious entertainment of this design, and the fact that it was not carried out, are quite sufficient for Lyly's purpose, and qualify Mary for the part of Tellus' original far better than either of the two ladies hitherto proposed. If Mary cannot be credited with any special plots against Leicester, no more can Lady Essex, and hardly, Lady Sheffield. Much, too, may have passed in the way of political intrigue of which no trace remains to-day; and, in any case, Mary is in natural opposition to Leicester as a prominent member of Elizabeth's government[4]. The leniency of Tellus' treatment is abundantly reflected in that actually shown to Mary by Elizabeth, who, after the full discovery of Norfolk's conspiracy in 1572, refused to comply with the petition of Parliament that she should be proceeded against by Bill of Attainder, pleading that 'she could not put to death the bird that had flown to her for succour from the hawk[5],' and allowed her to continue in the custody of the

---

[1] It is further to be remarked, as against Halpin, that there is a singular impropriety in making Tellus (Lady Sheffield) confide her plots against Endimion to Floscula (her rival, Lady Essex); and that Cynthia's own kindly attitude to Floscula, pp. 60, 63, is quite inconsistent with the jealous anger Elizabeth cherished against Lady Essex as late as 1586. See Froude's *History of England*, xii. 170.

[2] Act v. sc. 1, pp. 66-7.

[3] See Froude's *History*, vii. chs. 41, 43, 44 (pp. 53, 183, 185, 269, 311, pop. ed.).

[4] See, too, what is said about the intrigue against Endimion below, pp. 98, 102.

[5] Froude, x. ch. 57, pp. 83-91 (pop. ed.). Again, after Parry's confession in

Catholic Earl of Shrewsbury. She was in fact looked upon at this time (1573 and 1574) as heir to the crown, and had, says Froude, 'all the enjoyments of English country life¹.' The comparative laxity of Shrewsbury's guardianship, which in 1569 had induced the Queen to associate the Earl of Huntingdon temporarily with him in the charge of her², is in exact accord with the indulgence shown to Tellus by Corsites, whose passion for his captive has also its counterpart in the slanders circulated at Court by Shrewsbury's Countess as to his improper intimacy with Mary³. The single point that makes against Tellus as Mary is her final marriage with her gaoler; but concluding marriages are a necessity of comedy, and can hardly be pleaded in bar of my interpretation. A further little sign of Tellus' rank and importance is that she is addressed by Floscula, p. 23, as 'Madame,' a title of respect elsewhere reserved, both in *Endimion* and *Sapho*, for the Queen herself⁴.

There could scarcely be stronger evidence of error in Halpin's choice of Lady Sheffield for Tellus, than that it leads him to that of Sir Edward Stafford for Corsites. Corsites is a soldier, whose great physical strength⁵, 'tough and unsmoothed nature⁶,' and honest simplicity of character⁷, are variously dwelt upon. Appointed gaoler of Tellus, his passion for her leads him to relax her confinement; and her blandishments induce him further to undertake an office vaguely hostile to Endimion, but foredoomed, as she knows, to failure. He is attacked and punished by fairies, but united in the end to Tellus. Sir Edward Stafford satisfies no single one of these conditions, saving that of marriage with Tellus⁸,

Corsites.

Feb. 1585 of his plot to assassinate Elizabeth with the design of placing Mary on the throne, a motion was made in Parliament to revive the proceedings against her which had been dropped in 1572, but was again damped by Elizabeth, who in the speech from the throne at the close of the session defended her indulgent policy (Id. xi. 544-6). This recent instance of the Queen's generosity, or hesitation, is, I believe, alluded to by Panelion and Zontes (v. 3, p. 71), who discuss the treatment of Tellus as though it were a parallel, and not the identical case:—' *Pan*. I maruell what Cynthia will determine in this cause? *Zon*. I feare, as in all causes, heare of it in iustice, and then iudge of it in mercy: for howe can it be that shee that is vnwilling to punish her deadliest foes with disgrace, will reuenge iniuries of her trayne with death?'

¹ *History*, xi. 70.
² Froude, viii. 433, 480, 490, &c., and article 'Hastings, Henry, 3rd Earl of Huntingdon,' in *Dict. Nat. Biog*.
³ Camden's *Elizabeth*, 1582. In a letter to Walsingham, dated Oct. 18, 1582, Shrewsbury writes, 'Among the rest of my false accusations, your Honour knoweth that I have been touched with some undutiful respects touching the Queen of Scots, but I am very well able to prove she hath shewed herself an enemy to me, and to my fortune; and that I trust will sufficiently clear me.' (Lodge's *Illustrations*, ii. 239 : see also pp. 243, 275.)
⁴ In view of Mary's position in 1585, ii. 3. 15-6 cannot be urged against this.
⁵ Act iv. sc. 3. 13, 135.   ⁶ P. 61.   ⁷ P. 54.
⁸ By way of strengthening his case Halpin suggests (*Oberon's Vision*, p. 63) that Lady Sheffield *may* have been committed to Stafford's custody *by Leicester* previously, for better concealment of her marriage with himself, but offers no grounds for such a supposition save Elizabeth's general dislike of marriages made without her consent. With regard to her union with Stafford, whose second wife

a match probably due, as suggested above, to the necessity of pairing the characters of the comedy. Stafford was not a soldier but a diplomatist (a character in which a rugged honesty and simplicity are not as a rule leading constituents), who conducted the negotiations about the Anjou match in 1579–82, and in 1583 was appointed resident ambassador to France, where he remained till the end of 1590[1]. A far more suitable original for Corsites is found in the stern and rigidly honest Sir Amyas Paulet, a zealous Puritan and favourer of the Huguenots, who, after a term as governor of Jersey, occupied the post of French ambassador from 1576–9. His stern demeanour was displeasing to Leicester, but on Walsingham's suggestion he was appointed to the custody of the Queen of Scots, an office which he assumed on April 17, 1585, and executed with such close watchfulness and unswerving fidelity as won him due reward after Mary's death [2]. The Queen of Scots made a vain endeavour to corrupt his honesty, hinting that if ever she came to the throne 'he might have another manner of assurance of that island than ever was given to an English subject[3]'; but Paulet told her plainly that he was not to be seduced from his allegiance. This incident, which affords a parallel for Tellus' deceptive promises to Corsites (iv. 1. p. 54), is related by Froude as occurring at the commencement of Paulet's appointment in 1585. Among other details of his guardianship of Mary, Froude relates that when she wished her apartments, which looked upon the castle court, changed to others commanding a view of the open country, Paulet refused, from a conviction that she would use the opportunity thus afforded to exchange signals with some of the messengers ever on the watch to carry communications to her friends [4]. This detail is probably the suggestion of Tellus' remark—'I maruell Corsites giueth me so much libertie: all the world knowing his charge to bee so high, and his nature to bee most straunge; who hath so ill intreated Ladies of great honour, that he hath not suffered them to *look out of windowes*, much lesse to walke abrode': and her further remark at the end of the scene, 'I will in, and laugh with *the other Ladies* at Corsites sweating,' probably has reference to the mischievous enjoyment by Mary and her train of their continual efforts to elude her gaoler's vigilance [5].

she was, Halpin shows (p. 39) that Sussex could not have pleaded on Leicester's behalf that 'no man was to be troubled for a lawful marriage' (i.e. to Lettice), had not Lady Sheffield previously withdrawn her claim to be Leicester's wife. On the authority of Dugdale he tells us that she was induced to do so at an interview with Leicester 'in the close arbour of the Queen's garden at Greenwich,' on consideration of receiving from Leicester £700 a year; and that she probably married Stafford about this time, i.e. autumn of 1579.

[1] *Dict. of Nat. Biog.*, art. 'Stafford, Sir Edward.'
[2] *Dict. of Nat. Biog.*, art. ' Paulet, Sir Amyas.'
[3] Froude, xi. ch. 67, p. 576. The attempt was made on the suggestion of Morgan, Mary's agent in Paris.
[4] Ibid., p. 579.
[5] Act iv. sc. 1, pp. 52, 54. The anxious attention of Parliament and the nation,

CORSITES A COMBINATION

Of course, however, I have to admit that Sir Amyas' severity is an ill representative of Corsites' indulgence and amorous weakness for his captive. Of this inconsistency I offer the following defence. In the first place, if my identification of Tellus with Mary be correct, it was desirable for Lyly to give us ocular illustration of the fatal power of her seductions and that universal attraction of which Tellus boasts[1]: and if he has to some extent falsified facts in doing so, the falsification stops with itself, and leaves the issue quite untouched. Tellus knows, and explicitly forewarns us, that Corsites' attempt on Endimion will be void of effect; and, if we must acknowledge here some defect of dramatic construction, the episode at least serves the purpose of introducing the ballet of Fairies, a welcome *divertissement* which Lyly has employed before in *Gallathea*[2], without, however, in that case taking the necessary trouble to give them a proper connexion with the action. But I believe the episode may be shown to have its proper place in the allegory itself, if we remember the compression and recombination of events imposed on the historic, still more perhaps on the allegorical, dramatist. Tellus (Mary) is the real centre of the plot. The extraordinary indulgence of Elizabeth's treatment of her, the absence of anything like undue severity or oppression in her confinement, this was what was filling men's minds in 1585, this is the point on which the Court dramatist could without flattery insist. Now much in Corsites that is hardly true of Sir Amyas Paulet is abundantly true of Mary's former gaoler, the Earl of Shrewsbury, as I indicated above when dealing directly with Tellus[3]. Shrewsbury, her custodian from 1569 to August, 1584, though on the whole faithful to Elizabeth, seems not to have been quite unsusceptible to Mary's charms, or at least to her influence. In April, 1571, at the time of Norfolk's conspiracy, Ridolfi actually reported to Alva that Shrewsbury was privy to the plot to rescue Mary and place her upon the throne, and had promised to protect her until the Scotch army came to the rescue[4]. This was probably an exaggeration; at any rate, from the time of the discovery of the conspiracy in October, 1571, there was no wavering in Shrewsbury's loyalty to Elizabeth, and his surveillance over Mary became much more strict[5]. But by-and-by when it was ascertained that Elizabeth would not, perhaps dared not, adopt those extreme measures against her which Parliament desired, the Queen of Scots again became a centre of influence and intrigue; and Shrewsbury, who favoured the idea of her succession, did not wholly escape implication. It was said that he had promised

As Tellus' gaoler, he combines Shrewsbury and Paulet.

concentrated at this time (1585) upon Mary and her schemes, would ensure such details being promptly reported and repeated at Court, and the allusions in the play would count as very palpable hits. The apparent dissociation of the first from Tellus herself is a transparent device to secure the author, like the speech of Zontes quoted in note 5 on p. 90 above.
[1] Act iv. sc. 1, p. 52.   [2] Act ii. sc. 3. 5.   [3] P. 91, and note 3.
[4] Froude, x. 203: cf. Act iv. sc. 1. 36.   [5] Id., x. 295–6.

her that, on the Queen's death, he would himself place the crown upon her head[1]. At any rate he allowed himself to be drawn by Mary and his Countess into a scheme by which Mary's brother-in-law, Lord Charles Stuart, was secretly married to Elizabeth Cavendish, Lady Shrewsbury's daughter by a former husband; a marriage which, as strengthening Mary's family connexion in England, gave the direst offence to Elizabeth, causing her to commit Lady Lennox (the bridegroom's mother, and a party to the plot) to the Tower, and bringing down on Shrewsbury a severe rebuke, under which he tried to excuse himself by laying the blame upon his wife. Here we have an adequate original for Corsites' temporary and partial disloyalty to Cynthia under Tellus' promptings; and even some connexion with Endimion is supplied in that bad entertainment of Leicester at Chatsworth and Buxton, when on a sanatory visit to the baths, of which Elizabeth complained in a sarcastic letter to the Shrewsburies dated June 4, 1577[2]. At a later period too, 1582-4, we get those distinct slanders about the intimacy between Shrewsbury and Mary which his Countess, who was at enmity with him from 1580 to 1586, circulated about the Court, and which Lyly probably intends to represent by the Fairies' pinches, from whose effects he may recover by the use of lunary[3], i.e. by direct appeal to Elizabeth. It is then, as I believe, rather the relations between Mary and her former gaoler that Lyly has in mind in this amorous weakness of Corsites. In Tellus' gaoler he attempts to embody the general treatment of Mary in her captivity; though in his native character and in certain allusions Corsites represents exclusively her gaoler at the time of writing, Sir Amyas Paulet. Such transference assists the partial mystification which has to be maintained; and leaves Lyly free to represent in Geron and Dipsas the relations between Shrewsbury and his Countess, and the royal displeasure under which the former especially rested.

Eumenides.   But of all Halpin's identifications that of Sussex with Eumenides is probably the one that will least commend itself to the student. The leading features of the character are that he is the chivalrous and devoted friend of Endimion, the chivalrous and devoted lover of Semele; that his unselfish desire to aid his friend entails on him a long absence from the Court, and that a noble sacrifice of his love to friendship is instrumental in bringing about Endimion's restoration; that he offers his tongue to ransom Semele's, and finally obtains his mistress' hand. To represent all this chivalrous devotion Halpin selects Leicester's most bitter opponent, Sussex, on the sole ground that, in the affair of Simier's revelation, which he regards as the main subject of the play, Sussex with no less justice

[1] Froude, xi. 71.
[2] Froude gives this letter as if it were the sequel or conclusion of this secret marriage plotted between Mary, Lady Lennox, and the Shrewsburies, vol. x. ch. 60, pp. 398–402 (pop. ed.).
[3] Act iv. sc. 3, p. 62.

than generosity pleaded against too harsh a treatment of the favourite[1]. But Eumenides is obviously young, as his talk with Geron implies; while Sussex, born '1526?'[2], died at the age of say fifty-five in 1583, an additional argument against him, if my date (1585) for the play be correct. There is one name that rises instinctively to the lips when acts that are lovely and noble and of good report are mentioned—one that still falls upon the ear like refreshing music in this hard heart-wearying age of brass, even as its bearer softens and shames with his mild lustre the coarser fames and gaudier heroics of that iron time—the name of

'that pensive Hesper light
O'er Chivalry's departed sun,'

Sir Philip Sidney. Can the relations of Eumenides in the play be made to square with him? It would seem that he particularly suits them. Supposing Endimion's slumber and estrangement from Cynthia to represent the disfavour of Leicester during his opposition to the Anjou match, we find that Leicester's policy was fully endorsed by his nephew Sidney, who ventured early in 1580 his well-known letter to the Queen against the match, and as a consequence was compelled to spend seven months of that year in retirement at Wilton, his return to Court coinciding with Leicester's restoration to favour[3]. Again towards the end of 1584 Sidney wrote a formal *Defence of Leicester* in answer to the attack by the Jesuit, Parsons, entitled *Leicester's Commonwealth*; and though the *Defence* was not printed before 1746, its contents were probably well known at Court. At the very time when *Endimion* was probably produced (Feb. 2, 1586) Sidney is serving with his uncle in the Netherlands, having left England as governor of Flushing on November 16. Sidney thus affords a sufficiently close parallel for Eumenides' championship of his friend and exile from Court on that account. The question of his postponement of love to friendship brings us to Semele.

Halpin identifies her with Frances Sidney, Sir Philip's cousin; a selection made, apparently, because Frances was the second wife of Sussex, whom he has already selected for Eumenides, though he tries to strengthen it by the suggestion that Semele's petulance with Endimion[4] may represent

Semele.

---

[1] Mr. Baker argues in Halpin's support that—'The two men were not friends, but they were fellow-councillors' (*Endymion*, p. lvii); reasoning which reminds us of that by which he essays to prove an early connexion between Leicester and Lyly, namely, that Lyly was an undergraduate of the university of which Leicester was Chancellor, that he was still at Oxford at the date of the Kenilworth festivities (1575), and that Leicester was the general patron of men of wit! (pp. xxxv, lxxiii).
[2] *Dict. Nat. Biog.*, art. 'Radcliffe, Thos., 3rd Earl of Sussex.'
[3] 'In the course of the summer (1580) Leicester left his retirement and returned to Court. It was understood that though still not liking the French match, he would in future offer no opposition to the queen's wishes; and on these terms he induced Philip also to make his peace with her Majesty. We find him [Sidney], accordingly, again in London before the autumn.' (*English Men of Letters—Sidney*, by J. A. Symonds, p 97.)
[4] Act iii. 1, p. 40, iv. 3, p. 60 and *Oberon's Vision*, p. 65.

Frances' annoyance at Leicester's marriage as likely to deprive Sir Philip of his succession to Leicester's property. As with Tellus and Corsites, Halpin's interpretation here owns a needless constraint in the pairing of Semele and Eumenides at the end; a match which, as in that case, may be regarded as merely a stage-necessity. My own suggestion for Semele, who is distinguished in the play by her long coldness to her lover, by her waspish tongue and the displeasure it brings upon her, is Philip's flame, Lady Penelope Devereux, the daughter of the Earl of Essex, who became Lady Rich in 1581, with the result, apparently, of increasing Philip's passion [1]. I do not know whether waspishness can correctly be attributed to Stella: beauty and coquetry certainly can; and a match between her and Philip had been arranged as far back as 1576, but was broken off by Philip's father, Sir Henry Sidney, after Essex's death at Dublin on September 21 of that year, probably because Leicester, the Sidneys' near relation, was darkly associated in popular suspicion with Essex's end [2]. I suggest that this probable reason for the breach of Philip's engagement offers us our required parallel for Eumenides' postponement of love to friendship; that the length of his connexion with Penelope is reflected by the seven years of silent worship of which Eumenides speaks [3]; and that the offer of his tongue to ransom Semele's is an allusion to the *Astrophel and Stella* sonnets, or at least that such allusion is found in Cynthia's reply 'What! should'st thou liue wanting a tongue to blaze the beauty of Semele [4]?'

Finally, the possible severance about this time of Lyly's relations with the Earl of Oxford, relations which we know to have been clouded in 1582 [5], may perhaps have driven him into the arms of the Leicester faction; and, if this be true, he would find additional reason for a flattering

---

[1] Symonds' *Sidney*, pp. 96, 37.
[2] But the acknowledged opposition between Leicester and Essex would constitute reason enough, without the suggestion of foul play in the latter's death. Halpin (*Oberon's Vision*, p. 35) tells us that the intrigue between Leicester and Lady Essex began in 1574, and that Essex on his return from Ireland in 1575 did not attempt to conceal his indignation against the favourite. He suspects the honesty of the verdict of natural death returned at the inquest on Essex held by Sir Henry Sidney's direction as Lord Deputy of Ireland; and refers us to Camden's *Annals of Elizabeth*, 1576, and Parsons' *Secret Memoirs*, p. 31.
For the breaking off of Philip's engagement to Penelope see Symonds' *Sidney*, pp. 35-6. Symonds suggests an old grudge entertained by Sir Henry against Essex.
[3] Act iii. sc. 4. 52-6. 'Howe hardly hath shee rewarded thee, without cause or colour of despight! Howe secrete hast thou beene these seauen yeeres, that hast not, nor once darest not to name her, for discontenting her. Howe faythfull! that hast offered to die for her, to please her.'
[4] Act v. sc. 3. 230. '*Astrophel and Stella* had circulated among its author's private friends for at least four years when Zutphen [Sept. 22, 1586] robbed England of her poet-hero' (Symonds' *Sidney*, p. 95).
[5] Letter of Lyly to Burleigh, July 1582 (*Lansdowne MS.* 36, *Art.* 76), quoted in Life, vol. i. p. 28.

SHREWSBURY AND HIS COUNTESS

portrait of Sir Philip in the latter's violent quarrel with Oxford in September 1579[1].

With regard to Geron and Dipsas I have already admitted that no better counterpart for their relations can be found than those of the Earl and Countess of Shrewsbury, which Halpin suggests. 'Bess of Hardwick' was the most notable shrew of her time; and Lodge's *Illustrations* teems with evidence of her quarrel with and slander of her husband[2], a quarrel not made up (by the Queen) until 1586, and not finally then[3]. Shrewsbury's long absence from Court during his custody of Mary is, no doubt, the original of Geron's exile. On Aug. 5, 1582, he writes to the Queen ' Having these ten years been secluded from your most gracious sight and happy presence, which more grieveth me than any travel or discommodity that I have suffered in this charge that it hath pleased your Majesty to put me in trust withal, I have taken the boldness' to beg a fortnight's leave of absence from his post in order to come to Court and clear himself of malicious accusations[4]. Not till the autumn of 1584, after he had been released from his charge, was the opportunity granted him; when ' being lately come unto the Court,' at a meeting of the Privy Council at which Burleigh, Leicester, the elder Sidney, Hatton and Walsingham were present, he refused to take his seat amongst them as a privy councillor until he was cleared by them of disloyalty in the execution of his charge; and the Council, readily acceding, recorded a special minute to that effect, which Dugdale speaks of as 'a memorable Testimonial[5].' These vague charges disseminated by Shrewsbury's wife are, as Halpin perceived, very like the vague displeasure of Cynthia under which Geron rests and which is due to Dipsas' arts[6]; and Dares' mention of a pathetic speech made by Geron on his return to Court[7] is surely an allusion to this scene in the Privy Council, of which Lyly may

Geron and Dipsas.

---

[1] Symonds (*Sidney*, pp. 57-8) quotes Greville's detailed account of the quarrel.
[2] The difference seems to have commenced in 1577, when she wished him to move with Mary from Sheffield to Chatsworth. In 1579 his allowance from the Treasury was reduced by about one quarter. Towards the close of 1583 the Countess left her husband (*Dict. Nat. Biog.*, art. 'Talbot, Elizabeth, Countess of Shrewsbury'). On Oct. 13, 1582, Shrewsbury writes to Walsingham defending himself against the charge of disaffection to Elizabeth and 'undutiful respects' with which he has been touched 'touching the queen of Scots' (Lodge's *Illustrations*, ii. 239). On Aug. 8, 1584, he writes to Leicester, alluding to 'my wicked and malicious wife,' and his son's partisanship with her (Id., ii. 243): while on Nov. 9, 1585, there is allusion in a further letter to 'my wife and her imps' (Id., ii. 275).
[3] *Calendar of State Papers* (Domestic), 1581-90, pp. 451-5. In 1589 the Queen again writes desiring him to allow his wife access.
[4] Lodge's *Illustrations*, ii. 228.
[5] Lodge's *Illustrations*, ii. 247; the minute is dated 'At Oatlands 15 Sept. 1584' (No. 189).
[6] Cf. Act iii. sc. 4, p. 52 'vnto Cynthia must I discouer all my sorrowes, who also must worke in mee a contentment,' and v. 3, p. 72.
[7] Act v. sc. 1, p. 63 (after a remark on Eumenides' strange tale) 'The other old man, what a sad speech vsed he, that caused vs almost all to weepe.'

well enough have heard some account. There is, perhaps, little historical warrant for crediting Lady Shrewsbury with special hostility to Leicester, unless it was she who informed Simier of his marriage with Lettice: but it is to be noted that the action of Dipsas against Endimion is undertaken with reluctance and purely at Tellus' prompting, 'for,' says Dipsas, 'from her gather wee all our simples to maintaine our sorceries[1]'; while in the marriage of Lord Charles Stuart, referred to above [2], we have a definite plot organized between Mary and the Countess (Tellus and Dipsas) which gave the greatest displeasure to the Queen. The intrigue against Endimion, indeed, is scantly supported in the Court history by any similar intrigue of moment against Leicester; and if this point of the parallel were to be pressed, we should rather have to identify Dipsas with Catherine de' Medici, as standing behind Simier in his revelation of Leicester's marriage. This, however, would deprive us of the obvious correspondence of Geron and Dipsas to the Shrewsbury couple; and it is far more probable that the plot against Endimion is, chiefly, the author's device for linking together the different personages of his plot, while it serves to enlist sympathy for his hero, the favourite.

Floscula and Bagoa. Of the remaining characters Floscula and Bagoa alone are of any importance to the allegory, though Sir Tophas may possibly claim a definite original. Floscula appears to hold the post of confidential attendant to Tellus, though she does not accompany her in exile. Bagoa is maid to Dipsas, and entirely subject to her authority. Both women feel a warm sympathy for Endimion. Floscula, after a vain endeavour to dissuade Tellus, dissociates herself definitely from her schemes [3]. Bagoa, used as an instrument, betrays the plot to Cynthia's councillors, is changed to an aspen by Dipsas, but retransformed by Cynthia. Floscula's feeling for Endimion is the subject of a suspicious question by Cynthia [4], and of a slighting remark by Eumenides [5]; while Endimion on his recovery assures her of the continuance of his 'former affections [6]': but as an agent in his restoration she takes no part. I confess I am tempted by Halpin's identification of her with Lady Essex, and of both with Shakespeare's 'little western flower'; for Shakespeare, it is clear, knew Lyly's work through and through, and the translation of Lyly's Cynthia, Tellus, and Floscula into his own 'cold moon,' 'the earth,' and the 'little western flower [7],' is both literal and quite consistent with the other contents of Oberon's speech, especially if Lyly's Tellus be Mary Queen of Scots. Nor need we be disturbed by the specific epithet 'western,'

---

[1] Act ii. sc. 3. 38. It is probably an allusion to the allowance the Shrewsburies received for Mary's support.
[2] p. 94.
[3] Act i. sc. 4. 5 'I will in this case neither giue counsell nor consent.'
[4] Act iv. sc. 3. 61 'Are you in loue with his person?'
[5] Act v. sc. 1. 148 'Doe not that wrong to the setled friendship of a man, as to compare it with the light affection of a woman.'
[6] Act v. sc. 3. 197.   [7] *Oberon's Vision*, p. 87.

which seems at first to justify Boaden in pointing to Amy Robsart; for, accompanied as it is by the 'fair vestal throned by the west,' 'western' need mean no more than 'English.' Shakespeare, at any rate, who follows Lyly in this allegory as in several other points of the *Midsummer Night's Dream*[1], may well have believed that Lettice was meant. Certainly no other passion of Leicester's is of such historical importance as to entitle its subject to a mention along with Mary and Elizabeth; and if the flower be allegorical at all, the line

'Before milk-white, now purple with love's wound,'

is beautifully applicable in Halpin's sense, though we may not like to see our favourite poet making courtly allusions to criminal intrigue. It is significant, too, that Floscula, whose confessed 'goodwill' to him Endimion owns, in Cynthia's absence, to be 'better then I haue deserued[2],' remains, like Cynthia, unpaired at the close; while Tellus, Semele, Bagoa and Dipsas all find a mate. Halpin tells us that Leicester regained Elizabeth's favour in 1579 by denying on oath that he was married to Lettice[3]; and Lyly may be adopting the view which the Queen preferred, in public, to accept. Cynthia's dispassionate tone to Floscula[4], and her insignificance to the action, are not out of harmony with such a view: yet as they are quite irreconcileable with the real facts as regards Lady Essex, I suggest as an alternative Frances Howard, third daughter of Lord Howard of Effingham. On May 11, 1573, Gilbert Talbot writes to his father the Earl of Shrewsbury that the sisters, Lady Sheffield and Frances Howard, are both 'very far in love' with Leicester[5], and the latter's active sympathy with him at the period of his disgrace is shown by the part she took in a ruse to revive Elizabeth's tenderness for him. A beseeching letter, addressed by Leicester to Burleigh, but meant for the royal eye, was handed by her to Burleigh in the presence-chamber, and dropped in the handing, with the expected result that the Queen demanded to see it[6]. Floscula's superfluousness to the action is some reason for supposing that she was not the mere creature of the author's brain, but had a definite original: yet the effort to identify every character may well be vain where so many of the lines in the maze of Court intrigue must have been effaced by time.

For Bagoa, who is far more important than Floscula, not indeed to

[1] See essay on 'Lyly as a Playwright,' vol. ii. pp. 297-8.
[2] Act v. sc. 1. 152. [3] *Oberon's Vision*, p. 40.
[4] Act iv. sc. 3, p. 63 '*Flosc.* O Endimion, could spight itself deuise a mischiefe so monstrous?... Where others number their yeeres, their houres, their minutes, and steppe by staires, thou onely hast thy yeeres and times in a· cluster, being olde before thou remembrest thou wast younge. *Cynth.* No more Floscula, pittie doeth him no good: I would any thing els might,' &c.
[5] Lodge's *Illustrations*, ii. 100.
[6] I am indebted for this incident to Mr. Baker's introduction (*Endymion*, pp. lxix–lxx). He quotes it from Parsons' *Memoirs of Robert Dudley*, iv. 19, 20, but without applying it to the allegory.

ON THE ALLEGORY IN ENDIMION

Endimion's restoration, but to the discovery of Tellus' intrigue, no original has hitherto been suggested. If I am right in regarding the plot of Mary and Lady Shrewsbury for the marriage of Lord Charles Stuart in 1574 as the original of the alliance between Tellus and Dipsas, a natural representative for Bagoa presents herself in Lady Lennox, the third party to that plot, who is found writing excuses on the subject to the Queen's ministers, represented in the play by Panelion and Zontes, in the winter of that year [1]. This attitude of submission and excuse, really dictated by her fears of Elizabeth, who, says Froude, sent her to the Tower, is represented in the play by Dipsas' transformation of her to a quivering aspen-tree, from which by favour of Cynthia she is restored to her former shape. Lady Lennox, the mother of Darnley and Lord Charles Stuart, is certainly an old woman, while Sir Tophas' reversion to her from the crone Dipsas implies Bagoa's comparative youth; but otherwise Lady Lennox fairly fulfils the requirements of the part.

Sir Tophas.   For Sir Tophas Halpin suggests Stephen Gosson, who sought to inspire his 'schoole' with military ardour as a diversion from 'stage plaies'; but he acknowledges that too little of Gosson's verse survives to allow us to compare it with Lyly's parody [2]. Beyond the general ground of Gosson's attack upon the stage in *The Schoole of Abuse* in 1579, there seems no reason why Lyly should satirize him; and the complimentary reference in *Euphues and his England* [3] to Gosson's defence of *The Schoole*, entitled *The Ephemerides of Phialo*, makes against such an idea. Much more probable is Professor Ward's suggestion [4], which by an odd mistake he attributes to Halpin, of Gabriel Harvey. From a passage in *Pappe with a Hatchet* [5] we know that Lyly had long cherished a grudge against this 'old acquaintance': the scoffing allusion to Sir Tophas' verses is appropriate to Harvey's experiments in metre: his patronizing self-sufficiency, his affectation of learning [6], his grammatical jokes [7], his flow of quotations, and Epiton's remark 'Nothing hath made my master a foole but flat schollership [8],' are all reflective of the pedant; and his behaviour to two lively girls, brought in for the express purpose of rallying

---

[1] See the dialogue between Panelion and Zontes about Bagoa, Act v. sc. 3. p. 71. Lady Lennox's part in the transaction is related by Froude, x. ch. 60, pp. 398 sqq., pop. ed. On Dec. 3, 1574, she writes to Burleigh lamenting the Queen's displeasure in the matter, and enclosing copy of a former letter to Leicester on the same subject. On Dec. 10 she again writes to Burleigh from Hackney, excusing herself for visiting the Countess of Shrewsbury and consenting to the marriage. On Dec. 22 Walsingham writes to the Earl of Huntingdon with questions to be put to Lady Lennox's secretary about the marriage. (*Calendar of State Papers, Domestic*, 1547–80, p. 489.)
[2] *Oberon's Vision*, p. 75; and cf. Act iv. sc. 2. p. 55.   [3] Vol. ii. p. 99, l. 17.
[4] *English Dramatic Literature*, i. 292 (ed. 1899).
[5] *Pappe* (vol. iii) 'for this tenne yeres haue I lookt to lambacke him'—written in the autumn of 1589.
[6] Act i. sc. 3. 91, 102 'all Mars and Ars': 'the Latine hath saued your liues.'
[7] Act iii. sc. 3. 5–19.   [8] Act v. sc. 2. 38.

him [1], looks like a personal reminiscence. Doubtless it is vain to seek in this academic personage any analogy to Sir Tophas' burlesque passion for Dipsas or his marriage with Bagoa, but Sir Tophas lies so much away from the plot that this matters little; nor was Gabriel Harvey so entirely without Court influence but that he was able to give Spenser an introduction to Sir Philip Sidney [2].

To attempt an identification of the remaining characters is needless, and would probably be vain, since they have no real part in the action nor any distinguishing marks. We therefore present our amended cast for comparison with Halpin's.

	(HALPIN)	(BOND)
Endimion	(the Earl of Leicester)	the Earl of Leicester
Eumenides	(the Earl of Sussex)	Sir Philip Sidney
Corsites	(Sir Edward Stafford)	{ Sir Amyas Paulet
Geron	(the Earl of Shrewsbury)	{ the Earl of Shrewsbury
Panelion } Zontes }	(unidentified)	? { Lord Burleigh ? { Sir Francis Walsingham
Sir Tophas	(Stephen Gosson)	Gabriel Harvey
Cynthia	(Queen Elizabeth)	Queen Elizabeth
Tellus	(Lady Sheffield (née Howard))	Mary Queen of Scots
Semele	(Frances Sidney)	Lady Rich (née Penelope Devereux)
Floscula	(Lady Essex)	Lady Essex, or Frances Howard
Bagoa	(unidentified)	? the Countess of Lennox
Dipsas	(the Countess of Shrewsbury)	the Countess of Shrewsbury

If the above cast be accepted, it is clear that the general scope of the play must be widened far beyond the bounds of Halpin's interpretation. His theory of its subject as Leicester's imprisonment consequent on Simier's revelation concentrates attention on what was, in fact, only a brief incident in a much longer period of Court disfavour caused by his opposition to the Anjou match, and elevates into political importance two ladies who were really of but slight significance. It was perfectly admissible for a dramatist to do this, but it would have been most impolitic in a Court dramatist. The introduction of people like Lady Sheffield or Lady Essex as direct competitors with the Queen was a piece of audacity that could hardly fail to be displeasing to Elizabeth; and, when we

[1] Act ii. sc. 2.
[2] It is, however, faintly possible that Lyly's late master, Oxford, is intended; in which case Epiton will be Lyly himself.

remember how sharp was the wound to her feelings caused by Leicester's marriage, it is all but incredible that either Leicester or Lyly would dream of venturing to dramatize the subject before the whole Court, even if we could conceive Leicester willing, as Mr. Baker imagines, to represent his wife as a poor dupe, the mere cloak to cover his real passion for Elizabeth. I doubt if his marriage has any place in the piece whatever. The tissue of vulgar intrigue disclosed to us in the pages of Mr. Halpin's essay is not a story of which Elizabeth, either as an injured woman or as the crowned representative of Chastity, could have wished to be reminded. Much more probable is it that Lyly, recently appointed as caterer for her amusement and casting about for means to flatter his mistress, turned his attention to the royal prisoner, so long Elizabeth's rival, the fear of whose machinations was urgent in all men's hearts in 1585. This rivalry, these machinations, together with the equally perennial royal affection for Leicester, are the most salient features in the domestic annals of the reign; and a sufficient warrant for their dramatic connexion was supplied by the match actually contemplated between Mary and the favourite in 1563–1565. These two, then, must be regarded as the double subject of the piece; and they are supplemented by two subordinate ones (1) the quarrel between the Shrewsburies, (2) the relations of Sir Philip Sidney with his uncle and his mistress. This explanation, while it allows us to keep four or five of Halpin's identifications, gives us, I think, a fuller and more probable explanation of their functions in the piece, and supplements them by other figures more conspicuous than those Halpin selects. Its weak point is, doubtless, the want of any definite intrigue against Leicester by Mary or Lady Shrewsbury; but the same weakness is inherent in the theory of Mr. Halpin, and in Mr. Baker's emendation of it. Neither Lady Sheffield nor Lady Essex can properly be credited with any intrigue against him: indeed, in spite of a widespread feeling of hatred and jealousy of the all-powerful favourite, it is difficult to point to any distinctly hostile action except that of Simier in the August of 1579. There are, as shown above, strong reasons against taking that incident as the chief subject of the play[1]. General considerations, no less than the identification of particular characters, require us to widen its scope. With that widening of scope there is imposed upon the dramatist the necessity of some invention for the securing of unity. He obtains it by making Mary and Lady Shrewsbury the direct causes of Leicester's disgrace, and thus enlisting for the favourite, his hero and perhaps his patron,

---

[1] It is likely enough, however, that representing as it does the acutest phase of the royal disfavour, it is alluded to in the Three Ladies of the first part of Endimion's dream, which differs considerably in purport from the action of the play as a whole. I take the lady with the knife and the looking-glass to be Elizabeth herself (cf. especially the flattering language used in describing the victory of mercy over her anger; v. 1. 96–100), the prompter of cruelty to be Lady Sheffield or Lady Shrewsbury, and the sympathetic lady to be Lady Essex.

a sympathy which neither on grounds of fact or character did he at all deserve.

I will close this essay with the briefest reference to a far greater poet than Lyly. Mr. Colvin in his monograph on Keats (*English Men of Letters*), p. 93, says 'In his own special range of Elizabethan reading, he was probably acquainted with Lyly's Court comedy of *Endimion*, in prose, which had been edited, as it happened, by his friend Dilke a few years before [i.e. in *Old Plays*, vol. i. 1814]: but in it he would have found nothing to his purpose.' Yet on p. 95 Mr. Colvin adds 'it is the passion of the human soul for beauty which he attempts, more or less consciously, to shadow forth in the quest of the shepherd-prince after his love': and since this ideal aspect of love, and the contrast of such with more earthly passion, certainly forms one aspect of Lyly's play (see above, p. 83), I think we are justified in claiming the latter as among the possible formative influences in Keats' poem. Michael Drayton's *Man in the Moone*[1], to which Mr. Colvin also refers in regard to Keats, cannot, I think, be said to owe anything to Lyly, except perhaps the title: nor do I trace any connexion between Drayton's poem and *The Woman in the Moone*.

[1] *Poemes Lyrick and pastorall. Odes, Eglogs, The Man in the Moone. By Michaell Drayton, Esquier. At London, Printed by R. B. for N. L. and I. Flasket.* n. d. [1604 or 1605]. The *Man in the Moone* was adapted from an earlier and, I think, better poem—about 1000 rhymed heroics—entitled *Endimion and Phœbe. Ideas Latmvs*, which appeared without date in 1594. It describes how Phœbe lulled her shepherd to sleep for 'thirty yeeres' that she might descend to him at will; and promises to relate elsewhere 'what in vision there to him befell.' The *Man in the Moone* has an allusion to lunary :

> 'As my great brother, so have I a flower
> To me peculiar, that doth ope and close
> When as I rise, and when I me repose.'

MIDAS

EDITIONS

'4to octobris 1591 mystres Broome Wydowe Late Wyfe of William Broome Entred for her copies vnder the hand of the Bishop of London: Three Comedies plaied before her maiestie by the Children of Paules th one Called . Endimion. Th other . Galathea and th other, Midas ... xviij^d.' *Sta. Reg.* ii. p. 596 (ed. Arb.).

Q. *Midas . | Plaied before | the Qveenes Maiestie | vpon Twelfe Day at | night, By the Children | of Paules . | London | Printed by Thomas Scarlet for I. B. | and are to be sold in Paules Churchyard at | the signe of the Bible . | 1592 . | 4to.* A, A 2, A-G 4 in fours. No colophon. (*Br. Mus.* : *Bodl.* : *Dyce Coll. S. Kensington.*)

Under date 23 Aug. 1601 *Midas*, together with *Camp., Sapho and Phao, Gallathea and Endim.*, is transferred to George Potter (*Sta. Reg.* iii. p. 191, ed. Arb., quoted under CAMPASPE-*Editions*).

The *Sixe Covrt Comedies* are entered to Edward Blount under date 9 Jan. 1628 (*Sta. Reg.* iv. p. 192, ed. Arb., quoted under CAMPASPE-*Editions*).

Second ed. (Blount's).   *MYDAS . | Played before the Queenes | Maiestie vpon Twelfe | Day at Night . | By the Children of | Pavls . | London, | Printed by William Stansby, | for Edward Blount . | 1632. |* 12mo, occupying sigs. S 12-Z 3, in twelves, of the *Sixe Covrt Comedies*.

Also in *Old English Plays*, vol. i (1814), with Introduction and Notes by C. W. Dilke; and in Fairholt's edition of Lyly's *Dramatic Works*, vol. ii (1858).

MIDAS

Argument. — Bacchus, in return for the hospitality of Midas, king of Phrygia, offers to grant him anything he may desire. Eristus advises him to ask his mistress; Martius, the sovereignty of the world; but Midas prefers the advice of a third councillor Mellacrites, and asks that his touch may turn everything to gold. A brief exercise of this power, which operates on his food, wine and raiment, reduces him to beg to be released from it. By the god's advice he bathes in the Pactolus, and transfers to its waters the fatal gift. A mood of sullen discontent follows (iv. 1, p. 141, v. 3, p. 159). As he is hunting in a wood on Mount Tmolus he comes upon the gods Pan and Apollo about to engage in a musical competition, of which the Nymphs are to be umpires. Associated with them in this function Midas decides for Pan, and his crass judgement is punished by Apollo with asses' ears. For a time he contrives to conceal them beneath a tiara; but the Nymphs have spread the news of his disgrace, and the words 'Midas the king hath asses' ears,' spoken by shepherds, are reproduced by some reeds as they wave in the wind. This prodigy is reported to the king by his discreet and affectionate daughter Sophronia, by whose advice he seeks Apollo's oracle at Delphi. There on his acknowledgement of folly and profession of repentance the curse is removed, and he returns to Phrygia vowing to relinquish those designs of conquest, especially against the heroic islanders of Lesbos, his ill-success in which has supplied the undercurrent of his thoughts throughout the play.

Comic relief is sought in the relations between some Court-pages and the royal barber Motto, who, robbed by them of the golden beard he has cut from Midas' chin, recovers it by curing Petulus' toothache; but is afterwards entrapped into treasonable utterance of the secret of the asses' ears, and compelled to surrender the beard as the price of their silence.

Text. — The text followed is that of the first and only known quarto, of 1592, which is unusually pure, presenting only eight positive errors, besides one or two of punctuation, though it lacks the four songs and a few indispensable stage-directions.

Blount gives us the missing songs, and corrects one of the quarto's errors, 'querenda,' p. 117; but introduces six others, besides omitting a word in six places.

Dilke, who rightly follows the quarto rather than Blount and, further, supplies some half-dozen needed stage-directions, modernizes the text in about a dozen places, e. g. p. 134 'travail' for 'trauel,' 154 'bauble' for 'Bable,' 157 'own' for 'owe,' makes eight other alterations which may be classed as emendations, and about a score which are quite the reverse, e. g. p. 118 'statute,' p. 120 'no other,' p. 137 'forward,' p. 140 'Ah' for 'I' (pron.), 141 'ears,' 'swan' for the jesting 'goose,' and p. 157 'dente' for Motto's mistake 'dento.'

Fairholt as usual follows Blount, correcting three of his corruptions, and adding two corrections of the original text; but making twelve corruptions of his own, e. g. pp. 126 'admit' for 'omit,' 131 'use' for 'lose, 141 'they' for 'there,' 147 'Min.' for 'Lic.'

I have adopted all clear emendations made by others, and added three (pp. 118, 136, 138), with one or two further stage-directions; reporting all variants in the footnotes.

Authorship. — Lyly's name is not on the title-page of the quarto: but the performance of the play by the Paul's boys, its inclusion by Blount, its marked style, and about a dozen reminiscences of *Euphues* (though these are fewer and fainter than formerly, and the play contains very few allusions to natural history), are sufficient to prove his authorship.

Sources and Allegory. — Dilke's introduction to the play says 'For the subject and incidents of this Comedy Lyly was indebted to Ovid, Galtruchius, and "The Golden Ass" of Apuleius; in the latter work the story is related at large.' It is unfortunate for this statement that Pierre Gautruche or Gaultruche, the author of *L'Histoire Poétique* (first translated into English, 1671, 8vo) was only born, at Caen, in 1602: and, further, that the *De Asino* of Apuleius, whose popular title seems so happily to combine the two instances of Midas' folly, contains no mention of Midas whatever; the Ass being of course Lucius, the hero of Apuleius' tale and of Lucian's Λούκιος ἢ Ὄνος, and the epithet 'golden' being merely the tribute of appreciative posterity. The error, which has survived till quite

INTRODUCTION

a recent year, is ultimately traceable to Langbaine (*English Dramatick Poets*, Oxford, 1691, 8vo, p. 329).

There remains as Lyly's sole source Ovid's *Metamorphoses*, xi. 85–193, which he closely follows. The only differences are that in Ovid Bacchus is under obligation for a service rendered to Silenus rather than to himself; that in Ovid no motive for Midas' desire of gold is suggested, while Lyly (as Hense suggests) supplies one in the thirst for conquest; that after ridding himself of the fatal gift Midas betakes himself to a rural life, represented in Lyly by his hunting expedition; that in the contest between Pan and Apollo, though Nymphs are present, it is Tmolus, the Genius of the mountain, who acts as umpire and whose decision is gratuitously contravened by Midas; that it is Midas' barber, alone cognizant of the ears, who whispers the secret into a hole he digs in the ground, afterwards filling in the soil, above which reeds spring up to repeat his words when stirred by the wind; and finally that Ovid mentions no expedition of Midas to Delphi, and no remission of the punishment; nor is any such recorded by Hyginus, whose 191st Fable relates both incidents, with the omission of the barber and the reeds.—A few words in iv. 2, p. 145 seem indebted to a chapter about Midas in *The Diall of Princes* (see note ad loc.).

Lyly, then, has added the comic elements of the Pages and Pipenetta and the Huntsman, and the contest between the former and the barber for the possession of the golden beard. He has added, too, the characters of Midas' daughter and her ladies, and of Midas' three councillors; and has credited Midas with ambitious designs on the territories of his neighbours, particularly on the island of Lesbos. Dilke (1814) was the first to observe that in this respect the play is intended as a satire on Philip II of Spain, representing 'the produce of his mines in S. America by his desire to turn everything about him into gold; and the defeat of the Armada by the fruitless attempts of Midas to subdue the Island of Lesbos.' Halpin in *Oberon's Vision* (Shakespeare Soc. 1843), p. 104, offers the following conjectural key:

Midas, king of Phrygia = Philip of Spain.
Isles north of Phrygia = British Isles. Lesbos = England.
Getulia, Lycaonia, Sola, &c. = Portugal, the Netherlands, and other countries cruelly tyrannized over by Philip.
Bacchus (the presiding deity of India) = the Genius of the Indies.
The golden gift = the influx of precious metals into Spain.

Pactolus (with golden sands) = the Tagus.
The contest in music = the controversy of the Reformation.
Tmolus = (probably) Trent.
Pan ('all'—Catholic) = Papal Supremacy.
Apollo (the antagonistic principle) = Protestant Sovereignty.
Syrinx = the Roman Catholic Faith.
Daphne = the Protestant Faith.
Motto (who betrays the ears of Midas) = Anthonio Perez, Philip's secretary, banished for betraying secrets.
Sophronia (daughter and successor of Midas) = Isabella, Philip's daughter, to whom, on her marrying the Archduke Albert, he resigned the sovereignty of the Netherlands.

Martius   ⎫   the Dukes of Medina Sidonia and D'Alva;
Mellicrates   ⎬ =   and Ruy Gomez de Libra [given in this
Eristus (probably) ⎭   order].

The golden beard perhaps alludes to the order of the Golden Fleece.

Probably most people will think that Halpin carries the allegory somewhat further than the author intended: especially we may note that Philip's decision for Catholicism as against Protestantism can hardly be represented as a secret that Midas long conceals from his daughter and his councillors (pp. 149–52, 158–9), a concealment for which, indeed, there is no adequate dramatic motive, seeing that his punishment is soon declared. But there can be little doubt about the identification of Martius, whose 'counsell hath shed as much bloud as would make another sea,' pp. 132, 161 (v. 3. 111), with the pitiless Alva; and the play abounds in allusions to Philip's covetousness, treachery and tyranny, and to current events such as the bloodshed in the Netherlands, p. 130, the defeat of the Armada, p. 131, the expedition of Drake and Norreys, iv. 4. 12, and other points illustrated in the Notes.

Date. — Obviously the play is written after the defeat of the Armada in 1588, and before its entry in the Stationers' Register on Oct. 4, 1591. The allusion to Drake and Norreys' expedition to Portugal (Act iv. sc. 4, p. 149 'suffers the enemies to bid vs good morrowe at our owne doors') which sailed Ap. 18, 1589 and returned in the middle of July, enables us to bring the upward limit down to May of that year; while a passage in Harvey's *Advertisement to Papp-Hatchett*, which forms the second Book of *Pierce's Supererogation* and is dated 'At Trinitie Hall: the fift of Nouember: 1589,' supplies us with the downward limit: 'Faith, quoth himselfe,

INTRODUCTION

thou wilt be caught by the stile: Indeede what more easie, then to finde the man by his humour, the *Midas* by his eares, the Calfe by his tongue, the goose by his quill, the Playmaker by his stile, the hatchet by the Pap[1].' Two other allusions, confirming Harvey's, occur in Nash's *An Almond for a Parrat*, written probably in January or February, 1589-90[2]. On p. 4 of Petheram's Reprint of that pamphlet we find 'for now a dayes, a man can not haue a bout with a Balletter or write *Midas habet aures asininas* in great Romaine letters, but hee shall bee in daunger of a further displeasure': and on p. 41 'Pen. [i.e. Penry] with Pan, hath contended with Appollo, and you lyke Midasses, haue ouerprised his musick.'

From these allusions it would appear that the play was composed between May and September, 1589. The title-page announces it as 'played before the Queenes Maiestie vpon Twelfe Day at Night. By the Children of Pavls.' In Chalmers' list of payments made to the master of the Paul's Boys (*Boswell's Malone*, iii. 425) is one on March 10, 1589-90 'for three plays on Sunday after Christmas-day, New Year's Day and Twelfth Day.' The last of these was probably *Midas*, performed at Court, therefore, on January 6, 1590.

Stage-History, Imitations. — Collier (*Hist. Dram. Poet.* i. 277) quotes the following from a tract printed abroad in 1592, with the title *A Declaration of the true causes of the greate troubles supposed to be intended against the Realme of England*, &c.—' And therefore as an introduction hereunto, to make him [the King of Spain] odious unto the people, certain players were suffered to scoffe and jeast at him vpon their common stages; and the like was used in the contempt of his Religion, first by making it no better then Turkish, by annexing unto the Psalmes of Dauid . . . this ensuinge meeter,' &c. Since the doggrel given is obviously not Lyly's, *Midas* can hardly be the particular play referred to: but there seems considerable probability that, as Halpin suggests (*Oberon's Vision*, p. 104, note),

---

[1] Brydges' *Archaica*, ii. 139. Before reading Mr. Baker's Biographical Introduction to his edition of *Endymion*, p. cl, I had not, I think, recognized the bearing of this passage on the date of *Midas*. Gabriel Harvey, writing at his Cambridge rooms, must have seen the play during the long vacation on the St. Paul's stage, where its performance would serve as rehearsal for its production at Court.

[2] Martin was, we are told, '*not many months since* most wittily scofte at by the extemporall endeuour of the pleasant author of Pap with a hatchet' (Petheram's Reprint, p. 12).

it may have been one of them; and Nash's remark in the *Almond*, quoted above, even seems to imply that Lyly's play had, early in 1590 or before, attracted official attention and remonstrance.

Midas' asses' ears as the punishment of arrogance and folly are, no doubt, the original of Bottom's ass-head in *A Midsummer Night's Dream*.

The relation between Motto and the Court-pages is probably the original of that between Vertigo, the tailor, and the courtiers in Fletcher and Rowley's *Maid in the Mill*.

A burlesque entitled *Midas*, by Kane O'Hara, was produced at Covent Garden in 1764, and reprinted several times in the succeeding years. In it Midas, introduced as an English squire and J. P., allies himself with an old tippler, Pan, to outwit Apollo, who, disguised as a shepherd, has won the hearts of a farmer's two daughters, Daphne and Nysa. Bribed by Mysis, the girls' mother, he decides at a musical contest for Pan's bagpipes against Apollo's guitar. Apollo reveals himself, punishes Midas with asses' ears, and reascends to heaven. The burlesque must have been popular, though I can find but little of the wit and humour which Dilke in his prefatory note to our play took occasion to eulogize.

Place and Time. — The expedition to Delphi in v. 3 violates the Unity of Place, which otherwise we might, by locating the palace at Sardis (mentioned Ovid, *Met.* xi. 137) instead of in Phrygia proper, claim to be observed in this as in all other of Lyly's comedies except *Endimion*. No instance occurs of a transfer of place in the middle of a scene; though, to avoid such, we have to suppose the locality of the reeds, where the shepherds are wandering in ii. 2, to be within easy distance of the palace in iv. 4 and v. 1.

Unity of Time is violated by Sophronia's remark at the beginning of Act v, that the wonder of the ears is 'nine dayes past,' and by the expedition to Delphi: but the general aim at continuity of scene within the limits of the single Act is quite clear (see ii. 2 end, Petulus' excuse for not going to Bacchus' temple with the lords at end of ii. 1; and iv. 2 end 'I heare some comming'), though it is violated by the compression necessary for the hunting described in Act iii p. 139, by the opening words of iv. 4 about Midas being 'melancholy since his hunting,' and by the changes of scene in Act v. Acts ii and iii are closely continuous.

MIDAS.

PLAIED BEFORE THE QVEENES MAIESTIE VPON TVVELFE DAY AT night, By the Children of Paules.

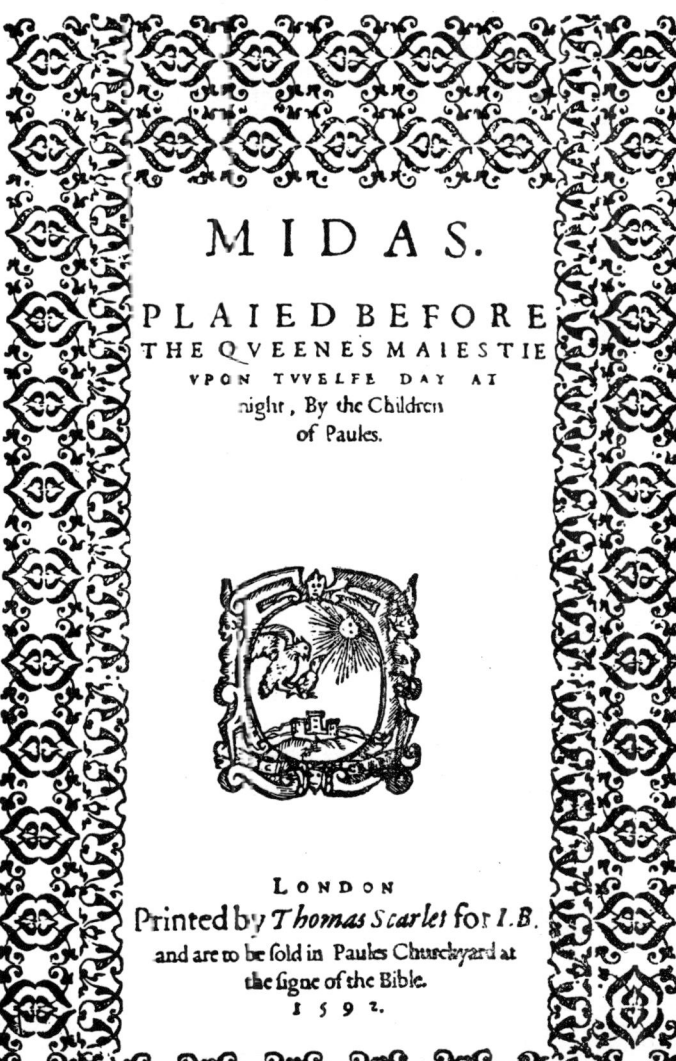

LONDON
Printed by *Thomas Scarlet* for I.B.
and are to be sold in Paules Churchyard at
the signe of the Bible.
1592.

⟨DRAMATIS PERSONÆ.

BACCHUS.
APOLLO.
PAN.
MIDAS, *King of Phrygia.*
ERISTUS,
MARTIUS, } *Councillors of Midas.*
MELLACRITES,
LICIO, *Page to Cælia.*
PETULUS, *Page to Mellacrites.*
MINUTIUS, *another Page.*
MOTTO, *a Barber.*
DELLO, *his Boy.*
MENALCAS,
CORYN,
CELTHUS, } *Shepherds.*
DRYAPON,
AMYNTAS,
Huntsman.
ERATO, *a Nymph.*
Other Nymphs.
SOPHRONIA, *Daughter of Midas.*
CÆLIA, *Daughter of Mellacrites.*
CAMILLA,
AMERULA, } *other Ladies of the Court.*
SUAVIA,
PIPENETTA, *Maid to Cælia.*

SCENE—*Phrygia and Delphi.*⟩

DRAMATIS PERSONÆ] *list first supplied* Dil., F. *adding* ERATO. *I have made their descriptions more precise* 6 Councillors &c.] Gentlemen of the Court *Dil. F.* 8 LICIO, Page to Cælia] *Dil. F. simply bracket* Licio, Petulus *and* Minutius *as* 'Servants' 22 CÆLIA, Daughter of Mellacrites] *Dil. F. simply bracket her with the three following as* 'Ladies of the Court' 26 PIPENETTA, Maid to Cælia] *Dil. F. describe her as* 'a Servant' SCENE—Phrygia and Delphos *suppl. F.*

THE PROLOGVE
IN PAVLES.

GEntlemen, so nice is the world, that for apparrel there is no fashion, for Musick no instrument, for diet no delicate, for playes no inuention, but breedeth sacietie before noone, and contempt before night.

5 *Come to the Tayler, hee is gone to the Paynters, to learne howe more cunning may lurke in the fashion, then can bee expressed in the making. Aske the Musicions, they will say their heads ake with deuising notes beyonde Ela. Enquire at Ordinaries, there must be sallets for the Italian; picktooths for the Spaniard; pots for the*
10 *German; porriage for the Englishman. At our exercises, Souldiers call for Tragedies, their obiect is bloud: Courtiers for Commedies, their subiect is loue; Countriemen for Pastoralles, Shepheards are their Saintes. Trafficke and trauell hath wouen the nature of all Nations into ours, and made this land like Arras, full of deuise, which*
15 *was Broade-cloth, full of workemanshippe.*

Time hath confounded our mindes, our mindes the matter; but all commeth to this passe, that what heretofore hath beene serued in seuerall dishes for a feaste, is now minced in a charger for a Gallimaufrey. If wee present a mingle-mangle, our fault is to be excused,
20 *because the whole worlde is become an Hodge-podge.*

Wee are ielous of your iudgementes, because you are wise; of our owne performance, because we are vnperfect; of our Authors deuice, because he is idle. Onelie this doeth encourage vs, that presenting our studies before Gentlemen, though they receiue an inward mislike, wee
25 *shall not be hist with an open disgrace.*

Stirps rudis vrtica est: stirps generosa, rosa.

---

3 satietie *Bl. mods*   9 Sallads *Bl. mods.*   10 porridge] Pottage *Bl. F., cf. Euph. p.* 189, *l.* 33

MIDAS

ACTUS PRIMUS.

SCÆNA PRIMA.—⟨*Gardens before* MIDAS' *Palace.*⟩

⟨*Enter*⟩ BACCHUS, MYDAS, ERISTUS, MARTIUS. ⟨*and* MELLACRITES⟩.

Bacchus. MIdas, where the Gods bestowe benefits they aske thankes, but where they receiue good turns, they giue rewards. Thou hast filled my belly with meate, mine eares with musicke, mine eies with wonders. *Bacchus* of all the Gods is the best fellow, and *Midas* amongst men a king of fellows. All thy grounds are vineyards, thy corne grapes, thy chambers sellers, thy houshold stuffe standing cuppes: and therfore aske any thing it shalbe graunted. Wouldest thou haue the pipes of thy conducts to run wine, the vdders of thy beasts to drop nectar, or thy trees to bud ambrosia? Desirest thou to be fortunate in thy loue, or in thy victories famous, or to haue the yeres of thy life as many as the haires on thy head? Nothing shalbe denied, so great is *Bacchus*, so happie is *Midas*.

Mid. *Bacchus*, for a king to begge of a God it is no shame, but to aske with aduise, wisdom; geue me leaue to consult: least desiring things aboue my reach, I bee fiered with *Phaeton:* or against nature, I be drowned with *Icarus:* & so perishing, the world shal both laugh and wonder, crying, *Magnis tamen excidit ausis*.

Bacchus. Consult, *Bacchus* will consent.

Mid. Now my Lords, let me heare your opinions, what wish may make *Mydas* most happie and his Subiects best content?

Erist. Were I a king I would wish to possesse my mistresse, for what sweetnes can there be found in life, but loue? whose wounds the more mortall they are to the heart, the more immortal they make

---

ACTUS PRIMUS . . . MIDAS' Palace: *the quarto's division into Acts and Scenes is retained. The localities of the scenes are first marked in this edition* S. D. [*and* MELLACRITES] *inserted Dil.* 8 conducts] Conduits *Bl. mods.* 17 I] & *all eds.*

the possessors: and who knoweth not that the possessing of that must bee most pretious, the pursuing whereof is so pleasing.

Mar. Loue is a pastime for children, breeding nothing but follie, and nourishing nothing but idlenes. I would wish to be monarch of the world, conquering kingdomes like villages, and being greatest on the earth be commaunder of the whole earth: for what is there that more tickles the mind of a king, then a hope to bee the only king, wringing out of euery countrie tribute, and in his owne to sit in triumph? Those that call conquerors ambitious, are like those that tearme thrift couetousnes, clenlines pride, honestie precisenes. Commaund the world, *Midas*, a greater thing you cannot desire, a lesse you should not.

Mid. What say you *Mellacrites*?

Mel. Nothing, but that these two haue said nothing. I would wish that euerie thing I touched might turne to gold: this is the sinewes of warre, and the sweetnesse of peace. Is it not gold that maketh the chastest to yeeld to lust, the honestest to lewdnes, the wisest to follie, the faithfullest to deceit, and the most holy in heart, to be most hollow of hart? In this word Gold are all the powers of the gods, the desires of men, the woonders of the worlde, the miracles of nature, the losenes of fortune and triumphs of time. By gold may you shake the courts of other Princes, and haue your own setled; one spade of gold vndermines faster then an hundred mattocks of steele. Would one be thought religious & deuout? *Quantum quisque sua nummorum seruat in arca, tantum habet & fidei:* Religions ballance are golden bags. Desire you vertue? *quærenda pecunia primum est, virtus post nummos:* the first staire of vertue is money. Doeth anie thirst after gentrie, and wish to be esteemed beautiful? *& genus & formam regina pecunia donat:* king Coin hath a mint to stamp gentlemen, and art to make amiablenes. I denie not but loue is sweet, and the marrowe of a mans minde, that to conquere kings is the quintessence of the thoughts of kings: why then follow both, *Aurea sunt verè nunc sæcula, plurimus auro venit honos, auro conciliatur amor:* it is a world for gold; honor and loue are both taken vp on interest. Doth *Midas* determine to tempt the mindes of true Subiectes? to drawe them from obedience to trecherie, from their allegiance and othes to treason and periurie? *quid non mortalia pectora cogit auri sacra fames?* what holes doth

---

50 ballance are *so all, and again p.* 118, *l.* 92; *cf. End.* v. 3. 191 quærenda *Bl. F.*: querenda *Q Dil.*   57 vero *Dil. misled by turned* e *in Q*

not gold bore in mens hearts? Such vertue is there in golde, that being bred in the barrennest ground, and troden vnder foote, it mounteth to sit on Princes heads. Wish gold *Midas,* or wish not to be *Midas.* In the councel of the gods, was not *Anubis'* with his long nose of gold, preferred before *Neptunes,* whose statua was but brasse? And *Æsculapius* more honored for his golden beard, then *Apollo* for his sweet harmonie?

Erist. To haue gold and not loue, (which cannot be purchast by gold) is to be a slaue to gold.

Mar. To possesse mountains of gold, and a mistresse more precious then gold, and not to commaunde the world, is to make *Mydas* new prentise to a mint, and Iorneiman to a woman.

Mel. To enioy a faire Ladie in loue, and wante faire gold to geue: to haue thousands of people to fight, and no peny to paye—wil make ones mistresse wilde, and his soldiers tame. *Iupiter* was a god, but he knew gold was a greater: and flewe into those grates with his golden winges, where he coulde not enter with his Swannes wings. What staide *Atalantas* course with *Hippomanes?* an apple of gold: what made the three goddesses striue? an apple of gold. If therfore thou make not thy mistres a goldfinch, thou mayst chance to find her a wagtaile: beleeue me, *Res est ingeniosa dare.* Besides, how many gates of cities this golden key hath opened, we may remember of late, and ought to feare hereafter. That iron world is worne out, the golden is now come. *Sub Ioue nunc mundus, iussa sequare Iouis.*

Erist. Gold is but the guts of the earth.

Mel. I had rather haue the earthes guttes, then the Moones braines. What is it that gold cannot cōmand, or hath not conquered? Iustice her selfe, that sitteth wimpled about the eyes, doth it not because shee will take no gold, but that she would not be seene blushing when she takes it: the ballance she holdeth are not to weie the right of the cause, but the weight of the bribe: she wil put vp her naked sword if thou offer her a golden scabberd.

Mid. Cease you to dispute, I am determined. It is gold, *Bacchus,* that *Mydas* desireth, let euery thing that *Mydas* toucheth be turned to gold, so shalt thou blesse thy guest, and manifest thy godhead. Let it be golde *Bacchus.*

Bacchus. Midas thy wish cleaueth to thy last word. Take vp this stone.

66 counsell *Bl. F.*: council *Dil.*   Anubis *all eds.*   67 Neptune *Dil. F.* statua] stature *Q Bl. F.*: statute *Dil.*   70 by] with *Dil.*   80 Atlantas *Q Bl. Dil.*

Mid. Fortunate *Mydas!* It is gold *Mellacrites!* gold! it is gold!

Mel. This stick.

Mid. Gold *Mellacrites!* my sweet boy al is gold! for euer 105 honoured be *Bacchus*, that aboue measure hath made *Mydas* fortunate.

Bacchus. If *Mydas* be pleased *Bacchus* is, I will to my temple with *Silenus*, for by this time there are many to offer vnto me sacrifices: *Pœnam pro munere poscis.* ⟨*Exit* BACCHUS.⟩

110 *Mid.* Come my Lords, I wil with golde paue my court, and deck with gold my turrets, these petty ilands neer to Phrygia shal totter, and other kingdoms be turned topsie turuie: I wil commaund both the affections of men, and the fortunes. Chastitie wil growe cheape where gold is not thought deere; *Celia*, chast *Celia* shall yeeld. 115 You my Lords shall haue my handes in your houses, turning your brasen gates to fine gold. Thus shal *Mydas* be monarch of the world, the darer of fortune, the commander of loue. Come let vs in.

Mel. We follow, desiring that our thoughtes may be touched with thy finger, that they also may become gold.

120 *Erist.* Wel I feare the euent, because of *Bacchus* last words, *pœnam pro munere poscis.*

Mid. Tush, he is a dronken god, els he woulde not haue geuen so great a gift. Now it is done, I care not for any thing he can doe.

Exeunt.

SCE. 2.—⟨ *The same.* ⟩

⟨*Enter*⟩ LICIO. PETULUS.

Licio. THou seruest *Mellacrites*, and I his daughter, which is the better man?

Pet. The Masculin gender is more worthy then the feminine, therfore *Licio*, backare.

5 *Licio.* That is when those two genders are at iarre, but when they belong both to one thing, then—

Pet. What then?

Licio. Then they agree like the fiddle and the stick.

Pet. Pulchrè sanè. Gods blessing on thy blewe nose! but *Licio*, 10 my mistres is a proper woman.

113 the[2]] their *Bl. F.*   114 not *om. Bl. F.*   119 fingers *F.*   1 Licio] Lit. *Q*

Licio. I but thou knowest not her properties.
Pet. I care not for her qualities, so I may embrace her quantitie.
Licio. Are you so peart?
Pet. I and so expert, that I can aswel tel the thoughts of a womans heart by her eyes, as the change of the weather by an almanack.
Licio. Sir boy you must not be saucie.
Pet. No, but faithful and seruiceable.
Licio. Lock vp your lips or I wil lop them off. But sirrha, for thy better instructions I wil vnfold euery wrinkle of my mistres disposition.
Pet. I pray thee doe.
Licio. But for this time I wil only handle the head and purtenance.
Pet. Nothing els?
Licio. Why, wil not that be a long houres work to describe, that is almost a whole daies work to dresse?
Pet. Proceed.
Licio. First, she hath a head as round as a tennis ball.
Pet. I would my bed were a hazard.
Licio. Why?
Pet. Nothing, but that I would haue her head there among other balles.
Licio. Video, pro Intelligo. Then hath she an haukes eye.
Pet. O that I were a partridge head.
Licio. To what end?
Pet. That she might tire with her eyes on my countenance.
Licio. Wouldst thou be hanged?
Pet. Scilicet.
Licio. Well, she hath the tongue of a Parrat.
Pet. Thats a leaden dagger in a veluette sheath, to haue a black tongue in a faire mouth.
Licio. Tush, it is not for the blacknesse, but for the babling, for euerie houre she wil crie 'walk knaue, walke.'
Pet. Then will I mutter, 'a rope for Parrat, a rope.'
Licio. So maist thou be hanged, not by the lippes, but by the neck. Then, sir, hath she a calues tooth.
Pet. O monstrous mouth! I would then it had been a sheepes eye, and a neates tongue.

11 not her] no other *Dil.*   44–5 *inv. commas first in Dil.: itals. F.*

SC. II]   MIDAS   121

50 *Licio.* It is not for the bignes, but the sweetnes: all her teeth are as sweet as the sweet tooth of a calfe
   Pet. Sweetly meant.
   Licio. She hath the eares of a Want.
   Pet. Doth she want eares?
55 *Licio.* I say the eares of a Want, a Mole, thou dost want wit to vnderstand me. She wil heare though she be neuer so low on the grounde.
   Pet. Why then if one aske her a question, it is likely she wil hearken to it.
60 *Licio.* Hearken thou after that. Shee hath the nose of a sowe.
   Pet. Then belike there she weares her wedding ring.
   Licio. No, she can smel a knaue a mile off.
   Pet. Let vs go farther *Licio*, she hath both vs in the wind.
   Licio. She hath a bettle brow.
65 *Pet.* What is she beetle browed?
   Licio. Thou hast a beetle head! I say the brow of a beetle, a little flie, whose brow is as black as veluet.
   Pet. What lips hath she?
   Licio. Tush, the lips are no part of the head, only made for
70 a double leafe dore for the mouth.
   Pet. What is then the chin?
   Licio. That is only the threshold to the dore.
   Pet. I perceiue you are driuen to the wall that stands behind the dore, for this is ridiculous: but now you can say no more of the head,
75 begin with the purtenances, for that was your promise.
   Licio. The purtenances! it is impossible to reckon them vp, much lesse to tell the nature of them. Hoods, frontlets, wires, caules, curling-irons, perriwigs, bodkins, fillets, hairlaces, ribbons, roles, knotstrings, glasses, combs, caps, hats, coifes, kerchers, clothes,
80 earerings, borders, crippins, shadowes, spots, and so many other trifles, as both I want the words of arte to name them, time to vtter them, and witte to remember them: these be but a fewe notes.
   Pet. Notes quoth you, I note one thing.
85 *Licio.* What is that?
   Pet. That if euerie part require so much as the head, it wil make the richest husband in the world ake at the heart.

60 that. Shee] that, shee *previous eds.*   61 there *om. Dil.*   64 bettle *Q*: beetle *Bl. mods.*

Enter PIPENETTA.

Licio. But soft, here comes *Pipenetta* : what newes ?

Pip. I would not be in your coats for any thing.

Licio. Indeed if thou shouldest rigge vp and downe in our iackets, thou wouldst be thought a very tomboy.

Pip. I meane I would not be in your cases.

Pet. Neither shalt thou *Pipenetta,* for first, they are too little for thy bodie, and then too faire to pull ouer so fowle a skinne.

Pip. These boyes be droonk ! I would not be in your takings.

Licio. I thinke so, for we take nothing in our hands but weapons, it is for thee to vse needles and pinnes, a sampler, not a buckler.

Pip. Nay then wee shall neuer haue done ! I meane I would not be so courst as you shalbe.

Pet. Worse and worse ! Wee are no chase (prettie mops,) for Deere we are not, neither red nor fallowe, because we are Batchelers and haue not *cornu copia,* we want heads : Hares we cannot be, because they are male one yere, and the next female, wee change not our sex : Badgers we are not, for our legs are one as long as another : and who wil take vs to be Foxes, that stand so nere a goose, and bite not ?

Pip. Fooles you are, and therefore good game for wise men to hunt : but for knaues I leaue you, for honest wenches to talke of.

Licio. Nay stay sweet *Pipenetta,* we are but disposed to be merrie.

Pip. I maruel how old you wil be before you be disposed to be honest. But this is the matter, my master is gone abroad, and wants his page to wayt on him : my mistresse would rise, and lacks your worshippe to fetch her haire.

Pet. Why, is it not on her head ?

Pip. Me thinks it should, but I meane the haire that she must weare to day.

Licio. Why, doth she weare any but her owne ?

Pip. In faith sir no, I am sure it is her owne when shee paies for it. But do you heare the strange newes at the Court ?

Pet. No, except this be it, to haue ones haire lie all night out of the house from ones head.

100 curst *Bl. F.*: coursed *Dil.*   102 Deere we] Deere, we *Bl.*: Deere; we *F.*   103 cannot be] are not *Dil.*   109 for¹ *om. Bl. F.*   117 that *om. Dil.*   120 it is] its *Bl. F.*

Pip. Tush! euerie thing that *Mydas* toucheth is gold.
Pet. The deuil it is!
Pip. Indeed gold is the deuil.
Licio. Thou art deceiued wench, angels are gold. But is it true?
Pip. True? Why the meat that he tutcheth turneth to gold, so doth the drinke, so doth his raiment.
Pet. I would he would geue me a good boxe on the eare, that I might haue a golden cheeke.
Licio. How happie shal we be if hee woulde but stroke our heads, that we might haue golden haires. But let vs all in, least he lose the vertue of the gift before wee taste the benefit.
Pip. If he take a cudgel and that turn to gold, yet beating you with it, you shal only feele the weight of gold.
Pet. What difference to be beaten with gold, and to be beaten gold?
Pip. As much as to say, drinke before you goe, and goe before you drinke.
Licio. Come let vs goe, least we drinke of a drie cuppe for our long tarrying. *Exeunt.*

ACTUS. 2.

SCÆ. 1.—⟨*The same.*⟩

ERISTUS, CÆLIA, SOFHRONIA, MELLACRITES. MARTIUS.

⟨*Enter* ERISTUS *and* CÆLIA.⟩

Erist. FAire *Cælia*, thou seest of gold there is sacietie, of loue there cannot.
Cæl. If thou shouldst wish that whatsoeuer thou thoughtest might be loue, as *Mydas* what euer he toucht might be gold, it may be loue would bee as lothsome to thine eares, as gold is to his eyes, and make thy heart pinch with melancholie, as his guts doe with famine.
Erist. No, sweet *Cælia*, in loue there is varietie.
Cæl. Indeed men varie in their loue.
Erist. They varie their loue, yet change it not.
Cæl. Loue and change are at variance, therefore if they varie, they must change.
Erist. Men change the manner of their loue, not the humor: the

1 satiety *Bl. mods.*

meanes how to obteine, not the mistresse they honor. So did *Iupiter*, that could not intreat *Danae* by golden words, possesse his loue by a golden shoure, not altering his affection, but vsing art.

Cæl. The same *Iupiter* was an Ægle, a Swan, a Bull; and for euerie Saint a new shape, as men haue for euery mistres a new shadow. If you take example of the gods, who more wanton, more wauering? if of your selues, being but men, who wil think you more constant then gods? *Eristus*, if gold could haue allured mine eies, thou knowest *Mydas* that commaundeth all thinges to bee gold, had conquered: if threats might haue feared my heart, *Mydas* being a king, might haue commaunded my affections: if loue, golde, or authoritie might haue inchaunted me, *Mydas* had obteyned by loue, golde, and authoritie, *Quorum si singula nostram flectere non poterant, potuissent omnia mentem.*

Erist. Ah, *Cælia*, if kinges saye they loue and yet dissemble, who dare say that they dissemble, and not loue? They commaunde the affections of others yeeld, and their owne to be beleeued. My teares which haue made furrowes in my cheekes, and in mine eyes fountaines: my sighes, which haue made of my heart a furnace, and kindled in my head flames: my body that melteth by peecemeale, and my mind that pineth at an instant, may witnesse that my loue is both vnspotted, & vnspeakeable, *Quorum si singula duram flectere non poterant, deberent omnia mentem.* But soft, here commeth the Princesse, with the rest of the Lords.

Enter SOPHRONIA. ⟨MELLACRITES, MARTIUS, *and other courtiers*⟩.

Soph. Mellacrites, I cannot tell whether I should more mislike thy councell, or *Mydas* consent, but the couetous humor of you both I contemne and wonder at, being vnfit for a king, whose honor should consiste in liberalitie, not greedines; and vnworthy the calling of *Mellacrites*, whose fame should rise by the Souldiers god, *Mars*, not by the merchants god, Gold.

Mel. Madam, things past cannot be recalled, but repented; and therfore are rather to be pittied than punished. It now behoueth vs how to redresse the miserable estate of our king, not to dispute of the occasion. Your highnes sees, and without griefe you cannot see, that his meat turneth to massie gold in his mouth, and his wine slideth downe his throte like liquide golde: if he touch his roabes

25 nostrum *Bl. F.*   29 to. *before* yeeld *Bl. mods.*   S.D. Enter SOPHRONIA: *thus far* Q *Bl. F.*; *Dilke adding* MELL. *and* MART.   45 to consider *before* how *Dil.*

they are turned to gold, and what is not that toucheth him, but becommeth golde?

Erist. I *Mellacrites*, if thy tongue had been turned to gold before thou gauest our king such councel, *Mydas* heart had been ful of ease, and thy mouth of gold.

Mar. If my aduise had taken place, *Mydas* that now sitteth ouer head and eares in crownes, had worn vpon his head many kings crownes, and been conquerour of the world, that now is commaunder of drosse. That greedines of *Mellacrites*, whose heart-stringes are made of *Plutus* purse-stringes, hath made *Mydas* a lumpe of earth, that should be a god on earth; and thy effeminate minde *Eristus*, whose eyes are stitcht on *Cælias* face, and thoughts gyude to her beautie, hath bredde in all the court such a tender wantonnes, that nothing is thoght of but loue, a passion proceeding of beastly lust, and coloured with a courtlie name of loue. Thus whilest we follow the nature of things, we forget the names. Since this vnsatiable thirst of gold, and vntemperat humor of lust crept into the kings court, Souldiers haue begged almes of Artificers, and with their helmet on their head been glad to follow a Louer with a gloue in his hatte, which so much abateth the courage of true Captaines, that they must account it more honorable, in the court to be a cowarde, so rich and amorus, than in a campe to be valiant, if poore and maimed. He is more fauoured that pricks his finger with his mistres needle, then hee that breakes his launce on his enemies face: and he that hath his mouth full of fair words, than he that hath his bodie ful of deep scarres. If one be olde, & haue siluer haires on his beard, so he haue golden ruddocks in his bagges, he must be wise and honourable. If young and haue curled locks on his head, amarous glaunces with his eyes, smooth speeches in his mouth, euerie Ladies lap shalbe his pillow, euery Ladies face his glasse, euery Ladies eare a sheath for his flatteries; only Souldiers, if they be old, must beg in their owne countries; if yong, trie the fortune of warres in another. Hee is the man, that being let bloud caries his arme in a scarfe of his mistres fauour, not he that beares his legge on a stilt for his Countries safetie.

Soph. Stay *Martius*, though I know loue to growe to such losenes, and hoarding to such miserie, that I maye rather grieue at both, than remedie either: yet thy animating my father to continuall armes, to

49 there *before* not *Dil.* 57 of[2] *om. F.* 60 gyude] guide *Bl.*: gyved *Dil.*: gyvde *F. rightly*

conquere crowns, hath only brought him into imminent danger of
his owne head. The loue hee hath followed—I feare vnnaturall, the
riches he hath got—I know vnmeasurable, the warres he hath leuied—
I doubt vnlawfull, hath drawn his bodie with graie haires to the 90
graues mouth; and his minde with eating cares to desperate deter-
minations: ambition hath but two steps, the lowest bloud; the
highest enuie: both these hath my vnhappie father climbde, digging
mines of gold with the liues of men, and now enuied of the whole
world, is enuironed with enemies round about the world, not know- 95
ing that ambition hath one heele nayled in hell, though she stretch
her finger to touch the heauens. I woulde the Gods would remoue
this punishment, so that *Mydas* would be penitent. Let him thrust
thee, *Eristus* with thy loue, into Italie, where they honour lust for
a God, as the Ægyptians did dogs: thee, *Mellacrites* with thy greedi- 100
nes of gold, to the vtmost partes of the West, where all the guts of
the earth are gold: and thee, *Martius*, that soundest but bloud and
terror, into those barbarous Nations, where nothing is to be found
but bloud and terror. Let Phrygia be an example of chastitie, not
luste; liberalitie, not couetousnes; valor, not tyrannie. I wish not 105
your bodies banisht, but your mindes, that my father and your king
may be our honor, and the worlds wonder. And thou, *Cælia*, and
all you Ladies, learn this of *Sophronia*, that beautie in a minute is
both a blossome and a blast: Loue, a worme which seeming to liue
in the eye, dies in the hart. You be all yong, and faire, endeuor all 110
to be wise & vertuous, that when, like roses, you shal fall from the
stalke, you may be gathered & put to the still.

    Cæl. Madam, I am free from loue, and vnfortunate to be beloued.

    Erist. To be free from loue is strange, but to thinke scorne to be
beloued, monstrous. 115

    Soph. *Eristus*, thy tongue doth itch to talke of loue, and my eares
tingle to heare it. I charge you all, if you owe any duetie to your
king, to goe presently vnto the temple of *Bacchus*, offer praise-giftes,
and sacrifice, that *Mydas* may be released of his wish, or his life:
this I entreate you, this *Mydas* commaunds you. Iarre not with 120
your selues, agree in one for your king, if euer you took *Mydas* for
your lawful king.

    Mel. Madam we will goe, and omit nothing that duety may per-
forme, or paynes.

    Soph. Goe speedelie, least *Mydas* die before you returne: and 125

    118 praise-giftes *Q Bl. F.*: praise, gifts, *Dil.*   123 admit *F.*

you, *Cælia*, shal go with me, that with talk we may beguyle the time, and my father think of no meat.

Cæl. I attend. *Exeunt.*

Scæna 2.—⟨*The same.*⟩

⟨*Enter*⟩ Licio, Petulus, Pipenetta.

Licio. AH my girle, is not this a golden world?

Pip. It is all one as if it were lead with mee, and yet as golden with mee as with the king, for I see it, and feele it not, hee feeles it, & enioyes it not.

5   *Licio.* Gold is but the earths garbadge, a weed bred by the sunne, the very rubbish of barren ground.

Pet. Tush *Licio*, thou art vnlettered! al the earth is an egge: the white, siluer; the yolk, gold.

Licio. Why thou foole, what hen should lay that egge?

10   *Pip.* I warrant a Goose.

Licio. Nay I beleeue a Bull.

Pet. Blirt to you both! it was layd by the Sunne.

Pip. The Sun is rather a cock than a hen.

Licio. Tis true girle, els how could *Titan* haue troaden *Daphne*?

15   *Pet.* I weep ouer both your wits! if I proue in euerie respect no difference between an egge and golde, wil you not then graunt gold to be an egge?

Pip. Yes, but I beleue thy idle imagination wil make it an addle egge.

20   *Licio.* Let vs heare. Proceed Doctor egge.

Pet. Gold wil be crackt: A common saying, a crackt crowne.

Pip. I, thats a broken head.

Pet. Nay then I see thou hast a broken wit.

Licio. Wel, suppose gold wil crack.

25   *Pet.* So wil an eg.

Licio. On.

Pet. An egge is rosted in the fire.

Pip. Well.

Pet. So is gold tried in the fire.

30   *Licio.* Foorth.

Pet. An egge (as Physicions say) will make one lustie.

S. D. *The three councillors are not, as usual in the old eds., enumerated with the servants at the head of the scene: their entry is duly notified at the proper place*

Pip. Conclude.

Pet. And who knowes not that gold will make one frolike?

Licio. *Pipenetta* this is true, for it is called egge, as a thing that doth egge on, so doth gold. 35

Pip. Let vs heare all.

Pet. Egges potcht are for a weake stomach, & golde boyld, for a consuming bodie.

Licio. Spoken like a Physicion.

Pip. Or a foole of necessitie. 40

Pet. An egge is eaten at one sup, and a portague lost at one cast.

Licio. Gamester-like concluded.

Pet. Egs make custards, and gold makes spoones to eat them.

Pip. A reason dowe-baked. 45

Licio. O! the ouen of his wit was not throwly heated.

Pet. Only this ods I finde betweene mony and egs, which makes me wonder, that being more pence in the world than egs, that one should haue three egges for a peny, and not three pence for an egge. 50

Pip. A wonderful matter! but your wisdome is ouershotte in your comparison, for egs haue chickens, gold hath none.

Pet. Mops I pittie thee! gold hath egs; change an angel into ten shillings, and all those peeces are the angels egges.

Licio. He hath made a spoke, wilt thou eat an egge? but soft, here 55 come our masters, let vs shrinke aside.

Enter MELLACRITES, MARTIUS, ERISTUS.

Mel. A short answere, yet a sound, *Bacchus* is pithy and pitifull.

⟨*Reads the*⟩ *Oracle.*

In Pactolus goe bathe thy wish, and thee,
Thy wish the waues shal haue, and thou be free.

Mar. I vnderstand no Oracles! shal the water turne euery thing 60 to gold? what then shal become of the fish? shal he be free from gold? what then shal become of vs, of his crowne, of our Countrie? I like not these riddles.

Mel. Thou *Martius* art so warlike, that thou wouldest cut of the wish with a sworde, not cure it with a salue: but the Gods that can 65 geue the desires of the heart, can as easilie withdraw the torment.

56 comes *Dil.* . s. d. [Reads the Oracle] *F.*: *Q Bl. Dil.* have simply Oracle

Suppose *Vulcan* should so temper thy sword, that were thy heart neuer so valeant, thine arme neuer so strong, yet thy blade shoulde neuer draw bloud, wouldest not thou wish to haue a weaker hand, and a sharper edge?

Mar. Yes.

Mel. If *Mars* should answere thee thus, goe bath thy sword in water, and wash thy hands in milke, and thy sword shal cleaue adamant, and thy heart answere the sharpnes of thy sword, wouldst not thou trie the conclusion?

Mar. What els?

Mel. Then let *Mydas* beleeue til he haue tried, and thinke that the Gods rule as wel by geuing remedies, as graunting wishes. But *Eristus* is mum.

Mar. Cœlia hath sealed his mouth.

Erist. Cœlia hath sealed her face in my heart, which I am no more ashamed to confesse, than thou that *Mars* hath made a scarre in thy face *Martius*. But let vs in to the king. Sir boies you wait wel!

Pet. We durst not go to *Bacchus*, for if I see a grape, my head akes.

Erist. And if I finde a cudgell Ile make your shoulders ake.

Mel. And you *Licio*, wait on your selfe.

Licio. I cannot chuse sir, I am alwaies so neer my selfe.

Mel. Ile be as neere you as your skin presently.   *Exeunt.*

ACTUS 3.

Scæ. 1.—⟨ *The same.* ⟩

⟨*Enter*⟩ MYDAS, MELLACRITES, MARTIUS, ERISTUS.

Midas ⟨reading the Oracle⟩.

IN *Pactolus* go bathe thy wish and thee,
  Thy wish the waues shal haue, and thou be free.

Miserable *Mydas*, as vnaduised in thy wish, as in thy successe vnfortunat. O vnquenchable thirst of gold, which turneth mens heads to lead, and makest them blockish; their hearts to iron, and

S. D. [reading the Oracle] *added F.*   1 bathe *Q mods.*: bath *Bl.*

makest them couetous; their eyes to delight in the view, and makest them blinde in the vse. I that did possesse mynes of golde, could not bee contented till my minde were also a myne. Could not the treasure of Phrygia, nor the tributes of Greece, nor mountaines in the East, whose guts are gold, satisfie thy minde with gold? Ambition eateth gold, & drinketh blood; climeth so high by other mens heads, that she breaketh her owne necke. What should I doo with a world of ground, whose bodie must be content with seauen foote of earth? or why did I couet to get so manie crownes, hauing my self but one head? Those that tooke small vessels at the sea, I accompted Pyrates; and my selfe that suppressed whole Fleetes, a Conquerour: as though robberies of *Mydas* might masque vnder the names of triumphs, and the traffique of other Nations bee called treacherie. Thou hast pampred vp thy selfe with slaughter, as *Diomedes* did his horse with blood; so vnsatiable thy thirst, so heauie thy sword. Two bookes haue I alwaies carried in my bosome, calling them the dagger, and the sword; in which the names of all Princes, Noblemen, and Gentlemen were dedicated to slaughter, or if not (which worse is) to slauerie. O my Lords, when I call to minde my cruelties in Lycaonia, my vsurping in Getulia, my oppression in Sola: then do I finde neither mercies in my conquests, nor colour for my warres, nor measure in my taxes. I haue written my lawes in blood, and made my Gods of golde; I haue caused the mothers wombes to bee their childrens tombes, cradles to swimme in blood like boates, and the temples of the Gods a stewes for strumpets. Haue not I made the sea to groane vnder the number of my ships: and haue they not perished, that there was not two left to make a number? Haue I not thrust my subiects into a Camp, like oxen into a Cart; whom hauing made slaues by vniust warres, I vse now as slaues for all warres? Haue not I entised the subiects of my neighbor Princes to destroy their natural Kings? like moaths that eate the cloth in which they were bred, like vipers that gnawe the bowels of which they were borne, and like woormes that consume the wood in which they were ingendred? To what kingdome haue not I pretended clayme? as though I had been by the Gods created heire apparant to the world, making euerie trifle a title; and all the territories about me, traitours to me. Why did I wish that all might bee gold I toucht,

8 also] all *Dil.*   10 East *so all*   thy] my *Dil.*   14 feet *Dil.*
17 kingdoms *before* Midas *Dil.*   20 horses *Dil.*   37 clothes *Dil.*

but that I thought all mens hearts would bee touched with gold,
that what pollicie could not compasse, nor prowes, gold might haue
commaunded, and conquered? A bridge of gold did I mean to
make in that Iland where all my nauie could not make a breach.
Those Ilandes did I long to touch, that I might turne them to
gold, and my selfe to glorie. But vnhappie *Mydas*, who by the
same meanes perisheth himself, that he thought to conquere others:
being now become a shame to the world, a scorne to that petie
Prince, and to thy self a consumption. A petie Prince, *Mydas*? no,
a Prince protected by the Gods, by Nature, by his own vertue, and
his Subiects obedience. Haue not all treasons beene discouered by
miracle, not counsell? that doo the Gods chalenge. Is not the
Countrie walled with huge waues? that dooth Nature claime. Is
hee not through the whole world a wonder, for wisdome and temper-
ance? that is his owne strength. Doe not all his Subiects (like
Bees) swarme to preserue the King of Bees? that their loyaltie
mainteineth. My Lords, I faint both for lack of food, & want of
grace. I will to the riuer, where if I be rid of this intollerable disease
of gold, I will next shake off that vntemperat desire of gouernment,
and measure my Territories, not by the greatnesse of my minde, but
the right of my Succession.

Mar. I am not a little sorrie, that because all that your Highnesse
toucheth turneth to pure golde, therefore all your Princely affections
should be conuerted to drosse. Doeth your Maiestie begin to melt
your owne Crowne, that should make it with other Monarchies
massie? Begin you to make incloasure of your minde, and to
debate of inheritance, when the sworde proclaimes you conqueror?
If your Highnes heart be not of kingdome proofe, euery pelting
Prince will batter it. Though you lose this garish golde, let your
minde be still of steele, and let the sharpest sword decide the right
of Scepters.

Mid. Euerie little king is a king, and the title consisteth not in
the compasse of grounde, but in the right of inheritance.

Mar. Are not conquests good titles?

Mid. Conquests are great thefts.

Mar. If your Highnesse would be aduised by mee, then would
I rob for kingdomes, and if I obteyned, fain woulde I see him that
durste call the Conquerour a theefe.

66 and *before* therefore *old eds. F.*   71 of *om. Dil.*   72 lose] use *F.*
this *om. Dil.*

Mid. *Martius*, thy councell hath shed as much bloud as would make another sea. Valor I cannot call it, and barbarousnesse is a worde too milde. Come *Mellacrites*, let vs goe, and come you *Eristus*, that if I obteine mercie of *Bacchus*, wee may offer Sacrifice 85 to *Bacchus*. *Martius*, if you be not disposed to goe, dispose as you will of your selfe.

Mar. I will humbly attend on your Highnesse, as still hoping to haue my hearts desire, and you your height of honor. *Exeunt.*

SCÆ. 2.—⟨*The same.*⟩

LICIO, PETULUS, DELLO, MOTTO.

⟨*Enter* LICIO *and* PETULUS.⟩

Pet. AH *Licio*, a bots on the Barbar! euer since I cosened him of the golden beard I haue had the toothach.

Licio. I think *Motto* hath poysoned thy gummes.

Pet. It is a deadlie paine.

Licio. I knew a dog run mad with it. 5

Pet. I beleeue it *Licio*, and thereof it is that they cal it a dogged paine. Thou knowest I haue tried all old womens medicins, and cunning mens charms, but *interim* my teeth ake.

Enter DELLO *the barbers boy.*

Dello ⟨*aside*⟩. I am glad I haue heard the wags, to be quittance for ouer-hearing vs. We wil take the vantage, they shall finde vs 10 quick Barbers. Ile tel *Motto* my master, and then we will haue *Quid pro quo*, a tooth for a beard. *Exit.*

Pet. *Licio*, to make me merrie I pray thee go forward with the description of thy mistres: thou must beginne now at the paps.

Licio. Indeed (*Petulus*) a good beginning for thee, for thou canst 15 eat pappe now, because thou canst bite nothing els. But I haue not mind on those matters. If the king lose his golden wish, wee shall haue but a brasen Court;—but what became of the beard, *Petulus?*

Pet. I haue pawnd it, for I durst not coyn it. 20

Licio. What doest thou pay for the pawning?

Pet. Twelue pence in the pound for the moneth.

S. D. Enter DELLO . . . boy *Q Bl. F.*: DELLO enters behind them *Dil.* 16 not] no *Dil.*

Licio. What for the herbage?

Pet. It is not at herbage.

Licio. Yes *Petulus*, if it be a beard it must be at herbadge, for a beard is a badge of haire; and a badge of haire, hairbadge.

Enter MOTTO *with* DELLO.

Motto. *Dello*, thou knowest *Mydas* toucht his beard, and twas gold.

Dello. Well.

Motto. That the Pages cosend me of it.

Dello. No lie.

Motto. That I must be reuenged.

Dello. In good time.

Motto. Thou knowest I haue taught thee the knacking of the hands, the tickling on a mans haires, like the tuning of a Cittern.

Dello. True.

Motto. Besides, I instructed thee in the phrases of our eloquent occupation, as 'how sir will you be trimmed? wil you haue your beard like a spade, or a bodkin? a penthouse on your vpper lip, or an allie on your chin? a lowe curle on your head like a Bull, or dangling lock like a spaniel? your mustachoes sharp at the endes, like shomakers aules, or hanging down to your mouth like Goates flakes? your loue-locks wreathed with a silken twist, or shaggie to fal on your shoulders?'

Dello. I confesse you haue taught me *Tullie de oratore*, the very art of trimming.

Motto. Wel for all this I desire no more at thy hands, than to keep secrete the reuenge I haue prepared for the Pages.

Dello. O sir, you know I am a Barber, and cannot tittle tattle, I am one of those whose tongues are swelde with silence.

Motto. Indeed thou shouldst be no blab, because a barber, therefore be secret.—(*Louder.*) Was it not a good cure *Dello*, to ease the toothach and neuer touch the tooth?

Dello. O master, he that is your patient for the toothach, I warrant is patient of all aches.

Motto. I did but rub his gummes, and presentlie the rewme euaporated.

Licio. *Deus bone*, is that worde come into the Barbers bason?

38–44 'how ... shoulders?' *inv. commas first F.*   56 rheume *Bl. mods.*

Dello. I sir and why not? My master is a Barber and a Surgeon.

Licio. In good time. 60

Pet. O *Motto*, I am almost dead with the toothach, al my gummes are swollen, and my teeth stande in my head like thornes.

Motto. It may be that it is only the breding of a beard, and being the first beard, you shall haue a hard trauel.

Pet. Old foole, doest thou thinke haires will breede in my teeth? 65

Motto. As likelie sir, for any thing I know, as on your chinne.

Pet. O teeth! ô torments!—ô torments! ô teeth!

Motto ⟨*aside to his boy*⟩. May I but touch them *Dello*, Ile teach his tong to tel a tale, what villenie it is to cosen one of a bearde, but stand not thou nigh, for it is ods when he spits, but that all his teeth 70 flie in thy face.

Licio. Good *Motto* geue some ease, for at thy comming in, I ouer-heard of a cure thou hadst done.

Pet. My teeth! I wil not haue this paine, thats certain!

Motto. I, so did you ouer-heare me, when you cosened me of 75 a beard: but I forget all.

Dello. My master is mild and mercifull: and mercifull, because a Barber, for when he hath the throat at commaund, you know hee taketh reuenge but on a sillie haire.

Motto. How now *Petulus*, do they still ake? 80

Pet. I *Motto*.

Motto. Let me rub your gummes with this leafe.

Pet. Doe *Motto*, and for thy labor I wil requite thee. ⟨*Under pretence of easing* MOTTO *hurts him.*⟩ Out rascal! what hast thou done? all my nether teeth are lose, and wag like the keyes of a paire 85 of virginals.

Dello. O sir, if you wil, I will sing to them, your mouth beeing the instrument.

Pet. Doe *Dello*.

Dello. Out, villen! thou bitest. I cannot tune these virginal keyes. 90

Pet. They were the Iackes aboue, the keyes beneath were easie.

Dello. A bots on your Iacks and Iawes too!

Licio. They were virginalls of your masters making.

Pet. O my teeth! good *Motto* what wil ease my pain?

Motto. Nothing in the world, but to let me lay a golden beard to 95 your chinne.

64 travail *Dil.*   68 [aside &c.] *Dil. suppl.* (aside)   S. D. [Under ... hurts him.] MOTTO rubs his gums *inserted Dil.*

Pet. It is at pawne.

Motto. You are like to fetch it out with your teeth, or goe without your teeth.

Pet. Motto withdraw thy selfe, it may be thou shalt drawe my teeth; attend my resolution. ⟨MOTTO *and* DELLO *retire.*⟩ A doubtfull dispute, whether I were best to loose my golden beard, or my bone tooth? Helpe me *Lycio* to determine.

Licio. Your teeth ake *Petulus,* your beard doth not.

Pet. I but *Lycio,* if I part from my beard, my heart will ake.

Licio. If your tooth be hollow it must be stopt, or puld out; and stop it the Barbar wil not, without the beard.

Pet. My heart is hollow too, and nothing can stop it but gold.

Licio. Thou canst not eate meate without teeth.

Pet. Nor buy it without money.

Licio. Thou maist get more gold; if thou loose these, more teeth thou canst not.

Pet. I but the golden beard will last me ten yeres in porredge, and then to what vse are teeth?

Licio. If thou want teeth, thy toung will catch cold.

Pet. Tis true, and if I lacke money my whole bodie may go naked. But *Lycio,* let the Barbar haue his beard, I will haue a deuice (by thy helpe) to get it againe, & a cousenage beyond that, maugre his beard.

Licio. Thats the best way, both to ease thy paines, and trie our wits.

Pet. Barber, eleuen of my teeth haue gone on a Iury, to trie whether the beard bee thine, they haue chosen my tongue for the foreman, which cryeth guiltie.

Motto. Guilded, nay boy, al my beard was gold. It was not guilt, I wil not be so ouer-matcht.

Dello. You cannot pose my master in a beard. Come to his house you shall sit vpon twentie, all his cushions are stuft with beards.

Licio. Let him goe home with thee, ease him, and thou shalt haue thy beard.

Motto. I am content, but I wil haue the beard in my hand to be sure.

Pet. And I thy finger in my mouth to be sure of ease.

Motto. Agreed.

S. D. [MOTTO ... retire] *first in Dil.*: *om. F.*   120 to *before* try *Bl. F.*

Pet. *Dello*, sing a song to the tune of my teeth do ake.
Dello. I will.

THE SONG.

Pet. O My Teeth! deare Barber ease me,
　　　Tongue tell mee, why my Teeth disease mee,
　O! what will rid me of this paine? 140
Motto. Some Pellitory fetcht from Spaine.
Licio. Take Masticke else.
Pet. 　　　　　Mastick's a patch.
Masticke does many a fooles face catch.
If suche a paine should breed the Horne,
Twere happy to be Cuckolds borne. 145
Should Beards with such an ach begin,
Each Boy to th' bone would scrub his chin.
Licio. His Teeth now ake not.
Motto. 　　　　Caper then,
And cry vp checkerd-apron men:
　There is no Trade but shaues, 150
　For, Barbers are trimme Knaues,
Some are in shauing so profound,
By trickes they shaue a Kingdome round.
　　　　　　　　　　　　　Exeunt.

SCÆ. 3.—⟨*The same.*⟩

⟨*Enter*⟩ SOPHRONIA, CÆLIA, CAMILLA, AMERULA SUAUIA.

Soph. Ladies, here must we attend the happy return of my father, but in the mean season what pastime shal we vse to passe the time? I wil agree to any, so it be not to talke of loue.

Sua. Then sleepe is the best exercise. 5

Soph. Why *Suauia*, are you so light, that you must chat of loue; or so heauie, that you must needes sleepe? *Penelope* in the absence of her Lord beguyled the daies with spinning.

Sua. Indeed she spun a faire threed, if it were to make a string to the bow wherin she drew her woers. 10

Soph. Why *Suauia*, it was a bow which she knew to be aboue their strength, and therein she shewde her wit.

Sua. Qui latus arguerit corneus arcus erat: it was made of horne madam, and therin she shewde her meaning.

Soph. Why, doest thou not think she was chast? 15

s.d. The song *so Q, without giving the words, which first appear in Bl.* 12 their] thy *Q Bl. F.*: her *Dil.*　　13 arguerit *so all*

SC. III]   MIDAS   137

Sua. Yes, of all her woers.

Soph. To talke with thee is to lose time, not well to spend it: how say you, *Amerula*, what shal we do?

Ame. Tel tales.

20   *Soph.* What say you *Cælia*?

Cæl. Sing.

Soph. What think you *Camilla*?

Cam. Daunce.

Soph. You see *Suauia*, that there are other things to keep one
25 from idlenes, besides loue: nay that there is nothing to make idlenes, but loue.

Sua. Well, let mee stande by and feede mine owne thoughts with sweetenes, whilest they fil your eyes and eares with songs and dauncings.

30 *Soph. Amerula*, begin thy tale.

Ame. There dwelt somtimes in Phrygia, a Lady very fair, but passing froward, as much maruelled at for beutie, as for peeuishnes misliked. Hie she was in the instep, but short in the heele; strait laced, but loose bodied. It came to passe, that a gentleman, as
35 yong in wit as yeres, and in yeres a very boy, chanced to glaunce his eies on her, & there were they dazeled on her beautie, as larkes that are caught in the Sunne with the glittering of a glasse. In her faire lookes were his thoughts intangled, like the birdes of Canarie, that fal into a silken net. Dote he did without measure,
40 and die he must without her loue. She on the other side, as one that knew her good, began to looke askaunce, yet felt the passions of loue eating into her heart, though shee dissembled them with her eyes.

Sua. Ha, ha, he!

Soph. Why laughest thou?

45 *Sua.* To see you (Madame) so tame as to be brought to heare a tale of loue, that before were so wylde you would not come to the name; and that *Amerula* could deuise how to spend the time with a tale, onely that she might not talke of loue, and now to make loue onely her tale.

50 *Soph.* Indeed I was ouershot in iudgement, and she in discretion. *Amerula*, another tale or none, this is too louely.

Sua. Nay let me heare anie woman tell a tale of x lines long without it tend to loue, & I wil be bound neuer to come at the

32 forward *Dil.*   36 on²] with *Dil.*   43 he *old eds. Dil.*: ha *F.*   52
x *Q*: tenne *Bl. mods.*

Court. And you *Camilla* that would fain trip on your petitoes; can you perswade me you take delight to dance, & not loue? or you that cannot rule your feet, can guid your affections, hauing the one as vnstaid as the other vnsteadie: dauncing is loue sauce, therefore I dare be so sawcie, as if you loue to daunce, to say you daunce for loue. But *Cælia* she will sing, whose voice if it should vtter her thoughts, would make the tune of a hart out of tune. She that hath crochets in her head, hath also loue conceipts. I dare sweare she harpeth not onely on plaine song: & before you (*Sophronia*) none of them all vse plaine dealing; but because they see you so curious they frame themselues counterfet. For my selfe, as I knowe honest loue to bee a thing inseperable from our sex, so doo I thinke it most allowable in the Court; vnlesse we would haue all our thoughts made of Church-worke, and so carrie a holiė face, and a hollow hart.

Soph. Ladies, how like you *Suauia* in her louing vaine?

Cæl. Wee are content at this time to sooth her in her vanitie.

Ame. Shee casts all our mindes in the mould of her owne head, and yet erreth as farre from our meanings, as she doth from her owne modestie.

Sua. *Amerula*, if you were not bitter, your name had been ill bestowed: but I think it as lawfull in the Court to bee counted louing and chast, as you in the Temple to seeme religious, and be spitefull.

Cam. I meruaile you will reply anie more *Amerula*, her toung is so nimble it will neuer lye still.

Sua. The liker thy feete *Camilla*, which were taught not to stand still.

Soph. So, no more Ladies: let our comming to sport not tourne to spight. Loue thou *Suauia*, if thou thinke it sweete: sing thou *Cælia* for thine owne content: tell thou tales, and daunce thou *Camilla*: and so euerie one vsing hir own delight, shall haue no cause to be discontent. But here cōmeth *Martius* & the rest.

⟨*Enter* MARTIUS, MELLACRITES, *and others.*⟩

What newes *Martius* of my Soueraigne and Father *Mydas*?

Mar. Madam, he no sooner bathed his lims in the riuer, but it turnde to a golden stream, the sands to fine gold, and all to gold

---

54 Camilla *Dil.*: Cælia Q Bl. F. *Cf. ll.* 23, 79 (*pp.* 137, 138) to *previous eds. from subsequent* to *ll.* 21, 82 (*pp.* 137, 138) 55 you[2]] her *om. Dil.* 59 Cælia *Dil.*: Camilla Q Bl. F. *Cf.* s. d. [Enter MARTIUS ... others] *Dilke only*

that was cast into the water. *Mydas* dismaid at the sodaine alteration, assaied againe to touch a stone, but he could not alter the
nature of the stone. Then went we with him to the Temple of
Bacchus, where we offred a launce wreathed about with yuie,
Garlands of ripe grapes, and skinnes of Wolues and Panthers, and
a great standing cup of the water, which so lately was turnd to
golde. *Bacchus* accepted our giftes, commaunding *Mydas* to honour
the Gods, and also in wishing to bee as wise, as he meant to haue
made him fortunate.

Soph. Happie *Sophronia*, thou hast liued to heare these newes,
and happie *Mydas*, if thou liue better to gouern thy fortune. But
what is become of our king?

Mel. Mydas ouerioyed with this good fortune, determined to vse
some solace in the woods; where, by chaunce we roused a great
bore: he eager of the sport, outrid vs; and wee thinking hee had
been come to his Pallace some other way, came our selues the next
way. If he be not returned, he cannot be long: we haue also lost
our pages, which we thinke are with him.

Soph. The Gods shield him from all harmes: the woods are full
of Tygers, and he of courage: wilde beasts make no difference between a king & a clowne; nor hunters in the heat of their pastime,
feare no more the fiersnes of the boare, thā the fearfulnes of the
hare. But I hope well, let vs in to see all well. *Exeunt.*

ACTUS 4.

SCÆNA 1.—⟨*Glade in a Forest on Mount Tmolus.*⟩

APOLLO. PAN. MYDAS. Nymphes.

⟨*Enter* APOLLO, PAN, ERATO *and* Nymphs.⟩

Apollo. PAn wilt thou contend with *Apollo*, who tunes the heauens,
and makes them all hang by harmony? *Orpheus* that
caused trees to moue with the sweetnes of his harp, offreth yerely
homage to my lute: so doth *Arion*, that brought Dolphins to his
sugred notes; and *Amphion*, that by musicke reard the walls of
Thebes. Onely *Pan* with his harsh whistle (which makes beasts

98 these] this *Dil.* 103 bore:] bore, *Q Bl. F.* 111 I *om. Bl. F.*

shake for feare, not men dance for ioy) seekes to compare with *Apollo*.

Pan. *Pan* is a God, *Apollo* is no more. Comparisons cannot bee odious, where the Dieties are equall. This pipe (my sweete pipe) was once a Nymph, a faire Nymph; once my louely Mistres, now my heauenly musicke. Tell mee *Apollo*, is there anie instrument so sweete to play on as ones Mistres? Had thy lute been of lawrell, and the strings of *Daphnes* haire, thy tunes might haue beene compared to my noates: for then *Daphne* would haue added to thy stroake sweetnes, & to thy thoughts melodie.

Apollo. Doth *Pan* talke of the passions of loue? of the passions of deuine loue? O, how that word *Daphne* wounds *Apollo*, pronounced by the barbrous mouth of *Pan*. I feare his breath will blaste the faire Greene, if I dazel not his eyes, that he may not behold it. Thy pipe a Nimph? some hag rather, hanting these shady groues, and desiring not thy loue, but the fellowship of such a monster. What God is *Pan* but the god of beastes, of woods, and hilles? excluded from heauen, and in earth not honoured. Breake thy pipe, or with my sweet lute will I breake thy heart. Let not loue enter into those sauage lips, a word for *Ioue*, for *Apollo*, for the heauenlie gods, whose thoughts are gods, & Gods are all loue.

Pan. *Apollo*, I tolde thee before that *Pan* was a God, I tell thee now againe, as great a god as *Apollo*, I had almost said a greater: and because thou shalt know I care not to tel my thoghts, I say a greater. *Pan* feeles the passions of loue deeply engrauen in his heart, with as faire Nimphs, with as great fortune, as *Apollo*, as *Neptune*, as *Ioue;* and better than *Pan* can none describe loue. Not *Apollo*, not *Neptune*, not *Ioue!* My Temple is in Arcadie, where they burne continuall flames to *Pan*. In Arcadie is mine Oracle, where *Erato* the Nymphe geeueth aunsweres for *Pan*. In Arcadie the place of Loue, is the honour of *Pan*. I but I am God of hilles. So I am, *Apollo!* and that of Hilles so high, as I can prie into the iugling of the highest Gods. Of woods! So I am *Apollo!* of woods so thicke, that thou with thy beames canst not pierce them. I knew *Apolloes* prying, I knewe mine owne iealouzie. Sunne and shadow cousen one another. Be thou Sun still, the shadow is fast at thy heeles *Apollo*. I as neere to thy loue, as thou to mine. A Carter with his whistle & his whip in

7 shake om. *Bl.*   21 haunting *Dil.*   41 Apollo *Dil.*   43 I] Ah, *Dil. perh. by misprint for* Ay,

true eare, mooues as much as *Phœbus* with his fierie chariot, and winged horses. Loue-leaues are as wel for countrie porridge, as heauenly nectar. Loue made *Iupiter* a goose, and *Neptune* a swine, and both for loue of an earthlie mistresse. What hath made *Pan*, or any God on earth (for gods on earth can change their shapes) turne themselues for an heauenly Goddesse? Beleeue me *Apollo*, our groues are pleasanter than your heauens, our Milk-maides than your Goddesses, our rude ditties to a pipe than your sonnets to a lute. Heere is flat faith *amo amas;* where you crie, *ô vtinam amarent vel non amassem.* I let passe (*Apollo*) thy hard words, as calling *Pan* monster; which is as much, as to call all monsters: for *Pan* is all, *Apollo* but one. But touch thy strings, and let these Nymphs decyde.

Apollo. Those Nymphes shall decide, vnlesse thy rude speach haue made them deafe: as for anie other aunswere to *Pan*, take this, that it becommeth not *Apolio* to aunswere *Pan*. *Pan* is all, and all is *Pan;* thou art *Pan* and all, all *Pan* and tinkerly. But to this musick, wherin all thy shame shall be seene, and all my skill.

Enter MYDAS.

Mid. In the chase, I lost all my companie, and missed the game too. I thinke *Mydas* shall in all things be vnfortunate.

Apollo. What is he that talketh?

Mid. Mydas the vnfortunate King of Phrygia.

Apollo. To be a King is next being to a God. Thy fortune is not bad: what is thy follie?

Mid. To abuse a God.

Apollo. An vngratefull part of a King. But, *Mydas*, seeing by chaunce thou art come, or sent by some God of purpose; none can in the earth better iudge of Gods, than Kings. Sit downe with these Nymphes. I am *Apollo*, this *Pan*, both Gods. We contend for souereigntie in Musicke. Seeing it happens in earth, we must be iudged of those on earth; in which there are none more worthie than Kings and Nymphes. Therefore giue eare, that thy iudgement erre not.

Mid. If Gods you be, althogh I dare wish nothing of Gods, being so deeply wounded with wishing; yet let my iudgement preuaile before these Nymphes, if we agree not, because I am a King.

45 ears *Dil.*   47 goose] swan *Dil.*   58 Those] These *F.*   67 being to *old eds.*: to being *Dil. F.*   75 there] they *F.*

Pan. There must be no condition, but iudge *Mydas*, and iudge Nymphes.

Apollo. Then thus I begin both my song and my play.

         A SONG *of* DAPHNE *to the Lute.*

Apollo. MY *Daphne's* Haire is twisted Gold,
     Bright starres a-piece her Eyes doe hold,   85
My *Daphne's* Brow inthrones the Graces,
My *Daphne's* Beauty staines all Faces,
On *Daphne's* Cheeke grow Rose and Cherry,
On *Daphne's* Lip a sweeter Berry,
Daphne's snowy Hand but touch'd does melt,   90
And then no heauenlier Warmth is felt,
My *Daphne's* voice tunes all the Spheres,
My *Daphne's* Musick charmes all Eares.
Fond am I thus to sing her prayse;
These glories now are turn'd to Bayes.   95

Nymph Erato. O diuine *Apollo,* ô sweete consent!

Tha. If the God of Musicke should not be aboue our reach, who should?

Mid. I like it not.

Pan. Now let me tune my pipes. I cannot pipe & sing, thats the 100 ods in the instrument, not the art: but I will pipe and then sing; and then iudge both of the art and instrument.

      He pipes, and then sings.

         SONG.

Pan. PAn's *Syrinx* was a Girle indeed,
    Though now shee's turn'd into a Reed,
From that deare Reed *Pan's* Pipe does come,   105
A Pipe that strikes *Apollo* dumbe;
Nor Flute, nor Lute, nor Gitterne can
So chant it, as the Pipe of *Pan;*
Cross-gartred Swaines, & Dairie girles,
With faces smug, and round as Pearles,   110
When *Pans* shrill Pipe begins to play,
With dancing weare out Night and Day:
The Bag-pipes Drone his Hum layes by,
When *Pan* sounds vp his Minstrelsie,

   S. D. A song . . . Lute *so* Q, *but without giving the words, which first appear in Bl.*   90 Daphne's snowy] My Daphne's *Dil. metr. gra.*   97 Tha. *Dil.*: Thia *Q Bl. F.*   S. D. He pipes, and then sings *so Q Bl. but Blount first gives the words*

His Minstrelsie! O Base! This Quill
Which at my mouth with winde I fill,
Puts me in minde, though Her I misse,
That still my *Syrinx* lips I kisse.

Apollo. Hast thou done *Pan*?

Pan. I, and done well, as I thinke.

Apollo. Now Nymphes, what say you?

Erato. Wee all say that *Apollo* hath shewed himselfe both a God, and of musicke the God; *Pan* himselfe a rude Satyre, neither keeping measure, nor time; his piping as farre out of tune, as his bodie out of forme. To thee diuine *Apollo*, wee giue the prize and reuerence.

Apollo. But what saies *Mydas*?

Mid. Mee thinkes theres more sweetnesse in the pipe of *Pan*, than *Apolloes* lute; I brooke not that nice tickling of strings, that contents mee that makes one starr. What a shrilnes came into mine eares out of that pipe, and what a goodly noise it made! *Apollo*, I must needes iudge that *Pan* deserueth most praise.

Pan. Blessed be *Mydas*, worthie to be a God: these girles, whose eares doo but itch with daintines, geue the verdit without weying the virtue; they haue been brought vp in chambers with soft musicke, not where I make the woods ring with my pipe, *Mydas*.

Apollo. Wretched, vnworthie to bee a King, thou shalt know what it is to displease *Apollo*. I will leaue thee but the two last letters of thy name, to be thy whole name; which if thou canst not gesse, touch thine eares, they shall tell thee.

Mid. What hast thou done *Apollo*? the eares of an Asse vpon the head of a King?

Apollo. And well worthie, when the dulnes of an asse is in the eares of a King.

Mid. Helpe *Pan!* or *Mydas* perisheth.

Pan. I cannot vndoo what *Apollo* hath done, nor giue thee anie amends, vnlesse to those eares thou wilt haue added these hornes.

1 *Nymph.* It were verie well, that it might bee hard to iudge whether he were more Ox or Asse.

Apollo. Farewell *Mydas*. ⟨*Exit.*⟩

Pan. Mydas farewell. ⟨*Exit.*⟩

2 *Nymph.* I warrant they bee daintie eares, nothing can please them but *Pans* pipe.

134 geue *Q*: giue *Bl. F.*: gave *Dil.*

Erato. He hath the aduantage of all eares, except the mouse; for els theres none so sharpe of hearing, as the Asse. Farewell *Mydas.*

2 Nymph. Mydas farewell.

3 Nymph. Farewell *Mydas.*   *Exeunt* ⟨ERATO *and* Nymphs⟩.

Mid. Ah *Mydas*, why was not thy whole bodie metamorphosed, that there might haue been no parte left of *Mydas*? Where shall I shrowd this shame? or how may I bee restored to mine olde shape? *Apollo* is angrie: blame not *Apollo*, whom being God of musick thou didst both dislike and dishonour; preferring the barbarous noyse of *Pans* pipe, before the sweete melodie of *Apolloes* lute. If I returne to Phrygia, I shall bee pointed at; if liue in these woods, sauage beasts must be my cōpanions: & what other companions should *Mydas* hope for than beasts, being of all beasts himselfe the dullest? Had it not bin better for thee to haue perished by a golden death, than now to lead a beastly life? Vnfortunat in thy wish, vnwise in thy iudgmēt; first a golden foole, now a leaden asse. What wil they say in Lesbos (if happely these newes come to Lesbos)? If they come *Mydas*? yes, report flies as swift as thoghts, gathering wings in the aire, & dubling rumors by her owne running, insomuch as hauing here the eares of an asse, it wil there be told, all my haires are asses eares. Then will this bee the by-word; Is *Mydas* that sought to bee Monarch of the world, become the mock of the world? are his goldē mynes turnd into water, as free for euery one that wil fetch, as for himself, that possessed thē by wish? Ah poore *Mydas!* are his conceipts become blockish, his counsells vnfortunate, his iudgements vnskilfull? Ah foolish *Mydas!* a iust reward, for thy pride to wexe poore, for thy ouerweening to wexe dull, for thy ambition to wexe humble, for thy crueltie to say, *Sisq̃ miser semper, nec sis miserabilis vlli.* But I must seeke to couer my shame by arte, least beeing once discouered to these pettie Kings of Mysia, Pisidia and Galatia, they all ioyne to adde to mine Asses eares, of all the beasts the dullest, a sheepes heart, of all the beasts the fearfullest: and so cast lots for those Kingdomes, that I haue won with so manie liues, & kept with so manie enuies.   *Exit.*

164 melolodie *Q*   165 I *before* liue *Dil. F.*   171 happily *Bl. F.*:
haply *Dil.*   these] this *Dil.*

ScÆ. 2.—⟨*A reedy place.*⟩

Enter 5. *shepheards;* MENALCAS, CORYN, CELTHUS, DRIAPON, AMYNTAS.

Menal. I Muse what the Nymphs ment, that so sang in the groues, *Mydas* of Phrygia hath Asses eares.

Cor. I maruel not, for one of them plainly told me he had Asses eares.

5 *Cel.* I, but it is not safe to say it : he is a great King, & his hands are longer than his eares : therefore for vs that keep sheepe, it is wisedome enough to tell sheepe.

Drya. Tis true, yet since *Mydas* grew so mischeuous, as to blurre his diademe with blood, which should glister with nothing but pittie;
10 and so miserable, that hee made gold his god, that was framde to be his slaue, manie broad speeches haue flowen abroad : in his owne Countrey they sticke not to call him Tyrant, and else where vsurper. They flatly say, that he eateth into other dominions, as the sea doth into the land, not knowing, that in swallowing a poore Iland
15 as big as Lesbos, he may cast vp three territories thrice as big as Phrygia: for what the sea winneth in the marshe, it looseth in the sand.

Amynt. Take me with you, but speak softlie, for these reedes may haue eares, and heare vs.

20 *Menal.* Suppose they haue, yet they may be without tongues, to bewray vs.

Cor. Nay, let them haue tongues too, wee haue eyes to see that they haue none, and therfore if they heare, & speak, they know not from whence it comes.

25 *Amynt.* Well, then this I say, when a Lion doeth so much degenerat from Princely kind, that he wil borow of the beasts, I say he is no Lion, but a monster; peec'd with the craftines of the fox, the crueltie of the tyger, the rauening of the woolfe, the dissembling of Hyena, he is worthie also to haue the eares of an
30 asse.

Menal. He seekes to conquere Lesbos, and like a foolish gamester, hauing a bagfull of his owne, ventures it all to winne a groat of another.

Cor. Hee that fishes for Lesbos, muste haue such a woodden net,

S. D. Draipon *Bl.*   27 craftinesses *F.*   29 the *before* Hyena *Dil. F.* (*see note*)

as all the trees in Phrygia wil not serue to make the cod, nor all the 35
woods in Pisidia prouide the corks.

Drya. Nay, he meanes to angle for it with an hook of gold and
a bait of gold, and so to strike the fish with a pleasing bait, that wil
slide out of an open net.

Amynt. Tush! tush! those Ilanders are too subtil to nibble at 40
craft, and too riche to swallowe treasure: if that be his hope, he
may as wel diue to the bottome of the sea, and bring vp an Anchor
of a thousand weight, as plod with his gold to corrupt a people so
wise. And besides, a Nation (as I haue heard) so valiant, that are
redier to strike than ward. 45

Cel. More than al this *Amintas* (though we dare not so much as
mutter it), their king is such a one as dazeleth the cleerest eyes with
Maiestie, daunteth the valiantest hearts with courage, and for vertue
filleth all the world with wonder. If beautie goe beyond sight,
confidence aboue valour, and vertue exceed miracle, what is it to 50
be thought, but that *Mydas* goeth to vndermine that by the simplicitie of man, that is fastened to a rock, by the prouidence of
the gods.

Menal. We poore commons (who tasting warre, are made to
rellish nothing but taxes) can do nothing but grieue, to see things 55
vnlawful practised, to obtein things impossible. All his mines doe
but gilde his combe, to make it glister in the warres, and cut oures
that are forced to follow him in his warres.

Cor. Well, that must be borne, not blam'd, that cannot be
changed: for my part, if I may enioy the fleece of my sillie flock 60
with quietnes, I will neuer care three flocks for his ambition.

Menal. Let this suffice, we may talke too much, and being ouer-
heard, be all vndone. I am so iealous, that me thinks the very
reedes bow downe, as though they listned to our talke: and soft!
I heare some comming, let vs in, and meet at a place more meet. 65
Exeunt.

Scæ. 3.—⟨*The same.*⟩

⟨*Enter*⟩ Licio, Petulus, Minutius, Huntsman.

Licio. IS not hunting a tedious occupation?
Pet. I and troublesome, for if you call a dog a dog, you
are vndone.

43 plod *so all*

Hunts. You be both fooles! and besides, base-minded: hunting is for kings, not peasants. Such as you are vnworthie to be hounds, much lesse huntsmen, that know not when a hound is fleet, faire flewde, and well hangd, being ignorant of the deepenesse of a houndes mouth, and the sweetnes.

Min. Why I hope sir a curres mouth is no deeper than the sea, nor sweeter than a hony combe.

Hunts. Prettie cockscombe! a hound wil swalow thee as easilie, as a great pit a small pibble.

Min. Indeed hunting were a pleasant sport, but the dogges make such barking, that one cannot heare the hounds crie.

Hunts. Ile make thee crie! If I catch thee in the forest thou shalt be leasht.

Min. Whats that?

Licio. Doest thou not vnderstand their language?

Min. Not I!

Pet. Tis the best Calamance in the world, as easilie deciphered, as the characters in a nutmeg.

Min. I pray thee speake some.

Pet. I will.

Hunts. But speake in order or Ile pay you.

Licio. To it *Petulus*.

Pet. There was a boy leasht on the single, because when he was imbost, he tooke soyle.

Licio. Whats that?

Pet. Why, a boy was beaten on the taile with a leathern thong, bicause when he fomde at the mouth with running, he went into the water.

Hunts. This is worse than fustian! mumme! you were best! Hunting is an honorable pastime, and for my part I had as leife hunt a deere in a parke, as court a Ladie in a chamber.

Min. Geue mee a pastie for a Parke, and let mee shake off a whole kennel of teeth for hounds, then shalt thou see a notable champing, after that will I carouse a boule of wine, and so in the stomack let the Venison take soyle.

Licio. He hath laid the plot to be prudent: why tis pastie crust, eat enough and it will make you wise, an olde prouerb.

16, 26 lashte *Bl. F.*   28 Licio] Min. *F.*   32 This is . . fustian! *assigned without authority or comment as separate speech to Minutius F*   39 prudent; *Dil.*: prudent, Q *Bl. F.*   40 eat . . . wise] *in inverted commas F. More correctly* 'why . . . wise'

Pet. I, and eloquent, for you must tipple wine freely, *& fæcundi calices quem non fecere disertum?*

Hunts. *Fecere dizardum!* Leaue off these toyes, and let vs seek out *Mydas*, whom we lost in the chase.

Pet. Ile warrant hee hath by this started a couey of Bucks, or roused a scull of Phesants.

Hunts. Treason to two braue sports, hauking & hunting, thou shouldest say, start a hare, rowse the deere, spring the partridge.

Pet. Ile warrant that was deuised by some Country swad, that seeing a hare skip vp, which made him start, he presently said, he started the hare.

Licio. I, and some lubber lying besides a spring, & seeing a partridge come by, said he did spring the partridge.

Hunts. Well, remember all this!

Pet. Remember all? nay then had we good memories, for there be more phrases than thou hast haires! but let me see, I pray thee whats this about thy neck?

Hunts. A bugle.

Pet. If it had stoode on thy head I should haue called it a horne. Wel, tis hard to haue ones browes imbroidered with bugle.

Licio. But canst thou blowe it?

Hunts. What els?

Min. But not away.

Pet. No, twil make *Boreas* out of breath, to blow his hornes away.

Licio. There was good blowing Ile warrant before they came there.

Pet. Well, tis a shrowd blow.

Hunts. Spare your windes in this, or Ile winde your neckes in a cord: but soft, I heard my masters blaste.

Min. Some haue felt it!

Hunts. Thy mother, when such a flyblow was buzd out! but I must be gone, I perceiue *Mydas* is come.   *Exit.*

Licio. Then let not vs tarrie, for now shal we shaue the Barbars house. The world will grow full of wyles seeing *Mydas* hath lost his golden wish.

Min. I care not, my head shall dig deuises, and my tongue stampe them; so as my mouth shall be a mynt, and my braynes a myne.

56 haires *so all*   68 shrewd *Dil.*

Licio. Then help vs to cousen the Barbar.

80 *Min.* The Barbar shal know euerie haire of my chin to be as good as a choakpeare for his purse. ⟨*Exeunt.*⟩

Scæna 4.—⟨*The same.*⟩

⟨*Enter*⟩ Mellacrites. Martius. Eristus.

Erist. I Maruell what *Mydas* meaneth to bee so melancholy since his hunting.

Mel. It is a good word in *Mydas*, otherwise I should tearme it in another blockishnes. I cannot tell whether it bee a sowernesse 5 commonly incident to age, or a seuerenesse perticular to the Kings of Phrygia, or a suspition cleauing to great Estates; but mee thinkes he seemeth so iealous of vs al, and becomes so ouerthwart to all others, that either I must coniecture his wits are not his owne, or his meaning verie hard to some.

10 *Mar.* For my part, I neither care nor wonder, I see all his expeditions for warres are laid in water: for now when he should execute, he begins to consult; and suffers the enemies to bid vs good morrowe at our owne doores, to whom wee long since might haue giuen the last Good night in their owne beds. Hee weareth (I know 15 not whether for warmth or wantonnes) a great Tyara on his head, as though his head were not heauie enough, vnlesse hee loaded it with great rolles: an attyre neuer vsed (that I could heare of) but of old women, or pelting priestes. This will make Pisidia wanton, Lycaonia stiffe, all his Territories wauering; and hee that hath 20 coutcht so manie Kingdomes in one Crowne, wil haue his Kingdome scattered into as manie Crownes as hee possesseth Countries. I will rouse him vp, and if his eares be not Asses eares, I will make them tingle. I respect not my life, I knowe it is my duetie, and certainly I dare sweare Warre is my profession.

25 *Erist. Martius*, we will all ioyne: and though I haue been (as in Phrygia they tearme) a braue Courtier, that is, (as they expound it) a fine Louer; yet will I set both aside, Loue and Courting, and followe *Martius:* for neuer shall it bee sayd, *Bella gerant alij, semper Eristus amet.*

30 *Mel.* And I (*Martius*) that honored gold for a god, and accounted

20 coutcht *Bl. F.*: coutched *Dil.*   Kingdome] Kingdomes *Bl. F.*

all other gods but lead, wil follow *Martius*, and say; *Vilius argentum est auro, virtutibus aurum.*

Mar. My Lords, I giue you thankes, and am glad: for there are no stouter soldiers in the world, than those that are made of louers, nor anie more liberall in wars, than they that in peace haue beene 35 couetous. Then doubt not, if courage and coyne can preuaile, but wee shall preuaile; & besides, nothing can preuaile but fortune. But here comes *Sophronia*, I wil first talk with her.

Enter SOPHRONIA, CAMILIA, AMERULA.

Madame, either our King hath no eares to heare, or no care to consider, both in what state we stand beeing his subiects, and what 40 danger he is in being our King. Dutie is not regarded, courage contemned; altogether careles of vs, and his owne safetie.

Soph. Martius, I mislike not thy plaine dealing: but pittie my Fathers traunce; a traunce I must call that, where nature cannot moue, nor counsaile, nor musick, nor phisicke, nor daunger, nor death, 45 nor all. But that which maketh me most both to sorrow and wonder, is that musick (a methridat for melancholy) should make him mad; crying still, *Uno namqʒ modo Pan & Apollo nocent.* None hath accesse to him but *Motto*, as thogh melancholy were to be shau'n with a razor, not cur'd with a medicin. But stay, what noise is this 50 in those reedes?

Mel. What sound is this? who dares vtter that he heares?

Soph. I dare *Mellacrites*, the words are plaine,—*Mydas* the King hath asses eares.

Cam. This is strange, and yet to be told the King. 55

Soph. So dare I *Camilla:* for it concerneth me in dutie, & vs all in discretion. But soft, let vs hearken better.

The Reedes. Mydas of Phrygia hath asses eares.

Erist. This is monstrous, & either portends some mischiefe to the king, or vnto the state confusion. *Mydas* of Phrygia hath asses 60 ears? It is vnpossible let vs with speed to the king to know his resolutiō, for to some oracle he must send. Til his maiesty be acquainted with this matter, wee dare not roote out the reedes; himselfe must both heare the sound, and gesse at the reason.

Soph. Vnfortunate *Mydas*, that beeing so great a king, there 65 should out of the earth spring so great a shame.

Mar. It may bee that his wishing for golde, being but drosse of the world, is by all the Gods accounted foolish, and so discouered out of the earth: for a King to thirst for golde in steede of honour, to preferre heapes of worldly coyne before triumphes in warlike Conquests, was in my minde no Princely minde.

Mel. Let vs not debate the cause, but seeke to preuent the snares; for in my minde it foretelleth that which woundeth my minde. Let vs in. *Exeunt.*

ACTUS 5.

Scæna 1.—⟨ *The reedy place.* ⟩

⟨*Enter*⟩ Mydas. Sophronia. Mellicrates. Martius.

Mid. Sophronia, thou seest I am become a shame to the world and a wonder. Mine eares glowe. Mine eares? Ah miserable *Mydas!* to haue such eares as make thy cheekes blush, thy head monstrous, and thy hart desperate? Yet in blushing I am impudent, for I walke in the streetes; in deformitie I seeme comely, for I haue left off my Tyara; and my heart the more heauie it is for griefe, the more hope it conceiueth of recouerie.

Soph. Dread Soueraigne and louing Syre, there are nine dayes past, and therefore the wonder is past; there are manie yeares to come, and therefore a remedie to bee hoped for. Though your eares be long, yet is there roome left on your head for a diademe: thogh they resemble the eares of the dullest beast, yet should they not daunt the spirit of so great a King. The Gods dally with men, kings are no more: they disgrace kings, lest they shuld be thoght gods: sacrifice pleaseth them, so that if you know by the Oracle what God wrought it, you shall by humble submission, by that God be released.

Mid. Sophronia, I commend thy care and courage, but let me heare these reedes, that these lothsome eares may be glutted with the report, and that is as good as a remedie.

The reedes. Mydas of Phrygia hath asses eares.

Mid. Mydas of Phrygia hath asses eares? So he hath, vnhappie *Mydas.* If these reedes sing my shame so lowde, wil men whisper it softly? No, all the world alreadie rings of it: and as impossible it is to staye the rumor, as to catch the wind in a nette that bloweth in the aier; or to stop the wind of al mens mouthes that breathe out

73 my[1] *om. Bl. F.*

aier. I will to *Apollo*, whose Oracle must be my doome, and I fear me, my dishonor, because my doom was his, if kings may disgrace gods: and gods they disgrace, when they forget their dueties.

Mel. What saith *Mydas*?

Mid. Nothing, but that *Apollo* must determine al, or *Mydas* see ruine of al. To *Apollo* wil I offer an Iuory lute for his sweet harmonie, and berries of baies as blacke as ieat, for his loue *Daphne*, pure simples for his physicke, and continuall incense for his prophecying.

Mar. Apollo may discouer some odde riddle, but not geue the redresse; for yet did I neuer heare that his oracles were without doubtfulnes, nor his remedies without impossibilities. This superstition of yours is able to bring errors among the common sort, not ease to your discontented mind.

Mid. Dost thou not know *Martius*, that when *Bacchus* commaunded mee to bathe my selfe in Pactolus, thou thoughtedst it a meere mockerie, before with thine eyes thou sawest the remedie.

Mar. I, *Bacchus* gaue the wish, and therefore was like also to geue the remedie.

Mid. And who knowes whether *Apollo* gaue me these eares, and therefore may release the punishment? Wel, replie not, for I wil to Delphos: in the meane time let it be proclaimed, that if there be any so cunning, that can tell the reason of these reedes creaking, he shal haue my daughter to his wife, or if she refuse it, a Dukedome for his paines: and withal, that whosoeuer is so bolde as to say that *Mydas* hath asses eares, shal presently lose his.

Soph. Deare father then go forwards, prepare for the sacrifice, and dispose of *Sophronia* as it beste pleaseth you.

Mid. Come let vs in. *Exeunt.*

SCÆNA 2.—⟨ *Gardens before the Palace.* ⟩

⟨*Enter*⟩ LICIO. PETULUS.

Pet. WHat a rascall was *Motto* to cosen vs, and say there were thirtie men in a roome that would vndoe vs, and when all came to all, they were but table-men.

Licio. I, and then to geeue vs an inuentorie of all his goods, only to redeeme the beard! but we will be euen with him; and Ile be forsworne but Ile be reuenged.

28 dishonor,] *Bl. om. comma*

Pet. And here I vow by my conceald beard, if euer it chaunce to be discouered to the worlde, that it maye make a pike deuant, I wil haue it so sharp poynted, that it shall stab *Motto* like a poynado.

Licio. And I protest by these haires on my head, which are but casualties,—for alas who knowes not how soone they are lost, Autumne shaues like a razor:—if these locks be rooted against winde and weather, spring and fall, I sweare they shal not be lopped, till *Motto* by my knauerie be so bauld, that I may write verses on his scalpe. In witnesse whereof I eate this haire: now must thou *Petulus* kisse thy beard, for that was the book thou swarest by.

Pet. Nay I woulde I coulde come but to kisse my chinne, which is as yet the couer of my booke! but my word shall stand. Now let vs read the inuentorie, weele share it equally.

Licio. What els?

Pet. ⟨*reading*⟩. 'An inuentorie of all *Mottoes* moueable baddes and goods, as also of such debts as are owing him, with such houshold stuffe as cannot be remoued. *Inprimis*, in the bed-chamber, one fowl wife, & fiue smal children.'

Licio. Ile not share in that.

Pet. I am content, take thou all. These be his moueable baddes.

Licio. And from me they shall be remoueables.

Pet. '*Item* in the seruants chamber, two paire of curst queanes tongues.'

Licio. Tongs thou wouldst say.

Pet. Nay they pinch worse than tongs.

Licio. They are moueables Ile warrant.

Pet. '*Item*, one pair of hornes in the bridechamber, on the beds head.'

Licio. The beasts head, for *Motto* is stuft in the head, and these are among vnmoueable goods.

Pet. Wel, *Fœlix quem faciunt aliena pericula cautum*, happie are they whom other mens hornes do make to beware. '*Item*, a broken pate owing me by one of the Cole house, for notching his head like a ches-boorde.'

Licio. Take thou that, and I geue thee al the rest of his debts.

⟨*Makes as to strike him.*⟩

17 swarest *Q Bl.*: swearedst *Dil.*: swearest *F.*   22–46 *inv. com. Dil. only*   22 moueable *Q Bl. F.*: moveables *Dil.*   24 Imprimis *Dil.*   42 Licio] *F. only: prev. eds. append* Take . . . debts *to Petulus' preceding speech, though foll. by fresh prefix* Pet.

Pet. *Noli me tangere,* I refuse the executorship, because I wil not meddle with his desperate debts. '*Item,* an hundred shrewd turnes owing me by the Pages in the Court, because I will not trust them for trimming.'

Licio. Thats due debt.

Pet. Wel, because *Motto* is poore, they shalbe paid him *cum recumbentibus.* All the Pages shall enter into recognisance, but *ecce, Pipenetta* chaunts it.

Enter PIPENETTA *singing.*

SONG.

Pip. 1.   'L As! How long shall I
          And my Mayden-head lie
    In a cold Bed all the night long,
       I cannot abide it,
       Yet away cannot chide it,
    Though I find, it does me some wrong

    2.   Can any one tell
    Where this fine Thing doth dwell,
    That carries nor forme, nor fashion?
       It both heates and cooles,
       Tis a Bable for Fooles,
    Yet catch'd at in euery Nation.

    3.   Say a Maide were so crost,
       As to see this Toy lost,
    Cannot Hue and Cry fetch it agen?
       'Las! No, for tis driuen
       Nor to Hell, nor to Heauen;
    When tis found, tis lost euen then.

Pip. Hey ho! would I were a witch, that I might be a Dutchesse.

Pet. I know not whether thy fortune is to be a Dutches, but sure I am thy face serues thee wel for a witch: whats the matter?

Pip. The matter? marry 'tis proclaymde, that who soeuer can tell the cause, and the reeds song, shal either haue *Sophronia* to wife, or (if she refuse it) a Dukedome for his wisdome. Besides, whosoeuer saith, that *Mydas* hath asses eares, shal lose theirs.

Licio. Ile be a Duke, I finde honor to bud in my head, and mee thinkes euerie ioynt of mine armes, from the shoulder to the

---

s. D. Enter Pipenetta singing *so old eds. though Bl. first gives* Song *and words*
61 bauble *Dil. modernizing*   73 cause, and *Q Bl.*: cause of *Dil. F. perh. rightly (F. wrongly reports Q as reading* of)

little finger, saies send for the Herauld. Mine armes are all armarie, gules, sables, azure, or, vert, pur, post, pare, &c.

80 *Pet.* And my heart is like a harth where *Cupid* is making a fire, for *Sophronia* shalbe my wife: me thinks *Venus* and Nature stande with each of them a paire of bellowes, the one cooling my lowe birth, the other kindling my loftie affections.

Pip. Apollo wil help me because I can sing.

85 *Licio.* Mercurie me, because I can lie.

Pet. All the Gods me, because I can lie, sing, sweare, and loue. But soft, here comes *Motto*, now shal we haue a fit time to be reuenged, if by deuise we can make him say, *Mydas* hath asses eares.

Enter MOTTO ⟨*and* DELLO⟩.

90 *Licio.* Let vs not seeme to bee angrie about the Inuentorie, and you shall see my wit to bee the hangman for his tongue.

Pip. Why fooles, hath a Barbar a tongue?

Pet. Weele make him haue a tongue, that his teeth that looke lyke a combe shall bee the cizzars to cut it off.

95 *Pip.* I pray let mee haue the odde endes. I feare nothing so much as to be tongue tawde.

Licio. Thou shalt haue all the shauings, and then a womans tongue ympt with a Barbars, will prooue a razor or a raser.

Pet. How now, *Motto*, what all a mort?

100 *Motto.* I am as melancholy as a cat.

Licio. Melancholy? marie gup, is melancholy a word for a barbars mouth? thou shouldst say, heauie, dull and doltish: melancholy is the creast of Courtiers armes, and now euerie base companion, beeing in his muble fubles, sayes he is melancholy.

105 *Pet.* Motto, thou shouldst say thou art lumpish. If thou encroach vpon our courtly tearmes, weele trouce thee: belike if thou shouldst spit often, thou wouldst call it the rewme. *Motto*, in men of reputation & credit it is the rewme; in such mechanicall mushrumpes, it is a catarre, a pose, the water euill. You were best weare a veluet
110 patch on your temples too.

Motto ⟨*aside*⟩. What a world it is to see egges forwarder than cocks! these infants are as cunning in diseases, as I that haue runne them ouer all, backward and forward.—I tell you boyes, it is melancholy that now troubleth me.

96 tongue taw'de *Bl. F.*: tongue-tied *Dil.*   107 the *om. Bl. Dil. F.*   108 mushrooms *Dil.*

Dello. My master could tickle you with diseases, and that olde ones, that haue continued in his Auncestors boanes these three hundred yeres. He is the last of the familie that is left vneaten.

Motto. What meanst thou *Dello?*

Pet. He meanes you are the last of the stocke aliue, the rest the wormes haue eaten.

Dello. A pox of those sawcie wormes, that eate men before they be dead.

Pet. But tell vs *Motto*, why art thou sad?

Motto. Because al the Court is sad.

Licio. Why are they sad in Court?

Motto. Because the King hath a paine in his eares.

Pet. Belike it is the wennes.

Motto. It may be, for his eares are swolne verie big.

Pet. ⟨*to* LIC.⟩. Ten to one *Motto* knowes of the asses eares.

Licio. If he know it, we shall: for it is as hard for a barbar to keepe a secrete in his mouth, as a burning coale in his hand. Thou shalt see mee wring it out by wit. *Motto*, twas told me that the King will discharge you of your office, because you cut his eare when you last trimd him.

Motto. Tis a lye; and yet if I had, he might wel spare an inch or two.

Pet. ⟨*to* LIC.⟩. It will out, I feele him comming.

Dello ⟨*aside to* MOTTO⟩. Master, take heed, you will blab al anone, these wags are craftie.

Motto. Let me alone!

Licio. Why *Motto*, what difference between the kings eares, and thine?

Motto. As much as betweene an asses eares and mine.

Pet. O, *Motto* is modest; to mitigate the matter, hee calls his owne eares, asses eares.

Motto. Nay, I meane the Kings are asses eares.

Licio. Treason, treason!

Dello. I told you, master! you haue made a faire hand; for now you haue made your lips cizars to cut off your eares.

Motto. Perij! vnles you pitie me, *Motto* is in a pit.

Pet. Nay *Motto*, treson is a worse pain than toothach.

129 S. D. [to LIC.] *suppl. Dil. Such directions are never marked in the old eds.*
S. D. [aside to MOTTO] *supplied Dil.*   148 you¹] your *Bl.*

Licio. Now *Motto*, thou knowest thine eares are ours to commaund.

Motto. Your seruants, or handmaides.

Pet. Then will I lead my maide by the hand.

He pulls him by the eares.

Motto. Out villen! thou wringst too hard.

Dello. Not so hard as he bit me.

Motto. Thou seest boy we are both mortall. I enioye mine eares, but *durante placite ;* nor thou thy finger, but *fauente dento.*

Pet. Yea *Motto*, hast thou Latin?

Motto. Alas! hee that hath drawen so manie teeth, and neuer askt Latin for a tooth, is ill brought vp.

Licio. Well *Motto*, let vs haue the beard, without couin, fraud, or delay, at one entier paiment, & thou shalt scape a paiment.

Motto. I protest by cizars, brush and combe; bason, ball and apron; by razor, eare-pike and rubbing cloathes; and all the *tria sequuntur triaes* in our secret occupation (for you knowe it is no blabbing arte) that you shall haue the beard, in manner and forme following. Not onely the golden beard and euerie haire, (though it be not haire,) but a dozen of beards, to stuffe two dozen of cushions.

Licio. Then they be big ones.

Dello. They be halfe a yeard broad, and a nayle, three quarters long, and a foote thicke; so sir shall you finde them stufte enough, and soft enough. All my mistres lynes that she dryes her cloathes on, are made only of Mustachio stuffe. And if I durst tell the truth, as lustie as I am heere, I lye vppon a bed of beards; a bots of their bristles, and they that owe them! they are harder than flockes.

Pet. A fine discourse! well *Motto*, we giue thee mercie, but we will not loose the beard. Remember nowe our Inuentorie. *Item*, wee will not let thee goe out of our hands, till we haue the beard in our hands.

Motto. Then followe. *Exeunt.*

---

159 dento *Q Bl. F.*: dente *Dil. stupidly without autho-*
rity   173 nayle,] *Dil. om. comma*   166 tria] tira *F. without authority*   178 owe] *Dil. modernizes to* own

SCÆN. 3.—⟨*Delphi. Before Apollo's Temple.*⟩

⟨*Enter*⟩ MYDAS. SOPHRONIA. MELLICRATES. MARTIUS.

Mid. THis is *Delphos*. Sacred *Apollo*, whose Oracles be all diuine, though doubtfull : aunswere poore *Mydas*, and pitie him. ⟨*A pause.*⟩

Soph. I maruell there is no answere.

Mid. Fond *Mydas*, how canst thou aske pitie of him whom thou hast so much abusde ; or why doost thou abuse the world, both to seeme ignorant in not acknowledging an offence ; and impudent, so openly to craue pardon ? *Apollo* will not aunswere, but *Mydas* must not cease. *Apollo,* diuine *Apollo, Mydas* hath asses eares, yet let pitie sinke into thine eares, and tell when he shall be free from this shame, or what may mittigate his sinne ? 5

⟨*A pause.*⟩ 10

Mar. Tush ! *Apollo* is tuning his pipes, or at barly-breake with *Daphne,* or assaying on some Shepheardes coate, or taking measure of a serpents skinne. Were I *Mydas*, I would rather cut these eares off close from my head, than stand whimpring before such a blinde God. 15

Mid. Thou art barbrous not valiant. Gods must bee entreated, not commanded : thou wouldst quench fire with a sword, and ad to my shame (which is more than any Prince can endure) thy rudenesse, (which is more than any sensible creature would folow). Diuine *Apollo*, what shal become of *Mydas?* Accept this lute, these berries, these simples, these tapers ; if *Apollo* take any delight in musick, in *Daphne,* in phisicke, in eternitie. 20

APOLLO *his Oracle.*

When *Pan Apollo* in musick shall excell,
Mydas of Phrygia shall lose his Asses eares ;
Pan did *Apollo* in musick farre excell,
Therefore king *Mydas* weareth Asses eares :
Vnlesse he shrinke his stretching hand from Lesbos,
His eares in length, at length shal reach to Delphos. 25

Mel. It were good, to expound these oracles, that the learned men in Phrygia were assembled ; otherwise the remedie wil be as impossible to be had, as the cause to be sifted. 30

s. D. Apollo his Oracle *Q Bl. both printing the words of the oracle as here*

Mar. I foresaw some old saw, which should be doutfull. Who would gad to such gods, that must be honored if they speake without sence: and the Oracle wondred at, as though it were aboue sence?

Mid. No more *Martius!* I am the learnedst in Phrygia to interpret these Oracles: and though shame hath hetherto caused me to conceale it, now I must vnfould it by necessitie. Thus destinie bringeth me, not only to be cause of all my shame, but reporter. Thou *Sophronia*, and you my Lordes, hearken; When I had bathed my self in Pactolus, and saw my wish to float in the waues, I wished the waues to ouerflow my bodie, so melancolie my fortune made me, so mad my follie: yet by hunting I thought to ease my heart. And comming at last to the hill Tmolus, I perceyued *Apollo* and *Pan* contending for excellencie in musick: among Nimphs they required also my iudgement. I (whom the losse of gold made discontent, and the possessing desperate) eyther dulled with the humors of my weak brain, or deceaued by thicknes of my deaffe eares, prefer'd the harsh noyse of *Pans* pipe, before the sweete stroke of *Apollos* Lute, which caused *Phœbus* in iustice (as I now confesse, and then as I sawe in anger) to set these eares on my head, that haue wroong so many teares from mine eyes. For stretching my hands to Lesbos, I find that all the Gods haue spurnde at my practises, and those Ilandes scornd them. My pride the gods disdaine; my pollicie men: my mines haue bin emptied by souldiers, my souldiers spoyled by warres, my wars without successe, because vsurping, my vsurping without end, because my ambition aboue measure. I wil therfore yeeld my self to *Bacchus*, and acknowledge my wish to be vanitie: to *Apollo*, and confesse my iudgement to be foolish: to *Mars*, and say my warres are vniust: to *Diana*, and tell my affection hath been vnnaturall. And I doubt not, what a God hath done to make me know my selfe, al the gods wil help to vndo, that I may come to my selfe.

Soph. ⟨*aside*⟩. Is it possible that *Mydas* should be so ouershot in iudgement? Vnhappy *Mydas*, whose wits melt with his gold, and whose gold is consumed with his wits.

Mid. What talketh *Sophronia* to her selfe?

Soph. Nothing, but that since *Mydas* hath confessed his fault to vs, he also acknowledge it to *Apollo*.

---

33 Mar.] Mel. *Bl.*   44.Timolus *Dil.*   45-6 musick: among Nimphs they *so punctuated* Q *Bl.*: music among nymphs; they *Dil. F., the latter placing comma at* musique   58-9 acknowledged *F.*

Mid. I wil *Sophronia.* Sacred *Apollo,* things passed cannot be 70
recalled, repented they may be: behold, *Mydas* not only submitting
himselfe to punishment, but confessing his peeuishnes, being glad
for shame to call that peeuishnes, which indeed was follie. Whatsoeuer *Apollo* shal commaund, *Mydas* will execute.

Apollo ⟨from the Temple⟩. Then attend *Mydas.* I accept thy sub- 75
mission, and sacrifice, so as yerelie at this temple thou offer Sacrifice
in submission: withal, take *Apollos* councel, which if thou scorne,
thou shalt finde thy destinie. I will not speake in riddles, all
shalbe plaine, because thou art dul, but all certaine, if thou be
obstinate. 80

      Weigh not in one ballance gold and iustice.
      With one hand wage not war and peace.
      Let thy head be glad of one Crowne.
      And take care to keep one frend.
      The frend that thou wouldst make thy foe, 85
      The kingdome thou wouldst make the world,
      The hand that thou doest arme with force,
      The gold that thou doest think a god,
      Shall conquere, fall, shrinke short, be common:
      With force, with pride, with feare, with traffick. 90
      If this thou like, shake off an Asses eares:
      If not, for euer shake an Asses eares.

Soph. *Apollo* will not reply.

Mid. It may be *Sophronia,* that neither you, nor anie els, vnderstand *Apollo,* because none of you haue the hart of a king: but my 95
thoughts expound my fortunes, and my fortunes hang vpon my
thoughts. That great *Apollo,* that ioynd to my head Asses eares,
hath put into my heart a Lions minde. I see that by obscure
shadows, which you cannot discerne in fresh colours. *Apollo* in the
depth of his darke answere, is to mee the glistering of a bright sunne. 100
I perceiue (and yet not too late) that Lesbos wil not be touched by
gold, by force it cannot: that the Gods haue pitched it out of the
world, as not to bee controlde by any in the world. Though my
handé bee golde, yet I must not thinke to span ouer the maine
Ocean. Though my souldiers be valiant, I must not therfore thinke 105
my quarrels iust. There is no way to nayle the crowne of Phrygia

    93 Soph. *F. only, prev. eds. printing the speech as closing line of the oracle*
    97 That] The *Dil.*

SC. III] MIDAS 161

fast to my daughters head but in letting the crownes of others sitte in quiet on theirs.

Mar. Mydas!

110 *Mid.* How darest thou replie seeing me resolued? thy counsell hath spilt more bloud than all my souldiers lances! let none be so hardie as to looke to crosse me. Sacred *Appollo*, if sacrifice yerely at thy temple, and submission hourely in mine owne Court, if fulfilling thy counsell, and correcting my councellors, may shake off
115 these Asses eares, I heere before thee vow to shake off al enuies abrode, and at home all tyrannie.

The eares fall off.

Soph. Honored be *Apollo*, *Mydas* is restored.

Mid. Fortunate *Mydas*, that feelst thy head lightned of dul eares, and thy heart of deadly sorows. Come my Lords, let vs repaire
120 to our Palace, in which *Apollo* shall haue a stately statue erected: euery month will we solemnize there a feast, and here euery yere a sacrifice. Phrygia shalbe gouerned by Gods, not men, leaste the Gods make beasts of men. So my counsell of warre shal not make conquests in their owne conceiptes, nor my councellers in peace
125 make me poor, to enrich them selues. So blessed be *Apollo*, quiet be Lesbos, happie be *Mydas*: and to begin this solemnitie, let vs sing to *Apollo*, for, so much as Musick, nothing can content *Apollo*.

They sing all.

SONG.

Sing to *Apollo*, God of Day,
130   Whose golden beames with morning play,
And make her eyes so brightly shine,
Aurora's face is call'd Diuine.
Sing to *Phœbus*, and that Throne
Of Diamonds which he sits vpon;
    Iô Pæans let vs sing,
135   To Physickes, and to Poesies King.

---

120 statue] palace *Dil.*   S. D. They sing all. Exeunt. *so Q, omitting the words of the song, which are first given in Bl.*

Crowne all his Altars with bright fire,
Laurels bind about his Lire,
A *Daphnean* Coronet for his Head,
The Muses dance about his Bed;
When on his rauishing Lute he playes, 140
Strew his Temple round with Bayes.
Iô Pæans let vs sing,
To the glittering Delian King.

Exeunt.

FINIS.

MOTHER BOMBIE

EDITIONS

'xviij Junij 1594 Cuthbert Burby . Entred for his copie vnder th and of master warden Cawood a booke intituled mother Bumbye beinge an enterlude ... vj^d C.' *Stationers' Register*, ii. 654 (ed. Arb.). ('C' indicates the warden, Cawood; just as 'S' and 'A,' on pp. 631, 614, indicate the wardens Styrrop and Allen.)

Q^1.   *Mother | Bombie. | As it was sundrie times plaied by | the Children of Powles. | London, | Imprinted by Thomas Scarlet | for Cuthbert Burby. | 1594. | 4to. A–I 3 in fours: no col. (Br. Mus.: Bodl.)*

Q$^.$ *Mother | Bombie. | As it was sundrie times | plaied by the Children of Powles. | London | Printed by Thomas Creede, for Cuthbert | Burby. 1598. | 4to. A–H in fours: no col. (Br. Mus.: Bodl.: Dyce Coll. S. Kens.)*

The *Sixe Covrt Comedies* are entered to Blount under date 9 Jan. 1628. (*Sta. Reg.* iv. p. 192, Arb.—entry quoted under CAMPASPE Eds.)

Third ed.   *Mother | Bombie. | As it was sundry times | Played by the Children | of Pavls. | (Blount's)   London, | Printed by William Stansby, | for Edward Blount. | 1632. | 12mo, occupying Z 4–D d 12, in twelves, of the Sixe Covrt Comedies.*

Also contained in Dilke's *Old English Plays*, vol. i. 1814, 8vo: and in Fairholt's edition of Lyly's *Dramatic Works*, vol. ii. 1858, sm. 8vo.

MOTHER BOMBIE

Argument. — Two wealthy old men, Memphio and Stellio, each ignorant of mental defect in the other's child (named Accius and Silena respectively), scheme to cheat each other into matching them. Two other old men, Sperantus and Prisius, opposing the union of their son and daughter Candius and Livia, scheme to marry them to the foolish children of their wealthier neighbours. The pages of all four, allies in mischief, are privy to their schemes, and possess the further knowledge of weak wits in Accius and Silena. To befool their masters, they plot to forward alike the undesirable match between these two, and the love-match between Candius and Livia. After a first meeting between the fools, interrupted by the parents before the defect is discovered to be mutual, they arrange for a second, at which either parent supposes his imbecile child to be personated by some one better qualified for courting. But the fools, though disguised in Candius' and Livia's attire, betray their identity to his or her parent, and their folly to the parent of the other. Meantime Candius and Livia, disguised as Accius and Silena, have effected their marriage with the connivance of their unsuspecting fathers, who, though they see their ambitions thus thwarted, are still resolved to prevent their own children's union. Discovering that they have been duped, they at length determine to forgive the offenders and their accomplices. Memphio and Stellio are similarly persuaded that a match between the two fools will be better than no union for them at all; but the marriage is prevented by the discovery that they are really the children of an old nurse Vicinia, who changed them at birth for the rich men's real offspring, Maestius and Serena. An unnatural passion between these latter is thus rendered legitimate; Memphio and Stellio engage still to support the crazed couple; the rascally pages are forgiven, and the general goodwill enhanced by the amicable adjustment of a side-quarrel between the latter and a horse-dealer. Mother Bombie, who gives a title to the piece, is a 'wise woman' to whom the different characters resort for advice or prognostication, and who prophesies in popular doggrel form the actual issue in each case; but she affects the plot only as inducing Vicinia's confession at the close.

Text and Bibliography. — The text followed is that of Q^1, which however corrupt· is by far the best, and well printed. It exhibits some seventy errors, ten occurring in classical quotations (e.g. on pp. 181, 186, 192, 206), ten being omissions of speeches, important words, or stage-directions for entry and exit (e.g. on pp. 189, 217, 222), ten or twelve others being mistakes that cause confusion (e.g. on pp. 196, 205, 210, 212, 221), and the rest comparatively unimportant.

Q^2 corrects only twenty of the seventy mistakes of Q^1, only six of which corrections are important, the rest being of such errors as could cause no misapprehension; while on the other hand it introduces sixty-seven corruptions, including six important omissions (on pp. 182, 183, 193, 202, 211, 218) and fifteen other important errors (on pp. 178, 184 (two), 190, 192 (two), 193 (two), 196, 197, 204, 211, 212, 216 and 222).

Blount prints from Q^2 and perpetuates most of its errors, making altogether only twelve corrections and sixteen fresh corruptions. But he inserts all the songs except 'The Love-knot,' v. 3. 21.

Dilke seems to have had both quartos before him, though in two instances, i. 3. 169, ii. 1. 12, he fails to insert three words found only in the first. He makes sixteen corrections and eleven corruptions —distinctly the next best text to Q^1, though modernized in places.

Fairholt merely reprinted Blount, making only five original corrections and introducing twenty corruptions. His notes, in which one or two of the worst omissions and errors are pointed out and emended, show that he had both QQ, as well as Dilke's edition, before him; but he made no thorough collation of the text, so that the great majority of its errors were reproduced. By returning to Q^1 we eliminate the whole after-growth of corruption, while we have attempted to emend its original errors.

Authorship. — The evidence of Lyly's authorship of the play is its performance by the Paul's boys; its scene laid in his county of Kent; its strong resemblance in plot-construction and handling to his other plays, in spite of his abandonment here of a mythological, allegorical or ideal treatment for a realistic one; its repetition of many phrases, proverbs, &c. used by him elsewhere—though the euphuistic style is almost entirely abandoned; and lastly, its inclusion by Blount in the *Sixe Court Comedies* of 1632. His name, however, appears on the title-page of neither quarto edition.

Source. — There appears to be no direct source for the plot—the only one of Lyly's plays of which this can be said: but the general model—the idea of rascally servants aiding their young masters in marriage-schemes against their parents' wishes—is obviously Terence. Of Roman comedy also is the motive of child-changing, and the solution of the plot by the discovery of such. In my note on Italian influence (vol. ii. pp. 473 sqq.) I have already stated that I attach little importance to Herr L. L. Schücking's claim that the piece is indebted to Ariosto's *Suppositi*, to Cecchi's comedies, or to the *Antivalomeni* of Cinthio; though doubtless Lyly had read Gascoigne's *Supposes*, which could yield him next to nothing for our play. In the Hackneyman and the Fortune-teller we have English national types for which Lyly's own experience could furnish him with far better and more abundant models than possibly could the Italian extemporal stage.

Date. — The play in spite of its contemporary character contains nothing that may help us to date it save the statement on the title-page of the first quarto (1594) that it was 'sundrie times plaied by the Children of Powles.' This must be before their long inhibition, our earliest evidence of which is the entry of *Endimion*, *Gallathea* and *Midas* in the Stationers' Register Oct. 4, 1591, coupled with the allusion of the printer in his prefatory note to *Endimion*, 1591:—'Since the Plaies in Paules were dissoulued there are certaine Commedies come to my handes by chaunce,' &c. *Midas* was performed at Court on Jan. 6, 1590, and there is no necessity to suppose the inhibition earlier than 1591. Fleay dates *Mother Bombie* 1588-9 or possibly 1589-90. But it is scarcely conceivable that a play of contemporary life, written by the topical Lyly in the year of the Armada, and with the scene laid in Kent, should contain no faintest echo of the great struggle which then absorbed all men's thoughts; while in 1589 Lyly was probably too busy to write it, for he sat in Parliament from Feb. 4 to March 29, and composed both *Midas* and *Pappe*, and probably one of the lost Anti-Martinist comedies, in the same year. There are strong reasons for supposing it later than *Midas* in (1) the rarity of reminiscences of *Euphues* and the few traces of euphuistic style; (2) the far greater skill in weaving a plot, a point in which we have already watched his gradual advance; lastly, (3), an argument well urged by Mr. Baker (*Endymion*, p. clii), its character as a new departure, an essay in Terentian comedy, after which Lyly would be less likely to return to the more conventional allegorical fashion of *Midas* and the three preceding plays. I should, therefore, date its composition and production in 1590. The reason why it is not included among those announced for publication by Widow Broome in 1591, is, perhaps, its more popular character, which would give it a better chance of acceptance at other theatres.

Time and Place. — Some two days altogether are occupied, from the middle of Monday to the middle of Wednesday. The continuity of Acts i and ii is shown at the beginning of ii. 1, where Riscio meets Dromio, whom he set out to seek at the end of i. 2. At the end of ii. 1 the four wags adjourn to the tavern, and on issuing from it agree to meet 'to morrow' (ii. 4. 24). In iii. 2 they do so meet, having in the interim fixed the second encounter of Accius and Silena for that evening ('I told him this wooing should be to night' (iii. 2. 36). Just before that second encounter, occurs the troth-plight of Candius and Livia and their immediate adjournment to church (iv. 1. 58). Towards the close of this same second day the wags adjourn with the Sergeant, Hackneyman and Scrivener to the tavern (iv. 2. 242), whence they are seen issuing in v. 1. A night intervenes, and then in v. 2 Mother Bombie promises Vicinia a solution of her difficulties 'before this daie end,' which corresponds with her promise to Mæstius and Serena on the preceding day (iii. 1. 40) that they should 'be married to morow.' Immediately after enter the fiddlers (v. 3) to salute the newly-married pair, Candius and Livia, with morning music; and at the close of the long *dénouement* the four old men agree to feast at their respective houses on that and the three following days, 'and euen so spend this weeke in good cheere.'

So that Acts i, ii occupy the latter part of Monday.
„ „ iii, iv, v. 1 occupy the whole of Tuesday.
„ „ v. 2, 3 occupy the first part of Wednesday.

INTRODUCTION

In the matter of Place Lyly strictly follows his Roman model, Terence. Whatever improbabilities are involved, the stage represents throughout one and the same place, an open square, namely, or street, wherein are situated the houses of the four old men, of Mother Bombie and of the Scrivener, and also the tavern to which the different characters repair; nor is there anything in the dialogue requiring an imaginary transfer in the middle of a scene. The proof of this identity of scene is as follows: the near neighbourhood of Memphio's and Stellio's houses is implied in iii. 3 and iv. 2, where, after their first and second encounters, the parents call their half-witted children in. That Sperantus' house is hard by is evident from v. 3, where the fiddlers pass from it to Memphio's, and are greeted from upper windows by Sperantus and Memphio in turn. That Mother Bombie's house is also there is clear from ii. 3, where Silena, seen issuing 'out of Stellio's house' at the beginning of the scene, summons the wise woman forth to speak with her near the end of it. That Prisius' house is also near is shown in iii. 4, where his servants Rixula and Lucio have evidently just come out of it, and visit Mother Bombie in the same scene. (Note that Rixula, hearing from Mother Bombie the whereabouts of the spoon she has lost, wants to run at once and see if it is still there iii. 4. 153–7.) The presence of the tavern and the Scrivener's house is evident from the end of iv. 2, a scene already shown to be laid before the houses of Memphio and Stellio.

MOTHER BOMBIE.

As it was sundrie times plaied by the Children of Powles.

LONDON,
Imprinted by Thomas Scarlet
for Cuthbert Burby.
1594.

⟨DRAMATIS PERSONÆ.

MEMPHIO, *an avaricious Old Man.*
STELLIO, *a wealthy Husbandman.*
PRISIUS, *a Fuller.*
SPERANTUS, *a Farmer.*
CANDIUS, *Son to Sperantus.* 5
MÆSTIUS, *Son to Memphio; supposed Son to Vicinia.*
ACCIUS, *supposed Son to Memphio.*
DROMIO, *a Boy, Servant to Memphio.*
RISCIO, *a Boy, Servant to Stellio.*
HALFPENNY, *a Boy, Servant to Sperantus.* 10
LUCIO, *a Boy, Servant to Prisius.*
LIVIA, *Daughter to Prisius.*
SERENA, *Daughter to Stellio; supposed Daughter to Vicinia.*
SILENA, *supposed Daughter to Stellio.*
VICINIA, *a Nurse, Mother to Accius and Silena.* 15
MOTHER BOMBIE, *a Fortune-teller.*
RIXULA, *a Servant-girl to Prisius.*
SYNIS,
NASUTUS, } *three Fiddlers.*
BEDUNENUS, 20
Hackneyman.
Sergeant.
Scrivener.

SCENE—*Rochester: an open square or street.*⟩

DRAM. PERS.] *the list first in Dilke, descriptions in Fairholt.*   3-4 PRISIUS, a Fuller; SPERANTUS, a Farmer] *Fairholt described them as* 'old countrymen': *but see pp.* 178 *top,* 182 *ll.* 184, 189, 194 *l.* 62, 221 *l.* 144   SCENE—Rochester &c.] *Fairholt first gave the scene* 'Rochester'

A PLEASANT CONCEITED COMŒDIE

CALLED

MOTHER BOMBIE

ACTUS PRIMUS

Scena Prima.

⟨*Enter*⟩ Memphio, Dromio.

Memphio. BOY, there are three thinges that make my life miserable; a threed bare purse, a curst wife, & a foole to my heire.

Dro. Why then, sir, there are three medicines for these three 5 maladies; a pike-staffe to take a purse on the high way, a holly wand to brush cholar frō my mistres tong, and a young wench for my yong master: so that as your Worship being wise begot a foole, so he beeing a foole may tread out a wise man.

Memp. I, but, *Dromio,* these medicines bite hot on great mis10 chiefs; for so might I haue a rope about my necke, hornes vpon my head, and in my house a litter of fooles.

Dro. Then, sir, you had best let some wise man sit on your sonne, to hatch him a good wit: they saie, if rauens sit on hens egs, the chickens will be black, and so forth.

15 *Memp.* Why boy, my sonne is out of the shell, and is growen a pretie cocke.

Dro. Carue him, master, & make him a capon, els all your breed will proue cockescombes.

Memp. I maruell he is such an asse, hee takes it not of his 20 father.

Dro. He may for anie thing you know.

Memp. Why, villain, dost thou think me a foole?

Dro. O no, sir, neither are you sure that you are his father.

Actus ... Prima] *the division into Acts and Scenes is that of the oldest and all succeeding editions*   5 mala-ladies Q^1 holy Q^1 6 choler *Bl.* *Dil. F.*   14 chichens Q^2 15 growne Q^2 *rest*

Memp. Rascall, doest thou imagine thy mistres naught of her bodie?

Dro. No, but fantasticall of her mind; and it may be, when this boy was begotten shee thought of a foole, & so conceiued a foole, your selfe beeing verie wise, and she surpassing honest.

Memp. It may be; for I haue heard of an Aethiopian, that thinking of a faire picture, brought forth a faire ladie, and yet no bastard.

Dro. You are well read, sir; your sonne may be a bastard, and yet legitimate; your selfe a cuckold, & yet my mistres vertuous; all this in conceit.

Memp. Come, *Dromio*, it is my grief to haue such a sonne that must inherit my lands.

Dro. He needs not, sir, Ile beg him for a foole.

Memp. Vile boy! thy yong master?

Dro. Let me haue in a deuice.

Memp. Ile haue thy aduice, and if it fadge, thou shalt eate till thou sweate, play till thou sleep, and sleepe till thy bones ake.

Dro. I marie, now you tickle me, I am both hungrie, gamesome, & sleepie, and all at once. Ile breake this head against the wal, but Ile make it bleed good matter.

Memp. Then this it is, thou knowest I haue but one sonne, and he is a foole.

Dro. A monstrous foole!

Memp. A wife, and she an arrand scold.

Dro. Ah, master, I smell your deuice, it will be excellent!

Memp. Thou canst not know it till I tell it.

Dro. I see it through your braines, your haire is so thin, and your scull so transparant, I may sooner see it than heare it.

Memp. Then, boy, hast thou a quicke wit, and I a slow tongue: but what ist?

Dro. Marie, either you would haue your wiues tong in your sons head, that he might bee a prating foole; or his braines in hir brain pan, that she might be a foolish scold.

Memp. Thou dreamst, *Dromio*, there is no such matter. Thou knowest I haue kept him close, so that my neighbors thinke him to be wise, and her to be temperate, because they neuer heard them speake.

30 ladie *so all*: *qy.?* babie (*P. A. Daniel*)   40–1 eate till thou] eate, thou shalt *all eds.: see note*   48 arrand *QQ Bl.*   59 him[1]] them *Dil. phps. rightly*

Dro. Well!

Memp. Thou knowest that *Stellio* hath a good farme and a faire daughter; yea so faire that she is mewed vp, and onely looketh out at the windows, least she should by some roisting courtier be stollen away.

Dro. So, sir.

Memp. Now if I could compasse a match between my sonne and *Stellios* daughter, by conference of vs parents, and without theirs, I should be blessed, he coosned, and thou for euer set at libertie.

Dro. A singular conceit.

Memp. Thus much for my sonne. Nowe for my wife; I would haue this kept from her, else shal I not be able to keepe my house from smoake; for let it come to one of her eares, & then wo to both mine: I would haue her goe to my house into the Countrie whilest we conclude this; and this once done, I care not if her tong neuer haue done: these if thou canst effect, thou shalt make thy master happie.

Dro. Thinke it done, this noddle shall coin such new deuice as you shall haue your sonne marryed by to morrow.

Memp. But take heed that neither the father nor the maide speak to my sonne, for then his folly will marre all.

Dro. Lay all the care on mee, *Subleuabo te onere*, I will rid you of a foole.

Memp. Wilt thou rid me for a foole?

Dro. Tush! quarrell not.

Memp. Then for the dowrie, let it bee at least two hundreth ducats, and after his death the farme.

Dro. What else?

Memp. Then let vs in, that I may furnish thee with some better counsell, and my son with better apparell.

Dro. Let me alone.—⟨*Aside.*⟩ I lacke but a wagge more to make of my counsell, and then you shall see an exquisite coosnage, & the father more foole than the sonne.—But heare you, sir, I forgot one thing.

Memp. Whats that?

Dro. Nay, *Expellas furca licet, vsque recurret*.

Memp. Whats the meaning?

67 So,] No, *F.*   70 coosned *QQ Bl. F.*: coz'ned *Dil.*   75 woe *Bl. Dil. F.*   81 by] py *Q¹*   88 hundreth *QQ Bl.*: hundred *Dil.*: hundredth *F.*

Dro. Why though your sons folly bee thrust vp with a paire of 100
hornes on a forke, yet being naturall, it will haue his course.
Memp. I praie thee no more, but about it. *Exeunt.*

Sce. 2.

⟨*Enter*⟩ Stellio, Riscio.

Stel. *Risio*, my daughter is passing amiable, but verie simple.
Ris. You meane a foole, sir.
Stel. Faith I implie so much.
Ris. Then I apply it fit: the one shee takes of her father, the
other of her mother: now you may bee sure she is your owne. 5
Stel. I have penned her vp in a chamber, hauing onely a windowe
to looke out, that youthes seeing her fayre cheekes, may be ena-
moured before they heare her fond speech. How likest thou this
head?
Ris. There is verie good workmanship in it, but the matter is but 10
base; if the stuffe had bene as good as the mold, your daughter had
bene as wise as she is beautifull.
Stel. Doest thou thinke she tooke her foolishnes of mee?
Ris. I, & so cunningly, that she toke it not frō you.
Stel. Well, *Quod natura dedit, tollere nemo potest.* 15
Ris. A good euidence to proue the fee-simple of your daughters
folly.
Stel. Why?
Ris. It came by nature, and if none can take it awaie, it is per-
petuall. 20
Stel. Nay, *Riscio*, she is no natural foole, but in this consisteth her
simplicitie, that she thinketh her selfe subtile; in this her rudenesse,
that she imagines she is courtly; in this the ouershooting of her selfe,
that she ouerweeneth of her selfe.
Ris. Well, what followes? 25
Stel. *Risio*, this is my plot. *Memphio* hath a pretie stripling to his
sonne, whom with cockring he hath made wanton: his girdle must
be warmde, the ayre must not breath on him, he must lie a bed til
noon, and yet in his bed breake his fast: that which I doe to con-

101 his] its *F.*   102 no] no no Q^2 *Bl.*   Sce. 2] *old eds. prefix an erroneous* Act 2   s. d. Riscio *QQ, though elsewhere often* Risio. *I follow their various spelling only in dialogue and old stage-directions*   22 selfe *twice* Q^1 subtile; in *Dil.*: subtile in *QQ Bl. F.*

ceale the folly of my daughter, that doth hee in too much cockering of his sonne. Now, *Risio*, how shall I compasse a match betweene my girle and his boy?

Ris. Why with a payre of compasses, and bring them both into the circle, Ile warrant the'il match themselues.

Stel. Tush! plot it for me that neuer speaking one to another, they be in loue one with another: I like not solemne woing, it is for courtiers; let countrie folkes beleeue others reports as much as their own opinions.

Ris. O then, so it be a match you care not.

Stel. Not I, nor for a match neither, were it not I thirst after my neighbors farme.

Ris. ⟨*aside*⟩. A verie good nature.—Well, if by flat wit I bring this to passe, whats my rewerd?

Stel. Whatsoeuer thou wilt aske.

Ris. Ile aske no more than by my wit I can get in the bargaine.

Stel. Then about it.   *Exit.*

Ris. If I come not about you neuer trust mee. Ile seeke out *Dromio*, the counseller of my conceit.   ⟨*Exit.*⟩

Sce. 3.

⟨*Enter*⟩ Prisius, Sperantus.

Pris. It is vnneighbourly done to suffer your son since hee came from schoole, to spende his time in loue; and vnwisely done to let him houer ouer my daughter, who hath nothing to her dowrie but her needle, & must proue a Sempster; nor he any thing to take to but a Grammer, and cannot at the best be but a schoolemaster.

Spe. Prisius, you bite and whine, wring me on the withers, and yet winch your selfe; it is you that goe about to match your girle with my boy, shee beeing more fit for seames than for marriage, and hee for a rod than a wife.

Pris. Her birth requires a better bridegrome than such a groome.

Spe. And his bringing vp another gate marriage than such a minion.

Pris. Marie gup! I am sure he hath no better bread than is

---

41 farme] fame *Bl. F.*   43 rewerd Q^1: reward Q^2 *Bl. mods.*   48 Dromio Q^1 *mods.*: Romio Q^2 *Bl.*   4 to² Q^1 *Dil.*: too Q^2 *Bl. F.*   7 wince *Dil.*
your girle] my girle Q^1 12 gates Q^2 *Bl. Dil.*: gate's *F.*!

made of wheat, nor worne finer cloth than is made of woll, nor
learned better manners than are taught in schooles.

Spe. Nor your minxe had no better grandfather than a Tailer, who (as I haue heard) was poore and proud: nor a better father than your selfe, vnlesse your wife borrowed a better, to make her daughter a Gentlewoman.

Pris. Twit not me with my ancestors, nor my wiues honestie; if thou doest—— ⟨*threatening him.*⟩

Spe. Hold thy hands still, thou hadst best; & yet it is impossible now I remēber, for thou hast the palsy.

Pris. My handes shake so, that wert thou in place where, I would teach thee to cog.

Spe. Nay, if thou shake thy hands, I warrant thou canst not teach anie to cog. But, neighbour, let not two olde fooles fall out for two yong wantons.

Pris. In deed it becōmeth men of our experience to reason, not raile: to debate the matter, not to combat it.

Spe. Wel, then this Ile tel thee friendly, I haue almost these two yeres cast in my head, how I might match my princockes with *Stellios* daughter, whom I haue heard to be verie faire, and know shal be verie rich: she is his heire; he doats, he is stooping old, and shortly must die; yet by no meanes, either by blessing or cursing can I win my sonne to be a woer, which I know proceeds not of bashfulnesse but stubbornnesse; for hee knowes his good though I saie it, he hath wit at wil: as for his personage, I care not who sees him, I can tell you he is able to make a Ladies mouth water if she winke not.

Pris. Stay, *Sperantus,* this is like my case, for I haue bene tampering as long to haue a marriage cōmitted betweene my wench and *Memphios* only son: they saie he is as goodly a youth as one shall see in a Summers daie, and as neate a stripling as euer went on neats leather; his father will not let him be forth of his sight, he is so tender ouer him; he yet lies with his mother for catching cold. Now my pretie elfe, as proud as the day is long, she wil none of him, she forsooth wil choose her owne husband; made marriages proue mad marriages; shee will choose with her eie, and like with her heart, before she consent with her tong; neither father nor mother,

15 woll Q^1: wol Q^2: wooll *Bl. F.*: wool *Dil.*   19 her Q^1: your *rest*
21 with *before* my^2 *F.*   for *before* if Q^2 *Bl. mods.*   25 shake, so that
Bl. F.   46 be] he *Bl.*: hie *F.*

kith nor kin, shalbe her caruer in a husband, shee will fall too where she likes best; and thus the chicke scarce out of the shell, cackles as though she had bene troden with an hundreth cockes, and mother of a thousand egges.

Spe. Well then, this is our best, seeing we knowe each others minde, to deuise to gouerne our owne children: for my boy, Ile keepe him to his bookes, & studie shall make him leaue to loue: Ile breake him of his will, or his bones with a cudgell.

Pris. And Ile no more dandle my daughter; shee shall prick on a clout till her fingers ake, or Ile cause her leaue to make my heart ake. But in good time, though with ill lucke, beholde if they be not both together; let vs stand close and heare all, so shall we preuent all. ⟨*They stand aside.*⟩

Enter CANDIUS *and* LIUIA.

Spe. ⟨*aside*⟩. This happens pat, take heed you cough not, *Prisius*.

Pris. Tush! spit not you, & Ile warrant, I, my beard is as good as a handkerchiefe.

Livia. Sweet *Candius*, if thy father should see vs alone, would he not fret? The old man me thinkes should be full of fumes.

Cand. Tush! let him fret one heart string against another, he shall neuer trouble the least vaine of my little finger. The old churle thinkes none wise, vnles he haue a beard hang dagling to his wast: when my face is bedaubed with haire as his, then perchance my conceit may stumble on his staiednes.

Pris. ⟨*aside*⟩. I, in what booke read you that lesson?

Spe. I know not in what booke hee read it, but I am sure he was a knaue to learne it.

Cand. I beleeue, faire *Liuia*, if your soure sire shuld see you with your sweet heart, he would not be verie patient.

Livia. The care is taken. Ile aske him blessing as a father, but neuer take counsel for an husband; there is as much oddes between my golden thoughts, & his leaden aduice, as betweene his siluer haires, and my amber lockes; I know hee will cough for anger that I yeeld not, but he shall cough mee a foole for his labour.

Spe. ⟨*aside to* PRIS.⟩. Where pickt your daughter that worke, out of broad-stitch?

---

58 him¹ *Q*¹ *only*   60 dandle] dandie *F.*   S. D. [They stand aside] *suppl. Dil.*   67 handkercheffe *Q*².

Pris. Out of a flirts sampler; but let vs stay the end, this is but the beginning, you shall heare two children well brought vp!

Cand. Parents in these daies are growen pieuish, they rocke their children in their cradles till they sleepe, and crosse them about their bridals till their hearts ake. Marriage among them is become a market. What will you giue with your daughter? What Ioynter will you make for your sonne? And many a match is broken off for a penie more or lesse, as though they could not afford their children at such a price; when none should cheapen such ware but affection, and none buy it but loue.

Spe. ⟨*aside*⟩. Learnedly and scholerlike!

Livia. In deed our parents take great care to make vs aske blessing, and say grace when as we are lyttle ones, and growing to yeeres of iudgement, they depriue vs of the greatest blessing, and the most gracious things to our mindes, the libertie of our minds: they giue vs pap with a spoon before we can speak, and when wee speake for that wee loue, pap with a hatchet: because their fansies beeing growen musty with hoarie age, therefore nothing can relish in their thoughtes that sauours of sweet youth: they studie twentie yeeres together to make vs grow as straight as a wande, and in the ende by bowing vs, make vs as crooked as a cammocke. For mine owne part (sweet *Candius*) they shall pardon me, for I will measure my loue by min owne iudgement, not my fathers purse or peeuishnes. Nature hath made me his child, not his slaue: I hate *Memphio* and his son deadly, if I wist he would place his affection by his fathers appointment.

Pris. ⟨*aside*⟩. Wittily but vnciuily!

Can. Be of that minde still, my faire *Liuia*: let our fathers lay their purses together, we our harts. I wil neuer woo where I cannot loue: let *Stellio* inioy his daughter. But what haue you wrought here?

Livia. Flowers, fowles, beasts, fishes, trees, plants, stones, and what not. Among flowers, cowslops & lillyes, for our names *Candius* and *Liuia*. Among fowles, Turtles and Sparrowes, for our truth and desires. Among beasts, the foxe and the Ermin, for beautie and policie. And among fishes, the cockle & the Tortuse, because of *Venus*. Among trees, the vine wreathing about the elme, for our

100 as Q^1 *only*   106 twentie] 20 Q^2 108 make vs Q^1 *only*   116 woo] woe *Bl. F.*   124 Venus; among trees, the *Dil.*: Venus among trees, the Q^1: Venus among trees: the Q^2 *Bl. foll. by F.*!

embracings. Among stones, Abeston, which being hot wil neuer be colde, for our constancies. Among plants, Time and harts-ease, to note that if we take time, we shall ease our hearts.

Pris. ⟨*aside*⟩. Theres a girle that knowes her lerripoope.

Spe. ⟨*aside*⟩. Listen, & you shall heare my sons learning.

Livia. What booke is that?

Can. A fine pleasant poet, who entreateth of the arte of Loue, and of the remedie.

Livia. Is there arte in loue?

Can. A short art & a certain, three rules in 3 lines.

Livia. I praie thee repeat them.

*Can. Principio quod amare velis reperire labora,
Proximus huic labor est placidam exorare puellam,
Tertius vt longo tempore duret amor.*

Livia. I am no Latinist, *Candius,* you must conster it.

Can. So I will, and pace it too: thou shalt be acquainted with case, gender, and number. First, one must finde out a mistres whom before all others he voweth to serue. Secondly, that he vse al the means that he may to obtaine her. And the last, with deserts, faith, and secrecie, to studie to keepe her.

Livia. Whats the remedie?

Can. Death.

Livia. What of all the booke is the conclusion?

Can. This one verse, *Non caret effectu quod voluere duo.*

Livia. Whats that?

Can. Where two are agreed, it is impossible but they must speed.

Livia. Then cannot we misse: therefore giue mee thy hand, *Candius.*

Pris. ⟨*advancing*⟩. Soft, *Liuia,* take mee with you, it is not good in lawe without witnes.

Spe. And as I remember, there must be two witnesses; God giue you ioy, *Candius,* I was worth the bidding to dinner, though not worthy to be of the counsell.

Pris. I thinke this hot loue hath prouided but cold cheere.

Spe. Tush! in loue is no lacke; but blush not, *Candius,* you neede not bee ashamed of your cunning: you haue made loue a booke case, and spent your time well at schoole, learning to loue

---

125 Abestor *old eds. F.*: asbestos *Dil.* 134 3 Q^1: three $Q^2 Bl.$ *mods.*
137 exorare *Dil. F.*: euorare *old eds.* 138 duret *Dil.*: ducet *old eds. F.*
140 pace *old eds. F.*: parse *Dil.* 148 effectu *Dil. F.*: effertu *old eds.* 150 are] is $Q^2 Bl. F.$ 160 you QQ: and *Bl. Dil. F.*

by arte, and hate against nature. But I perceiue, the worser childe the better louer.

Pris. And my minion hath wrought well, where euery stitch in her sampler is a pricking stitch at my heart: you take your pleasure on parents, they are peeuish, fooles, churles, ouergrowen with ignorance, because ouerworne with age: litle shalt thou know the case of a father, before thy selfe be a mother, when thou shalt breed thy childe with continuall paines, and bringing it foorth with deadly pangs, nurse it with thine owne paps, and nourish it vp with motherly tendernes; and then finde them to curse thee with their hearts, when they shoulde aske blessing on their knees, and the collop of thine owne bowels to be the torture of thine owne soul; with teares trickling downe thy cheeks, and drops of bloud falling from thy heart, thou wilt in vttering of thy minde wish them rather vnborne than vnnatural, & to haue had their cradles their graues rather than thy death their bridals. But I will not dispute what thou shouldst haue done, but correct what thou hast done: I perceiue sowing is an idle exercise, and that euerie daie there come more thoughtes into thine head, than stitches into thy worke; Ile see whether you can spin a better mind than you haue stitched, and if I coope you not vp, then let me be the capon.

Spe. As for you, sir boy, in stead of poaring on a booke, you shall holde the plough; Ile make repentance reape what wantonnesse hath sowen. But we are both well serued: the sonnes must bee masters, the fathers gaffers; what wee get together with a rake, they cast abroade with a forke; and wee must wearie our legges to purchase our children armes. Well, seeing that booking is but idlenesse, Ile see whether threshing be anie occupation: thy minde shall stoope to my fortune, or mine shall break the lawes of nature. How like a micher he standes, as though he had trewanted from honestie! Get thee in, and for the rest let me alone. In villaine!

Pris. And you, pretie minx, that must be fed with loue vpon sops, Ile take an order to cram you with sorrowes: get you in without looke or reply.
Exeunt CANDIUS, LIUIA.

Spe. Let vs follow, and deale as rigorously with yours, as I will with mine, and you shall see that hot loue wil wax soone colde. Ile

---

162 arte] heart *F.* 169 bringing it foorth Q^1 *only* 172 collops
Q^2 *rest* 174 cheeks] checkes Q^1 178 sewing *Dil.* 179 comes
Q^2 *rest* 183 poring *Dil.* 189 stoupe Q^2 *Bl. F.*

tame the proud boy, and send him as far from his loue, as hee is from his duetie.

200 *Pris.* Let vs about it, and also go on with matching them to our mindes: it was happie that we preuented that by chance, which we could neuer yet suspect by circumstance. *Exeunt.*

ACT. 2.

Sce. 1.

⟨*Enter at opposite sides*⟩ Dromio, Risio.

Drom. Now, if I could meete with *Risio*, it were a world of waggery.

Ris. Oh that it were my chance, *Obuiam dare Dromio*, to stumble vpon *Dromio*, on whome I doo nothing but dreame.

5 *Dro.* His knauerie and my wit, should make our masters that are wise, fooles; their chidren that are fooles, beggers; and vs two that are bond, free.

Ris. He to cosin, & I to coniure, would make such alterations, that our masters shuld serue themselues; the ideots, their children,
10 serue vs; and we to wake our wits betweene them all.

Dro. *Hem quàm opportune*, looke if he drop not ful in my dish.

Ris. *Lupus in fabula*, *Dromio* imbrace me, hugge me, kisse my hand, I must make thee fortunate.

Dro. *Risio*, honor me, kneele downe to mee, kisse my feet, I must
15 make thee blessed.

Ris. My master, olde *Stellio*, hath a foole to his daughter.

Dro. Nay, my master, old *Memphio*, hath a foole to his sonne.

Ris. I must conuey a contract.

Dro. And I must conuey a contract.

20 *Ris.* Betweene her and *Memphios* sonne, without speaking one to another.

Dro. Betweene him and *Stellios* daughter, without one speaking to the other.

Ris. Doest thou mocke me, *Dromio?*

25 *Dro.* Thou doest me else.

Ris. Not I, for all this is true.

3 obvium *Dil.*   9 idiots *Bl. mods.*   12-3 kisse my hand, *Q*¹ *only*   26 this] that *Dil.*

Dro. And all this.

Ris. Then are we both driuen to our wits endes, for if either of them had bin wise, wee might haue tempered, if no marriage, yet a close marriage.

Dro. Well, let vs sharpen our accounts; ther's no better grindstone for a young mans head than to haue it whet vppon an olde mans purse. Oh thou shalt see my knauerie shaue lyke a rasor!

Ris. Thou for the edge, and I the point, wil make the foole bestride our mistres backs, and then haue at the bagge with the dudgin hafte, that is, at the dudgen dagger, by which hanges his tantonie pouch.

Dro. These old huddles haue such strong purses with locks, when they shut them they go off like a snaphance.

Ris. The olde fashion is best, a purse with a ring round about it, as a circle to course a knaues hande from it. But, *Dromio*, two they saie may keep counsell if one be awaie: but to conuey knauerie, two are too few, and foure too many.

Dro. And in good time, looke where *Halfepenie, Sperantus* boy, commeth; though bound vp in *decimo sexto* for carriage, yet a wit in *folio* for coosnage. Single *Halfepenie*, what newes are now currant?

Enter HALFEPENIE.

Half. Nothing, but that such double coystrels as you be, are counterfeit.

Ris. Are you so dapper? weele sende you for an Halfepenie loafe.

Half. I shall goe for siluer though, when you shall bee nailed vp for slips.

Dro. Thou art a slipstring Ile warrant.

Half. I hope you shall neuer slip string, but hang steddie.

Ris. Dromio, looke heere, now is my hand on my halfepenie.

Half. Thou lyest, thou hast not a farthing to laie thy hands on, I am none of thine: but let mee bee wagging, my head is full of hammers, & they haue so maletted my wit, that I am almost a malcontent.

Dro. Why, whats the matter?

---

34 wil] we'll *F.*   36 is, at] *comma in all eds.*   40 olde] olke *Q²*
41 as *Q¹*: is *rest*   course *all eds.*   42 if] is *Q¹*   conuay *Bl. F.*   46 in (*roms.*) *QQ*: in (*itals.*) *Bl. F.*: in folio (*roms.*) *Dil.*   coosonage *Q²*: coosenage *Bl. F.*: cozenage *Dil.*

Half. My master hath a fine scholer to his sonne, *Prisius* a fayre lasse to his daughter.

Dro. Well!

Half. They two loue one another deadly.

Ris. In good time.

Half. The fathers haue put them vp, vtterly disliking the match, and haue appointed the one shall haue *Memphios* sonne, the other *Stellios* daughter; this workes lyke waxe, but how it will fadge in the end, the hen that sits next the cocke cannot tell.

Ris. If thou haue but anie spice of knauery, wele make thee happie.

Half. Tush! doubt not of mine, I am as full for my pitch as you are for yours; a wrens egge is as ful of meat as a goose eg, though there be not so much in it: you shal find this head wel stuft, though there went little stuffe to it.

Dro. Laudo ingenium, I lyke thy sconce, then harken: *Memphio* made me of his counsell about marriage of his sonne to *Stellios* daughter; *Stellio* made *Riscio* acquainted to plot a match with *Memphios* sonne. To be short, they be both fooles.

Half. But they are not fooles that bee short; if I thought thou meantst so, *Senties qui vir sim,* Thou shouldst haue a crow to pull.

Ris. Be not angrie, *Halfepenie;* for fellowship we will be all fooles, and for gaine all knaues. But why doest thou laugh.

Half. At mine owne conceit and quicke censure.

Ris. Whats the matter?

Half. Sodainly me thought you two were asses, and that the least asse was the more asse.

Ris. Thou art a foole, that cannot be.

Half. Yea, my yong master taught me to proue it by learning, and so I can out of *Ouid* by a verse.

Ris. Prethee how?

Half. You must first for fashion sake confes your selues to be asses.

Dro. Well.

Half. Then stand you here, and you there.

Ris. Go to.

Half. Then this is the verse as I point it, *Cum mala per longas inualuêre moras.* So you see the least asse is the more asse.

77 Lando Q^2 *Dil.* Memphios Q^2 *Bl.*: Memphio's *Dil. F.*   82 meantst QQ: meanest *Bl. F.*: mean'st *Dil.*   97 too Q^2 *Bl. F.*

Ris. Weele bite thee for an ape, if thou bob vs lyke asses. But to end all, if thou wilt ioyne with vs, we will make a match betweene the two fooles, for that must be our tasks; and thou shalt deuise to couple *Candius* & *Liuia*, by ouer-reaching their fathers.

Half. Let me alone, *Non enim mea pigra iuuentus*, there's matter in this noddle.

Enter LUCIO.

But looke where *Prisius* boy comes, as fit as a pudding for a dogs mouth.

Lucio. Pop three knaues in a sheath, Ile make it a right Tunbridge case, and be the bodkin.

Ris. Nay, the bodkin is heere alreadie, you must be the knife.

Half. I am the bodkin, looke well to your eares, I must boare them.

Dro. Mew thy tongue, or weele cut it out; this I speake representing the person of a knife, as thou didst that in shadow of a bodkin.

Lucio. I must be gone; *Tædet*, it irketh, *Oportet*, it behoueth: my wits worke like barme, alias yest, alias sizing, alias rising, alias Gods good.

Half. The new wine is in thine head, yet was hee faine to take this metaphor from ale; and now you talke of ale, let vs all to the wine.

Dro. Foure makes a messe, and wee haue a messe of masters that must be cosned; let vs lay our heads together, they are married and cannot.

Half. Let vs consult at the Tauerne, where after to the health of *Memphio*, drinke we to the life of *Stellio*, I carouse to *Prisius*, & brinch you mas *Sperantus*; we shall cast vp our accounts, and discharge our stomackes, like men that can disgest any thing.

Lucio. I see not yet what you go about.

Dro. Lucio, that can pearce a mud wall of twentie foote thicke, would make vs beleeue he cannot see a candle through a paper lanthorne; his knauerie is beyond *Ela*, & yet he sayes he knowes not *Gam vt*.

---

100 thee *Q* only   104 iuuentus] *i. e.* juventus: inuentus *old eds. F.* (*a turned* u): *hence* inventio *Dil.*   108, 116 Luc. *Dil. F.*: Liu. *old eds.*   116 irketh, Q^1 *Dil.*: liketh. Q^2 *Bl. F.*   117 to *before* worke Q^2 *Bl. ṁods., owing to Q^1 om. stop at* behoueth   123 cosned Q^1: cosoned Q^2: coozened *Bl. F.*: cozened *Dil.*   127 cast vp *Bl. mods.*: cast vs *QQ*; *but cf.* v. 1. 3.

Lucio. I am readie: if anie cosnage be ripe, Ile shake the tree.

Half. Nay, I hope to see thee so strong, to shake three trees at once.

Dro. Wee burne time, for I must giue a reckning of my dayes worke; let vs close to ⟨to⟩ the bush *ad deliberandum*.

Half. In deede *Inter pocula philosophandum*, it is good to plea among pots.

Ris. Thine will be the worst; I feare we shall leaue a halfepenie in hand.

Half. Why sayest thou that? thou hast left a print deeper in thy hand alreadie than a halfpenie canne leaue, vnles it should sing worse than an hot yron.

Lucio. All friendes, and so let vs sing: tis a pleasant thing to goe into the tauerne cleering the throate.

SONG.

Omnes.	*Iô Bacchus!* To thy Table	
	Thou call'st euery drunken Rabble,	
	We already are stiffe Drinkers,	
	Then seale vs for thy iolly Skinckers.	
Dro.	Wine, O Wine!	
	O Iuyce Diuine!	
	How do'st thou the Nowle refine!	
Ris.	Plump thou mak'st mens Rubie faces,	
	And from Girles canst fetch embraces.	
Half.	By thee our Noses swell,	
	With sparkling Carbuncle.	
Luc.	O the deare bloud of Grapes,	
	Turnes us to Anticke shapes	
	Now to shew trickes like Apes.	
Dro.	Now Lion-like to rore.	
Ris.	Now Goatishly to whore.	
Half.	Now Hoggishly ith' mire.	
Luc.	Now flinging Hats ith' fire.	
Omnes.	*Iô Bacchus!* at thy Table,	
	Make vs of thy Reeling Rabble.	

Exeunt ⟨*into tavern*⟩.

140 philosophandum, *Bl. mods.*: philosophundum *QQ*   144 Why, sayest thou that thou *all eds.*   S. D. SONG, &c. *first in Blount.*   *QQ have not even* Song

SCE. 2.

Enter MEMPHIO *alone.*

Memp. I maruell I heare no newes of *Dromio;* either he slackes the matter, or betrayes his master; I dare not motion anie thing to *Stellio*, till I knowe what my boy hath don; Ile hunt him out, if the loitersacke be gone springing into a tauerne, Ile fetch him reeling out. *Exit* ⟨*into tavern*⟩. 5

Enter STELLIO *alone.*

Stel. Without doubt *Risio* hath gone beyond himselfe, in casting beyond the Moone; I feare the boy be runne mad with studying, for I know hee loued me so well, that for my fauour hee will venture to runne out of his wits; and it may be, to quicken his inuention, hee is gone into this Iuy-bush, a notable neast for a grape owle. Ile 10 firret him out, yet in the end vse him friendly: I cannot be merrie till I heare whats done in the marriages. *Exit* ⟨*into tavern*⟩.

Enter PRISIUS *alone.*

Pris. I thinke *Lucio* be gone a squirelling, but Ile squirell him for it: I sent him on my arrande, but I must goe for an answere my selfe. I haue tied vp the louing worme my daughter, and will see 15 whether fansie can worme fansie out of her head. This green nosegaie I feare my boy hath smelt to, for if he get but a penny in his purse, he turnes it sodainly into *Argentum potabile;* I must search euery place for him, for I stand on thornes till I heare what he hath done. *Exit* ⟨*into tavern*⟩. 20

Enter SPERANTUS *alone.*

Spe. Well, be as bee may is no banning. I thinke I haue charmde my yong master: a hungry meale, a ragged coate, & a drie cudgell, haue put him quite beside his loue and his logick too besides his pigsnie is put vp, & therefore now Ile let him take the aire, and follow *Stellios* daughter with all his learning, if he meane to be my 25 heire. The boy hath wit sance measure, more than needs; cats meat & dogs meate inough for the vantage. Well, without *Halfepenie* all my witte is not woorth a dodkin: that mite is miching in this groue, for as long as his name is *Halfepenie*, he will bee banquetting for the other *Halfpenie*. *Exit* ⟨*into tavern*⟩. 30

5 S.D. Exeunt Q^2 *Bl.*   11 firret *old eds.* *F.*: ferret *Dil.*   17 to] too Q^2 *Bl. F.*   18 so *before* suddainly Q^2: so suddenly *Bl. mods.*   23 too] to Q^1 24 his Q^1 *only*   26 sance *old eds.* *F.*: sans *Dil.*   30 the other *Bl. mods.*: thether Q^1: thother Q^2

Sce. 3.

CANDIUS, SILENA.

⟨*Enter* CANDIUS.⟩

Can. He must needs goe that the deuill driues! a father? a fiend! that seekes to place affection by appointment, & to force loue by compulsion. I haue sworne to woo *Sylena*, but it shall be so coldly, that she shall take as small delight in my wordes, as I do
5 contentment in his commandement.   Ile teach him one schoole tricke in loue. But behold, who is that that commeth out of *Stellios* house? it should seem to be *Silena* by her attire.

Enter SILENA.

By her face I am sure it is she, oh faire face! oh louely countenance! How now, *Candius*, if thou begin to slip at beautie on
10 a sodaine, thou wilt surfet with carousing it at the last. Remēber that *Liuia* is faithfull; I, and let thine eyes witnesse *Silena* is amiable! Heere shall I please my father and my selfe: I wyll learne to be obedient, & come what will, Ile make a way; if shee seeme coy, Ile practise all the arte of loue, if I ⟨finde⟩ her coming, all
15 the pleasures of loue.

Sil. My name is *Silena*, I care not who knowe it, so I doo not: my father keeps me close, so he does; and now I haue stolne out, so I haue, to goe to olde *Mother Bombie* to know my fortune, so I wil; for I haue as fayre a face as euer trode on shoo sole, and as
20 free a foote as euer lookt with two eyes.

Can. ⟨*aside*⟩. What? I thinke she is lunatike or foolish! Thou art a foole, *Candius*; so faire a face cannot bee the scabbard of a foolish minde; mad she may bee, for commonly in beautie so rare, there fals passions extreame. Loue and beautie disdaine a meane,
25 not therefore because beautie is no vertue, but because it is happines; and we schollers know that vertue is not to be praised, but honored. I wil put on my best grace.—⟨*To* SILENA.⟩ Sweete wench, thy face is louely, thy bodie comely, & all that the eyes can see inchanting! you see how, vnacquainted, I am bold to
30 boord you.

---

4 shall *Q¹ only* 13 a way *Dil. F.* : away *old eds.* 14 if I finde her coming] if I her cunning *old eds.* : if cunning *Dil. F., the former proposing* coming *for* cunning *in a note* 18 Mother *Q¹ only* 21 lunatike *old eds.* : lunatic *Dil.* : a lunaticke *F.*

Sil. My father boordes mee alreadie, therefore I care not if your name were *Geoffrey*.

Can. Shee raues, or ouer-reaches.—I am one, sweet soule, that loues you, brought hether by reporte of your beautie, and here languisheth with your rarenesse.

Sil. I thanke you that you would call.

Can. I will alwaies call on such a saint that hath power to release my sorrowes; yeeld, fayre creature, to loue.

Sil. I am none of that sect.

Can. The louing sect is an auncient sect, and an honorable, and therefore ⟨loue⟩ should bee in a person so perfect.

Sil. Much!

Can. I loue thee much, giue mee one worde of comfort.

Sil. I faith, sir, no! and so tell your master.

Can. I haue no master, but come to make choise of a mistres.

Sil. A ha, are you there with your beares?

Can. ⟨*aside*⟩. Doubtles she is an idiot of the newest cut! Ile once more trye hir.—I have loued thee long, *Silena*.

Sil. In your tother hose.

Can. ⟨*aside*⟩. Too simple to be naturall: too senslesse to bee arteficiall.—You sayd you went to know your fortune: I am a scholler, and am cunning in palmistry.

Sil. The better for you, sir; heres my hand, whats a clocke?

Can. The line of life is good, *Venus* mount very perfect; you shall haue a scholler to your first husband.

Sil. You are well seene in cranes durt, your father was a poulter. Ha, ha, ha!

Can. Why laugh you?

Sil. Because you should see my teeth.

Can. ⟨*aside*⟩. Alas, poore wench, I see now also thy folly; a fayre foole is lyke a fresh weed, pleasing leaues and soure iuyce. I will not yet leaue her, shee may dissemble.—⟨*Aloud.*⟩ I cannot choose but loue thee.

Sil. I had thought to aske you.

Can. Nay then farewell, either too proud to accept, or too simple to vnderstand.

Sil. You need not bee so crustie, you are not so hard bakt.

---

40 The Q^1: Thy *rest*   41 loue *here first*   47 [aside] *this and the two asides below marked first in Dilke*   56 cranes] carnes Q^1 61 leaues] leaues, Q^2 *Bl. F. spoiling sense*   65 too¹] to Q^1 67 bakt] *so I correct* backt *of old eds.* F.: baked *Dil.*

Can. Now I perceiue thy folly, who hath rakt together all the odde blinde phrases, that helpe them that knowe not howe to dis-
70 course; but when they cannot aunswere wisely, eyther with gybing couer their rudenesse, or by some newe coyned by-word bewraie theyr peeuishnesse. I am glad of this: now shall I have coulour to refuse the match, and my father reason to accept of *Liuia*: I will home, and repeate to my father oure wise incounter, and hee shall
75 perceiue there is nothing so fulsome as a shee foole. *Exit.*

Sil. Good God, I thinke Gentlemen had neuer lesse wit in a yeere. Wee maides are madde wenches; we gird them and flout them out of all scotch and notch, and they cannot see it. I will knowe of the olde woman whether I bee a maide or no, and then,
80 if I bee not, I must needes be a man. ⟨*Knocks at* MOTHER BOMBIE'S *door.*⟩ God be heere.

Enter MOTHER BOMBIE.

Bom. Whose there?

Sil. One that would be a maide.

Bom. If thou be not, it is impossible thou shuldst be, and a shame
85 thou art not.

Sil. They saie you are a witch.

Bom. They lie, I am a cunning woman.

Sil. Then tell mee some thing.

Bom. Holde vp thy harde; not so high:—
90   Thy father knowes thee not,
    Thy mother bare thee not,
    Falsely bred, truely begot:
    Choise of two husbands, but neuer tyed in bandes,
    Because of loue and naturall bondes.

95 *Sil.* I thanke you for nothing, because I vnderstand nothing: though you bee as olde as you are, yet am I as younge as I am, and because that I am so fayre, therefore are you so fowle; & so farewell frost, my fortune naught me cost. *Exit.*

Bom. Farewell faire foole, little doest thou know thy hard fortune,
100 but in the end thou shalt, & that must bewraie what none can discouer: in the mean season I wil professe cunning for all commers.
                                                                            Exit.

---

68 rackt Q^2 *Bl. F.*: raked *Dil.*   71 by-word *Bl. mods.*: buy worde *QQ*
76 Sil. *Dil. F.*: Liu. *old eds.*   84 shuldst Q^1: should Q^2 *Bl. F.*: *Dil. italicizes* be not, shouldst be, *and* art not   90–4 Thy father . . . bondes] *this and the other oracles of Mother Bombie* (iii. 1 *and* 4, v. 2), *printed as continuous prose in old eds., were arranged according to the doggrel rhyme by Dilke in* 1814   92 falsely *QQ Dil.*: falsly *Bl.*: Fastly *F.*

SCE. 4.

⟨*Enter*⟩ DROMIO, RISIO, LUCIO, HALFEPENIE.

Dro. We were all taken tardie.

Ris. Our masters will be ouertaken if they tarry.

Half. Now must euerie one by wit make an excuse, and euerie excuse must bee coosnage.

Lucio. Let vs remember our complot. 5

Dro. We will all plod on that; oh the wine hath turnd my wit to vineger.

Ris. You meane tis sharpe.

Half. Sharpe? Ile warrant twill serue for as good sauce to knauerie as— 10

Lucio. As what?

Half. As thy knauerie meat for his wit.

Dro. We must all giue a reckning for our dayes trauell.

Ris. Tush! I am glad we scapt the reckning for our liquor. If you be examined how we met, sweare by chance; for so they met, 15 and therefore will beleeue it: if how much we drunke, let them answere them selues; they know best because they paid it.

Half. We must not tarry, *abeundum est mihi*, I must go and cast this matter in a corner.

Dro. *I præ, sequar*; a bowle, and Ile come after with a broome; 20 euerie one remember his que.

Ris. I, and his k, or else we shall thriue ill.

Half. When shall we meete?

Ris. To morrow, fresh and fasting.

Dro. Fast eating our meate, for we haue drunke for to morow, 25 & to morow we must eat for to day.

Half. Away, away, if our masters take vs here, the matter is mard.

Lucio. Let vs euerie one to his taske. *Exeunt.*

SCE. 5.

⟨*Enter*⟩ MEMPHIO, STELLIO, PRISIUS, SPERANTUS.

Memp. How luckily we met on a sodaine in a tauerne, that drunke not together almost these thirtie yeeres.

---

1 were Q^1: are *rest*   12 knauerie QQ: knauerie's *rest*   20 Dro. *om.*
old eds.: *supplied Dil. F.*   1 presequar Q^1: Ipresequam Q^2 *Bl.*: I, præ sequar
Dil. F.   21 cue *Dil.*   29 vs *om. Dil.*   1 luckily Q^1: quickly *rest*

Stel. A tauerne is the Randeuous, the Exchange, the staple for good fellowes: I haue heard my great grandfather tell how his great grandfather shoulde saie, that it was an olde prouerbe, when his greate grandfather was a childe, that it was a good winde that blew a man to the wine.

Pris. The olde time was a good time! Ale was an ancient drinke, and accounted of our ancestors autentical; Gascone wine was liquor for a Lord, Sack a medicine for the sicke; and I may tell you, he that had a cup of red wine to his oysters, was hoysted in the Queenes subsidie booke.

Spe. I, but now you see to what loosenes this age is growen, our boies carouse sack like double beere, and saith that which doth an old man good, can do a yong man no harme: old men (say they) eat pap, why shoulde not children drinke sacke? their white heads haue cosned time out of mind our yōg yeres.

Memp. Well! the world is wanton since I knew it first; our boyes put as much nowe in their bellies in an houre, as would cloath theyr whole bodies in a yeere: wee haue paide for their tipling eight shillinges, and as I haue hearde, it was as much as bought *Rufus*, sometime king of this land, a paire of hose.

Pris. Ist possible?

Stel. Nay, tis true; they saie Ale is out of request, tis hogges porredge, broth for beggers, a caudle for cunstables, watchmens mouth glew; the better it is, the more like bird lime it is, and neuer makes one staid but in the stockes.

Memp. Ile teach my wag-halter to know grapes from barley.

Pris. And I mine to discerne a spigot from a faucet.

Spe. And I mine to iudge the difference between a black boule and a siluer goblet.

Stel. And mine shall learne the oddes betweene a stand and a hogs-head; yet I cannot choose but laugh to see how my wag aunswered mee, when I strok$e$ him for drinking sacke.

Pris. Why what sayd he?

Stel. 'Master, it is the soueraigntest drinke in the world, and the safest for all times and weathers; if it thunder, though all the Ale and Beere in the towne turne, it will be constant; if it lighten, and that any fire come to it, it is the aptest wine to burn, and the most wholesomest when it is burnt. So much for Summer. If it freeze, why it is so hot in operation, that no Ise can congeale it; if it rayne, why then he that cannot abide the heate of it, may put in water. So much for winter.' And so ranne his way, but Ile ouer-take him.

Spe. Who woulde thinke that my hoppe on my thumbe, *Halfpenie*, scarse so high as a pint pot, wold reason the matter? but hee learnde his leere of my sonne, his young master, whom I haue brought vp at Oxford, and I thinke must learne heere in Kent at Ashford.

Memp. Why what sayd he?

Spe. Hee boldly rapt it out, *Sine Cerere & Baccho friget Venus*, without wine and sugar his veins wold waxe colde.

Memp. They were all in a pleasant vaine! But I must be gone, and take account of my boyes businesse; farewell, neighbours, God knowes when we shall meete againe!—⟨*Aside.*⟩ Yet I have dis-couered nothing: my wine hath been my wittes friende, I longe to heare what *Dromio* hath done. *Exit.*

Stel. I cannot staie, but this good fellowshippe shall cost mee the setting on at our next meeting.—⟨*Aside.*⟩ I am gladde I blabd nothing of the marriage, now I hope to compas it. I know my boy hath bin bungling about it. *Exit.*

Pris. Let vs all goe, for I must to my clothes that hang on the tenters: ⟨*Aside.*⟩ my boy shall hang with them, if hee aunswere mee not his dayes worke. *Exit.*

Spe. If all bee gone, Ile not staie: *Halfepenie* I am sure hath done mee a pennie woorth of good, else Ile spend his bodie in buying a rod. *Exit.*

ACT. 3.

Sce. 1.

⟨*Enter*⟩ Mæstius. Serena.

Mæstius. Sweet sister, I know not how it commeth to passe, but I finde in my selfe passions more than brotherly.

Ser. And I, deare brother, finde my thoughts intangled with

49 at Q^1: of *rest*   51 Cerere *Dil.*: Cere *old eds. F.*   55-63 *the asides here first marked in Dilke*

affections beyonde nature, which so flame into my distempered head,
that I can neither without danger smother the fire, nor without
modestie disclose my furie.

Mæst. Our parents are pore, our loue vnnaturall: what can then
happen to make vs happie?

Ser. Onely to be content with our fathers mean estate, to combat
against our own intemperate desires, and yeld to the succes of
fortune, who though she hath framd vs miserable, cannot make vs
monstrous.

Mæst. It is good counsel, faire sister, if the necessitie of loue
could be releeued by counsell. Yet this is our comfort, that these
vnnaturall heates haue stretched themselues no further than thoughts.
Vnhappie me that they should stretch so!

Ser. That which nature warranteth laws forbid. Straunge it
seemeth in sense, that because thou art mine, therefore thou must
not be mine.

Mæst. So it is, *Serena;* the neerer we are in bloud, the further
wee must be from loue; and the greater the kindred is, the lesse
the kindnes must be; so that between brothers & sisters superstition
hath made affection cold, between strangers custome hath bred loue
exquisite.

Ser. They say there is hard by an old cunning woman, who can
tell fortunes, expound dreames, tell of things that be lost, and deuine
of accidents to come: she is called the good woman, who yet neuer
did hurt.

Mæst. Nor anie good, I thinke, *Serena;* yet to satisfie thy minde
we will see what she can saie.

Ser. Good brother let vs.

Mæst. Who is within?

Enter MOTHER BOMBIE.

Bom. The dame of the house!

Mæst. She might haue said the beldam, for her face, and yeeres,
and attire.

Ser. Good mother tell vs, if by your cunning you can, what shall
become of my brother and me.

4 into] in *Dil.* 5 without²] with *Dil.* 9 comhat Q^1 17–9 Ser.
That ... be mine. Q^1 *only. Dil. suspecting error in Q^2 Bl. prefixed* Ser. *to* Yet
this ... stretch so *in preceding speech. F. gave the true reading from Q^1 in his
notes*

Bom. Let me see your hands, and looke on me stedfastly with your eyes.

You shall be married to morow hand in hand, 40
By the lawes of God, Nature, & the land,
Your parents shall be glad, & giue you their lande,
You shal each of you displace a foole.
& both together must releeue a foole.
If this be not true, call me olde foole. 45

Mæst. This is my sister, marrie we cannot: our parents are poore, and haue no land to giue vs: each of vs is a foole to come for counsell to such an olde foole.

Ser. These doggrell rimes and obscure words, comming out of the mouth of such a weather-beatē witch, are thought diuinations 50 of some holy spirite, being but dreames of decayed braines: for mine owne parte, I would thou mightest sit on that stoole, till he & I marrie by lawe.

Bom. I saie *Mother Bombie* neuer speakes but once, and yet neuer spake vntruth once. 55

Ser. Come, brother, let vs to our poore home; this is our comfort, to bewraie our passions, since we cannot inioy our loue.

Mæst. Content, sweet sister; and learne of me hereafter, that these olde sawes of such olde hags, are but false fires to leade one out of a plaine path into a deepe pit. *Exeunt.* 60

Sce. 2.

Dromio. Risio. Halfepenie. Luceo.

⟨*Enter* Dromio *and* Riscio.⟩

Dro. *Ingenium quondam fuerat pretiosius auro:* the time was wherein wit would worke like waxe, and crock vp golde like honnie.

Ris. *At nunc barbaries grandis habere nihil,* but nowe wit and honestie buy nothing in the market.

Dro. What *Risio*, how spedst thou after thy potting? 5

Ris. Nay, my master rong all in the tauerne, & thrust all out in the house. But how spedst thou?

Dro. I, it were a dayes worke to discourse it: he spake nothing

---

41 by *QQ*: and by *Bl. mods.* God, nature *Q² Bl. mods.*: good nature *Q¹*
45 then *before* call *Q² Bl. mods.* 57 to bewraie *so all: qy.?* not to bewraie
inioy our loue *Q¹*: enioy them *rest* Sce. 2] Sce. 3 *Q² Bl.* 1
pretiosius *Bl. F.*: pretiotius *QQ*: pretiosus *Dil.* 3 barbaries] barbarie est
QQ Bl. F.: barbaria est *Dil.* . 6 rung *Bl. mods.*

but sentences, but they were vengible long ones, for when one word
was out, hee made pause of a quarter long, till he spake another.

Ris. Why what did he in all that time?

Dro. Breake interiections lyke winde, as *eho, ho, to.*

Ris. And what thou?

Dro. Aunswere him in his owne language, as *euax, vah, hui.*

Ris. These were coniunctions rather than interiections. But what of the plot?

Dro. As we concluded, I tolde him that I vnderstood that *Silena* was verie wise, and could sing exceedingly; that my deuise was, seeing *Accius* his sonne a proper youth, & could also sing sweetly, that he should come in the nicke when she was singing, and answere her.

Ris. Excellent!

Dro. Then hee asked how it should be deuised that she might come abroade: I tolde ⟨him⟩ that was cast alreadie by my meanes: then the song beeing ended, and they seeing one another, noting the apparell, and marking the personages, he should call in his sonne for feare he should ouer-reach his speech.

Ris. Very good.

Dro. Then that I had gotten a young Gentleman, that resembled his sonne in yeeres and fauour, that hauing *Accius* apparell should court *Silena;* whome shee finding wise, would after that by small intreatie be won without mo wordes; & so the marriage clapt vp by this cosnage, and his sonne neuer speake word for himselfe.

Ris. Thou boy! so haue I done in euerie point, for the song, the calling her in, & the hoping that another shall woo *Accius*, and his daughter wed him. I told him this wooing should be to night, and they early married in the morning, without anie wordes sauing to saie after the Priest.

Dro. All this fodges well! now if *Halfpenie* and *Luceo* haue playde theyr partes, wee shall haue excellent sporte—and here they come. Howe wrought the wine, my lads?

Enter HALFPENIE, LUCEO.

Half. How? like wine, for my bodie being the rundlet, and my mouth the vent, it wrought two daies ouer, till I had thought the hoopes of my head woulde haue flowen asunder.

10 a quarter long *so all, sc.* of an hour   12 eho, ho, to. (to *roms.*) *Bl.*: *and so QQ (all romans)*: eho, ho, o. *(all itals.) Dil.*   17 I² Q¹: we *rest*   19 & *om. Dil*   23 him *om. old eds. Dil.*   25 marking Q¹: thanking *rest*   31 mo Q¹: my Q² *Bl.*: any *Dil.*: many *F.*   32 spake *F.*   38 fodges QQ *here and pp.* 204, 210: fadges *Bl. mods.*   39 exccellent Q¹

Lucio. The best was, our masters were as well whitled as we, for yet they lie by it.

Ris. The better for vs! we dyd but a little parboile our liuers, they haue sod theyrs in sacke these fortie yeeres.

Half. That makes them spit white broth as they doo. But to the purpose. *Candius* and *Liuia* will send their attires, you must send the apparell of *Accius* and *Silena;* they wonder wherefore, but commit the matter to our quadrapertit wit.

Lucio. If you keepe promise to marrie them by your deuice, and their parents consent, you shall haue tenne pounds a peece for your paines.

Dro. If wee doo it not wee are vndone! for we haue broacht a cosnage alreadie, and my master hath the tap in his hand, that it must needs runne out. Let thē be ruld, and bring hether their apparell, and we wil determine; the rest commit to our intricate considerations: depart.

Exeunt HALFEPENIE, LUCEO.   *Enter* ACCIUS *and* SILENA.

Dro. Here comes *Accius* tuning his pipes. I perceiue my master keepes touch.

Ris. And here comes *Silena* with her wit of proofe! marie it will scarse holde out question shot: let vs in to instruct our masters in the que.

Dro. Come let vs be iogging: but wert not a world to heare them woe one another?

Ris. That shall be hereafter to make vs sport, but our masters shall neuer know it.   *Exeunt.*

SCE. 3.

ACCIUS *and* SILENA *singing.*

SONG.

Sil. O *Cupid!* Monarch ouer Kings,
       Wherefore hast thou feete and wings?
   It is to shew how swift thou art,
   When thou wound'st a tender heart:
   Thy wings being clip'd, and feete held still,
   Thy Bow so many could not kill.

---

51 quadrapertite *Bl. F.*: quadrupartite *Dil.*   53 their Q^1 *Dil.*: your *rest*
60 Masters *Bl.*: master's *F.*   63 out Q^1: our *rest*   64 the que *QQ F.*: the Q *Bl.*:
their cue *Dil.*   66 woo *Bl. mods.* to *before* another *Dil.*   S. D. Exeunt. Sc. 3...
singing. *I follow F.'s suggested emendation; QQ have* Exeunt. Memphio and
Stellio singing. Act. 3. Sc. 3. Memphio and Stellio *om. the song*: *Bl. Dil. F. insert
before announcing scene* Song *and words* (*first* 6 *ll. to* Memp., *rest to* Stel.)

Acc. It is all one in *Venus* wanton schoole,
Who highest sits, the wise man or the foole:
Fooles in loues colledge
Haue farre more knowledge,
To reade a woman ouer,
Than a neate prating louer.
Nay, tis confest,
That fooles please women best.

⟨*Enter*⟩ MEMPHIO *and* STELLIO.

Mem. *Accius* come in, and that quickly! what! walking without leaue?

Stel. *Silena*, I praie you looke homewards, it is a colde aire, and you want your mufler.   *Exeunt* ACCIUS & SILENA.

Mem. ⟨*aside*⟩. This is rat! if the rest proceed, *Stellio* is like to marrie his daughter to a foole; but a bargen is a bargen!

Stel. ⟨*aside*⟩. This frames to my wish! *Memphio* is like to marrie a foole to his sonne; *Accius* tongue shall tie all *Memphios* land to *Silenas* dowrie, let his fathers teeth vndoo them if hee can: but heere I see *Memphio*. I must seeme kind, for in kindnes lies cosnage.

Mem. ⟨*aside*⟩. Wel, here is *Stellio;* Ile talke of other matters, & flie from the marke I shoot at, lapwing-like flying far from the place where I nestle. ⟨*Aloud.*⟩ *Stellio*, what make you abroad? I heard you were sicke since our last drinking.

Stel. You see reports are no truths: I heard the like of you, & we are both well. I perceiue sober men tel most lies, for *in vino veritas.* If they had drunke wine, they would haue tolde the truth.

Mem. Our boies will be sure then neuer to lie, for they are euer swilling of wine: but *Stellio*, I must straine cursie with you; I haue busines, I cannot stay.

Stel. In good time, *Memphio!* for I was about to craue your patience to departe; it stands me vppon.—⟨*Aside.*⟩ Perhaps ⟨I may⟩ moue his patience ere it be long.

Mem. ⟨*aside*⟩. Good silly *Stel.* we must buckle shortly.

                                                         Exeunt.

---

18 your Q^1: a *rest*   28 makes *Dil.*   31 in (*romans*) *all eds.*   34 cursie old eds.: cursy *Dil.*: cur'sie *F.*   37 [I may] *F.'s insertion*   37, 39 *these two asides suppl. Dilke*

Sce. 4.

Halfepenie. Luceo. Rixula. Dromio. Risio.

⟨*Enter* Halfpenny *with clothes belonging to* Candius, Lucio *and* Rixula *with clothes belonging to* Livia.⟩

Lucio. Come, *Rixula*, wee haue made thee priuie to the whole packe, there laie downe the packe.

Rix. I beleeue vnlesse it be better handled, wee shall out of doores.

Half. I care not, *Omnem solum forti patria*, I can liue in christen- 5
dome as well as in Kent.

Lucio. And Ile sing *Patria vbicunque bene;* euerie house is my home, where I may stanch hunger.

Rix. Nay, if you set all on hazard, though I be a pore wench I am as hardie as you both; I cannot speake Latine, but in plaine 10
English, if anie thing fall out crosse, Ile runne away.

Half. He loues thee well that would runne after.

Rix. Why, *Halfpenie*, there's no goose so gray in the lake, that cannot finde a gander for her make.

Lucio. I loue a nutbrowne lasse, tis good to recreate. 15

Half. Thou meanest, a browne nut is good to crack.

Lucio. Why wold it not do thee good to crack such a nut?

Half. I feare she is worm-eaten within, she is so moth-eaten without.

Rix. If you take your pleasure of mee, Ile in and tell your 20
practises against your masters.

Half. In faith, soure heart, hee that takes his pleasure on thee is verie pleasurable.

Rix. You meane knauishly, and yet I hope foule water will quench hot fire as soone as fayre. 25

Half. Well then, let fayre wordes coole that cholar, which foule speeches hath kindled; and because we are all in this case, and hope all to haue good fortune, sing a roundelay, and weele helpe,—such as thou wast woont when thou beatedst hempe.

Lucio. It was crabbs she stampt, and stole away one to make her 30
a face.

Rix. I agree, in hope that the hempe shall come to your wearing:

---

1 the Q^1: our *rest* 5 omne *Dil. stupidly* 10 cannon Q^2 16
brawne *F.* 27 speeches Q^1: words *rest* 29 beatest QQ

a halfepenie halter may hang you both, that is, *Halfepeny* and you may hang in a halter.

35 *Half.* Well brought about.

Rix. Twill when tis about your necke.

Lucio. Nay, now shees in she will neuer out.

Rix. Nor when your heads are in, as it is lykely, they should not come out. But harken to my song.

Cantant.

SONG.

40 *Rix.*
FVll hard I did sweate,
When hempe I did beate,
Then thought I of nothing but hanging;
The hempe being spun,
My beating was done;
45 Then I wish'd for a noyse
Of crack-halter Boyes,
On those hempen strings to be twanging.
Long lookt I about,
The City throughout,—

50 *The Pages.* And fownd no such fidling varlets.

Rix. Yes, at last comming hither,
I saw foure together.

The Pages. May thy hempe choake such singing harlots.

Rix. To whit to whoo, the Owle does cry;
55 Phip, phip, the sparrowes as they fly;
The goose does hisse; the duck cries quack;
A Rope the Parrot, that holds tack.

The Pages. The parrat and the rope be thine

Rix. The hanging yours, but the hempe mine.

Enter DROMIO, RISIO *(carrying clothes of* ACCIUS *and* SILENA *respectively).*

60 *Dro.* Yonder stands the wags, I am come in good time.

Ris. All here before me! you make hast.

Rix. I beleeue, to hanging; for I thinke you haue all robd your masters: heres euery man his baggage.

Half. That is, we are all with thee, for thou art a verie 65 baggage.

Rix. Hold thy peace, or of mine honesty Ile buy an halfpenie purse with thee.

s. d. Cantant *QQ Bl. F.*: om. *Dil.*: *Bl. alone of old eds. gives the song*   50,
53, 58 The Pages] 4 Pag. *Bl.*: The Men *Dil.*: 2 Pag. *F.*   60 stand *Dil.*   66
Rix. *QQ Dil.*: Ri. *Bl.*: Ris. *F.*

Dro. In deed thats big inough to put thy honesty in. But come, shall we go about the matter?

Lucio. Now it is come to the pinch my heart pants. 70

Half. I for my part am resolute, *in utrumque paratus*, redie to die or to runne away.

Lucio. But, heare me! I was troubled with a vile dream, and therefore it is little time spent to let *Mother Bomby* expound it: she is cunning in all things. 75

Dro. Then will I know my fortune.

Rix. And Ile aske for a siluer spoone which was lost last daie, which I must pay for.

Ris. And Ile know what wil become of our deuices.

Half. And I! 80

Dro. Then let vs all go quickly; we must not sleep in this busines, our masters are so watchfull about it.

⟨*They knock at* BOMBIE'S *door. Enter* MOTHER BOMBIE.⟩

Bom. Why do you rap so hard at the doore?

Dro. Because we would come in.

Bom. Nay, my house is no Inne. 85

Half. Crosse your selues, looke how she lookes.

Dro. Marke her not, sheele turne vs all to Apes.

Bom. What would you with me?

Ris. They say you are cunning, & are called the good woman of Rochester. 90

Bom. If neuer to doo harme, be to doo good, I dare saie I am not ill. But whats the matter?

Lucio. I had an ill dream, & desire to know the significatiō.

Bom. Dreames, my sonne, haue their weight: though they be of a troubled minde, yet are they signes of fortune. Say on. 95

Lucio. In the dawning of the day,—for about that time by my starting out of my sleepe, I found it to bee,—mee thought I sawe a stately peece of beefe, with a cape cloke of cabidge, imbrodered with pepper; hauing two honorable pages with hats of mustard on their heades; himselfe in greate pompe sitting vppon a cushion of 100 white Brewish, linde with browne Breade; me thought being poudred, he was much trobled with the salt rume; & therfore there

---

70 pinch] pitch *F.* 71 utrumque *Dil.*: vtrancȝ. *old eds.* S. D. [They knock... MOTHER BOMBIE] *upplied Dil. printing speech as part of Half.'s* 87 Dro. Q^1 *F.*: *rest omit,* 93 an] a Q^1 102 rheum *Dil.*

stood by him two great flagons of sacke and beere, the one to drie vp his rume, the other to quench his cholar. I as one enuying his ambition, hungring and thirsting after his honor, began to pull his cushiō frō vnder him, hoping by that means to giue him a fall ; & with putting out my hand awakt, & found nothing in all this dreame about me but the salt rume.

Dro. A dreame for a butcher.

Lucio. Soft, let me end it !—then I slumbred againe, & me thought there came in a leg of mutton.

Dro. What ! all grosse meat ? a racke had bene daintie.

Lucio. Thou foole ! how could it come in, vnlesse it had bin a leg ? me thought his hose were cut & drawen out with parsly, I thrust my hand into my pocket for a knife, thinking to hoxe him, and so awakt.

Bom. Belyke thou wentst supperlesse to bed.

Lucio. So I doo euerie night but sundaies : *Prisius* hath a weake stomacke, and therefore we must starue.

Bom. Well, take this for answere, though the dream be fantasticall ;—

>They that in the morning sleep dream of eating,
>Are in danger of sicknesse, or of beating,
>Or shall heare of a wedding fresh a beating.

Lucio. This may be true.

Half. Nay then let me come in with a dreame, short but sweet, that my mouth waters euer since I wakt. Me thought there sate vpon a shelfe three damaske prunes in veluet caps and prest satten gownes like Iudges ; and that there were a whole handfull of curants to be araigned of a riot, because they clūged together in such clusters ; twelue raisons of the sunne were impannelled in a Iewry, and, as a leafe of whole mase, which was bailief, was carrying the quest to consult, me thoght ther came an angrie cooke, and gelded the Iewry of theyr stones, and swept both iudges, iurers, rebels, and bailiefe, into a porredge pot ; whereat I beeing melancholy, fetcht a deepe sigh, that wakt my selfe and my bed fellow.

Dro. This was deuisd, not dreamt ; and the more foolish being no dreame, for that dreames excuse the fantasticalnesse.

Half. Then aske my bed-felow, you know him, who dreamt that night that the king of diamonds was sicke.

---

103 sacke Q^1 : wine *rest*   106 cushing *Bl.*   107 I *bef.* awakt Q^2 *rest*
128 indges Q^1 129 a *QQ only*   clūged Q^1 : clunged Q^2 *Bl.* : clung *mods.*
131 whole *old eds. Dil.* : old *F.*

Bom. But thy yeeres and humours, pretie child, are subiect to 140
such fansies, which the more vnsensible they seeme, the more
fantasticall they are ; therefore this dream is easie.
  To children, this is giuen from the Gods
  To dream of milke, fruit, babies, and rods ;
  They betoken nothing, but that wantons must haue rods. 145
Dro. Ten to one thy dreame is true, thou wilt bee swinged.
Rix. Nay gammer, I pray you tell me who stole my spoone out
of the buttrie?
Bom. Thy spoone is not stolne but mislaide,
  Thou art an ill huswife, though a good maid, 150
  Looke for thy spoon where thou hadst like to be no maide.
Rix. Bodie of me! let me fetch the spoone! I remember the
place!
Lucio. Soft, swift ; the place if it be there now, will bee there to
morrowe. 155
Rix. I, but perchance the spoone will not.
Half. Wert thou once put to it?
Rix. No, sir boy, it was put to me.
Lucio. How was it mist?
Dro. Ile warrant for want of a mist. But whats my fortune, 160
mother?
Bom. Thy father doth liue because he doth die,
  Thou hast spent all thy thrift with a die,
  And so lyke a begger thou shalt die.
Ris. I woulde haue likte well if all the gerundes had beene 165
there, *di, do,* and *dum*; but all in die, thats too deadly.
Dro. My father indeed is a diar, and I haue ben a dicer, but to
die a beggar, giue mee leaue not to beleeue, *Mother Bombie ;* and
yet it may bee. I haue nothing to liue by but knauery, and if the
world grow honest, welcome beggerie. But what hast thou to say, 170
Risio?
Ris. Nothing, till I see whether all this bee true that she hath
sayd.
Half. I, *Risio* would faine see thee beg.
Ris. Nay, mother, tell vs this, What is all our fortunes? we are 175
about a matter of legerdemaine, howe will it fodge?

141 vnsensible Q^1: vincible *rest*: *Dil. proposing to transpose* fantasticall *and*
vincible   147 gammer Q^1 *Dil.*: grammer *rest*   154 will] it will Q^1
165 I] I I Q^2: I, I *Bl. F.*: Ah! I *Dil.*   167 diar QQ: Dyar *Bl. F.*: dyer
Dil.   and *Dil. F.*: but *old eds.*   176 fadge *Bl. mods.*

Bom. You shall all thriue like coosners,
That is, to bee coosned by coosners :
All shall ende well, and you bee found coosners.

180 *Dro.* Gramercie! *Mother Bombie*, we are all pleasd, if you were for your paines. ⟨*Offering money.*⟩

Bom. I take no monie, but good wordes. Raile not if I tell true ; if I doe not, reuenge. Farewell.

Exit Bom.

Dro. Now haue we nothing to doe but to go about this busines.
185 *Accius* apparell let *Candius* put on ; and I wyll aray *Accius* with *Candius* clothes.

Ris. Heere is *Silenas* attire ; *Lucio*, put it vpon *Liuia*, and give me *Liuias* for *Silena :* this done, let *Candius* & *Liuia* come foorth, and let *Dromio* and mee alone for the rest.

190 *Half.* What shall become of *Accius* and *Silena ?*

Dro. Tush ! theyr turne shall bee next, all must bee done orderly : lets to it, for nowe it workes. *Exeunt.*

ACT. 4.

Sce. 1.

Candius, Liuia, Dromio, Risio, Sperantus, Prisius.

⟨*Enter* Candius *and* Livia, *in the clothes of* Accius *and* Silena, *respectively.*⟩

Livia. This attyre is verie fit. But how if this make me a foole, and *Silena* wise? you will then woo mee, and wedde her.

Can. Thou knowest that *Accius* is also a foole, and his raiment fits me : so that if apparell be infectious, I am also lyke to be a foole,
5 and hee wise ; what would be the conclusion, I meruaile.

Enter Dromio, Risio.

Livia. Here comes our counsellers.

Dro. Well sayd ; I perceiue turtles flie in couples.

Ris. Else how should they couple?

Livia. So do knaues go double, else how should they be so
10 cunning in doubling?

187 Lucio] Linceo Q^1 4-5 foole, and hee wise ; what] fool ; and he wise, what *Dil.*: foole, and hee wist what *QQ Bl. F.*

Can. *Bona verba, Liuia.*
Dro. I vnderstand Latine: that is, *Liuia* is a good worde.
Can. No, I byd her vse good wordes.
Ris. And what deeds?
Can. None but a deed of gift.
Ris. What gift?
Can. Her heart.
Dro. Giue mee leaue to pose you, though you bee a graduate; for I tell you we in Rochester spurre so many hackneys, that we must needs spurre schollers, for wee take them for hackneys.
Livia. Why so, sir boy?
Dro. Because I knew two hired for ten grotes a pece to saie seruice on sunday, and thats no more than a post horse from hence to Canterbury.
Ris. Hee knowes what hee sayes, for hee once serued the post-master.
Can. In deed I thinke hee serued some poast to his master, but come *Dromio post me.*
Dro. You saie you would haue her heart for a deed.
Can. Well.
Dro. If you take her hart for *cor*, that heart in her bodie, then know this: *Molle eius leuibus, cor enim violabile telis:* a womans heart is thrust through with a feather: if you meane she should giue a heart named *Ceruus*, then are you worse, for *cornua ceruus habet*, that is, to haue ones heart growe out at his head, which wyll make one ake at the heart in their bodie.

Enter PRISIUS, SPERANTUS.

Livia. I, beshrew your hearts, I heare one comming: I know it is my father by his comming.
Can. What must we doo?
Dro. Why, as I tolde you: and let me alone with the olde men: fall you to your bridall.
Pris. Come, neighbor, I perceiue the loue of our children waxeth key colde.
Spe. I thinke it was neuer but luke warme.
Pris. Bauins will haue their flashes, and youth their fansies; the one as soone quenched as the other burnt. But who be these?

32 Molle... Cor enim inuiolabile Q^1: *hence* Male... inuiolabile Q^2 *Bl. F.*: *Dil. lengthens* cor *reading* molle... levibus, cor est violabile (*so Lov. Met.* v. 2. 11)
38 comming] coughing *Dil.*   43 key colde Q^1: cold *rest*

Can. Here I do plight my faith, taking thee for the staffe of my age, and of my youth my solace.

Livia. And I vow to thee affection which nothing can dissolue, neither the length of time, nor mallice of fortune, nor distance of place.

Can. But when shall we be married?

Livia. A good question, for that one delay in wedding, brings an hundred dangers in the Church: we will not be askt, and a licence is too chargeable, and to tarrie til to morrow too tedious.

Dro. There's a girle stands on pricks till she be married.

Can. To auoid danger, charge, and tediousnesse, let vs now conclude it in the next Church.

Livia. Agreed

Pris. What be these that hasten so to marrie?

Dro. Marrie sir, *Accius*, sonne to *Memphio*, and *Silena*, *Stellios* daughter.

Spe. I am sorrie, neighbour, for our purposes are disappointed.

Pris. You see marriage is destinie; made in heauen, though consumated on earth.

Ris. How like you them? be they not a pretie couple?

Pris. Yes: God giue them ioye, seeing in spite of our hearts they must ioyne.

Dro. I am sure you are not angrie, seeing things past cannot be recald; and being witnesses to their contract, will be also welwillers to the match.

Spe. For my part I wish them well.

Pris. And I: and since there is no remedie, I am glad of it.

Ris. But will you neuer heereafter take it in dugeon, but vse them as well as though your selues had made the marriage?

Pris. Not I.

Spe. Nor I.

Dro. Sir, heres two old men are glad that your loues, so long continued, is so happily concluded.

Can. Wee thanke them; and if they will come to *Memphios* house, they shall take parte of a bad dinner.—⟨*Aside.*⟩ This cottons, and workes like waxe in a sowes eare.

Exeunt CANDIUS, LIUIA.

53 bringeth *Q*² *Bl. mods. at* Church   55 too¹] to *Q*¹.   73 that *before* I am *old eds.*   78 heres] heere *Q*² *Bl.* : here *Dil.*   love *F.*   79 is] are *Dil.*   81 bad *Q*¹ : hard *rest*
54 dangers: in *Dil. deleting the comma of old eds.*

Pris. Well, seeing our purposes are preuented, wee must lay other plots, for *Liuia* shall not haue *Candius*.

Spe. Feare not, for I haue sworne that *Candius* shall not haue *Liuia*. But let not vs fall out because our children fall in.

Pris. Wilt thou goe soone to *Memphios* house?

Spe. I, and if you will, let vs; that we may see how the young couple bride it, and so we may teach our owne. *Exeunt.*

Sce. 2.

Accius, Silena, Linceo, Halfepenie.

⟨*Enter* Lucio *and* Halfpenny.⟩

Lucio. By this time I am sure the wagges haue playde their parts; there rests nothing now for vs but to match *Accius* and *Silena*.

Half. It was too good to be true, for we should laugh heartily, and without laughing my spleene would split; but whist! here comes the man,

Enter Accius ⟨*in* Candius' *clothes*⟩.

and yonder the maide: let vs stand aside.

Enter Silena ⟨*in* Livia's *clothes*⟩.

Accius. What meanes my father to thrust mee forth in an other boies coate? Ile warrant tis to as much purpose as a hem in the forehead.

Half. There was an auncient prouerbe knockt in the head.

Accius. I am almost come into my nonage, and yet I neuer was so farre as the prouerbes of this citie.

Lucio. Theres a quip for the suburbes of Rochester.

Half. Excellently applyed.

Sil. Well, though this furniture make mee a sullen dame, yet I hope in mine owne I am no saint.

Half. A braue fight is lyke to bee betweene a cocke with a long combe, and a hen with a long leg.

Lucio. Nay, her wits are shorter than her legs.

Half. And his combe longer than his wit.

Accius. I haue yonder vncouered a faire girle: Ile be so bolde as spurre her, what might a bodie call her name?

84 other Q^1 *only* anothers boyes Q^1 88 will let *all eds.*   12 mine Q^1 4 was] would be *Dil.*   8-9

Sil. I cannot help you at this time, I praie you come againe to morrow.

Half. I, marie sir!

Accius. You neede not bee so lustye, you are not so honest.

Sil. I crie you mercy, I tooke you for a ioynd stoole.

Lucio. Heeres courting for a conduit or a bakehouse.

Sil. But what are you for a man? me thinks you loke as pleaseth God.

Accius. What doo you giue me the boots?

Half. Whether will they? here be right coblers cuts!

Accius. I am taken with a fit of loue: haue you anye minde of marriage?

Sil. I had thought to haue askt you.

Accius. Vpon what acquaintance?

Sil. Who would haue thought it?

Accius. Much in my gascoins, more in my round hose; all my fathers are as white as daisies, as an egge full of meate.

Sil. And all my fathers plate is made of Crimosin veluet.

Accius. Thats braue with bread!

Half. These two had wise men to theyr Fathers.

Lucio. Why?

Half. Because when their bodies were at worke about houshold stuffe, their mindes were busied about commonwealth matters.

Accius. This is pure lawne: what call you this, a pretie face to your haire?

Sil. Wisely! you haue pickt a raison out of a fraile of figges.

Accius. Take it as you list, you are in your owne clothes.

Sil. Sauing a reuerence, thats a lie! my clothes are better, my father borrowed these.

Accius. Long may hee so doe. I could tell that these are not mine, if I would blab it lyke a woman.

Sil. I had as liefe you should tell them it snowd.

Lucio. Come let vs take them off, for we haue had the creame of them.

Half. Ile warrant if this bee the creame, the milke is verie flat: let vs ioyne issue with them.

---

33 Whether *i.e.* Whither *as Dil.*   39 hose] house *Bl. Dil.*   41 crimson Q^2 *rest*   42 Thats] That Q^1 43 two *Dil. F.*: three *old eds.*   49 haire] heir *Dil.*   50 Wisely you *all eds.*   56 liefe] leaue *Bl. mods.*

Lucio. To haue such issues of our bodies, is worse than haue an issue in the bodie. ⟨*To* SILENA.⟩ God saue you, prety mouse.

Sil. You may command and go without.

Half. Theres a glieke for you, let me haue my girde.—⟨*To* SIL.⟩ On thy conscience tell me what tis a clocke?

Sil. I cry you mercie, I haue kild your cushion.

Half. I am paid and stroke dead in the neast.—I am sure this soft youth who is not halfe so wise as you are faire, nor you altogether so faire as he is foolish, will not be so captious.

Accius. Your eloquence passes my recognoscence.

Enter MEMPHIO, STELLIO ⟨*severally, behind*⟩.

Lucio. I neuer heard that before, but shal we two make a match betweene you?

Sil. Ile know first who was his father.

Accius. My father? what need you to care? I hope he was none of yours!

Half. A hard question, for it is oddes but one begate them both; hee that cut out the vpper leather, cut out the inner, & so with one awl stitcht two soles together.

Stel. ⟨*aside to* LUC.⟩. What is she?

Luc. Tis *Prisius* daughter.

Stel. In good time: it fodges.

Memp. ⟨*aside to* HALF.⟩. What is he?

Half. Sperantus sonne.

Memp. So: twill cotton.

Accius. Damsell, I pray you how olde are you?

Memp. ⟨*aside, alarmed*⟩. My sonne would scarce haue askt such a foolish question.

Sil. I shall be eighteene next beare-baiting.

Stel. ⟨*aside, alarmed*⟩. My daughter woulde haue made a wiser aunswere.

Half. ⟨*to* LUC.⟩. O how fitly this comes off!

Accius. My father is a scolde, whats yours?

Memp. My heart throbs,—I⟨'ll⟩ looke him in the face: and yonder I espie *Stellio*.

61 issues] issue Q^2 *rest*   64 a glieke] glicke Q^2 *rest, which Dil. explains as* '*to gibe*'   65 tis] it is Q^2 *rest*   70 passe QQ 77 that] hath *F.*   79–84 Stel. [aside to Luc.] *this and the five following prefixes are misplaced in all eds.* Memp. Half. Memp. Stel. Luc. Stel. *See note*   81 fadges *Bl. mods.*   91 off] of Q^1 93 I'll] I *of all eds. is prob. mistake for* Ile *due to* l *in* looke

95   *Stel.* My minde misgiues mee—but whist, yonder is *Memphio.*
     Accius ⟨*to* MEMP.⟩. In faith I perceiue an olde sawe and a rustie, no foole to the old foole. I praie you wherefore was I thrust out lyke a scar-crow in this similitude?
     Memp. My sonne! and I ashamd! *Dromio* shall die.
100 *Sil.* Father, are you sneaking behind? I pray you what must I doe next?
     Stel. My daughter! *Risio* thou hast cosned mee.
     Lucio. Now begins the game.
     Memp. How came you hether?
105 *Accius.* Marrie, by the waie from your house hether.
     Memp. How chance in this attire?
     Accius. How chance *Dromio* bid me?
     Memp. Ah, thy sonne will bee begd for a concealde foole.
     Accius. Will I? I faith, sir, no.
110 *Stel.* Wherefore came you hether, *Silena*, without leaue?
     Sil. Because I dyd, and I am heere because I am.
     Stel. Poore wench, thy wit is improued to the vttermost.
     Half. I, tis an hard matter to haue a wit of the olde rent; euerie one rackes his commons so high.
115 *Memp.* ⟨*aside*⟩. *Dromio* tolde mee that one should meete *Stellios* daughter, and courte her in person of my sonne.
     Stel. ⟨*aside*⟩. *Risio* tolde me one shoulde meete *Memphios* sonne, and pleade in place of my daughter.
     Memp. ⟨*aside*⟩. But alas, I see that my sonne hath met wyth
120 *Silena* himselfe, and bewraid his folly.
     Stel. ⟨*aside*⟩. But I see my daughter hath pratled with *Accius*, and discouered her simplicitie.
     Lucio. A braue crie to heare the two olde mules weep ouer the young fooles.
125 *Memp. Accius*, how lykest thou *Silena*?
     Accius. I take her to be pregnant.
     Sil. Truly his talke is very personable.
     Stel. Come in, girle: this geare must be fetcht about.
     Memp. Come, *Accius*, let vs go in.
130 *Lucio* ⟨*to* STELLIO⟩. Nay, sir, there is no harme done; they haue

---

104 hither *Q² rest*   107 How chance? Dromio bid me. *Dil.*   111 am² *Q¹*: came *rest*   117 Stel. Risio . . . sonne *Q¹ only. The rest print* and pleade . . . daughter *as continuation of Memphio's preceding speech, old eds. placing fresh prefix* Memp. *before* But alas   123 to *before* weepe *Q² Bl. mods.*   126 pregnant *Q¹*: repugnant *rest*

neither bought nor solde: they may be twinnes for theyr wits and yeeres.

Memp. ⟨*to* HALFPENNY⟩. But why diddest thou tell mee it was *Sperantus* sonne?

Half. Because I thought thee a foole, to aske who thine owne sonne was.

Lucio ⟨*to* STELLIO⟩. And so, sir, for your daughter, education hath done much, otherwise they are by nature softe wytted inough.

Memp. Alas, theyr ioyntes are not yet tied, they are not yet come to yeeres and discretion.

Accius. Father, if my handes bee tyed, shall I growe wise?

Half. I, and *Silena* too, if you tie them fast to your tongues.

Sil. You may take your pleasure of my tongue, for it is no mans wife.

Memp. Come in, *Accius*.

Stel. Come in, *Silena*: I wyll talke with *Memphios* sonne; but as for *Risio*—!

Memp. As for *Dromio*—!

Exeunt MEMPHIO, ACCIUS, STELLIO, SILENA.

Half. Asse for you all foure!

Enter DROMIO, RISIO.

Dro. How goes the worlde now? We haue made all sure; *Candius* and *Liuia* are maryed, their fathers consenting, yet not knowing.

Lucio. We haue flat mard all! *Accius* and *Silena* courted one another; their fathers toke them napping; both are ashamd; and you both shall be swingd.

Ris. Tush! let vs alone: we will perswade them that all fals out for the best; for if vnderhande this match had bene concluded, they both had ben coosned; and now seeing they finde both to bee fooles, they may be both better aduised. But why is *Halfepenie* so sad?

Enter Hackneyman, Sergeant.

Half. Because I am sure I shall neuer bee a pennie.

Ris. Rather praie there bee no fall of monie, for thou wilt then go for a que.

---

134 Sperantus] Prisius *all eds. See my emendation of the prefixes* ll. 79–84 140 and *so all* 142 too Q^2 *rest* : to Q^1 150 worlde, now we *all eds.*, *Dil. F. om. comma at* world 156 vnderhande, Q^1: I vnderstand *rest*, *Dil. repeating* if *bef.* this 162 que *old eds. i. e.* q. *as Dil.* : farthing *F*.

Dro. But did not the two fooles currantly court one another?

Lucio. Verie good words, fitly applyed, brought in the nicke.

165 *Serg.* ⟨*laying hand on* Dromio⟩. I arest you.

Dro. Me, sir! why then didst not bring a stoole wyth thee, that I might sit downe?

Hack. Hee arests you at my suite for a horse.

Ris. The more Asse hee! if hee had arested a mare in stead of
170 an horse, it had bin but a slight ouersight; but to arest a man that hath no lykenesse of a horse, is flatte lunasie or alecie.

Hack. Tush! I hired him a horse.

Dro. I sweare then he was well ridden.

Hack. I think in two daies he was neuer baited.

175 *Half.* Why, was it a beare thou ridst on?

Hack. I meane he neuer gaue him bait.

Lucio. Why he tooke him for no fish.

Hack. I mistake none of you when I take you for fooles!—I say thou neuer gauest my horse meate.

180 *Dro.* Yes, in foure and fortie houres I am sure he had a bottle of hay as big as his belly.

Serg. Nothing else? thou shouldest haue giuen him prouender.

Ris. Why he neuer askt for anie.

Hack. Why, doest thou thinke an horse can speake?

185 *Dro.* No, for I spurd him till my heeles akt and hee sayd neuer a word.

Hack. Well, thou shalt paie sweetly for spoiling him! it was as lustie a nag as anie in Rochester, and one that would stand vpon no ground.

190 *Dro.* Then is he as good as euer he was. Ile warrant heele do nothing but lie downe.

Hack. I lent him thee gently.

Dro. And I restored him so gently, that hee neither would cry *wyhie*, nor wag the taile.

195 *Hack.* But why didst thou boare him thorough the eares?

Lucio. It may be he was set on the pillorie, because hee had not a true pace.

Half. No, it was for tyring.

Hack. He would neuer tire: it may be he would be so wearie
200 he would go no further, or so.

170 but[1] Q^1 *only*   183 Ris.] Dro. F. *wrongly reporting* Q^1 for *om.* Q^2
Bl. Dil.   190 is he Q^1: hee is *rest*   194 wyhie] *ital. first F.*

Dro. Yes, he was a notable horse for seruice; he wold tyre, and retire.

Hack. Doe you thinke Ile be iested out of my horse? Sergeant, wreake thy office on him.

Ris. Nay, stay, let him be baild.

Hack. So he shall when I make him a bargen.

Dro. It was a verie good horse, I must needs confesse; and now hearken to his qualities, and haue patience to heare them, since I must paie for him. He would stumble three houres in one mile, I had thought I had rode vpon addeces betweene this and Canterburie; if one gaue him water, why he would lie downe & bath himselfe lyke a hauke: if one ranne him, he woulde simper and mump, as though he had gone a wooing to a maltmare at Rochester: hee trotted before and ambled behinde, and was so obedient, that he would doo dutie euerie minute on his knees, as though euerie stone had bin his father.

Hack. I am sure he had no diseases.

Dro. A little rume or pose: hee lackt nothing but an handkercher.

Serg. Come, what a tale of a horse haue we here! I can not stay, thou must with me to prison.

Ris. If thou be a good fellow, Hacknyman, take all our foure bondes for the paiment: thou knowest wee are towne borne children, and wil not shrinke the citie for a pelting iade.

Half. Ile enter into a statute Marchant to see it aunswered. But if thou wilt haue bondes, thou shalt haue a bushell full.

Hack. Alas, poore Ant! thou bound in a statute marchant? a browne threed will bind thee fast inough. But if you will be content all foure ioyntly to enter into a bond, I will withdrawe the action.

Dro. Yes, Ile warrant they will. How say you?

Half. I yeeld.

Ris. And I.

Lucio. And I.

Hack. Well, call the Scriuener.

Serg. Heeres one hard by: Ile call him.

⟨*Knocks at a door.*⟩

---

204 thine Q^2 *Bl. mods.*   205 stay, Q^1 *only*   208 to[1] Q^1: of *rest*   210 addeces *QQ* (*i.e.* adzes): addices *rest*   218 rheume *Bl. mods.*   222 Ris.] Ri. Q^1: Li. Q^2 *Bl.*: Luc. *Dil. F.*   fellow Q^1 *only*   227 poore] poort Q^1 s. d. [Knocks at a door] *supplied Dil.*

[SC. II]

Ris. A scriueners shop hangs to a Sergeants mase, like a burre to a freese coate.

Scri. ⟨*within*⟩. Whats the matter?

240 *Hack.* You must take a note of a bond.

Dro. Nay, a pint of curtesie puls on a pot of wine. In this Tauerne weele dispatch.

Hack. Agreed. *Exeunt* ⟨*all but* RISCIO⟩.

Ris. Now if our wits be not in the waine, our knauery shall bee 245 at the full. They will ride them worse than *Dromio* rid his horse, for if the wine master their wits, you shall see them bleed their follyes. *Exit.*

ACT. 5.

SCE. 1.

⟨*Enter*⟩ DRO, RISIO, LUCIO, HALFPENIE.

Dromio. Euerie foxe to his hole, the houndes are at hande.

Ris. The Sergeants mase lyes at pawne for the reckning, and he vnder the boord to cast it vp.

Lucio. The Scriuener cannot keepe his pen out of the pot: euery 5 goblet is an inkhorne.

Half. The hackneyman hee whiskes with his wande, as if the Tauerne were his stable, and all the seruantes his horses: 'Iost there vp, bay Richard!'—and white loaues are horsebread in his eyes.

Dro. It is well I haue my acquitance, and hee such a bond as 10 shall doo him nc more good than the bond of a faggot. Our knaueries are now come to the push, and wee must cunningly dispatch all. Wee two will goe see howe wee may appease our masters, you two howe you may conceale the late marriage: if all fall out amisse, the worst is beating; if to the best, the worst 15 is lybertie.

Ris. Then lettes about it speedely, for so many yrons in the fire together require a diligent Plummer. *Exeunt.*

237 a *om.* Q^1 s. D. [all but Riscio] *added Dil.*   245 They] we *Dil.*
SCE. 1] Sce 8. Q^2 s. D. LUCIO] Linceo *old eds.*   7–8 *inv. commas first in Dil.*   9 acquitance] acquaintance Q^2 *Bl. F.*   such a bond Q^1: such bonds *rest*   13 the Q^1: your *rest*   16 fire *om.* Q^1

Sce. 2.

Vicinia. Bombie.

⟨*Enter* Vicinia.⟩

Vic. My heart throbbes, my eares tingle, my minde misgiues mee, since I heare such muttering of marryages in Rochester. My conscience, which these eighteene yeeres hath beene frosen with coniealed guiltynesse, beginnes nowe to thawe in open griefe. But I wil not accuse my selfe till I see more danger : the good olde woman *Mother Bombie* shall trie her cunning vpon me ; and if I perceiue my case is desperate by her, then wyll I rather preuent, although with shame, then report too late, and be inexcusable. ⟨*Knocks. Enter* Mother Bombie.⟩ God speed, good mother.

Bom. Welcome, sister.

Vic. I am troubled in the night with dreames, and in the daie with feares ; mine estate bare, which I cannot well beare ; but my practises deuillish, which I cannot recall. If therefore in these same yeeres there be anie deepe skill, tell what my fortune shall be, and what my fault is.

Bom. In studying to be ouernaturall,
    Thou art like to be vnnaturall,
    And all about a naturall :
    Thou shalt bee eased of a charge,
    If thou thy conscience discharge,
    And this I commit to thy charge.

Vic. Thou hast toucht mee to the quicke, mother ; I vnderstand thy meaning, and thou well knowest my practise. I will follow thy counsell. But what wyll bee the end?

Bom. Thou shalt know before this daie end : farewel.

Exit Bom.

Vic. Nowe I perceiue I must either bewraie a mischiefe, or suffer a continual inconuenience. I must hast homewardes, and resolue to make all whole : better a little shame, than an infinite griefe. The strangenes will abate the faulte, and the bewraying wipe it cleane away. *Exit.*

---

s. d. Vicinia *Q*¹, *here and below, ll.* 269, 272, 342 : Vicina *Q*² *rest*   2 such *Q*¹ : some *rest*   3 haue *Q*² *Bl. F.* : has *Dil.*   4 coniealed *QQ* : congealed *Bl. F.* : concealed *Dil.*   this *bef.* conicaled *Q*² *rest*   8 report *so all*   14 me *after* tell *Bl. mods.*   18 a *Q*¹ *only*

Sce. 3.

⟨*Enter*⟩ *Three* Fidlers, Synis, Nasutus, Bedunenus.

Syn. Come, fellowes, tis almost daie; let vs haue a fit of mirth at *Sperantus* doore, and giue a song to the bride.

Nas. I beleeue they are asleepe: it were pittie to awake them.

Bed. Twere a shame they shoulde sleepe the first night.

5 *Syn.* But who can tell at which house they lie? at *Prisius* it may be! weele trie both.

Nas. Come lets drawe lyke men.

Syn. Now, tune, tune, I saie! that boy, I thinke will neuer profit in his facultie! he looses his rosen, that his fiddle goes cush, cush, 10 like as one should go wet-shod; and his mouth so drie that he hath not spittle for his pinne as I haue.

Bed. Mary, sir, you see I go wetshod and dry mouthd, for yet could I neuer get newe shooes or good drinke; rather than Ile leade this life, I throw my fiddle into the leads for a hobler.

15 *Syn.* Boy, no more words! theres a time for al things. Though I say it that should not, I haue bene a minstrell these thirtie yeeres, and tickled more strings than thou hast haires, but yet was neuer so misused.

Nas. Let vs not brabble but play: to morrow is a new daie.

20 *Bed.* I am sorrie I speake in your cast. What shall wee sing?

Syn. The Loue-knot, for thats best for a bridall.

Sing.

Good morow, fayre bride, and send you ioy of your bridall.

Sperantus *lookes out.*

Spe. What a mischiefe make the twanglers here? we haue no trenchers to scrape: it makes my teeth on edge to heare such grating. 25 Get you packing! or Ile make you weare double stockes, and yet you shall bee neuer the warmer.

Syn. We come for good will, to bidd the bride and bridegroome, God giue them ioy.

Spe. Heres no wedding.

---

s. d. Bedunenus] Bedvnens Q^1 9 roson Q^2: Rozen *Bl.*: rosin *Dil.*: razon *F.*   14 I Q^1: Ile Q^2 *Bl. F.*: I'll *Dil.*   15 theres a Q^1: there is rest   s. d. Sing.] *roms. all ees.*: *at end of line* Q^1. *Prob. stage-direction as F. first suggests*   22 Good] God QQ. *Dil. assigns* Good ... bridall *to Nas.*   23 makes *Dil.*   twangers Q^2 *Bl. mods.*   29 Heres] Hers Q^1

Syn. Yes, your sonne and *Prisius* daughter were maryed : though you seeme strange, yet they repent it not, I am sure.

Spe. My sonne, villaine ! I had rather hee were fairely hanged.

Nas. So he is, sir ; you haue your wish.

Enter CANDIUS.

Can. Here, fidlers, take this, and not a worde : heere is no wedding, it was at *Memphios* house ; yet, gramercy ! your musicke, though it mist the house, hit the minde ; we were a preparing our wedding geare.

Syn. I crie you mercie, sir, I thinke it was *Memphios* sonne that was married. ⟨*Exit* CANDIUS.⟩

Spe. O ho, the case is altered ! goe thether then, and be haltered for me.

Nas. Whats the almes ?

Syn. An Angell.

Bed. Ile warrant thers some worke towards : ten shillings is money in master Maiors purse.

Syn. Let vs to *Memphios* and share equally ; when we haue done all, thou shalt haue new shooes.

Bed. I, such as they cry at the Sizes, a marke in issues, and marke in issues, and yet I neuer sawe so much leather as would peece ones shooes.

Syn. No more ! thers the mony.

Bed. A good handsell, and I thinke the maidenhead of your liberalitie.

Nas. Come, heres the house : what shall we sing ?

Syn. You know *Memphio* is verie rich and wise, and therefore let vs strike the gentle stroke, and sing a catch. *Sing.*

SONG.

All 3. THe Bride this Night can catch no cold ;
No cold, the Bridegroome's yong, not old,
Like Iuie he her fast does hold,

1 *Fid.*   And clips her,
2 „   And lips her.
3 „   And flips her too.
All 3. Then let them alone, they know what they doe.

S. D. [Exit CANDIUS] *om. all eds. though they record his re-entry below*   40
Spe. *om.* Q^2 48 and *om. Bl. Dil.*   50 ones Q^1 : my *rest*   S. D. Sing.]
as stage-direction Q^1 : *as text, rest. Bl. alone of old eds. gives the words*

	1 *Fid.*	At laugh and lie downe, if they play,
65	2 ,,	What Asse against the sport can bray?
	3 ,,	Such Tick-tacke has held many a day,
	1 ,,	And longer.
	2 ,,	And stronger.
	3 ,,	It still holds too.
70	*All* 3.	Then let them alone, they know what they doe.

<pre>
                    This Night,
                    In delight
                Does thump away sorrow.
                    Of billing
                    Take your filling,
                So good morrow, good morrow.
</pre>

Nas. Good morrowe, mistres bride, and sende you a huddle.

Memp. ⟨*above*⟩. What crouding knaues haue we there? case vp your fiddles, or the cunstable shall cage you vppe! What bride talke you of?

Syn. Heres a wedding in Rochester, and twas tolde me first that *Sperantus* son had married *Prisius* daughter. We were there, and they sent vs to your worshippe, saying your son was matched with *Stellios* daughter.

Memp. Hath *Sperantus* that churle nothing to doe but mocke his neighbours? Ile bee euen with him! And get you gone, or I sweare by the roodes bodie Ile laye you by the heeles.

Nas. Sing a catch? heres a faire catch in deed! sing til we catch colde on our feet, and bee cald knaue tyll our eares glowe on our heades! Your worshippe is wise, sir.

Memp. Dromio, shake off a whole kennel of officers, to punish these iarring rogues. Ile teach them to stretch theyr dried sheepes guts at my doore, and to mock one that stands to be maior.

Dro. ⟨*above*⟩. I had thought they had beene sticking of pigs, I heard such a squeaking. I go, sir.

Syn. Let vs be packing.

Nas. Where is my scabberde? euerye one sheath his science.

Bed. A bots on the shoomaker that made this boote for my fiddle: tis too straight.

Syn. No more wordes! twill bee thought they were the foure waites, and let them wring; as for the wagges that set vs on worke, wele talke with them. *Exeunt.*

77 Good] God *QQ* with *before* his *Q*² *Bl. mods.* 78 [above] *Dil. suppl.* Memphio looks out 85 92 rogues *Q*¹: tongues *rest*

⟨*Enter*⟩ MEMPHIO, DROMIO.

Dro. They be gone, sir.

Memp. If they had stayed, the stockes shoulde haue staied them. But, sirra, what shall we now doo?

Dro. As I aduised you, make a match; for better one house be cumbred with two fooles than two.

Memp. Tis true: for it beeing bruted that eache of vs haue a foole, who will tender marriage to anie of them, that is wise? besides, fooles are fortunate, fooles are faire, fooles are honest.

Dro. I, sir, and more than that, fooles are not wise: a wise man is melancholy for moone-shine in the water; carefull, building castles in the ayre; & commonly hath a foole to his heyre.

Memp. But what sayest thou to thy dames chafing?

Dro. Nothing, but all her dishes are chafing dishes.

Memp. I would her tongue were in thy belly.

Dro. I had as liefe haue a rawe neates tongue in my stomacke.

Memp. Why?

Dro. Marie, if the clapper hang within an inch of my heart, that makes mine eares burne a quarter of a mile off, do you not thinke it would beate my heart blacke and blew?

Memp. Well, patience is a vertue, but pinching is worse than any vice! I wil breake this matter to *Stellio*, and if he be willing, this day shall be their wedding.

Dro. Then this day shall be my libertie.

Memp. I, if *Stellios* daughter had beene wise, and by thy meanes cosned of a foole.

Dro. Then, sir, Ile reuolt, and dash out the braines of your deuises.

Memp. Rather thou shalt be free. *Exeunt.*

⟨*Enter*⟩ SPERANTUS, HALFEPENIE, PRISIUS, LUCIO.

Spe. Boy, this smoake is a token of some fire, I lyke not the lucke of it. Wherefore should these minstrelles dreame of a marryage?

Half. Alas, sir, they rustle into euery place. Giue credit to no such wordes.

Spe. I will to *Prisius:* I cannot be quiet—and in good time I meet him. Good morow, neighbor.

---

106 aduise Q^2 *Bl. mods.*　　109 wise?] wise, *old eds.* : wise; *Dil. F.*　　120 off, do *Dil.*: off. Do *old eds. F.*　　S. D. LUCIO] Linceo Q^1: Lincio Q^2 *Bl.*　　131 a Q^1 *only*　　lucke] look *Dil.*　　136 Good *mod. eds.*: God *QQ Bl.*

Pris. I cast the morrow in thy face, & bid good night to all neighborhood.

Spe. This is your olde tricke, to pick ones purse & then to picke quarrels: I tell thee, I had rather thou shouldest rob my chest, than imbesell my sonne.

Pris. Thy sonne? my daughter is seduced! for I hear say she is married, and our boyes can tell.—⟨*To* LUCIO.⟩ How sayest thou? tell the truth or Ile grinde thee to pouder in my mill. Be they married?

Lucio. True it is they were both in a church.

Pris. Thats no fault, the place is holy.

Half. And there was with them a priest.

Spe. Why what place fitter for a priest than a church?

Lucio. And they tooke one another by the hand.

Pris. Tush! thats but common curtesie.

Half. And the priest spake many kinde wordes.

Spe. That shewed hee was no dumbe minister. But what sayde they? diddest thou heare anie wordes betweene them?

Lucio. Faith there was a bargaine during life, and the clocke cryed, God giue them ioy.

Pris. Villaine! they be married!

Half. Nay, I thinke not so.

Spe. Yes, yes! God giue you ioy is a binder! Ile quickly be resolud. *Candius,* come forth.

⟨*Re-*⟩*Enter* CANDIUS.

Pris. And Ile be put out of doubt. *Liuia,* come forth.

⟨*Enter*⟩ LIUIA.

Spe. The micher hangs downe his head!

Pris. The baggage begins to blush!

Half. Now begins the game!

Lucio. I beleeue it will be no game for vs.

Spe. Are you married, yong master?

Can. I cannot denie it, it was done so lately.

Spe. But thou shalt repent it was done so soone.

Pris. Then tis bootlesse to aske you, *Liuia.*

Livia. I, and needlesse to be angrie.

137 face] fate Q^1 141 imbeasell *Bl. F.*: embezzle *Dil.*   144 powdeded Q^2 155 clocke] clerk *Dil. without authority, but perhaps rightly*

Pris. It shall passe anger; thou shalt finde it rage.

Livia. You gaue your consent.

Pris. Impudent giglot, was it not inough to abuse me, but also to belie me?

Can. You, sir, agreed to this match. 175

Spe. Thou brasen face boy, thinkest thou by learning to persuade me to that which thou speakest? Where did I consent, when, what witnes?

Can. In this place yesterday before *Dromio* and *Risio*.

Pris. I remember we heard a contract between *Memphios* sonne 180 and *Stellios* daughter; and that our good wils being asked, which needed not, wee gaue them, which booted not.

Can. Twas but the apparell of *Accius* and *Silena*; we were the persons.

Pris. O villany not to be borne! ⟨*To* Lucio.⟩ Wast thou priuie 185 to this practise?

Lucio. In a manner.

Pris. Ile pay thee after a manner.

Spe. And you, oatemeale groate! you were acquainted with this plot. 190

Half. Accessarie, as it were.

Spe. Thou shalt be punished as principal: here comes *Memphio* and *Stellio*; they belike were priuie, and all theyr heads were layde together to grieue our heartes.

Enter Memphio, Stellio, ⟨Dromio, Riscio⟩.

Memp. Come, *Stellio*, the assurance may be made to morrow, and 195 our children assured to day.

Stel. Let the conueyance runne as we agreed.

Pris. You conuey cleanely in deede, if coosnage bee cleane dealing, for in the apparell of your children you haue conuaide a match betweene ours, which grieues vs not a little. 200

Memp. Nay, in the apparel of your children, you haue discouerd the folly of ours, which shames vs ouermuch.

Stel. But tis no matter; though they bee fooles they are no beggers.

Spe. And thogh ours be disobedient, they be no fools. 205

Dro. So now they tune theyr pipes.

188 pay] pray Q^2 *Bl.* S. D. [Dromio, Riscio] *supplied Dil.* 202 shames] shame *F.*

Ris. You shal heare sweet musicke betweene a hoarse rauen and a schritch owle.

Memp. Neighbours, let vs not vary : our boyes haue playd theyr
210 cheating partes. I suspected no lesse at the Tauerne, where our foure knaues met together.

Ris. If it were knauery for foure to meet in a Tauerne, your worships wot well there were other foure.

Stel. This villaine cals vs knaues by craft.

215 *Lucio.* Nay, truly, I dare sweare hee vsed no crafte, but meanes plainly.

Spe. This is worse! come, *Halfepenie*, tel truth & scape the rod.

Half. As good confesse heere beeing trust, as at home with my
220 hose about my heeles.

Dro. Nay, Ile tell thee, for twill neuer become thee to vtter it.

Memp. Well, out with it.

Dro. Memphio had a foole to his sonne, which *Stellio* knew not ; *Stellio* a foole to his daughter, vnknowen to *Memphio ;* to coosen
225 eache other, they dealte with theyr boyes for a match ; we met with *Lucio* and *Halfepenie* who told the loue betweene their masters children, the youth deeply in loue, the fathers vnwilling to consent.

Ris. Ile take the tale by the end,—then wee foure met, which
230 argued we were no mountaines ; and in a tauern we met, which argued we were mortall ; and euery one in his wine told his dayes worke, which was a signe we forgot not our busines ; and seeing all our masters troubled with deuises, we determined a little to trouble the water before they dronke ; so that in the attire of your children
235 our masters wise children bewrayed theyr good natures ; and in the garments of our masters children yours made a marriage ; this all stoode vppon vs poore children, and your yong children, to shewe that olde folkes may be ouertaken by children.

Pris. Heres a children indeed ! Ile neuer forget it.

240 *Memp.* I will ! *Accius,* come forth.

Stel. I forgiue all ! *Silena,* come forth.

210 cheating] chearing Q^2 *Bl. Dil.*   210–1 our foure] foure foure QQ 213 worships *Dil. F.* : wor. *old eds.*   217 Halfepenie *Bl. mods.* : Half. QQ 219 honfesse Q^1 trust *all eds. for* trussed   226 Lucio] Lincio *old eds.*   227 unwilling *Dil.* : vnwitting *old eds. F.*   239 a QQ *only*

⟨*Enter* ACCIUS *and* SILENA.⟩

Spe. Neighbor, these things cannot be recald, therefore as good consent; seeing in all our purposes also we mist the marke, for they two will match their children.

Pris. Well of that more anone: not so sodainely, least our vngratious youths thinke we dare do no other; but in truth their loue stirres vp nature in me.

Memp. Come, *Accius*, thou must be marryed to *Silena*. How art thou minded?

Accius. What for euer and euer?

Memp. I, *Accius*, what els?

Accius. I shall neuer be able to abide it, it will be so tedious.

Stel. Silena, thou must be betrothed to *Accius*, & loue him for thy husband.

Sil. I had as liefe haue one of clouts.

Stel. Why, *Silena*?

Sil. Why looke how he lookes.

Accius. If you will not, another will.

Sil. I thanke you for mine olde cap.

Accius. And if you be so lustie, lend me two shillings.

Pris. ⟨*to* SPE.⟩. We are happie we mist the foolish match.

Memp. Come, you shall presently be contracted.

Dro. Contract their wits no more, they bee shronke close already.

Accius. Well, father, heeres my hande; strike the bargaine.

Sil. Must he lie with me?

Stel. No, *Silena*, lie by thee.

Accius. I shall giue her the humble-bees kisse.

Enter VICINIA, ⟨MÆSTIUS, *and* SERENA⟩.

Vic. I forbid the banes.

Ris. What, doest thou thinke them rattes, and fearest they shall be poisoned?

Memp. You, *Vicinia*? wherefore?

Vic. Hearken!—about eighteene yeeres agoe, I nurst thee a sonne, *Memphio*, and thee a daughter, *Stellio*.

Stel. True.

Memp. True.

S. D. VICINIA *QQ*: Vicina *Bl. mods.*   S. D. [MÆSTIUS and SERENA] *supplied Dil.*   272 Vicina *Q² Bl. mods.*

Vic. I had at that time two children of mine owne; and being poore, thought it better to change them than kill them. I imagined if by deuice I coulde thrust my children into your houses, they should be wel brought vp in their youth, and wisely prouided for in their age: nature wrought with me, and when they were weaned, I sent home mine in sted of yours, which hetherto you haue kept tenderly as yours: growing in yeres I founde the children I kept at home to loue dearely, at first lyke brother and sister, which I reioyced at, but at length too forward in affection; which although inwardly I could not mislike, yet openly I seemed to disallowe. They increased in their louing humours; I ceased not to chastise them for theyr loose demeanors. At last it came to my eares, that my sonne that was out with *Memphio* was a foole; that my daughter with *Stellio* was also vnwise; and yet beeing brother and sister, there was a match in hammering betwixt them.

Memp. What monstrous tale is this?

Stel. And I am sure incredible.

Spe. Let her end her discourse.

Accius. Ile neuer beleeue it!

Memp. Holde thy peace!

Vic. My verie bowels earned within me, that I shuld be author of such vilde incest, an hinderance to lawfull loue. I went to the good olde woman, *Mother Bombie*, to knowe the euent of this practise; who tolde mee this day I might preuent the danger, and vpon submission escape the punishment. Hether I am come to claime my children, though both fooles, and to deliuer yours, both louing.

Memp. Is this possible? how shall we beleeue it?

Stel. It cannot sinke into my head.

Vic. This triall cannot faile. Your sonne *Memphio*, had a moale vnder his eare: I framed one vnder my childes eare by arte; you shall see it taken away with the iuyce of mandrage; beholde nowe for your sonnes, no hearbe can vndo that nature hath done. Your daughter, *Stellio*, hath on her wrist a moale, which I counterfeted on my daughters arme, & that shall you see taken away as the other. Thus you see I doe not dissemble, hoping you will pardon me, as I haue pittied them.

279 should Q^1: would *rest mods.* 288 demeanor *F.* 297 earned] yearned *mods.* 298 vilde *QQ*: vile *Bl. mods.* an] and *Dil. perhaps rightly* 299 good olde] gold *Bl.*: good *Dil.* 302-3 your both louing Q^1: yours both liuing Q^2 *rest, Dil. inserting comma at* yours

Memp. This is my sonne. O fortunate *Memphio!*
Stel. This is my daughter, more than thrice happie *Stellio!* 315
Mæst. How happie is *Mæstius*, how blessed *Serena*, that being neither children to poore parents, nor brother and sister by nature, may inioye their loue by consent of parents and nature.
Accius. Soft, Ile not swap my father for all this.
Sil. What, do you thinke Ile bee cosned of my father? me thinkes 320 I should not! *Mother Bombie* tolde me 'my father knew mee not, my mother bore mee not, falsely bred, truly begot,'—a bots on *Mother Bomby!*
Dro. *Mother Bombie* tolde vs we should be founde coosners, and in the end be cosned by cosners: wel fare *Mother Bomby!* 325
Ris. I heard *Mother Bomby* saie that thou shalt die a beggar: beware of *Mother Bomby!*
Pris. Why haue you all bene with *Mother Bomby*?
Lucio. All, and as farre as I can see ⟨she⟩ foretolde all.
Memp. In deed she is cunning and wise, neuer doing harme, but 330 still practising good. Seeing these things fall out thus, are you content, *Stellio*, the match goe forward?
Stel. I, with double ioye, hauing found for a foole a wise maide, and finding betweene them both exceeding loue.
Pris. Then to end all iars, our childrens matches shall stand 335 with our good liking. *Liuia*, inioy *Candius*.
Spe. *Candius*, inioy *Liuia*.
Can. How shall we recompence fortune, that to our loues hath added our parents good wills?
Mæst. How shall wee requite fortune, that to our loues hath 340 added lawfulnesse, and to our poore estate competent liuing?
Memp. *Vicinia*, thy fact is pardoned; though the law would see it punisht. Wee be content to keepe *Silena* in the house with the new married couple.
Stel. And I doo maintaine *Accius* in our house. 345
Vic. Come, my children, though fortune hath not prouided you landes, yet you see you are not destitute of friends. I shall be eased of a charge both in purse and conscience: in conscience, having reuealed my lewd practise; in purse, hauing you kept of almes.
Accius. Come, if you bee my sister, its the better for you. 350

316 how] thou *all eds.*, *Dil. placing comma at* blessed 321-2 *inv. com. first F.*
325 wel fare *F.*: welfare *old. eds.*: farewell *Dil.* Bomby] Bom. *Bl. Dil.*
329 [she] *inserted Dil.* 342 Vicina Q^2 *Bl. mods.* 348 having *mods.*:
haue *old eds.* 350 its Q^1: tis Q^2 *rest*

Sil. Come, brother, me thinkes its better than it was: I should haue beene but a balde bride. Ile eate as much pie as if I had bene marryed.

Memp. Lets also forgiue the knauerie of our boyes, since all turnes to our good haps.

Stel. Agreed: all are pleased nowe the boyes are vnpunisht.

Enter Hackneyman, Sergeant, Scriuener.

Hack. Nay, softe, take vs with you, and seeke redresse for our wrongs, or weele complaine to the Maior.

Pris. Whats the matter?

Hack. I arested *Memphios* boye for an horse. After much mocking, at the request of his fellowe wagges, I was content to take a bonde ioyntlye of them all: they had me into a tauerne; there they made me, the Scriuener, and the Sergeant, dronke, paunde his mase for the wine, and seald mee an obligation nothing to the purpose: I pray you, reade it.

Memp. What wags be these! Why by this bond you can demand nothing; and thinges done in drinke may be repented in sobernes, but not remedyed.

Dro. Sir, I haue his acquittaunce: lette him sue his bonde.

Hack. Ile crie quittance with thee.

Serg. And I, or it shall cost me the laying on freelie of my mase.

Scri. And Ile giue thee such a dash with a pen as shall cost thee many a pound, with such a *Nouerint* as Cheapside can shew none such.

Half. Doe your worst; our knaueries will reuenge it vpon your childrens children.

Memp. Thou boy! ⟨*To* Hackneyman.⟩ We wil paie the hire of the horse: be not angrie; the boyes haue bene in a merrie cosning vaine, for they haue serued their masters of the same sorte; but all must be forgotten. Now all are content but the poore fidlers: they shal be sent for to the marriage, & haue double fees.

Dro. You need no more send for a fidler to a feast, than a begger to a fayre.

Stel. This daie we will feast at my house.

Memp. To morrow at mine.

351 its *QQ*: 'tis *Bl. F.*: it is *Dil.*   360 horse after *old eds. F.*: horse; after *Dil.*   363 pawnde *Q² Bl. F.*: pawned *Dil.*   369 acquaittance *Bl.*   370 I'ld *F.*   373 cheap side *old eds.*   375 renenge *Q¹*   377 Thou boy!] Then, boy, *Dil.*   378 cosning *Q¹*: cousning *Q²*: cousening *Bl. F.*: cozening *Dil.*

Pris. The next day at mine.

Spe. Then at mine the last day, & euen so spend this weeke in good cheere.

Dro. Then we were best be going whilest euery one is pleasd: and yet these couples are not fully pleasde, till the priest haue done his worst.

Ris. Come, Sergeant, weele tosse it this weeke, and make thy mase arest a boild capon.

Serg. No more words at the wedding: if the maior shuld know it, I were in danger of mine office.

Ris. Then take heed how on such as we are, you shew a cast of your office.

Half. If you mace vs, weele pepper you.

Accius. Come, sister, the best is, we shall haue good chere these foure dayes.

Lucio. And be fooles for euer.

Sil. Thats none of our vpseekings.

⟨*Exeunt.*⟩

FINIS.

387 day Q^1 *only*

THE WOMAN IN THE MOONE

EDITIONS

'xxij die Septembris . 1595. Robert Fynche. Entred for his Copie vnder th andes of bothe the wardens a booke intituled a woman in the moone ... vj^d.' *Sta. Reg.* iii. 48 (ed. Arb.). This is the only entry in the whole Register concerning Robert Finch, all note of transference of rights in *The Woman* to William Jones, the actual publisher, being wanting.

Q. *The Woman | in the Moone. | As it was presented before | her Highnesse. | By Iohn Lyllie maister | of Artes. | Imprinted at London for William | Iones, and are to be sold at the signe of the | Gun, neere Holburne Conduict. | 1597. |* 4to. A-G 2 in fours, G 2 verso blank. No col. (*Br. Mus.: Bodl.: Dyce Coll. S. Kensing.*)

The play is not included among the *Sixe Covrt Comedies*, its second publication being that of Fairholt's edition of the *Dramatic Works*, vol. ii. 1858.

THE WOMAN IN THE MOONE

Argument. — Nature on the petition of the shepherds of Utopia creates a woman for their comrade, and dowers her with the several excellences of the gods who preside over the Seven Planets. The latter, filled with envy, determine to work her ruin by subjecting her in turn to their influence. Under that of *Saturn* she repays with a moody discourtesy the service rendered by Gunophilus (the Clown of the piece), and the admiration of the shepherds. Under that of *Jupiter* she rejects contemptuously the love proffered by the god and the sceptre she at first requested; she exacts exaggerated demonstrations of respect from Gunophilus, and delights in exercising the shepherds in dangerous tasks. When *Mars* assumes the ascendant, he brings the shepherds to blows over the boar they have killed; but Pandora mingles in the fray, and puts them all to rout. *Sol*, succeeding, makes her sweet-tempered and poetical: she apologizes to Gunophilus and her suitors, selects Stesias as her husband, and prophesies their happiness in oracular verse. Next, *Venus*, aided by Cupid and Joculus, renders her wanton: she makes love in turn to Gunophilus and the three other shepherds, Learchus, Melos, and Iphicles, and invites them to a banquet. Gunophilus, jealous of the shepherds, posts Stesias in wait in a cave, but, failing to give the signal till the banquet with its jealousies and recriminations is over, only receives a beating for his pains. *Mercury*, assuming sovereignty, fills Pandora with the spirit of lying and theft; while the shepherds, changed also to intriguers under his influence, betray her conduct to Stesias. Warned by Gunophilus, Pandora parries Stesias' reproaches by a feigned swoon, and represents the shepherds' reports as caused by jealousy and disappointed love. She revenges herself on them by pretended assignations, at which Stesias, in his wife's clothes, meets and cudgels them; while she herself elopes with Gunophilus, carrying her husband's treasure along with her. On their way to the coast, however, *Luna* assumes sway, causing her purpose to change and her wits to wander. Stesias overtakes them; but she soon

INTRODUCTION

breaks away from him, and finally lies down to sleep. Stesias, again assured by the shepherds of her treachery, determines to kill her: from this, however, he is dissuaded by the Planets, and finally Nature assigns her a place in the Moon, with special influence over women; while Stesias, appointed to attend on her as the Man in the Moon, in his anger rends Gunophilus, who has been changed into a hawthorn, to form the bush at his back.

Text.—I follow that of the Quarto, which is far better than Fairholt's reprint of it, correcting its errors, and inserting many necessary stage-directions. It presents about twenty mistakes in the text, and seventeen important omissions of stage-directions for entry or exit, especially the latter. Yet it is distinguished from the quarto editions of the other plays by a much greater fullness and frequency of other stage-directions: the metre, too, is well preserved, requiring correction in only three instances—a circumstance due no doubt to the end-stopped character of Lyly's blank verse.

Fairholt corrects seventeen errors of Q; but introduces twenty-five corruptions, many of them more serious than those which he corrects, e. g. pp. 249, 'Calisco' for 'Calisto'; 253, 'where thy' for 'were they'; 259, 'Utopia' for 'Vtopiæ'; 260, 'fortunæ' for 'fortuna'; 268, '*Gun.*' for '*Pan.*'; 270, 'love' for 'Ioue'; 274, 'protenus' for 'protervus'; 282, 'Musk white' for 'Milke white,' 'breach' for 'breath.' Yet since in this case we are spared the intervention of Blount's carelessly-printed edition, Fairholt's text is better for this play than for most of the rest; though we have lost the two Songs in i. 1, which Blount would doubtless have given.

Authorship.—(a) 'By Iohn Lyllie maister of Artes' (title-page of Q); (b) the allusion 'Ceres and her sacred Nymphes,' iii. 1. 50, is probably to the Nymphs of Ceres in *Loves Metamorphosis*, asserted to be Lyly's on its title-page; and in iii. 2. 21–4 there is a notable reproduction of an opinion strongly emphasized by Lyly in *Euphues and his England*, vol. ii. p. 160, about women's attitude towards a man's love.

Date.—The downward limit may, in the case of a play, be considered as supplied by the entry to Robert Finch in the *Stationers' Register*, under date Sept. 22, 1595, of a 'booke intituled a woman in the moone,' which was followed in due course by its publication in 1597 'for William Iones.'

For the upward limit, the similarity noted above between Venus' speech, iii. 2. ll. 21–4, and the argument on p. 160 of *Euphues and his England* (1580) cannot safely be taken as evidence that the play was not written before 1580, since the passage in the novel might be developed from that in the play. A line in the Prologue describing the play as the author's dream,

> The first he had in Phœbus holy bowre,

has sometimes been interpreted as meaning absolutely the first play [1]; but the more natural meaning is, surely, the first attempt at a play in verse, and there is much to support the idea of a late date. To begin with, the absence in this single case of the name of the Paul's boys from the title-page suggests its production after their inhibition in 1591, an inhibition which lasted till 1599. Then the mention of Ceres' nymphs, iii. 1. 50, who play no part in the classical myth of the goddess, points to a date of composition later than that of at least the earliest form of *Loves Metamorphosis*, where such nymphs figure prominently—a play produced, probably, before the suppression of the Paul's boys; and perhaps later than Sept. 1592, the date of the entertainment at Bisham, another work of Lyly, wherein Ceres and her nymphs also appear [2]. In iii. 1. 53, 63 are two uncommon words, 'demeane' and 'depart,' used as substantives, which Lyly almost certainly borrowed from the *Faerie Queene* (1590), ii. 9. 40, 'modest of demayne,' and iii. 7. 20, 'lament for her depart.' The only earlier instances quoted by Murray of 'demeane' as a noun are of 1450 and 1534, the only earlier one of 'depart' is c. 1330 in the romance *Arthur and Merlin*—none of which seem likely to have crossed Lyly's eye. Further, my later study of the play induces me to class it as dramatically one of the best and most skilfully constructed of all Lyly's efforts. Euphuism, too, is entirely absent: the wretched puns are gone, and are replaced by a far more natural humour. It is in this last respect particularly, and only I think in this play, that we may trace in our author the reciprocal influence of Shakespeare. Fairholt has noticed as common to this work and the *Midsummer Night's Dream* the apology for the play as merely the author's dream, and the introduction of the man in the moon with his bush. These were

---

[1] To suppose it his first literary work of any kind is absolutely prohibited by the words at the beginning of the dedication of *Euph. and his Eng.*—' In the like manner fareth it with me (Right Honourable) who *neuer before handling the pensill*, did for my fyrst counterfaite, coulour mine owne Euphues,' &c.

[2] See vol. i. p. 476 l. 2. Compare, too, ' Maremaydes glasse,' iii. 2. 162, with the stage-direction for the Siren in *Loves Met.* iv. 2, p. 322.

INTRODUCTION

points which I believe Shakespeare to have borrowed from Lyly; and he may further have found in Pandora's passion for Gunophilus under malign influence (pp. 262, 280), especially Luna's, the suggestion of Titania's grotesque amour with Bottom in his asshead; in the lines spoken by the amatory shepherds,

'When will the sun go downe? flye Phœbus flye!
Oh that thy steeds were wing'd with my swift thoughts: ...
Come night, come gentle night, for thee I stay' (iv. 1. 248-54),

an anticipation of Juliet's speech in the orchard (iii. 2),

'Gallop apace, you fiery-footed steedes;
To Phœbus mansion . . . . . .
And send in cloudie night immediately' (1st Quarto 1597);

and in some lines in iii. 2. 166-9 a hint for 'Under the greenwood tree' in *As You Like It*. But it has not been noticed that in *The Woman* we get, in far more pronounced degree than in Manes in *Campaspe*, the exact presentment of the early Shakespearean Clown of the type of Costard and Launce. Hitherto Lyly has distributed his comic matter among a group of pages with their butt or butts: here he concentrates it in the person of Gunophilus, with just that admixture of shrewd rustic comment on the action and rueful reflection on his own mishaps which is so familiar to us in Shakespeare (see pp. 247, 251-2, 265-6, 267, 278, 282-3). *Love's Labour's Lost*, *The Two Gentlemen*, and *The Comedy of Errors* were all produced probably 1590-1592, and Lyly may well have witnessed all three.

Connected with this last argument is the character of the blank verse, which is certainly not that of an early date like 1580-1586, but evinces the skill more appropriate to a time when it was winning, or had won, general acceptance as the right dramatic vehicle. It is true that smooth and moderately good end-stopped blank verse had been written much earlier, e. g. *Gorboduc*, 1561, *Jocasta*, 1566, *Tancred and Gismunda*, 1568, *The Arraignment of Paris* (pub. 1584) and *The Misfortunes of Arthur*, 1587: but not one of these, with the possible and partial exception of Peele's *Arraignment*, exhibits the ease and strength so noticeable throughout *The Woman in the Moone*; still less does any of them approach the delicate poetic fancy displayed in many of Lyly's lines. Moreover, a close examination of these lines shows him not unaffected by the improvements—the variety of cadence, the departures from the normal decasyllabic line—which are generally accredited to Marlowe's *Tamburlaine*, 1587. I have counted over thirty lines in the play where such irregularities appear, and they are seldom such as can be attributed to mistakes in printing, e. g. :

 iii. 2. 4. Wanton discourses, musicke and merrie songes
 iii. 2. 65. And of them all Stesias deserues the least
 iii. 2. 128. Then shepheard this kisse shalbe our nuptials
 iii. 2. 238. Bring Iphicles and Melos with thee, and tell them
 iv. 1. 10. Theeuish, lying, subtle, eloquent
 v. 1. 107. Milke white Squirrels, singing Popiniayes
 iv. 1. 24. She singing on her Lute, and Melos being the note
 v. 1. 324. Fantasticall, childish, and folish, in their desires

Moreover, as I have shown under 'Sources' below, the play is probably indebted to the example of Greene's *Planetomachia*, published in black-letter quarto by Thos. Cadman, 1585; and to the dramatic example of *The Rare Triumphs of Love and Fortune*, pub. 1589. Finally the Latin lines, iii. 1. 111–5, are a later adaptation of an effect already employed by him in the *Elvetham Entertainment*, 1591 : vol. i. p. 445. On all these grounds I incline, then, to reverse my earlier judgement (*Quarterly Review*, Jan. 1896) that *The Woman* is Lyly's earliest play, 1578–81, and to pronounce it his latest conception (followed only by the revised form of *Loves Metamorphosis*), composed 1591–3, probably nearer the end than the beginning of that period, but earlier than *A Midsummer Night's Dream*, which dates about 1594.

Sources.—The story of the creation of Pandora is original in Hesiod's Ἔργα καὶ Ἡμέραι, ll. 69–82 :

Ὣς ἔφαθ'· οἱ δ' ἐπίθοντο Διὶ Κρονίωνι ἄνακτι.
Αὐτίκα δ' ἐκ γαίης πλάσσε κλυτὸς Ἀμφιγυήεις
παρθένῳ αἰδοίῃ ἴκελον, Κρονίδεω διὰ βουλάς·
ζῶσε δὲ καὶ κόσμησε θεὰ γλαυκῶπις Ἀθήνη·
ἀμφὶ δέ οἱ Χάριτές τε θεαὶ καὶ πότνια Πειθὼ
ὅρμους χρυσείους ἔθεσαν χροΐ· ἀμφὶ δὲ τήνγε
Ὧραι καλλίκομοι στέφον ἄνθεσιν εἰαρινοῖσι·
[πάντα δέ οἱ χροῒ κόσμον ἐφήρμοσε Παλλὰς Ἀθήνη.]
Ἐν δ' ἄρα οἱ στήθεσσι διάκτορος Ἀργειφόντης
ψεύδεά θ' αἱμυλίους τε λόγους καὶ ἐπίκλοπον ἦθος
τεῦξε Διὸς βουλῇσι βαρυκτύπου· ἐν δ' ἄρα φωνὴν
θῆκε θεῶν κῆρυξ· ὀνόμηνε δὲ τήνδε γυναῖκα
Πανδώρην, ὅτι πάντες Ὀλύμπια δώματ' ἔχοντες
δῶρον ἐδώρησαν, πῆμ' ἀνδράσιν ἀλφηστῇσιν.

See also the *Theogony* 570–612.

INTRODUCTION 235

The following is the version of Hyginus, Fab. 142, *Pandora* :
'Prometheus Iapeti filius, primus homines ex luto finxit, postea Vulcanus Iouis iussu ex luto mulieris effigiem fecit, cui Minerva animam dedit, caeterique Dii alius aliud donum dederunt, ob id Pandoram nominarunt, ea data in coniugium Epimetheo fratri, inde nata est Pyrrha, quae mortalis dicitur prima esse creata.'

Lyly may have read the latter, and had probably read the former passages; but I have found a still closer resemblance in some words in the third of Geoffrey Fenton's *Certeine Tragicall Discourses written oute of Frenche*, &c., *London* . . . 1567, B. L. 4º, being thirteen tales translated from Belleforest's *Histoires Tragiques*, which came originally from Bandello's Italian. The third of Fenton's *Discourses* is about 'A younge Ladye of Myllan,' who is named Pandora, and 'longe abused the vertue of her youth and honor of mariage with an vnlawfull haunte of diuerse yonge Gentlemen' (from the 'Table'). On fol. 62 it is said of her, 'This Pandora . . . gaue manyfest signes during the tyme of her Infansye of her future disposition, arguinge the poysined Clymatte whiche first gettynge domynion ouer the yonge yeares of her grene vnderståding dyrected after ye whole seaquel of her life by the dyal of a cursed constellacion . . . for she was disdaynfull without respect, spytefull without measure, honge altogether full of the fethers of folyshe pryde, so wholly giuen to wallowe in dilycacie that she detested al exercises of vertue' &c. : while on fol. 66 occurs the following in a letter written to Pandora by her lover Parthenope—'The curious Artificer and coninge worke woman Dame Nature . . . was not so careful to worke you in her semelie frame of all perfecticns, as the powers deuine and disposers of the daungerous and loftye planets, assistinge her endeuour with certaine peculier ornaments of their speciall grace weare redye to open their golden vessell of precious treasur.'

The idea of conflict between the Planets in regard to their influence on human affairs appears in actual dialogue-form in Greene's *Planetomachia* (1585), of which the following is the title :—

'Planetomachia : Or the first parte of the generall opposition of the seuen Planets : wherein is Astronomically described their essence, nature, and influence : Diuersly discouering in their pleasaunt and Tragicall histories, the inward affections of the mindes, and painting them out in such perfect Colours, as youth may perceiue what fond fancies their florishing yeares doe foster : and age clerely see what doting desires their withered heares doe afforde. Conteyning also a briefe Apologie of the sacred and misticall Science of Astronomie : By Robert Greene, Master of Arts and student in Phisicke. 1585. Imprinted at London for Thomas Cadman, dwelling at the great North doore of S. Paules, at the signe of the Byble. 1585.' (6 fols. then A, B, *B*—I 3 in fours, bl. lett. 4º.) The book represents a quarrel between Venus and Saturn as to whose astrological influence is the more pernicious, in which Mars and Mercury take Venus' part, while Jupiter and Luna side with Saturn, and Sol, whose sphere lies midmost of the Seven, is appointed 'moderator' between them. Venus then gives a general statement of the melancholy influence exercised by Saturn on those born under his star, and illustrates it by 'a pleasant though Tragical History' (occupying 14 fols.) of the loves of Rodento and Pasylla, daughter of Valdracko Duke of Ferrara, and their unfortunate issue owing to the Duke's enmity with Rodento's father, Count Celio. Then the dialogue between the Planets is resumed (sig. F 3), and Luna gives an 'Astronomicall description of Venus,' which is followed by 'Saturnes Tragedie,' closing the book with the story of Rhodope, the Egyptian courtesan, and the evils attending those who surrender themselves to Venus' influence. The book is redolent of *Euphues*, but shows no knowledge of Lyly's play, which, as the more elaborate, is the more likely to be derived, though close parallels are lacking. He may have found a closer model in the play called *The Rare Triumphs of Love and Fortune*, pub. 1589, 4º; the first Act of which is occupied by a council of the gods to set the action in motion ; in the second, third, and fourth Fortune and Venus alternately dominate the lives of two lovers, Hermione and Fidelia ; while in the fifth, by Jupiter's command, they combine to secure their happiness. For Mézières' suggestion of Pandora or Luna as a satirical allegory of the Queen, a suggestion I hesitate to accept, see the Essay, vol. ii. p. 256 note, and Life and Appendix, vol. i. pp. 63–4, 383, 389–90.

Stage-History. — The quarto's use of a smaller roman type for five particular stage-directions (Act i. ll. 31, 57, 224; Act ii. ll. 201, 203) may point to additions on the MS. in another hand, made, at a later performance than that before the Queen, by some stage-manager to whom Lyly had sold the play ; or, since it is not said to have been acted by the Paul's or Chapel Children, to additions made by the stage-manager (other than Lyly) of the first performance. The greater frequency of stage-directions in this, as compared with the

INTRODUCTION

other plays, favours the idea that Lyly had no hand in the actual production, and, in this case, wrote instructions he could not give orally.

Imitations. — Besides the suggestions afforded by this play to Shakespeare, as enumerated under 'Date' above (and cf. Essay, vol. ii. pp. 297–8), it undoubtedly contributed something to a poem of uncertain date, but originally dedicated to Prince Henry (ob. 1612) by William Basse, entitled *Vrania the Woman in the Moone*; wherein two gods, sent by Jupiter to report on the state of the world, fall in love with an Ethiopian woman, who having extracted from them the secret by which they are able to reascend, flies to Olympus, and on her arrival is banished by the Immortals to the Moone. Cynthia's indignation at the comparion thus forced upon her is made to explain the common lunar phenomena, and especially the subjection to her influence of all women, whom she afflicts

> With fancyes, frenzies, lunacyes, with strange
> Feares, fashions, factions, furyes, & affections,
> With fondnes, fayntnes, fugacy, and change
> Of mindes, moodes, habits, houses, freindes, complections:
>   In breife she raignes o're Women as a Queene.
>   In her their state, in them her power, is seene.

See my edition of William Basse's *Poetical Works*, p. 308 (Ellis and Elvey, 1893), and compare the closing lines of Lyly's play.

Place and Time. — In this his latest play but one we have the same indeterminate treatment, the same hovering between rule and licence, as in earlier works. In his one drama of contemporary life, however, *Mother Bombie*, he observed the Unities more strictly; and in this play, his next composition, it is natural to find a greater effort at conformity. Yet, while taking the Unities for his working-plan, he allows inconsistency to creep in. As regards Place, the presence of the balcony, occupied continuously by one or other of the Planets, really fixes the scene at one spot; but, while in iv. 1. 165 Pandora appoints to meet Iphicles 'on Enipeus sedgy bankes,' later on *in the same scene*, l. 292, Stesias entering as her substitute says, 'This is Enipeus banke.' Just before that point Pandora and Gunophilus have crossed the stage on their way 'vnto the sea side,' l. 270; while at the beginning of Act v. l. 10, evidently representing a later moment of the same expedition, Gunophilus says, 'We are almost at the sea side.' Evidently there is an imaginary transfer of scene, the difficulty presented by the continuous use of the balcony being obviated by the reflection that it stands in this play for the heavens or actual planetary spheres, which would be equally present at different spots in the same neighbourhood. Several similar imaginary transfers occur in *Campaspe*, one in *Endimion*, pp. 60–1, and one in *Loves Metamorphosis*, Act ii. As regards Time, he is stricter than in any other play. Though the notes of it are not very precise, he intends the action to occupy no more than the single day allowed for Comedy. Acts iv and v are, as I have shown, continuous, and early in Act iv (l. 103, 'ere the sunne go doun') Pandora alludes to the approach of evening. The inference is that the earlier part of the day has been occupied by the preceding Acts; for the plan of the piece seems to require that if Mercury and Luna, who dominate the Fourth and Fifth Act respectively, hold sway only for a few hours, the ascendency of the preceding Planets shall not be of very much longer or shorter duration. The banquet that occupies the second scene of Act iii thus falls appropriately about the middle of the single day occupied by the whole piece; and we may note that the division of this Third Act into two scenes involves no real interval, since Gunophilus executes in the second scene, l. 68, a commission (to fetch a herb) imposed on him in the first, ll. 65–71. Similarly the sway of Luna, or moon-rise, comes near the end of the piece. We are, then, to disregard the inconsistencies which Lyly, whether carelessly or deliberately, left in the text, of which the chief are the words of Pandora, ii. 1. 8–9 :

> By day I thinke of nothing but of rule,
> By night my dreames are all of Empery—

words used immediately after Jupiter has assumed ascendency, and the recital by the shepherds, iv. i. 21 sqq., of past favours she has shown to them; which would properly require the lapse of a considerable interval.

THE WOMAN
in the Moone.

As it was prefented before
her Highneſſe.

By IOHN LYLLIE maiſter
of Artes.

Imprinted at London for William
Iones, and are to be ſold at the ſigne of the
Gun, neere Holburne Conduict.
1597.

⟨DRAMATIS PERSONÆ

NATURE.
CONCORD, ⎫
DISCORD, ⎭ *her handmaids.*
SATURN,
JUPITER,
MARS,
SOL, *the Seven Planets.*
VENUS,
MERCURY,
LUNA,
JUNO.
GANYMEDE, *attending on Jupiter* (*mute*).
CUPID, ⎱ *attending on Venus.*
JOCULUS, ⎰
PANDORA, *the Woman.*
STESIAS,
LEARCHUS, ⎱ *Utopian Shepherds.*
MELOS,
IPHICLES,
GUNOPHILUS, *Servant to Pandora.*

SCENE—*Utopia.*⟩

DRAM. PERS.] *list supplied F.*   11 JUNO *om. F.*   21 SCENE—Utopia *suppl. F.*

Prologus

Ovr Poet slumbring in the Muses laps,
    Hath seene a Woman seated in the Moone,
A point beyond the aunctient Theorique:
And as it was so he presents his dreame,
Here in the bounds of fayre Vtopia,   5
Where louely Nature being onely Queene,
Bestowes such workmanship on earthly mould
That Heauens themselues enuy her glorious worke.
But all in vaine: for (malice being spent)
They yeeld themselues to follow Natures *doom;*   10
And fayre Pandora *sits in* Cynthias *orbe.*
This, but the shadow of our Authors dreame,
Argues the substance to be neere at hand:
At whose appearance I most humbly craue,
That in your forehead she may read content.   15
If many faults escape in her discourse,
Remember all is but a Poets dreame,
The first he had in Phœbus *holy bowre,*
But not the last, vnlesse the first displease.

THE WOMAN IN THE MOONE

⟨ACT I⟩

Enter NATURE, *with her two maidens* CONCORD *and* DISCORD.

NATURE.

Nature descends from farre aboue the spheeres,
 To frolicke heere in fayre Vtopia,
Where my chiefe workes do florish in their prime,
And wanton in their first simplicitie.
Heere I suruey the pictured firmament, 5
With hurtlesse flames in concaue of the Moone;
The liquid substance of the welkins waste,
Where moystures treasurie is clouded vp;
The mutuall Ioynter of all swelling seas,
And all the creatures which their waues conteine; 10
Lastly the rundle of this Massiue earth,
From vtmost face vnto the Centers point:
All these, and all their endlesse circumstance,
Heere I suruey, and glory in my selfe.
But what meanes *Discord* so to knit the browes, 15
With sorrowes clowde ecclipsing our delights?
Discord. It grieues my hart, that still in euery worke,
My fellow *Concorde* frustrates my desire,
When I to perfect vp some wondrous deed,
Do bring forth good and bad, or light and darke, 20
Pleasant and sad, moouing and fixed things,
Fraile and immortall, or like contraries:
She with her hand vnites them all in one,
And so makes voide the end of mine attempt.

S. D. ACT I: *om.* Q. *The division of the play into Acts, and of the Third Act into scenes, is reproduced from Q F.*   S. D. Enter Nature, &c.: *this and all unbracketed stage-directions, more full and numerous for this play, are, as usual, from the Q*   6 Moone;] *the stops at end of ll.* 6, 8, 10, 12 *are represented by commas in Q; F. substituting full stop only at* conteine

Nat. I tell thee *Discord* while you twaine attend 25
 On *Natures* traine, your worke must prooue but one;
 And in your selues though you be different,
 Yet in my seruice must you well agree.
 For *Nature* workes her will from contraries,—
 But see where our Vtopian Shepheards come. 30

Enter STESIAS, LEARCHUS, MELOS, IPHICLES, *all clad in Skins.*
    They kneele downe.

Stesias. Thou Soueraigne Queene and Author of the world,
 Of all that was, or is, or shall be framde,
 To finish vp the heape of thy great gifts,
 Vouchsafe thy simple seruants one request.
Nat. Stand vp, and tell the sum of your desire, 35
 The boone were great that *Nature* would not graunt:
 It euer was and shall be still my ioy,
 With wholesome gifts to blesse my workemanship.
Iphicles. We craue, fayre goddesse, at thy heauenly hands,
 To haue as euery other creature hath, 40
 A sure and certaine meanes among our selues,
 To propagate the issue of our kinde:
 As it were comfort to our sole estate,
 So were it ease vnto thy working hand.
 Each Fish that swimmeth in the floating sea, 45
 Each winged fowle that soareth in the ayre,
 And euery beast that feedeth on the ground,
 Haue mates of pleasure to vpholde their broode:
 But thy Vtopians, poore and simple men,
 As yet bewaile their want of female sex. 50
Nat. A female shall you haue, my louely swaines,
 Like to your selues, but of a purer moulde:
 Meane while go hence, and tend your tender flocks,
 And while I send her, see you holde her deare.
    Exeunt Shepheards, *singing a roundelay in praise of* NATURE.
 Now Virgins put your hands to holy worke, 55
 That we may frame new wonders to the world.
    They draw the Curtins from before NATURES shop, where
    stands an Image clad and some vnclad, they bring forth the
    cloathed image.

S. D. They kneele downe] *the change of type here and in four places below, ll.* 57, 224; *Act* ii. 201, 203, *is reproduced from Q. See under Stage-History, p.* 236

When I arayde this lifelesse Image thus,
It was decreed in my deepe prouidence,
To make it such as our Vtopians craue,
A merror of the earth, and heauens dispight : 60
The matter first when it was voyde of forme,
Was purest water, earth, and ayre, and fyre,
And when I shapt it in a matchlesse mould,
(Whereof the lyke was neuer seene before)
It grew to this impression that you see, 65
And wanteth nothing now but life and sowle.
But life and soule I shall inspire from heauen,
So hold it fast, till with my quickning breath,
I kindle inward seeds of sence and minde.
Now fire be turnd to choler, ayre to bloud, 70
Water to humor purer then it selfe,
And earth to flesh more cleare then Christall rock.
And *Discord* stand aloofe, that *Concords* hands
May ioyne the spirit with the flesh in league.
      CONCORD *fast imbraceth the Image.*
Concord. Now do I feele how life and inward sence, 75
 Imparteth motion vnto euery limme.
Nat. Then let her stand or moue or walke alone.
      The Image walkes about fearefully.
Herein hath *Nature* gone beyond her selfe,
And heauen will grudge at beautie of the earth,
When it espies a second sonne belowe. 80
Dis. Now euerie part performes her functions dew,
 Except the tongue whose strings are yet vntyed.
Nat. Discorde, vnlose her tongue, to serue her turne,
 For in distresse that must be her defence :
 And from that roote will many mischiefes growe, 85
 If once she spot her state of innocence. *Image speakes.*
Pandora kneeling. Haile heauenly Queene, the author of all good,
 Whose wil hath wrought in me the fruits of life,
 And fild me with an vnderstanding soule,
 To know the difference twixt good and bad. 90
Nature lifting her vp. I make thee for a solace vnto men,
 And see thou follow our commaunding will.
 Now art thou *Natures* glory and delight,
 Compact of euery heauenly excellence :

Thou art indowd with *Saturns* deepe conceit, 95
Thy minde as hawte as *Iupiters* high thoughts,
Thy stomack Lion-like, like *Mauors* hart,
Thine eyes bright beamde, like *Sol* in his array,
Thy cheekes more fayre, then are faire *Venus* cheekes,
Thy tongue more eloquent then *Mercuries*, 100
Thy forehead whiter then the siluer Moones:
Thus haue I robd the Planets for thy sake.
Besides all this, thou hast proud *Iunoes* armes,
Auroraes hands, and louely *Thetis* foote:
Vse all these well, and *Nature* is thy friend, 105
But vse them ill, and *Nature* is thy foe.
Now that thy name may suite thy qualities,
I giue to thee *Pandora* for thy name.
⟨*During the following dialogue* PANDORA *sits apart.*⟩
Enter the seuen Planets.

Saturn. What creature haue we heere? a new found gawde?
A second man, lesse perfect then the first? 110
Mars. A woman this forsooth, but made in hast,
To robbe vs Planets of our ornaments.
Jupiter. Is this the Saint, that steales my *Iunoes* armes?
Sol. Mine eyes? then gouerne thou my daylight carre.
Venus. My cheekes? then *Cupid* be at thy commaund. 115
Mercury. My tongue? thou pretty Parrat speake a while.
Luna. My forehead? then faire *Cynthia* shine by night.
Nat. What foule contempt is this you Planets vse,
Against the glory of my words and worke?
It was my will, and that shall stand for lawe, 120
And she is framd to darken all your prides.
Ordeynd not I your motions, and your selues?
And dare you check the author of your liues?
Were not your lights contriude in *Natures* shop?
But I haue meanes to end what I begun, 125
And make Death triumphe in your liues decay:
If thus you crosse the meede of my deserts,
Be sure I will dissolue your harmonie,
When once you touche the fixed period:
Meane while I leaue my worthy workmanship, 130
Here to obscure the pride of your disdaine. *Exit.*

97 Mauors] Mars's *F.*, *misreporting Q as reading* Manor's

Sat. Then in reuenge of *Nature* and her worke,
   Let vs conclude to shew our Emperie:
   And bend our forces gainst this earthly starre.
   Each one in course shall signorize awhile,   135
   That she may feele the influence of our beames,
   And rue that she was formde in our dispight:
   My turne is first, and *Saturne* will begin.   *He ascends.*
Jup. And Ile begin where *Saturne* makes an end,
   And when I end, then *Mars* shall tyrrannize,   140
   And after *Mars* then *Sol* shall marshall her,
   And after *Sol* each other in his course:
   Come let vs go, that *Saturne* may begin.
          ⟨*Exeunt all the* Planets *except* SATURNE.⟩
Sat. I shall instill such melancholy moode,
   As by corrupting of her purest bloud,   145
   Shall first with sullen sorrowes clowde her braine,
   And then surround her heart with froward care:
   She shalbe sick with passions of the hart,
   Selfwild, and toungtide, but full fraught with teares.

          Enter GUNOPHILUS.

⟨*Gun.*⟩ Gratious *Pandora*: *Nature* thy good friend   150
   Hath sent *Gunophilus* to waite on thee:
   For honors due that appertaines her will,
   And for the graces of thy louely selfe,
   Gunophilus will serue in humble sorte,
   And is resolud to liue and die with thee.   155
Pan. If *Nature* wild, then do attend on me,
   But little seruice haue I to commaund,
   If I my selfe might choose my kinde of life,
   Nor thou, nor any else should stay with me,
   I finde my selfe vnfit for company.   160
Gun. How so faire Mistres in your flouring youth,
   When pleasures ioy should sit in euery thought?
Pan. Auaunt sir sawce! play you the Questionest?
   Whats that to thee, if I be sick or sad?
   Eyther demeane thy selfe in better sort,   165
   Or get thee hence, and serue some other where.

          136 our] her *Q F.*

Gun. ⟨*aside*⟩. A sowre beginning: but no remedy,
Nature hath bound me, and I must obey:
I see that seruants must haue Marchants eares,
To beare the blast and brunt of euery winde. 170
Pan. What throbs are these that labour in my brest?
What swelling clouds, that ouercast my braine?
I burst, vnlesse by teares they turne to raine.
I grudge and grieue, but know not well whereat:
And rather choose to weepe then speake my minde, 175
For fretfull sorrow captiuates my tongue.
She playes the vixen with euery thing about her ⟨*and finally resumes her seat*⟩.

Enter STESIAS, MELOS, LEARCHUS, *and* IPHICLES.

Ste. See where she sits, in whom we must delight.
Beware! she sleepes: no noyse for waking her!
Iphi. A sleepe? why see how her alluring eyes,
With open lookes do glaunce on euery side. 180
Melos. O eyes more fayre then is the morning starre!
Lear. Nature her selfe is not so louely fayre!
Ste. Let vs with reuerence kisse her Lillie hands,
They all kneele to her.
And by deserts in seruice win her loue.
Sweete Dame, if *Stesias* may content thine eye, 185
Commaund my Neate, my flock, and tender Kids,
Whereof great store do ouerspred our plaines.
Graunt me sweet Mistresse but to kisse thy hand.
She hits him on the lips.
Lear. No *Stesias* no, *Learchus* is the man:
Thou myrror of Dame *Natures* cunning worke, 190
Let me but hold thee by that sacred hand,
And I shall make thee our *Vtopian* Queene,
And set a guilded Chapplet on thy head,
That Nymphes and Satyrs may admyre thy pompe.
She strikes his hand. He riseth.
Gun. These twaine and I haue fortunes all alyke. 195
Melos. Sweet *Natures* pride, let me but see thy hand,
And servant lyke, shall *Melos* waite on thee,
And beare thy traine: as in the glorious heauens,
Perseus supports his loue *Andromeda*:

  Whose thirty starres, whether they rise or fall,   200
 He falles or ryseth, hanging at her heeles.
        She thrusts her hands in her pocket.
Iphi. O then to blesse the loue of *Iphicles*,
 Whose heart dooth hold thee deerer then himselfe,
 Do but behold me with a louing looke,
 And I will leade thee in our sollemne daunce,   205
 Teaching thee tunes, and pleasant layes of loue.
         She winkes and frownes.
Ste. No kisse? nor touche? nor friendly looke?
 What churlish influence depriues her minde?
 For *Nature* sayd, that she was innocent,
 And fully fraught with vertuous qualities: 210
 But speake sweete loue: thou canst not speake but well.
Gun. She is not tongue tyde, that I know by proofe.
Melos. Speake once *Pandora* to thy louing friends.
Pan. Rude knaues, what meane you thus to trouble me?
 Gun. She spake to you my maisters, I am none of your company.   216
Lear. Alas! she weeping sounds: *Gunophilus*
 O helpe to reare thy Mistresse from the ground.
Gun. This is the very passion of the heart,
 And melancholy is the ground thereof.   220
Ste. O then to sift that humor from her heart,
 Let vs with Rundelayes delight her eare:
 For I haue heard that Musick is a meane,
 To calme the rage of melancholy moode.   *They sing.*
   She starteth vp and runs away at the end of the Song saying.
Pan. What songs? what pipes? & fidling haue we here?   225
 Will you not suffer me to take my rest?   *Exit.*
Melos. What shal we do to vanquish her disease?
 The death of that were life to our desires:
 But let vs go, we must not leaue her thus.   *Exeunt.*
     SATURNE *descendeth on the stage.*
Sat. Saturne hath layd foundation to the rest,   230
 Whereon to build the ruine of this dame,
 And spot her innocence with vicious thoughts;
 My turne is past, and *Iupiter* is next.   *Exit.*
     Actus primi finis.

ACT. 2.

Scena. 1.

Enter IUPITER.

⟨*Iup.*⟩ *A Ioue principium, sunt & Iouis omnia plena.*
    Now *Iupiter* shall rule *Pandoraes* thoughts,
    And fill her with Ambition and Disdaine :
    I will inforce my influence to the worst, 4
    Least other Planets blame my regiment.   ⟨*He ascends.*⟩

Enter PANDORA *and* GUNOPHILUS.

Pan. Though rancor now be rooted from my hart,
    I feele it burdened in an other sort :
    By day I thinke of nothing but of rule,
    By night my dreames are all of Empery.
    Mine eares delight to heare of Soueraingtie, 10
    My tongue desires to speake of princely sway,
    My eye would euery obiect were a crowne.
Jup. ⟨*aside*⟩. *Danae* was fayre, and *Læda* pleasd me well,
    Louely *Calisto* set my hart on fyre :
    And in mine eye *Europa* was a gemme, 15
    But in the beauty of this Paragon,
    Dame *Nature* far hath gone beyond her selfe,
    And in this one are all my loues conteind.
    And come what can come, *Iupiter* shall prooue,
    If fayre *Pandora* will accept his loue : 20
    But first I must discusse this heauenly clowde
    That hydes me from the sight of mortall eyes.
    Behold *Pandora* where thy louer sits, ⟨*Discovers himself.*⟩
    High *Ioue* himselfe, who rauisht with thy blaze,
    Receiues more influence then he powers on thee, 25
    And humbly sues for succour at thy hands.
Pan. Why what art thou ? more then *Vtopian* swaines ?
Jup. The king of Gods, one of immortall race,
    And he that with a beck controules the heauens.
Pan. Why then *Pandora* dooth exceed the heauens, 30
    Who neither feares nor loueth *Iupiter*.

S. D. [He ascends] *required by ll.* 60, 173 S. D.   14 Calisco *F. misled by
a battered letter in* Q

Jup. Thy beauty will excuse what ere thou say,
  And in thy lookes thy words are priuiledgd.
  But if *Pandora* did conceiue those gifts,
  That *Ioue* can giue, she would esteeme his loue ; 35
  For I can make thee Empresse of the world,
  And seate thee in the glorious firmament.
Pan. The words of Empresse and of firmament,
  More please mine eares then *Jupiter* mine eyes :
  Yet if thy loue be lyke to thy protest, 40
  Giue me thy golden scepter in my hand.
  But not as purchase of my precious loue,
  For that is more then heauen it selfe is worthe.
Jup. There, hold the scepter of Eternall *Ioue*,
        ⟨*Hands it from the balcony.*⟩
  But let not Maiestie encrease thy pride. 45
Pan. What lack I now but an imperiall throne,
  And *Ariadnæs* star-lyght Diadem.

Enter IUNO.

Juno. False, periurd *Iupiter* and full of guile,
  Are these the fruites of thy new gouernment?
  Is *Iunoes* beauty and thy wedlock vowe, 50
  And all my kindnesse troden vnder foote?
  Wast not enough to fancie such a trull,
  But thou must yeeld thy scepter to her hand?
  I thought that *Ganimede* had wened thy hart,
  From lawlesse lust of any womans loue : 55
  But well I see that euery time thou strayest,
  Thy lust but lookes for strumpet stars belowe.
Pan. Why know, *Pandora* scornes both *Ioue* and thee,
  And there she layes his scepter on the ground.
Juno ⟨*picking it up*⟩. This shall with me to our Celestiall court,
  Where gods (fond *Iupiter*) shall see thy shame, 61
  And laugh at Loue for tainting Maiestie :
  And when you please, you will repaire to vs :
  But as for thee, thou shamelesse counterfet,
  Thy pride shall quickly loose her painted plumes, 65
  And feele the heauy weight of *Junoes* wrath.   *Exit* IUNO.

  49 governments? *F. mistaking battered interrogation point of Q*   53
sceptet *Q*

Pan. Let *Iuno* fret, and mooue the powers of heauen,
Yet in her selfe *Pandora* stands secure:
Am I not *Natures* darling and hir pride?
Hath she not spent her treasure all on me?   70
Jup. Yet be thou wise (I counsell thee for loue)
And feare displeasure at a goddesse hand.
Pan. I tell thee *Iupiter*, *Pandoras* worth
Is farre exceeding all your goddesses:
And since in her thou dost obscure my prayse,   75
Here (to be short) I do abiure thy loue.
Jup. I may not blame thee, for my beames are cause
Of all this insolence and proud disdaine:
But to preuent a second raging storme,
If iealious *Iuno* should by chaunce returne,   80
Here ends my loue: *Pandora* now farewell.   *Exit ⟨above⟩.*
Pan. And art thou clouded vp? fare as thou list,
Pandoraes hart shall neuer stoope to *Ioue:*
Gunophilus, base vassaile as thou art,
How haps when *Iuno* was in presence here,   85
Thou didst not honor me with kneele and crowche,
And lay thy hands vnder my precious foote,
     He powres downe a number of curtesies.
To make her know the height of my desart?
Base pesaunt, humbly watch my stately lookes,
And yeeld applause to euery word I speake: 90
Or from my seruice Ile discarde thee quite.
     GUNOPHILUS *on his knees.*
Gun. Fayre and dread Soueraigne! Lady of the world!
Euen then when iealous *Iuno* was in place,
As I beheld the glory of thy face,
My feeble eyes admiring maiestie,   95
Did sinke into my hart such holly feare,
That very feare amazing euery sence,
Withheld my tongue from saying what I would,
And freezd my ioynts from bowing when they should.
Pan. I now *Gunophilus* thou pleasest me,   100
These words and cursies prooue thee dutifull.

   93 place,] place: *Q*

Enter STESIAS, LEARCHUS, MELOS, *and* IPHICLES.

Ste. Now *Stesias* speake.
Lear.   *Learchus*, plead for loue.
Iphi. Now Cyprian Queene, guider of louing thoughts,
  Helpe *Iphicles*.
Melos.   *Melos* must speed, or dye.
Gun. ⟨*intervening between the* Shepherds *and* PANDORA⟩. Whether
   now my maisters in such post hast?   105
  Her excellence is not at leisure now.
Ste. O sweet *Gunophilus* further our attempts.
Iphi. And we shall make thee riche with our rewards.
Gun. Stay heere vntill I know her further pleasure:
            ⟨*Turning to* PAN.⟩
  Stesias & his felows humbly craue accesse to your excellēce. 110
Pan. I now thou fittest my humor: Let them come.
  Gun. Come on maisters.   ⟨*The* Shepherds *approach.*⟩
Ste. Tel me my deare, when comes that happy houre,
  Whereon thy loue shall guerden my desire.
Lear. How long shall sorows winter pinche my hart?   115
  And luke warme hopes be child with freezing feare,
  Before my suite obteyne thy sweete consent?
Iphi. How long shall death, incroching by delayes,
  Abridge the course of my decaying life,
  Before *Pandora* loue poore *Iphicles*?   120
Melos. How long shall cares cut off my flowring prime,
  Before the haruest of my loue be in?
Ste. O speake! sweete loue.
Iphi.   Some gentle words, sweete loue.
Lear. O let thy tongue first salue *Learchus* wound,
  That first was made with those immortall eyes.   125
Melos. The only promise of thy future loue,
  Will drowne the secret heapes of my dispayre
  In endlesse Ocean of expected ioyes.
Pan. Although my brest yet neuer harbored loue,
  Yet should my bountie free your seruitude: 130
  If loue might well consort our Maiestie,
  And not debase our matchlesse dignitie.
Ste. Sweet hony words, but sawst with bitter gawle.

   113 me] on *Q F. prob. for* one, *the compositor mistaking* me   114 thy] my *F.*

Iphi. They drawe me on, and yet they put me back.
Lear. They hold me vp, and yet they let me fall. 135
Melos. They giue me life, and yet they let me dye.
Ste. But as thou wilt, so giue me sweet or sowre :
  For in thy pleasure must be my content.
Iphi. Whether thou drawe me on, or put me back,
  I must admyre thy beauties wildernesse. 140
Lear. And as thou wilt, so let me stand or fall :
  Loue hath decreed thy word must gouerne me.
Melos. And as thou wilt, so let me liue or dye,
  In life or death I must obey thy wyll.
Pan. I please my selfe in your humility, 145
  Yet will I make some triall of your faith,
  Before I stoope to fauour your complaints :
  For wot ye well *Pandora* knowes her worth.
  He that will purchase things of greatest prize,
  Must conquer by his deeds, and not by words : 150
  Go then all foure, and slay the sauadge Boare,
  Which roauing vp and downe with ceaselesse rage,
  Destroyes the fruit of our *Vtopian* fields,
  And he that first presents me with his head,
  Shall weare my gloue in fauour of the deed. 155
Melos. We go *Pandora.*
Lear.   Nay we runne !
Ste.   We flye !
            ⟨*Exeunt* Shepherds.⟩
Pan. Thus must *Pandora* exercise these swaines,
  Commaunding them to daungerous exploits :
  And were they kings my beautie should commaund.
  Sirra *Gunophilus* beare vp my traine. 160
            Exit PANDORA *and* GUNOPH.

              Enter MARS.

Mars. Mars comes intreated by the Queene of heauen,
  To summon *Ioue* from this his regiment :
  Such iealious humor croweth in her braine,
  That she is mad till he returne from hence.
  ⟨*Louder.*⟩ Now Soueraigne *Ioue* king of immortal kings, 165

    139 thou] they *F.*   159 were they] where thy *F.*

Thy louely *Iuno* long hath lookt for thee,
And till thou come thinkes euery howre a yeere.

⟨*Re-enter* JUPITER *above, with* GANYMEDE.⟩

Jup. And *Ioue* will go the sooner to asswage
  Her franticke, idle, and suspitious thoughts,
  For well I know *Pandora* troubles her, 170
  Nor will she calme the tempest of her minde,
  Til with a whirlwinde of outragious words,
  She beat mine eares, and weep curst hart away.
      He descends ⟨*with* GANYMEDE⟩.
  Yet will I go, for words are but a blast,
  And sun-shine wil insue when stormes are past. 175
      Exit with GANIMEDE. ⟨MARS *ascends.*⟩
MARS *in his seate.* Now bloudy *Mars* begins to play his part,
  Ile worke such warre within *Pandoraes* brest,
  (And somewhat more for *Iunoes* fayre request)
  That after all her churlishnesse and pride
  She shall become a vixen Martialist. 180
    Enter the foure Shepheards *with the Boares head.*
Ste. Heere let vs stay till fayre *Pandora* come,
  And then shal *Stesias* haue his due rewarde.
Iphi. And why not *Iphicles* as well as you?
Melos. The prize is mine, my sword cut off his head.
Lear. But first my speare did wound him to the death. 185
Ste. He fell not downe till I had goard his side.
Lear. Content you all, *Learchus* did the deed,
  And I will make it good who eare sayes nay.
Melos. Melos will dye before he lose his right.
Iphi. Nay then tis time to snatch, the head is mine. 190
Ste. Lay downe, or I shal lay thee on the earth. *They fight.*

    Enter PANDORA *and* GUNOPHILUS.

Pan. I, so, fayre and far off, for feare of hurt,
  See how the cowards counterfet a fray:
  Strike home you dastard swaines, strike home, I say!
  Fight you in iest? let me bestur me then, 195
  And see if I can cudgel yee all foure.
    She snatcheth the speare out of STESIAS *hand & layes about her.*

S. D. [Re-enter JUP. &c.] *required by ll.* 81 S. D., 175 S. D.

Gun. What? is my mistresse mankinde on the sudden?
Lear. Alas! why strikes *Pandora* her best friends?
Pan. My friends? base pesants! My friends would fight like men:
    Auaunt! or I shall lay you all for dead.   200
                          Exeunt, all sauing STESIAS.
Ste. See cruell fayre, how thou hast wrongd thy friend,
                              He sheweth his shirt all bloudy.
    To spill his bloud that kept it but for thee.
    Thers my desart: And here is my rewarde,
        Pointing first to the head on the ground: and then to his wound.
    I dare not say of an ingratefull minde,
    But if *Pandora* had been well aduisd,   205
    This dare I say, that *Stesias* had been sparde.
Pan. Begon I say, before I strike againe.
Gun. O stay sweet mistresse and be satisfied.
Pan. Base vassall, how darst thou presume to speake?   209
    Wilt thou incounter any deed of mine?   *She beats him.*
    How long haue you beene made a counseller?
                        Exit GUNOPH., *running away.*
Ste. Here strike thy fill, make lauish of my life,
    That in my death my loue may finde reliefe:
    Launce vp my side, that when my heart leapes out,
    Thou maist behold how it is scorcht with loue,   215
    And euery way croswounded with desire:
    There shalt thou read my passions deepe ingrauen,
    And in the midst onely *Pandoraes* name.
Pan. What telst thou me of loue and fancies fire?
    Fyre of debate is kindled in my hart,   220
    And were it not that thou art all vnarmd,
    Be sure I should make tryall of thy strength:
    But now the death of some fierce sauadge beast,
    In bloud shall end my furies tragedie,   224
    For fight I must, or else my gall will burst.   *Exit* PAND.
Ste. Ah ruthlesse hart! harder then Adamant,
    Whose eares are deafe against affections plaints,
    And eyes are blinde, when sorrow sheds her teares:
    Neither contented that I liue nor dye.

---

    199 My friends would ... men *as separate line in Q F.*   S. D. Exeunt, all
sauing STESIAS—*i. e. the other three shepherds*

But fondling as I am, why grieue I thus? 230
Is not *Pandora* mistris of my life?
Yes, yes, and euery act of hers is iust.
Her hardest words are but a gentle winde:
Her greatest wound is but a pleasing harme: 234
Death at her hands is but a second life. *Exit* STESI.

MARS *descendeth*.

Mars. *Mars* hath inforst *Pandora* gainst her kinde,
   To manage armes and quarrell with her friends:
   And thus I leaue her, all incenst with yre:
   Let *Sol* coole that which I haue set on fire. *Exit.*
Actus 2. *finis.*

ACT. 3.

SCENA. 1.

Enter SOL *and take his seate.*

Sol. In looking downe vpon this baser worlde,
   I long haue seene and rude *Pandoraes* harmes;
   But as my selfe by nature am inclinde,
   So shall she now become, gentle and kinde,
   Abandoning all rancour, pride, and rage, 5
   And changing from a Lion to a Lambe;
   She shalbe louing, liberall, and chaste,
   Discreete and patient, mercifull and milde,
   Inspired with poetry and prophesie,
   And vertues apperteyning womanhoode. 10

Enter PANDORA *with* GUNOPHILUS

Pan. Tell me *Gunophilus* how doth *Stesias* now?
   How fares he with his wound? vnhappy me,
   That so vnkindely hurt so kind a friende!
   But *Stesias*, if thou pardon what is past,
   I shall rewarde thy sufferaunce with loue, 15
   These eyes that were like two malignant starres,
   Shall yeeld thee comfort with their sweet aspect;

2 rued *F.*   17 thee] their *Q F.*

And these my lippes that did blaspheme thy loue,
Shall speake thee fayre and blesse thee with a kisse;
And this my hand that hurt thy tender side,   20
Shall first with herbes recure the wound it made,
Then plight my fayth to thee in recompence.
And thou *Gunophilus* I pray thee pardon me,
That I misdid thee in my witles rage,
As time shall yeelde occasion, be thou sure   25
I will not fayle to make thee some amends.
Gun. I so content me in this pleasaunt calme,
That former stormes are vtterly forgot.

Enter (the) foure Shepherdes.

Lear. We follow still in hope of grace to come.
Iphi. O sweete *Pandora!* deigne our humble suites.   30
Melos. O graunt me loue or wound me to the death!
Pan. Stand vp: *Pandora* is no longer proud,
But shames at folly of her former deedes.
But why standes *Stesias* like a man dismayde?
Draw neare, I say, and thou, with all the rest,   35
Forgiue the rigour of *Pandoraes* hand,
And quite forget the faultes of my disdayne.
Now is the time if you consent all foure,
Wherein Ile make amends for olde offence.
One of you foure shalbe my wedlocke mate,   40
And all the rest my welbeloued friendes:
But vowe you here in presence of the Gods,
That when I choose, my choyse shall please you all.
Ste. Then make I vowe, by *Pallas* shepherds Queene,
That *Stesias* will alowe *Pandoraes* choyse.   45
But if he speede that lesse deserues then I,
Ile rather dye, then grudge or make complaynt.
Melos. I sweare the like by all our country gods.
Iphi. And I by our *Dianes* holy head.
Lear. And I by *Ceres* and her sacred Nymphes.   50
Pan. Then loue and *Hymen* blesse me in my choyse.
You all are young and all are louely fayre,
All kinde, and curteous and of sweete demeane,

35 rest. *Q*   44 Pallas' *F.*

All right and valiaunt, all in flowring prime;
But since you graunt my will his libertie, 55
Come *Stesias* take *Pandora* by the hand,
And with my hand I plight my spotles fayth.
Ste. The word hath almost slayne me with delight.
Lear. The worde with sorowe killeth me outright.
Melos. O happy *Stesias*, but vnhappy me! 60
Iphi. Come let vs goe, and weepe our want els where:
Stesias hath got *Pandora* from vs all.
                    Exeunt ⟨LEARCHUS, MELOS, *and* IPHICLES⟩.
Pan. Their sad depart would make my hart to earne,
Were not the ioyes that I conceaue in thee:
Go, go, *Gunophilus* without delay, 65
Gather me balme and cooling Violets,
And of our holly hearbe Nicotian,
And bring with all pure hunny from the hyue,
That I may heere compound a wholsome salue,
To heale the wound of my vnhappy hand. 70
Gun. I goe. ⟨*Exit.*⟩
Ste. Blest be the hand that made so happy wound,
For in my sufferance haue I wonne thy loue;
And blessed thou, that hauing tryed my faith,
Hast giuen admittance to my harts desert: 75
Now all is well, and all my hurt is whole,
And I in paradise of my delight.
Come, louely spouse, let vs go walke the woods,
Where warbling birds recorde our happines,
And whisling leaues make musick to our myrthe, 80
And *Flora* strews her bowre to welcome thee.
Pan. But first sweet husband, be thou ruld by me:
Go make prouision for some holy rytes,
That zeale may prosper our new ioyned loue,
And by and by my selfe will follow thee. 85
Ste. Stay not my deere, for in thy lookes I liue. *Exit.*
Pan. I feele my selfe inspyrd, but wot not how,
Nor what it is, vnlesse some holy powre:
My heart foretels me many things to come,
And I am full of vnacquainted skil, 90

64 Were not the *Q F.* (*F. misreporting Q as* Where not the)   85 follw *Q*

Yet such as wil not issue from my tongue,
But like *Sibillaes* goulden prophesies,
Affecting rather to be clad in verse
(The certaine badge of great *Apolloes* gift)
Then to be spred and soyld in vulgar words; 95
And now to ease the burden of my bulke,
Like *Sibill*, thus *Pandora* must begin.

Enter STESIAS.

Ste. Come my *Pandora*, *Stesias* stayes for thee.
Pan. Peace man, with reuerence here & note my words,
 For from *Pandora* speakes the Lawreat God. 100
 Vtopiæ Stesias Phœnici soluit amorem,
 Numina cælorum dum pia præcipiunt.
 And backward thus the same, but double sence.
 Præcipiunt pia dum celorum Numina, amorem
 Soluit Phœnici Stesias Vtopiæ. 105

He soberly repeating these verses, first forward and then backward,
 sayeth.

Ste. If *soluere amorem* signifie to loue,
 Then meanes this prophesie good to Stesias:
 But if it signifie to withdrawe loue,
 Then is it ill aboadement to vs both:
 But speake *Pandora* while the God inspyres. 110
Pan. *Idaliis prior hic pueris est: æquoris Alti*
 Pulchrior hec nymphis, & prior Aoniis.
 And backward thus, but still all one in sense.
 Aoniis prior, & nymphis hec pulchrior alti
 Æquoris est: pueris hic prior Idaliis. 115

He soberly repeating these also, backward and forward, sayeth
Ste. Forward and back, these also are alike,
 And sence all one, the pointing only changd:
 They but import *Pandoraes* praise and mine.
Pan. Euen now beginneth my furie to retyre,
 And now with *Stesias* hence wil I retyre. *Exeunt.* 120

92 Siballaes *Q F.*   101 soluit *Q F.*; *query?* soluet   105 Utopia *F.*
117 the] this *F.*

Scen. 2.

Enter Venus ⟨*with* Cupid *and* Joculus⟩.

⟨*Venus.*⟩ *Phœbus* away, thou makst her too precise,
Ile haue her wittie, quick, and amorous,
Delight in reuels and in banqueting,
Wanton discourses, musicke and merrie songes.
⟨Sol *descends.*⟩
Sol. Bright Cyprian Queene, intreate *Pandora* fayre.　　　5
For though at first *Phœbus* enuied her lookes,
Yet now doth he admire her glorious hew,
And sweares that neyther *Daphne* in the spring,
Nor glistering *Thetis* in her orient robe,
Nor shamefast morning gert in siluer cloudes,　　　10
Are halfe so louely as this earthly sainte.
Venus. And being so fayre my beames shall make her light,
For Leuety is Beauties wayting mayde.
Sol. Make Chastity *Pandoraes* wayting mayde,
For modest thoughtes beseemes a woman best.　　　15
Venus. Away with chastity and modest thoughts,
Quo mihi fortunâ si non conceditur vti?
Is she not young? then let her to the worlde:
All those are strumpets that are ouer chaste,
Defying such as keepe their company.　　　20
Tis not the touching of a womans hand,
Kissing her lips, hanging about her necke,
A speaking looke, no, nor a yeelding worde,
That men expect; beleeue me *Sol* tis more,
And were *Mars* here he would protest as much.　　　25
Sol. But what is more then this is worse then nought:
⟨*Aside.*⟩ I dare not stay least she infect me too.　　　*Exit.*
Venus. What, is he gone? then light foote *Ioculus,*
Set me *Pandora* in a dauncing vayne.
Joc. Fayre mother I will make *Pandora* blyth,　　　30
And like a Satyre hop vpon these playnes.　　　*Exit.*
Venus. Go *Cupid* giue her all the golden shafts,

---

s. d. [with Cupid and Joc.] *required by ll. 30 and 34*　　s. d. [Sol descends]
om. Q F.　　13 Leuety *F.*: Lenety *Q* (*turned* u)　　17 fortuna *Q*: fortunæ *F.*: *see note*　　32 the *Q F.*: *qy.?* thy

And she will take thee for a forrester.
Cupid. I will and you shall see her streight in loue. *Exit.*
  VENUS *ascendeth.*
Venus. Here *Venus* sit, and with thy influence
  Gouerne *Pandora, Natures* miracle.

  Enter PANDORA ⟨*with* CUPID⟩ *and* IOCULUS.

Pan. Prethee be quiet, wherefore should I daunce?
Joc. Thus daunce the Satyrs on the euen lawnes.
Pan. Thus, prety Satyr, will *Pandora* daunce.
Cupid. And thus will *Cupid* make her melody.
  He shootes.

  ⟨*They dance and sing as follows*⟩

Joc. Were I a man I could loue thee.
Pan. I am a mayden, wilt thou haue me?
Joc. But *Stesias* saith you are not.
Pan. What then? I care not.
Cup. Nor I.
Joc. Nor I.
Pan. Then merely
  Farewell my maydenhead.
  These be all the teares Ile shed;
  Turne about and trippe it.

Venus. Cupid and *Ioculus*, come leaue her now.
  Exeunt ⟨CUP. *and* JOC.⟩.
Pan. The boyes are gone and I will follow them.
  I will not follow them, they are to young.
  What hony thoughts are in *Pandoraes* brayne?
  Hospitis est tepedo necte recepta sui.
  Ah I enuie her, why was not I so?
  And so will I be: where is *Iphicles,*
  Melos, Learchus? any of the three?
  I cure the sicke? I study Poetry?
  I thinke of honour and of chastitie?
  No: loue is fitter then *Pandoraes* thoughts;

s. D. [They dance and sing &c.] *not in Q F. which print song as prose*   46
merely *i.e.* merrily   54 necte : *both in Br. Mus. copy and in Dyce copy the first*
e *is a little blurred or buttered. In Br. Mus. it is more like* e *than* o, *while in the
Dyce copy an original* c *seems to have been inked with a pen into an* e. *Both copies
read* tepedo *quite clearly*   60 then *Q F.* : *qy. ?* for

Yet not the loue of *Stesias* alone;
Learchus is as fayre as *Stesias*,
And *Melos* loulier then *Learchus* farre,
But might I chose, I would haue *Iphicles*,
And of them all *Stesias* deserues the least.   65
Must I be tyde to him? no Ile be loose,
As loose as *Helen*, for I am as fayre.

Enter GUNOPHILUS.

⟨*Gun.*⟩ Mistresse, here be the hearbs for my maisters wound.
Pan. Prety *Gunophilus*, give me the hearbs:
Where didst thou gather them my louely boye?   70
Gun. Vpon *Learchus* plaine.
Pan. I feare me *Cupid* daunst vpon the plaine,
I see his arrow head vpon the leaues.
Gun. And I his golden quiuer and his bowe.
Pan. Thou doost dissemble, but I meane good sooth.   75
These hearbes haue wrought some wondrous effect:
Had they this vertue from thy Lilly hands?
Lets see thy hands my fayre *Gunophilus*.
Gun. It may be they had, for I haue not washt them this many
    a day.   80
Pan. Such slender fingers hath *Ioues Ganymede*:
Gunophilus, I am loue sick for thee.
Gun. O that I were worthy you should be sick for me!
Pan. I languish for thee, therefore be my loue.
Gun. Better you languish, then I be beaten! Pardon me, I dare
not loue, because of my Maister.   86
Pan. Ile hide thee in a wood, and keepe thee close.
Gun. But what if he come a hunting that way?
Pan. Ile say thou art a Satyre of the woods.
Gun. Then I must haue hornes.   90
Pan. I, so thou shalt, Ile giue thee *Stesias* hornes.
Gun. Why he hath none.
Pan. But he may haue shortly.
Gun. Yee say true, and of that condition I am yours.

Enter LEARCHUS.

Lear. I may not speake of loue, for I haue vowd   95
Nere to sollicit her, but rest content;

Therefore onely gaze, eyes, to please your selues,
Let not my inward sence know what you see,
Least that my fancie doate vpon her still.
Pandora is diuine, but say not so,　　　　　　　　　100
Least that thy heart heare thee and breake in twaine.
I may not court her: what a hell is this!
Pan. *Gunophilus*: Ile haue a banquet streight,
Goe thou, prouide it, and then meete me here.
Gun. I will; but by your leaue Ile stay a while.　　105
Lear. Happy are those that be *Pandoraes* guestes.
Pan. Then happy is *Learchus*, he is my guest.
Lear. And greater ioy doe I conceaue therein,
Then *Tantalus* that feasted with the Gods.
Gun. Mistres, the banquet.　　　　　　　　　　　110
Pan. What of the banquet?
Gun. You haue bid no body to it.
Pan. Whats that to you? Goe and prepare it.
Gun. And in the meane time you will be in loue with him.
I pray let me stay, and bid him prepare the banquet.　115
Pan. Away, ye peasant!
Gun. Now she begins to loue me.　　　　　⟨*Exit.*⟩
Pan. *Learchus* had I markt this golden hayre,
I had not chosen *Stesias* for my loue,
But now—— ⟨*sighs*⟩.　　　　　　　　　　　　120
Lear. Louely *Pandora*, if a shepherds teares
May moue thee vnto rueth, pity my state.
Make me thy loue, though *Stesias* be thy choyse,
And I in steade of loue will honour thee.
Pan. ⟨*aside*⟩. Had he not spoke I should haue courted him: 125
Wilt thou not say *Pandora* is to light,
If she take thee insteede of *Stesias*?
Lear. Rather ile dye then haue but such a thought.
Pan. Then shepheard this kisse shalbe our nuptials.
Lear. This kisse hath made me welthier then *Pan.*　130
Pan. Then come agayne: Now be as great as *Ioue*.
Lear. Let *Stesias* neuer touch these lippes agayne.
Pan. None but *Learchus*: Now sweet loue begone,
Least *Stesias* take thee in this amarous vayne;
But go no farther then thy bower my loue,　　　　　135
Ile steale from *Stesias* and meete thee streight.

Lear. I will *Pandora*, and agaynst thou comst,
  Strew all my bower with flagges and water mints. *Exit.*
Pan. A husband? what a folish word is that!
  Giue me a louer, let the husband goe. 140

Enter MELOS ⟨*and* IPHICLES⟩.

Melos. O *Iphicles* beholde the heauenly Nymphe.
Iphi. We may beholde her, but she scornes our loue.
Pan. Are these the shepherds that made loue to me?
Melos. Yea, and the shepherds that yet loue thee still.
Iphi. O that *Pandora* would regard my suite! 145
Pan. They looke like water Nymphes, but speake like men:
  Thou should be *Nature* in a mans attire,
  And thou young *Ganimayde* Minion to *Ioue.*
Melos. Then would I make a worlde and giue it thee.
Iphi. Then would I leaue great *Ioue*, to follow thee. 150
Pan. ⟨*aside*⟩. *Melos* is loueliest, *Melos* is my loue;
  Come hether *Melos* I must tell thee newes,
  Newes tragicall to thee and to thy flock.
  She whispers in his eare.
  Melos, I loue thee, meete me in the vale.
  She speakes aloude.
  I saw him in the Wolues mouth, *Melos* flye. 155
Melos. O that so fayre a Lambe should be deuoured:
  Ile goe and rescue him. ⟨*Exit* MELOS.⟩
Iphi. Could *Iphicles* goe from thee for a Lambe?
  The wolfe take all my flocke, so I haue thee!
  Will me to diue for pearle into the sea, 160
  To fetch the fethers of the Arabian bird,
  The Golden Apples from the Hesperian wood,
  Maremaydes glasse, *Floras* abbiliment,
  So I may haue *Pandora* for my loue.
Pan. He that would do all this, must loue me well; 165
  And why should he loue me and I not him?
  Wilt thou for my sake goe into yon groue,
  And we will sing vnto the wilde birdes notes,
  And be as pleasant as the Western winde,

---

s. d. [and IPHICLES] *added F.*   163 The *before* Maremaydes *F.*: *but the word is meant as trisyllable*

That kisses flowers and wantons with their leaues. 170
Iphi. Will I? O that *Pandora* would!
Pan. I will! and therefore followe, *Iphicles.*   *Exeunt.*

Enter STESIAS *with* GUNOPHILUS.

Ste. Did base *Learchus* court my heauenly loue?
 Pardon me *Pan* if, to reuenge this deed,
 I shed the blood of that desembling swaine. 175
 With Iealous fire my heart begins to burne.
 Ah bring me where he is, *Gunophilus*,
 Least he intice *Pandora* from my bower.
Gun. I know not where he is, but here heele be:
 I must prouide the banquet, and be gone. 180
Ste. What! will the shepherds banquet with my wife?
 O light *Pandora* canst thou be thus false?
 Tell me where is this wanton banquet kept?
 That I may hurle the dishes at their heades,
 Mingle the wine with blood, and end the feast 185
 With Tragicke outcries, like the Theban Lord
 Where fayre *Hippodamia* was espousd.
Gun. Here in this place, for so she poynted me.
Ste. Where might I hide me to behold the same?
Gun. O, in this caue, for ouer this theyle sitte. 190
  ⟨*Pointing to a trapdoor.*⟩
Ste. But then I shall not see them when they kisse.
 Gun. Yet you may here what they say; if they kisse ile hollow.
Ste. But do so then my sweete *Gunophilus*;
 And as a stronge winde bursting from the earth, 195
 So will I rise out of this hollow vault,
 Making the woods shake with my furious wordes.
 Gun. But if they come not at all, or when they come do vse themselues honestly, then come not out, least you seeming Iealious make her ouer hate you. 200
Ste. Not for the worlde vnles I heare thee call,
 Or els their wanton speech prouoke me forth.
 Gun. Well, in then! ⟨STESIAS *descends through the trap.*⟩ Wert not a prety iest to bury him quicke? I warrant it would be a good

189 hehold *Q*   195 bursting *F.*: brusing *Q*

while eare she would scratch him out of his graue with her nayles, 205
and yet shee might too, for she hath digd such vaults in my face that
ye may go from my chinne to my eyebrowes betwixt the skin and
the flesh! wonder not at it, good people! I can proue there hath
bene two or three marchantes with me to hire romes to lay in wine:
but that they doe not stand so conueniently as they wold wish, (for 210
indeed they are euery one too neare my mouth, and I am a great
drinker) I had had a quarters rent before hand. Wel, be it knowne
vnto all men that I haue done this to cornute my mayster, for yet
I could neuer have opportunitie. You would litle thinke, my necke
is growne awry with loking back as I haue been a kissing, for feare 215
he should come, and yet it is a fayre example; beware of kissing,
bretheren! ⟨*The trap rises slightly.*⟩ What! doth the caue open?
ere she and he haue done heele picke the lock with his horne.

Enter PANDORA.

Pan. Now haue I playde with wanton *Iphicles*,
 Yea, and kept touch with *Melos*, both are pleased;   220
 Now, were *Learchus* here!—but stay, me thinkes
 Here is *Gunophilus*, Ile goe with him.
Gun. ⟨*speaking low*⟩. Mistres, my mayster is in this caue thinking
to meete you and *Learchus* here.
Pan. ⟨*same tone*⟩. What, is he Iealious? come *Gunophilus*   225
 In spite of him Ile kisse thee twenty times.
Gun. O looke how my lippes quiuer for feare!
Pan. ⟨*louder, for* STESIAS' *ear*⟩. Where is my husband? speake
 Gunophilus.
Gun. He is in the woods, and will be here anon.
Pan. ⟨*lower*⟩. I, but he shall not.   230
 ⟨*Louder, as before.*⟩ His fellow swaines will meete me in this
  bower,
 Who for his sake I meane to entertayne,
 If he knew of it he would meete them here.
 Ah! where so ere he be, safe may he be!
 Thus hold I vp my hands to heauen for him,   235
 Thus weepe I for my deere loue *Stesias!*
Gun. When will the shepheards come?
Pan. Imediately; prepare the banquet streight:

215 awry *F.*: away *Q*

Meane time Ile pray that *Stesias* may be here.
⟨*Lower again.*⟩ Bring *Iphicles* and *Melos* with thee, and tell
    them   240
Of my husband *Descendit ad inferos.*
Gun. Youle loue them then?
Pan. No, onely thee, yet let them sitte with me.
Gun. Content, so you but sit with them.   *Exit.*

                Enter LEARCHUS.

Lear. Why hath *Pandora* thus deluded me?   245
Pan. Learchus, whist! my husbands in this caue,
    Thinking to take vs together here!
Lear. Shall I slay him, and enioy thee still?
Pan. No! let him liue, but had he *Argos* eyes,
    He should not keepe me from *Learchus* loue: 250
    Thus will I hang about *Learchus* necke,
    And sucke out happinesse from forth his lippes.
Lear. And this shalbe the heauen that Ile ayme at.

        Enter GUNOPHILUS ⟨*with glasses, &c. for banquet*⟩.

Gun. Sic vos non vobis, sic vos non vobis.
Lear. What meanst thou by that?   255
Gun. Here is a coment vpon my wordes,
            He throwes the Glasse downe and breakes it.
Pan. Wherefore doest thou breake the glasse?
Gun. Ile answere it: shall I prouide a banquet and be cosend
of the best dish? I hope, syr, you haue sayde grace, and now
may I fall too.   260
    He takes his mistres by the hand and imbraceth her.
Lear. Away, base swayne!
Gun. Sir, as base as I am, Ile goe for currant here.
Lear. What? will *Pandora* be thus light?
Gun. O! you stand vpon the weight! wel if she were twenty
graines lighter I would not refuse her, prouided alwayes she be
not clipt within the ringe.   266
Pan. Gunophilus, thou art too malepert!
    ⟨*Aside to* LEARCHUS.⟩ Thinke nothing, for I can not shift him
        off.

247 vs] *qy. ?* vs both *metr. gra.*   248 and] *qy. ?* and so *metr. gra.*   thee
Q: the *F.*   250 not *Q*: no *F.*   258 it:] it, *Q F.*

⟨*To* Gun.⟩ Sirra, prouide the banquet you are best.
Gun. I will! and that incontinently! for indeed I cannot abstein. *Exit.*
Pan. Here, take thou *Melos* fauours, keep it close,
For he and *Iphicles* will streight be here;
I loue them not, they both importune me,
Yet must I make as if I loue them both;
Here they come.
Welcome *Learchus* to *Pandoraes* feast.
⟨*Re-enter* Gunophilus *with viands, &c.*⟩

Enter Melos *and* Iphicles ⟨*meeting*⟩.

Melos. What makes *Learchus* here?
Iphi. Wherefore should *Melos* banquet with my loue?
Lear. My heart ryseth agaynst this *Iphicles.*
Pan. Melos, my loue! Sit downe, sweete *Iphicles.*
⟨*Confers with* Iphi. *apart.*⟩
Melos. She daunts *Learchus* with a strange aspect.
Lear. I like not that she whispers vnto him.
Iphi. ⟨*aside to* Pand.⟩. I warrant you.
Pan. Her⟨e'⟩s to the health of *Stesias* my loue,
Would he were here to welcome you all three.
Melos. I will go seeke him in the busky groues.
Gun. You lose your labour then, he is at his flocke.
Pan. I, he wayes more his flocke then me.
⟨*Lear.*⟩ She weepes.
Iphi. Weepe not *Pandora,* for he loues thee well.
Pan. And I loue him.
Iphi. But why is *Melos* sad?
Melos. For thee I am sad, thou hast iniured me.
Pan. Knowes not *Melos* I loue him?
Iphi. Thou iniurest me, and I wilbe reuenged!
Pan. Hath *Iphicles* forgot my wordes?
Gun. ⟨*aside*⟩. If I should hollow they were all vndone.
Lear. ⟨*aside*⟩. They both are Iealious, yet mistrust me not!
Iphi. Here, *Melos!*
Melos. I pledge thee, *Iphicles.*

285 Here's] Hers *Q*: Her's *F.*   289 Pan. *Q*: Gun. *F.*   She weepes.] *itals. without cap. S in one line with preceding, Q: as stage-direction, F.: but required in text to complete the line. I prefix* Lear.

Pan. ⟨*aside to* LEAR.⟩. *Learchus* goe, thou knowst my minde. 300
Lear. ⟨*aside*⟩. Shall I sit here thus to be made a stale?
Louely *Pandora* meanes to follow me:
Farewell this feast, my banquet comes not yet. *Exit.*
Iphi. Let him goe.
Melos. Pandora go with me to *Stesias.* 305
Iphi. No, rather goe with me.
Melos. Away, base *Iphicles!*
Iphi. Coward! hand of! or els Ile strike thee downe!
Pan. My husband heres you!—⟨*Louder.*⟩ Will you striue for wine?
Giue vs a fresh cup, I will haue ye friends. 310
Melos. I defie thee, *Iphicles!*
Iphi. I thee, *Melos!*
Gun. Both of them are drunke!
Melos ⟨*to* PAND.⟩. Is this thy loue to me?
 Pan. Nay, if you fall out, farewell. ⟨*Aside.*⟩ Now will I goe meet *Learchus.* *Exit* PAND. 316
Iphi. I see thy Iugling, thou shalt want thy will.
Melos. Follow me if thou darst, and fight it out.
Iphi. If I dare? Yes I dare, and will! Come thou.
⟨*Exeunt* MEL. *and* IPH.⟩
Gun. Hollow! hollow! 320
STESIAS *riseth out of the caue.*
Ste. Where is the villayne that hath kist my loue?
Gun. No body, mayster.
Ste. Why striue they then?
Gun. Twas for a cup of wine, they were all drunke.
Ste. Whither is my wife gone? 325
Gun. To seeke you.
 Ste. Ah! *Pandora,* pardon me! thou art chaste. Thou madst me to suspect her, take thou that. ⟨*Beating* GUN.⟩
 Gun. O mayster! I did for good will to you!
 Ste. And I beat thee for good will to her. What hast thou to doe betwixt man and wife?
 Gun. Too much with the man, too litle with the wife. 332
Exeunt.

Finis Actus tertij.

320 S. D. Stesias *F.*: He *Q*

ACT. 4.

SCEN. 1 ⟨*with transfer at l.* 294⟩.

Enter MERCURY.

Mer. Empresse of loue, giue *Hermes* leaue to reigne,
  My course comes next, therefore resigne to me.
                    Descend VENUS.
Venus. Ascend, thou winged purseuant of *Ioue.*
Mer. Now shall *Pandora* be no more in loue;
  And all these swaines that were her fauorits   5
  Shall vnderstand their mistres hath playde false,
  And lothing her blab all to *Stesias.*
  Now is *Pandora* in my regiment,
  And I will make her false and full of slights,
  Theeuish, lying, suttle, eloquent;   10
  For these alone belong to *Mercury.*

         Enter MELOS, LEARCHUS, IPHICLES.

Iphi. Vnkind *Pandora* to delude me thus.
Lear. Too kinde *Learchus* that hath loude her thus.
Melos. Too foolish *Melos* that yet dotes on her.
Lear. Blacke be the Iuory of her tysing face.   15
Melos. Dimde be the sun shine of her rauishing eyes.
Iphi. Fayre may her face be, beautifull her eyes!
Lear. O *Iphicles* abiure her, she is false!
Iphi. To thee *Learchus* and to *Melos* false.
Melos. Nay, to vs all too false and full of guile. 20
Lear. How many thousand kisses gaue she me,
  And euery kisse mixt with an amorous glaunce.
Melos. How oft haue I leand on her siluer breast,
  She singing on her Lute, and *Melos* being the note.
Iphi. But waking, what sweete pastime haue I had, 25
  For loue is watchfull, and can neuer sleepe.
Melos. But ere I slept—
Lear.   When I had list—
Iphi.   What then?

  3 Ioue *Q*: love *F.*   5 her *Q*: were *F.*   6 there *Q F.*

Melos. Cætera quis nescit?
Lear. *Melos* preuents me that I should haue sayd.
Iphi. Blush *Iphicles* and in thy Rosie cheekes 30
   Let all the heat that feeds thy heart appeare.
Lear. Droope not fayre *Iphicles* for her misdeeds:
   But to reuenge it hast to *Stesias*.
Melos. Yea he shall know she is lasciuious.
Iphi. In this complaint Ile ioyne with thee, let vs go. 35
Lear. Stay, heere he comes.

   Enter STESIAS *with* GUNOPHILUS.

Ste. O *Stesias* what a heauenly loue hast thou!
   A loue as chaste as is *Apolloes* tree:
   As modest as a vestall Virgins eye,
   And yet as bright as Glow wormes in the night, 40
   With which the morning decks her louers hayre.
   O fayre *Pandora*, blessed *Stesias*!
Iphi. O foule *Pandora*, cursed *Stesias*!
Ste. What meanst thou *Iphicles*?
Melos. Ah! is she fayre that is lasciuious? 45
   Or that swaine blest that she makes but a stale?
Lear. He meanes thy loue, vnhappy *Stesias*.
Ste. My loue? no, Shepheards, this is but a stale,
   To make me hate *Pandora* whom I loue:
   So whispered late the false *Gunophilus*; 50
   Let it suffice that I beleeue you not.
Iphi. Loue is deafe, blinde, and incredulous;
   I neuer hung about *Pandoraes* neck,
   She neuer termd me fayre and thee black swaine.
Melos. She playd not vnto *Melos* in her bowre, 55
   Nor is his greene bowre strewd with Primrose leaues.
Lear. I kist her not, nor did she terme me loue;
   Pandora is the loue of *Stesias*.
   ⟨*Exeunt* LEAR. IPH. *and* MEL.⟩
Ste. Sirra! bid your Mistres come hether. 59
Gun. I shall syr.   *Exit.*
Ste. 'I neuer hung about *Pandoraes* neck,'—
   'She playde not vnto *Melos* in her bower,'—

S. D. [Exeunt LEAR. &c.] *suggested F.*   61–3 'I neuer &c.'] *quotation-marks suppl. F.*

'I kist her not, nor did she terme me loue;'—
These wordes argue *Pandora* to be light.
She playde the wanton with these amarous swaines, 65
By all these 'streames that interlaced these floodes,
Which may be venom to her thirstie soule,
Ile be reuenged as neuer shepherd was!
Now foule *Pandora*, wicked *Stesias*.

Enter GUNOPHILUS *and* PANDORA.

Gun. Mistres tis true, I hard them, venter not. 70
Pan. Fenced with her tongue, and garded with her wit,
Thus goeth *Pandora* vnto *Stesias*.
Ste. Detested falsor! that to *Stesias* eyes
Art more infestious then the Basiliske.
Pan. Gunophilus, *Pandora* is vndone! 75
Her loue, her ioy, her life hath lost his wits!
Offer a Kyd in *Esculapius* fane,
That he may cure him, least I dye outright.
Gun. ⟨*aside*⟩. Ile offer it *Esculapius*, but he shall not haue him,
for when he comes to him selfe I must answer it. 80
Pan. Go, I say!
Ste. Stay! I am well, tis thou that makst me raue.
Thou playdst the wanton with my fellow swaynes.
Pan. Then dye, *Pandora!* art thou in thy wits, 84
And calste me wanton? *She fals downe.*
Gun. O Maister! what haue you done?
Ste. Diuine *Pandora!* rise and pardon me!
Pan. I cannot but forgiue thee *Stesias*,
But by this light, if——
Gun. ⟨*aside*⟩. Looke how she winkes.
Ste. O stay, my loue! I know twas their deuise. 90
Pan. He that will winne me must haue *Stesias* shape,
Such golden hayre, such Alabaster lookes;
Wilt thou know why I loued not *Iupiter*?
Because he was vnlike my *Stesias*.
Ste. Was euer silly shepherd thus abusd? 95
All three afirmd *Pandora* held them deare.

66 interlaced *so Q F.*   71 Fenced *F.*: Fence *Q*   74 insestious *Q (compositor picking up long* s *for* f) *F.*   77 Esculapias *Q F.*   88 cannot, but *F.*
89 Looke *Q* : Looke, *F*: *qy.?* Looke you

Pan. It was to bring me in disgrace with thee,
   That they might haue some hope I would be theirs.
   I cannot walke but they importune me.
   How many amarous letters haue they sent!
   What giftes! yet all in vayne: to proue which true,
   Ile beare this slaunder with a patient minde,
   Speeke them all fayre, and ere the sunne go downe,
   I'le bring thee where they vse to lie in wait,
   To robbe me of my honour in the groues.
Ste. Do so sweete wife, and they shall buy it deare.
   I cannot stay, my sheepe must to the fould.   *Exit.*
Pan. Go *Stesias* as simple as a sheepe;
   And now *Pandora* summon all thy wits,
   To be reuenged vpon these long-toungd swaynes.
   Gunophilus beare *Iphicles* this ring:
   Tell him I raue and languish for his loue:
   Will him to meete me in this meade alone,
   And sweare his fellowes haue deluded him.
   Beare this to *Melos* ⟨*handing a bloody napkin*⟩ ; say that for his
      sake
   I stabd my selfe, and hadst not thou been neare,
   I had bene dead, but yet I am aliue,
   Calling for *Melos* whom I onely loue.
   And to *Learchus* beare these passionate lines,
   Which, if he be not flint, will make him come.
Gun. I will, and you shall see how cunningly Ile vse them;
stay here, and I will send them to you one after another, and then
vse them as your wisdome shall thinke good.   *Exit.*
Pan. That letter did I pen doubting the worst,
   And dipt the Napking in the Lambkins blood.
   For *Iphicles* were he compact of Iron,
   My ring is Adamant to drawe him foorth,
   Let women learne by me to be reuengd.
   Ile make them bite their tongues and eate their wordes,
   Yea sweare vnto my husband all is false.
   My wit is plyant and inuention sharpe,
   To make these nouises that iniure me.
         ⟨*Aside, as she sees* IPH. *approaching.*⟩

104 wait] weight *Q F.*   112 languish] language *Q F.*   S. D. [handing
&c.] *required by ll.* 125, 171

Young *Iphicles* must boast I fauourd him,
Here I protest as *Helen* to her loue:
    Oscula luctanti tantummodo pauca proteruus   135
    abstulit: vlterius, nil habet ille mei.
And whats a kisse? too much for *Iphicles!*
                                      ⟨*Enter* IPHICLES.⟩
Iphi. ⟨*aside*⟩. *Melos* is wily, and *Learchus* false,
Here is *Pandoraes* ring, and she is mine!
It was a stratagem layde for my loue.   140
O foolish *Iphicles*, what hast thou done?
Must thou betray her vnto *Stesias?*
Pan. ⟨*as if alone*⟩. Here will I sit till I see *Iphicles*,
Sighing my breath, out weeping my heart bloud.
Go, soule, and flye vnto my leefest loue,   145
A fayrer subiect then Elysium.
Iphi. ⟨*aside*⟩. Can I heare this? can I view her? O no!
Pan. But I will view thee, my sweet *Iphicles!*
Thy lookes are physicke, suffer me to gaze,
That for thy sake am thus distempered.   150
Iphi. Pale be my lookes to witnesse my amisse.
Pan. And mine to shew my loue; louers are pale.
Iphi. And so is *Iphicles.*
Pan. And so *Pandora;* let me kisse my loue,
And adde a better couler to his cheekes.   155
Iphi. O bury all thy anger in this kisse,
And mate me not with vttering my offence.
Pan. Who can be angrie with one whom she loues?
Rather had I to haue no thoughts at all,
Then but one ill thought of my *Iphicles:*   160
Go vnto *Stesias* and deny thy words,
For he hath thrust me from his cabanet.
And as I haue done, I will loue thee still:
Delay no time, hast, gentle *Iphicles:*
And meete me on Enipeus sedgy bankes.   165
Iphi. When shall I meet thee? tell me my bright loue.
Pan. At midnight, *Iphicles;* till then farewell!
Iphi. Farewell *Pandora!* Ile to *Stesias.*   *Exit.*

    135 proteruus] proternus *Q* (*turned* u): *hence* protenus *F., who gratuitously transfers* abstulit *to end of this line*   163 And *Q*: For *F.*   165 Enipeus] Enepeus *Q F.*

Pan. Thus will I serue them all; now, *Melos*, come,
   I loue thee too, as much as *Iphicles*.   170

       Enter MELOS ⟨*with the bloody napkin*⟩.

Melos. This is *Pandoraes* blood; hast, *Melos*, hast!
   And in her presence launce thy flesh as deepe:
   Wicked *Learchus*, subtill *Iphicles*:
   You haue vndone me by your reaching wit.
Pan. Gunophilus! where is *Gunophilus*?   175
   Giue me the knife thou pulledst from my brest:
   Melos is gone, and left *Pandora* here;
   Witnesse yee wounds, witnesse yee siluer streames,
   That I am true, to *Melos* onely true,
   And he betrayde me vnto *Stesias*.   180
Melos. Forgiue me, loue, it was not I alone,
   It was *Learchus*, and false *Iphicles*.
Pan. Tis not *Learchus*, nor that *Iphicles*,
   That greeues me, but that *Melos* is vnkinde;
   Melos, for whom *Pandora* straynd her voyce,   185
   Playing with euery letter of his name:
   Melos, for whom *Pandora* made this wounde:
   Melos, for whom *Pandora* now will dye!
Melos. Diuine *Pandora*, stay thy desperat hand!
   May summers lightning burne our Autumne crop,   190
   The thunders teeth plowe vp our fayrest groues,
   The scorching sun-beames dry vp all our springs,
   And ruffe windes blast the beauty of our plaines,
   If *Melos* loue not thee, more then his heart.
Pan. So *Melos* sweares, but tis a louers othe.   195
Melos. Once guiltie, and suspected euermore!
   Ile nere be guiltie more, suspect me not.
Pan. Nor I suspect thee more, mistrust me not:
   Learchus neuer toucht *Pandoraes* lips,
   Nor *Iphicles* receaud a friendly word: 200
   Melos hath al my fauours, and for all
   Doe onely this, and Ile be onely thine.
   Go vnto *Stesias* and deny thy wordes,
   And as the sunne goes downe Ile meete thee heare.

      202 this,] *F. transferred comma from end of preceding line*

Melos. I will *Pandora;* and to cure thy wound, 205
  Receiue these vertuous hearbes which I haue found.
⟨*Exit* MELOS.⟩
Pan. A prety swayne worthy *Pandoraes* loue!
  But I haue written to *Learchus,* I,
  And I will keepe my promise though I dye;
    Enter LEARCHUS *with a letter, and* GUNOPHILUS.
  Which is to cozen him as he did me. 210
Lear. ⟨*reading*⟩. '*Learchus*, my loue *Learchus!*' O the iteration of my name argues her affection. 'Was it my desert? thine, alas! *Pandora.*' It was my destiny to be credulous to these miscreants.
Gun. Looke, looke, she is writing to you agayne. 215
Pan. What, is he come? then shall my tongue declayme.
  Yet am I bashfull and afeard to speake.
Lear. Blush not, *Pandora;* who hath made most fault?
Pan. I that sollicit thee which loues me not.
Lear. I that betrayd thee, which offended not. 220
Pan. Learchus pardon me!
Lear. Pandora pardon mee!
  Gun. ⟨*aside*⟩. All friendes! and so they kist.
Pan. I can but smile to thinke thou wast deceiud.
  Learchus thou must to my husband streight, 225
  And say that thou art sory for thy wordes,
  And in the euening ile meete thee agayne,
  Vnder the same groue where we both sat last.
Lear. I will, *Pandora;* but looke where he comes.
Pan. Then giue me leaue to desemble. 230
  ⟨*Louder*⟩. Tis not thy sorrow that can make amends;
  Were I a man thou shouldst repent thy wordes!
⟨*Enter* STESIAS.⟩
Ste. Learchus will you stand vnto your wordes?
Lear. O, *Stesias!* pardon me: twas their deceite.
  I am sory that I iniurd her. 235
Ste. They lay the fault on thee, and thou on them;
  But take thee that. ⟨*Striking him.*⟩
Pan. Ah, *Stesias*, leaue; you shall not fight for me.

211 [reading] *suppl. F. The quarto prints speech as four lines of verse:* Learchus ... Learchus,—O the ... affection,—Was it ... Pandora,—It was ... miscreants. *Inv. com. suppl. by F.*   213 to² *Q :* on *F.*   224 wast *Q, slightly smeared :* was't *F.*   237 thee so *Q F.*   S. D. [Striking him] *suppl. F.*

Go, goe, *Learchus*, I am *Stesiasses*.
Lear. Art thou? 240
Gun. No, no, *Learchus*, she doth but say so.
Ste. Out of my ground *Learchus*, from my land,
And from hence forward come not neare my lawnes.
Pandora come: *Gunophilus* away! 244
Pan. ⟨*aside to* LEAR.⟩. *Learchus* meete me straight, the time
drawes nigh. ⟨*Exit* PAND. *after* STES. *and* GUN.⟩
Lear. The time draws nigh,—O that the time were now!
I go to meete *Pandora* at the groue. *Exit.*

Enter MELOS.

Melos. When will the sun go downe? flye *Phœbus* flye!
O, that thy steeds were wingd with my swift thoughts:
Now shouldst thou fall in *Thetis* azure armes; 250
And now would I fall in *Pandoraes* lap.

Enter IPHICLES.

Iphi. Wherefore did *Iupiter* create the day?
Sweete is the night when euery creature sleepes.
Come night, come gentle night, for thee I stay.
Melos. Wherefore dooth *Iphicles* desire the night? 255
Iphi. ⟨*starting*⟩. Whose that? *Melos?* thy words did make me
afeard;
I wish for midnight but to take the Wolfe,
Which kils my sheepe, for which I make a snare:
Melos farewell, I must go watch my flocks.
Exit IPHICLES.
Melos. And I my loue! here she will meet me streight. 260
See where she comes, hiding her blushing eyes.

Enter STESIAS *in womans apparell.*

Melos. My loue *Pandora* for whose sake I liue!
Hide not thy beauty which is *Melos* sunne.
Here is none but vs two, lay aside thy vale.
Ste. Here is *Stesias; Melos* you are deceaud. 265
He striketh MELOS.
Melos. Pandora hath deceau'd me, I am vndone! ⟨*Exit.*⟩
Ste. So will not I, syr: I meane simply.
Exit ⟨*pursuing him*⟩.

s. d. Exit IPH. *follows l.* 260 *Q F.*   264 two *F.*: too *Q*

Enter PANDORA *with* GUNOPHILUS.

Pan. Come hast thou all his Iewels and his pearles?
Gun. I, all! but tell me which way shall we go?
Pan. Vnto the sea side, and take shipping streight.   270
   Gun. Well I am reuengd at last of my Maister; I pray God I may be thus euen with all mine enemyes, onely to runne away with their wiues.
Pan. Gunophilus, for thee I haue done this.
   Gun. I, and for your selfe too: I am sure you wil not beg by the way.
Pan. For thee Ile beg and dye *Gunophilus!*
   Gun. I, so I thinke; the world is so hard, that if yee beg yee may be sure to be starud.
Pan. I prythee be not so churlish.   280
   Gun. O this is but myrthe; do you not know
         Comes facetus est tanquam vehiculus in via?
A merry companion is as good as a Wagon, for you shalbe sure to ryde though yee go a foote.
Pan. Gunophilus, setting this mirth aside,   285
   Dost thou not loue me more then all the world?
   Gun. Be you as stedfast to me as Ile be to you, and we two wil goe to the worlds end; and yet we cannot, for the world is round, and seeing tys round, lets daunce in the circle: come, turne about.
⟨*They dance.*⟩
Pan. When I forsake thee, then heauen it selfe shal fall.   290
   Gun. No, God forbid, then perhaps we should haue Larkes.
Exeunt.

Enter STESIAS ⟨*as before*⟩.

Ste. This is Enipeus banke, here she should be.

Enter IPHICLES.

Iphi. What, is it midnight? time hath bene my friend,
   Come sweete *Pandora* all is safe and whist:
   Whither flyes my loue?   295
Ste. Follow me, follow me; here comes *Stesias!*
Iphi. She hath betrayd me: whither shall I flye?
Ste. Eyther to the riuer, or els to thy graue.
            He strikes IPHICLES.

s. d. [as before] *not in* Q F.   Q *has* Enter Stesias, and Iphicles, *repeating* Enter Iphicles *bef. l.* 293   s. d. He strikes IPH. *precedes l.* 298 Q

Enter LEARCHUS.

Lear. The euenings past, yea, midnight is at hand.
And yet *Pandora* comes not at the groue. 300
Ste. But *Stesias* is her deputy, he comes;
And with his shephcoke greetes *Learchus* thus.
He layes about.
Lear. Pardon me *Stesias*, twas *Pandoraes* wiles,
That hath betrayd me; trust her not, she is false. 304
Ste. Why doest thou tell me the contrary? take that; she is honest, but thou wouldst seduce her. Away from my groue, out of my land; did I not giue thee warning?
Exit (driving them out).

ACT. 5.

Enter LUNA.

Lu. Now other planets influence is done,
To *Cynthia* lowest of the erring starres,
Is beautious *Pandora* giuen in charge.
And as I am, so shall *Pandora* bee,
New fangled, fyckle, slothfull, foolish, mad, 5
In spight of *Nature*, that enuies vs all.
⟨*Enter* PANDORA *and* GUNOPHILUS.⟩
Gun. Come, come, *Pandora*, we must make more hast,
Or *Stesias* will ouertake vs both.
Pan. I cannot go no faster, I must rest. ⟨*She lies down.*⟩
Gun. We are almost at the sea side: I pray thee ryse. 10
Pan. O I am faynt and weary, let me sleepe.
Gun. Pandora, if thou loue me, let vs goe.
Pan. Why doest thou waken me? ile remember this.
Gun. What, are you angry with me?
Pan. No, with my selfe for louing such a swayne. 15
What fury made me doate vpon these lookes?
Like winters picture are his withered cheekes,
His hayre as rauens plumes; ah! touch me not!
His handes are like the finnes of some foule fish;

305-7 Why ... warning?] *Q F. print as verse* 'Why ... that,—She ... her.—
Away ... land,—Did ... warning?' 6 nature *Q* 14 What are *Q*

Looke how he mowes, like to an aged ape!
Ouer the chayne, Iacke! or ile make thee leape!
Gun. What a suddayne change is here?
Pan. Now he sweares by his ten bones; downe, I say!
Gun. Did I not tell you I should haue Larkes?
Pan. Where is the larks? come, weel go catch some streight!
No, let vs go a fishing with a net!
With a net? no, an angle is enough:
An angle, a net, no none of both,
Ile wade into the water, water is fayre,
And stroke the fishes vnder neath the gilles.
But first Ile go a hunting in the wood;
I like not hunting; let me haue a hawke.
What wilt thou say and if I loue thee still?
Gun. Any thing, what you will!
Pan. But shall I haue a gowne of oken leaues,
A chaplet of red berries, and a fanne
Made of the morning dewe to coole my face?
How often will you kisse me in an houre?
And where shall we sit till the sunne be downe?
For *Nocte latent mendæ.*
Gun.   What then?
Pan. I will not kisse thee till the sunne be downe;
That art deformd, the nyght will couer thee;
We women must be modest in the day:
O tempt me not vntill the euening come.
Gun.   *Lucretia toto*
    Sis licet vsque die: Thaida nocte volo.
Hate me a dayes, and loue me in the nyght.
Pan. Calst thou me *Thais?* goe, and loue not me;
I am not *Thais,* Ile be *Lucretia,* I;
Giue me a knife, and for my chastety
Ile dye to be canonized a saynt.
Gun. But you will loue me when the sun is downe?
Pan. No, but I will not!
Gun.   Did you not promise me?
Pan. No, I! I saw thee not till now.

---

36 fanne *F.*: *Q turning the* n, faune   39 we *F.*: me *Q*   45-6 Lucretia
toto sis &c.] Lucretiæ tota sis &c. *Q*: Lucretia tota sis &c. *F.—both giving
the whole as one line*   54 No, I! *F.*: No I, *Q, i.e. perh.* No, ay! *but qy.?* Not I!

Gun.   Do you see me now?
Pan. I! and loth thee!
Gun. Belike I was a spirit all this while?
Pan. A spirit! a spirit! whither may I flye?

         Enter STESIAS ⟨*in his own attire*⟩.

Ste. I see *Pandora* and *Gunophilus*.
Pan. And I see *Stesias*; welcome, *Stesias*!
Ste. *Gunophilus*, thou hast inveigled her,
   And robd me of my treasure and my wife.
   Ile strippe thee to the skinne for this offence,
   And put thee in a wood to be deuourd
   Of emptie Tygres, and of hungry Wolues,
   Nor shall thy sad lookes moue me vnto rueth.
Gun. Pardon me, mayster; she is Lunaticke,
   Foolish and franticke, and I followed her,
   Onely to saue the goods and bring her backe:
   Why thinke you I would runne away with her?
Pan. He neede not, for Ile runne away with him;
   And yet I will go home with *Stesias*:
   So I shall haue a white lambe coloured blacke,
   Two little sparrowes, and a spotted fawne.
Ste. I feare it is too true that he reportes.
Gun. Nay, stay a while, and you shall see her daunce.
Pan. No, no, I will not daunce, but I will sing: ⟨*Sings.*⟩

      Stesias hath a white hand,
        But his nayles are blacke;
      His fingers are long and small,
        Shall I make them cracke?
      One, two, and three;
      I loue him, and he loues me.
      Beware of the shephooke;
        Ile tell you one thing,
        If you aske me why I sing,
      I say yee may go looke.

Ste. *Pandora* speake; louest thou *Gunophilus*?
Pan. I, if he be a fish, for fish is fine;
   Sweete *Stesias* helpe me to a whiting moppe.

  60 has *F.*   77 Stesias &c.] *song printed without change of type, and first six lines as three Q F.*   88 is *Q*: are *F.*

Ste. Now I perceiue that she is lunaticke: 90
  What may I do to bring her to her wits?
Gun. Speake, gentle maister, and intreat her fayre.
Ste. *Pandora,* my loue *Pandora!*
Pan. Ile not be fayre; why call you me your loue
  Loue is a little boy, so am not I! 95
Ste. I will allure her with fayre promises;
  And when I haue her in my leauie bower,
  Pray to our water Nimphes and Siluane gods,
  To cure her of this piteous lunacye.
Pan. Giue me a running streame in both my hands, 100
  A blew kings fisher, and a pible stone,
  And Ile catch butter flies vpon the sand,
  And thou *Gunophilus* shalt clippe their wings.
Ste. Ile giue thee streames whose pibble shalbe pearle,
  Loue birdes whose feathers shalbe beaten gold, 105
  Musk flyes with amber berries in their mouthes,
  Milke white Squirrels, singing Popiniayes,
  A boat of deare skins, and a fleeting Ile,
  A sugar cane, and line of twisted silke.
Pan. Where be all these? 110
Ste. I haue them in my bower; come, follow me.
  Pan. Streames with pearles? birdes with golden feathers? Musk flyes, and amber berries? white Squirrels, And singing Popiniayes? a boat of deare skins? Come, Ile goe! Ile go! *Exeunt* ⟨STES. PAND.⟩.
  Gun. I was nere in loue with her till now. O absolute *Pandora!* because folish, for folly is womens perfection. To talke Idely, to loke wildly, to laugh at euery breath and play with a feather, is that would make a Stoyke in loue, yea, thou thy selfe, 118
  O Marce fili annum iam audientem Cratippum idque Athenis.
  Grauity in a woman is like to a gray beard vpon a breaching boies chinne, which a good Scholemaister would cause to be clipt, and the wise husband to be avoyded.

Enter MELOS *and the rest.*

Melos. *Gunophilus,* where is thy Mistresse?
Gun. A ketching a blew kings fisher.

107 Milke *Q*: Musk *F.* 112-4 Streames . . . go!] *as verse Q F.* Streames . . . feathers?—Musk . . . Squirrels,—And . . . deare skins?—Come . . . go. 117 breath] breach *F. misled by battered* t *of Q* 118 selfe. *Q F.* 119 Marce] Marci *Q F.* (*see note*) 119 Athænis *Q* : Athœnis *F.*

Iphi. Tell vs where is she? 125
Gun. A gathering little pibles.
Lear. What! dost thou mocke vs?
Gun. No: but if she were here she would make mowes at the proudest of you.
Melos. What meanest thou by this? 130
Gun. I meane my mistres is become folish.
Iphi. A iust reward for one so false as shee.
Melos. Such hap betide those that intend vs ill.
Lear. Neuer were simple shepherdes so abusd.
Iphi. *Gunophilus* thou hast betrayd vs all. 135
Thou broughtest this ring from her which made me come.
Melos. And thou this bloody napkin vnto me.
Lear. And thou this flattering letter vnto me.
Gun. Why I brought you the ring thinking you and shee should be maried togeather. And being hurt, as she told me, I had thought she had sent for you as a surgeon. 141
Lear. But why broughtest thou me this letter?
Gun. Onely to certifie you that she was in health, as I was at the bringing hereof. And thus being loth to trouble you, I commit you to God. Yours, as his owne, *Gunophilus.* *Exit.*
Melos. The wicked youngling flouteth vs; let him goe! 146
Lear. Immortall *Pan,* where ere this lad remayres,
Reuenge the wrong that he hath done thy swaines.
Melos. O that a creature so diuine as she,
  Whose beauty might inforce the heauens to blush, 150
  And make fayre *Nature* angry at the hart
  That she hath made her to obscure her selfe,
  Should be so fickle and so full of slightes,
  And fayning loue to all, loue none at all.
Iphi. Had she been constant vnto *Iphicles,* 155
  I would haue clad her in sweete *Floraes* roabes:
  Haue set *Dianaes* garland on her head,
  Made her sole mistres of my wanton flocke,
  And sing in honour of her diety,
  Where now with teares I curse *Pandoraes* name. 160
Lear. The springs that smild to see *Pandoraes* face,
  And leapt aboue the bankes to touch her lippes;

143-5 Onely ... Gunophilus] *as verse Q*: Onely ... health,—As I ... hereof. —And thus ... God.—Yours ... Gunophilus.

The proud playnes dauncing with *Pandoraes* weight;
The Iocund trees that vald when she came neare,
And in the murmur of their whispering leaues,   165
Did seeme to say, '*Pandora* is our Queene!'
Witnesse how fayre and beautifull she was,
But now alone how false and treacherous!
Melos. Here I abiure *Pandora*, and protest
To liue for euer in a single life.   170
Lear. The like vow makes *Learchus* to great *Pan*.
Iphi. And *Iphicles;* though soare agaynst his will.
Lear. In witnesse of my vow I rend these lines;—
O thus be my loue disperst into the ayre!
Melos. Here lie the bloody Napkin which she sent,   175
And with it my affection, and my loue.
Iphi. Breake, breake, *Pandoraes* ring; and with it breake
Pandoraes loue, that almost burst my heart.

Enter Stesias, Pandora, *and* Gunophilus.

Ste. Ah whither runnes my loue *Pandora*? stay,
Gentle *Pandora* stay; runne not so fast.   180
Pan. Shall I not stamp vpon the ground? I will!
Who sayth *Pandora* shall not rend her hayre?
Where is the groue that askt me how I did?
Giue me an angle, for the fish will bite.
Melos. Looke how *Pandora* raues! now she is starke mad.   185
Ste. For you she raues, that meant to rauish her;
Helpe to recouer her or els yee dye!
Lear. May she with rauing dye! do what thou darst.
Iphi. She ouer reacht vs with deceitfull guile;
And *Pan*, to whom we prayed, hath wrought reuenge.   190
Pan. Ile haue the Ocean put into a glasse,
And drinke it to the health of *Stesias*.
Thy head is full of hediockes *Iphicles*,
So, shake them of; now let me see thy hand;
Looke where a blasing starre is in this line,   195
And in the other two and twenty sonnes.
Ste. Come, come, *Pandora;* sleepe within my armes.
Pan. Thine armes are firebrandes! whers *Gunophilus*?
Go kisse the eccho, and bid loue vntrusse;

166 *inv. com. first F.*   188 dye? *Q, i.e.* dye! *as usual*: dye; *F.*   190 had *F.*

sc. I]   THE WOMAN IN THE MOONE   285

 Go fetch the blacke Goat with the brazen heele, 200
 And tell the Bell-wether I heare him not.
 Not, not, not, that you should not come vnto me
 This night, not at all, at all, at all. *Dormit.*
Gun. She is a sleepe, mayster; shall I wake her?
Ste. O no *Gunophilus;* there let her sleepe, 205
 And let vs pray that she may be recurd.
Lear. *Stesias* thou pittiest her that loues thee not.
Melos. The wordes we told thee *Stesias* were too true.
Iphi. Neuer did *Iphicles* desemble yet:
 Beleeue me *Stesias* she hath been vntrue. 210
Ste. Yet will you slay me with your slaunderous words?
 Did you not all sweare for her chastety?
Lear. It was her subtle wit that made vs sweare;
 For, *Stesias,* know she shewed loue to vs all,
 And seuerally sent for vs by this swayne. 215
 And vnto me he brought such hony lines,
 As ouercomd, I flew vnto her bower;
 Who, when I came, swore she loud me a lone,
 Willing me to deny the wordes I spoke,
 And she at night would meete me in the groue. 220
 Thus meaning simply, lo! I was betrayd.
Melos. *Gunophilus* brought me a bloody cloth,
 Saying for my loue she was almost slayne;
 And when I came she vsed me as this swaine,
 Protesting loue, and poynting me this place. 225
Iphi. And by this bearer I receiued a ring,
 And many a louing word that drew me foorth.
 O that a woman should desemble so!
 She then forswore *Learchus* and this swaine,
 Saying that *Iphicles* was onely hers; 230
 Whereat I promised to deny my wordes,
 And she to meete me at Enipeus bankes.
Ste. Wert thou the messenger vnto them all?
Gun. I was, and all that they haue sayde is true;
 She loud not you, nor them, but me alone. 235
 How oft hath she runne vp and downe the lawnes,
 Calling aloud—'Where is *Gunophilus?*'

232 Enipeus] Enepius Q F. 235 loud] loue Q : lov'd F. 237 *vnv. com. first F.*

Ste. ⟨*aside*⟩. Ah! how my hart swels at these miscreants wordes!
Melos. Come let vs leaue him in this pensiue mood.
Lear. Fret, *Stesias*, fret; while we daunce on the playne. 240
Melos. Such fortune happen to incredulus swaines.
Iphi. Sweete is a single life; *Stesias* farewell.
       Exeunt ⟨IPH. MEL. *and* LEAR.⟩.
Ste. Go life, flye soule; go, wretched *Stesias!*
 Curst be Vtopia for *Pandoraes* sake!
 Let wild bores with their tuskes plow vp my lawnes, 245
 Deuouring Wolues come shake my tender lambes,
 Driue vp my goates vnto some steepy rocke,
 And let them fall downe headlong in the sea.
 She shall not liue, nor thou *Gunophilus*,
 To triumph in poore *Stesias* ouerthrow. 250

    Enter the seauen Planets.

Sat. Stay shepherd, stay!
Jup. Hurt not *Pandora*, louely *Stesias*.
    She awakes and is sober.
Pan. What meanes my loue, to looke so pale and wan?
Ste. For thee, base strumpet, am I pale and wanne.
Mer. Speake mildly, or Ile make thee, crabbed swaine! 255
Sol. Take her agayne, and loue her, *Stesias*.
Ste. Not for Vtopia! no, not for the world!
Venus. Ah! canst thou frowne on her that lookes so sweet?
Pan. Haue I offended thee? Ile make amends.
Mer. And what canst thou demaund more at her hand? 260
Ste. To slay her selfe, that I may liue alone.
Luna. Flint harted shepherd, thou deseruest her not.
Ste. If thou be *Ioue*, conuey her from the earth,
 And punish this *Gunophilus* her man.
 Gun. O *Ioue!* let this be my punishment, to liue still with
Pandora. 266
    Enter NATURE.

Nat. Enuious planets, you haue done your worst.
 Yet in despight of you *Pandora* liues;
 And seeing the shepherds haue abiurd her loue,
 She shalbe placed in one of your seauen orbs. 270
 But thou that has not serud her as I wild,

    262 deserveth *F.*

  Vanish into a Haythorne as thou standst,
Neare shalt thou wait vpon *Pandora* more.
Exit GUNOPHILUS.

Sat. O *Nature!* place *Pandora* in my sphere,
 For I am old, and she will make me young.   275
Jup. With me! and I will leaue the Queene of heauen.
Mars. .With me! and *Venus* shall no more be mine.
Sol. With me! and Ile forget fayre *Daphnes* loue.
Venus. With me! and ile turne *Cupid* out of doores.
Mer. With me! and ile forsake *Aglauros* loue.   280
Luna. No! fayre *Pandora*, stay with *Cynthia*,
 And I will loue thee more then all the rest:
 Rule thou my starre, while I stay in the woods,
 Or keepe with *Pluto* in the infernall shades.
Ste. Go where thou wilt so I be rid of thee.   285
Nat. Speake, my *Pandora* ; where wilt thou be ⟨placed⟩?
Pan. Not with old *Saturne* for he lookes like death.
 Nor yet with *Iupiter*, least *Iuno* storme;
 Nor with thee *Mars*, for *Venus* is thy loue;
 Nor with thee *Sol*, thou hast two Parramours,   290
 The sea borne *Thetis* and the rudy morne.
 Nor with thee *Venus*, least I be in loue
 With blindfold *Cupid* or young *Ioculus ;*
 Nor with thee *Hermes*, thou art full of slightes,
 And when I need thee *Ioue* will send thee foorth.   295
 Say *Cynthia*, shall *Pandora* rule thy starre,
 And wilt thou play *Diana* in the woods,
 Or *Hecate* in *Plutos* regiment?
Luna. I, *Pandora!*
Pan. Fayre *Nature* let thy hand mayd dwell with her,   300
 For know that change is my felicity,
 And ficklenesse *Pandoraes* proper forme.
 Thou madst me sullen first, and thou *Ioue*, proud;
 Thou bloody minded ; he a Puritan :
 Thou *Venus* madst me loue all that I saw,   305
 And *Hermes* to deceiue all that I loue ;
 But *Cynthia* made me idle, mutable,
 Forgetfull, foolish, fickle, franticke, madde ;

---

277 Mars. *F.*: Mer. *Q*   286 placed *required by metre*   291 seabore *F.*   308 Forgetfull *misplaced at the end of preceding line Q F.*

These be the humors that content me best,
And therefore will I stay with *Cynthia*.

Nat. And *Stesias* since thou setst so light on her,
Be thou her slaue, and follow her in the Moone.

Ste. Ile rather dye then beare her company!

Jup. *Nature* will haue it so, attend on her.

Nat. Ile haue thee be her vassaile, murmur not.

Ste. Then, to reuenge me of *Gunophilus*,
Ile rend this hathorne with my furious hands,
And beare this bush; if eare she looke but backe,
Ile scratch her face that was so false to me.

Nat. Now rule, *Pandora*, in fayre *Cynthias* steede,
And make the moone inconstant like thy selfe;
Raigne thou at womens nuptials, and their birth;
Let them be mutable in all their loues,
Fantasticall, childish, and folish, in their desires,
Demaunding toyes:
And starke madde when they cannot haue their will.
Now follow me ye wandring lightes of heauen,
And grieue not, that she is not plast with you;
All you shall glaunce at her in your aspects,
And in coniunction dwell with her a space.

Ste. O that they had my roome!

Nat. I charge thee follow her, but hurt her not.

⟨*Exeunt.*⟩

Finis.

326 And starke madde *placed as completion of preceding line* Q F. *This rare irregularity suggests the loss of some words*   329 All Q: And F.

LOVES METAMORPHOSIS

EDITIONS

'43 Regine. 25 Novembris 1600 william wood Entred for his Copie vnder the handes of Master Pasfeild and the wardens A booke Called Loves metamorphesis wrytten by master John Lylly and playd by the Children of Paules . . vj^d.' *Stationers' Register,* iii. 176 (ed. Arb.).

Q. *Loves Meta-|morphosis. | A | Wittie and Courtly | Pastorall, | Written by | Mr. Iohn Lyllie. | First playd by the Children of Paules, and now | by the Children of the Chappell. | London | Printed for William Wood, dwelling at the West end of | Paules, at the signe of Time .* 1601. | 4to. A (verso blank), B–F 4 in fours, G (verso blank). No col. (Br. Mus.: Bodl.: Magd. Coll. Camb.: Dyce Coll S. Kensing.)

Not included among the *Sixe Covrt Comedies*, its second publication being that of Fairholt's edition of the *Dramatic Works,* vol. ii. 1858.

LOVES METAMORPHOSIS

Argument.—Erisichthon, a wealthy farmer, jealous of honours paid to Ceres by her nymphs, destroys a tree sacred to the goddess; and in so doing kills another nymph of Ceres, Fidelia, who has found protection in that shape from the pursuit of a satyr. Ceres in revenge commissions Famine to prey on the offender, who is speedily reduced by his insatiable hunger to poverty, and sells his daughter, Protea, to a merchant. Her appeal to Neptune enables her to elude her purchaser in the form of a fisherman; and by a second transformation to the likeness of Ulysses she rescues her lover, and father's benefactor, Petulius, from the dangerous fascinations of a Siren. Meantime Ceres' three nymphs, Nisa, Celia, and Niobe, to whose information the farmer owed his punishment, have themselves incurred the displeasure of Cupid by disdainful treatment of three admiring foresters; and at the latters' request the god transforms them respectively into a rock, a rose, and a bird. Ceres' petition for their release is used by Cupid to extort from her the pardon of Erisichthon, whose daughter's faithful love has given her a claim on his protection. The nymphs recover their shape on condition of their acceptance of the amorous foresters, and the wedding-feast is held at Erisichthon's house.

Text.—I follow the original quarto edition of 1601, which has few serious errors, the chief being pp. 303, 'constancie' for 'inconstancie,' 305 'Miretia' for 'Mirrha,' 325 'fames' for 'formes,' 330 'Nisa' for 'Niobe,' and one or two scenes misnumbered. The fourteen Latin quotations are given with unusual accuracy: probably the author gave more personal attention to the printing. But there is the same paucity of stage-directions, due probably to the fact that he himself supervised its production and instructed the actors by word of mouth; while to a similar cause may be assigned (Essay, vol. ii. 265) the loss of the four songs, indicated in i. 2 the Nymphs, iii. 1 Niobe and Silvestris, and iv. 2 two by the Siren.

Fairholt's text, escaping in this instance the unfortunate intervention of Blount, who does not include the play in the *Sixe Covrt Comedies*, is much better than usual. It corrects the mistake on p. 325, and the numbering of the scenes, and it sometimes emends the punctuation: but it leaves the other errors unrepaired; it omits half a line p. 321, a speech of Petulius p. 328, and 'take' on p. 331; it introduces some half-dozen stupid mis-spellings, and some other errors, e.g. pp. 311 'No' for 'Not,' 314 'garland' for 'garlands,' 318 'fond' for 'found,' 329 'And' for 'Are'; and it fails to supply some needed stage-directions, though those required for iii. 1 and iv. 2 are suggested in a note.

Authorship.—Lyly's authorship is proved by his own name, and those of the two Children's companies with which he was connected, on the title-page; by the generally euphuistic character of the speeches (cf. i. 1, i. 2 p. 305, iv. 1 pp. 319–20, v. 1 p. 325, v. 3, v. 4 p. 329), by ten distinct echoes of *Euphues* itself (given in the notes), and by the ample use made of his favourite Latin poet Ovid.

Sources.—For the somewhat slender scaffolding which, in virtue of its prior introduction and the larger share of dialogue allotted to it, pretends to the position of main plot—that, namely, which deals with the loves of Ceres' nymphs and the three foresters—Lyly seems to have had no other source than his own invention; though the same book of the *Metamorphoses*, from which he drew the by-plot, contains transformations of Nisus into a bird, of Naiads into islands, and of Philemon and Baucis into trees, while Bk. vi. 146–312 relates that of 'Niobe in marmor [1].' In the by-plot, which is interwoven with considerable skill, he follows very closely Ovid's *Metamorphoses*, viii. 738–878. There we read how Erisichthon, jealous of Ceres' honours, attacks her sacred oak, hung with garlands 'memoresque tabellae,' under which 'Dryades festas duxere choreas' (cf. i. 1 and 2). The blows of his axe are followed by a flow of blood and a voice from an unnamed nymph of Ceres confined in the tree, who at the moment of her death prophesies Erisichthon's punishment. Ceres, informed

[1] See, however, what is said about a possible suggestion for Nisa and her transformation in Sannazarro's *Eclogae Piscatoriae* and Boccaccio's *Ameto*, below, p. 295.

by the Dryads, devises his destruction by Famine, the allegorical description of whom is almost verbally copied by Lyly:

> Quae quatenus ipsi
> Non adeunda Deae (neque enim Cereremque Famemque
> Fata coire sinunt), montani numinis unam
> Talibus agrestem compellat, Oreada, dictis:
> Est locus extremis Scythiae glacialis in oris,
> Triste solum, sterilis, sine fruge, sine arbore, tellus;
> Frigus iners illic habitant, Pallorque, Tremorque,
> Et ieiuna Fames: ea se in praecordia condat
> Sacrilegi scelerata, iube: nec copia rerum
> Vincat eam; superetque meas certamine vires.

The Oread (unnamed by Ovid, 'Tirtena' in Lyly—from 'Tirrena' in Sannazarro's *Arcadia*?) obeys:

> Quaesitamque Famem lapidoso vidit in agro,
> Vnguibus, et raras vellentem dentibus herbas.
> Hirtus erat crinis; caua lumina; pallor in ore;
> Labra incana situ; scabri rubigine dentes;
> Dura cutis, per quam spectari viscera possent;
> Ossa sub incuruis extabant arida lumbis;
> Ventris erat pro ventre locus: pendere putares
> Pectus, et a spinae tantummodo crate teneri.
> Auxerat articulos macies, genuumque rigebat
> Orbis, et immodico prodibant tubere tali.
> Hanc procul ut vidit (neque enim est accedere iuxta [cf. Act ii. sc. 1.
> Ausa) refert mandata Deae; &c.   l. 32].

As in Lyly Erisichthon exhausts his patrimony in the endeavour to assuage his hunger, and finally sells his daughter (Metra, unnamed by Ovid, who merely calls her 'Autolyci coniux'):

> Tandem, demisso in viscera censu,
> Filia restabat, non illo digna parente.
> Hanc quoque vendit inops. Dominum *generosa* recusat; [cf.
>   Protea's 'Gentleman,' &c. iii. 2. 41].
> Et vicina suas tendens super aequora palmas,
> Eripe me domino, qui raptae praemia nobis
> Virginitatis habes, ait. (Haec Neptunus habebat.)
> Qui prece non spreta, quamuis modo visa sequenti
> Esset hero [i.e. domino], formamque nouat, vultumque virilem
> Induit, et cultus piscem capientibus aptos:

in which shape she eludes her purchaser's inquiries, and returns to her father.

Lyly is original only in making Erisichthon a farmer, in the motive of a satyr's pursuit for the change of Fidelia into a tree, in the names Protea (borrowed from the transformations of Proteus summarized by Ovid just before, l. 730-7) and Petulius (for Ovid's 'Autolycus'), whom he represents as Protea's suitor and her father's benefactor, rather than as her husband, and in the pardon accorded to Erisichthon, who in Ovid perishes by devouring his own flesh: little changes subserving the purpose of dramatic unity. Also, for variety's sake and to give Protea opportunity for a new transformation, he adds the Siren, suggested perhaps by their conjunction with Ceres in *Metamorph.* v. 557-63[1] and Hyginus' *Fable CXLI*, where 'Cereris voluntate, quod Proserpinae auxilium non tulerant, volaticae sunt factae'; mingling the classical conception with the Teutonic and Northern superstition of mermaids, just as in *The Woman in the Moone* he mingles the classical divinities with the mediaeval notion of planetary influence.

I have exhibited his debt to Ovid thus fully because of the natural temptation to connect the play rather with Spenser's *Faerie Queene*, the first three books of which appeared in 1590. The striking incident of Fidelia bears considerable resemblance to that of Fradubio and Fraclissa, borrowed from Ariosto in Bk. i, canto 2[2]; while the description of Famine might be modelled on Spenser's similar pictures of Idleness, Gluttony, Wrath, &c., in Bk. i, c. 4, or on those of Doubt, Danger, Fear, &c., in the masque of Cupid, Bk. iii, c. 12; though Spenser's whole poem contains no specific description of Famine like that in Lyly's play. In the *Quarterly Review* for Jan. 1896[3], I suggested that Lyly might have founded the latter on some stanzas in Sackville's Induction to *The Mirrour for Magistrates*, quoted in the notes. But the extracts from Ovid given above leave no doubt that he, and not Spenser nor Sackville, was Lyly's true original in this description. In two points, however, Fidelia's speech does seem to me to indicate a knowledge of Spenser's Third Book; the idea, namely, not in Ovid, of Fidelia's attempted rape by a satyr (cf. *F. Q.* iii. c. 10), and the mention together (i. 2, p. 305) of Daphne and Myrrha as instances of flight, two cases hardly parallel, which Spenser also combines:

[1] Or perhaps by the allusions to them in Sannazarro's *Eclogae Piscatoriae*: cf. below, p. 295.
[2] For the transformation into a tree, of which Lyly has two other instances, some example was afforded by Gascoigne's show in the *Princely Pleasures of Kenilworth*, 1576; cf. vol. ii. p. 477, note 5.
[3] Article *John Lyly: Novelist and Dramatist*, p. 133.

> Not halfe so fast the wicked Myrrha fled
> From dread of her revenging father's hond;
> Nor halfe so fast to save her maydenhed
> Fled fearfull Daphne on th' Aegean strond,
> As Florimell fled, &c. *F. Q.* iii. 7. 26.

Under this head of sources should be mentioned the close connexion of this play in subject and treatment with the earlier pastoral *Gallathea*. Both celebrate the triumph of true love over a false ideal of chastity which declines and mocks at marriage[1]. The stuff of both consists in great part of the relations between a presiding goddess (Diana or Ceres) and her nymphs, who become subject to the power of Cupid; and there is accordingly the same conceited dialogue on the subject of love (cf. *Gall.* i. 2, iv. 2 with *Loves Met.* ii. 2, iv. 1). If that in the later play shows as a fainter reflection of the former, yet Nisa's spirited exposure of poetic fictions on the subject (p. 308) affords us compensation. In two passages our play actually alludes to *Gallathea*, as has been pointed out in the one case by Steinhäuser, in the other by Fleay[2]. Then we have the same angry figure in the background (Neptune or Erisichthon) to serve as moving cause of the action; the same idea of filial sacrifice by reluctant parents and of the evasion thereof: the same introduction of a genuine tragic note in Hæbe and Fidelia, neither of whom is dramatically essential; the same solution by a compromise between rival deities; the same general idea of locality, woods near a seacoast, and especially, the same tree occupying a conspicuous position on the stage and often referred to; and even the same series of musical puns (cf. iii. 1. 122–7 with *Gall.* v. 3. 188–93). But the play is far from being a mere repetition. The attitude towards love of Ceres and her nymphs, respectively, is almost a reversal of that of Diana and hers: and Cupid is no longer a petulant boy, playing truant, making mischief, caught and punished for it; but a great god with a temple at which Ceres offers homage, and wielding a dread power of physical punishment. Here too, if there is no

---

[1] '"Gallathea" und "Love's Metamorphosis" können als allegorische Verherrlichung des Sieges wahrer Liebe über die falsche Keuschheit bezeichnet werden, welche auch die Ehe für verwerflich hält, und deren—wenigstens öffentliche—Hauptvertreterin in England Elisabeth war' (Steinhäuser, *John Lily als Dramatiker*, p. 21).

[2] Act ii. sc. 1. l. 77: 'Diana's Nymphes were as chast as Ceres virgines, as faire, as wise: how Cupid tormented them, I had rather you should heare then feele; but this is truth, they all yeelded to loue.' Act v. sc. 1. ll. 18–9: 'Diana hath felt some motions of loue, Vesta doth, Ceres shall.'

comic element, the by-plot is far better interwoven with the main action, and may boast a greater variety in itself.

Lastly, just as *Gallathea* and the pastoral scenes in *Midas* may owe something to Sannazarro's *Arcadia*, so this play may confess, perhaps, a hint or two from his *Eclogae Piscatoriae*, in the introduction of a Siren (they are associated with Sannazarro's scene, the Naples coast) and consequently of Ulysses, and in the stony-hearted Nisa's transformation; e. g. cf. v. 4. 68 and 116 with

> Sirenes, mea cura, audite haec ultima vota.
> Aut revocet iam Nisa suum, nec spernat Iolam,
> Aut videat morientem. Haec saxa impulsa marinis
> Fluctibus, haec misero vilis dabit alga sepulchrum. (*Ecl.* iii. 50–3.)

Boccaccio's *Ameto* has, in the story of Acrimonia, faint suggestions of Lyly's nymphs and their punishment, and of Protea's proposed voyage. See note, vol. ii. pp. 473 sqq.

Date.—The date is perhaps harder to fix than that of any other play of Lyly. Could we judge simply by the year of its publication, we should have to regard it as much the latest, written and produced a year or two before November, 1600; for it is not entered on the Stationers' Register till November 25, 1600, and not issued till the following year. But a difficulty occurs in the statement of the Register, repeated on the title-page, that it had been played by the Paul's Boys. This company was suspended from acting, temporarily perhaps in the autumn of 1589 (see note on *Pappe*, ad med.), but permanently before October 4, 1591, when three of its plays are entered for publication: and Collier considers the suspension to have lasted till about 1600[1]. The title-page says it was 'first playd by the Children of Paules, and now [i.e. 1601] by the Children of the Chappell.' The latter company were under inhibition probably from 1583 till 1597, when a new writ was issued to Nathaniel Giles, their master, to take up boys for the chapel service, which must be understood as including the removal of the prohibition on their acting[2]. There seem, then, prima facie grounds for supposing that

---

[1] *History of Dramatic Poetry*, i. 272.
[2] The wording of these writs to choir-masters nowhere contemplates a dramatic function for the boys so 'taken up'; but from the very interesting petition, published in the *Athenaeum* for Aug. 10, 1889, by Mr. James Greenstreet and printed by Mr. Fleay, it seems clear that the Queen winked at the practice of so employing them. See Fleay's *History of the Stage*, pp. 126 sqq., where Giles, Robinson, and Evans, against whose proceedings the petition protests, are stated to have said that 'yf the Queene ... would not beare them furth in that accion [of practically kidnapping boys, who were not musical, simply to turn them into actors], she

the Paul's Boys first produced the play before 1591, and that the Chapel Children after the removal of their inhibition revived it in 1598–1600. True, the Stationers' Register (November 25, 1600) only names the Paul's Boys in connexion with it; and as there seems no good reason why these should not have recommenced acting as early as 1599—the printing of *The Maydes Metamorphosis* in 1600 'as it hath bene sundrie times Acted by the Children of Powles' favours the idea—they may have played it in 1599 or early in 1600, before transferring it to the Chapel Children[1]. But strong arguments for a much earlier date exist in the markedly euphuistic character of the dialogue, far more noticeable than in *Midas* or *Mother Bombie*; in a reference to 'Ceres and her sacred Nymphes' in *The Woman*, iii. 1. 50, which was entered for publication in 1595; and in the general connexion of subject and treatment which unites the three plays *Sapho and Phao*, *Gallathea*, and *Loves Metamorphosis*, in all of which Cupid plays a prominent part, while there are references in *Gallathea* to *Sapho*, and in *Loves Metamorphosis* to *Gallathea*. Mr. Baker[2] even considers this connexion ground for placing the composition of the play before 1584, i.e. before the earlier inhibition of the Paul's Boys, though he doubts if it was acted then. But there seems no cogent reason why plays connected in subject or treatment should be written in immediate succession: and though the points of connexion enumerated under 'Sources' prove it subsequent to *Gallathea*, the very number and close resemblance of these points, especially the series of musical puns, make against its immediate succession; for Lyly, of all authors, would shun the charge of poverty of invention. Mr. Fleay's opinion, that it was acted at Court by the Paul's Boys 'no doubt in 1588–9[3],' escapes this objection; and might find a vague support in the record in the Council Registers, quoted by Chalmers[4], of a payment on March 23, 1588–9, of £30 to Thomas Giles, master of the Paul's Boys, 'for sundry plays in the Christmas holydays.' Mr. Fleay further considers that it was revived by the Chapel Children *circ.* 1529 before the Paul's Boys recommenced.

I believe we may accept, roughly, Mr. Fleay's dates. But I find

should gett another to execute her commission for them' (p. 130); and 'were yt not for the benefit they made by the sayd play howse [Blackfriars], whoe would should serve the Chappell wth childeren for them' (p. 131).

[1] See vol. i, Life, pp. 72–4.
[2] Introduction to his edition of *Endymion*, p. xcviii.
[3] *Biographical Chronicle*, ii. 41.
[4] Boswell's *Malone's Shakespeare*, iii. 425.

strong reason for supposing that the play as revived, whether by the Paul's or Chapel Children, was an alteration from that originally produced. (1) Firstly, it is remarkable for its brevity, caused by the absence of the farcical element found in all the other plays. It is quite possible that such element existed in the earlier form, and that it contained some matter, perhaps of Anti-Martinist tendency, which was sufficient to prevent the play obtaining its licence for printing along with *Endimion*, *Gallathea*, and *Midas* in 1591, but which was excised before its revival. Compare, too, the 'thicke mist' of iv. 1. 109 (see note ad loc.); also Tirtena in v. 1, p. 324. (2) Secondly, it is unlikely that the last twelve years of Lyly's life (ob. 1606) should have been quite unoccupied with dramatic work[1]; and it exhibits an improved skill in dramatic construction—it is better woven than any except *Mother Bombie*, and of more varied interest than any—and a more evident effort to give characteristic distinction to the individual members of the groups of nymphs and foresters than is noticeable in earlier work. (3) Thirdly, there are the points of connexion with the *Faerie Queene* (Bk. iii, published 1590) which I have noted under 'Sources.' (4) Fourthly, I would suggest the possibility of allegorical allusion in Erisichthon to Elizabeth's relations with her favourite Essex. That the Queen is represented in the person of Ceres has been generally allowed. Her attitude towards love is here largely modified from that of Diana in *Gallathea*; but even here we get a reflection of the old jealousy of marriage without her consent in v. 4. 12—'You might haue made me a counsell of your loues,' and 20-2, which probably allude to Southampton's stolen match with Elizabeth Vernon, her maid of honour, in 1598. The Queen's displeasure was enhanced by Essex's appointment of Southampton to be General of the Horse in Ireland in 1599; and I think it very possible that in Erisichthon, so ungrateful for the bounty Ceres has showered upon him, we have allusion to Essex himself, and his presumptuous attitude towards the Queen in 1598, 1599, and 1600[2]. (5) Lastly, revival of *Loves Metamorphosis* in a revised form, and especially without a previously existing farcical element, would be consistent with an allusion in the Induction to Jonson's *Cynthia's Revels*, produced by the Chapel Children in the same year

---

[1] I find, later, that there was probably some masque-work within this period.

[2] Compare, especially, Elizabeth's saying, in regard to the monopoly of sweet wines for which Essex in 1600 sought a renewal, that 'an ungovernable Beast must be stinted in his provender, that he may be the better manag'd' (Camden's Annals of Eliz. 1600, in the fol. *Hist. of Eng.* ii. p. 626).

—'the *umbrae* or ghosts of some three or four plays departed a dozen years since, have been seen walking on your stage here,' &c.

I consider, then, that an earlier form of the play was produced by the Paul's Boys in 1586–8; that it was revived by them in its present form in 1599 or early in 1600, and transferred to the Chapel Children before the year was far advanced.

Place and Time.—The number of scenes cannot be reduced below three: 1. At Ceres' Tree. 2. Before Cupid's Temple. 3. Seashore near Erisichthon's Farm. The distinction between these is shown in iv. 1, p. 320, where the foresters, in front of Cupid's Temple, discuss whether they shall go to look for the nymphs at Ceres' Tree, or visit Erisichthon; and again in v. 1, p. 325, where Ceres leaves Cupid's Temple to fetch Erisichthon. This distinction of the localities involves one imaginary transfer in the middle of Act ii—a single scene, at the commencement of which Ceres is lamenting over her fallen tree, but proposes, p. 307, to visit Cupid's Temple, and after some talk, during which they are supposed to be proceeding thither, remarks p. 308 'This is the temple.' Compare, too, iii. 1. 150–7 ' Here is the tree.' Several similar transfers occurred in *Campaspe* (see *Place and Time* in the introduction to that play), one in *Endimion*, Act iv. 3, pp. 60–1, and one in *The Woman*, Act iv.

As regards Time, the action of the play requires at least several days to allow for the operation of famine on Erisichthon, the sale of his goods, p. 315, the appointment of 'day' and 'hower' with the Merchant, p. 316, Petulius' aid mentioned iv. 2. 37, and the revenge of the foresters on the nymphs. The intervals should be arranged to fall between the Acts, and some time may consistently be supposed to elapse between Acts i and ii, and Acts ii and iii: yet though the adventure of Protea with the Merchant, and the infliction and repentance of their revenge by the foresters, require some time, the last three Acts are represented as continuous—Acts iii and iv being connected by the visit to Cupid announced iii. 1, and carried out in iv. 1, while Acts iv and v are placed in close connexion by the 'straunge discourse' of Protea, begun iv. 2. 100, and just concluded v. 2, p. 325. So that in this, as in preceding plays, especially *Midas*, there is visible an attempt at close continuity of action irreconcileable with the lapse of time which the plot requires, a circumstance which, when contrasted with the greater care exercised in *Mother Bombie* and *The Woman*, constitutes yet another argument for an early date.

LOVES META-
MORPHOSIS.

A Wittie and Courtly Pastorall,

WRITTEN BY
Mr. Iohn Lyllie.

First playd by the Children of Paules, and now by the Children of the Chappell.

LONDON
Printed for William Wood, dwelling at the West end of Paules, at the signe of Time. 1601.

⟨DRAMATIS PERSONÆ.

CUPID.
RAMIS,   ⎫ Foresters   ⎧ Nisa.
MONTANUS, ⎬ in love, re- ⎨ Celia.
SILVESTRIS, ⎭ spectively, with ⎩ Niobe.
ERISICHTHON, *a churlish Husbandman.*   5
PETULIUS, *in love with Protea.*
Merchant.
CERES.
NISA,   ⎫
CELIA,   ⎬ *Nymphs of Ceres.*   10
NIOBE,   ⎪
TIRTENA,   ⎭
FIDELIA, *a Nymph of Ceres transformed into a Tree.*
PROTEA, *Daughter to Erisichthon.*
Siren.   15
          SCENE—*Arcadia.*⟩

DRAM. PERS.] *list supplied by F., whom I follow with but trifling change*
SCENE—Arcadia] *suppl. F.*

LOUES METAMORPHOSIS

⟨ACTUS PRIMUS.

Scæna Prima.—*At Ceres' Tree.*⟩

⟨*Enter*⟩ Ramis, Montanus, Siluestris.

⟨*Ramis.*⟩ I Cannot see, *Montanus,* why it is fain'd by the Poets, that Loue sat vpon the Chaos and created the world ; since in the world there is so little loue.

Mon. *Ramis,* thou canst not see that which cannot with reason
5 be imagined; for if the diuine vertues of Loue had disperst themselues through the powers of the world so forcibly as to make them take by his influence the formes and qualities imprest within them, no doubt they could not cause but sauour more of his Diuinitie.

Sil. I doe not thinke Loue hath any sparke of Diuinitie in him ;
10 since the end of his being is earthly. In the bloud he is begot by the fraile fires of the eye, & quencht by the frayler shadowes of thought. What reason haue we then to soothe his humor with such zeale, and folow his fading delights with such passion ?

Ramis. We haue bodies, *Siluestris,* and humane bodies ; which
15 in their owne natures being much more wretched then beastes, doe much more miserably then beasts pursue their owne ruines : And since it will aske longer labour and studie to subdue the powers of our bloud to the rule of the soule, then to satisfie them with the fruition of our loues, let vs bee constant in the worlds errours, and
20 seeke our owne torments.

Mon. As good yeeld indeed submissiuely, and satisfie part of our affections ; as bee stubburne without abilitie to resist, and enioy none of them. I am in worst plight, since I loue a Nymph that mockes loue.

---

s. d. Act I. Scene I. *supplied F. The division into Acts and Scenes is that of the quarto and F. The localities of the several scenes are first marked in this edition* 1 [Ramis] *supplied F.*

Ramis. And I one that hates loue.

Sil. I, one that thinkes her selfe aboue loue.

Ramis. Let vs not dispute whose mistris is most bad, since they be all cruell; nor which of our fortunes be most froward, since they bee all desperate. I will hang my Skutchin on this tree in honour of *Ceres*, and write this verse on the tree in hope of my successe. *Penelopen ipsam perstes modo tempore vinces.* *Penelope* will yeeld at last: continue and conquer.

Mon. I this: *Fructus abest facies cum bona teste caret.* Faire faces lose their fauours, if they admit no louers.

Ramis. But why studiest thou? What wilt thou write for thy Lady to read?

Sil. That which necessitie maketh me to indure, loue reuerence, wisdome wonder at. *Riualem patienter habe.*

Mon. Come, let vs euerie one to our walkes, it may be we shall meete them walking.   *Exeunt.*

SCENA SECVNDA.—⟨*The same.*⟩

NISA, CELIA, NIOBE, FIDELIA, ERISICTHON.

⟨*Enter* NISA, CELIA, NIOBE.⟩

Nisa. It is time to hang vp our Garlands, this is our haruest holyday, wee must both sing and daunce in the honour of *Ceres:* of what colours or flowers is thine made of, *Niobe?*

Niobe. Of Salamints, which in the morning are white, red at noone, and in the Euening purple, for in my affections shall there be no staiednesse but in vnstaiednes: but what is yours of, *Nisa?*

Nisa. Of Hollie, because it is most holy, which louely greene neither the Sunnes beames, nor the winds blasts can alter or diminish. But, *Celia,* what Garland haue you?

Celia. Mine all of Cypres leaues, which are broadest and beautifullest, yet beareth the least fruit; for beautie maketh the brightest shew, being the slightest substance; and I am content to wither before I bee worne, and depriue my selfe of that which so many desire.

Niobe. Come, let vs make an end, lest *Ceres* come and find vs slacke in performing that which wee owe. But soft, some haue beene here this Morning before vs.

31 perstes *foll. by comma* Q F.

Nisa. The amorous Foresters, or none; for in the woods they haue eaten so much wake-Robin, that they cannot sleepe for loue.

Celia. Alas poore soules, how ill loue sounds in their lips, who telling a long tale of hunting, thinke they haue bewray'd a sad passion of loue!

Niobe. Giue them leaue to loue, since we haue libertie to chuse, for as great sport doe I take in coursing their tame hearts, as they doe paines in hunting their wilde Harts.

Celia. Niobe, your affection is but pinned to your tongue, which when you list you can vnloose. But let vs read what they haue written: *Penelopen ipsam perstes modo tempore vinces.* That is for you Nisa, whome nothing will mooue, yet hope makes him houer.

Nisa. A fond Hobbie to houer ouer an Eagle.

Niobe. But Forresters thinke all Birds to be Buntings. What's the next? *Fructus abest facies cum bona teste caret.* Celia, the Forrester giues you good counsel, take your penniworth whiles the market serues.

Celia. I hope it will be market day till my deathes day.

Nisa. Let me read to. *Riualem patienter habe.* Hee toucheth you, Niobe, on the quicke, yet you see how patient he is in your inconstancie.

Niobe. Inconstancie is a vice, which I will not swap for all the vertues; though I throwe one off with my whole hand, I can pull him againe with my little finger; let vs encourage them, and write something; if they censure it fauourably, we know them fooles; if angerly, we wil say they are froward.

Nisa. I will begin. *Cedit amor rebus, res age, tutus eris.*

Celia. Indeed better to tell stars then be idle, yet better idle then ill employed. Mine this: *Sat mihi si facies, sit bene nota mihi.*

Niobe. You care for nothing but a Glasse, that is, a flatterer.

Nisa. Then all men are Glasses.

Celia. Some Glasses are true.

Niobe. No men are; but this is mine: *Victoria tecum stabit.*

Nisa. Thou giuest hope.

Niobe. He is worthy of it, that is patient.

Celia. Let vs sing, and so attend on *Ceres;* for this day, although into her heart neuer entred any motion of loue, yet vsually to the Temple of *Cupid,* shee offereth two white Doues, as entreating his

fauour, and one Eagle, as commaunding his power. *Præcibusq,*
minas regaliter addet. *Cantant & Saltant.*

⟨*Enter* ERISICHTHON.⟩

Eris. What noyse is this, what assembly, what Idolatrie? Is the
modestie of virgins turnd to wantonnesse? The honour of *Ceres*
accompted immortal? And *Erisicthon* ruler of this Forrest, esteemed 60
of no force? Impudent giglots that you are, to disturb my game,
or dare doe honour to any but *Erisicthon.* It is not your faire faces
as smooth as Ieate, nor your entysing eyes, though they drew yron
like Adamants, nor your filed speeches, were they as forcible as
Thessalides, that shall make me any way flexible. 65

Niobe. *Erisicthon,* thy sterne lookes ioynd with thy stout speeches,
thy words as vnkembd as thy lockes, were able to affright men of
bold courage, and to make vs silly girles franticke, that are full of
feare; but knowe thou, *Erisicthon,* that were thy hands so vnstaied
as thy tongue, and th' one as ready to execute mischiefe as the other 70
to threaten it, it should neither moue our hearts to aske pittie, or
remooue our bodies from this place; wee are the handmaides
diuine *Ceres;* to faire *Ceres* is this holy tree dedicated, to *Ceres,* by
whose fauour thy selfe liuest, that art worthy to perish.

Eris. Are you addicted to *Ceres,* that in spight of *Erisicthon* you 75
wil vse these sacrifices? No, immodest girles, you shal see that
I haue neither regard of your sexe which men should tender, nor of
your beautie which foolish loue would dote on, nor of your goddesse,
which none but pieuish girles reuerence. I will destroy this tree in
despite of all, and that you may see my hand execute what my heart 80
intendeth, and that no meane may appease my malice, my last
word shall bee the beginning of the first blowe.

⟨*Smites the trunk with his axe.*⟩

Celia. Out, alas! what hath he done?

Niobe. Our selues, I feare, must also minister matter to his
furie. 85

Nisa. Let him alone: but see, the tree powreth out bloud, and
I heare a voice.

Eris. What voice? if in the tree there be any bodie, speake
quickly, lest the next blow hit the tale out of thy mouth.

Fide. ⟨*from the trunk*⟩. Monster of men, hate of the heauens, and 90

---

57 addet *so* Q F., *as Lyly may have written* 60 immortal?] F. *queries*
immoral? 65 Thessalides Q F.: *query?* Messalinas 88 anybodies *F.*

to the earth a burthen, what hath chast *Fidelia* committed? It is thy spite, *Cupid*, that hauing no power to wound my vnspotted mind, procurest meanes to mangle my tender body, and by violēce to gash those sides that enclose a heart dedicate to vertue: or is it that sauage Satire, that feeding his sensuall appetite vpon lust, seeketh now to quench it with bloud, that being without hope to attaine my loue, hee may with cruelty end my life? Or doth *Ceres*, whose nymph I haue beene many yeares, in recompence of my inuiolable faith, reward me with vnspeakable torments? Diuine *Phœbus*, that pursued *Daphne* till shee was turned to a Bay tree, ceased then to trouble her; I, the gods are pittifull: and *Cinyras*, that with furie followed his daughter *Mirrha*, till shee was chaunged to a Mirre tree, left then to prosecute her; yea, parents are naturall: *Phœbus* lamented the losse of his friend, *Cinyras* of his child: but both gods and men either forgot or neglect the chaunge of *Fidelia*; nay, follow her after her chaunge, to make her more miserable: so that there is nothing more hatefull then to be chast, whose bodies are followed in the world with lust, and prosecuted in the graues with tyrannie; whose minds the freer they are from vice, their bodies are in the more daunger of mischiefe; so that they are not safe when they liue, because of mens loue; nor being chaunged, because of their hates; ncr being dead, because of their defaming. What is that chastitie which so few women study to keep, and both gods and men seeke to violate? If onely a naked name, why are we so superstitious of a hollow sound? If a rare vertue, why are men so carelesse of such an exceeding rarenesse? Goe, Ladies, tell *Ceres* I am that *Fidelia*, that so long knit Garlands in her honour, and chased with a Satyre, by praier to the gods became turned to a tree, whose body now is growne ouer with a rough barke, and whose golden lockes are couered with greene leaues; yet whose mind nothing can alter, neither the feare of death, nor the torments. If *Ceres* seeke no reuenge, then let virginitie be not only the scorne of Sauage people, but the spoyle. But alas, I feele my last bloud to come, & therfore must end my last breath. Farewel Ladies, whose liues are subiect to many mischieues; for if you be faire, it is hard to be chast; if chast, impossible to be safe; if you be young, you will quickly bend; if bend, you are suddenly broken. If you be foule, you shall seldome be flattered; if you be not flattered, you

95 Satire *F.*: satire *Q* 101, 104 Cineras *Q F.* 102 Mirrha] Miretia *Q F.* 115 verture *F.*

will euer bee sorrowfull. Beautie is a firme ficklenes, youth a feeble
staiednesse, deformitie a continuall sadnesse.   ⟨*Dies.*⟩ 130
  Niobe. Thou monster, canst thou heare this without griefe?
  Eris. Yea, and double your griefes with my blowes.
            ⟨*He proceeds to fell the tree to the ground.*⟩
  Nisa. Ah poore *Fidelia*, the expresse patterne of chastitie, and
example of misfortune.
  Celia. Ah, cruel *Erisicthon*, that not onely defaceth these holy 135
trees, but murtherest also this chast nimph.
  Eris. Nimph, or goddesse, it skilleth not, for there is none that
Erisicthon careth for, but *Erisicthon :* let *Ceres*, the Lady of your
haruest, reuenge when shee will, nay, when shee dares ! and tell her
this, that I am *Erisicthon*. 140
  Niobe. Thou art none of the gods.
  Eris. No, a contemner of the gods.
  Nisa. And hopest thou to escape reuenge, being but a man?
  Eris. Yea, I care not for reuenge, beeing a man and *Erisicthon*.
  Nisa. Come, let vs to *Ceres*, and complaine of this vnacquainted 145
and incredible villaine : if there bee power in her deitie, in her mind
pittie, or vertue in virginitie, this monster cannot escape.   *Exeunt.*

ACTVS SECVNDVS.

SCENA PRIMA.—⟨*At* CERES' *Tree, with transfer to* CUPID'S
Temple, ll. 39–80.⟩

CERES, NIOBE, NISA, CUPID, TIRTENA.

⟨*Enter* CERES, NIOBE, NISA, *and* TIRTENA.⟩

  Ceres. Doth *Erisicthon* offer force to my Nymphs, and to my
deitie disgrace? Haue I stuffed his barnes with fruitfull graine, and
doth hee stretch his hand against me with intolerable pride? So it
is, *Ceres*, thine eyes may witnesse what thy Nymphes haue told ;
heere lyeth the tree hackt in peeces, and the bloud scarce cold of 5
the fairest virgine. If this bee thy crueltie, *Cupid*, I will no more
hallow thy temple with sacred vowes : if thy cankred nature,
Erisicthon, thou shalt find as great miserie, as thou shewest
malice : I am resolued of thy punishment, and as speedie shall bee
my reuenge, as thy rigour barbarous.   *Tirtena*, on yonder hill 10

10 Tirtenæ *Q*

ACT II, SC. I]   LOUES METAMORPHOSIS   307

where neuer grew graine nor leafe, where nothing is but barren-
nesse and coldnesse, feare and palenesse, lyeth famine; goe to her,
and say that *Ceres* commaundeth her to gnaw on the bowels of
Erisicthon, that his hunger may bee as vnquenchable as his furie.

15 *Tir.* I obey; but how should I know her from others?

Ceres. Thou canst not misse of her, if thou remember but her
name; and that canst thou not forget, for that comming neere to the
place, thou shalt find gnawing in thy stomacke. Shee lyeth gaping,
and swalloweth nought but ayre; her face pale, and so leane, that
20 as easily thou maiest through the verie skinne behold the bone, as in
a glasse thy shadow; her haire long, blacke and shaggie; her eyes
sunke so farre into her head, that shee looketh out of the nape of
her necke; her lips white and rough; her teeth hollow and red with
rustinesse; her skin so thin, that thou maiest as liuely make an
25 Anatomie of her body, as shee were cut vp with Chirurgiōs; her
maw like a drie bladder, her heart swolne bigge with wind, and all
her bowels like Snakes working in her body. This monster when
thou shalt behold, tell her my mind, and returne with speed.

Tir. I goe, fearing more the sight of famine, then the force.

30 *Ceres.* Take thou these few eares of corne, but let not famine so
much as smell to them; and let her goe aloofe from thee. ⟨*Exit*
TIRTENA.⟩ Now shall *Erisicthon* see that *Ceres* is a great goddesse,
as full of power as himselfe of pride, and as pittilesse as he presumptuous: how thinke you Ladies, is not this reuenge apt for so
35 great iniurie?

Niobe. Yes Madam: To let men see, they that contend with the
gods doe but confound themselues.

Ceres. But let vs to the Temple of *Cupid* and offer sacrifice; they
that thinke it straunge for chastitie to humble it selfe to *Cupid*,
40 knowe neither the power of loue, nor the nature of virginitie: th'
one hauing absolute authoritie to commaund, the other difficultie to
resist: and where such continuall warre is betweene loue and vertue,
there must bee some parlies, and continuall perils: *Cupid* was neuer
conquered, and therefore must be flattered; Virginitie hath, and
45 therefore must be humble.

Nisa. Into my heart, Madam, there did neuer enter any motion
of loue.

Ceres. Those that often say, they cannot loue, or will not loue,
certainely they loue. Didst thou neuer see *Cupid?*

50 *Nisa.* No: but I haue heard him described at the full, and, as

I imagined, foolishly. First, that he should bee a god blind and naked, with wings, with bowe, with arrowes, with fire-brands; swimming sometimes in the Sea, & playing sometimes on the shore; with many other deuices, which the Painters, being the Poets Apes, haue taken as great paines to shaddow, as they to lie. Can I thinke that gods that commaund all things, would goe naked? What should he doe with wings that knowes not where to flie? Or what with arrowes, that sees not how to ayme? The heart is a narrow marke to hit, and rather requireth *Argus* eyes to take leuel, then a blind boy to shoote at randome. If he were fire, the Sea would quench those coles, or the flame turne him into cinders.

Ceres. Well *Nisa*, thou shalt see him.

Nisa. I feare *Niobe* hath felt him.

Niobe. Not I, Madam, yet must I confesse, that oftentimes I haue had sweete thoughts, sometimes hard conceites; betwixt both, a kind of yeelding; I know not what. But certainely I thinke it is not loue: sigh I can, and find ease in melancholly; smile I doe, and take pleasure in imagination; I feele in my selfe a pleasing paine, a chill heate, a delicate bitternesse, how to terme it I know not; without doubt it may be loue, sure I am it is not hate.

Nisa. *Niobe* is tender hearted, whose thoughts are like water, yeelding to euerie thing, and nothing to bee seene.

Ceres. Well, let vs to *Cupid;* and take heede that in your stubbernesse you offend him not, whome by entreaties you ought to follow. *Dianas* Nymphes were as chast as *Ceres* virgines, as faire, as wise: how *Cupid* tormented them, I had rather you should heare then feele; but this is truth, they all yeelded to loue: looke not scornefully, my Nymphes, I say they are yeelded to loue. This is the temple. ⟨*The temple-doors open.*⟩ Thou great god *Cupid*, whome the gods regard, and men reuerence, let it bee lawfull for *Ceres* to offer her sacrifice.

Cupid. Diuine *Ceres*, *Cupid* accepteth any thing that cometh from *Ceres;* which feedeth my Sparrowes with ripe corne, my Pigeons with wholsome seedes; and honourest my Temple with chast virgines.

Ceres. Then, Loue, to thee I bring these white and spotlesse Doues, in token that my heart is as free from any thought of loue, as these from any blemish, and as cleare in virginitie, as these perfect

61 these *F*.

in whitenesse. But that my Nymphes may know both thy power and thy lawes, and neither erre in ignorance nor pride, let me aske some questions to instruct them that they offend not thee, whome resist they cannot. In virgines what dost thou chiefest desire?

Cupid. In those that are not in loue, reuerent thoughts of loue; in those that be, faithfull vowes.

Ceres. What doest thou most hate in virgines?

Cupid. Pride in the beautifull, bitter taunts in the wittie, incredulitie in all.

Ceres. What may protect my virgines that they may neuer loue?

Cupid. That they be neuer idle.

Ceres. Why didst thou so cruellie torment all *Dianas* Nymphes with loue?

Cupid. Because they thought it impossible to loue.

Ceres. What is the substance of loue?

Cupid. Constancie and secrecie.

Ceres. What the signes?

Cupid. Sighes and teares.

Ceres. What the causes?

Cupid. Wit and idlenesse.

Ceres. What the meanes?

Cupid. Oportunitie and Importunitie.

Ceres. What the end?

Cupid. Happinesse without end.

Ceres. What requirest thou of men?

Cupid. That onely shall be knowne to men.

Ceres. What reuenge for those that will not loue?

Cupid. To be deceiued when they doe.

Ceres. Well, *Cupid*, increate my Nymphes with fauour, and though to loue it be no vice, yet spotlesse virginitie is the onely vertue: let me keepe their thoughtes as chast as their bodies, that *Ceres* may be happie, & they praised.

Cupid. Why, *Ceres*, doe you thinke that lust followeth loue? *Ceres*, louers are chast: for what is loue, diuine loue, but the quintescens of chastitie, and affections binding by heauenly motions, that cannot bee vndone by earthly meanes, and must not be comptrolled by any man?

Ceres. Wee will honour thee with continuall sacrifice, warme vs with mild affections; lest being too hotte, wee seeme immodest like wantons, or too cold, immoueable like stockes.

Cupid. *Ceres*, let this serue for all; let not thy Nymphes be light 130
nor obstinate, but as virgines should be, pittifull and faithfull; so
shall your flames warme, but not burne, delight, and neuer discomfort.

Ceres. How say you, my Nymphs, doth not *Cupid* speake like
a god? Counsel you I will not to loue, but coniure you I must 135
that you be not disdainefull. Let vs in, and see how *Erisicthon*
speedeth; famine flieth swiftly, and hath already seyzed on his
stomacke. *Exeunt.*

ACTVS TERTIVS.

SCENA PRIMA.—⟨*A Glade in the Forest, with transfer
to the Tree,* l. 157.⟩

RAMIS, NISA, MONTANUS, CELIA, SILUESTRIS, NIOBE.

⟨*Enter* RAMIS, *pursuing* NISA.⟩

Ramis. Stay, cruell *Nisa*, thou knowest not from whome thou
fliest, and therefore fliest; I come not to offer violence, but that
which is inuiolable: my thoughts are as holy as thy vowes, and I as
constant in loue as thou in crueltie: lust followeth not my loue as
shadowes doe bodies, but truth is wouen into my loue, as veines 5
into bodies: let me touch this tender arme, and say my loue is
endlesse.

Nisa. And to no end.

Ramis. It is without spot.

Nisa. And shall be without hope. 10

Ramis. Dost thou disdaine Loue and his lawes?

Nisa. I doe not disdaine that which I thinke is not, yet laugh at
those that honour it if it be.

Ramis. Time shall bring to passe that *Nisa* shall confesse there
is loue. 15

Nisa. Then also will loue make me confesse that *Nisa* is a foole.

Ramis. Is it folly to loue, which the gods accompt honourable,
and men esteeme holy?

Nisa. The gods make any thing lawfull, because they be gods,
and men honour shadowes for substance, because they are men. 20

Ramis. Both gods and men agree that loue is a consuming of the
heart and restoring, a bitter death in a sweete life.

22 restoring,] *comma misplaced at* heart *Q F.*

Nisa. Gods doe know, and men should, that loue is a consuming of wit, and restoring of folly, a staring blindnesse, and a blind gazing.
Ramis. Wouldst thou allot me death?
Nisa. No, but discretion.
Ramis. Yeeld some hope.
Nisa. Hope to dispaire.
Ramis. Not so long as *Nisa* is a woman.
Nisa. Therein, *Ramis* you show your selfe a man.
Ramis. Why?
Nisa. In flattering your selfe that all women wil yeeld.
Ramis. All may.
Nisa. Thou shalt sweare that we cannot.
Ramis. I will follow thee, and practise by denials to bee patient, or by disdaining die, and so be happie. *Exeunt.*

⟨*Enter* Montanus, *pursuing* Celia.⟩

Mon. Though thou hast ouer-taken me in loue, yet haue I ouer-taken thee in running: faire *Celia*, yeelde to loue, to sweete loue.
Celia. *Montanus*, thou art mad, that hauing no breath almost in running so fast, thou wilt yet spend more in speaking so foolishly: yeeld to loue I cannot, or if I doe, to thy loue I will not.
Mon. The fairest Wolfe chuseth the foulest, if he bee faithfullest, and he that indureth most griefe, not hee that hath most beautie.
Celia. If my thoughts were woluish, thy hopes might be as thy comparison is, beastly.
Mon. I would thy words were, as thy lookes are, louely.
Celia. I would thy lookes were, as thy affection is, blind.
Mon. Faire faces should haue smoothe hearts.
Celia. Fresh flowres haue crooked rootes.
Mon. Womens beauties will waine, and then no art can make them faire!
Celia. Mens follies will euer waxe, and then what reason can make them wise?
Mon. To be amiable and not to loue, is like a painted Lady, to haue colours, and no life.

30 Not *Q*: No *F*.   35 we *Q F*.: *qy. ?* one

Celia. To bee amorous, and not louely, is like a pleasant foole, full of words, and no deserts.

Mon. What call you deserts, what louely?

Celia. No louelier thing then wit, no greater desert then patience.

Mon. Haue not I an excellent wit?

Celia. If thou thinke so thy selfe, thou art an excellent foole.

Mon. ⟨*with heat*⟩. Foole? no, *Celia*, thou shalt find me as wise, as I doe thee proud, and as little to disgest thy taunts, as thou to brooke my loue.

Celia. I thought, *Montanus*, that you could not deserue, when I told you what it was, Patience.

Mon. Sweete *Celia*, I will be patient and forget this.

Celia. Then want you wit, that you can be content to be patient.

Mon. A hard choyse, if I take all well, to be a foole; if find fault, then to want patience.

Celia. The fortune of loue, and the vertue, is neither to haue successe nor meane.   Farewel! ⟨*Exit.*⟩

Mon. Farewell? nay, I will follow! and I know not how it commeth to passe, disdaine increaseth desire; and the further possibilitie standeth, the neerer approacheth hope. I follow!

⟨*Exit.*⟩

⟨*Enter* SILVESTRIS *and* NIOBE.⟩

Sil. *Polypus*, *Niobe*, is euer of the colour of the stone it sticketh to, and thou euer of his humor thou talkest with.

Niobe. Find you fault that I loue?

Sil. So many.

Niobe. Would you haue me like none?

Sil. Yes, one.

Niobe. Who shall make choyse but my selfe?

Sil. My selfe.

Niobe. For another to put thoughts into my head were to pull the braynes out of my head; take not measure of my affections, but weigh your owne; the Oake findeth no fault with the dewe, because it also falleth on the bramble. Beleeue me, *Siluestris*, the onely way to be mad, is to bee constant. Poets make their wreathes of Lawrell, Ladies of sundrie flowers.

Sil. Sweete *Niobe*, a ryuer running into diuers brookes becommeth shallow, and a mind diuided into sundrie affections, in the end will

---

60 foole, *comma inserted* F.   64 I not F.   75 vertue, *no comma* Q F.:
F. *also om.* Q's *comma at* loue   76, 79 S. D. (*bis*) [Exit] *om.* Q: Exeunt. F.

haue none. What joy can I take in the fortune of my loue, when I shall know many to haue the like fauours? Turtles flocke by couples, and breede both ioy and young ones.

Niobe. But Bees in swarmes, and bring forth waxe and honie.

100 *Sil.* Why doe you couet many, that may find sweetnesse in one?

Niobe. Why had *Argus* an hundred eyes, and might haue seene with one?

Sil. Because whilest he slept with some, he might wake with other some.

105 *Niobe.* And I loue many, because, being deceiued by the inconstancie of diuers, I might yet haue one.

Sil. That was but a deuice of *Iuno*, that knewe *Iupiters* loue.

Niobe. And this a rule of *Venus*, that knew mens lightnes.

Sil. The whole heauen hath but one Sunne.

110 *Niobe.* But starres infinite.

Sil. The Rainebow is euer in one compasse.

Niobe. But of sundrie colours.

Sil. A woman hath but one heart.

Niobe. But a thousand thoughts.

115 *Sil.* My Lute, though it haue many strings, maketh a sweete consent; and a Ladies heart, though it harbour many fancies, should embrace but one loue.

Niobe. The strings of my heart are tuned in a contrarie keye to your Lute, and make as sweete harmonie in discords, as yours in 120 concord.

Sil. Why, what strings are in Ladies hearts? Not the base.

Niobe. There is no base string in a womans heart.

Sil. The meane?

Niobe. There was neuer meane in womans heart.

125 *Sil.* The treble?

Niobe. Yea, the treble double and treble; and so are all my heartstrings. Farewell!

Sil. Sweete *Niobe*, let vs sing, that I may die with the Swanne.

Niobe. It will make you sigh the more, and liue with the Salamich.

130 *Sil.* Are thy tunes fire?

Niobe. Are yours death?

Sil. No; but when I haue heard thy voice, I am content to die.

Niobe. I will sing to content thee.

Cantant ⟨then exit NIOBE⟩.

126 treble¹] treble, *F.*

Sil. Inconstant *Niobe!* vnhappie *Siluestris!* yet had I rather shee should rather loue all then none: for nowe though I haue no certaintie, yet doe I find a kinde of sweetnesse.

⟨*Re-enter* RAMIS.⟩

Ramis. Cruell *Nisa*, borne to slaughter men!

⟨*Re-enter* MONTANUS.⟩

Mon. Coy *Celia*, bred vp in skoffes!

Sil. Wauering, yet wittie *Niobe!* But are wee all met?

Ramis. Yea, and met withall, if your fortunes be answerable to mine, for I find my Mistris immoueable, and the hope I haue is to despaire.

Mon. Mine in pride intolerable, who biddeth me looke for no other comfort then contempt.

Sil. Mine is best of all, and worst; this is my hope, that either shee will haue many or none.

Ramis. I feare our fortunes cannot thriue, for *Erisicthon* hath felled downe the holy tree of *Ceres*, which will encrease in her choler, and in her Nymphes crueltie: let vs see whether our Garlands bee there which we hanged on that tree; and let vs hang our selues vpon another.

Sil. A remedie for loue irremoueable; but I will first see whether all those that loue *Niobe* do like: in the meane season I will content my selfe with my share.

Mon. Here is the tree. O mischiefe scarce to be beleeued, impossible to be pardoned!

Ramis. Pardoned it is not, for *Erisicthon* perisheth with famine, and is able to starue those that looke on him. Here hang our Garlands: something is written; read mine.

Sil. Cedit amor rebus, res age, tutus eris.

Mon. And mine.

Sil. Sat mihi si facies, sit bene nota mihi.

Now for my selfe,

Victoria tecum stabit—scilicet.

Mon. You see their posies is as their hearts; and their hearts as their speeches, cruell, proud, and wauering: let vs all to the Temple of *Cupid*, and intreate his fauour, if not to obtaine their loues, yet to reuenge their hates: *Cupid* is a kinde god, who, knowing our vnspotted thoughts, will punish them, or release vs. Wee will

149 garland *F*.   150 the *F*.   164 scilicet *as part of quotation Q F*.

170 studie what reuenge to haue, that our paines proceeding of our owne minds, their plagues may also proceed from theirs. Are you all agreed?

Sil. I consent; but what if *Cupid* denie helpe?

Mon. Then he is no god.

175 *Sil.* But if he yeeld, what shall we aske?

Ramis. Reuenge.

Mon. Then let vs prepare our selues for *Cupids* sacrifice.

Exeunt.

SCENA SECVNDA.—⟨ *Seashore near* ERISICHTHON'S *Farm.*⟩

ERISICTHON, PROTEA, Marchant.

⟨*Enter* ERISICHTHON *and* PROTEA.⟩

Eris. Come, *Protea*, deare daughter, that name must thou buy too deare; necessitie causeth thee to be sold, nature must frame thee to be contented. Thou seest in how short a space I haue turned all my goods into my guts, where I feele a continuall fire, which
5 nothing can quench: my famine increaseth by eating, resembling the Sea, which receiueth all things, and cannot bee filled: life is sweete, hunger sharpe; betweene them the contention must bee short, vnlesse thou, *Protea*, prolong it. I haue acknowledged my offence against *Ceres;* make amends I cannot, for the gods holding
10 the ballance in their hands, what recompence can equally weigh with their punishments? Or what is hee that hauing but one ill thought of *Ceres*, that can race it with a thousand cutifull actions? such is the difference, that none can find defence: this is the ods, we miserable, and men; they immortall, and gods.

15 *Pro.* Deare father, I will obey both to sale and slaughter, accompting it the onely happinesse of my life, should I liue an hundred yeares, to prolong yours but one mynute: I yeeld, father, chop and chaunge me, I am readie; but first let mee make my prayers to *Neptune*, and withdraw your selfe till I haue done: long it shall not
20 bee, now it must be.

Eris. Stay, sweete *Protea*, and that great god heare thy prayer, though *Ceres* stop her eares to mine.

⟨ERISICHTHON *retires.*⟩

Pro. Sacred *Neptune*, whose godhead conquered my maiden-head, bee as ready to heare my passions, as I was to beleeue thine, and
5 performe that now I intreate, which thou didst promise when thy

selfe didst loue. Let not me bee a pray to this Marchaunt, who knowes no other god then Gold, vnlesse it bee falsely swearing by a god to get gold; let me, as often as I be bought for money, or pawnd for meate, be turned into a Bird, Hare, or Lambe, or any shape wherin I may be safe; so shall I preserue mine owne honour, my fathers life, and neuer repent me of thy loue: and now bestirre thee, for of all men, I hate that Marchant, who, if he find my beautie worth one pennie, will put it to vse to gaine ten, hauing no Religion in his mind, nor word in his mouth but money. *Neptune*, heare now or neuer. Father, I haue done.

Eris. ⟨*advancing*⟩. In good time, *Protea*, thou hast done; for loe, the Marchant keepeth not onely day, but hower.

Pro. If I had not beene here, had I beene forfeited?

Eris. No, *Protea*, but thy father famished. ⟨*Enter a* Merchant.⟩ Here, Gentleman, I am ready with my daughter.

Pro. Gentleman?

Mar. Yea, Gentleman, faire maide! my conditions make me no lesse.

Pro. Your conditions in deed brought in your obligations, your obligations your Vsurie, your Vsurie your Gentrie.

Mar. Why, doe you iudge no Marchants Gentlemen?

Pro. Yes, many, and some no men!

Mar. You shall be well intreated at my hands.

Pro. It may. Commaunded I will not be.

Mar. If you be mine by bargaine, you shall.

Pro. Father, hath this Marchant also bought my mind?

Eris. He cannot buy that, which cannot be sold.

Mar. Here is the money.

Eris. Here the maide: farewell, my sweete daughter; I commit thee to the gods, and this mans curtesie, who I hope will deale no worse with thee, then hee would haue the gods with him. I must bee gone, lest I doe starue as I stand. *Exit.*

Pro. Farewell, deare Father, I will not cease continually to pray to *Ceres*, for thy recouerie.

Mar. You are now mine, *Protea*.

Pro. And mine owne.

Mar. In will, not power.

Pro. In power if I will.

59 thy *om. F.*

Mar. I perceiue Nettles, gently touched, sting; but roughly handled, make no smart.

Pro. Yet roughly handled, Nettles are Nettles, and a Waspe is a Waspe, though shee lose her sting.

Mar. But then they doe no harme.

Pro. Nor good.

Mar. Come with me, and you shall see that Marchaunts know their good as well as Gentlemen.

Pro. Sure I am, they haue Gentlemens goods. *Exeunt.*

ACTVS QVARTVS.

SCENA PRIMA.—⟨*Before the Temple of* CUPID.⟩

RAMIS, MONTANUS, SILUESTRIS, CUPID.

⟨*Enter the three* Foresters *with offerings.*⟩

Ramis. This is the Temple of our great god, let vs offer our sacrifice.

Mon. I am readie.

Sil. And I. *Cupid,* thou god of loue, whose arrowes haue pierced our hearts, giue eare to our plaints.

⟨*The temple-doors open.*⟩

Cupid. If you come to *Cupid,* speake boldly, so must louers; speake faithfully, so must speeders.

Ramis. These euer burning Lampes are signes of my neuer to be quenched flames; this bleeding heart, in which yet stickes the head of the golden shaft, is the liuely picture of inward torments: mine eyes shall bedewe thine Altars with teares, and my sighes couer thy Temple with a darke smoake: pittie poore *Ramis.*

Mon. With this distaffe haue I spun, that my exercises bee as womanish as my affections, and so did *Hercules:* and with this halter will I hang my selfe, if my fortunes answere not my deserts, and so did *Iphis.* To thee, diuine *Cupid,* I present not a bleeding, but a bloudlesse heart, dried onely with sorrow, and worne with faithfull seruice.

This picture I offer, carued with no other instrument then Loue; pittie poore *Montanus.*

Sil. This fanne of Swans and Turtles feathers is token of my truth and iealousie: iealousie, without which loue is dotage, and with

which loue is madnesse; without the which loue is lust, and with
which loue is folly. This heart, neither bleeding nor bloudlesse, but
swolne with sighes, I offer to thy godhead, protesting that all my
thoughts are, as my words, without lust, and all my loue, as my
fortune, without sweetnesse. This Garland of flowers, which hath
all colours of the Rainebowe, witnesseth that my heart hath all
torments of the world: pittie poore *Siluestris*.

Cupid. I accept your offers, not without cause; and wonder at
your loues, not without pleasure: but bee your thoughts as true as
your words?

Ramis. Thou *Cupid*, that giuest the wound, knowest the heart;
for as impossible it is to conceale our affections, as to resist thy
force.

Cupid. I know that where mine arrowe lighteth, there breedeth
loue; but shooting euerie minute a thousand shafts, I know not on
whose heart they light, though they fall on no place but hearts.
What are your mistresses?

Ramis. Ceres maidens: mine most cruell, which shee calleth
constancie.

Mon. Mine most faire, but most proud.

Sil. Mine most wittie, but most wauering.

Cupid. Is the one cruell, th' other coye, the third inconstant?

Ramis. Too cruell!

Mon. Too coye!

Sil. Too fickle!

Cupid. What do they thinke of *Cupid*?

Ramis. One saith hee hath no eyes, because he hits hee knowes
not whome.

Mon. Th' other, that he hath no eares, to heare those that call.

Sil. The third, that he hath no nose, for sauours are not found
of louers.

Ramis. All, that hee hath no taste, because sweete and sower is
all one.

Mon. All, that hee hath no sence, because paines are pleasures,
and pleasures paines.

Sil. All, that he is a foolish god, working without reason, and
suffering the repulse without regard.

Cupid. Dare they blaspheme my god-head, which *Ioue* doth

52 found *Q*: fond *F*.

worship, *Neptune* reuerence, and all the gods tremble at? To make them loue were a reuenge too gentle for *Cupid:* to make you hate, a recompence too smal for louers. But of that anon: what haue you vsed in loue?

65 *Ramis.* All things that may procure loue,—giftes, words, othes, sighs, and swounings.
Cupid. What said they of gifts?
Mon. That affection could not bee bought with gold.
Cupid. What of words?
70 *Ramis.* That they were golden blastes, out of Leaden bellowes.
Cupid. What of othes?
Sil. That *Iupiter* neuer sware true to *Iuno.*
Cupid. What of sighes?
Sil. That deceipt kept a forge in the hearts of fooles.
75 *Cupid.* What of swounings?
Mon. Nothing, but that they wished them deathes.
Cupid. What reasons gaue they, not to loue?
Sil. Womens reasons ; they would not, because they would not.
Cupid. Well, then shall you see *Cupid* requite their reasons
80 with his rigour. What punishment doe you desire, that *Cupid* will denie?
Ramis. Mine being so hard as stone, would I haue turned to stone; that being to louers pittilesse, shee may to all the world be sencelesse.
85 *Mon.* Mine being so faire and so proud, would I haue turned into some flower; that shee may know beautie is as fading as grasse, which being fresh in the morning, is withered before night.
Sil. Mine, diuine *Cupid,* whose affection nothing can make staied, let her be turned to that Bird that liueth only by ayre, and dieth if
90 shee touch the earth, because it is constant. The bird of Paradise, *Cupid,* that, drawing in her bowels nothing but ayre, shee may know her heart fed on nothing but ficklenesse.
Cupid. Your reuenges are reasonable, and shall bee graunted. Thou *Nisa,* whose heart no teares could pearce, shalt with continuall
95 waues be wasted: in stead of thy faire haire, shalt thou haue greene mosse; thy face of flint, because thy heart is of marble; thine eares shall bee holes for fishes, whose eares were more deafe then fishes. Thou *Celia,* whome beautie made proud, shalt haue the fruite of beautie, that is, to fade whiles it is flourishing, and to blast
100 before it is blowne. Thy face, as faire as the Damaske rose, shall

perish like the Damaske rose; the canker shall eate thee in the bud, and euerie little wind blow thee from the stalke, and then shall men in the morning weare thee in their Hats, and at night cast thee at their heeles. Thou *Niobe,* whome nothing can please, (but that which most displeaseth *Cupid,* inconstancie) shalt only breathe and sucke ayre for foode, and weare feathers for silke, beeing more wauering then ayre, and lighter then feathers. This will *Cupid* doe. Therefore, when next you shall behold your Ladies, doe but send a faithfull sigh to *Cupid,* and there shall arise a thicke mist which *Proserpine* shall send, and in the moment you shall be reuenged, and they chaunged, *Cupid* proue himselfe a great god, and they peeuish girles.

Ramis. With what sacrifice shall wee shewe our selues thankfull, or how may we requite this benefit?

Cupid. You shal yerely at my Temple offer true hearts, and howerly bestow all your wits in louing deuices; thinke all the time lost, that is not spent in loue; let your othes be without number, but not without truth; your words full of alluring sweetnesse, but not of broad flatterie; your attires neate, but not womanish; your giftes of more price for the fine deuice, then the great valewe, and yet of such valew that the deuice seeme not beggerly, nor your selues blockish; be secrete, that worketh myracles; bee constant, that bringeth secrecie; this is all *Cupid* doth commaund. Away!

Ramis. And to this we all willingly consent.

⟨ *The temple-doors close.* ⟩

Nowe what resteth but reuenge on them that haue practised malice on vs? let mine be any thing, seeing shee will not be onely mine.

Mon. Let vs not now stand wishing, but presently seeke them out, vsing as great speed in following reuenge as we did in pursuing our loue: certainely wee shall find them about *Ceres* tree, singing or sacrifizing.

Sil. But shall we not goe visit *Erisicthon?*

Mon. Not I, lest hee eate vs, that deuoureth all things; his lookes are of force to famish: let vs in, and let all Ladies beware to offend those in spight, that loue them in honour; for when the Crow shall set his foote in their eye, and the blacke Oxe tread on their foote, they shall finde their misfortunes to be equall with their deformities, and men both to loath and laugh at them.   *Exeunt.*

129 pursuing *Q*: pursing *F*.

SCENA SECVNDA.—⟨*Seashore near* ERISICHTHON'S *Farm.*⟩

ERISICTHON, PROTEA, PETULIUS, Syren.

⟨*Enter* ERISICHTHON *and* PROTEA.⟩

Eris. Come, *Protea*, tell me, how didst thou escape from the Marchant?

Pro. Neptune, that great god, when I was ready to goe with the Marchaunt into the ship, turned me to a Fisherman on the shore, with an Angle in my hand, and on my shoulder a net; the Marchaunt missing me, and yet finding me, asked me who I was, and whether I saw not a faire maiden? I answered, no! Hee marueiling and raging, was forced either to lose his passage, or seeke for mee among the Pebbles! To make short, a good wind caused him to goe I know not whither, and me (thanks be to *Neptune*) to returne home.

Eris. Thou art happie, *Protea*, though thy Father bee miserable: and *Neptune* gracious, though *Ceres* cruell: thy escape from the Marchaunt breedeth in me life, ioy, and fulnesse.

Pro. My father cannot be miserable, if *Protea* be happie; for by selling me euerie day, hee shall neuer want meate, nor I shiftes to escape. And, now, Father, giue me leaue to enioy my *Petulius*, that on this vnfortunate shore still seekes me sorrowing.

Eris. Seeke him, deare *Protea*; find and enioy him; and liue euer hereafter to thine owne comforts, that hast hitherto beene the preseruer of mine. *Exit.*

Pro. Aye me, behold, a Syren haunts this shore! the gods forbid shee should entangle my *Petulius*. Syren ⟨*appears*⟩.

Syren. Accursed men! whose loues haue no other meane then extremities, nor hates end but mischiefe.

Pro. Vnnaturall monster! no maide, that accuseth men, whose loues are built on truth, and whose hearts are remoued by curtesie: I will heare the depth of her malice.

Syren. Of all creatures most vnkind, most cunring, by whose subtilties I am halfe fish, halfe flesh, themselues being neither fish nor flesh; in loue luke warme, in crueltie red hot; if they praise, they flatter; if flatter, deceiue; if deceiue, destroy.

Pro. Shee rayles at men, but seekes to intangle them: this slight

SCENA PRIMA *Q, corrected F.* S. D. Syren appears *F.*: *Q simply* Syren *in middle of page* 26-7 whose loues ... truth, *and om. F.*

is prepared for my sweete *Petulius* ; I will withdraw my selfe close,
for *Petulius* followeth : hee will without doubt be enamored of her, 35
enchaunted hee shall not be, my charmes shall counteruaile hers ;
it is he hath saued my Fathers life with money, and must prolong
mine with loue.

⟨*Enter* PETULIUS.⟩

Pet. I maruaile *Protea* is so farre before me : if shee runne, ile
flie : sweete *Protea*, where art thou ? it is *Petulius* calleth *Protea*. 40

Syren. Here commeth a braue youth. Now *Syren*, leaue out
nothing that may allure—thy golden lockes, thy entising lookes, thy
tuned voice, thy subtile speeche, thy faire promises, which neuer
missed the heart of any but *Vlisses*.

Sing with a Glasse in her hand and a Combe.

Pet. What diuine goddesse is this ? What sweete harmonie ? my 45
heart is rauished with such tickling thoughts, and mine eyes stayed
with such a bewitching beautie, that I can neither find the meanes
to remoue my affection, nor to turne aside my lookes.

Sing againe Syren.

I yeeld to death, but with such delight, that I would not wish to
liue, vnlesse it were to heare thy sweete layes. 50

Syren. Liue still, so thou loue me ! why standest thou amazed at
the word Loue?

Pro. ⟨*behind*⟩. It is high time to preuent this mischiefe. Nowe,
Neptune, stand to thy promise, and let me take suddenly the shape
of an olde man ; so shall I marre what shee makes. 55

⟨*Exit into the structure at back.*⟩

Pet. Not yet come to my selfe, or if I bee, I dare not credit mine
eares. Loue thee, diuine goddesse ? Vouchsafe I may honour
thee, and liue by the imagination I haue of thy words and worthinesse.

Syren. I am ⟨not⟩ a goddesse, but a Ladie and a virgine, whose 60
loue if thou embrace, thou shalt liue no lesse happie then the gods
in heauen.

⟨*Re-enter* PROTEA *as an old man.*⟩

Pro. Beleeue not this Inchauntresse (sweete youth) who retaineth
the face of a Virgine, but the heart of a Fiend, whose sweet tongue 65
sheadeth more drops of bloud then it vttereth sillables.

S. D. Sing *Q*: Sings *F*.   56 mine] my *F*.

Pet. Out, dottrell! whose dimme eyes cannot discerne beautie, nor doting age iudge of loue.

Pro. If thou listen to her words, thou shalt not liue to repent: for her malice is as suddaine as her ioyes are sweete.

70 *Pet.* Thy siluer haires are not so precious as her golden lockes, nor thy crooked age of that estimation as her flowring youth.

Syren. That old man measureth the hot assault of loue with the cold skirmishes of age.

Pro. That young cruell resembleth old Apes, who kill by culling: 75 from the top of this Rocke whereon shee sitteth, will shee throw thee headlong into the Sea, whose song is the instrument of her witchcraft, neuer smiling but when shee meaneth to smite, and vnder the flatterie of loue practiseth the sheading of bloud.

Pet. What art thou, which so blasphemest this diuine creature?

80 *Pro.* I am the Ghost of *Vlisses*, who continually houer about these places, where this *Syren* haunteth, to saue those which otherwise should be spoyled: stop thine eares, as I did mine, and succour the faire, but, by thy folly, the most infortunate *Protea*.

Pet. Protea? What dost thou heare, *Petulius?* Where is 85 *Protea?*

Pro. In this thicket, ready to hang her selfe, because thou carest not for her, that did⟨st⟩ sweare to follow. Curse this hag, who onely hath the voice and face of a Virgine, the rest all fish and feathers, and filth; follow me, and strongly stoppe thine eares, lest the second 90 encounter make the wound incurable.

Pet. Is this a *Syren*, and thou *Vlisses?* Cursed be that hellish carkas, and blessed be thy heauenly spirit.

Syren. I shrinke my head for shame. O *Vlisses!* is it not enough for thee to escape, but also to teach others? Sing and die, nay die, 95 and neuer sing more.

Pro. Followe me at this doore, and out at the other.

⟨*They pass through the central structure,* PROTEA *emerging in her own character.*⟩

Pet. How am I deliuered! the old man is vanished, and here for him stands *Protea*.

Pro. Here standeth *Protea*, that hath saued thy life, thou must 100 also prolong hers: but let vs into the woods, and there I will tell thee howe I came to *Vlisses*, and the summe of all my fortunes, which happily will breed in thee both loue and wonder.

75 sittith *F.*   87 that didst] *F. in note proposed* that thou didst

Pet. I will, and onely loue *Protea*, and neuer cease to wonder at
Protea. *Exeunt.*

ACTVS QVINTVS.

Scena Prima.—⟨*Before the Temple of* Cupid.⟩

⟨*Enter*⟩ Ceres, Cupid, Tirtena.

Ceres. *Cupid*, thou hast transformed my Nymphes and incensed me; them to shapes vnreasonable, me to anger immortall, for at one time I am both robd of mine honour and my Nymphes.

Cupid. *Ceres*, thy Nymphes were stubborne, and thy selfe, speaking so imperiously to *Cupid*, somewhat stately. If you aske the cause in choller, *Sic volo, sic iubeo*: if in curtesie, *Quæ venit ex merito pœna dolenda venit.* They were disdainefull, and haue their deserts; thou *Ceres*, doest but gouerne the guts of men, I the hearts: thou seekest to starue *Erisicthon* with thy minister, famine, whome his daughter shall preserue by my vertue, loue.

Ceres. Thou art but a god, *Cupid*.

Cupid. No *Ceres*, but such a god that maketh thunder fall out of *Ioues* hand, by throwing thoughts into his heart, and to bee more terrified with the sparkling of a Ladies eye, then men with the flashes of his lightning: such a god that hath kindled more fire in *Neptunes* bosome, then the whole Sea which he is king of can quench: such power haue I, that *Plutoes* neuer dying fire doth but scorch in respect of my flames. *Diana* hath felt some motions of loue, *Vesta* doth, *Ceres* shall.

Ceres. Art thou so cruell?

Cupid. To those that resist, a Lyon; to those that submit, a Lambe.

Ceres. Canst thou make such difference in affection, and yet shall it all be loue?

Cupid. Yea, as much as betweene sicknesse and health, though in both bee life: those that yeeld and honour *Cupid*, shall possesse sweete thoughts and enioy pleasing wishes: the other shall bee tormented with vaine imaginations and impossible hopes.

Ceres. How may my Nymphes be restored?

Cupid. If thou restore *Erisicthon*, they embrace their loues, and all offer sacrifice to me.

s. d. Tirtena. *Q F. See note* 9 ministred *Q F.*

Ceres. *Erisicthon* did in contempt hewe downe my sacred tree.

Cupid. Thy Nymphes did in disdaine scorne my constant love.

Ceres. He slew most cruelly my chast *Fidelia*, whose bloud lieth
35 yet on the ground.

Cupid. But *Diana* hath chaunged her bloud to freshe flowers, which are to be seene on the ground.

Ceres. What honour shal he doe to *Ceres* ? What amends can he make to *Fidelia* ?

40 *Cupid.* All *Ceres* groue shall he decke with Garlands, and accompt euerie tree holy ; a stately monument shall hee erect in remembraunce of *Fidelia*, and offer yearely sacrifice.

Ceres. What sacrifice shall I and my Nymphes offer thee? for I will doe any thing to restore my Nymphes, and honour thee.

45 *Cupid.* You shall present in honour of my mother *Venus*, Grapes and Wheate ; for *Sine Cerere & Baccho friget Venus*. You shall suffer your Nymphes to play, sometimes to be idle, in the fauour of *Cupid* ; for *Otia si tollas, periere Cupidinis arcus*. So much for *Ceres*. Thy Nymphes shall make no vowes to continue Virgins,
50 nor vse words to disgrace loue, nor flie from oportunities that kindle affections : if they be chast, let them not bee cruell ; if faire, not proud ; if louing, not inconstant. Crueltie is for Tygers, pride for Peacockes, inconstancie for fooles.

Ceres. Cupid, I yeeld, and they shall : but sweete *Cupid*, let
55 them not be deceiued by flatterie, which taketh the shape of affection, nor by lust, which is clothed in the habit of loue ; for men haue as many slights to delude, as they haue words to speake.

Cupid. Those that practise deceit shall perish : *Cupid* fauoureth none but the faithfull.

60 *Ceres.* Well, I will goe to *Erisicthon,* and bring him before thee.

Cupid. Then shall thy Nymphes recouer their formes, so as they yeeld to loue.

Ceres. They shall. *Exeunt.*

SCENA SECVNDA.—⟨ *The same.* ⟩

⟨*Enter*⟩ PETULIUS, PROTEA.

Pet. A straunge discourse, *Protea*, by which I find the gods amorous, and Virgines immortall, goddesses full of crueltie, and men of vnhappinesse.

61 formes *F*.: fames *Q*   SCENA PRIMA *Q, corr. F.*   2 immortall,
F. rightly transfers Q's comma from goddesses

Pro. I haue told both my Fathers misfortunes, grown by stoutnesse, and mine by weaknesse; his thwarting of *Ceres*, my yeelding to *Neptune*.

Pet. I know, *Protea*, that hard yron, falling into fire, waxeth soft; and then the tender heart of a Virgine being in loue, must needes melt: for what should a faire yong, and wittie Ladie answere to the sweete inticements of loue, but,

Molle meum leuibus cor est violabile telis?

Pro. I haue heard too, that hearts of men stiffer then steele, haue by loue beene made softer then wooll, and then they crie,

Omnia vincit amor, & nos cedamus amori.

Pet. Men haue often fained sighs.

Pro. And women forged teares.

Pet. Suppose I loue not.

Pro. Suppose I care not.

Pet. If men sweare and lie, how will you trie their loues?

Pro. If women sweare they loue, how will you trie their dissembling?

Pet. The gods put wit into women.

Pro. And nature deceite into men.

Pet. I did this but to trie your patience.

Pro. Nor I, but to prooue your faith. But see, *Petulius*, what miraculous punishments here are for deserts in loue: this Rocke was a Nymph to *Ceres*; so was this Rose; so that Bird.

Pet. All chaung'd from their shapes?

Pro. All chaung'd by *Cupid*, because they disdain'd loue, or dissembl'd in it.

Pet. A faire warning to *Protea*; I hope shee will loue without dissembling.

Pro. An Item for *Petulius*, that hee delude not those that loue him; for *Cupid* can also chaunge men. Let vs in. *Exeunt.*

SCENA TERTIA.—⟨*The same.*⟩

⟨*Enter*⟩ RAMIS, SILUESTRIS, MONTANUS.

Ramis. This goeth luckily, that *Cupid* hath promised to restore our mistresses: and *Ceres*, that they shall accept our loues.

Mon. I did euer imagine that true loue would end with sweete ioyes, though it was begun with deepe sighs.

10 leuibus ... telis Q (*Cf. M. Bomb.* iv. 1. 35): lenibus ... telit *F*. SCENA QVARTA Q, *corrected F*.

Sil. But how shall we looke on them when we shal see them smile? We must, and perchaunce they will, frowne.

Ramis. Tush! let vs indure the bending of their faire browes, and the scorching of their sparkling eyes, so that we may possesse at last the depth of their affections.

Mon. Possesse? Neuer doubt it; for *Ceres* hath restored *Erisicthon*, and therefore will perswade with them, nay, commaund them.

Sil. If it come by commaundement of *Ceres*, not their owne motions, I rather they should hate: for what ioye can there be in our liues, or in our loues sweetnesse, when euerie kisse shall bee sealed with a curse, and euerie kind word proceed of feare, not affection? enforcement is worse then enchantment.

Ramis. Art thou so superstitious in loue, that wast wont to be most carelesse? Let them curse all day, so I may haue but one kisse at night.

Mon. Thou art worse then *Siluestris*; hee not content without absolute loue, thou with indifferent.

Sil. But here commeth *Ceres* with *Erisicthon*: let vs looke demurely; for in her heart shee hates vs deeply.

SCENA VLTIMA.—⟨*The same.*⟩

CUPID, CERES, Nymphes, ERISICTHON, PETULIUS, PROTEA.

⟨*Enter, to the* Foresters, CERES *and* ERISICTHON.⟩

Eris. I will hallow thy woods with solemne feastes, and honour all thy Nymphes with due regard.

Ceres. Well, doe so; and thanke *Cupid* that commands; nay, thanke my foolish Nymphes, that know not how to obey; here be the louers ready at receipt. How now, Gentlemen, what seeke you?

Ramis. Nothing but what *Ceres* would find.

Ceres. *Ceres* hath found those that I would shee had lost, vaine louers.

Ramis. *Ceres* may lose that that *Cupid* would saue, true louers.

Ceres. You thinke so one of another.

Sil. *Cupid* knoweth so of vs all.

Ceres. You might haue made me a counsell of your loues.

Mon. I madame, if loue would admit counsell.

18 wast *Q*: was *F*.   SCENA VLTIMA *Q F*.

⟨ *The temple-doors open.* ⟩

Ceres. *Cupid*, here is *Erisicthon* in his former state; restore my Nimphs to theirs, then shal they embrace these louers, who wither out their youth.

⟨ *Enter* PETULIUS *with* PROTEA. ⟩

Eris. Honoured bee mightie *Cupid*, that makes me liue!

Pet. Honoured bee mightie *Cupid*, that makes me loue.

Pro. And me!

Ceres. What, more louers yet? I thinke it bee impossible for *Ceres* to haue any follow her in one hower, that is not in loue in the next.

Cupid. *Erisicthon*, bee thou carefull to honour *Ceres*, and forget not to please her Nymphs. The faithfull loue of thy daughter *Protea*, hath wrought both pittie in me to graunt her desires, and to release thy punishments. Thou *Petulius* shalt enioy thy loue, because I know thee loyall.

Pet. Then shall *Petulius* be most happie.

Pro. And *Protea* most fortunate.

Cupid. But doe you, *Ramis*, continue your constant loue? and you, *Montanus*? and you, *Siluestris*?

Ramis. Nothing can alter our affections, which encrease while the meanes decrease, and waxe stronger in being weakened.

Cupid. Then, *Venus*, send downe that showre, wherewith thou wert wont to wash those that doe thee worship; and let loue by thy beames bee honoured in all the world, and feared, wished for, and wondred at: here are thy Nymphs, *Ceres*.

Ramis. Whome doe I see? *Nisa*?

Mon. Diuine *Celia*, fairer than euer shee was!

Sil. My sweete *Niobe*!

Ceres. Why stare you, my Nymphs, as amazed? triumph rather because you haue your shapes: this great god *Cupid*, that for your prides and follies changed, hath by my praier and promise restored you.

Cupid. You see, Ladies, what it is to make a mocke of loue, or a scorne of *Cupid:* see where your louers stand; you must now take them for your husbands; this is my iudgement, this is *Ceres* promise.

Ramis. Happie *Ramis!*

17 liue *Q*: loue *F*.   18 Pet. Honoured ... loue *om. F.*   25 relase *F.*

Mon. Happie *Montanus!*
Sil. Happie *Siluestris!*
Ceres. Why speake you not, Nymphes? This must bee done, and you must yeeld.
Nisa. Not I!
Niobe. Nor I!
Celia. Nor I!
Ceres. Not yeeld? Then shal *Cupid* in his furie turne you againe to sencelesse and shamefull shapes.
Cupid. Will you not yeeld? How say you, *Ramis?* Doo your loues continue? Are your thoughts constant? & yours *Montanus?* And yours *Siluestris?*
Ramis. Mine most vnspotted!
Mon. And mine!
Sil. And mine, *Cupid*, which nothing can alter!
Cupid. And will you not yeeld, Virgins?
Nisa. Not I, *Cupid:* neither doe I thanke thee that I am restored to life, nor feare againe to be chaunged to stone: for rather had I beene worne with the continuall beating of waues, then dulled with the importunities of men, whose open flatteries make way to their secret lustes, retaining as little truth in their hearts as modestie in their words. How happie was *Nisa*, which felt nothing; pined, yet not felt the consumption! vnfortunate wench, that now haue eares to heare their cunning lies, and eyes to behold their dissembling lookes! turne me, *Cupid*, againe, for loue I will not!
Ramis. Miserable *Ramis!* vnhappie to loue; to chaunge the Ladie, accurst; and now lose her, desperate!
Celia. Nor I, *Cupid:* well would I content my selfe to bud in the Summer, and to die in the Winter: for more good commeth of the Rose, then can by loue: when it is fresh, it hath a sweete sauour; loue, a sowre taste: the Rose, when it is old, loseth not his vertue; loue, when it is stale, waxeth loathsome. The Rose, distilled with fire, yeeldeth sweete water: loue, in extremities, kindles iealousies: in the Rose, how euer it be, there is sweetnes; in loue nothing but bitternesse. If men looke pale, and sweare, & sigh, then forsooth women must yeeld, because men say they loue, as though our hearts were tied to their tongues, and we must chuse them by appointment, our selues feeling no affection, and so haue our

60 Are] And *F.*   71-2 pined yet, *Q*

thoughtes bound prentises to their words : turne me againe. Yeeld I will not!

Mon. Which way shalt thou turne thy selfe, since nothing will turne her heart? Die, *Montanus*, with shame and griefe, and both infinite!

Niobe. Nor I, *Cupid!* let me hang alwayes in the ayre, which I found more constant then mens words : happie *Niobe*, that touched not the ground where they goe, but alwayes holding thy beake in the ayre, didst neuer turne backe to behold the earth. In the heauens I saw an orderly course, in the earth nothing but disorderly loue, and pieuishnesse : turne me againe, *Cupid*, for yeeld I will not!

Sil. I would my selfe were stone, flower, or fowle; seeing that *Niobe* hath a heart harder then stone, a face fairer then the Rose, and a mind lighter then feathers.

Cupid. What haue we here? Hath punishment made you peruerse? *Ceres*, I vowe here by my sweete mother *Venus*, that if they yeeld not, I will turne them againe, not to flowers, or stones, or birds, but to monsters, no lesse filthie to bee seene then to bee named hatefull: they shall creepe that now stand, and be to all men odious, and bee to themselues (for the mind they shall retaine) loathsome.

Ceres. My sweete Nymphs, for the honor of your sex, for the loue of *Ceres*, for regard of your own countrie, yeeld to loue; yeeld, my sweete Nymphes, to sweete loue.

Nisa. Shall I yeeld to him that practised my destruction, and when his loue was hotest, caused me to bee chaunged to a rocke?

Ramis. *Nisa*, the extremitie of loue is madnesse, and to be mad is to bee sencelesse; vpon that Rocke did I resolue to end my life: faire *Nisa*, forgiue him thy chaunge, that for himselfe prouided a harder chaunce.

Celia. Shall I yeeld to him that made so small accompt of my beautie, that he studied how he might neuer behold it againe?

Mon. Faire Ladie, in the Rose did I alwayes behold thy colour, and resolu'd by continuall gazing to perish, which I could not doe when thou wast in thine owne shape, thou wast so coy and swift in flying from me.

Niobe. Shall I yeeld to him that caused me haue wings, that I might flie farther from him?

101 Niobe] Nisa *Q F.*

Sil. Sweete *Niobe*, the farther you did seeme to bee from me, the neerer I was to my death, which, to make it more speedy, wisht thee wings to flie into the ayre, and my selfe lead on my heeles to sinke into the Sea.

Ceres. Well, my good Nymphes, yeeld; let *Ceres* intreat you yeeld.

Nisa. I am content, so as *Ramis*, when hee finds me cold in loue, or hard in beliefe, hee attribute it to his owne folly; in that I retaine some nature of the Rocke he chaunged me into.

Ramis. O, my sweete *Nisa!* bee what thou wilt, and let all thy imperfections bee excused by me, so thou but say thou louest me.

Nisa. I doe.

Ramis. Happie *Ramis!*

Celia. I consent, so as *Montanus*, when in the midst of his sweete delight, ⟨he⟩ shall find some bitter ouerthwarts, impute it to his folly, in that he suffered me to be a Rose, that hath prickles with her pleasantnes, as hee is like to haue with my loue shrewdnes.

Mon. Let me bleed euerie minute with the prickles of the Rose, so I may enioy but one hower the sauour; loue, faire *Celia*, and at thy pleasure comfort, and confound.

Celia. I doe.

Mon. Fortunate *Montanus!*

Niobe. I yeelded first in mind though it bee my course last to speake: but if *Siluestris* find me not euer at home, let him curse himselfe that gaue me wings to flie abroad, whose feathers if his iealousie shall breake, my policie shall imp.

Non custodiri, ni velit, vlla potest.

Sil. My sweete *Niobe!* flie whither thou wilt all day, so I may find thee in my nest at night, I will loue thee, and beleue thee.

Sit modo, non feci, dicere lingua memor.

Cupid. I am glad you are all agreed; enioy your loues, and euerie one his delight. Thou, *Erisicthon*, art restored of *Ceres*, all the louers pleased by *Cupid*, shee ioyfull, I honoured. Now, Ladies, I will make such vnspotted loue among you, that there shall bee no suspition nor iarre, no vnkindnesse nor iealousie: but let all Ladies heereafter take heede that they resist not loue, which worketh wonders.

Ceres. I will charme my Nymphes, as they shall neither be so stately as not to stoope to loue, nor so light as presently to yeeld.

152 imp] nip *Q F.*   155 beleue] beloue *Q F.*   162 take *om. F.*

Cupid. Here is none but is happie: but doe not as *Hippomanes* did, when by *Venus* ayd hee wonne *Atlanta*, defile her Temple with vnchast desires, and forgot to sacrifice vowes. I will soare vp into heauen, to settle the loues of the gods, that in earth haue dispos'd the affections of men. 170

Ceres. I to my haruest, whose corne is now come out of the blade into the eare; and let all this amorous troupe to the temple of *Venus*, there to consummate what *Cupid* hath commaunded.

Eris. I, jn the honour of *Cupid* and *Ceres*, will solemnize this feast within my house; and learne, if it be not too late, againe to 175 loue. But you Forresters were vnkind, that in all my maladies would not visit me.

Mon. Thou knowest, *Erisicthon*, that louers visit none but their mistresses.

Eris. Well, I wil not take it vnkindly, since all ends in kind- 180 nesse.

Ceres. Let it bee so :——these louers mind nothing what we say.

Ramis. Yes, we attend on *Ceres*.

Ceres. Well, doe. *Exeunt.*

FINIS.

167 Atalanta *F.*   168 forget *F.*

THE MAYDES METAMORPHOSIS
⟨DOUBTFUL⟩

EDITIONS

The Maydes Metamorphosis. As it hath bene sundrie times Acted by the Children of Powles. London: *Printed by Thomas Creede, for Richard Oliue, dwelling in long Lane.* 1600. 4°.

Reprinted in *A Collection of Old Plays*, vol. i, 1882, 4°, pp. 99-164, with Introduction and Notes by A. H. Bullen.

I add here the title of the other play once claimed for Lyly (see below, p. 334)—

A Warning for Faire Women, containing The most Tragicall and Lamentable Murther of Master George Sanders, of London, Marchant, nigh Shooters Hill; consented unto by his owne wife, acted by M. Browne, Mistris Drewry and Trusty Roger, agents therin: with thier seuerall ends. As it hath beene lately diuerse times acted by the right Honorable the Lord Chamberlaine his Seruantes. Printed at London by Valentine Sims for William Apsley. 1599. 4°.

Reprinted in *The School of Shakspere*, vol. ii, 1878, 8°, with Introduction and Notes by Richard Simpson.

THE MAYDES METAMORPHOSIS

INTRODUCTORY NOTE

Two anonymous plays were included by Wood (*Athenae Oxon.*, 1691, ed. Bliss, i. 676) in the list of Lyly's pieces: 1. *A Warning for Faire Women*, pub. 1599; 2. *The Maydes Metamorphosis*, pub. 1600. The assignment of the first seems to have originated with Milton's nephew, Edward Phillips, in his *Theatrum Poetarum* (1675), p. 113; that of the second with William Winstanley, *Lives of the English Poets* (1687), p. 97, where, as he mentions every play of Lyly's save *Loves Metamorphosis*, it is probably a mistake for the latter.

The first, though accepted by Winstanley and Wood, was rejected by Langbaine in his *English Dramatick Poets*, Oxf., 1691; since when the attribution to Lyly has found, as it deserves, no support. The play, a domestic tragedy of the type of *Arden of Feversham*, presents, in speech or conduct, no resemblance whatever to Lyly's work.

The second appears to have passed unquestioned as Lyly's down to the present century; being accepted by Langbaine, by Reed in his continuation of Baker's *Biographia Dramatica*, 1782, and by Dilke in his *Old English Plays*, 1814, vol. i. p. 201. The first indication of doubt seems to have come from Collier, who in his *History of Dramatic Poetry*, iii. p. 12, speaks of it as 'attributed doubtfully to Lyly,' though on an earlier page (p. 4) he acknowledges that there is 'no sufficient reason to deprive him of it, unless that it is better in some respects than his other plays, and sketches its contents with some approval. But Fairholt, in 1858, pronounced decidedly against it, and rejected it from his edition of the plays. Two years later Bodenstedt (*Shakespeare's Zeitgenossen und ihre Werke*, iii. 50) impugned his decision, but only on the grounds of a general ascription to Lyly and the great likeness of the fairy-songs to others of his. Mr. Gosse assigned it to Day, an assignment supported by Mr. A. H. Bullen, who reprinted it in his *Collection of Old Plays*, vol. i. 1882. Since then it has been generally rejected; though Mr. Fleay, in 1891, while assigning the greater part of it to Daniel, considers the prose bits (the boys Mopso and Frisco, ii. 2, iii. 2), and especially the Fairies in ii. 2, 'almost certainly by Lyly' (*Biog. Chron.* ii. 324). Mr. Baker,

THE MAYDES METAMORPHOSIS

weighing the question in his edition of *Endimion*, 1894, pp. clxxvi-ix, decides once more against Lyly's authorship; and the balance of evidence, as of modern opinion, is in my judgement quite with him.

The Argument is briefly as follows. Two courtiers, Phylander and Orestes, charged by Duke Telemachus to kill a 'mayd of meane discent,' Eurymine, who is beloved by the Prince Ascanio, after a dramatic revelation to her of their purpose by means of a feigned tale, are finally moved to spare her on condition that she conceals herself. They satisfy the duke by presenting him with a kid's heart for hers, together with a piece of lawn from her dress; while Eurymine, now the object of competition between a forester and a shepherd, accepts a cottage from the one and a flock to tend from the other. Ascanio, after dispatching his comic page Joculo in search of her, is visited in sleep, under Juno's direction, by Morpheus in the shape of Eurymine, who advises him to repair for news of her to a certain hermit. Meanwhile the god Apollo, vainly urging on the beautiful shepherdess his own passion, is challenged by her to prove his boasted deity by changing her into a man, and, in his anger, actually does so. The hermit, an exiled prince, Aramanthus, who has studied astrology, informs Ascanio that the object of his love is a man; but when at length the pair meet, the prince recognizes Eurymine notwithstanding her male dress, obtains assurance of her continued regard, and repairs to the Graces to entreat their intercession with Apollo, who at last consents to her retransformation. Apollo further discovers to Aramanthus that Eurymine is his long-lost daughter; while the Duke, relenting, learns the deception practised on him and invites the lovers to return to Court. The pastoral element is supported by choruses led by Gemulo the shepherd and Silvio the ranger; while comic relief is supplied in the intercourse of their respective boys, Mopso and Frisco, with Joculo and with some Fairies, and in the scene where Iris rouses Somnus to procure the vision for Ascanio.

The rhymed heroics in which the piece is, with the exception of the comic prose passages, almost entirely composed, are not without a share, in places, of lyric beauty; and the songs are graceful and pretty enough.

The following details are suggestive of Lyly:—

Act i. 1. 56 'within his fathers Court | *The Saint was shrinde*' (cf. *Euph.* i. 215 l. 1).

Act i. 1. 229 'record' = remember (*Euph.* i. 303 l. 31, ii. 25 l. 14, 35 l. 19, 185 l. 8); iv. 1. 13, 2. 42 = 'sing' (*Woman*, iii. 1. 79, *Euph.* ii. 58 l. 7).

Act i. 1. 309 'I haue a garden full of Bees' (cf. Fidus in *Euph.* ii. 44).

Act i. 1. 320 'Why, hunting is a pleasure for a King' (cf. *Mid.* iv. 3. 5 'hunting is for kings, not peasants').

Act ii. 1. 62 Joculo's aside to the audience (cf. Gunophilus, *Woman*, iii. 2. 208; Cupid, *Gall.* ii. 2. 13).

Act iii. 2. 28 Joculo's pun 'a Kitchen God, Pan' (cf. *Mid.* iv. 1. 61

'all Pan and tinkerly'); and later in the scene his pun on 'poynts' (cf. *Gall.* i. 4. 42, ii. 3. 42).

Act iv. 1. 71 the making the good Aramanthus 'Prince of Lesbos Ile' (cf. *Midas*, iii. 1. 53, iv. 2. 31 sqq.).

Act v. 1. 113 the musical reference—the brook as a bass to the birds' voices.

In the conduct of the action, too, though the reader will be reminded most of Spenser's *Faerie Queene*, on which the verse too is often modelled, yet there are several points in which it can be paralleled from Lyly's dramatic work, e. g. in the title as compared with that of *Loves Metamorphosis*; in the use made of Ovid's *Metamorphoses* in regard to Somnus and his three sons (ii. 1) and Apollo and Hyacinth (iii. 1); in the imaginary transfer of scene to Somnus' cave (ii. 1. 139–49) and its subsequent contradiction (ll. 185–6) by the continued presence of the sleeping Ascanio; in the successive exits at the end of iii. 2 and iv. 1, as in *Mother Bombie*, ii. 2 and ii. 5 (cf. Sperantus' 'If all bee gone, Ile not staie' with Joculo's 'Nay let them go a Gods name, one by one'); in the change effected in the heroine's sex, as in *Gallathea*; in the vain suit of shepherds and foresters to her, as in *The Woman* and *Loves Metamorphosis*; in the sleep of the hero like that of Endimion; in the appeal of the several characters to the wizard or astrologer living a hermit's life in a cave, like Cassander, or Sybilla, or Mother Bombie, and in the considerable likeness of the scene between Aramanthus and the boys (iii. 2) to that between Mother Bombie and the wags in that play (iii. 4); in the interview between Aramanthus and Ascanio (iv. 1), which a little resembles that between Geron and Eumenides, while his wrapt absent manner at its commencement is very like that of the Alchemist and Astronomer in *Gallathea*; in the employment of servant-boys to make fun; in the introduction of fairies (whose dialogue with the boys, as Bullen notes, is a little like that of Shakespeare's fairies with Bottom); and in the large intervention of the classical deities. The last three points, however, are fairly common by 1596 or 1600[1]; while the others, though characteristic of Lyly, may nevertheless indicate some younger playwright, familiar with the work of previous years. The conduct of the opening scene and of that where Apollo changes Eurymine have, for me, an abruptness and direct force wholly foreign to Lyly's manner or genius; while Aramanthus' connexion with Eurymine is more lamely and casually treated than it would have been in his hands. The pastoral contains no compliments to Elizabeth; and the recourse to the *démodé* vehicle of the rhymed couplet seems unlikely in one who had written such good blank verse as is to be found

---

[1] Joculo's remark in iv. 1. 157 'Maister be contented, this is leape yeare,' may suggest one or other of these years as that of the play's original production, or may have been added on Lyly's revival of it in 1600, to which date '1599' of the Table (vol. ii. p. 230) should perhaps be altered.

in *The Woman in the Moone*. It is true that Lyly, in the Prologue to *The Woman*, had spoken of writing another verse-play; but, if this is the fulfilment of the promise, why does his name not appear on the title-page, as on those of *The Woman*, 1597, and *Loves Metamorphosis*, 1601?

So far as the actual verse is concerned little argument can be drawn from the disappearance of the peculiar 'mechanical devices' of Lyly's style. Absent from the blank verse of *The Woman*, they would still more naturally be absent from a novel experiment in rhymed heroics. But in the matter and sentiment, as apart from the conduct of the action, I find nothing specially characteristic of him beyond the few faint echoes cited above: and the general texture of the verse appears to me too thin and slight, and sometimes too prosy and obvious, in spite of Spenserian passages of poetic merit, to be the product of Lyly's brain [1]—even the songs are too simple and spontaneous, too artless, for him; though I should admit the possibility of his authorship of the Fairies' songs in Act ii, of the duet between Gemulo and Silvio in Act iv, and of the closing song in Act v. But in the two prose-scenes between Joculo, Mopso and Frisco (ii. 2, iii. 2) I do feel that there is a sufficient likeness, a sufficient amount of antithesis and word-play, to make his *late* authorship of these possible; though I am by no means sure that there is more than might easily be acquired by a young playwright imitating a popular predecessor, and I do not think it very probable that one in Lyly's rather distinct position would be found collaborating at all. They might, however, be added by him on the occasion of his coaching the Paul's Boys in the performance of the play, in 1599 or 1600.

Disbelieving, then, in his authorship of the whole, and admitting only a possibility of his authorship of the two prose-scenes, ii. 2 (containing the Fairies) and iii. 2 (with its considerable resemblance to iii. 4 of *Mother Bombie*), and perhaps of the duet in Act iv and the closing song of Act v, I have decided to print the play in a category apart as 'doubtful,' that the reader may be able to verify all that is here said and judge for himself.

Mr. Fleay (*Biograph. Chronicle*, ii. 324) says 'the style of most of the play is just that of Daniel's earlier dramatic work.' Now Daniel's earliest dramatic works were the strict Senecan tragedies *Cleopatra* and *Philotas*, pub. 1594 and 1605 respectively, in verse rhymed for the most part alternately, not in couplets, and far stronger, more regular, of a more ethical and intellectualized cast than is that of the *Maydes Metamorphosis*, which is written and conducted throughout in the freer spirit of the Romantic drama. Also, Mr. Fleay urges, in 1604 Daniel published *The Vision of the Twelve Goddesses*, in which Juno, Iris and Somnus are introduced as in ii. 1 of *M. M.*, and 'some of the very words are repeated.'

[1] The tameness, however, of some of the verse in my lately-identified *Entertainments* as well as in the *Poems*, weakens the force of this argument.

For particular expressions, however, affording ground for comparison, I look in vain; nor could anything be farther from the dignified conduct and diction of Daniel's *Vision* than the comic or serio-comic treatment of Juno, Iris and Somnus in *M. M.* Mr. Fleay rightly urges that the Prologue of *M. M.* is more appropriate to some private occasion like a wedding than to a public audience; but the line of Daniel's first sonnet from which he says ' Then to the boundlesse Ocean of your woorth,' Prol. l. 9, is taken, really runs ' Unto the boundless ocean of thy beauty'; and the mere fact that at the end of the play the Muses dance to Apollo's music is certainly not sufficient to identify it with the masque performed at the wedding of Lord Herbert with Anne Russell on June 16, 1600, where Muses did the same thing [1]. Some general likeness, however, may be admitted between our play and Daniel's *Vision*, which, further, carries something of the same sense of being written by one influenced by Lyly's work [2].

Mr. Gosse and Mr. Bullen pronounce for Day's authorship; and Mr. Bullen, Day's editor in 1881, cites a parallel in his *Humour out of Breath* for ' the merciless harrying of the word *kind*' at the beginning of Act v, and in *Law Trickes*, v. 1, for the echo-scene in iv. 1 of our play, while he considers ' the amœbæan rhymes between Gemulo and Silvio (Act i) in their sportive quaintness, as like Day's handiwork as they are unlike Lyly's.' Mr. Bullen here, and still more in his Introduction to Day, p. 33, is somewhat less than just to Lyly; but, putting that aside, one may acknowledge that the general style of *The Maydes Metamorphosis* is more like Day. Day, when he wrote verse, generally chose the rhymed couplet, which there is no instance of Lyly's using: and the chief metrical characteristics of this play, (1) a noticeable carelessness about the rhymes chosen; (2) the frequent leaving of a line unrhymed in the middle of a rhymed passage; (3) a tendency to run into twelve syllables [3], and especially to do this where the line is divided between two characters, e. g. iii.

---

[1] See however above, vol. i. p. 381 note, where I have followed Fleay so far as to suppose that our play may have been given on the Tuesday or Wednesday night of the same occasion, and that the last line of the Epilogue may *refer* to the masque of the preceding Monday night, June 16.

[2] The *Vision* was composed as a masque, and represented January 8, 1604-5, not 1603-4 as Fleay asserts (*Biog. Chron.* i. 90). Before the end of Jan. an unauthorized quarto without author's name was issued by Edw. Allde, with title *The Trve Discription of a Royall Masque. Presented at Hampton Court, vpon Sunday night, being the eight of Ianuary*, 1604. *And Personated by the Queenes most Excellent Majestie, attended by Eleuen Ladies of Honour. London Printed by Edward Allde, and are to be solde at the Long Shoppe, adjoyning vnto S. Mildreds Church in the Poultrye* 1(60)4. (3 copies are in the Br. Mus.), which compelled Daniel to issue a correct ed. in 8vo entitled *The Vision of the Twelve Goddesses presented in a masque at Hampton Court, the 8 of January, &c.* Printed by *T. C. for Simon Waterson*. 1604. A copy exists in the Bodleian. See E. Law's ed. of the 4° of 1623, (1880), Introd. pp. 49-50.

[3] Instances are not unknown in Lyly, e. g. vol. i. 479 l. 15 and *Woman*, iv. 1. 24.

1. 76, 79, 83, 131 ; iv. 2. 91 ; v. 1. 42 ; (4) a certain confusion or misapprehension in the use of double-rhymes, e. g. iii. 1. 21–2, 178–9 ; iv. 2. 65–6 (cf. Day's *Parliament of Bees*, p. 49, 'A pirate' with 'hate'); are all paralleled in Day's work[1]. In Day's *Law Trickes* there is a page named Joculo: in *The Ile of Gvls* a girl named Mopsa. The resemblances to Lyly's work in the conduct of *The Maydes Metamorphosis* may be referable to a conscious or unconscious imitation by Day of the older dramatist, of his familiarity with whose work I can point to two rather striking instances, (1) *Law Trickes*, iii. p. 41, ' doost see Vulcan with the *horning parenthesis* in his forehead,' a joke inexplicable save by reference to that of the smith Calypho in *Sapho and Phao*, iii. 2. 47 sqq. ; (2) *The Ile of Gvls*, ii. 1. p. 48, Violetta's remarks about 'maydenhead' are exactly parallel to Pipenetta's song on the same subject in *Midas*, v. 2. p. 154 :—

> ' But in the allowed opinion of most,
> Tis neuer truly had till it be lost.
> . . . .
> And in my dreame me thought twas too much wrong
> A prettie maid should lie alone so long.'

On the whole, then, without feeling quite convinced, I am content to acquiesce in the view that this play is an early work by that author, probably touched and added to by Lyly in the course of his rehearsal of it with the Paul's Boys in 1599 or 1600.

I reprint it *literatim et punctuatim* from the quarto, using conical brackets for one or two trifling additions, and appending the quarto reading in a footnote in the few cases where I have emended the text. A number of explanatory or illustrative notes, some from Mr. Bullen, will be found at the end, though I have not treated the play quite so elaborately as those in which Lyly's hand is undoubted.

[1] Instances in Lyly are vol. i. 476 ll. 30–1 ; 483 ll. 3–4 ; 468 ll. 7–8.

THE Maydes Metamorphosis.

As it hath bene sundrie times Acted by the Children of Powles.

LONDON

Printed by Thomas Creede, for Richard Oliue, dwelling in long Lane.
1600.

The Prologue

THe manifold great fauours we haue found,
  By you, to vs poore weaklings still extended:
Whereof your vertues haue bene only ground,
And no desert in vs to be so friended:
Bindes vs some way or other to expresse, 5
(Though all our all be else defeated quite
Of any meanes) saue duteous thankefulnes,
Which is the vtmost measure of our might:
Then to the boundlesse Ocean of your woorth,
This little drop of water we present: 10
Where though it neuer can be singled foorth,
Let zeale be pleader for our good intent.
   Drops not diminish, but encrease great floods:
   And mites impaire not, but augment our goods.

The Maydes Metamorphosis.

⟨ACT I.⟩

⟨SCENE I.⟩

Enter Phylander, Orestes, Eurymine.

Eurymine.

P *Hylander,* and *Orestes,* what conceyt
   Troubles your silent mindes? Let me intreat
   Since we are come thus farre, as we do walke
   You would deuise some prettie pleasant talke:
   The aire is coole, the euening high and faire,   5
   Why should your cloudie lookes, then shew dispaire?
Phy. Beleeue me faire *Eurimine*, my skill
   Is simple in discourse, and vtterance ill:
   Orestes if he were disposde to trie,
   Can better manage such affaires than I.   10
Eu. Why then *Orestes* let me craue of you
   Some olde, or late done story to renew:
   Another time you shall request of me
   As good, if not, a greater curtesie.
Or. Trust me as now (nor can I shew a reason)   15
   All mirth vnto my mind comes out of season:
   For inward I am troubled in such sort,
   As all vnfit I am to make report
   Of any thing may breed the least delight,
   Rather in teares, I wish the day were night: 20
   For neither can my selfe be merry now,
   Nor treat of ought that may be likte of you.
Eu. Thats but your melancholike old disease,
   That neuer are disposde but when ye please.
Ph. Nay mistresse, then since he denies the taske   25
   My selfe will strait ⟨ac⟩complish what ye aske:
   And though the pleasure in my tale be small,
   Yet may it serue to pass the time withall.

Eu. Thanks good *Phylander,* when you please say on,
  Better I deeme a bad discourse, then none.   30
Phy. Sometime there liu'd a Duke not far from hence,
  Mightie in fame, and vertues excellence,
  Subiects he had, as readie to obey
  As he to rule: beloued euery way,
  But that which most of all he gloried in,   35
  (Hope of his age, and comfort of his kin,)
  Was the fruition of one onely sonne,
  A gallant youth, inferior vnto none
  For vertue, shape, or excellence of wit,
  That after him vpon his throne might sit.   40
  This youth when once he came to perfect age,
  The Duke would faine haue linckt in marriage
  With diuers dames of honourable blood,
  But stil his fathers purpose he withstood.
Eu. How, was he not of mettal apt to loue?   45
Phy. Yes apt enough, as wil the sequel proue.
  But so the streame of his affection lay,
  As he did leane a quite contrary way,
  Disprouing still the choyce his father made,
  And oftentimes the matter had delaid: 50
  Now giuing hope he would at length consent,
  And then again, excusing his intent.
Eu. What made him so repugnant in his deeds?
Phy. Another loue, which this disorder breeds:
  For euen at home within his fathers Court   55
  The Saint was shrinde, whom he did honor most:
  A louely dame, a virgin pure and chaste,
  And worthy of a Prince to be imbrac'te.
  Had but her birth (which was obscure they said)
  Answerd her beautie, this their opinion staid.   60
  Yet did this wilful youth affect her still,
  And none but she was mistres of his will.
  Full often did his father him disswade,
  From liking such a mean and low borne mayde.
  The more his father stroue to change his minde,   65
  The more the sonne became with fancy blinde.
Eu. Alas, how sped the silly Louers then?
Phy. As might euen grieue the rude vnciuel'st men.
  When hereupon to weane his fixed heart
  From such dishonour, to his high desert,   70
  The Duke had labourd, but in vaine did striue,
  Thus he began his purpose to contriue:

Two of his seruants of vndoubted troth,
He bound by vertue of a solemne oath,
To traine the silly damzel out of sight, 75
And there in secret to bereaue her quite
Eu. Of what, her life?
Phy.   Yes Madame of her life,
Which was the cause of all the former strife.
Eu. And did they kill her?
Phy.   You shall heare anon:
The question first must be discided on 80
In your opinion, whats your iudgement? say,
Who were most cruell: those that did obay,
Or he that gaue commandment for the fact?
Eu. In each of them it was a bloody act:
Yet they deserue (to speake my mind of both) 85
Most pardon, that were bound thereto by oath.
Phy. It is enough, we do accept your doome,
To passe vnblam'd, what ere of you become.
Eu. To passe vnblamde, what ere become of me?
What may the meaning of these speeches be? 90
Phy. Eurymine, my trembling tongue doth faile,
My conscience yrkes, my fainting sences quaile:
My faltring speech bewraies my guiltie thought,
And stammers at the message we haue brought.
Eu. Ay me, what horror doth inuade my brest? 95
Or. Nay then *Phylander* I will tell the rest.
Damzell thus fares thy case, demand not why,
You must forthwith prepare your selfe to dye.
Therefore dispatch, and set your mind at rest.
Eu. Phylander is it true? or doth he iest? 100
Phy. There is no remedie but you must dye:
By you I framde my tragicke history.
The Duke my maister, is the man I meant,
His sonne, the Prince, the mayd of meane discent
Your selfe, on whom *Ascanio* so doth doate, 105
As for no reason may remoue his thought:
Your death the Duke determines by vs two,
To end the loue betwixt his sonne and you:
And for that cause we trainde you to this wood,
Where you must sacrifice your dearest blood. 110
Eur. Respect my teares.
Orest.   We must regard our oath.
Eur. My tender yeares.
Or.   They are but trifles both.

Eu. Mine innocency.
Or. That would our promise breake,
Dispatch forthwith, we may not heare you speake.
Eu. If neither teares nor innocency moue, 115
Yet thinke there is a heauenly power aboue.
Orest. A done, and stand not preaching here all day.
Eu. Then since there is no remedie, I pray
Yet good my maisters, do but stay so long
Till I haue tane my farewell with a song, 120
Of him whom I shall neuer see againe.
Phy. We will affoord that respit to your paine.
Eu. But least the feare of death appall my mind,
Sweet gentlemen let me this fauour find.
That you wil vale mine eye-sight with this scarfe: 125
That when the fatall stroke is aymde at me,
I may not start, but suffer patiently.
Orest. Agreed, giue me, Ile shadow ye from feare,
If this may do it.
Eu. Oh I would it might
But shadowes want the power to do that right. 130
Shee sings.
Ye sacred Fyres, and powers aboue,
Forge of desires working loue,
Cast downe your eye, cast downe your eye
Vpon a Mayde in miserie.
My sacrifice is louers blood: 135
And from eyes salt teares a flood:
All which I spend, all which I spend
For thee *Ascanio*, my deare friend:
And though this houre I must feele
The bitter sower of pricking steele, 140
Yet ill or well, yet ill or well
To thee *Ascanio* still farewell.
*Orestes offers to strike her with his Rapier, and is stayed
by Phylander.*
Orest. What meanes *Phylander*?
Phy. Oh forbeare thy stroke,
Her piteous mone and gesture might prouoke
Hard flints to ruthe. 145
Orest. Hast thou forgot thy oath?
Phy. Forgot it? no.
Or. Then wherfore doest thou interrupt me so?
Phy. A sudden terror ouercomes my thought.
Or. Thē suffer me, that stands in fear of nought.

Phy. Oh hold *Orestes*, heare my reason first. 150
Or. Is all religion of thy vowe forgot?
  Do as thou wilt, but I forget it not.
Phy. *Orestes*, if thou standst vpon thine oath,
  Let me alone, to answere for vs both.
Or. What answer canst thou giue? I wil not stay. 155
Phy. Nay villain, then my sword shall make me way.
Or. Wilt thou in this, against thy conscience striue?
Phy. I will defend a woman while I liue.
  A virgin, and an innocent beside,
  Therefore put vp, or else thy chaunce abide. 160
Or. Ile neuer sheath my sword, vnles thou show,
  Our oath reserued, we may let her go.
Phy. That will I do, if truth may be of force.
Or. And then wil I be pleasd to graunt remorse.
Eu. Litle thought I when out of doore I went, 165
  That thus my life should stand on argument.
Phy. A lawfull oath in an vnlawfull cause,
  Is first dispenc't withall, by reasons lawes:
  Then next, respect must to the end be had,
  Because th' intent, doth make it good or bad. 170
  Now here th' intent is murder as thou seest,
  Which to performe, thou on thy oath reliest:
  But since the cause is wicked and vniust,
  Th' effect must likewise be held odious.
  We swore to kill, and God forbids to kill: 175
  Shall we be rulde by him, or by mans will?
  Beside it is a woman is condemde:
  And what is he that is a man indeed,
  That can endure to see a woman bleed?
Or. Thou hast preuaild, *Eurymine* stand vp, 180
  I will not touch thee for a world of gold.
Phy. Why now thou seemst to be of humane mould.
  But on our graunt faire mayd that you shall liue,
  Will you to vs your faithfull promise giue,
  Henceforth t'abandon this your Country quite, 185
  And neuer more returne into the sight
  Of fierce *Telemachus*, the angry Duke,
  Whereby we may be voyd of all rebuke?
Eur. Here do I plight my chaste vnspotted hand,
  I will abiure this most accursed land: 190
  And vow henceforth what fortune ere betide,
  Within these woods and desarts to abide.

Phy. Now wants there nothing, but a fit excuse,
To sooth the Duke, in his conceiu'd abuse:
That he may be perswaded she is slaine, 195
And we our wonted fauour still maintaine.
Orest. It shall be thus, within a Lawne hard by,
Obscure with bushes, where no humane eye,
Can any way discouer our deceite:
There feeds a heard of Goates, and country neate. 200
Some Kidde, or other youngling, will we take,
And with our swords dispatch it for her sake.
And hauing slaine it, rip his panting breast,
And take the heart of the vnguiltie beast:
Which to th'intent, our counterfeit report 205
May seeme more likely, we will beare to court:
And there protest with bloody weapons drawne,
It was her heart.
Phy. Then likewise take this Lawne,
Which well *Telemachus* did know she wore:
And let it be all spotted too with gore. 210
How say you mistresse, will you spare that vale?
Eur. That or what else, to verifie your tale:
And thankes *Phylander*, and *Orestes* both,
That you preserue me from a Tyrants wroth.
Phy. I would it were within my power, I wis, 215
To do you greater curtesie then this:
But what we cannot by our deeds expresse
In heart we wish to ease your heauinesse.
Eur. A double debt, yet one word ere ye go,
Commmend me to my deare *Ascanio*: 220
Whose loyall loue, and presence to forgoe,
Doth gall me more then all my other woe.
Orest. Our liues shall neuer want to do him good.
Phy. Nor yet our death, if he in daunger stood:
And mistresse, so good fortune be your guide. 225
Or. And ought that may be fortunate beside.
                                              (*Exeunt.*

Eu. The like I wish vnto your selues againe:
And many happie dayes deuoyd of paine.
And now *Eurymine* record thy state,
So much deiected, and opprest by fate: 230
What hope remaines? wherein hast thou to ioy?
Wherein to tryumph, but thine owne annoy?
If euer wretch might tell of miserie,
Then I alas, poore I, am only she:

Vnknowne of parents, destitute of friends, 235
Hopefull of nought, but what misfortune sends.
Banisht, to liue a fugitue alone,
In vncoth paths, and regions neuer knowne.
Behold *Ascanio*, for thy only sake,
These tedious trauels I must vndertake: 240
Nor do I grudge, the paine seemes lesse to mee,
In that I suffer this distresse for thee.

Enter Siluio, a Raunger.

Sil. Wel met fair Nymph, or Goddesse if ye bee:
Tis straunge me thinkes, that one of your degree
Should walk these solitary groues alone. 245
Eu. It were no maruell if you knew my mone.
But what are you that question me so far?
Sil. My habit telles you that, a Forrester:
That hauing lost a heard of skittish Deere,
Was of good hope, I should a found them heere. 250
Eu. Trust me, I saw not any, so farewell.
Sil. Nay stay: and further of your fortunes tell:
I am not one that meanes you any harme.

Enter Gemulo the shepheard.

Ge. I thinke my Boy be fled away by charme.
Raunger well met: within thy walke I pray, 255
Sawst thou not *Mopso*, my vnhappie Boy?
Sil. Shepheard not I, what meanst to seeke him here?
Ge. Because the wagge, possest with doubtfull feare,
Least I would beate him for a fault he did:
Amongst those Trees, I do suspect hees hid. 260
But how now Raunger? you mistake I trowe,
This is a Lady, and no barren Dowe.
Sil. It is indeede, and as it seemes, distrest,
Whose griefe to know, I humbly made request:
But she as yet will not reueale the same. 265
Ge. Perhaps to me she will: speak gentle dame?
What daunger great hath driuen ye to this place?
Make knowne your state, and looke what slender grace,
A Shepheards poore abilitie may yeeld,
You shall be sure of, ere I leaue the feeld. 270
Eur. Alas good Sir, the cause may not be knowne,
That hath inforste me to be here alone.
Sil. Nay feare not to discouer what you are:
It may be we may remedie your care.

256 Mopso] Moyso *Q*

Eu. Since needs you will, that I renew my griefe, 275
Whether it be my chance to finde reliefe
Or not, I wreake not: such my crosses are,
As sooner *I* expect to meete dispaire.
Then thus it is: not farre from hence do dwell
My parents, of the world esteemed well: 280
Who with their bitter threats, my graũt had won,
This day to marrie with a neighbours son.
And such a one, to whom I should be wife,
As *I* could neuer fancie in my life.
And therefore to auoyd that endlesse thrall, 285
This morne I came away and left them all.
Sil. Now trust me virgin, they were much vnkind,
To seeke to match you so against your minde.
Ge. It was beside, vnnaturall constraint:
But by the tenure of your iust complaint, 290
It seemes you are not minded to returne,
Nor any more to dwell where you were borne.
Eu. It is my purpose, if I might obtaine
A place of refuge where I might remaine.
Sil. Why go with me, my Lodge is not far off, 295
Where you shall haue such hospitalitie
As shall be for your health and safetie.
Ge. Soft Raunger, you do raunge beyond your skill,
My house is nearer: and for my good will,
It shall exceed a woodmans woodden stuffe: 300
Then go with me, Ile keep you safe enough.
Sil. Ile bring her to a bower beset with greene.
Ge. And I an arbour, may delight a Queene.
Sil. Her dyet shalbe Venson at my boord.
Ge. Yong Kid and Lambe, we shepheards can affoord. 305
Sil. And nothing else?
Ge.   Yes, raunging now and then,
A Hog, a Goose, a Capon, or a Hen.
Sil. These walkes are mine, amongst the shadie trees.
Ge. For that I haue, a garden full of Bees,
Whose buzing musick with the flowers sweet, 310
Each euen and morning, shall her sences greet.
Sil. The Nightingale is my continuall clocke.
Ge. And mine the watchfull, sin-remembring cocke.
Sil. A hunts vp, I can tune her with my hounds.
Ge. And I can shew her meads, and fruitfull grounds. 315
Sil. Within these woods are many pleasant springs.
Ge. Betwixt yond dales, the Eccho daily sings.

Sil. I maruell that a rusticke shepheard dare
  With woodmen thus audaciously compare?
  Why, hunting is a pleasure for a King, 320
  And Gods themselues sometime frequent the thing.
  Diana with her bowe and arrowes keene,
  Did often vse the Chace, in Forrests greene.
  And so alas, the good Athenian knight,
  And swift *Acteon* herein tooke delight: 325
  And *Atalanta* the Arcadian dame,
  Conceiu'd such wondrous pleasure in the game:
  That with her traine of Nymphs attending on,
  She came to hunt the Bore of *Calydon*.
Ge. So did *Apollo* walk with shepheards crooke, 330
  And many Kings their scepters haue forsooke:
  To lead the quiet life we shepheards know
  Accounting it a refuge for their woe.
Sil. But we take choice of many a pleasant walke
  And marke the Deare how they begin to stalke, 335
  When each according to his age and time,
  Pricks vp his head, and beares a Princely minde:
  The lustie Stag conductor of the traine,
  Leads all the heard in order downe the plaine:
  The baser rascalls scatter here and there, 340
  As not presuming to approach so neere.
Ge. So shepheards sometime sit vpon a hill,
  Or in the cooling shadow of a mill:
  And as we sit, vnto our pipes we sing,
  And therewith make the neighboring groues to ring. 345
  And when the sun steales downward to the west,
  We leaue our chat, and whistle in the fist:
  Which is a signall to our stragling flocke,
  As Trumpets sound to men in martiall shocke.
Sil. Shall I be thus out-faced by a swaine? 350
  Ile haue a guard to wayt vpon her traine,
  Of gallant woodmen, clad in comely greene:
  The like whereof, hath sildome yet bene seene.
Ge. And I of shepheards such a lustie crew,
  As neuer Forrester the like yet knew: 355
  Who for their persons and their neate aray,
  Shalbe as fresh, as is the moneth of May.

319 thus] then *Q*   332 know] *I correct* tooke. of the *Q*   336 *Bullen queries* kinde, *but* time *is perhaps better sense, and an assonance or annomination (like* fist *and* west, *l.* 346) *often satisfies the author instead of a rhyme*

Where are ye there, ye merry noted swaines?
Draw neare a while, and whilst vpon the plaines
Your flocks do gently feed, lets see your skill,
How you with chaunting, can sad sorrow kill.

Enter shepheards singing.

Sil. Thinks *Gemulo* to beare the bell away?
By singing of a simple Rundelay?
No, *I* haue fellowes, whose melodious throates
Shall euen as far exceed those homely notes
As doth the Nightingale in musicke passe,
The most melodious bird that euer was.
And for an instance, here they are at hand,
When they haue done, let our deserts be scand.

Enter wood-men, and sing.

Eu. Thanks to you both, you both deserue so well,
As I want skill your worthinesse to tell:
And both I do commend for your good will,
And both Ile honor, loue and reuerence still:
For neuer virgin had such kindnes showne,
Of straungers, yea, and men to her vnknowne.
But more, to end this sudden controuersie,
Since I am made an vmpier in the plea,
This is my verdite: Ile intreate of you
A Cottage for my dwelling: and of you,
A flocke to tend: and so indifferent
My gratefull paines on either shalbe spent.
Sil. I am agreed, and for the loue I beare
Ile boast, I haue a Tenant is so faire.
Ge. And I wil hold it as a rich possession,
That she vouchsafes to be of my profession.
Sil. Thē for a sign that no man here hath wrong
From hence lets all conduct her with a song.

The end of the first Act.

ACTUS SECUNDUS.

⟨Scene I.⟩

Enter Ascanio, and Ioculo his Page.

Asca. Away *Ioculo.*
Io. Here sir, at hand.
Asca. Ioculo, where is she?
Io. I know not.
Asca. When went she?

Io. I know not.
Asca. Which way went she?
Io. I know not.
Asca. Where should I seeke her?
Io. I know not.
Asca. When shall I find her?
Io. I know not.
Asca. A vengeance take thee slaue, what dost thou know?
Io. Marry sir, that I doo know.
Asca. What villaine?
Io. And you be so testie, go looke: What a coyles here with you? If we knew where she were, what need we seeke her? I thinke you are lunaticke: where were you when you should haue lookt after her? now you go crying vp and downe after your wench, like a Boy had lost his horne booke.
Asca. Ah my sweet Boy.
Io. Ah my sweet Maister: nay I can giue you as good words as you can giue me: alls one for that.
Asca. What canst thou giue me no reliefe?
Io. Faith sir, there comes not one morsel of comfort from my lips, to sustaine that hungry mawe of your miserie, there is such a dearth at this time, God amend it.
Asca. A *Ioculo*, my breast is full of griefe,
And yet my hope, that only wants reliefe.
Io. Your brest and my belly, are in two contrary kaies, you walke to get stomacke to your meate, and I walke to get meate to my stomacke: your breast's full, and my belli's emptie. If they chance to part in this case, God send them merry meeting: that my belly be ful, and your brest empty.
Asca. Boy, for the loue that euer thou didst owe,
To thy deare master, poore *Ascanio*,
Racke thy proou'd wits, vnto the highest straine,
To bring me backe *Eurymine* againe.
Io. Nay master, if wit could do it, I could tell you more: but if it euer be done, the very legeritie of the feete must do it: these ten nimble bones must do the deed: Ile trot like a little dog: theres not a bush so big as my beard, but Ile be peeping in it: theres not a Coate but Ile search euery corner: if she be aboue, or beneath, ouer the ground, or vnder, Ile finde her out.
Asca. Stay *Ioculo*: alas it cannot be:
If we should part, I loose both her and thee:
The woods are wide: and wandring thus about,
Thou maist be lost: and not my Loue found out.

16–63 *All Joculo's speeches within these limits as verse in* Q

Io. I pray you let me goe.
Asca. I pray thee stay.
Io. Ifaith ile runne.
Asca. And doest not know which way.
Io. Any way: alls one, ile drawe drie foote: if you send not to seeke 50
her, you may lye here long enough, before she come to seeke you: she
litle thinkes that you are hunting for her in these quarters.
    Asca. Ah *Ioculo*, before I leaue my Boy,
Of this worlds comfort, now my only ioy:
Seest thou this place? vpon this grassie bed, 55
With sommers gawdie dyaper bespred.
        He lyes downe.
Vnder these shadowes shall my dwelling be:
Till thou returne, sweete *Ioculo* to me.
Io. And if my Conuoy be not cut off by the way, it shall not be long
before I be with you.
       He speakes to the people. 60
Well, I pray you looke to my maister: for here *I* leaue him amongst you:
and if *I* chaunce to light on the wench, you shall heare of me by the
next winde.
       Exit Ioculo, Ascanio solus.
    Asca. In vaine I feare, I beate my braines about,
Proouing by search, to finde my mistresse out: 65
Eurymine, Eurymine, retorne:
And with thy presence guild the beautious morne:
And yet I feare to call vpon thy name,
The prattling Eccho, should she learne the same,
The last words accent sheele no more prolong, 70
But beare that sound vpon her airie tong.
Adorned with the presence of my Loue,
The woods I feare, such secret power shal proue
As they'll shut vp each path: hide euery way,
Because they still would haue her go astray: 75
And in that place would alwaies haue her seene,
Only because they would be euer greene:
And keepe the wingged Quiristers still there,
To banish winter cleane out of the yeare.
But why persist I to bemone my state, 80
When she is gone, and my complaint too late?
A drowsie dulnes closeth vp my sight,
O powerfull sleepe, I yeeld vnto thy might.
       He falles a sleepe.

       Enter Iuno, and Iris.
Iuno. Come hither *Iris.*
Iris. Iris is at hand,

  To attend *Ioues* wife: great *Iunos* hie command.   85
Iuno. *Iris* I know I do thy seruice proue,
 And euer since I was the wife of *Ioue*
 Thou hast bene readie when I called still,
 And alwayes most obedient to my will:
 Thou seest how that imperiall Queene of loue,   90
 With all the Gods, how she preuailes aboue,
 And still against great *Iunos* hests doth stand,
 To haue all stoupe and bowe, at her command:
 Her Doues and Swannes, and Sparrowes, must be graced,
 And on Ioues Aultars, must be highly placed.   95
 My starry Peacocks, which doth beare my state:
 Scaresly alowed within his pallace gate:
 And since her selfe, she thus preferd doth see,
 Now the proud huswife will contend with mee:
 And practiseth her wanton pranckes to play   100
 With this *Ascanio*, and *Eurymine*.
 But Loue shall know, in spight of all his skill,
 Iuno's a woman, and will haue her will.
Iris. What is my Goddesse will? may *Iris* aske?
Iuno. *Iris*, on thee *I* do impose this taske,   105
 To crosse proud *Venus*, and her purblind Lad,
 Vntill the mother, and her brat be mad,
 And with each other, set them so at ods,
 Till to their teeth they curse, and ban the Gods.
Iris. Goddes, the graunt consists alone in you,   110
Iuno. Then mark the course which now you must pursue.
 Within this ore-growne Forrest, there is found
 A duskie Caue, thrust lowe into the ground:
 So vgly darke, so dampie and ⟨so⟩ steepe,
 As for his life the sunne durst neuer peepe   115
 *I*nto the entrance: which doth so afright
 The very day, that halfe the world is night.
 Where fennish fogges, and vapours do abound:
 There *Morpheus* doth dwell within the ground,
 No crowing Cocke, nor waking bell doth call,   120
 Nor watchfull dogge disturbeth sleepe at all.
 No sound is heard in compasse of the hill,
 But euery thing is quiet, whisht, and still.
 Amid this Caue, vpon the ground doth lie,
 A hollow plancher, all of Ebonie   125
 Couer'd with blacke, whereon the drowsie God,
 Drowned in sleepe, continually doth nod:

  95 Ioues *required by context*: Loues Q *by a common mistake*

Go *Iris* go, and my commaundment take,
And beate against the doores till sleepe awake,
Bid him from me, in vision to appeare, 130
Vnto *Ascanio* that lieth slumbring heare.
And in that vision, to reueale the way,
How he may finde the faire *Eurymine*.
Iris. Madam, my seruice is at your command,
Iuno. Dispatch it then, good *Iris* out of hand. 135
My Peacocks and my Charriot shall remaine,
About the shore, till thou returne againe. *Exit Iuno.*
Iris. About the businesse now that *I* am sent,
To sleepes blacke Caue, *I* will incontinent:
And his darke cabine, boldly will *I* shake, 140
Vntill the drowsie lumpish God awake:
And such a bounsing at his Caue Ile keepe,
That if pale death, seaz'd on the eyes of sleepe,
Ile rowse him vp, that when he shall me heare,
Ile make his locks stand vp on end with feare. 145
Be silent aire, whil'st *Iris* in her pride
Swifter then thought, vpon the windes doth ride.
What *Somnus*, what *Somnus*, *Somnus*. *Strikes.*
   Pauses a litle.
What wilt thou not awake? art thou still so fast?
Nay then yfaith, Ile haue an other cast. 150
  What Somnus Somnus *I* say?
   Strikes againe.
 Som. Who calles at this time of the day?
  What a balling dost thou keepe?
  A vengeance take thee, let me sleepe.
Iris. Vp thou drowsie God, *I* say, 155
  And come presently away,
  Or *I* will beate vpon this doore,
  That after this, thou sleep'st no more.
Som. *I*le take a nap, and come annon.
Iris. Out you beast, you blocke, you stone: 160
  Come, or at thy doore *I*le thunder,
  Til both heauen and hel do wonder,
  Somnus, I say!
Som. A vengeance split thy chaps asunder. 164
Iris. What *Somnus*? *Enter Somnus.*
Som. *Iris I* thought it should be thee.
 How now mad wench, what wouldst with me?
Iris. From mightie I*uno*, I*oues* immortal wife,
 Somnus I come: to charge thee on thy life,

 That thou vnto this Gentleman appeere,   170
 And in this place, thus as he lyeth heere,
 Present his mistres to his inward eies,
 In as true manner, as thou canst deuise.
Som. I would thou wert hangd for waking me.
 Three sonnes I haue, the eldest *Morpheus* highte: 175
 He shewes of man, the shape or sight.
 The second *Icelor*, whose beheasts
 Doth shewe the formes of birds and beasts.
 Phantasor for the third, things lifeles hee;
 Chuse which like thee of these three.   180
Iris. *Morpheus*: if he in humane shape appeare.
Som. *Morpheus* come forth in perfect likenes heere,
 Of, how call ye the Gentlewoman?
Iris.   *Eurymine.*
Som. Of *Eurymine*: and shewe this Gentleman,
 What of his mistres is become.   185
       Kneeling downe by Ascanio.

   Enter Eurymine, to be supposed Morpheus.

Mor. My deare *Ascanio*, in this vision see,
 Eurymine doth thus appeare to thee:
 As soone as sleepe hath left thy drowsie eies,
 Follow the path that on thy right hand lies,
 An aged Hermit thou by chaunce shalt find,   190
 That there hath bene, time almost out of mind:
 This holy man, this aged reuerent Father,
 There in the woods, doth rootes and simples gather:
 His wrinckled browe, tells strengths past long ago:
 His beard as white, as winters driuen snow.   195
 He shall discourse the troubles I haue past,
 And bring vs both togither at the last.
 Thus she presents her shadow to thy sight,
 That would her person gladly if she might.
Iris. See how he catches to imbrace the shade.   200
Mor. This vision fully doth his powers inuade.
 And when the heate shall but a litle slake:
 Thou then shalt see him presently awake.
Som. Hast thou ought else, that I may stand in sted?
Iris. No *Somnus*, no: go back vnto thy bed: 205
 Iuno she shall reward thee for thy paine.
Som. Then good night, *Iris*, Ile to rest againe.
Iris. *Morpheus* farwell: to *Iuno* I will flie.
Mor. And *I* to sleepe, as fast as *I* can hie.   *Exeunt.*

Ascanio starting, sayes.

Eurymine: Ah my good Angell stay: 210
O vanish not so suddenly away.
O stay my Goddes, whither doest thou flie?
Returne my sweet *Eurymine*, tis *I*.
Where art thou speake? Let me behold thy face:
Did *I* not see thee, in this very place 215
Euen now? Here did *I* not see thee stand?
And here thy feete did blesse the happie land?
Eurymine: Oh wilt thou not attend?
Flie from thy foe: *Ascanio* is thy friend.
The fearfull Hare, so shuns the labouring hound, 220
And so the Dear eschues the Hunts-man wound.
The trembling Foule, so flies the Falcons gripe:
The Bond-man, so, his angry maisters stripe.
I follow not, as *Phœbus Daphne* did:
Nor as the Dog pursues the trembling Kid. 225
Thy shape it was: alas *I* sawe not thee:
That sight were fitter for the Gods then mee.
But if in dreames, there any truth be found,
Thou art within the compas of this ground.
*I*le raunge the woods, and all the groues about, 230
And neuer rest, vntill *I* find thee out.   *Exit.*

⟨SCENE II.⟩

Enter at one doore, Mopso singing.

Mop. Terlitelo, Terlitelo, terlitelee, terlo,
So merrily this shepheards Boy
His horne that he can blow,
Early in a morning, late, late, in an euening,
And euer sat this little Boy, 5
So merrily piping.

Enter at the other doore, Frisco singing.

Fris. Can you blow the little horne?
Weell, weell, and very weell.
And can you blow the little horne,
Amongst the leaues greene? 10

Enter Ioculo in the midst singing.

Io. Fortune my foe, why doest thou frowne on mee?
And will my fortune neuer better bee:
Wilt thou I say, for euer breed my paine?
And wilt thou not restore my Ioyes againe?

Frisco. Cannot a man be merry in his owne walke, but a must be thus encombred?

Io. I am disposed to be melancholly, and I cannot be priuate, for one villaine or other.

Mop. How the diuel stumbled this case of rope-ripes in- into my way?

Fris. Sirrha, what art thou? and thou?

Io. I am Page to a Courtier.

Mop. And I a Boy to a Shepheard.

Fris. Thou art the Apple-squier to an Eawe, and thou sworne brother to a bale of false dice.

Io. What art thou?

Fris. I am a Boy to a Raunger.

Io. An Out-lawe by authoritie: one that neuer sets marke of his own goods, nor neuer knowes how he comes by other mens.

Mop. That neuer knowes his cattell, but by their hornes.

Fris. Sirrha, so you might haue said of your masters sheep.

Io. I marry: this takes fier like touch powder, and goes off with a huffe.

Fris. They come of crick-cracks, and shake their tayles like a squib.

Io. Ha you Rogues, the very steele of my wit, shall strike fier from the flint of your vnderstandings: haue you not heard of me?

Mop. Yes, if you be that *Ioculo* that I take you for, we haue heard of your exployts, for cosoning of some seuen, and thirtie Alewiues, in the Villages here about.

Io. A wit, as nimble as a Sempsters needle, or a girles finger at her Buske poynt.

Mop. Your iest goes too low sir.

Fris. O but tis a tickling iest.

Io. Who wold haue thought to haue found this in a plaine villaine, that neuer woare better garment, then a green Ierkin?

Frisco. O Sir, though you Courtiers haue all the honour, you haue not all the wit.

Mop. Soft sir, tis not your witte can carry it away in this company.

Io. Sweet Rogues, your companie to me, is like musick to a wench at midnight: when she lies alone, and could wish, yea marry could she.

Fris. And thou art as welcom to me, as a new poking stick to a Chamber mayd.

Mop. But soft, who comes here?

Enter the Faieries, singing and dauncing.

By the Moone we sport and play,
With the night begins our day:
As we daunce the deaw doth fall,
Trip it little vrchins all:

Lightly as the little Bee,
Two by two, and three by three:
And about go we, and about go wee.
Io. What Mawmets are these?
Fris. O they be the Fayries that haunt these woods.
Mop. O we shall be pincht most cruelly.
1 *Fay.* Will you haue any musick Sir?
2 *Fay.* Will you haue any fine musicke?
3 *Fay.* Most daintie musicke?
Mop. We must set a face on't now, theres no flying. No Sir: we are very merry I thanke you.
1 *Fay.* O but you shall Sir.
Fris. No, I pray you saue your labour.
2 *Fay.* O Sir, it shall not cost you a penny.
Io. Where be your Fiddles?
3 *Fay.* You shall haue most daintie Instruments Sir.
Mop. I pray you, what might I call you?
1 *Fay.* My name is *Penny*.
Mop. I am sory I cannot purse you.
Fris. I pray you sir, what might I call you?
2 *Fay.* My name is *Cricket*.
Fris. I would I were a Chimney for your sake.
Io. I pray you, you prettie litle fellow, what's your name?
3 *Fay.* My name is litttle, little *Pricke*.
Io. Little, little *Pricke*? ô you are a daungerous Fayrie, and fright all the little wenches in the Country, out of their beds. I care not whose hand I were in, so I were out of yours.
1 *Fay.* I do come about the coppes,
Leaping vpon flowers toppes:
Then I get vpon a flie,
Shee carries me aboue the skie:
And trip and goe.
2 *Fay.* When a deawe drop falleth downe,
And doth light vpon my crowne,
Then I shake my head and skip:
And about I trip.
3 *Fay.* When I feele a gyrle a sleepe,
Vnderneath her frock I peepe,
There to sport, and there I play,
Then *I* byte her like a flea:
And about *I* skip.
Io. I, I thought where I should haue you.
1 *Fay.* Wilt please you daunce sir?
Io. Indeed sir, I cannot handle my legges.

2 *Fay.* O you must needs daunce and sing:
   Which if you refuse to doo,
   We wil pinch you blacke and blew.
   And about we goe.
They all daunce in a Ring, and sing as followeth.
Round about, round about, in a fine Ring a: 105
Thus we daunce, thus we daunce, and thus we sing a.
Trip and go, too and fro, ouer this Greene a:
All about, in and out, for our braue Queene a.

Round about, round about, in a fine Ring a:
Thus we daunce, thus we daunce, and thus we sing a.   110
Trip and go, too and fro, ouer this Greene a:
All about, in and out, for our braue Queene a.

We haue daunc't round about, in a fine Ring a:
We haue daunc't lustily, and thus we sing a:
All about, in and out, ouer this Greene a: 115
Too and fro, trip and go, to our braue Queene a.

ACTUS TERTIUS.

Scena I.

Enter Appollo, *and three Charites.*

1 *Cha.* No no great *Phœbus*, this your silence tends,
   To hide your griefe from knowledge of your friends,
   Who if they knew the cause in each respect,
   Would shewe their vtmost skill to cure th'effect.
Ap. Good Ladyes, your conceites in iudgement erre,   5
   Because you see me dumpish, you referre
   The reason to some secret griefe of mine:
   But you haue seene me melancholy many a time,
   Perhaps it is the glowing weather now,
   That makes me seeme so ill at ease to you.   10
1. Fine shifts to colour what you cannot hide,
   No *Phœbus*, by your lookes may be discride
   Some hid conceit, that harbors in your thought,
   Which hath therein, some straunge impression wrought:
   That by the course thereof, you seeme to mee,   15
   An other man then you were wont to bee.
Ap. No Ladies, you deceiue your selues in mee:
   What likelihood or token do ye see,
   That may perswade it true that you suppose?
2. *Appollo*, hence a great suspition growes,   20

Ye are not so pleasaunt now, as earst in companie,
Ye walke alone, and wander solitarie.
The pleasaunt toyes we did frequent sometime,
Are worne away, and growne out of prime.
Your Instrument hath lost his siluer sound, 25
That rang of late, through all this grouie ground.
Your bowe wherwith the chace you did frequent,
Is closde in case, and long hath bene vnbent.
How differ you from that *Appollo* now,
That whilom sat in shade of Lawrell bowe, 30
And with the warbling of your Iuorie Lute,
T'alure the Fairies for to daunce about.
Or from *Th'appollo* that with bended bowe,
Did many a sharp and wounding shaft bestowe.
Amidst the Dragon *Pithons* scalie wings, 35
And forc't his dying blood to spout in springs.
Beleeue me *Phebus*, who sawe you then and now,
Would thinke there were a wondrous change in you.

Ap. Alas faire dames, to make my sorows plain,
Would but reuiue an aunciente wound again. 40
Which grating presently vpon my minde,
Doth leaue a scar of former woes behinde.

3. *Phœbus*, if you account vs for the same,
That tender thee, and loue *Appollos* name,
Powre forth to vs the fountaine of your woe, 45
Frõ whence the spring of these your sorows flowe?
If we may any way redresse your mone,
Commaund our best, harme will we do you none.

Ap. Good Ladies, though I hope for no reliefe,
Ile shewe the ground of this my present griefe. 50
This time of yeare, or there about it was,
Accursed be the time, tenne times alas:
When I from *Delphos* tooke my iourney downe,
To see the games in noble *Sparta* Towne,
There saw I that, wherein I gan to ioy, 55
Amyclas' sonne a gallant comely boy,
Hight (*Hiacinth*) full fifteene yeares of age,
Whom I intended to haue made my Page,
And bare as great affection to the boy,
As euer *Ioue*, in *Ganimede* did ioy. 60
Among the games, my selfe put in a pledge,
To trie my strength in throwing of the sledge,

56 Q *misprints* Amilchars

SC. 1] THE MAYDES METAMORPHOSIS

 Which poysing with my strained arme I threw
So farre, that it beyond the other flew.
My *Hiacinth*, delighting in the game,   65
Desierd to proue his manhood in the same:
And catching ere the sledge lay still on ground,
With violent force, aloft it did rebound
Against his head, and battered out his braine:
And so alas, my louely boy was slaine.   70
1. Hard hap O *Phœbus*, but sieth it's past & gone,
We wish ye to forbeare this frustrate mone.
Ap. Ladies, I know my sorrowes are in vaine,
And yet from mourning can I not refraine.
1. *Eurania* some pleasant Song shall sing.   75
To put ye from your dumps.
Ap.   Alas, no Song will bring
The least reliefe to my perplexed minde.
2. No *Phœbus*? what other pastime shal we finde,
To make ye merry with?
Ap.   Faire dames I thanke you all,
No sport nor pastime can release my thrall: 80
My grief's of course, when it the course hath had,
I shall be merrie, and no longer sad.
1. What will ye then we doo?
Ap.   And please ye, you may goe,
And leaue me here to feed vpon my woe.
2. Then *Phebus*, we can but wish ye wel again.   85
           Exeunt Charites.

Ap. I thanke ye gentle Ladies for your paine.
O *Phœbus* wretched thou thus art thou faine
With forg'de excuses, to conceale thy paine.
O *Hyacinth*, I suffer not these fits
For thee my Boy, no, no, another sits   90
Deeper then thou, in closet of my brest:
Whose sight so late, hath wrought me this vnrest.
And yet no Goddesse, nor of heauenly kinde
She is, whose beautie thus torments my minde.
No Fayrie Nymph, that haunts these pleasaunt woods,   95
No Goddesse of the flowres, the fields, nor floods:
Yet such an one, whom iustly I may call
A Nymph, as well as any of them all.
Eurymine, what heauen affoords thee heere?
So may I say, because thou com'st so neere?   100
And neerer far vnto a heauenly shape,
Then she of whom *Ioue* triumph't in the Rape.

Ile sit me downe, and wake my griefe againe,
To sing a while, in honour of thy name.

The Song.

Amidst the mountaine *Ida* groues, 105
Where *Paris* kept his Heard:
Before the other Ladies all,
He would haue thee preferd.
Pallas for all her painting than,
Her face would seeme but pale: 110
Then *Iuno* would haue blusht for shame,
And *Venus* looked stale.
Eurymine thy selfe alone,
Shouldst beare the golden ball:
So far would thy most heauenly forme, 115
Excell the other all.
O happie *Phœbus*, happie then,
Most happie should I bee:
If faire *Eurymine* would please,
To ioyne in loue with mee. 120

Enter Eurymine.

Eu. Although there be such difference in the chaunge,
To liue in Court, and desart woods to raunge,
Yet in extremes, wherein we cannot chuse,
An extreame refuge is not to refuse.
Good gentlemen, did any see my heard? 125
I shall not finde them out, I am afeard:
And yet my maister wayteth with his bowe,
Within a standing, for to strike a Doe.
You saw them not? Your silence makes me doubt:
I must goe further, till I finde them out. 130
Ap. What seek you prettie Mayde?
Eu.   Forsooth my heard of Deere.
Ap. I sawe them lately, but they are not heere.
Eu. I pray Sir, where?
Ap.   An houre agoe or twaine,
I sawe them feeding all aboue the plaine.
Eu. So much the more my toile to fetch them in. 135
I thanke ye Sir.
Ap.   Nay stay sweet Nymph with mee.
Eu. My busines, cannot so dispatched bee.
Ap. But praye ye Maide, it will be verie good,
To take the shade, in this vnhaunted wood:

This flowring bay with branches large and great, 140
Will shrowd ye safely, from the parching heat.
Eu. Good sir, my busines calls me hence in hast.
Ap. O stay with him, who conquered thou hast.
With him, whose restles thoughts do beat on thee:
With him that ioyes, thy wished face to see. 145
With him whose ioyes surmount all ioyes aboue:
If thou wouldst thinke him worthie of thy loue.
Eu. Why Sir, would you desire another make?
And weare that garland for your Mistres sake?
Ap. No Nymph, although I loue this lawrel tree, 150
My fancy ten times more affecteth thee:
And as the bay is alwaies fresh and greene,
So shall my loue as fresh to thee be seene.
Eu. Now truly Sir, you offer me great wrong,
To hold me from my busines here so long. 155
Ap. O stay sweet Nymph, with more aduisement view,
What one he is, that for thy grace doth sue:
I am not one that haunts on hills or Rocks,
I am no shepheard wayting on my flocks.
I am no boystrous Satyre, no nor Faune, 160
That am with pleasure of thy beautie drawne.
Thou dost not know God wot, thou dost not kno,
The wight, whose presence thou disdainest so.
Eu. But I may know, if you wold please to tell.
Ap. My father in the highest heauens doth dwel: 165
And I am knowne the sonne of *Ioue* to bee,
Whereon the folke of *Delphos* honor mee.
By me is knowne what is, what was, and what shall bee,
By me are learnde the rules of harmonie.
By me the depth of Phisicks lore is found: 170
And power of hearbes that grow vpon the ground.
And thus by circumstances maist thou see,
That I am *Phœbus*, who doth fancie thee.
Eu. No sir, by these discourses may I see,
You mock me with a forged pedegree. 175
If sonne you be to *Ioue*, as erst ye said,
In making loue vnto a mortall maide,
You worke dishonour to your deitie:
I must be gone: I thanke ye for your curtesie
Ap. Alas, abandon not thy Louer so. 180
Eu. I pray sir hartily, giue me leaue to goe.
Ap. The way ore-growne, with shrubs and bushes thick,
The sharpned thornes, your tender feete will prick.

The brambles round about, your traine will lappe,
   The burs and briers, about your skirts will wrappe. 185
Eu. If *Phœbus*, thou of *Ioue* the ofspring be,
   Dishonor not thy deitie so much,
   With profered force, a silly mayd to touch:
   For doing so, although a god thou bee,
   The earth, and men on earth, shall ring thy infamie. 190
Ap. Hard speech to him that loueth thee so well.
Eu. What know I that?
Ap.   I know it, and can tell:
   And feele it too.
Eu.   If that your loue be such,
   As you pretend, so feruent and so much,
   For proofe thereof, graunt me but one request. 195
Ap. I will, by *Ioue* my father, I protest:
   Prouided first, that thy petition bee,
   Not hurtfull to thy selfe, nor harme to mee.
   For so sometimes did *Phaeton* my sonne,
   Request a thing, whereby he was vndonne. 200
   He lost his life through crauing it, and I
   Through graunting it, lost him my sonne thereby.
Eu. Then *Phœbus* thus it is, if thou be hee,
   That art pretended in thy pedegree,
   If sonne thou be to *Ioue* as thou doest faine, 205
   And chalengest that tytle not in vaine:
   Now heer bewray some signe of godhead than?
   And chaunge me straight, from shape of mayd to man?
Ap. Alas, what fond desire doth moue thy minde
   To wish thee altered from thy natiue kinde? 210
   If thou in this thy womans forme canst moue,
   Not men but gods, to sue and seeke thy loue:
   Content thy selfe with natures bountie than,
   And couet not to beare the shape of man.
   And this moreouer will I say to thee, 215
   Fairer man then mayde, thou shalt neuer bee.
Eu. These vaine excuses, manifestly showe,
   Whether you vsurp *Appollos* name or no.
   Sith my demaund so far surmounts your Art,
   Ye ioyne exceptions, on the other part. 220
Ap. Nay then my doubtles Deitie to proue,
   Although thereby for euer I loose my Loue,
   I graunt thy wish, thou art become a man:
   I speake no more, then well performe I can.
   And though thou walke in chaunged bodie now, 225

This pennance shall be added to thy vow:
Thy selfe a man, shalt loue a man, in vaine:
And louing, wish to be a maide againe.
Eu. Appollo, whether I loue a man or not,
   I thanke ye, now I will accept my lot: 230
And sith my chaunge hath disappointed you,
Ye are at libertie to loue anew.   *Exit.*
Ap. If euer I loue, sith now I am forsaken,
Where next I loue, it shall be better taken:
But what so ere my fate in louing bee,   235
Yet thou maist vaunt, that *Phœbus* loued thee.   *Exit Appollo.*

⟨SCENE II.⟩

*Enter Ioculo, Frisco, and Mopso, at three
seuerall doores.*

Mop. Ioculo, whither iettest thou? hast thou found thy Maister?
Io. Mopso wel met, hast thou found thy mistresse?
Mop. Not I by Pan.
Io. Nor I by Pot.
Mop. Pot? what god's that?   5
Io. The next god to a Pan, and such a pot it may be,
That as he shall haue moe seruants then all the Pannes in a Tinkers shop.
Mop. Frisco, where hast thou bene frisking? hast thou found?
Fris. I haue found.
Io. What hast thou found *Frisco*?   10
Fris. A couple of crack-roapes.
Io. And I.
Mop. And I.
Fris. I meane you two.
Io. I you two   15
Mop. And I you two.
Fris. Come, a trebble coniunction: all three, all three.
        They all embrace each other.
Mop. But *Frisco*, hast not found the faire shepheardesse, thy Maisters Mistresse?
Fris. Not I by God, *Priapus* I meane.   20
Io. Priapus quoth a? Whattin a God might that bee?
Fris. A plaine God, with a good peg to hang a shepheardresse bottle vpon.
Io. Thou being a Forresters Boy, shouldst sweare by the God of the woods.   25
Fris. My Maister sweares by *Siluanus*, I must sweare by his poore neighbour.

Io. And heer's a shepheards swaine, sweares by a Kitchen God, *Pan.*

Mop. *Pan's* the shepheardes God, but thou swearest by Pot, what God's that? 30

Io. The God of good-fellowship: well, you haue wicked Maisters, that teach such little Boyes as you are to sweare so young.

Fris. Alas good old great man, wil not your master swear?

Io. I neuer heard him sweare six sound oaths in all my life.

Mop. May hap he cannot, because hees diseasd. 35

Fris. Peace *Mopso*, I will stand toot, hee's neither braue Courtier, bouncing Caualier, nor boone Companion, if he sweare not sometime: for they will sweare, forsweare, and sweare.

Io. How? sweare, forsweare, and sweare? how is that?

Fris. They'le sweare at dyce, forsweare their debts: and sweare 40 when they loose their labour in loue.

Io. Well, your maisters haue much to answere for, that bring ye vp so wickedly.

Fris. Nay my maister is damn'd Ile be sworne, for his very soule burnes in the firie eye of his faire mistresse. 45

Mop. My maister is not damn'd, but he is dead, for he hath buried his ioyes in the bosome of his faire mistresse.

Io. My maister is neither damnde nor dead, and yet is in the case of both your maisters: like a woodden shepheard, and a sheepish wood-man, for he is lost in seeking of a lost sheepe, and spent in 50 hunting a Doe that hee would faine strike.

Fris. Faith and I am founderd with a flinging too and fro, with Ches-nuts, Hazel-nuts, Bullaze, and wildings, for presents from my maister to the faire shepherdesse.

Mop. And I am tierd like a Calfe, with carrying a Kidde euery weeke 55 to the Cottage of my maisters sweete Lambkin.

Io. I am not tierd, but so wearie I cannot goe, with following a maister, that followes his mistresse, that followes her shadow, that followes the sunne, that followes his course.

Fris. That follows the colt, that followed the mare, the man rode on 60 to Midleton: shall I speake a wise word?

Mop. Do and wee will burne our caps.

Fris. Are not we fooles?

Io. Is that a wise word?

Fris. Giue me leaue: are not we fooles to weare our yong feete to old 65 stumps, when there dwells a cunning man in a Caue hereby, who for a bunch of rootes, a bagge of nuts, or a bushell of crabs, will tell vs, where thou shalt finde thy maister, and which of our maisters shall win the wenches fauour?

36 *Bullen corrects to* too't

Io. Bring me to him *Frisco*, Ile giue him all the poynts at my hose, to poynt me right to my maister.

Mop. A bottle of whey shall be his meed, if he saue me labour for posting with presents.

Enter Aramanthus, *with his Globe, &c.*

Fris. Here he comes, offend him not *Ioculo*, for feare he turne thee to a Iacke an Apes.

Mop. And thee to an Owle.

Io. And thee to a Wood-cocke.

Fris. A Wood-cocke, an Owle, and an Ape?

Mop. A long bill, a broade face, and no tayle?

Io. Kisse it *Mopso*, and be quiet, Ile salute him ciuilly. Good speed good man.

Aram. Welcome bad boy.

Fris. He speakes to thee *Ioculo*.

Io. Meaning thee *Frisco*.

Aram. I speake, and meane not him, nor him, nor thee,
But speaking so, I speake and meane, all three.

Io. If ye be good at Rimes and Riddles old man, expound me this.
These two serue two, those two serue one,
Assoyle me this, and I am gone.

Aram. You three serue three: those three do seeke to one,
One shall her finde, he comes, and she is gone.

Io. This is a wise answer: her going causd his comming, for if she had nere gone, he had nere come.

Mop. Good maister wizard, leaue these murlemewes, and tel *Mopso* plainly, whether *Gemulo* my maister, that gentle shepheard, shall win the loue of the faire shepherdesse his flock-keeper or not, and Ile giue ye a bottell of as good whey, as ere ye laid lips too.

Fris. And good father Fortune-teller, let *Frisco* knowe, whither *Siluio* my maister that lustie Forrester, shal gaine that same gay shepherdesse or no? Ile promise ye nothing for your paines, but a bag full of nuts: if I bring a crab or two in my pocket, take them for aduantage.

Io. And gentle maister wise-man, tell *Ioculo*, if his noble Maister *Ascanio*, that gallant Courtier, shalbe found by me, and she found by him, for whom, he hath lost his fathers fauour, and his owne libertie, and I my labour, and Ile giue ye thankes: for we Courtiers, neither giue nor take bribes.

Aram. I take your meaning better then your speech,
And I wil graunt the thing you doo beseech:
But for the teares of Louers be no toyes,
Ile tell their chaunce in parables to Boyes.

74-5, 92-3, *as verse*, Q

Fris. In what ye will, lets heare our maisters luck.
Aram. Thy maisters Doe, shall turne vnto a Buck.
                    To Mopso.
          Thy maisters Eawe, be chaunged to a Ram,
                    To Ioculo.
          Thy maister seeks a maide, and findes a man.
          Yet for his labor shall he gaine his meede,   115
          The other two shall sigh, to see him speede.
Mop. Then my maister shall not win the shepheardesse?
Aram. No: hast thee home, and bid him right his wrong,
          The shepheardesse wil leaue his flock ere long.
Mop. Ile run to warne my master of that.   *Exit.*   120
Fris. My maister wood-man, takes but woodden paines to no purpose
I thinke, what say ye, shall he speede?
Aram. No: tell him so, and bid him tend his Deare:
          And cease to woe, he shall not wed this yeare.
Fris. I am not sorie for it, farewell *Ioculo.*   *Exit.*   125
Io. I may goe with thee, for I shall speed euen so too, by staying behinde.
Aram. Better my Boy, thou shalt thy maister finde,
          And he shall finde the partie he requires:
          And yet not finde the summe of his desires.   130
          Keep on that way, thy maister walkes before,
          Whom when thou find'st, loose him good Boy no more.
                                                          Exit ambo.

ACT. 4.

⟨SCENE I.⟩

Enter Ascanio, and Ioculo.

Asca. Shall then my trauell euer endles proue?
  That I can heare no tydings of my Loue?
  In neither desart, groue, nor shadie wood,
  Nor obscure thicket, where my foote hath trod?
  But euery plough-man, and rude shepheard swain,   5
  Doth still reply vnto my greater paine?
  Some Satyre then, or Goddesse of this place,
  Some water Nymph, vouchsafe me so much grace
  As by some view, some signe, or other sho,
  I may haue knowledge if she liue or no.   10
Eccho. No.
Asca. Then my poore hart is buried too in wo:
  Record it once more, if the truth be so?
Eccho. So.

Asca. How, that *Eurymine* is dead, or liues?   15
Eccho. Liues.
Asca. Now gentle Goddesse thou redeem'st my soule
  From death to life: Oh tell me quickly where?
Eccho. Where?
Asca. In some remote far region, or else neere?   20
Eccho. Neere.
Asca. Oh what conceales her from my thirstie eies?
  Is it restraint? or some vnknowne disguise?
Eccho. Disguise.
Io. Let me be hangd my Lord, but all is lyes.   25
Eccho. Lyes.
Io. True, we are both perswaded thou doest lye.
Eccho. Thou doest lye.
Io. Who I?
Eccho. Who I?   30
Io. I thou.
Eccho. I thou.
Io. Thou dar'st not come and say so to my face.
Eccho. Thy face.
Io. Ile make you then for euer prating more.   35
Eccho. More.
Io. Will ye prate more? Ile see that presently.
Ascha. Stay *Ioculo*, it is the Eccho Boy,
  That mocks our griefe, and laughes at our annoy.
  Hard by this groue there is a goodly plaine   40
  Betwixt two hils, still fresh with drops of raine:
  Where neuer spreading Oake nor Poplar grew,
  Might hinder the prospect or other view,
  But all the country that about it lyes,
  Presents it selfe vnto our mortall eyes: 45
  Saue that vpon each hill, by leauie trees,
  The Sun at highest, his scorching heat may leese.
  There languishing my selfe I will betake,
  As heauen shall please, and only for her sake.
Io. Stay maister, I haue spied the fellow now, that mockt vs all this
  while: see where he sits.   51

Aramanthus sitting.

Asca. The very shape my Vision told me off,
  That I should meet with as I strayd this way.
Io. What lynes he drawes? best go not ouer farre.
Asca. Let me alone, thou doest but trouble mee.   55
Io. Youle trouble vs all annon, ye shall see.

Asca. God speed faire Sir.
Io.   My Lord doo ye not marke?
   How the skie thickens, and begins to darke?
Asca. Health to ye Sir.
Io.   Nay then God be our speed.
Ara. Forgiue me Sir, I sawe ye not in deed.   60
Asca. Pardon me rather, for molesting you.
Io. Such another face I neuer knew.
Ara. Thus studious I am wont to passe the time,
   By true proportion, of each line from line.
Io. Oh now I see he was learning to spell,   65
   Theres A. B. C. in midst of his table.
Asca. Tel me I pray ye sir, may I be bold to craue
   The cause of your abode within this Caue?
Ara. To tell you that in this extreme distresse,
   Were but a tale of Fortunes ficklenesse.   70
   Sometime I was a Prince of *Lesbos* Ile,
   And liu'd belou'd, whilst my good stars did smile:
   But clowded once with this worlds bitter crosse,
   My ioy to grife, my gaine conuerts to losse.
Asca. Forward I pray ye, faint not in your tale.   75
Io. It will not all be worth a cup of Ale.
Ara. A short discourse of that which is too long
   How euer pleasing, can neuer seeme but wrong:
   Yet would my tragicke story fit the stage,
   Pleasaunt in youth, but wretched in mine age.   80
   Blinde Fortune setting vp and pulling downe,
   Abusde by those my selfe raisde to renowne:
   But y^t which wrings me neer, and wounds my hart,
   Is a false brothers base vnthankfull part.
Asc. A smal offence comparde with my disease,   85
   No doubt ingratitude in time may cease
   And be forgot: my grief out-liues all howres:
   Raining on my head, continual haplesse showers.
Ara. You sing of yours, and I of mine relate:
   To euery one, seemes worst his owne estate.   90
   But to proceed, exiled thus by spight,
   Both country I forgoe, and brothers sight:
   And comming hither where I thought to liue,
   Yet here I cannot but lament and greeue.
Asca. Some comfort yet in this there doth remaine: 95
   That you haue found a partner in your paine.
Ara. How are your sorrowes subiect, let me heare?
Asca. More ouerthrowne, and deeper in dispaire

| Than is the manner of your heauie smart,
| My curelesse griefe, doth ranckle at my hart. 100
| And in a word, to heare the summe of all,
| I loue, and am belou'd: but there-withall
| The sweetnesse of that banquet must forgo,
| Whose pleasant tast is chaungde with bitter wo.
Ara. A conflict, but to try your noble minde, 105
  As common vnto youth, as raine to winde.
Asca. But hence it is that doth me treble wrong,
  Expected good, that is forborne so long:
  Doth loose the vertue which the vse would proue.
Ara. Are you then sir, despised of your Loue? 110
Asca. No, but depriued of her company.
  And for my careles negligence therein:
  Am bound to doo this penaunce for my sin.
  That if I neuer finde where she remaines,
  I vowe a yeare shalbe my end of paines. 115
Ara. Was she then lost within this Forrest here?
Asc. Lost or forlorn, to me she was right deere.
  And this is certaine, vnto him that could
  The place where she abides to me vnfold:
  For euer I would vow my selfe his friend, 120
  Neuer reuolting till my life did end.
  And therefore sir, (as well as I know your skill)
  If you will giue me phisicke for this ill,
  And shewe me if *Eurymine* do liue,
  It were a recompence for all my paine, 125
  And *I* should thinke my ioyes were full againe.
Ara. They know the want of health that haue bene sick,
  My selfe sometime acquainted with the like
  Do learne in dutie of a kinde regard,
  To pittie him whose hap hath bene so hard. 130
  How long *I* pray ye hath she absent beene?
Asca. Three dayes it is since that my Loue was seene.
Io. Heer's learning for the nonce, that stands on ioynts:
  For all his cunning, ile scarse giue two poynts.
Ara. Mercurio regnante virum, subsequente Luna, 135
  Fœminam designat.
Io. Nay and you go to latin, then tis sure, my maister shall finde her, if he could tell when.
Ara. I cannot tell what reason it should bee,
  But loue and reason here doo disagree. 140

107 it is] *Q misprints* it it   127 want] *qy.?* worth   136 Fœminum *Q and Bullen*   138 when] where *Bull., by oversight, as he makes no note*

> By proofe of learned principles I finde,
> The manner of your loue's against all kinde.
> And not to feed ye with vncertaine ioy,
> Whom you affect so much, is but a Boy.

Io. A Riddle for my life, some Antick Iest, did I not tell ye what his cunning was? 146
Asca. I loue a Boy?
Ara.   Mine Art doth tell me so.
Asca. Adde not a fresh increase vnto my woe.
Ara. I dare auouch what lately I haue saide,
   The loue that troubles you, is for no maide. 150
Asca. As well I might be said to touch the skie,
   Or darke the horizon with tapestrie :
   Or walke vpon the waters of the sea,
   As to be haunted with such lunacie.
Ara. If it be false, mine Art I will defie. 155
Asca. Amaz'de with griefe, my loue is then transform'd.
Io. Maister be contented, this is leape yeare,
   Women weare breetches, petticoats are deare.
   And thats his meaning, on my life it is.
Asc. Oh God, and shal my torments neuer cease? 160
Ara. Represse the fury of your troubled minde :
   Walke here a while, your Lady you may finde.
Io. A Lady and a Boy, this hangs wel together :
   Like snow in haruest, sun-shine and foule weather.

            Enter Eurymine singing.
Since hope of helpe my froward starres denie, 165
Come sweetest death, and end my miserie.
He left his country, I my shape haue lost,
Deare is the loue, that hath so dearly cost.
Eu. Yet can I boast, though *Phœbus* were vniust
   This shift did serue, to barre him from his lust. 170
   But who are these alone? I cannot chuse
   But blush for shame, that any one should see,
   Eurymine in this disguise to bee.
Asca. It is, it is not my loue, *Eurymine.*
Eury. Hark, some one hallows: gentlemen adiew, 175
   In this attire I dare not stay their view.   *Exit.*
Asca. My loue, my ioy, my life,
   By eye, by face, by tongue, it should be shee.
   Oh I, it was my loue, Ile after her,

  145–6 *as verse,* Q   165–8 Q *prints the four lines in romans like the rest, but its prefix at the fifth seems to mark transition from song to speech. I italicize them after Bullen*   174 *Bullen corrects to* It is (is't not?) &c.

And though she passe the Eagle in her flight, 180
Ile neuer rest, till I haue gain'd her sight. *Exit.*
Ara. Loue carries him, and so retains his mind,
That he forgets how I am left behind:
Yet will I follow softly as I can
In hope to see the fortune of the man. *Exit.* 185
Io. Nay let them go a Gods name, one by one,
With ⟨all⟩ my heart *I* am glad to be alone.
Heres old transforming, would with all his Art,
He could transforme this tree into a tart.
See then if *I* would flinch from hence or no: 190
But for it is not so, *I* needs must go. *Exit.*

⟨SCENE II.⟩

Enter Siluio *and* Gemulo.

Sil. Is it a bargaine *Gemulo*, or not?
Ge. Thou neuer knew'st me breake my word *I* wot,
Nor will *I* now, betide me bale or blis.
Sil. Nor *I* breake mine, and here her cottage is:
Ile call her forth.
Ge.   Will *Siluio* be so rude? 5
Sil. Neuer shall we betwixt our selues conclude
Our controuersie, for we ouerweene.
Ge. Not I, but thou, for though thou iet'st in greene,
As fresh as Meadow in a morne of May,
And scorn'st the shepheard, for he goes in gray. 10
But Forrester, beleeue it as thy Creede,
My mistresse mindes my person, not my weede.
Sil. So 'twas I thought, because she tends thy sheepe
Thou thinkst in loue of thee she taketh keepe:
That is as townish damzels lend the hand, 15
But send the heart to him aloofe doth stand.
So deales *Eurymine* with *Siluio*.
Ge. Albe she looke more blithe on *Gemulo*,
Her heart is in the dyall of her eye,
That poynts me hers.
Sil.   That shall we quickly trye. 20
Eurymine.
Ge.   *Erynnis* stop thy throte,
Vnto thy hound thou hallowst such a note:
I thought that shepheards had bene mannerlesse,
But Wood-men are the ruder groomes I guesse.

Sil. How shuld I cal her Swain, but by her name? 25
Ge. So *Hobinoll* the plow-man, calls his dame.
Call her in Carroll from her quiet coate.
Sil. Agreed: but whether shall begin his note.
Ge. Draw cuttes.
Sil.   Content, the longest shall begin.
Ge. Tis mine.
Sil.   Sing loude, for she is farre within. 30
Ge. Instruct thy singing in thy Forrest waies.
Shepheards know how to chant their roundelaies.
Sil. Repeat our bargain, ere we sing our Song.
Least after wrangling, should our mistresse wrong.
If me she chuse, thou must be well content: 35
If thee she chuse, I giue thee like consent.
Ge. Tis done: now *Pan* pipe on thy sweetest Reede,
And as *I* loue, so let thy seruaunt speede.

      As little Lambes lift vp their snowie sides,
      When mounting Larke salutes the gray-eyed morne: 40
Sil. *As from the Oaken leaues the honie glides,*
      Where Nightingales record vpon the thorne.
Ge. So rise my thoughts.
Sil.   So all my sences cheere.
Ge. When she surueyes my flocks.
Sil.   And she my Deare.
Ge.   Eurymine. 45
Sil.   Eurymine.
Ge. Come foorth.
Sil.   Come foorth.
Ge.   Come foorth and cheere these plaines.
And both sing this togither, when they haue sung it single.
Sil. The Wood-mans Loue.
Ge.   And Lady of the Swaynes.

      Enter Eurymine.

Faire Forester and louely shepheard Swaine,
Your Carrolls call *Eurymine* in vaine: 50
For she is gone, her Cottage and her sheepe,
With me her brother, hath she left to keepe:
And made me sweare by *Pan*, ere she did go,
To see them safely kept, for *Gemulo*.
   They both looke straungely vpon her, apart each from other.
Ge. What? hath my Loue a new come Louer than? 55
Sil. What? hath my Mistresse got another man?

   39 *Only the first four lines are italicized in* Q

Ge. This Swayne will rob me of *Eurymine*.
Sil. This youth hath power to win *Eurymine*.
Ge. This straungers beautie beares away my prize.
Sil. This straunger will bewitch her with his eies. 60
Ge. It is *Adonis*.
Sil.   It is *Ganymede*.
Ge. My blood is chill.
Sil.   My heart is cold as Leade.
Eu. Faire youthes, you haue forgot for what ye came.
 You seeke your Loue, shee's gone.
Ge.   The more too blame.
Eu. Not so, my sister had no will to go: 65
 But that our parents dread commaund was so.
Sil. It is thy scuse, thou art not of her kin,
 But as my Ryuall, com'ste my Loue to win.
Eu. By great *Apollos* sacred Deitie,
 That shepheardesse so neare is Sib to me, 70
 As I ne may (for all this world) her wed:
 For she and I in one selfe wombe were bred.
 But she is gone, her flocke is left to mee.
Ge. The shepcoat's mine, and I will in and see.
Sil. And I.   *Exeunt* Siluio *and* Gemulo.
Eu.   Go both, cold comfort shall you finde, 75
 My manly shape, hath yet a womans minde:
 Prone to reueale what secret she doth know,
 God pardon me, I was about to show
 My transformation: peace they come againe.

    Enter Siluio, *and* Gemulo.

Sil. Haue ye found her?
Ge.   No, we looke in vaine. 80
Eu. I told ye so.
Ge.   Yet heare me, new-come Swayne.
 Albe thy seemly feature set no sale
 But honest truth vpon thy nouell tale,
 Yet (for this world is full of subtiltie)
 We wish thee goe with vs for companie 85
 Vnto a Wise-man wonning in this wood,
 Hight *Aramanth*, whose wit and skill is good:
 That he may certifie our mazing doubt,
 How this straunge chaunce and chaunge hath fallen out.
Eu. I am content: haue with ye, when ye will. 90
Sil. Euen now.
Eu.   Hee'le make ye muse, if he haue any skill. *Exeunt.*

ACT. 5.

⟨Scene I.⟩

Enter Ascanio, and Eurymine.

Asca. *Eurymine*, I pray if thou be shee,
Refraine thy haste, and doo not flie from mee.
The time hath bene my words thou wouldst allow,
And am I growne so loathsome to thee now?
Eu. *Ascanio*, time hath bene I must confesse,
When in thy presence was my happinesse:
But now the manner of my miserie,
Hath chaung'd that course, that so it cannot be.
Asca. What wrong haue I contriued? what iniurie
To alienate thy liking so from me?
If thou be she whom sometime thou didst faine,
And bearest not the name of friend in vaine,
Let not thy borrowed guise of altred kinde,
Alter the wonted liking of thy minde:
But though in habit of a man thou goest,
Yet be the same *Eurymine* thou wast.
Eu. How gladly would I be thy Lady still,
If earnest vowes might answere to my will?
Asca. And is thy fancie alterd with thy guise?
Eu. My kinde, but not my minde in any wise.
Asca. What though thy habit differ from thy kind:
Thou maiest retain thy wonted louing mind.
Eu. And so I doo.
Asca.   Then why art thou so straunge?
Or wherefore doth thy plighted fancie chaunge?
Eu. *Ascanio*, my heart doth honor thee.
Asc. And yet continuest stil so strange to me?
Eu. Not strange, so far as kind wil giue me leaue.
Asca. Vnkind that kind, that kindnesse doth bereaue:
Thou saist thou louest me.
Eu.   As a friend his friend:
And so I vowe to loue thee to the end.
Asca. I wreake not of such loue, loue me but so
As faire *Eurymine* lou'd *Ascanio*.
Eu. That loue's denide vnto my present kinde.
Asca. In kindly shewes, vnkinde I doo thee finde:
I see thou art as constant as the winde.

Eu. Doth kind allow a man to loue a man?
Asca. Why art not thou *Eurymine*?
Eu.   I am.
Asca. Eurymine my Loue?
Eu.   The very same.
Asca. And wast not thou a woman then?
Eu.   Most true.
As. And art thou changed from a woman now?   40
Eu. Too true.
Asc.   These tales my mind perplex:
  Thou art *Eurymine*.
Eu.   In name, but not in sexe.
Asca. What then?
Eu.   A man.
Asca.   In guise thou art I see.
Eu. The guise thou seest, doth with my kinde agree.
Asca. Before thy flight thou wast a woman tho.   45
Eu. True *Ascanio*.
Asca.   And since art thou a man?
Eu. Too true deare friend.
Asca.   Then haue I lost a wife.
Eu. But found a friend, whose dearest blood and life,
  Shalbe as readie as thine owne for thee:
  In place of wife, such friend thou hast of mee.   50
            Enter Ioculo, and Aramanthus.
Io. I here they are: maister well ouertane,
  I thought we two should neuer meete againe:
  You went so fast, that I to follow ye,
  Slipt ouer hedge and ditch, and many a tall tree.
Ara. Well said my Boy, thou knowest not how to lie.   55
Io. To lye Sir? how say you was it not so?
  You were at my heeles, though farre off, ye know:
  For maister, not to counterfayt with ye now,
  Hee's as good a footeman as a shackled sow.
Asca. Good Sir y'are welcome, sirrha hold your prate.   60
Ara. What speed in that I told to you of late?
Asca. Both good and bad, as doth the sequell proue,
  For (wretched) I haue found, and lost my Loue.
  If that be lost which I can nere enioy.
Io. Faith Mistresse y'are too blame to be so coy.   65
  The day hath bene, but what is that to mee:
  When more familiar with a man you'ld bee.
Ara. I told ye you should finde a man of her:
  Or else my rule did very straungely erre.

Asca. Father, the triall of your skill I finde, 70
My Loue's transformde into another kinde:
And so I finde, and yet haue lost my Loue.
Io. Ye cannot tell, take her aside and proue.
A*sca.* But sweet *Eurymine* make some report
Why thou departedst from my fathers Court? 75
And how this straunge mishap to thee befell,
Let me intreat thou wouldst the processe tell.
Eu. To shew how I arriued in this ground,
Were but renewing of an auncient wound :
Another time that office ile fulfill, 80
Let it suffice, I came against my will.
And wandring here about this Forrest side,
It was my chaunce of *Phœbus* to be spide.
Whose loue because I chastly did withstand,
He thought to offer me a violent hand. 85
But for a present shift to shun his rape,
I wisht my selfe transformde into this shape :
Which he perform'd (God knowes) against his wil :
And I since then, haue wayld my fortune still.
Not for misliking ought I finde in mèe, 90
But for thy sake, whose wife I meant to bee.
A*sca.* Thus haue you heard our woful destenie,
Which I in heart lament, and so doth she.
Ara. The fittest remedie that I can finde,
Is this, to ease the torment of your minde. 95
Perswade your selues that great A*pollo* can,
As easily make a woman of a man,
As contrariwise he made a man of her.
Asca. I thinke no lesse.
Ara.   Then humble suite preferre
To him : perhaps your prayers may attaine, 100
To haue her turnd into her forme againe.
Eu. But *Phœbus* such disdain to me doth beare,
As hardly we shall win his graunt I feare.
Ara. Then in these verdant fields al richly dide,
With natures gifts, and *Floras* painted pride : 105
There is a goodly spring whose christal streames
Beset with myrtles, keepe backe *Phœbus* beames :
There in rich seates all wrought of Iuory,
The Graces sit, listening the melodye :
The warbling Birds doo from their prettie billes 110
Vnite in corcord, as the brooke distilles.
Whose gentle murmure with his buzzing noates,

sc. I]   THE MAYDES METAMORPHOSIS   381

    Is as a base vnto their hollow throates.
    Garlands beside they weare vpon their browes,
    Made of all sorts of flowers earth allowes :   115
    From whence such fragrant sweet perfumes arise,
    As you would sweare that place is Paradise.
    To them let vs repaire with humble hart,
    And meekly shew the manner of your smart :
    So gratious are they in *Apollos* eies,   120
    As their intreatie quickly may suffice.
    In your behalfe, Ile tell them of your states,
    And craue their aides, to stand your aduocates.
Asca. For euer you shall bind vs to you than.
Ara. Come go with me : Ile doo the best I can.   125
                ⟨*Exeunt, except* JOCULO.⟩
Io. Is not this hard luck to wander so long,
    And in the end to finde his wife markt wrong.

              Enter Phylander.

    A proper iest as euer I heard tell,
    In sooth, me thinks the breech becomes her well :
    And might it not make their husbands feare them,   130
    Wold all the wiues in our town might wear them.
Phy. Tell me youth, art a straunger here or no?
Io. Is your commission sir, to examine me so?
Phy. What is it thou? now by my troth wel met.
Io. By your leaue, it's well ouertaken yet.   135
Phy. I litle thought I should a found thee here.
Io. Perhaps so sir.
Phy.   I prethee speake, what cheere?
Io. What cheere can here be hopte for in these woods?
    Except trees, stones, bryars, bushes, or buddes?
Phy. My meaning is, I faine would heare thee say,   140
    How thou doest man, why tak'st thou this another way.
Io. Why then sir, I doo as well as I may.
    And to perswade ye, that welcome ye bee,
    Wilt please ye sir, to eate a crab with mee?
Phy. Beleeue me *Ioculo*, reasonable hard cheere.   145
Io. Phylander, tis the best we can get heere.
    But when returne ye to the Court againe?
Phy. Shortly, now I haue found thee.
Io.   To requite your paine,

S. D. [Exeunt &c.] *omitted Q and Bullen*   130 them] *Bullen rightly corrects* then *of Q*   132 Phy.] *the prefix omitted in Q and Bullen*   141 tak'st thou] thou tak'st *Q Bull.*

Shall I intreat you beare a present from me?
Phy. To whom?
Io.   To the Duke.
Phy.   What shall it be?   150
Io. Because Venson so conuenient doth not fall,
  A pecke of Acornes to make merry withall.
Phy. What meanest thou by that?
Io.   By my troth sir as ye see,
  Acornes are good enough for such as hee.
  I wish his honour well, and to doo him good: 155
  Would he had eaten all the Acornes in th' wood.
Phy. Good words *Ioculo*, of your Lord & mine.
Io. As may agree with such a churlish swine.
  How dooes his honor?
Phy.   Indifferently well.
Io. I wish him better.
Phy.   How?
Io.   Vice-gerent in hell.   160
Phy. Doest thou wish so, for ought that he hath done?
Io. I for the loue he beares vnto his sonne.
Phy. Hees growne of late, as fatherly and milde,
  As euer father was vnto his childe:
  And sent me forth to search the coast about,   165
  If so my hap might be to finde him out.
  And if *Eurymine* aliue remaine,
  To bring them both vnto the Court againe.
  Where is thy maister?
Io.   Walking about the ground.
Phy. Oh that his Loue *Eurymine* were found.   170
Io. Why so she is, come follow me and see.
  Ile bring ye strait where they remaining bee.   *Exeunt.*

⟨SCENE II.⟩

*Enter three or foure Muses, Aramanthus, Ascanio, Siluio,
and Gemulo.*

Asca. Cease your contention for *Eurymine*.
  Nor wordes, nor vowes, can helpe her miserie:
  But he it is that did her first transforme,
  Must calme the gloomy rigor of this storme:
  Great *Phœbus*, whose Pallace we are neere,   5
  Salute him then in his celestiall sphere:
  That with the notes of cheerfull harmonie,
  He may be mou'd to shewe his Deitie.

[SC. II] THE MAYDES METAMORPHOSIS

Sil. But wheres *Eurymine*, haue we lost her sight?
As. Poore soule, within a caue, with fear affright   10
    She sits, to shun *Apollos* angry view,
    Vntill she see what of our prayers ensue:
    If we can reconcile his loue or no,
    Or that she must continue in her woe.
1. *Mu.* Once haue we tried *Ascanio*, for thy sake   15
    And once againe we will his power awake:
    Not doubting but as he is of heauenly race,
    At length he will take pitie on her case.
    Sing therefore, and each partie from his heart,
    In this our musicke, beare a chearefull part.   20

Song.

All haile faire Phœbus, *in thy purple throne,*
Vouchsafe the regarding of our deepe mone.
Hide not, oh hide not, thy comfortable face,
But pittie, but pittie, a virgins poore case.

Phœbus appeares.

1. *Muse.* Illustrate bewtie, Christall heauens eye,   25
    Once more we do entreat thy clemencie:
    That as thou art the power of vs all,
    Thou would'st redeeme *Eurymine* from thrall.
    Graunt gentle God, graunt this our small request,
    And if abilitie in vs do rest: 30
    Whereby we euer may deserue the same,
    It shalbe seene, we reuerence *Phœbus* name.
Phœ. You sacred sisters of faire *Helli(c)on*,
    On whom my fauours euermore haue shone,
    In this you must haue patience with my vow,   35
    I cannot graunt what you aspire vnto.
    Nor was't my fault, she was transformed so,
    But her owne fond desire, as ye well know.
    We told her too, before her vow was past,
    That cold repentance would ensue at last.   40
    And sith her selfe did wish the shape of man,
    She causde the abuse, digest it how she can.
2. *Muse.* Alas, if vnto her you be so hard,
    Yet of *Ascanio* haue some more regard,
    And let him not endure such endlesse wrong,   45
    That hath pursude her constant loue so long.

    21-4 All haile ... case] *the four lines are not italicized in* Q

Asca. Great God, the greeuous trauells I haue past,
   In restlesse search, to find her out at last:
   My plaints my toiles, in lieu of my annoy,
   Haue well deseru'd my Lady to enioy.   50
   Penance too much I haue sustaind before:
   Oh *Phœbus*, plague me not with any more.
   Nor be thou so extreame, now at the worst
   To make my torments greater than at the first.
   My Fathers late displeasure is forgot,   55
   And theres no let,' nor any churlish blot
   To interrupt our ioyes from being compleat,
   But only thy good fauour to intreat:
   In thy great grace it lyes to make my state
   Most happie now, or most infortunate.   60
1 *Mu.* Heauenly *Apollo*, on our knees I pray,
   Vouchsafe thy great displeasure to allay.
   What honor to thy Godhead will arise,
   To plague a silly Lady in this wise?
   Beside, it is a staine vnto thy Deitie,   65
   To yeeld thine owne desires the soueraigntie:
   Then shew some grace vnto a wofull Dame,
   And in these groues, our tongues shall sound thy fame.
Phœ. Arise deare Nourses of diuinest skill,
   You sacred Muses of *Pernassus* hill: 70
   Phœbus is conquerd by your deare respect,
   And will no longer clemency neglect.
   You haue not sude nor praide to me in vaine:
   I graunt your willes, she is a mayd againe.
Asca. Thy praise shal neuer die whilst I do liue.   75
2. *Mu.* Nor will we slack perpetual thankes to giue.
Phœ. Thalia, neare the Caue where she remaines
   The Fayries keepe, request them of their paines,
   And in my name, bid them forthwith prouide,
   From that darke place, to be the Ladies guide. 80
   And in the bountie of their liberall minde,
   To giue her cloathes according to her kinde.
1. *Mu.* I goe diuine *Apollo*.   *Exit.*
Phœ.   Haste againe.
   No time too swift, to ease a Louers paine.
Asca. Most sacred *Phœbus*, endles thankes to thee, 85
   That doest vouchsafe so much to pittie mee.
   And aged father, for your kindnesse showne,
   Imagine not your friendship ill bestowne.
   The earth shall sooner vanish and decay,

Than I will proue vnthankfull any way.	90

Ara. It is suffcient recompence to me,
If that my silly helpe haue pleasurde ye.
If you enioy your Loue and hearts desire,
It is enough: nor doo I more require.

Phœ. Graue *Aramanthus*, now I see thy face 95
I call to minde, how tedious a long space
Thou hast frequented these sad desarts here,
Thy time imployed, in heedfull minde I beare:
The patient sufferance of thy former wrong,
Thy poore estate, and sharp exile so long, 100
The honourable port thou bor'st sometime,
Till wrongd thou wast, with vndeserued crime
By them whom thou to honour didst aduance,
The memory of which thy heauy chance,
Prouokes my minde to take remorse on thee, 105
Father henceforth, my clyent shalt thou bee:
And passe the remnant of thy fleeting time,
With Lawrell wreath, amongst the Muses nine.
And when thy age hath giuen place to fate,
Thou shalt exchaunge thy former mortall state: 110
And after death, a palme of fame shalt weare,
Amongst the rest that liue in honor here.
And lastly know, that faire *Eurymine*
Redeemed now from former miserie
Thy daughter is, whom I for that intent 115
Did hide from thee, in this thy banishment:
That so she might the greater scourge sustaine,
In putting *Phœbus* to so great a paine.
But freely now, enioy each others sight:
No more *Eurymine*: abandon quite 120
That borrowed name, as *Atlanta*, she is calde,
And here she woman, in her right shape instalde.

Asca. Is then my Loue deriu'de of noble race?
Phœ. No more of that, but mutually imbrace.
Ara. Liues my *Atlanta*, whom the rough seas waue 125
I thought had brought vnto a timelesse graue?
Phœ. Looke not so straunge, it is thy fathers voyce.
And this thy Loue: *Atlanta* now reioyce.
Eu. As in another world of greater blis
My daunted spirits doo stand amazde at this. 130
So great a tyde of comfort ouerflowes,
As what to say, my faltering tongue scarse knowes:

      122 *Bullen corrects to* And here's the woman

But only this, vnperfect though it bee,
*I*mmortall thankes great *Phœbus* vnto thee.
Phœ. Well Lady, you are retransformed now,
But *I* am sure you did repent your vow.
Eury. Bright Lampe of glory, pardon my rashnesse past.
Phœ. The penance was your owne, though *I* did fast.

Enter Phylander, and Ioculo.

Asca. Behold deare, Loue, to make your ioyes abound,
Yonder *Phylander* comes.
Io.   Oh sir, well found.
But most especially it glads my minde,
To see my mistresse restorde to kinde.
Phy. My Lord & Madam, to requite your pain,
Telemachus hath sent for you againe.
All former quarrels now are trodden downe,
And he doth smile, that heretofore did frowne.
Asca. Thankes kinde *Phylander*, for thy friendly newes,
Like *Iunos* balme, that our lifes blood renewes.
Phœ. But Lady, first ere you your iourney take,
Vouchsafe at my request, one graunt to make.
Eu. Most willingly.
Phœ.   The matter is but small.
To weare a braunch of Lawrell in your Caull
For *Phœbus* sake, least else *I* be forgot,
And thinke vpon me, when you see me not.
Eu. Here while I liue a solemne oath I make,
To loue the Lawrell for *Apollos* sake.
Ge. Our suite is dasht, we may depart I see.
Phœ. Nay *Gemulo* and *Siluio*, contented bee:
This night let me intreate ye you will take,
Such cheare as I and these poore Dames can make.
To morrow morne weele bring you on your way.
Sil. Your Godhead shall commaund vs all to stay.
Phœ. Then Ladies gratulate this happie chaunce,
With some delightfull tune and pleasaunt daunce.
Meane space, vpon his Harpe will *Phœbus* play,
So both of them may boast another day
And make report, that when their wedding chaunc'te,
Phœbus gaue musicke, and the Muses daunc'te.

149 Phœ.] Phy. *Q, by mistake*

The Song.

Since painfull sorrowes date hath end,
And time hath coupled friend with friend: 170
Reioyce we all, reioyce and sing,
Let all these groaues of Phœbus *ring.*
Hope hauing wonne, dispaire is vanisht:
Pleasure reuiues, and care is banisht.
Then trippe we all this Roundelay,   175
And still be mindfull of the Bay.   *Exeunt.*

FINIS.

ANTI-MARTINIST WORK, ETC.

EDITIONS OF PAPPE

(1) A. Title as at p. 393, but having headpiece with bald-headed boy in centre and two creatures with horned yet human heads gallopping from him. 4° undated [1589]. (Bodleian—Douce, N. 252 (wanting fol. E 1): Trin. Coll. Camb.)

(2) B. Title as at p. 393, but having headpiece containing woman's head with ringlets in centre. 4° undated [1589].
(Brit. Mus. 2 copies, C. 37. d. 41 and 96. b. 15: King's Coll. Camb.)

(3) C. Title exactly as B. 4° undated [1589]. (Bodleian—Malone, 715.)

(4) With Introduction and Notes by John Petheram, forming No. 3 of the series *Puritan Discipline Tracts*, Lon. 1844, 12mo, printed from (2).

(5) Among *Elizabethan and Jacobean Pamphlets* (Pocket Library of English Literature, vol. iv. pp. 43–83), with brief introduction and notes by G. F. Saintsbury (Lon. Percival & Co. 1892. 16mo).

PAPPE WITH AN HATCHET

Text.—My collation of the two copies in the Bodleian and the two in the British Museum establishes clearly the existence of three editions, both British Museum copies (from one of which Petheram printed) being of the same. But in all copies the tract has but nineteen leaves, whose collation is the same, the number of words on a page never differing, though there is occasional slight variety in the internal arrangement. In all, the address 'To the Father,' &c. occupies the second and third leaves, that 'To the Indifferent Reader' (in smaller italics) the fourth, while the appended portion (from 'Here I was writing Finis and Funis') commencing on the verso of the sixteenth leaf extends for three leaves more. But the distinction between the three editions is established by the variety in the position of the signatures, and by a large number of orthographical differences, in addition to the points enumerated in the table below. It is almost impossible to fix their order with certainty; but I have noticed a large number of cases where B and C agree in spelling or pointing, and differ from A; ten or eleven points which are evidently corrections of B by C; and one (p. 398 l. 28) in which C corrects both A and B. As to the respective order of these latter, the character of the three cases in which B (followed by C) corrects A—pp. 395 l. 5, 405 l. 2, 406 l. 4—may be taken to establish B's later date, in spite of the ten cases (given below) in which, on that supposition, it corrupts A; for five of these are again corrected by C, while the other five perhaps should hardly be considered corruptions. The question is of no importance, as all three editions must have appeared close together. The text I have followed is that of C, errors being corrected from A or B and every variant of the least importance being given in the footnotes.

	A (Douce copy)	B (Brit. Mus. copies)	C (Malone copy)
P. 395 l. 5	the nephewe his ape	his nephewe the ape	his nephewe the ape
P. 398 l. 6	brake your fast	brake you fast	brake you fast
P. 398 l. 28	*Mart'ins . . ergo*	*Mart'ins . . ergo*	*Martins . . ergo* (for Martin's)
P. 399 l. 34	all is	alls	alls
P. 400 l. 4	abusde, for	abusde . for	abusde : for

P. 400 l. 4	vertuously	vertuousty	vertuously
P. 400 l. 39	Sainct *Martins*	Sainct *Martins*	Saincts *Martins*
P. 401 l. 11	(fol. B 4 recto, line 1) They venter (printed level with following line)	(printed level, as in A)	(indented the width of two letters to mark new paragraph)
P. 402 l. 19	set him to worke	set to him worke	set him to worke
P. 402 l. 33	perceiue	perceine	perceiue
P. 404 l. 24	*Martin*	*Mantin*	*Martin*
P. 405 l. 2	I (marie quoth the Iudge)	I marie (quoth the Iudge)	I marie (quoth the Iudge)
P. 405 l. 29	Wierdrawers	Wierdawers	Wierdawers
P. 405 l. 35	this gaming humour	his gaming humour	his gaming humour
P. 405 ll. 39-40	hath sod	had sod	hath sod
P. 406 l. 4	smile	simile	simile
P. 407 l. 30	not	nor	not
P. 409 l. 3	GOD saue	GOD sane	GOD saue
P. 410 l. 5	authoritie	authorie	authorie
P. 412 l. 3	hath	had	had
P. 412 l. 33	foole	foole	foale
P. 413 l. 2	you cannot	you cannot	thou cannot

Authorship.—Lyly's authorship cannot seriously be disputed. On p. 400 ll. 25 sqq. we have a passage referring to Gabriel Harvey, which called forth from the latter the *Advertisement to Papp-Hatchet*, dated Nov. 5, 1589, and printed as the second book of *Pierces Supererogation* in 1593. In this *Advertisement*, and again in the *Four Letters and certaine Sonnets* of 1592, Harvey expressly identifies Lyly as the author[1]; and though

---

[1] From the *Advertisement*, printed in Brydges' *Archaica*, vol. ii :—

'Pap-hatchet (for the name of thy good nature is pitifully grown out of request) thy old acquaintance in the Savoy, when young Euphues hatcht the eggs that his elder friends laid (Surely Euphues was some way a pretty fellow : would God Lilly had alwaies been Euphues and never Papp-hatchet), that old acquaintance now somewhat strangely saluted with a new remembrance, is neither lullabied with thy sweet Papp, nor scare-crow'd with thy sour Hatchett.' P. 81.

—' Euphues it is good to be merry, and Lyly it is good to be wise, and Papp-hatchet it is better to lose a new jest than an old friend.' P. 81.

—' Albeit every man cannot compete such grand volumes as Euphues, or reare such mighty tomes as Pap-hatchet ; yet he might have thought other poore men have tongues and pennes to speak something, when they are provoked unreasonably. But loosers may have their wordes and comedians their actes : such drie bobbers can lustily strike at other, and cunningly rapp themselves. He hath not played the Vicemaster of Poules, and the Foolemaster of the Theater for naughtes : himselfe a mad lad, as ever twangd, never troubled with any substance of witt, or circumstance of honestie, sometime the fiddlesticke of Oxford, now the very bable of London.' P. 137.

—' had I been Martin (as for a time I was vainly suspected by such mad

this identification might conceivably be mere conjecture on Harvey's part, yet it is confirmed by our knowledge of a previous quarrel between the two men of a date roughly corresponding with the 'tenne yeres' grudge to which *Pappe* (p. 400 l. 34) alludes. Moreover the attribution was never denied, either by Lyly himself or by Nash, his partner in the war against the Martinists. In *Strange Newes*, 1593, Nash twice alludes to the Harveys' attack on himself and Pap-hatchet; in *Pierce Pennilesse*, 1592, he anticipates that 'he also whom thou tearmest the vayn Paphatchet will haue a flurt at thee one day'; and in *Haue with you to Saffron Waldron*, 1596, he writes 'For Master Lillie (who is halues with me in this indignitie that is offred) [i. e. in *Pierces Supererogation*], I will not take the tale out of his mouth; for he is better able to defend himselfe than I am able to say he is able to defend himselfe, and in so much time as hee spendes in taking Tobacco one weeke, he can compile that which would make Gabriell repent himselfe all his life after. With a blacke sant he meanes shortly to bee at his chamber window, for calling him the Fiddlesticke of Oxford.' It is impossible to read these passages, and those from the *Advertisement* quoted below, and not feel that the Bishops' engagement of Lyly and Nash was an open secret; and there is nothing surviving (beyond the doubtful *Whip for an Ape* and *Mar-Martine*) that can be attributed to Lyly except *Pappe*, which, further, affords internal evidence of his authorship, both in matter consonant with our knowledge of Lyly, and in echoes of *Euphues*. Under the first head might be mentioned his allusions to Cambridge, pp. 398-9, and to Nash (his junior) as a 'little wag,' a 'boy,' p. 398, to the gambling in 'an Hospitall' (a reminiscence of the Savoy, p. 399 l. 14, to the violin, p. 413 l. 31; his knowledge of the Court, p. 397 l. 7, and of theatrical affairs, p. 408; and his sense of the contrast of style between *Pappe* and *Euphues*—'I was loath so to write as I haue done, but . . . who would currie an Asse with an Iuorie combe?' p. 394 ll. 27-30. Under the second head we get, for all he can do, a vast amount of punning and alliteration, and occasional antithetic passages: 'Faith,' he says, p. 401 l. 14 after such a lapse into euphuism, 'thou wilt bee caught by the stile'; and indeed one cannot

copesmates that can surmise anything for their purpose, howsoever unlikely or monstrous) I would have been so far from being moved by such a fantastical confuter, that it should have been one of my May-games or August triumphs to have driven officials . . . bishops and archbishops . . . to entertain such an odd light-headed fellow for their defence; a professed jester, a hick-scorner, a scoffmaster, a play-monger, an interluder; once the fool of Oxford, now the stale of London, and ever the apes-clog of the press, Cum privilegio perennitatis.' P. 86.
From the *Four Letters and certaine Sonnets* (Brydges' *Archaica*, ii. p. 17):—
—'And that was all the fleeting that ever I felt, saving that another company of special good fellows (whereof he was none of the meanest that brauely threatened to conjure up one which should massacre Martin's wit or should be lambacked himself with ten years provision) would needs forsooth very courtly persuade the Earle of Oxforde that something in those letters, and namely the Mirrour of Tuscanismo, was palpably intended against him,' &c.

believe that he was particularly anxious to avoid detection, having no such motive for concealment as had the Martinists. The idea (p. 395 l. 2) of riding the kickish wit of an opponent occurs again at the end of Act iv. Sc. 2 of *Mother Bombie*. The following particular echoes of *Euphues* are also clearly traceable (see notes) : ' addle egges ... idle heads,' p. 396 l. 30; the making of Sciron and Procrustes partners, ib. l. 31 ; ' mould ... mould,' p. 397 l. 3 ; ' such a warming as shall make all his deuices like wood,' p. 399 ll. 25-6 ; ' abiects ... subiects,' p. 411 l. 41 ; ' teare boughs ... hew tree,' ' wet feete ... care not how deepe they wade,' p. 412 ll. 1-2 ; a couple of natural history allusions, pp. 396 l. 16 (camel), 399 l. 29 (Estritch); and the passage ' Her sacred Maiestie,' &c., p. 409 ll. 5 sqq., which a little recalls Euphues' ' Glasse for Europe.'

For the occasion of the pamphlet and the Marprelate Controversy in general see Life, vol. i. pp. 49-60.

Date.—The composition of all except the closing pages preceded the appearance of Martin's *Protestatyon*, after which, at p. 410 l. 19, the pamphlet was resumed. An approximate date for that appearance is to be inferred from *The Returne of Pasquill* (D iii. verso), where just after ' Pasquil's Protestation,' which is dated ' 20 Octobris. Anno Millimo Quillimo Trillimo,' Nash says, ' Yester night late olde Martins Protestation in Octauo was brought vnto mee.' I see no reason to doubt that ' 20 Octobris ' represents the real date of Nash's writing, and therefore that the *Protestatyon* had appeared from the beginning to the middle of the same month. That being so, *Pappe*, which contains an appendix answering it, can hardly have appeared before the second or third week of October ; while a downward limit is found in the date affixed to Harvey's reply, the *Advertisement to Papp-Hatchett*—' At Trinitie hall : this fift of Nouember : 1589.'

Contents.—It is unnecessary to summarize its contents. It makes little attempt at serious argument, and indeed seems to disclaim any such (p. 410 ll. 4 sqq.). It is a mere farrago of abuse and scandal gleaned from Nash, which Gabriel Harvey (Brydges' *Archaica*, ii. p. 83) adequately described as ' alehouse and tinkerly stuff,' saying that a pamphlet ' so oddly huddled and bungled together, in so madbrain a sort and with so brainsick stuff,' was ' nothing worthy a scholar or a civil gentleman,' and ' one of the most paltry things that ever was published by graduate of either university ' (Brydges' *Archaica*, i. p. 141). Its apparent high spirits do not prevent an occasional indication that Lyly finds his task a bore, e. g. pp. 399 l. 34, 403 ll. 6, 18, 404 ll. 29, 36, 406 ll. 6-8, 413 l. 4. Mingled, however, with the ribaldry are one or two pertinent and well-told stories, e. g. pp. 402 ll. 12-26, 409 ll. 16-35 ; much that at first appears sheer nonsense is found on examination to possess some point ; and the *brochure*, whatever its defects, reached a third edition.

Pappe with an hatchet.
Alias,
A figge for my God sonne.
Or
Cracke me this nut.
Or
A Countrie cuffe, that is, a sound boxe of the
eare, for the idiot *Martin* to hold his peace,
seeing the patch will take no
warning.

VVritten by one that dares call a dog, a dog,
and made to preuent *Martins* dog daies.

Imprinted by *Iohn Anoke*, and *Iohn Astile*, for the
Bayliue of Withernam, *cum priuilegio perennitatis*, and are to bee sold at the signe of the
crab tree cudgell in thwack-
coate lane.

A sentence.

Martin hangs fit for my mowing.

To the Father and the two Sonnes, Huffe, Ruffe, and Snuffe,

the three tame ruffians of the Church, which take pepper
in the nose, because they can
not marre Prelates⟨,⟩
grating.

ROOME for a royster; so thats well sayd, itch a little further for a good fellowe. Now haue at you all my gaffers of the rayling religion, tis I that must take you a peg lower. I am sure you looke for more worke, you shall haue wood enough to cleaue, make your tongue the wedge, and your head the beetle, Ile make such a splinter runne into your wits, as shal make thē ranckle till you become fooles. Nay, if you shoot bookes like fooles bolts, Ile be so bold as to make your iudgements quiuer with my thunderbolts. If you meane to gather clowdes in the Commonwealth, to threaten tempests, for your flakes of snowe weele pay you with stones of hayle; if with an Easterlie winde you bring Catterpillers into the Church, with a Northerne wind weele driue barrennes into your wits.

We care not for a Scottish mist, though it wet vs to the skin, you shal be sure your cockscombs shall not be mist, but pearst to the skuls. I professe rayling, and think it as good a cudgell for a Martin, as a stone for a dogge, or a whippe for an Ape, or poyson for a rat.

Yet find fault with no broad termes, for I haue mesured yours with mine, & I find yours broader iust by the list. Say not my speaches are light, for I haue weighed yours and mine, and I finde yours lighter by twentie graines than the allowance. For number you exceede, for you haue thirtie ribauld words for my one, and yet you beare a good spirit. I was loath so to write as I haue done, but that I learnde, that he that drinkes with cutters, must not be without his ale dagger; nor hee that buckles with *Martin*, without his lauish termes.

Who would currie an Asse with an Iuorie combe? giue the beast thistles for prouender. I doo but yet angle with a silken flye, to see whether *Martins* will nibble; and if I see that, why then I haue wormes for the nonce, and will giue them line enough like a trowte, till they swallow both hooke and line, and then *Martin* beware your gilles, for Ile make you daunce at the poles end.

I knowe *Martin* will with a trice bestride my shoulders. Well, if he ride me, let the foole sit fast, for my wit is verie kickish ; which if he spurre with his copper replie, when it bleedes, it will all to besmeare their consciences.

If a *Martin* can play at chestes, as well as his nephewe the ape, he shall knowe what it is for a scaddle pawne, to crosse a Bishop in his owne walke. Such dydoppers must be taken vp, els theile not stick to check the king. Rip vp my life, discipher my name, fill thy answer as full of lies as of lines, swel like a toade, hisse like an adder, bite like a dog, & chatter like a monkey, my pen is prepared and my minde ; and if yee chaunce to finde any worse words than you brought, let them be put in your dads dictionarie. And so farewell, and be hangd, and I pray God ye fare no worse.

Yours at an houres warning
Double V.

5 the nephewe his ape *A*

TO THE
INDIFFERENT READER.

It is high time to search in what corner of the Church the fire is kindled, being crept so far, as that with the verie smoke the consciences of diuers are smothered. It is found that certaine *Martins,* if no mis- creants in religion (which wee may suspect) yet without doubt malecōtents (which wee ought to feare) haue throwen fire, not into the Church porch, but into the Chauncell, and though not able by learning and iudgement to displace a Sexton, yet seeke to remooue Bishops. They haue scattered diuers libels, all so taunting and slanderous, as it is hard to iudge, whether their lyes exceed their bitternesse, or their bitternesse their fables.

If they be answered by the grauitie of learned Prelates, they presentlie reply with railings; which argueth their intent to be as farre frō the truth of deuotion, as their writings from mildnes of spirit. It is said that camels neuer drinke, til they haue troubled the water with their feete, & it seemes these *Martins* cannot carouse the sapp of the Church, till by faction they make tumults in religion. Seeing thē either they expect no graue replie, or that they are settled with railing to replie; I thought it more conuenient, to giue them a whisk with their owne wand, than to haue them spurd with deeper learning.

The *Scithian* slaues, though they bee vp in armes, must bee tamde with whippes, not swords, and these mutiners in Church matters, must haue their mouthes bungd with iests, not arguments.

I seldome vse to write, and yet neuer writ anie thing, that in speech might seeme vndecent, or in sense vnhonest; if here I haue vsed bad tearmes, it is because they are not to bee answered with good tearmes: for whatsoeuer shall seeme lauish in this Pamphlet, let it be thought borrowed of *Martins* language. These *Martins* were hatcht of addle egges, els could they not haue such idle heads. They measure conscience by their owne yard, and like the theeues, that had an yron bed, in which all that were too long they would cut euen, all that were too short they would stretch out, and none escapte vnrackt or vnsawed, that were not iust of their beds length: so all that are not *Martins,* that is, of their peeuish mind, must be measured by them. If he come short of their religion, why he is but a colde Protestant, hee must bee pluckt out to

the length of a Puritane. If any be more deuout than they are, as to giue
almes, fast, and pray, then they cut him off close by the workes, and say
he is a Papist. If one be not cast in *Martins* mould, his religion must
needes mould. He saith he is a Courtier, I thinke no Courtier so peruerse, that seeing the streight rule of the Church, would goe about to
bend it. It may be he is some Iester about the Court, and of that I meruaile, because I know all the fooles there, and yet cannot gesse at him.
What euer he be, if his conscience be pind to his cognizance, I will
account him more politicke than religious, and more dangerous for ciuill
broyles, than the Spaniard for an open warre. I am ignorant of *Martin*
and his maintainer, but my conscience is my warrant, to care for neither.
For I knowe there is none of honour so carelesse, nor any in zeale so
peeuish, nor of nature any so barbarous, that wil succor those that be
suckers of the Church, a thing against God and policie; against God, in
subuerting religion; against policie, in altering gouernment, making in
the Church, the feast of the *Lapithees,* where all shall bee throwne on
anothers head, because euerie one would be the head. And these it is
high time to tread vnder foote: for who would not make a threshold of
those, that go about to make the Church a barne to thresh in. *Itaque sic
disputo.*

FINIS.

PAPPE WITH AN HATCHET.

GOOD morrow, goodman *Martin*, good morrow: will ye anie musique this morning? What fast a sleepe? Nay faith, Ile cramp thee till I wake thee. *O whose tat?* Nay gesse olde knaue and odd knaue: for Ile neuer leaue pulling, til I haue thee out of thy bed into the streete; and then all shall see who thou art, and thou know what I am. 5

Your Knaueship brake your fast on the Bishops, by breaking your iests on them: but take heed you breake not your owne necke. Bastard *Iunior* dinde vpon them, and cramde his maw as full of mallice, as his head was of malapertnesse. Bastard *Senior* was with them at supper, and I thinke tooke a surfet of colde and raw quipps. O what queasie girds 10 were they towards the fall of the leafe. Old *Martin*, neuer entaile thy wit to the eldest, for hee'le spend all he hath in a quire of paper.

Now sirs, knowing your bellies full of Bishops bobbs, I am sure your bones would be at rest: but wee'le set vp all our rests, to make you all restie. I was once determined to write a proper newe Ballet, entituled 15 *Martin and his Maukin*, to no tune, because *Martin* was out of all tune. *Elderton* swore hee had rimes lying a steepe in ale, which shoulde marre all your reasons: there is an olde hacker that shall take order for to print them. O how heele cut it, when his ballets come out of the lungs of the licour. They shall bee better than those of *Bonner*, or the ierkes for 20 a Iesuit. The first begins, Come tit me come tat me, come throw a halter at me.

Hee sweares by his mazer, that he will make their wits wet-shod, if the ale haue his swift current.

Then I thought to touch *Martin* with Logick, but there was a little wag in *Cambridge*, that swore by Saint *Seaton*, he would so swinge him with Sillogismes, that all *Martins* answeres should ake. The vile boy 25 hath manie bobbes, and a whole fardle of fallacies. He begins,

   Linquo coax ranis, cros coruis, vanaque vanis.
   Ad Logicam pergo, quæ Martin's non timet ergo.

And saies, he will *ergo Martin* into an ague. I haue read but one of his arguments. 30

   Tiburne stands in the cold,
   But Martins *are a warme furre:*
   Therefore Tiburne must be furd with
    Martins.

O (quoth I) boy thou wilt be shamed; tis neither in moode nor figure: 35

6 you *BC* 27 cros] *qy.?* crax *for* corax (κόραξ) 28 Mart'ins *AB*: Martins *C*

all the better, for I am in a moode to cast a figure, that shall bring them
to the conclusion. I laught at the boye, and left him drawing all the
lines of *Martin* into silogismes, euerie conclusion beeing this, *Ergo
Martin* is to bee hangd.

Nay, if rime and reason bee both forestalde, Ile rayle, if *Martin* haue
not barrelde vp all rakehell words: if he haue, what care I to knocke him
on the head with his owne hatchet. He hath taken vp all the words for
his obscenitie: obscenitie? Naie, now I am too nice, squirrilitie were
a better word: well, let me alone to squirrell them.

Martin, thinkst thou thou hast so good a wit, as none can outwrangle
thee? Yes *Martin*, wee will play three a vies wits: art thou so backt
that none dare blade it with thee? Yes *Martin*, we wil drop vie stabbes.
Martin sweares I am some gamester. Why, is not gaming lawful?
I know where there is more play in the compasse of an Hospitall, than
in the circuite of *Westchester*. One hath been an old stabber at passage:
the One that I meane, thrust a knife into ones thigh at *Cambridge*, the
quarrel was about cater-tray, and euer since hee hath quarrelled about
cater-caps.

I thought that hee which thrust at the bodie in game, would one day
cast a foyne at the soule in earnest. But hee workes closelie and sees
all, hee learnd that of old *Vidgin* the cobler, who wrought ten yeares
with spectacles, and yet swore he could see through a dicker of leather.
He hath a wanton spleene, but wee will haue it stroakt with a spurne,
because his eyes are bleard, hee thinkes to bleare all ours; but let him
take this for a warning, or else looke for such a warming, as shall make
all his deuices as like wood, as his spittle is like woodsere. Take away
the Sacke, and giue him some Cinamom water, his conscience hath
a colde stomacke. Cold? Thou art deceiued, twil digest a Cathedral
Church as easilie, as an Estritch a two penie naile.

But softe *Martins*, did your Father die at the *Groyne*? It was well
groapt at, for I knewe him sicke of a paine in the groyne. A pockes of
that religion, (quoth *Iulian Grimes* to her Father) when al his haires fell
off on the sodaine. Well let the olde knaue be dead. Whie are not the
spawnes of such a dog-fish hangd? Hang a spawne? drowne it; alls
one, damne it.

Ye like not a Bishops rochet, when all your fathers hankerchers were
made of his sweete harts smocke. That made you bastards, and your
dad a cuckold, whose head is swolne so big, that he had neede sende to
the cooper to make him a biggin: and now you talke of a cooper, Ile tell
you a tale of a tubb.

At *Sudburie*, where the Martin-mōgers swarmd to a lecture, like beares
to a honnie pot: a good honest strippling, of the age of fiftie yeares or

thereabout, that could haue done a worse act if companie had not been neere, askt his sweete sister, whether lecherie in her conscience were a sinne? In faith (quoth she) I thinke it the superficies of sinne, and no harme if the tearmes be not abusde: for you must say, vertuously done, not lustily done. Fie, this is filthie ribaldry. O sir, ther is no mirth without ribaldrie, nor ribaldrie without *Martin*, ask mine hostesse of the iuie bush in *Wye* for the one, & my old hostesse of the Swanne in *Warwicke* for the other. She is dead: the diuell shee is. You are too broad with *Martins* brood: for hee hath a hundred thousand that will set their handes to his Articles, and shewe the Queene. Sweeter and sweeter: for wee haue twentie hundred thousand handes to withstand them. I would it were come to the grasp, we would show them an Irish tricke, that when they thinke to winne the game with one man, wee'le make them holde out till wee haue but two left to carrie them to the gallowes: wel followed in faith, for thou saidst thou wert a gamester. All this is but bad English, when wilt thou come to a stile? *Martin* hath manie good words. Manie? Now you put me in minde of the matter, there is a booke cōming out of a hundred merrie tales, and the petigree of *Martin*, fetchte from the burning of *Sodome*, his armes shalbe set on his hearse, for we are prouiding his funerall, and for the winter nights the tales shall be told *secundum vsum Sarum:* the Deane of Salisburie can tell twentie. If this will not make *Martin* mad, malicious and melancholie (ô braue letter followed with a full crie) then will we be desperate, & hire one that shall so translate you out of French into English, that you will blush and lie by it. And one will we coniure vp, that writing a familiar Epistle about the naturall causes of an Earthquake, fell into the bowells of libelling, which made his eares quake for feare of clipping, he shall tickle you with taunts; all his works bound close, are at least six sheetes in quarto, & he calls them the first tome of his familiar Epistle: he is full of latin endes, and worth tenne of those that crie in London, *haie ye anie gold ends to sell*. If he giue you a bob, though he drawe no bloud, yet are you sure of a rap with a bable. If he ioyne with vs, *periisti Martin*, thy wit will be massacred: if the toy take him to close with thee, then haue I my wish, for this tenne yeres haue I lookt to lambacke him. Nay he is a mad lad, and such a one as cares as little for writing without wit, as *Martin* doth for writing without honestie; a notable coach companion for *Martin*, to drawe Diuinitie from the Colledges of *Oxford* and *Cambridge*, to Shoomakers hall in Sainct *Martins*. But we neither feare *Martin*, nor the foot cloth, nor the beast that weares it, be he horse or asse; nor whose sonne he is, be he *Martins*, sonne, *Iohns*, sonne, or *Richards*, sonne; nor of what occupation hee be, be a ship-wright, cart-wright, or tiburn-wright. If they

They are not so many, thei are all Centimani, an hundred hands a peece: so that in all they are but one thousand.

39 Sainct *AB*: Saincts *C*

bring seauen hundred men, they shall be boxt with fourteene hundred boyes. Nay we are growing to a secret bargaine. O, but I forgate a riddle ; *the more it is spied, the lesse it is seene.* Thats the Sunne : the lesse it is spied of vs, the more it is seene of those vnder vs. The Sunne ? Thou art an asse, it is the Father, for the old knaue, thinking by his bastardie to couer his owne heade, putteth it like a stagge ouer the pale. Pale ? nay I will make him blush as red as ones nose, that was alwaies washt in well water.

What newes from the Heraldes ? Tush, thats time enough to know to morrow, for the sermon is not yet cast. The sermon foole ? why they neuer studie, but cleaue to Christ his *dabitur in illa hora.* They venter to catch soules, as they were soles ; Doctors are but dunces, none sowes true stitches in a pulpet, but a shoomaker.

Faith, thou wilt bee caught by the stile. What care I to be found by a stile, when so many Martins haue been taken vnder an hedge ? If they cannot leuell, they will rone at thee, and anatomize thy life from the cradle to the graue, and thy bodie from the corne on thy toe, to the crochet on thy head. They bee as cunning in cutting vp an honest mans credit, as *Bull* in quartering a knaues bodie. Tush, (what care I) is my posie ; if hee meddle with mee, Ile make his braines so hot, that they shall crumble and rattle in his warpt scull, like pepper in a dride bladder. *Martin Iunior saies, hee found his fathers papers vnder a bush, the knaue was started frō his Fourme.*

I haue a catalogue of al the sheepe, and it shal goe hard, but I wil crosse the bel-weather. Why shuld I feare him that walkes on his neatsfeete. Neither court, nor countrie that shalbe free, I am like death, Ile spare none. There shall not misse a name of any, that had a Godfather ; if anie bee vnchristened, Ile nicke him with a name.

But whist ; beware an action of the case. Then put this for the case, whether it bee not as lawful to set downe the facts of knaues, as for a knaue to slander honest men. Alls as it is taken ; marie the diuell take al, if truth find not as many soft cushions to leane on, as trecherie.

Theres one with a lame wit, which will not weare a foure cornerd cap, then let him put on Tiburne, that hath but three corners ; & yet the knaue himselfe hath a pretie wench in euerie corner.

I could tickle *Martin* with a true tale of one of his sonnes, that hauing the companie of one of his sisters in the open fieldes, saide, hee woulde not smoother vp sinne, and deale in hugger mugger against his Conscience. In the hundred merrie tales, the places, the times, the witnesses and all, shall be put downe to the proofe, where I warrant you, the Martinists haue consciences of proofe. Doost think *Martin*, thou canst not be discouered ? What foole would not thinke him discouered that is balde ? Put on your night cap, and your holie day English, and the best wit you haue for high daies, all wil be little enough to keep you from *He calls none but the heaues to witnesse.*

39 Doest *A*

a knaues penance, though as yet you be in a fooles paradice. If you coyne words, as *Cankerburie, Canterburines*, &c. whie, I know a foole that shall so inkhornize you with straunge phrases, that you shall blush at your owne bodges. For Similes, theres another shal liken thee to anie thing, besides he can raile too. If *Martin* muzzle not his mouth, and manacle his hands, Ile blabb all, and not sticke to tell, that pewes and stewes are rime in their religion.

Scratch not thy head *Martin*, for be thou *Martin* the bird, or *Martin* the beast; a bird with the longest bill, or a beast with the longest eares, theres a net spread for your necke. *Martin*, Ile tell thee a tale woorth twelue pence, if thy witt bee woorth a pennie.

There came to a Duke in *Italie*, a large lubber and a beggerlie, saying hee had the Philosophers Stone, and that hee could make golde faster, than the Duke could spend it; The Duke askt him, why hee made none to mainteine himself? Because, quoth he, I could neuer get a secret place to worke in; for once I indeuoured, and the Popes holinesse sent for me, whom if he had caught, I should haue been a prentice to mainteine his pride. The Duke minding to make triall of his cunning, & eager of golde, set him to worke closely in a vault, where it was not knowen to his neerest seruaunts. This Alcumist, in short time consumed two thousande pound of the Dukes gold, and brought him halfe a Ducket: whie (quoth the Duke) is this all? All quoth he my Lord, that I could make by Art. Wel said the Duke, then shalt thou see my cunning: for I will boyle thee, straine thee, and then drie thee, so that of a lubber, that weighed three hundred weight, I will at last make a dram of knaues powder. The Duke did it.

Martin, if thou to cousen haue crept into the bosome of some great mē, saying thou hast the churches discipline, & that thou canst by thy faction & pollicie, pull down Bishops and set vp Elders, bring the lands of the Clergy, into the cofers of the Temporaltie, and repaire Religion, by impayring their liuings, it may bee, thou shalt bee hearkened too, stroakt on the head, greasd in the hand, fed daintelie, kept secretlie, and countenaunst mightelie. But when they perceiue, that all thy deuices bee but *Chymeraes*, monsters of thine owne imaginations, so farre from pulling downe a Cathedrall Church, that they cannot remooue a corner of a square cap, thē will they deale with thee, as the Duke did with the Alcumist, giue thee as many bobs on the eare, as thou hast eaten morsels of their meate, and make thee an example of sedition to be pointed at, that art now so mewde vp, that none can point where thou art. All this tale, with the application, was not of my penning, but found among loose papers; marie he that did it, dares stand to it. Now, because I haue nothing to doo betweene this and supper, Ile tell you another tale, and so begin Winter by time.

Martin & his mainteiner are both sawers of timber, but Martin stands in the pit, all the dust must fall in his eies, but he shal neuer walke on the boards.

19 to him *B*   33 perceine *B*

There was a libeller, who was also a coniurer, so that whatsoeuer casting of figures there was, he deceiued them; at the last, one as cunning as himself, shewed, wher he sate writing in a fooles coate, & so he was caught and whipt. *Martin*, there are figures a flinging, & ten to one thou wilt be found sitting in a Knaues skinne, and so be hangd.

Hollow there, giue me the beard I wore yesterday. O beware of a gray beard, and a balde head: for if such a one doo but nod, it is right dudgin and deepe discretion. But soft, I must now make a graue speach.

There is small difference between Swallowes & *Martins*, either in shape or nature, saue onely, that the *Martins*, haue a more beetle head, they both breed in Churches, and hauing fledgde their young ones, leaue nothing behind them but durt. Vnworthie to come into the Church porch, or to be nourished vnder anie good mans eues, that gnawe the bowels, in which they were bred, and defile the place, in which they were ingendred.

They studie to pull downe Bishopps, and set vp Superintendents, which is nothing else, but to raze out good *Greeke*, & enterline bad *Latine*. A fine period; but I cannot continue this stile, let me fal into my olde vaine. O doost remember, howe that Bastard *Iunior* complaines of brothells, and talkes of long *Megg* of *Westminster*. A craftie iacke, you thoght because you twitted *Mar-martin*, that none would suspect you; yes faith *Martin*, you shall bee thresht with your owne flaile.

It was one of your neast, that writt this for a loue letter, to as honest a womā as euer burnt malt. *Grace, mercie, and peace to thee (O widow) with feruent motions of the spirit, that it may worke in thee both to will and to doo. Thou knowest my loue to thee is, as* Paules *was to the* Corinthians; *that is, the loue of copulation.* *Hee thought Lais had still lien at Corinth as wel as Paul.*

How now holie *Martin*, is this good wooing? If you prophane the Scriptures, it is a pretie wit: if we but alledge Doctors to expound them, wee are wicked. If *Martin* oppresse his neighbor, why hee saith, it is his conscience; if anie else doo right, it is extremitie. *Martin* may better goe into a brothell house, then anie other go by it; he slides into a bad place like the Sunne, all others stick in it like pitch. If *Martin* speake broad bawdrie, why all the crue saies, your worship is passing merrie. *Martin* will not sweare, but with indeede, in sooth, & in truth, hee'le cogge the die of deceipt, and cutte at the bumme-carde of his conscience. O sweetelie brought in, at least three figures in that line, besides, the wit ant.

One there was, and such a one as *Martin* would make the eldest of his Elders, that hauing fortie angels sent him for a beneuolence, refusde to giue the poore fellowe a quittance for the receipt, saying, Christ had giuen his master a quittance, the same howre he told it out: & this was at his table, where he sate with no lesse than fortie good dishes of the greatest dainties, in more pompe than a Pope, right like a superintendant.

Now to the two bastards, what were you twins? It shuld seeme so, for there wēt but a paire of sheres betweene your knaueries. When the old henne hatcht such eggs, the diuel was in the cocks comb. Your father thrusts you forward, remember pettie *Martins Aesops* crab, the mother going backward, exhorted her sonnes to goe forward; doo you so first mother quoth they, and we will follow. Now the old cuckold hath puld in his hornes, he would make you creepe cleane out of the shell, & so both loose your houses, and shewe your nakednesse. You go about impossibilities, wele no such chāge, and if yee had it, yee would be wearie of it.

There was a man like *Martin*, that had a goose, which euerie daie laid him a golden egge; hee not content with the blessing, kild his goose, thinking to haue a mine of golde in her bellie, and finding nothing but dung, the gāder wisht his goose aliue. Martinists that liue well by the Church, & receiue great benefites of it, thinke if all Churches were downe, they should be much better, but when they shall see cōfusion in stead of discipline, & atheisme to be found in place of doctrine, will they not with sighs wish the Churches and Bishops in their wonted gouernmēt? Thou art well seen in tales, & preachest *Aesops fables*. Tush, Ile bring in *Pueriles*, and *Stans puer ad mensam*, for such vnmannerlie knaues as Martin, must bee set againe to their A.B.C. and learne to spell *Our Father* in a Horne booke. *Martin Iunior* giues warning that none write against reuerent *Martin*: yes, there are *a tribus ad centum*, from three to an hūdred, that haue vowed to write him out of his right wittes, and we are all *Aptots*, in all cases alike, til we haue brought *Martin* to the ablatiue case, that is, to bee taken away with *Bulls* voider.

O here were a notable full point, to leaue Martin in the hangmans apron. Nay, he would be glad to scape with hanging, weele first haue him lashte through the Realme with cordes, that when hee comes to the gallowes, he may be bleeding new.

The babie comes in with *Nunka, Neame*, and *Dad:* (Pappe with an hatchet for such a puppie) giue the infant a bibbe, he all to beslauers his mother tongue, if he driuell so at the mouth and nose, weele haue him wipte with a hempen wispe. *Hui?* How often hast thou talkt of haltring? Whie it runnes still in my minde that they must bee hangd. Hangde is the Que, and it comes iust to my purpose.

There was one endited at a Iaile deliuerie of felonie, for taking vp an halter by the high way. The Iurie gaue verdit and said guiltie. The Iudge an honest man, said it was hard to find one guiltie for taking vp a penie halter, and bad them consider, what it was to cast awaie a man.

24 Mantin *B*   33 Nuncka *A*

Quoth the foreman, we haue enquired throughly, and found there was a horse tied to the halter. I marie (quoth the Iudge) then let him be tied to the halter, and let the horse goe home. *Martin*, a Monarch in his owne moyst conceit, and drie counsell, saies he is enuied onelie, because he leuelleth at Bishops; & we say as the Iudge saith, that if there were nothing else, it were hard to persecute them to death; but when we finde that to the rule of the Church, the whole state of the Realme is linckt, & that they filching away Bishop by Bishop, seeke to fish for the Crown, and glew to their newe Church their owne conclusions, we must then say, let Bishops stand, & they hang; that is, goe home. Looke howe manie tales are in this booke, so manie must you abate of an hundred in the next booke, reckon this for one.

There came by of late a good honest Minister, with a cloake hauing sleeues: ah (quoth a Martinist, sitting on a bulke in Cheapside) he is a knaue I warrant you, a claspe would become one of his coate to claspe his cloak vnder his chinne. Where tis to be noted, that they come in with a sleeuelesse conscience, and thinke it no good doctrine, which is not preached with the cloak cast ouer each shoulder like a rippier.

Twas a mad knaue and a Martinist, that diuided his sermon into 34. parts for memorie sake, and would handle but foure for memorie sake, and they were, why Christ came, wherefore Christ came, for what cause Christ came, and to what end Christ came; this was all for memorie sake. If that *Martin* could thatch vp his Church, this mans scabship should bee an Elder, and Elders they may bee, which being fullest of spungie pith, proue euer the driest kixes. For in time you shall see, that it is but a bladder of worldlie winde which swells in their hearts, being once prickt, the humour will quicklie be remoued. O what a braue state of the Church it would be for all Ecclesiasticall causes to come before Weauers and Wierdrawers, to see one in a motlie Ierkin and an apron to reade the first lesson. The poore Church should play at vnequal game, for it should loose al by the *Elder* hand. Nay Mas Martin, weele make you deale, shuffle as well as you can, we meane to cut it.

If you had the foddring of the sheep, you would make the Church like Primero, foure religions in it, and nere one like another. I cannot out of this gaming humour. Why? Is it not as good as *Martins* dogged humour, who without reuerence, regard, or exception, vseth such vnfitting tearmes, as were hee the greatest subiect in England hee could not iustifie them.

Shut the doores (sirs) or giue me my skimmer, *Martins* mouth hath sod vnskimde these twelue months, and now it runnes ouer; yet let him alone, he makes but porredge for the diuell.

His Elderberrines though it be naught woorth, yet is it like an elder-

2 I (marie quoth *A*   29 Wierdawers *BC*   35 this *A* : his *BC*   39 had *B*

berrie, which being at the ripenes of a perfect black, yet brused staines
ones hands like bloud. They pretending grauitie in the rottennes of their
zeale, bee they once wrung, you shall finde them lighter than feathers.
Thats a simile for the slaues. Nay, Ile touch them deeper, and make
them crie, O my heart, there is a false knaue among vs.

Take awaie this beard, and giue mee a pikede vaunt, *Martin* sweares
by his ten bones: nay, I will make him mumpe, mow, and chatter, like
old Iohn of Paris garden before I leaue him.

If *Martin* will fight Citie fight, wee challenge him at all weapons, from
the taylors bodkin to the watchmans browne bil. If a field may be
pitcht, we are readie: if they scratch, wee will bring cattes: if scolde,
we will bring women: if multiplie words, we will bring fooles: if they
floute, we will bring quippes: if dispute the matter, we will bring
schollers: if they buffet, wee will bring fists. *Deus bone*, what a number
of we will brings be here? Nay, we will bring *Bull* to hang them.
A good note & signe of good lucke, three times motion of *Bull*. Motion
of *Bull*? Why, next olde *Rosses* motion of Bridewell, *Buls* motion fits
them best. *Tria sequuntur tria*, in reckoning *Bull* thrice, meethinkes
it should presage hanging. O bad application; Bad? I doo not thinke
there can be a better, than to applie a knaues necke to an halter. *Martin*
can not start, I am his shadowe, one parte of the daie before him, another
behinde him; I can chalke a knaue on his backe thrice a weeke, Ile let
him bloud in the combe.

Take heed, he will pistle thee. Pistle me? Then haue I a pestle so
to stampe his pistles, that Ile beate all his wit to powder. What will
the powder of *Martins* wit be good for? Marie blow vp a dram of it
into the nostrels of a good Protestant, it will make him giddie; but if
you minister it like *Tobacco* to a Puritane, it will make him as mad as
a *Martin*.

Goe to, a hatch before the doore, *Martin* smels thee, and wil not feare
thee; thou knowest how he dealeth with the Archbishop and a Counsellor,
hee will name thee and that broadlie. Name me? Mary, he and his
shall bee namefied, that's it I thirst after, that name to name, and knowing
one another, wee may in the streetes grapple; wee except none: wee
come with a verse in our mouthes, courage in our hearts, and weapons
in our hands, and crie

Discite iustitiam moniti, & non temnere diuos.

Martins conscience hath a periwig; therefore to good men he is more
sower than wig: a Lemman will make his conscience curd like a Posset.
Now comes a biting speach, let mee stroake my beard thrice like a
Germain, before I speak a wise word.

Martin, wee are now following after thee with hue and crie, & are hard

at thy heeles; if thou turne backe to blade it, wee doubt not but three honest men shall bee able to beate sixe theeues. Weele teach thee to commit sacriledge, and to robbe the Church of xxiiij. Bishops at a blowe. Doost thinke that wee are not men *Martin*, and haue great men to
5 defend vs which write? Yes, although with thy seditious cloase, thou would'st perswade her Maiestie, that most of the Gentlemen of account and men of honour, were by vs thought Puritanes. No, it is your poore Iohns, that with your painted consciences haue coloured the religion of diuers, spreading through the veynes of the Commonwealth like poyson,
10 the doggednes of your deuotions; which entring in like the smoothnes of oyle into the flesh, fretteth in time like quicksiluer into the bones.

When children play with their meate, tis a signe their bellies are full, & it must be taken away from them; but if they tread it vnder their feete, they ought to be ierkt. The Gospell hath made vs wantons, wee dallie
15 with Ceremonies, dispute of circumstances, not remembring that the Papists haue been making roddes for vs this thirtie yeares; wee shall bee swing'd by them, or worse by *Martin*, if *Martins* bee worse. Neuer if it, for they bee worse with a witnesse, and let the diuell be witnesse. Wee are so nice, that the Cap is a beame in our Church, the booke
20 of Common Praier a milstone, the *Pater noster* is not well pend by Christ. Well, either religion is but policie, or policie scarce religious.

If a Gentleman riding by the way with twentie men, a number of theeues should by deuise or force binde all his seruants; the good Iustice of Peace would thinke he should bee robd. When Martinists rancke
25 robbers of the Church shall binde the legges and armes of the Church, me thinkes the supreme head of the Church should looke pale.

They that pull downe the bells of a steeple, and say it is conscience, will blow vp the chauncell to make it the quintessence of conscience. Bir Ladie, this is a good settled speech, a Diuine might haue seemd to
30 haue said so much. O sir, I am not al tales, and riddles, and rimes, and iestes, thats but my Liripoope, if *Martin* knock the bone he shall find marrow, & if he looke for none, we'le knock the bone on his pate, and bring him on his marie bones.

I haue yet but giuen them a fillip on the conceipt, Ile fell it to the
35 ground hereafter. Nay, if they make their consciences stretch like chiuerell in the raine, Ile make them crumple like parchment in the fire.

I haue an excellent balme to cure anie that is bitten with *Martin mad-dog*.

I am worth twentie Pistle-penners; let them but chafe my penne, & it shal sweat out a whole realme of paper, or make the odious to the
40 whole Realme.

O but be not partial, giue them their due though they were diuels, so will I, and excuse them for taking anie money at interest.

4 Doest *A*   17 Martin] Martins *A*   30 not] nor *B*

There is a good Ladie that lent one of these Martinists fortie pounds, and when at the daie shee required her money, *Martin* began to storme, and said, he thought her not the child of God, for they must lend, looking for nothing againe, and so to acquite himselfe of the blot of vsurie, he kepte the principall.

These *Martins* make the Scriptures a Scriueners shop to drawe conueyances, and the common pleas of *Westminster* to take forfeitures. Theyle not sticke to outlaw a mans soule, and serue it presently with an execution of damnation, if one denie them to lie with his neighbours wife. If they bee drunke, they say, they haue *Timothie* his weake stomacke, which Saint *Paule* willeth to warme with wine.

They haue sifted the holie Bible, and left vs nothing as they say, but branne; they haue boulted it ouer againe and againe, and got themselues the fine meale; tis meale indeede, for with their wresting and shuffling holie Writ, they finde all themselues good meales, and stand at liuerie as it were, at other mens tables.

Sed heus tu, dic sodes, will they not bee discouraged for the common players? Would those Comedies might be allowed to be plaid that are pend, and then I am sure he would be decyphered, and so perhaps discouraged.

He shall not bee brought in as whilom he was, and yet verie well, with a cocks combe, an apes face, a wolfs bellie, cats clawes, &c. but in a cap'de cloake, and all the best apparell he ware the highest day in the yeare, thats neither on Christmas daie, Good fridaie, Easter daie, Ascension, nor Trinitie sundaie, (for that were popish) but on some rainie weeke daie, when the brothers and sisters had appointed a match for particular praiers, a thing as bad at the least as Auricular confession.

A stage plaier, though he bee but a cobler by occupation, yet his chance may bee to play the Kings part. *Martin*, of what calling so euer he be, can play nothing but the knaues part, *qui tantum constans in knauitate sua est.*

If it be shewed at Paules, it will cost you foure pence: at the Theater two pence: at Sainct Thomas a Watrings nothing.

Would it not bee a fine Tragedie, when *Mardocheus* shall play a Bishoppe in a Play, and *Martin Hamman*, and that he that seekes to pull downe those that are set in authoritie aboue him, should be hoysted vpon a tree aboue all other.

Though he play least in sight now, yet we hope to see him stride from Aldgate to Ludgate, and looke ouer all the Citie at London Bridge. Soft swift, he is no traytor. Yes, if it bee treason to encourage the Commons against the chiefe of the Clergie, to make a generall reuolt from the gouernment so wel established, so wisely maintained, and so long prospering.

Reade Martin Seniors Libell, and

Because they say, *Aue Cæsar*, therefore they meane nothing against Cæsar. There may bee hidden vnder their long gownes, short daggers, and so in blearing Cæsars eyes, conspire Cæsars death. God saue the

Queene; why it is the Que which they take from the mouthes of all traytors, who though they bee throughly conuinced, both by proofe and their owne confessions, yet at the last gaspe they crie, God saue the Queene. GOD saue the Queene (say I) out of their hands, in whose hearts (long may the Queene thus gouerne) is not engrauen.

you shall perceiue that he is able to teach Gracchus to speake seditiouslie.

Her sacred Maiestie hath this thirtie yeares, with a setled and princelie temper swayed the Scepter of this Realme, with no lesse content of her subiects, than wonder of the world. GOD hath blessed her gouernment, more by miracle thā by counsaile, and yet by counsaile as much as can come from policie. Of a State taking such deepe roote, as to be fastened by the prouidence of God, the vertue of the Prince, the wisedome of Counsellers, the obedience of subiects, and the length of time; who would goe about to shake the lowest bough, that feeles in his conscience but the least blessing. Heere is a fit roome to squese them with an Apothegme.

There was an aged man that liued in a well ordered Common-wealth by the space of threescore yeares, and finding at the length that by the heate of some mens braines, and the warmnes of other mens bloud, that newe alterations were in hammering, and that it grewe to such an height, that all the desperate & discontented persons were readie to runne their heads against their head; comming into the midst of these mutiners, cried as loude as his yeares would allow; Springalls and vnripened youthes, whose wisedomes are yet in the blade, when this snowe shall be melted (laying his hand on his siluer haires) then shal you find store of durt, and rather wish for the continuance of a long frost, than the comming of an vntimely thaw. Ile moralize this.

Ile warrant the good old man meant, that when the ancient gouernment of the state should be altered by faction, or newe lawes brought in that were deuised by nice heads, that there should followe a foule and slipperie managing; where if happelie most did not fall, yet all would bee tired. A settled raigne is not like glasse mettal, to be blowne in bignesse, length or fashion of euerie mans breath, and breaking to be melted againe, & so blowne afresh; but it is compared to the fastning of the Cedar, that knitteth it selfe with such wreaths into the earth, that it cannot be remooued by any violent force of the aire.

Martin, I haue taken an inuentorie of al thy vnciuill and rakehell tearmes, and could sute them in no place but in Bedlam and Bridewell, so mad they are, and so bad they are, and yet all proceedes of the spirit. I thinke thou art possest with the spirites of Iacke Straw & the Blacksmith, who, so they might rent in peeces the gouernment, they would drawe cuts for religion.

If all be conscience, let conscience bee the foundation of your building,

3 sane *B*

not the glasse, shew effects of conscience, mildnesse in spirit, obedience to Magistrates, loue to thy brethren. Stitch charitie to thy faith, or rip faith from thy works.

If thou wilt deale soberlie without scoffes, thou shalt be answered grauely without iests, yea and of those, whom thou canst not controll for learning, nor accuse for ill life, nor shouldst contemne for authoritie. But if like a restie Iade thou wilt take the bitt in thy mouth, and then runne ouer hedge and ditch, thou shalt be brokē as *Prosper* broke his horses, with a muzroule, portmouth, and a martingall, and so haue thy head runne against a stone wall.

If thou refuse learning, and sticke to libelling; if nothing come out of those lauish lips, but taunts not without bitternesse, yet without wit; rayling not without spite, yet without cause, then giue me thy hand, thou and I will trie it out at the cuckingstoole. Ile make thee to forget Bishops English, and weep Irish; next hanging there is no better reuenge on *Martin*, than to make him crie for anger; for there is no more sullen beast, than a he drab. Ile make him pull his powting croscloath ouer his beetle browes for melancholie, and then my next booke, shall be *Martin* in his mubble fubbles.

HERE I was writing *Finis* and *Funis*, and determined to lay it by, till I might see more knauerie filde in: within a while appeared olde *Martin* with a wit worn into the socket, twinkling and pinking like the snuffe of a candle; *quantum mutatus ab illo*, how vnlike the knaue hee was before, not for malice but for sharpnesse.

The hogshead was euen come to the hauncing, and nothing could be drawne from him but dregs: yet the emptie caske sounds lowder than when it was ful; and protests more in his waining, than he could performe in his waxing. I drew neere the sillie soule, whom I found quiuering in two sheetes of protestation paper. O how meager and leane hee lookt, so creast falne, that his combe hung downe to his bill, and had I not been sure it was the picture of enuie, I shoulde haue sworne it had been the image of death, so like the verie Anatomie of mischiefe, that one might see through all the ribbes of his conscience, I began to crosse my selfe, and was readie to say the *Pater noster*, but that I knewe he carde not for it, and so vsed no other wordes, but *abi in malam crucem*, because I knewe, that lookt for him. I came so neere, that I could feele a substantiall knaue from a sprites shadowe.

I sawe through his paper coffin, that it was but a cosening corse, and one that had learned of the holie maid of Kent, to lie in a trance, before

---

6 authoritie *A* : authorie *BC*   32 it had been the image . . . No more did one of his minions (*p.* 411 *l.* 35) *this portion, representing the whole of fol.* E *in the original quarto, is missing from A*

he had brought foorth his lie; drawing his mouth awrie, that could neuer speake right; goggling with his eyes that watred with strong wine; licking his lips, and gaping, as though he should loose his childes nose, if he had not his longing to swallowe Churches; and swelling in the paunch, as though he had been in labour of a little babie, no bigger than rebellion; but Truth was at the Bishops trauaile: so that *Martin* was deliuered by sedition, which pulls the monster with yron from the beastes bowells. When I perceiued that hee masked in his rayling robes, I was so bolde as to pull off his shrowding sheete, that all the world might see the olde foole daunce naked.

Tis not a peniwoorth of protestation that can buy thy pardon, nor al worth a penie that thou proclaimest. *Martin* comes in with bloud, bloud, as though hee should bee a martir. *Martins* are bad martirs, some of them burnt seauen yeares agoe, and yet aliue. One of them lately at *Yorke*, pulling out his napkin to wipe his mouth after a lie, let drop a surgeans caliuer at his foote where he stood; these fellowes can abide no pompe, and yet you see they cannot be without a little squirting plate: rub no more, the curtall wrinches.

They call the Bshops butchers, I like the Metaphore wel, such calues must be knockt on the head, and who fitter than the Fathers of the Church, to cut the throates of heresies in the Church. Nay, whē they haue no propertie of sheepe but bea, their fleece for flockes, not cloath, their rotten flesh for no dish, but ditches; I thinke them woorth neither the tarring nor the telling, but for their scabbednes to bee thrust from the pinfolde to the scaffold, and with an *Habeas corpus* to remooue them from the Shepheards tarre-boxe, to the hangmans budget.

I but he hath sillogismes in pike sauce, and arguments that haue been these twentie yeres in pickle. I, picke hell, you shall not finde such reasons, they bee all in *celarent*, and dare not shewe their heads, for wee will answere them in *ferio* and cut their combes. So say they, their bloud is sought. Their bloud? What should wee doo with it, when it will make a dogge haue the toothach to eate the puddings.

Martin tunes his pipe to the lamentable note of *Ora whine meg*. O tis his best daunce next shaking of the sheetes; but hee good man meant no harme by it. No more did one of his minions, that thinking to rap out an oath and sweare by his conscience, mistooke the word and swore by his concupiscence; not vnlike the theefe, that in stead of God speede, sayd stand, and so tooke a purse for God morowe.

Yet dooth *Martin* hope that all her Maiesties best subiects will become Martinists; a blister of that tongue as bigge as a drummes head; for if the Queenes Maiestie haue such abiects for her best subiects, let all true subiects be accompted abiects.

38 for a God morowe *A*

They that teare the boughs, will hew at the tree, and hauing once wet their feete in factions, will not care how deepe they wade in treason.

After *Martin* had racked ouer his protestation with a Iades pace, hee runnes ouer his fooleries with a knaues gallop, ripping vp the souterlie seames of his Epistle, botching in such frize iestes vppon fustion earnest, that one seeing all sortes of his shreddes, would thinke he had robd a taylors shop boord; and then hee concludes all doggedlie, with Doctor *Bullens* dogge *Spring*, not remembring that there is not a better Spanniell in England to spring a couie of queanes than *Martin*.

Hee sliues one, has a fling at another, a long tale of his talboothe, of a vulnerall sermon, and of a fooles head in souce. This is the Epistle which he woonders at himselfe, and like an olde Ape hugges the Vrchin so in his conceipt, as though it should shew vs some new tricks ouer the chaine: neuer wish it published *Martin*, we pitie it before it comes out. Trusse vp thy packet of flim flams, & roage to some Countrey Faire, or read it among boyes in the belfrie, neuer trouble the church with chattering; but if like dawes, you will be cawing about Churches, build your nests in the steeple, defile not the quier.

Martin writes merely, because (hee ·saies) people are carried away sooner with iest than earnest. I, but *Martin*, neuer put Religion into a fooles coate; there is great oddes betweene a Gospeller, and a libeller.

If thy vain bee so pleasant, and thy wit so nimble, that all consists in glicks and girds; pen some playe for the Theater, write some ballads for blinde *Dauid* and his boy, deuise some iestes, & become another *Scogen*; so shalt thou haue vent inough for all thy vanities, thy Printer shall purchase, and all other iesters beg.

For to giue thee thy due, thou art the best dyed foole in graine that euer was, and all other fooles lacke manie graines, to make them so heauie.

There is not such a mad foole in Bedlam, nor such a baudie foole in Bridewell, nor such a dronken foole in the stockes, nor such a scolding foole on the cucking-stoole, nor such a cosening foole on· the pillerie, nor such a roaging foole in the houses of correction, nor such a simple foole kept of alms, nor such a lame foole lying in the spittle, nor in all the world, such a foole, all. Nay for fooles set down in the scriptures, none such as *Martin*.

What atheist more foole, that saies in his heart, *There is no God?* What foole more proud, that stands in his own cōceit? What foole more couetous than he, that seekes to tedd abroad the Churches goods with a forke, and scratch it to himselfe with a rake.

Thou seest Martin, with a little helpe, to the foure & twentie orders of knaues, thou maist solder the foure and twentie orders of fooles, and

3 had] hath *A*   27 died *AB*   33 foole¹] foale *C*

so because thou saist thou art vnmarried, thou maist commit matrimonie, from the heires of whose incest, wee will say that which you cannot abide, *Good Lord deliuer vs.*

If this veyne bleede but sixe ounces more, I shall proue a pretie railer, and so in time may growe to bee a proper Martinist. Tush, I doo but licke ouer my pamphlet, like a Beares whelpe, to bring it in some forme; by that time hee replies, it will haue clawes and teeth, and then let him looke to bee scratcht and bitten too.

Thou seest *Martin* Molewarpe, that hetherto I haue named none, but markt them readie for the next market: if thou proceed in naming, be as sure as thy shirt to thy knaues skinne, that Ile name such, as though thou canst not blush, because thou art past shame, yet they shall bee sorie, because they are not all without grace.

Pasquil is comming out with the liues of the Saints. Beware my Comment, tis odds the margent shall bee as full as the text. I haue manie sequences of Saints; if naming be the aduantage, & ripping vp of liues make sport, haue with thee knuckle deepe, it shall neuer bee said that I dare not venter mine eares, where *Martin* hazards his necke.

Now me thinkes *Martin* begins to stretch himselfe like an old fencer, with a great conscience for buckler, and a long tongue for a sword. Lie close, you old cutter at the locke, *Nam mihi sunt vires, & mea tela nocent.* Tis ods but that I shall thrust thee through the buckler into the brain, that is through the conscience into the wit.

If thou sue me for a double maime, I care not though the Iurie allow thee treble damages, it cannot amount to much, because thy cōscience is without wit, and thy wit without conscience, & therefore both, not worth a penie.

Therefore take this for the first venew, of a yonger brother, that meanes to drie beate those of the *Elder* house. *Martin*, this is my last straine for this fleech of mirth. I began with God morrowe, and bid you God night. I must tune my fiddle, and fetch some more rozen, that it maie squeake out *Martins* Matachine.

FINIS.

Candidissimi Lectores, peto terminum ad libellandum.

Lectores.

Assignamus in proximum.

2-3 you cannot *AB*: thou cannot *C*　　　20 for a buckler *A*

A WHIP FOR AN APE

(DOUBTFUL)

EDITIONS

(1) *A | Whip for an Ape: | Or | Martin displaied. | Ordo Sacerdotum fatuo turbatur ab omni, | Labitur et passim Religionis honos.* | 4°, black letter, 4 leaves, paged. No date. *Brit. Mus.* (press-mark C. 37. d. 42): *Lambeth Palace Library*.

(2) *Rythmes against Martin Marre-Prelate. | Ordo Sacerdotum fatuo turbatur ab omni, | Labitur et passim Religionis honos.* 4°. No date. *Bodleian* (where it appears bound between *Mar-Martine* and *Marre-Mar-Martin*).

(3) Reprinted from (2) in D'Israeli's *Quarrels of Authors*, Lond. 1814, post 8vo, vol. iii. pp. 271–282.

(4) Reprinted from (1) in *The Bibliographical Miscellany*, No. 5, March 20th 1854, with a note or two by Edward F. Rimbault.

The present is a reprint of the first edition, collated with the second.

NOTE ON THE DATE AND AUTHORSHIP.

THIS lampoon, the best of the Anti-Martinist rhymes, has been claimed for both Lyly and Nash, to the latter of whom I preferred, until just lately, to assign it [1]. Its date is fixed as about April, 1589, (1) by the allusion of the penultimate stanza to the Martinist tract *Hay any work for Cooper?* which was issued about March 23, 1589 (see Depositions against Robert Waldegrave, *Harl. MS.* 7042, pp. 1–11, quoted in Arber's *Introd. Sketch* to the Controversy, p. 125); (2) by the following mention of it in *Martin's Months Minde* (the date of which is fixed by its allusion to *Countercuffe*, itself dated Aug. 8), where (sig. E 3 verso) Nash recounts as successive sufferings of Martin that he was 'drie beaten (marginal note, 'T. C.') then whipt that made him winse' (marg. note, 'A whip for an Ape'), then 'made a *Maygame* vpon the Stage' (marg. note, 'The Theater'), 'and at length cleane Marde' (marg. note, 'Marre-martin'). Points that seem to suggest Lyly's authorship are the words in Richard Harvey's dedication of *Plaine Perciual*, 'to all Whip Iohns and Whip Iackes'; and, internally, the use of the expression 'sweares by

[1] See vol. i. p. 57 footnote.

his ten bones' of the Ape (st. 4), as of Martin in *Pappe*, p. 406 l. 7 ; the uncommon form 'rent' (as present tense) for 'rend' (st. 12), as in *Pappe*, p. 409 l. 40 and elsewhere in Lyly (cf. Glossary) ; the mention of 'Bridewell and Bedlem' together (line 41) in connexion with Martin's railing (cf. *Pappe*, p. 409 l. 37, 412 l. 30) ; the allusion to 'Scoggins iests,' l. 56 (cf. *Pappe*, p. 412 l. 24); the assertion that the interests of Church and Crown are bound up together, ll. 79–84 (cf. *Pappe*, p. 405 ll. 7 sqq. ' to the rule of the Church, the whole state of the Realme is linckt, & that they filching away Bishop by Bishop, seeke to fish for the Crown,' and pp. 408 ll. 37 sqq., 412 ll. 1–2) ; and the comparison of Martin to Jack Straw, l. 89 (cf. *Pappe*, p. 409 l. 39). These points, it is true, are not conclusive, since *Pappe*, written towards the end of September (pp. 410, 392), may have borrowed from *A Whip*; and the Anti-Martinist partnership would favour an interchange of suggestion, especially in work which ignored art. Moreover the allusions to the stage in stanzas 1, 6, 8 and 9 would suit Nash as well as Lyly : his pamphlets have the same argument about the power of the Crown being endangered with that of the bishops, and the same charge against the Martinists of aiming at the destruction of the Universities, l. 78 (cf. *Countercuffe*, sig. A iij recto, ironically exhorting Martin Junior ' Downe with learning and Vniuersities') : while in *Martin's Months Minde*, besides the allusion already quoted, we get (sig. H 3) the following comment on l. 138 : ' because one saith that your workes should go the way of all wast writings you giue him his owne word againe and make him groome of a close stoole.' But my recent identification of a large quantity of poor verse as Lyly's (see Introd. to *Poems* below, and cf. especially the *Certaine Verses* of 1586, pp. 427–32 and Note on them vol. i. pp. 401–2) much lessens the hesitation I previously felt in attributing to him such work as the *Whip*. One should remember, too, that it does not aim at poetry ; and, while I find nothing which quite warrants the withdrawal of the epithet ' doubtful,' I now incline to his authorship rather than to that of Nash, and also to his authorship of such portions of *Mar-Martine* as I print below, the rest being possibly by Nash (cf. vol. i. pp. 387–8).

D'Israeli (*Quarrels of Authors*, 1814, vol. iii. 269) says of the *Whip* : ' It is an admirable political satire against a mob-government. In our poetical history this specimen too is curious, for it will show that the stanza in alternate rhymes, usually denominated Elegiac, is adapted to very opposite themes. The solemnity of the versification is impressive, and the satire equally dignified and keen.' This is much too high praise ; but there *is* interest in the manner of the vehicle's adaptation to its purpose of social or political satire, to which the closing couplet gives an edge. It reminds me of the early production of William Basse in the same metre, entitled *Sword and Bvckler: or Serving-Mans Defence*, 1602.

A Whip for an Ape:
Or
Martin displaied.

Ordo Sacerdotum fatuo turbatur ab omni,
Labitur & passim Religionis honos.

A WHIP FOR AN APE

⟨Sig. A 2 recto⟩

Since reason (Martin) cannot stay thy pen,
We'il see what rime will doo: haue at thee then.

A Dizard late skipt out vpon our Stage;
   But in a sacke, that no man might him sée:
And though we knowe not yet the paltrie page,
   Himselfe hath *Martin* made his name to bée.
A proper name, and for his feates most fit;   5
The only thing wherein he hath shew'd wit.

Who knoweth not, that Apes men *Martins* call;
   Which beast this baggage seemes as t'were himselfe:
So as both nature, nurture, name and all,
   Of that's expressed in this apish elfe.   10
Which Ile make good to *Martin* Marr-als face
In thrée plaine poynts, and will not bate an ace.

For first the Ape delights with moppes and mowes,
   And mocketh Prince and peasants all alike:
This iesting Jacke that no good manner knowes,   15
   With his Asse héeles presumes all States to strike.
Whose scoffes so stinking in each nose doth smell,
As all mouthes saie of dolts he beares the bell.

Sometimes his choppes doo walke in poynts too hie,
   Wherein the Ape himselfe a Woodcocke tries: 20
Sometimes with floutes he drawes his mouth awrie,
   And sweares by his ten bones, and falselie lies.
Wherefore be what he will I do not passe,
He is the paltriest Ape that euer was.

Such fléering, léering, iarring fooles bopéepe;   25
   Such hahaes, téehées, wéehées, wild colts play:
Such sohoes, whoopes and hallowes, hold and kéepe;
   Such rangings, ragings, reuelings, roysters ray,
With so foule mouth, and knaue at euery catch,
Tis some knaues neast did surely *Martin* hatch.   30

19 Chappes *in Bodleian copy*

A WHIP FOR AN APE

Now out he runnes with Cuckowe king of May,
   Then in he leapes with a wild Morrice daunce;
Now strikes he vp Dame *Lawsens* lustie lay;
   Then comes Sir *Ieffries* ale tub tapde by chaunce:
Which makes me gesse, (and I can shrewdly smell) 35
He loues both t'one and t'other passing well.

Then straight as though he were distracted quite,
   He chafeth like a cutpurse layd in Warde;
And rudely railes with all his maine and might,
   Against both Knights and Lords without regarde: 40
So as *Bridewell* must tame his dronken fits,
And *Bedlem* helpe to bring him to his wits.

But *Martin*, why in matters of such waight
   Doest thou thus play the Dawe and dancing foole?
O sir (quoth he) this is a pleasant baite 45
   For men of sorts, to traine them to my schoole.
Ye noble States how can you like hereof,
A shamelesse Ape at your sage heads should scoffe?

Good Noddie now leaue scribling in such matters,
   They are no tooles for fooles to tend vnto; 50
Wise men regard not what mad Monckies patters;
   Twere trim a beast should teach men what to do.
Now *Tarleton's* dead the Consort lackes a vice:
For knaue and foole thou maist beare pricke and price.

The sacred sect and perfect pure precise, 55
   Whose cause must be by *Scoggins* iests maintainde,
Ye shewe although that purple Apes disguise,
   Yet Apes ⟨ye⟩ are still, and so must be disdainde.
For though your Lyons lookes weake eyes escapes
Your babling bookes bewraies you all for Apes. 60

The next poynt is, Apes vse to tosse and teare
   What once their ficling fingers fasten on;
And clime aloft and cast downe euery where,
   And neuer staies till all that stands be gon.
Now whether this in *Martin* be not true, 65
You wiser heads marke here what doth ensue.

What is it not that *Martin* doth not rent?
   Cappes, Tippets, Gownes, blacke Chiuers, Rotchets white;
Communion bookes, and Homelies, yea so bent
   To teare, as womens wimples feele his spite. 70
Thus tearing all, as all Apes vse to doo;
He teares withall the Church of Christ in two.

Marke now what things he meanes to tumble downe,
  For to this poynt to looke is worth the while,
In one that makes no choyce twixt Cap and Crowne;   75
  Cathedrall Churches he would faine vntile,
And snatch vp Bishops lands, and catch away
All gaine of learning for his prouling pray.
And thinke you not he will pull downe at length
  Aswell the top from tower, as Cocke from stéeple?   80
And when his head hath gotten some more strength,
  To play with Prince as now he doth with people?
Yes, he that now saith, Why should Bishops bée?
Will next crie out, Why Kings? The Saincts are frée.
The *Germaine* Boores with Clergie men began,   85
  But neuer left till Prince and Péeres were dead:
Iacke Leydon was a holie zealous man,
  But ceast not till the Crowne was on his head.
And *Martins* mate *Iacke Strawe* would alwaies ring
  The Clergies faults, but sought to kill the King.   90
Oh that quoth *Martin* chwere a Noble man!
  A vaunt vile villaine: tis not for such swads.
And of the Counsell too; Marke Princes then:
  These roomes are raught at by these lustie lads.
For Apes must climbe, and neuer stay their wit,   95
Untill on top of highest hilles they sit.
What meane they els, in euery towne to craue
  Their Priest and King like Christ himselfe to be?
And for one Pope ten thousand Popes to haue,
  And to controll the highest he or she?   100
Aske *Scotland* that, whose King so long they crost
As he was like his Kingdome to haue lost.
Beware ye States and Nobles of this land,
  The Clergie is but one of these mens buts:
The Ape at last on masters necke will stand: 105
  Then gegge betime these gaping greedie guts,
Least that too soone, and then too late ye feele,
He strikes at head that first began with heele.
The third tricke is, what Apes by flattering waies
  Cannot come by, with ·biting they will snatch: 110
Our *Martin* makes no bones, but plainlie saies,
  Their fists shall walke, they will both bite and scratch.
He'il make their hearts to ake, and will not faile,
Where pen cannot, their penknife shall preuaile.

114 their *Q*: *qy.?* there

⟨Sig. A 3 verso. Page 6⟩

A WHIP FOR AN APE

But this is false, he saith he did but mocke: 115
  A foole he was that so his words did scan.
He only ment with pen their pates to knocke:
  A knaue he is, that so turnes cat in pan.
But *Martin* sweare and stare as déepe as hell,
Thy sprite thy spite and mischeuous mind doth tell. 120

The thing that neither Pope with Booke nor Bull,
  Nor *Spanish* King with ships could do without,
Our *Martins* here at home will worke at full;
  If Prince curbe not betimes that rabble rout.
That is, destroy both Church, and State, and all; 125
For if t'one faile, the other néedes must fall.

Thou *England* then whom God doth make so glad,
  Through Gospels grace and Princes prudent raigne:
Take heede least thou at last be made as sad,
  Through *Martins* makebates marring, to thy paine: 130
For he marres all, and maketh nought, nor will,
Saue lyes and strife, and workes for *Englands* ill.

And ye graue men that answere *Martins* mowes,
  He mockes the more, and you in vaine loose times:
Leaue Apes to dogges to baite, their skins to crowes, 135
  And let old *Lanam* lash him with his rimes.
The beast is proud when men wey his enditings:
Let his worke go the waie of all wast writings.

Now *Martin*, you that say you will spawne out
  Your broyling brattes in euery towne to dwell; 140
Wée will prouide in each place for your route
  A bell and whippe, that Apes do loue so well.
And if ye skippe and will not wey the checke,
We'il haue a springe and catch you by the necke.

(Sig. A 4 r.
P. 7)

And so adiew mad *Martin* marre the land, 145
  Leaue off thy worke, and more worke, hear'st thou me?
Thy work's nought worth, take better worke in hand:
  Thou marr'st thy worke, & thy worke will marre thée.
Worke not a newe, least it doth worke thy wracke,
And thou make worke for him that worke doth lacke. 150

---

135 Leaue] Leaues Q 138 *D'Israeli reprinting the 'Whip' in the
'Quarrels of Authors' reads* vast: *but Nash's comment on the line in '* Martin's
Months Minde,' *sig.* H 3 *verso, shows* wast (*i.e.* waste) *to be right*

And this I warne thée Martins Monckies face,
  Take héed of me, my rime doth charme thee bad:
I am a rimer of the Irish race,
  And haue alreadie rimde thée staring mad.
But if thou ceasest not thy bald iests still to spread,
Ile neuer leaue, till I haue rimde thée dead.

FINIS.

MAR-MARTINE,

⟨Title-page⟩

I know not why a trueth in rime set out
Maie not as wel mar Martine and his mates,
As shamelesse lies in prose-books cast about
Marpriests, & prelates, and subvert whole states.
For where truth builds, and lying overthroes,
One truth in rime, is worth ten lies in prose[1].

⟨1⟩

L⟨ORDES⟩ of our land, and makers of our Lawes,
Long may yee liue, Lawes many may you make,
This careful, kind, and country-louing clawse,
As from a faithfull friend, vouchsafe to take:
   Martine the merry, who now is *Mar-prelate*,   5
   Will proue madde *Martine*, and *Martine* mar-the-state.

⟨Title-page verso⟩

The wind doth first send forth a whistling sound,
Then fierce, and fearefull, hollow, thundering threates,
At length it riues the earth and rents the ground
And tumbles townes and cities from their seates,   10
   So he who first did laughing libells send,
   Will at the last procure a wreakefull end.

Women are woed to follow men precise
Young boies without experience hold the Gods,
Yea some for gaine, who are both olde and wise: 15
Thus merrie *Martine* sets the world at ods.
   The frozen snake for colde that cannot creepe
   Restorde to strength a stinging stur will keepe.

⟨*Poems*, 15 st. 5⟩

Let neighbour-nations learne vs to beware,
Let harmes at home teach vs for to take heede;   20
When *Browne* and *Barrowe* haue done what they dare,
Their hellish Hidraes heades will spring with speede:

---

[1] Undated, 4°, 4 leaves, cropped—no sigs. remaining. The several rhymes are unnumbered, without heading or signature, and separated only by a line across the page. *Press-mark* Br. Mus. 96. b. 15 (1); and 722. g. 20 (wanting first leaf).

Such men as *Martine* caused all these woes:
This poison still encreaseth as it goes.

Somewhat I hearde, and mickle haue I seene 25
It were too long to tell your Lordships what:
Somewhat I knowe, and somewhat haue I beene,
Yet this I saie, and this is also flat.
⟨*Euph.* ii.
172 l. 25⟩ Bridle the coltish mouth of Male-part
Or else his hoofe will hurte both head and hart. 30

Anglia Martinis parce favere malis.

⟨There follows (2) another rhyme in 16 6-line stanzas of shorter lines, (3) ten stanzas in Scotch dialect in the old 14-syllable rhymes of Golding and Phaer, and then⟩

⟨on verso
of 3rd leaf⟩

⟨4⟩

Anglia.

O England gemme of Europe, Angells land,
Blest for thy gospell, people, prince, and all,
And all through peace, let *Martins* vnderstand
The hony of thy peace, abhorre their gall. 35

Martinis.

Martins? what kind of creatures mought those bee?
Birds, beasts, men, Angels, Feends? Nay worse say we.
The feendes spake faire sometimes and honor gaue,
Curse and contempt is all that *Martins* haue.

Disce.

England if yet thou art to learne thy spell, 40
Learne other things, such doctrine is for hell.

⟨F⟩*avere.*

What favor would these *Martins?* Shall I say
As other birds wherwith yong children play.
Let them be cagd, and hempseed be their food
Hempseed the only meate to feede this broode. 45

Tuis.

Disclaime these monsters, take them not for thine
Hell was their wombe, and hell must be their shryne.

⟨5⟩

⟨*Pappe*,
p. 400
ll. 39-40⟩

Many would know the holy Asse,
  And who mought Martin been,
Plucke but the footecloth from his backe, 50
  The Asse will soone be seene.

⟨6⟩

My Lordes wise wittall Martins thinke,
  Your Lordships flie to hie:
Keepe on your flight aloft as yet,
  Lest Martins come too nie. 55

For were your winges a little clipt,
    They soone would plucke the rest:
    And then the place too high for you.
    Would be pure Martins nest.

⟨Then follow four other short rhymes in the same ballad metre.⟩

⟨11⟩ ⟨on recto of 4th leaf⟩

Wel maist thou marre but neuer canst thou marre,   60
This present state whereat thou so doost storme:
Nor they that thee vphold to make this iarre,
And would forsooth our English lawes deforme.
    Then be thou but *Marke-prelate* as thou art:
    Thou canst not marre though thou wouldst swelt thy hart.   65

⟨12⟩

In *Ammons* land pretended *Rephaims* dwelt,   *Deu.* 2. 20
That termd them-selues *Reformers* of the state,
These like *Zanzummins*, and *Deformers* dealte,
Among the people stirring vp debate.
    But when their vilenes, was espied and knowen: 70
    From *Ammons* land this Gyants broode, was throwen.
Our England, that for vnitie hath beene,
A glasse for *Europe*, hath such monsters bread,
That raile at Prelats, and oppugne their Queene,
Whole common wealthes, each beareth in his head.   75
    These *Rephaims*, for so the⟨y⟩ would be deemd :
    Are nothing lesse, then that they most haue seemd.
Then if we loue the gouernement of peace,
Which true *Reformers* from aboue maintaine,
And forraine force could never make it cease,   80
Nor these *Deformers*, can with vices staine:
    First let vs finde pretended *Rephaims* rowte,
    And like *Zanzummins*, let vs cast them out.

⟨13⟩

Martin had much a farther reach, then euery man can gesse,
Hee might haue cald himselfe Mar-preest, that hath bene somewhat lesse,
But seeking all to overthrowe, what ever high might be: 86
Mar-prelate he did call himselfe, a foe to high degree.

⟨The fourteenth rhyme, of four lines, has lost a line or two, being at bottom of page.⟩

⟨15⟩ ⟨on verso of 4th leaf⟩

If any mervaile at the man, and doe desire to see
The stile and phrase of *Martins* booke: come learne it here of mee.

Holde my cloke boy, chill haue a vling at *Martin*, O the boore ; 90
And if his horseplay like him well, of such he shall haue store.
He thus bumfeges his bousing mates, and who is *Martins* mate?
O that the steale-counters were knoune, chood catch them by the pate.
Th'vnsauorie snuffes first iesting booke, though clownish, knauish was:
But keeping still one stile, he prooues a sodden headed asse. 95
Beare with his ingramnesse a while, his seasoned wainscot face:
That brought that godly Cobler Cliffe, for to disproue his grace.

But (O) that Godly cobler Cliffe, as honest an olde lad,
As *Martin* (O the libeller) of hangbyes euer had.
If I berime thy worshipnes, as thou beliest thy betters: 100
For railing, see which of vs two shall be the greatest getters.
But if in flinging at such states, thy noddle be no slower:
Thy brother hangman will thee make, be pulde three asses lower.
Then mend these manners *Martin*, or in spite of *Martins* nose:
My rithme shall be as dogrell, as vnlearned is thy prose. 105

These tinkers termes, and barbers iestes first *Tarleton* on the stage,
Then *Martin* in his bookes of lies, hath put in euery page:
The common sort of simple swads, I can their state but pitie:
That will vouchsafe, or deygne to laugh, at libelles so vnwittie.
Let *Martin* thinke some pen as badde, some head to be as knauish:
Soome tongue to be as glibbe as his, some rayling all as lavish, 111
And be content : if not, because we know not where to finde thee:
We hope to se thee where deserts of treason haue assigned thee.

⟨16⟩

Cast of thy cloake and shriue thy selfe, in cloake-bagge, as is meete:

⟨*Whip*, l. 167⟩

And leaue thy flinging at the preest, as Iades doe with their feete.
The Preest must liue, the Bishop guide : 116
To teach thee how to leaue thy pride.

⟨17⟩

If Martin dy by hangmans hands, as he deserues no lesse,
This Epitaph must be engravde, his maners to expresse.
Here hangs knaue Martine *a traitrous Libeler he was* 120
Enemie pretended but in hart a friend to the Papa,

This bodg known to ⟨be⟩ his own.

Now made meat to the birdes that about his carkas are hagling.
Learne by his example yee route of Pruritan Asses,
Not to resist the doings of our most gratious Hester,
Martin *is hangd* ⟨*f*⟩*or the Master of al Hypocritical hangbies* ...

⟨It is uncertain whether one or more lines followed, for the pamphlet has been mutilated in the binding, or before, both at top, bottom, and side.⟩

108 their] there *Q*

CERTAINE[1]
ENGLISHE
Verses, presented vnto
𝔱𝔥𝔢 𝔔𝔲𝔢𝔢𝔫𝔢𝔰 𝔪𝔬𝔰𝔱 𝔢𝔵𝔠𝔢𝔩𝔩𝔢𝔫𝔱 𝔐𝔞𝔦𝔢𝔰𝔱𝔦𝔢, 𝔟𝔶 𝔞 𝔠𝔬𝔲𝔯-
tier: In ioy of the most happie disclosing, of the most dangerous conspiracie pretended by the late executed Traitours, against her royall person, and
the whole Estate.

[PRINTER'S DEVICE.]

AT LONDON
Printed by Hentie Haslop, and are to bee
sold in Paules Church-yard at the
signe of the Bible
1586.

---

[1] 4°, four leaves, A–A4, verso of title blank, no col. For the occasion of these verses, of Lyly's authorship of which the verification of the references I have inserted at ll. 15, 21, 71, 108, 113–4 will, I think, leave no doubt, see vol. i. p. 401.

THE TRIVMPHS OF TROPHES,

In Saphic verse of Iubiles.

Exultātes cantate Domino, & iubilate Deo Jacob. Psal. 80.

IF *DAVID* daunst for ioy before the Arke being a king
    If *Barac* sang when Israels foes were foild,
Then victors wee that *Deboras* song may sing
    Our *Iudith* stout *Holofernes* Mates hath spoild.

Psallite Domino in Cithara iucunda & voce carminis. Psal. 98.

If *Rome* of Romane Triumphes earst was oft so glad   5
    and likewise *Greece* of *Grecians Trophes* ioyed:
If *Iewes* of *Iubilees* their onlie mirth haue had
    then *England* leap, and laugh aloud for Queene enioyd.

Clangite tubam, sumite psalmū, & date tympanum cum nablo. Psal. 80.

Now *Baal* and *Bell*, now *Titanes* sonnes are slaine,
    their Prophets false their wicked Priests are kild   10
Their *Pluto* howles that *Babels* brood are taen,
    their Tower did fall that *Nimrods* Imps did build.

Tu deus dissipasti impios & cōfregisti capita draconū in aquis ps.

Sith *Nessus* brood and *Cassius* crue are knowen
    like *Siluane Centaures* conspirde your Realme to quaile,   14
Take courage Queene, for *Sinon* sleights abroad are blowen, ⟨*Euph.*i.23 l. 13, ii. 197
    the Traitours found, and yet the treasons faile. l. 9⟩

Demersæ sunt gente in foueā quam fecerunt.

These *Ciclopp*es seede which at your crowne doe kicke
    and frame a forme to make your kingdome bleed,
Like *Giants* seeke with stones the starres to strike
    but mist the marke and wound themselues in deed: 20

Sepulcrum patens guttur eorum. Psal. 5.

They vowd *Zopirus* vowes, to please *Darius* beck ⟨*Euph.* ii. 97 l. 30⟩
    they sought a new deuise which *Sphinx* of *Rome* thē taught,
They faine would finde, that *England* had one neck,
    that by a stroke the head might off they sought—

Gladiū strinxerunt.& arcū telēderunt impij, vt iugulent eos qui recto sunt corde. Vt darent cadauera tuorū in ci-

Their match was made, their wager was not wonne,   25
    their snares were laid, but yet their purpose mist,
Their day decreed, and yet the deed not done,
    a will they had you see, that wanted what they wis⟨h⟩t.
What thought *Pyragmons* sprats to doe, we know,
    their Romish *Iesabell Naboths* vineyard sought,   30

---

29 Pyragmons sprats Q: i.e. *Pyracmon's brood*, a variation on These Cicloppes seede *of* st. 5. Cf. vol. ii. 554

THE TRIVMPHS OF TROPHES

Who like *Medusa* bends her cursed Bow
   the onlie *Circes*, which hath this mischief wrought.

*bum auibus cœli. Psal.*79.

These vipers tend with *Briareus* hundred hands,
   with hundred *Argus* eies these Scorpions wait,
These busie *Basilisks* and brood of Cocatrice stands   35
   like *Nilus* Crocodiles hungrie for their bait.

Deus vltionum est Dominus. Psal. 94.

These sucking serpents, these monstrous snakish crewe,
   these blooddie Dragons like spiteful Asps are set,
With *Hidras* heads which erst *Alcides* slue
   are now of late with our *Bellona* mette.   40

Callidŭ excogitarunt consiliŭ contra dominŭ. Psal. 10. 2.

Of Canaan faine they would a *Chaos* make,
   and bring *Palladium* in, our *Ilion* to deface,
A spoile for *Hispaine*, a feat for *Fraunce* in hand they take
   and quite to make an end of *Brutus* race.

Vt Jerusalem ponerēt in aceruos ruinarum. Ps. 79.

Thus these climing mates *Enceladus* like attempt,   45
   in armes seeke *Ioue* from skies by force to take,
They seeke the Sun, the Moone, the Starres in great contempt
   to obscure their light a deadlie Eclips to make.

Via impiorum tenebrosa, nesciunt vbi corruant. Prou. 4.

They seeke with *Phaëton Phoebus* charge to rest,
   Vulcans net, *Gordian* knot they would vnknit   50
And breake their blooddie blades on *Pallas* breast,
   thus they couet much in Moses chaire to sit.

Sepè expugnauerūt me a iuuētute mea nunc dicat Jsrael. Psal. 129.

To wrest from *Hercules* hand his Club, who can?
   who may from *Ioue*, his lightning take by force?
Homers verse, who can disgrace? I say no man,   55
   who then can touch a sacred Princes coarse.

Though *Cæsar* was in Senate slaine by *Brute* his friend,
   Though *Cirus* head was bathd in blood luke warme,
No maruaile though, for blood requireth blood at thend
   but mercie too much thine, I feare doth harme,   60

Sanguis sanguinis merces Deus

For if *Laban* was for *Jacob* sake so blest,
   and *Putiphars* hap, by *Iosephs* meane no lesse
Our hap, our blisse, our ioyes wherein we rest,
   For whom it is, we must of force confesse.

Genes. 30. 39.

Who with *Ionas* gourd hath sau'de vs from the Sunne,   65
   Who with *Aser* shoes, hath kept vs from the mire?
Who hath with *Dauids* sling *Golias* mates vndone.
   our *Cynthia*, she who hath appeas'd *Iehouas* ire.

Tegmen a turbine & vmbraculum ab æstu dominus Deus (Is. xxv. 4.)

    40 meete *Q*   50 Gordious *Q*   65 gurth *Q*

Quærunt animā meā & meditati sunt tota die dolos Ps. 38.

These on *Bellerephons* horse do ride in skie,
   with *Icarus* wings to clime in cloudes is their drift,   70
These would make *Architas* woodden Doue to flie,   (*Camp.* v. 4 14–5)
   What blinde *Tiresias* doth not see their shift.   (*Euph.* ii 113 l. 26)

Pone eos domine vt clibanum ignis, in tempore iræ tuæ. Psal. 21.

In *Phætonissa* schoole, at *Endor* they were taught,
   with *Dracos* ink to write, with *Creons* seale to signe,
With *Iudas* kisse to kill, with *Hamons* haue they sought,   75
   both *Iudaes* spoyle, and *Sions* fall in fine.

These secret *Satires*, these cruell *Catelins* wait,
   these dogs of *Moabs* house greadie of their pray.
Like *Eumenides* whelpes tending on their bait,
   Vultures for *Prometheus* guts readie set in ray.   80

A periculis persequentium & conuentu malignantium tu salus mea. Eijce fulmen & dissipe eos: mitte sagittas tuas & disturba illos. Psal. (144.) *Leuate signū capta est Babilon, cōfusus est Bell.*

They ventured *Acherontas* depth to wade,
   they striued through *Stigias* streame to saile,
Mauger of *Megeras* head away they made,
   by *Carons* help, *Elisius* field to assaile.

To make spotted Ewes with *Iacobs* stick they sought,   85
   to walke vnseene, with *Giges* ring faine they would
Of *Simon Magus* these men would faine be taught,
   like Curres by *Circes* charm'd to be with Lions bold.

Circes cup is falne, *Calipsos* sauce is shed
   Balims brood is bar(e)d, their *Harpies* are descried,   90
Cerberus soppes are found, *Sirens* songs are red
   Thus is *Accaron* knowen, and *Romane* Idoll tried.

Carnes piorum bestijs terræ dederunt. Psal. 79.

Their drinke is blood, their bread is humane flesh,
   Consuls heads with Preachers tongues their food, & what
Is their daintiest dish? Princes harts I gesse,   95
   Thus like *Basan* Bulles, they feed their Pope with fat.

Conati sunt priuare me anima mea. Psal. 52.

But time decreed, how long should *Assur* liue,
   and God foretolde, when *Pharaoes* life should end,
To take thy life the man of sinne doth striue,
   in vaine O Queene, when Angels thee defend.   100

Non obueniet tibi malū, nec appropinquabit plaga tabernaculo tuo. Psal. 91. *Non est consiliū nec prudentia contra Dominū.*

Could *Ionas* in the raging Seas be drownd?
   could Lions *Daniel* in their Dennes deuoure?
Might *Misael* burne in firie furnace bound?
   durst Traitours blade attempt our sacred Princes bowre?

A blast of winde made *Th'assirians* hoast to flie,   105
   Earthen pots made *Madianites* to take their flight,
Hornes threw *Ierichoes* wall flat on ground to be,
   God makes Flies, Frogs, Rats and Lice, for him to fight.   (*Euph.* i. 249 ll. 28–

72 Teresias Q   77 seceet Q   91 Cirens Q

Cains curse, Herods death, I wish on them to fall,
   that seeke a sacred Prince with secret sword to kill,   110
Iudas death to good for Iudas mates I call,
   who bathes in blood, and drinke of blood their fill.

Euph. ii.
138 ll. 11–2)
Euph. ii.
77 l. 15)

But Serpents neuer build in Boxe, nor breede
   in *Cipres* tree, no Canker can the Emerald touch,
Euen so these hellish *Heliottes* cannot feed,   115
   on her whose vertues rare amaseth such.

These *Minotaurus* brood from *Rome*, from *Creete*,
   with sword and fire, in *Albion* swarme like Bees
Like *Sampsons* Foxes with fired tailes and feete,
   they dread no death to winne a Popish fees.   120

Euph. i.
52 l. 33)
Ib. l. 34)

In *Rhodes* was neuer seen, they say, an Eagles nest
   some hold it so, tha(t) *Creete* can breed no Owle,
And Crowes in *Athens* were neuer seen at least
   that England breedes no wolues, an error foule.

Cymerians blinde, that haunts *Trop⟨h⟩onius* Caue,   125
   could neuer bide the shining Sunne in sight,
Who still in darknesse dwell, the light doe neuer craue,
   but like *Cacus* Captiues shrouded aie with night.

Mid. iv.
47)

A simple Goat could asswage god *Faunus* ire,
   a grunting hog could *Neptunes* rage appease,   130
A seelie Cocke could coole *Asculapius* fire,
   but Lions cround, the bull of *Rome* must please.

His *Dan* and *Bethell*, sacred *Pantheon* cald,
   his sinagoge esteemes no Oxe, no Calfe, no Bull,
But blood of kings in Royall seates enstald,   135
   wherein *Perillus* part he plaies at full.

oems,
83 l. 3)

No fire in *Rome* could *Romulus* staffe consume,
   no meanes might make king *Pyrrhus* toes to burne
But Pope with *Nœuius* knife euer durst presume,
   with Briers and Brambles make Cædar trees to mourn. 140

But might these mates haue had but *Aarons* rod in hand
   or could haue borrowed *Elias* cloke no doubt,
They had made the Seas, on both sides for to stand,
   that *Fraunce* and *Spaine* might make the slaughter out.

Their *Dagon* fell, our sacred Arke stood vp,   145
   their *Pharao* myst, our Moses did preuaile,
Their crosse was downe, our crowne did neuer stoupe,
   Their Barge did sinke, our Ship top gallant saile,

Pone eos sicut rotam, & sicut stipulam ante ventum.

Intret gladius eorum in cor eorum. Psal. 37.

Profer lanceā, apprehēde clyp. & surge in auxiliū domine. Psal. 35.

Qui ambulat in tenebris odit lucem.

Dij Gentiū vani sunt. Deus noster cœlos fecit.

miserunt in Ignem sancta tua & polluerūt tabernaculum nominis tui. Psal. 74.

Anima nostra sicut passer erepta est ex laqueo venantium Psal. (124.)

Quis deus præter Dominum? quis fortis? sicut Deus noster (ii.) *Sam:* 22(.32.)

432 THE TRIVMPHS OF TROPHES

<small>Cadant a consilijs suis, quoniā rebelles sunt tibi. Psal. 5.</small>

<small>Regum 4. cap. 13 Act: cap. 5 Act. cap. 19</small>

Noughtie *Nabals* curse on *Dauid* neuer fell:
   Achitophels cruel counsaile did no good   150
to *Absalon*, when *Absalon* did rebell:
   Semei could doe no harme, when *Semei* God withstood.

Elizeus bones could raise the Dead from graue,
   Peters shadowe passing by, made sicke men hole.
Paules handkercher from death, did many saue,   155
   thus vertue deales to vertuous men her dole

<small>Spiritus procellarum erit pars callicis eorum. Psalm. (11.)</small>

<small>Pluet super impios laqueos, ignem & sulphur.</small>

But *Bulles* of *Rome* and Beares of *Hispaine* did more,
   they murther whom they will, and pardon whom they list,
Kings from crownes depriue, and Kings to crownes restore,
   thus to shadow *Cæsars* state, the Pope hath euer wisht.   160

If *Dathan* and *Abiron* sanke for treason wrought,
   if *Assur*, *Pharo* so enuied *Dauids* seat,
If Greekes Iewes and Gentiles *Iacobs* starre haue sought,
   these *Gorgons* would *Eliza* faine from Crowne defeat.

<small>Inueniet manus tua inimicos tuos. Psal. (21.)</small>

When *Perseus* sword shall snatch of *Medusas* head,   165
   when *Mercuries* whistle lulls *Argos* eies to sleep, <small>(*Euph*. ii. 197 ll. 14-5)</small>
When Phœbus faulchion kils monstrous *Python* dead,
   then shall *Eliza* make Romane *Cerberus* creepe.

Though still you beare the Oliue branch in breast,
   yet some wish you *Hermes Harpen* in your hand,   170
Though you the Lambe imbrace, the Lion is your beast,
   for mercie must with iustice ioine to rule a land.

<small>Dispelle eos sicut palea a facie venti. Psal. 1.</small>

Cleanse *Augeus* hall, destroy *Stymphalides* seede,
   your souldiers readie preast, do stand in aray,
Thunders, hailstones, brimstone, fier, your foes shal speede   175
   Angels armd, hosts from hie, God himself will say.

<small>Stent & saluët te augures cœli qui contemplātur sydera: Esa 47 Dux fœmina factum.</small>

To *Cumæ* trudge, of *Sibill* knowe your fates,
   to *Ammons* priests, at *Ammons* temple scrape.
To *Delphos* post, call and knock at *Phœbus* gates,
   to knowe of *Phœbus* how traitors best may scape.   180

No Iewell, Gemme, no goulde to giue I had,
   no Indian stones, no Persean gaze in hand.
No pearles from *Pactolus* to a Prince, yet glad,
   these happie *Halcions* daies to see in *Britaine* land.

FINIS q^d. L. L.

<small>160 Cæsar states Q   167 Phæbus Q   170 *i.e.* ἅρπην (*acc.*)   182 *marg.* factum Q</small>

POEMS

(DOUBTFUL)

List of Sources

WHENCE THE POEMS ARE TAKEN.

MSS.

Harleian 6910: Nos. 2-5, 22, 54, 64.
Egerton 923: No. 59.
Additional 15,227: Nos. 68-73.
　　,,　　15,232: No. 20.
　　,,　　22,601: Nos. 7-12, 16, 28, 57-8.
Rawlinson (Poetical) 85: Nos. 1, 65.
　　,,　　　,,　　148: Nos. 17, 60-3.

Anthologies.

A Handefull of Pleasant Delites, 1584: Nos. 18-9.
A Banquet of Daintie Conceits, 1588: Nos. 13-5.
The Phœnix Nest . . . 1593: Nos. 6, 23, 29-36.
Englands Helicon . . . 1600: Nos. 38-40.
A Poetical Rapsody . . . 1602: Nos. 41$^{1-2}$.

Song-Books.

William Byrd's　*Psalmes, Sonets, & songs* . 1588: No. 25.
　,,　　　,,　　*Songs of sundrie natures* . . 1589: Nos. 26-7.
John Dowland's　*First Booke of Songes or Ayres,* 1597: Nos. 37, 55-6.
　,,　　　,,　　*Second Booke　,,　,,　,,* 1600: Nos. 24, 42-3.
　,,　　　,,　　*Third and Last Booke　　,,* 1603: No. 44.
Thomas Morley's *First Booke of Balletts* . . 1600: No. 21.
Robert Jones'　*First Booke of Songes & Ayres,* 1600: Nos. 45-52,
　　　　　　　　　　　　　　　　　　　　　　　　　　　　66-7.
　,,　　　,,　　*Muses Gardin for Delights* . 1610: No. 53.

POEMS

(DOUBTFUL)

INTRODUCTION.

Lyly probably among the writers of anon. verse.

IT must have occurred to many students of the songs printed in Blount's *Sixe Covrt Comedies*—songs, every one of which, and nine besides, are announced, though not given in the quarto texts; while all together present a general resemblance, exhibiting only two or three alternative manners, and a great similarity of metrical forms, a large proportion being dialogue-songs closely connected by their contents with the plot and personages of the plays—it must, I say, have occurred to the readers of these songs, the Lylian authorship of which I see no sufficient reason to question, that so practised a song-writer probably left much other lyrical work, which either has never yet found its way into print, or else has appeared anonymously. A certain proportion of such, confirming his title to the songs in the plays, I am now for the first time presenting as Lyly's, in the various Entertainments which I have shown to be his: but there are other possible repositories, to which the reader's thoughts will naturally turn, in the shape of the MS. collections, the Music-Books, and the successive Anthologies published during Elizabeth's reign. In the MSS. poems are often variously, and generally uncertainly, assigned: in the Music-Books the names of the authors of the words are hardly ever given, partly because the composer was pre-occupied with his own art, partly owing to the modesty of the authors or their fashionable reluctance to appear in public as poets[1]: in the Anthologies, while much work is signed, much is anonymous, appearing either without

---

[1] Puttenham writes in 1589: 'Now also of such among the Nobilitie or gentrie as be very well seene in many laudable sciences, and especially in making or Poesie, it is so come to passe that they haue no courage to write and if they haue, yet are they loath to be a knowen of their skill. So as I know very many notable Gentlemen in the Court that haue written commendably and suppressed it agayne, or els suffred it to be publisht without their owne names to it: as if it were a discredit for a Gentleman, to seeme learned, and to shew himself amorous of any good Art.' *Arte of Poesie*, Bk. i. p. 37, ed. Arber, who quotes the passage in his ed. of *Tottell's Miscellany*, p. iii. So too Robert Jones in the address to the Reader prefixed to his *First Booke of Songes & Ayres*, 1600, says: 'I was not vnwilling to embrace the conceits of such gentlemen as were earnest to haue me apparel these ditties for them; which though they intended for their priuate recreation, neuer meaning that they should come into the light, yet were content vpon intreaty' to authorize their publication, but without their names: and again, 'seeing neither my cold ayres, nor their idle ditties (as they will needes haue me call them) haue hitherto been sounded in the eares of manie,' &c.

INTRODUCTION

subscription or else with various signatures such as 'Ignoto,' 'Incerto,' 'Anonimus,' and a large proportion is subscribed with initials merely; while the prefatory remarks of the editors, or the changes made in subsequent editions, cast some doubt upon the correctness of their attributions [1]. The complexity of the question is not lessened by the great similarity of manner which much of this work presents to the modern reader, a similarity due to the writers' working upon the same models and to their habit of free exchange of each others' verses: nor is the attempt to distinguish very inviting to one who, like myself, feels the bulk of this Elizabethan unsigned verse as dull, artificial and mechanical in the last degree. Did it often exhibit the qualities it sometimes reveals—were there anything like a plenitude of the spirit shown in one or two of the pieces commonly ascribed to Raleigh, such as 'The Lie [2]' or 'Now what is loue, I praie thee tell,' of the beauty of 'Weep ye no more, sad fountains,' in Dowland's *Third and Last Booke of Songs or Aires*, 1603, or of the style apparent in 'I saw my Lady weep' in his *Second Booke*, 1600 (given below, p. 471)—the task of selection and distinction, if not easier, would at least be more interesting. But, *me scilicet iudice*, it does not. On the contrary the bulk of it impresses me as journeywork, undertaken far more in obedience to a fashion than to any strong emotional impulse or even to delight in the exercise of the poetic craft; work put forth by men who were fighters, politicians, or amorists first, and poets only incidentally or because they believed the making of verse to be the gallant, the accomplished, or the gentlemanly thing to do; work rarely touched and consecrated by the inexplicable, imperishable breath, and whose average standard, whether of inspiration or technique, is in my judgement far surpassed by the average of work offered in our day to an entirely indifferent public, or withheld in despair of any genuine access to it [3]. I am glad to note that even so ardent an Elizabethan as Mr. A. H. Bullen, without whose accurate and invaluable labours in this field the task I have here attempted would have been much more difficult, is able to recognize

Mediocrity of this unsigned verse.

[1] For instance, Nicholas Ling who seems at least to have shared with 'A. B.' in collecting the materials for *Englands Helicon*, 1600, though he states in his Epistle to the Reader that no name has been affixed to any poem without the authority of 'some especial copy,' yet evidently feels that the attribution may sometimes be questionable, and anticipates complaints, from some that their work has been given to another, from others that he has violated an anonymity they wished preserved. In one or two cases in his volume 'Ignoto' printed on a slip has been pasted in so as to lie over previously printed initials: while among the large number of poems attributed in Davison's *Poetical Rapsody*, 1602, to 'Anomos' or 'Anonimos' (identified by Sir H. Nicholas (1826), or by Ritson earlier, with the 'A. W.' of Francis Davison's own list in *Harl. MS.* 280, ff. 102-6), are four from which the signature is withdrawn in later editions.
[2] In *Rawl. MS. Poet.* 172, f. 12, it is headed 'D^r. Latworthe lye to all estates.'
[3] Publication which, however costly, cannot ensure a pretty general *exhibition for sale*, is no real publication.

that most of the work in *The Phœnix Nest*, 1593, for example, is but poor stuff[1].

Its characteristics

Now to this large body of mediocre and discreetly anonymous verse I believe our author was a considerable contributor, a supposition rendered probable by the general marks which it exhibits. Among the most prominent of these are

(1) the continual strain after ingenious love-conceits, the Petrarcan manner naturalized by Wyatt and Surrey.

(2) the constant habit of buttressing or illustrating an argument by appeal to natural phenomena, real or supposed; an appeal that often leaves the reader with a feeling that the same illustration would have served as well to maintain the opposite, and actually invited replies in the same vein, which have in some cases survived: e.g. Nos. 11, 15, 18, 41$^{1-2}$, 53, 54.

(3) a proverbial and gnomic tendency, often verging on platitude: e.g. Nos. 7, 15-18, 54, &c.

(4) the use of antithesis.

(5) the habit of summing up in a final couplet the different parts, actions, or feelings touched on in the preceding lines: e.g. Nos. 30, 31, 43, 50, 63.

(6) the inartistic constructive trick of using the last word or words of one stanza or line as the starting-point of the next: e.g. the song about the Phœnix in *Cowdray*, vol. i. p. 426; No. 36 st. 4, and, in part, Nos. 31, 37—a method which, though perhaps suggested by the set French forms of the rondeau, villanelle, &c., seems, when used apart from them, to negative a proper unity and preconception, and prompts the offer to 'rhyme you so eight years together[2].'

(7) the sometimes tame finish, as though the poet were careless, or unable, to conceal his flagging inspiration: e.g. Nos. 6, 16, 25, 40, 45, 51, 58.

(8) the occasional accommodation of grammar to the exigencies of rhyme and metre, a defect not always explicable by altered grammatical rule: e.g. Nos. 8 l. 30, 15 st. 10 l. 26, 59 st. 5 l. 11. Cf. the similar use of an inexact word for the sake of rhyme: e.g. p. 454 l. 26 'pretence,' p. 458 l. 42 'surmise,' p. 476 l. 37 'all the rest,' p. 478 ll. 7-8, No. 48 st. 1 'prolong.'

---

[1] He abandoned the idea of reprinting that anthology, contenting himself with reproducing eight anonymous pieces, three of which, 'Those eies which set my fancie on a fire,' 'A Counterloue,' and 'The Description of Iealousie,' are given below, pp. 474, 476-7, and saying 'It will be found that there is not much spicery left in the Nest when we have rifled it of the poems that appear in *Englands Helicon* and in the following pages.' *Lyrics from the Romances*, p. xxviii.

[2] In looking through my selection I find the instances rarer and more fragmentary than I thought; but this method of obtruding rather than concealing the incidental suggestions that arise in course of composition, is a distinct note in the verse of the period.

INTRODUCTION

Of the first four of these methods, as will readily be acknowledged, Lyly is in prose the recognized high-priest. No one who has studied either his novels or plays could suppose him incapable of rivalling the most ingenious sonneteer who ever embroidered on the eternal theme of love; antithesis is the most strongly-marked of his formal or structural characteristics; while natural history allusions, and proverbs, are his most frequent methods of adornment. Even of the last three I fear instances could be supplied from the songs in the Plays or the Entertainments, though those in the former, especially the earlier ones, are marked by a freshness and vigour, besides an ingenuity, which little that I print here or in the Entertainments (except the Phillida and Coridon song of *Elvetham*, a song not certainly his) can boast. Some of the Entertainment songs, especially that of the Phœnix in *Cowdray*, and Apollo's 'My hart and tongue' and 'Hearbes, wordes and stones' in *Sudeley*, are at once very close to Lyly, and very like the generality of the unsigned verse I am discussing. Since ascertaining his authorship of those shows, therefore, I have renewed an investigation only cursorily performed before, and have selected from the various sources named above the following body of mostly unsigned verse to which I think he has considerable claims; though there is not much of it that I print with any pleasure, nor very many about which I entertain no personal doubt, among them being that on the Bee, which I had decided must be his, before I found it definitely assigned to him in *Rawlinson MS. Poet.* 148—the only case I know, outside the plays, of such an attribution. The body selected excludes many things that may probably be his, and some (among these) which I should have been glad to print as his, had their poetical merit been adequately supported in other ways. Those admitted have been chosen on grounds of strong general likeness in subject, sentiment and treatment, of special likeness in phrase or diction, and sometimes of similar collocation of ideas or allusions [1], in no case, of course, merely on grounds of poetical merit,—I include much that is more likely to injure than assist Lyly. In some cases, though I could not perceive, or succeed in verifying, any special likeness, I have felt the general likeness of tone so strong as to warrant inclusion in a 'Doubtful' list, especially where a poem adjoins another in the same MS. also felt to be probably Lyly's. In other cases the special likenesses, which carry a widely varying force, may seem to be merely commonplaces of love or life, or allusion to some common proverb; but this, while it weakens, does not destroy the argument. When a writer is perpetually harping on a particular sentiment, such as the unreliability of women; when he is for ever citing special proverbs like that about smoke and fire, or using certain imagery, e. g. baits and hooks, nettles and roses, storms and anchors, hearts and tongues, double or single, &c., the circumstance

are those of Lyly.

Grounds of choice.

[1] E. g. No. 18, 'A Warning for Wooers,' stanzas 4, 8, 10.

gives him a preferential claim to unsigned work in which such sentiments or imagery appear. So far as possible I have indicated cases of special likeness—generally far more individual than these [1]—in the margin; but the reader will be aware of the impossibility of verifying, in the large body of Lyly's work, all that recollection suggests, and I must trust largely to his own familiarity with the acknowledged text. Few, I believe, will be found to question the correctness of my attribution of the *Bee*, p. 494, *A Warning for Wooers* p. 465, the long poem on pp. 459–63, 'Compare the Bramble with the Cedar tree' p. 483, or 'Where lingring feare doth once posses the hart' p. 487, and the acceptance of these lends a separate probability to others. Nevertheless I am well aware of the extremely treacherous nature of the ground on which I am here treading. Though I have done my best to preclude mistake, a chance familiarity with some one or other of the obscurer poets of this prolific time may enable a reader to negative this or that suggestion. I trust that an effort undertaken with reluctance and diffidence, at the very close of a laborious task, because I felt it might possibly be demanded on the score of completeness, will not on account of its perhaps disappointing, or sometimes unconvincing, results, be allowed to discredit the other portions of my work; and that the reader will be able to feel that I have, in this section, added something to our definite knowledge of the author, though I may have somewhat lowered the reputation of the poet.

Sources.   I cannot pretend that my search has been exhaustive: though, so far as the MSS. in the British Museum are concerned, I should hardly expect a later investigator to add much to my list that had not already passed under my review; while I believe I have also gleaned all that the *Rawlinson MSS. (Poetical)* at the Bodleian have to yield [2]. Those which I deem most worth attention, and to which I have given the most thorough scrutiny, are *Harleian MS.* 6910, *Additional MSS.* 15,232, 22,601, and *Rawlinson MSS.* 85, 148, 172. I have also gone through all the printed Elizabethan Anthologies, most of the Music-Books before 1610, and some modern collections of ancient work [3]. I am satisfied that

---

[1] E. g. cf. No. 10 l. 17 with *Euph.* i. 225 l. 31 'I force not Philautus his fury,' and ii. 94 ll. 23–4 'I feare not thy force, I force not thy friendship': and No. 51 st. 2 ll. 27–8 with *Euph.* i. 250 ll. 8–10 'Thinke ... that Hiena, when she speaketh lyke a man deuiseth most mischiefe, y^t women when they be most pleasant, pretend most trecherie.'

[2] The chief MSS. which I have examined on this matter of anonymous poems, following the guidance of the descriptive Catalogues or the reff. of critics, are *Harleian MSS.* 367, 2127, 4064, 6910, 6917, 7312, 7332; *Lansdowne MS.* 740; *Egerton MSS.* 923, 2230; *Additional MSS.* 5956, 15,117, 15,118, 15,225, 15,226, 15,227, 15,232, 15,233, 21,433, 22,601, 22,602, 22,603, 25,707, 28,101, 33,963; *Rawlinson MSS. Poet.* 56, 66, 85, 92, 108, 112, 120, 148, 153, 160, 171, 172, 185, 212. The *Douce* and *Malone MSS.*, as summarized in Mr. Madan's Catalogue, promise nothing.

[3] Out of a thousand or possibly double that number of poems under review, I copied some two hundred, from which my selection has been made.

INTRODUCTION 439

nothing I here present has been claimed for Sidney, Greville, Dyer, Breton, Oxford, Essex[1], Raleigh[2], or Spenser. What I select forms, I think, a body of fairly homogeneous, though seldom more than mediocre, verse. It should be remembered that there is great inequality of merit among the songs in the Plays, some of which are almost a disgrace to the author of 'Cupid and my Campaspe.' It is clear that Lyly, while capable of the exquisite, could descend to the slipshod, though we might have expected better things from one of his evident artistic sense. I believe not only that with him, as with a famous modern Euphuist, John Ruskin, fluency and fullness of suggestion made him impatient of the delay and constraint of versification; but also, what could never be said of Ruskin, that his mind was strictly of a prosaic cast. His thought moved freely, but on the plain, never upon the peaks. The praise due to the very best of his songs is that of grace and daintiness whether of fancy or execution, of prettiness and ingenuity, and of freshness; never, I think, of power, awe, passion, or other than an earthly beauty. And he seems to have been aware of the inconstant and qualified nature of his impulse, and to have distrusted himself in this field. He describes himself in *Elvetham* as 'modicum poetam'; he does not print even the songs in the (prose) plays; his Prologue to the blank verse play, *The Woman*, 1593 (where two songs are allowed to appear in the quarto), is in the modest tone of a tyro; and in any other poems he may have written he remains anonymous. Probably he had imbibed, from early acquaintance with the classics, and with Sidney and Spenser in the Savoy, too high a respect for the poetic function to venture on it rashly, or to obtrude his efforts.

Lyly prosateur rather than poet.

A correct chronological arrangement of the pieces I print is probably unattainable. The dates of MSS. are too vague to guide us, and those on the title-pages of anthology or song-book afford only a downward limit. I have followed what seemed the probable order of production, qualifying this with some attempt to keep together poems taken from the same source or dealing with the same subject.

Grouping adopted.

I. Nos. 1–15. First come a few which I have classed as 'Early Autobiographical'; beginning with a set of hexameters on trees recalling some of Lyly's favourite illustrations and written probably in the days of Harvey's Areopagus, and continuing with some versification of special sentiments in *Euphues*, generally in Chaucer's seven-line stanza popularized by Sackville, which made way later for that formed by omission of its fifth line. The last three of this group are taken from Anthony Munday's *A Banquet of Daintie Conceits*, 1588, reprinted from a unique

From Munday's 'Banquet.'

---

[1] Except *The Bee*.
[2] Exceptions are to be found in 'Praisd be Dianas faire and harmles light' (No. 36), 'Hey downe a downe did Dian sing' (No. 38), 'Like to a Hermite,' &c. (No. 23), and the two poems after Marlowe's 'Come liue with me' (Nos. 39, 40).

copy in the *Harleian Miscellany*, vol. ix. Thomas Park, the editor, noted the likeness in the first to the speeches of Polonius, which I have shown to be founded on *Euphues* (vol. i. p. 165). The other two are more doubtful: their tone and subject are quite those of *Euphues*, Part I; but these commonplaces about youth and age and the fading of beauty might be perpetrated by any young writer, e. g. Munday himself. Still I know none to whom they would be half so appropriate as to Lyly. If his, I should, comparing them with the much more compact prose expression of the same sentiments in *Euphues*, suppose them to precede that work; though their smooth versification argues previous practice in rhyming.

II. Nos. 16-20. Next I place a group of 'Early Love-Poems,' mainly of rougher and poorer verse, but exhibiting, though drawn from different sources, a striking similarity of tone and manner, and that distinctly Lylian. The longest, No. 16, is from a MS. (*Addit.* 22,601) which has contributed several other poems in my selection, though generally with less certainty than this. The second of two poems in the same uncommon metre (Nos. 17, 18) is from Clement Robinson's *Handefull of Pleasant Delites*, 1584, and extremely euphuistic—a mosaic of proverbs: there is another of that metre in the same anthology, 'The Lover,' which fails to establish a claim to admission; but I have included, with some doubts, 'A Proper Sonet,' No. 19, and one, No. 20 (from another MS.), which resembles in tone No. 10.

From Cl. Robinson's 'Hande- full.'

III. Nos. 21-4. These are followed by four songs from different sources, inserted rather because they fit the place of some that are missing in the plays than because they are strikingly like Lyly, though they may be his.

IV. Nos. 25-53. Then comes by far the largest group, 'Later Love-Poems,' mostly of much better verse than that of groups I and II, and containing a good deal of which Lyly has no reason to be ashamed. This is the section to which exception may most easily be taken, though of course its contents do not stand or fall together. It includes

From W. Byrd.

(*a*) three, Nos. 25-7, from William Byrd's Song-Books of 1588 and 1589, which remind me of Lyly's phrases and ideas; and a fourth, No. 28, strikingly like him, from *Addit. MS.* 22,601;

From 'The Phœnix Nest.'

(*b*) eight, Nos. 29-36, from *The Phœnix Nest . . . set foorth by R. S. of the Inner Temple Gentleman . . .* 1593, from which I took two others, Nos. 6, 23. For the first seven of these eight, I can allege no very special likeness. They present a general resemblance both to each other and to Lyly; an impression that will be strengthened by a comparison of them with the three in *Cowdray*, which I do not doubt for his. I acknowledge their similarity also to much other ideal love-verse written about this time: they show, for instance, considerable likeness to the work of Lyly's friend, Thomas Watson. But three other poems in *The Phœnix Nest* appear with direct attribution to Watson; and, in view of his high repute as a poet, it seems more likely that these, if his, would have been similarly

INTRODUCTION

assigned. It should not be forgotten that in 1582 (Life, p. 27) Lyly promises to communicate to Watson certain love-poems written by himself, which he then disclaims all intention of printing. Even if these were the poor verses I have included under 'Early Love-Poems,' yet they were probably succeeded by later and more practised work; and the reluctance to print, felt in the first instance, may have disappeared in the interval, or have been ignored or overruled by R. S. *The Phœnix Nest*, at any rate, was, with the exception of Munday's *Banquet of Daintie Conceits*, 1588 (which has nothing I should claim, beyond the three already dealt with), the first collection since Robinson's in which they could appear; and the inclusion therein of the dialogue between Constancy and Inconstancy (or Liberty) from the Quarrendon Entertainment of the preceding year— a dialogue surely Lyly's, and not known to have existed save in MS. —suggests Lyly's acquaintance with 'R. S.,' and makes it probable that some poems in the *Nest* are also his [1].

(*c*) The eighth of the *Nest* group, No. 36, 'Praisd be Dianas faire and harmles light,' together with the next poem 'My thoughts are wingde with hopes,' &c., are also found in *Englands Helicon*, 1600, from which I have included (besides the five which found their way into that collection from the *Entertainments*) three more, Nos. 38–40—'Hey downe a downe did Dian sing,' and the two suggested by Marlowe's 'Come liue with me.' The second of this group of five, No. 37, 'My thoughts,' &c., was assigned by Francis Davison, in a private list of the *Helicon* contents (*Harl. MS.* 280, ff. 99-101) made, no doubt, in preparing his own *Rapsody*, to the 'Earle of Cumberland,' a patron I think of Lyly's, in whose literary performances I rather disbelieve [2]. Collier wrongly reported Dowland as giving it to Greville; and Grosart, while indicating his mistake, included it in Greville's *Works*, ii. 132 as 'much in the same vein.' I think the likeness to the diction of *Endimion* gives Lyly an infinitely better claim. All the other four, together with 'Like to a Hermite poore,' No. 23, from the *Nest*, have been claimed for Raleigh, a claim supported in the case of 'Praisd be Dianas,' &c. by the initials 'W. R.' affixed to the first line in Davison's MS. list above referred to. Davison, however, may have had no better reason than the signature 'Ignoto' attached to all four in *Englands Helicon* [3]—a signature which, though sometimes Raleigh's, is subscribed

From 'Englands Helicon.'

---

[1] That about Apelles, however (the last but one—'Sir painter, are thy colours redie set '), though reminiscent of *Campaspe* in its 4th and 10th stanzas, is not Lylian enough in manner, and is probably by some one else familiar with the play.
[2] See vol. i. Biog. App. p. 384, and Notes to Ents. p. 519.
[3] Yet Davison withholds the initials from the other three.—It has been alleged in regard to 'Praisd,' &c., and 'The Nimphs reply' that in ed. 1600 the initials 'S. W. R.' have first been printed on the page, and that afterwards a slip with 'Ignoto' printed on it has been attached at one side so as to lie over and cover the initials. This, while true of other poems in the *Helicon*, is, in the case of the Brit. Mus. copy of 1600, uncertain as regards 'Praisd,' &c., where is neither slip nor signature, only signs of some erasure, and incorrect as regards

in the same anthology to poems satisfactorily assigned to Barnfield, Dyer, Greville, and Lodge. Dr. Hannah[1] accepted the claim for Raleigh, made in the seventeenth century, of 'Like to a Hermite poore' and 'The Nimphs reply'; and also, but doubtfully, that of 'Praisd,' &c.; while he rejected 'Hey downe a downe' and the other Marlowe imitation. It seems to me that 'Praisd,' &c. is redolent of *Endimion*, presenting just that coadmixture of physical and mythological allegory which we have traced in that play (above, pp. 81–2) and which, if it occurs in anything like the same degree in any other Elizabethan work, has entirely escaped my notice. Similarly the language of 'Like to a Hermite poore' is sufficiently near that of *Endimion* to suggest Lyly's authorship, though the strength of the suggestion is not that of the former case. 'Hey downe a downe' is either modelled on, or model of, 'Phœbes Sonnet,' printed in the same collection from Lodge's *Rosalynde*, 1590; and the passages cited in the margin from *Euphues*, about an earlier age when love had not yet learned dissimulation, conjoined with the lectures of Diana in *Gallathea*, seem to give Lyly a prior claim. Izaak Walton gave 'The Nimphs reply' to Maudlin's mother to sing, with commendations, as 'made by Sir Walter Raleigh in his younger days'; but said nothing of the ‹other imitation. Mr. Bullen[2] does not hold either proven for Raleigh's. Both, I think, carry suggestions of Lyly: the first, of his habit of sermonizing to youth; the second, of the Entertainments and of *The Woman*, in which he was to some extent Marlowe's imitator—cf. especially Acts iii. 2. 167–70, v. 25–39, 96–109. In neither is the likeness to his manner very strong; but I wish to suggest his claim, which is perhaps better than any one else's. I have felt some doubt whether the similarly-signed allegorical poem, 'In Pescod time,' is not Lyly's; but there is no sufficient likeness of phrase or sentiment to justify its inclusion.

From 'A Poetical Rapsody.' (d) There remains of the Anthologies[3], Davison's *Poetical Rapsody*, 1602, whence two poems, the *Ode. Of Cynthia* and *Lottery*, to which Sir John Davies may dispute Lyly's claim, have already been given among the Entertainments (vol. i. 414, 499–504). Some of the 'A.W.' poems might on mere internal grounds be assigned to Lyly; but it is extremely un-

the Reply, where the word 'Ignoto' is printed fairly and cleanly on the original page, as it is in the case of the other Marlowe imitation and 'Hey downe a downe.'
[1] *Poems of Raleigh and Wotton*, 1875, pp. xxx, xxxi, 11, 12, 77.
[2] *Works of Marlowe*, 1885, vol. iii. p. 283.
[3] *Tottell's Miscellany*, 1557, is much too early: I find nothing to which Lyly can lay claim in Edwardes' *Paradyse of daynty deuises*, 1578, nor in *A gorgious Gallery of gallant Inuentions by T. P.* 1578: *The Welspring of wittie Conceites . . . Out of Italian by W. Phist*, 1584, is in prose: *Wits Commonwealth* [1597] is a mere collection of citations from the classics and the Fathers: *Wits Theater*, 1599, is a book of signed quotations, mostly ancient, in which Lyly's name does not appear: *Belvedere or the Garden of the Mvses*, 1600 (single lines and couplets only), does not include Lyly in its prefatory list of authors: and *Englands Parnassus*, 1600, is a book of longer signed extracts, wherein, among the few anonymous fragments, is nothing of his.

INTRODUCTION

likely that Davison in his private memorandum of those poems of a 'deere friend' (*Harl. MS.* 280, f. 102) would put down any but the writer's true initials; and, if 'Anonymous Writer' be inadmissible [1], 'Amicus Watsoni' or 'Alter Watsonus' would be equally so. Nor does examination of the poems here subscribed 'Ignoto,' or unsubscribed, suggest more than a possibility that Lyly might be the author of 'An Invective against Women [2],' which reminds one somewhat of Euphues' 'Cooling Card,' and of 'A Counterloue,' No. 33. But among the four from which the signature 'Anomos' is withdrawn in all editions after the first, is one (No. 41[2]) so thoroughly Lylian that I feel bound to include it. It purports to be a reply to two stanzas subscribed 'Incerto' in the first edition, but assigned in *Rawlinson MS. Poet.* 148, f. 50, to 'Mr Edward Dier,' beginning

> The lowest trees have tops; the ant her gall;
> The fly her spleen; the little sparks their heat:

and it is enumerated in Davison's 'A. W.' list as '116. Though lowest trees have tops, the ant her gall. Answer.' Though in printing the *Rapsody* itself Davison omits the first stanza, that is found with the other four in *Rawl. MS. Poet.* 148, f. 53, where the poem appears unsigned, but headed 'The aunswer to M^r: Diers ditie, in fol. 50.' My belief is that these five stanzas, the refrain of which embodies an opinion expressed by Alexander in *Campaspe*, ii. 2. 80 sqq., are Lyly's reply to Dyer's verses, elicited partly by the fact that the latter were practically a cento from *Euphues* [3]; and that Davison, who at first supposed them to be by 'A. W.' had ascertained his error before the second edition of his *Rapsody*, 1608. I am the more inclined to regard the answer as Lyly's, because the same Rawlinson MS. contains, not only the *Bee* with definite ascription to him, but several others included here on various grounds of likeness [4]. But though it contains the initial stanza, its text is so inferior that I prefer to print both poems from the first edition of the *Rapsody*, adding the stanza in a footnote. Another of the four poems from which the signature 'Anomos' is withdrawn after the first edition, 'It chanct of late a Shepheards swayne [5],' tempts me with an air of probability for subject and treatment; but, beyond the proverb of the last stanza, I see no special Lylian likeness of phrase or style.

(e) I have added to this group of 'Later Love-Poems' three (Nos. 42–4) *From John*

---

[1] I disbelieve in the use of 'anonymous' as an English epithet at this date.
[2] Vol. ii. 123, ed. Bullen; who, with Hannah, rejects the claim for Raleigh.
[3] Compare with the two lines quoted above *Euph.* ii. 90 l. 22 'I but Euphues, low trees haue their tops, smal sparkes their heat, the Flye his splene, ye Ant hir gall, Philautus his affection, which is neither ruled by reason, nor led by appointment.' See too the other references given in the margin. Even if Dyer's verses were written before the Second Part of *Euphues*, these passages show that they had attracted Lyly's notice, and might elicit a reply.
[4] See below, pp. 444–5.
[5] Vol. i. 37, ed. Bullen. Dr. Hannah rejected the claim of this poem for Raleigh.

Dowland and Robert Jones.

from John Dowland's Song-Books of 1600 and 1603, and as many as ten (Nos. 45–52, 66–7) from Robert Jones' *First Booke of Songes & Ayres*, 1600, with one from his *Muses Gardin for Delights*, 1610. One or two others are included later from the same composers, who with Byrd (three, Nos. 25–7), and Morley (one, No. 21), are the only ones laid under contribution. Though I have hunted through many other music-books—of Morley, Wilbye, Weelkes, N. Yonge, &c.—it seemed to me unlikely that Lyly's work would be found in many hands. It may be thought I have drawn too largely on the single book of Jones, 1600; but the Lylian impression of these pieces is to me very strong. In none of these music-books, nor anywhere else, have I come upon the faintest trace of any of the songs printed by Blount: nor, let me add, am I aware of any mention of Lyly as a poet pure and simple in any contemporary work.

V. Nos. 54–67. There remains the section headed 'Later Autobiographical,' wherein I have collected a number of pieces which seem to lament, no coldness or treachery of some mistress, real or ideal, but the continual thwarting of his material hopes. The superior sincerity of accent is obvious. Doubtless this vein of bitter complaint might be indulged by many others at Court; but the pieces I choose are either extremely Lylian, e. g. Nos. 54, 58, 59, or else are recommended by their appearance in a quarter where I have found others more evidently his. Perhaps there is least verbal evidence for those which are poetically the best, the four from the Song-Books, Nos. 55–6, 66–7. In support of the last, which reminds one rather of Nash, I would urge the marked rhythm of the fifth line in each stanza, repeated in the fifth lines of No. 59 which is more like Lyly. No. 65, from the same MS. as the hexameters on trees, is recommended by the musical imagery, by the puns in stanza 3, and by Lyly's favourite trick of exposing fictions, poetic or other[1]. The rest are taken from or found in the following three MSS. on which I have already made considerable drafts.

From Rawl. MS. Poet. 148.

(1) *Rawlinson MS. Poetical*, 148, 4°, 114 leaves, is dated in Mr. F. Madan's Catalogue as about 1600, and is bound with and following on a printed copy of Watson's *Hecatompathia*, 1582. It is all written in a single hand, that of John Lilliat, a clergyman who, one might conjecture from some details he gives of proceedings at Christ Church during a royal visit, resided at or near Oxford, and who signs his name, generally but not always in Greek characters, or prints it from a stamp, all over the MS. As the great majority of the poems bear his signature, we may reasonably infer that the unsigned ones are by others; and it seems to

---

[1] *Euph.* i. 195 drawbacks of wit, ii. 114–9 love-charms, *Camp.* Diogenes throughout, and iii. 3 Jupiter's character, *Saph.* ii. 3 Moluṣ on valiancy, *Gall.* Alchemist and Astronomer, *Loves Met.* ii. 1. 51–61 Nisa on poetic accounts of Love, *M. Bomb.* i. 3. 90–110 Candius and Livia on parents' affection, *Woman* Gunophilus' vein throughout.

INTRODUCTION

me probable that the five preceding the *Bee*, occupying ff. 31 v.–32 v., are all by Lyly; though as the two first of these, 'Who sees yᵉ sunne how soone it growes obscure' (5 stt.), and a sonnet 'Of a sealed doue,' present no special resemblances, I only copy the three fragments (Nos. 60-2) on f. 32 v.¹ Other poems in my selection also found in this MS. are Nos. 17 'Of lingeringe Loue' (f. 2), 50 'When loue on time, &c. (f. 59), and 63 'Ouer theis brookes,' &c. f. 46).

(2) *Additional MS.* 22,601, 12ᵐᵒ, 107 leaves, was acquired by the Museum at Dr. Bliss' sale, 1858, and formerly belonged to Andrews, a Bristol bookseller. It is a most interesting collection of poems, ballads, satirical pieces, &c., all transcribed in one very legible hand about 1603. The Percy Society printed twenty-two pieces from it under the title of *Poetical Miscellanies* in vol. xv of its collection of *Early English Poetry*. I have already claimed the fourth of these (No. 28), a sonnet said to be worked on a sampler, extremely Lylian in thought and diction, though of more pathos than he usually exhibits; four others, Nos. 7, 8, 10, 12, alike in their praise of independence, sincerity, and 'the mean'; and the long piece of poor verse (No. 16) which preaches Sybilla's lesson of bold wooing. Three of them are in octosyllabic metre, and should probably be placed before 1580, about the same time as 'Of lingeringe Loue' and 'A Warning for Wooers.' In the same MS., f. 49, are given the mottoes for the Lots of the *Harefield* Entertainment (vol. i. pp. 500-4).

From Add. MS. 22,601.

(3) *Harleian MS.* 6910 is a very large collection (190 leaves) of poems all copied in the same fine small hand; those occupying ff. 1-74 being all by Spenser, and followed in the MS. by 'finis 1596,' so that the succeeding ones, nearly all of them unsigned, were at least transcribed after that date². Its contents, which are of every shade of merit, range over the whole of Elizabeth's reign, and include poems in the old fourteener, though most are in stanzas of six or seven decasyllabic lines, e. g. there are long transcripts from Sackville's *Induction*. I have included from this MS. seven poems as possibly by our author, and have transcribed from other sources five besides the *Bee* (Nos. 23, 35, 41, 43, 59, 63) also found here.

From Harl. MS. 6910.

The long poem on the Bee claims special notice. It seems to have enjoyed a contemporary fame equal to that of 'Nowe what is loue' or *The Lie*, and is found in an even greater number of MSS., of which the list given below³ is probably far from complete. Its vogue may be partly

The Bee.

---

¹ Fol. 33, which would have contained the first four stt. of *The Bee*, and probably something else immediately preceding it, is lost.

² About one half of them can be definitely assigned. I should like to see this portion of the MS. ff. 74-190 edited by some one of full knowledge—and ample fortune.

³ Harl. MS. 6910, ff. 167-8 (14 stt., om. 5ᵗʰ) unsigned.
   Harl. MS. 2127, f. 58 (14 stt., om. 5ᵗʰ) unsigned, endorsed 'The Bees Songe.'
   Addit. MS. 5956, f. 25 (3 stt. 7, 10, 11, with two odd couplets) unsigned.
   (Dowland printed stt. 1-2, unsigned, as No. 18 of his *Third and Last Booke of Songs or Aires*, 1603.)

attributed to its, I believe, incorrect ascription to the Earl of Essex. In several MSS., notably in Harl. MS. 6910—almost the best—it is anonymous. Reading it there first I felt assured it must be Lyly's; and shortly afterwards found it in Rawl. MS. Poet. 148 actually subscribed 'q^d Mr John Lilly,' in a hand other than that of Lilliat, but still contemporary. Then, one after another, I came upon the MSS. with the Essex ascription, culminating in the Sloane MS. 1303 with a particularity (cf. note, below) that compels close examination. Park in his edition (1806) of Walpole's *Royal and Noble Authors*, ii. 107-14, printed it as by Essex; and Grosart, in his Fuller Worthies *Miscellanies* (1872-6), pp. 85-9. I submit that the contents of the poem are inapplicable to Essex, and are exactly applicable to Lyly, whose phrases and ideas, besides, the poem repeats. It laments under a thin allegorical veil the author's lack of all reward for his service; the last stanza in particular speaks of his having been sustained by false hopes and promises for ten years, and specifies money as the object of his dreams; while the third and fourth stanzas allude to the Queen's rejection with rebuke of some special application he had made to her. Now Essex came to Court in 1585, and had received almost continuous marks of royal favour. He was refused a command in 1594; but even in that year he won Elizabeth's regard by securing the conviction of the physician Lopez, and she began to treat him with a separate confidence that aroused a natural jealousy in the Cecils. The poem's complaint of utter neglect is not such as Essex could reasonably make, either in 1595 (ten years after coming to Court), or 1598 [1] (the date given by the Sloane

Rawl. MS. Poet. 148, ff. 34-5 (stt. 5-15 only—f. 33 missing), signed in another hand 'q^d M^r. Iohn Lilly.'
Addit. MS. 15,891, ff. 244-5 (12 stt., om. 5th, 14th, 15th), unsigned, but following letters between Essex and Egerton.
Tanner MS. 306, p. 249
Ashmole MS. 767, f. 1 } (14 stt., om. 5th), signed 'E' (?) headed 'The Buzzeinge Bee's Complaynt.'
Ashmole MS. 781, p. 132
Rawl. MS. Poet. 112, ff. 9-10 (14 stt., om. 5th), unsigned, but forming the first of two poems headed 'Verses or English Poemes written by the Lo: the E: of E:'
Rawl. MS. Poet. 172, ff. 13-4 (14 stt., om. 5th), unsigned, headed 'My Lord of Essex his Bee.'
Collier's MS. (15 stt.), subscribed 'R. Devereux, Essex,' headed 'Honi soit quy mal y pense.' (Bibl. Cat. ii. 189, where stt. 11, 12 are quoted.)
Sloane MS. 1303 (Tracts relating to the Earl of Essex), ff. 71-2 (15 stt.), subscribed 'Robert Deuoreux Earle of Essex and Ewe, Earle Marshall of Englande,' headed 'The Earle of Essex his Buzze wch he made vpon some discontentment he receiued, a litle before his iourney into Ireland. Año Dñi 1598.'
Egerton MS. 923, ff. 5-7 (15 stt.), unsigned, headed 'A Poem made on Robt Deuorex Earle of Essex by Mr Henry Cuff his Chaplaine.'
I have reported all variants of any importance, not every minute difference. The report of the Tanner and Ashmole MSS. is given from Grosart's Fuller Worthies *Miscellanies*, vol. iv. 85-91.

[1] By no straining could the scene in the Council in July, when Raleigh repeated an uncomplimentary remark of Essex, for which the Queen boxed the latter's ears,

MS.); nor is its piteous tone at all consistent with his pride or his position at any time. But to Lyly's position and fortunes it is absolutely applicable, forming a most natural expression of his reflections on the rejection of his First Petition, presented after ten years' service, i.e. in 1598[1]. It is the burthen of both petitions that he has been working hard and has received *nothing*. Tobacco is specially associated with Lyly in passages of Nash and Ben Jonson (Life, pp. 60-1): bees furnish probably his most frequent image in *Euphues* and elsewhere: and those who will verify the references in the margin will find many special likenesses. In view of the anonymity in regard to his poems, which he breaks only in the case of *The Woman*, it is easy to understand how this one, copied widely perhaps from some collection of Oxford's, might come to be associated with the figure who bulked so large in the popular mind at the close of the century. The MSS. which assert Essex's authorship are very faulty in text, though perhaps not much, if at all, later than the others. The Egerton MS., which alone assigns it to Henry Cuffe, Essex's secretary or chaplain, is dated in the Catalogue 'c. 1630-40.' Cuffe is not known as a maker of English verse. Though I disbelieve in its ascription, I print from this MS. as furnishing, though late, the best copy, possessing the 5th stanza, which Harl. MS. 6910, the next best copy, lacks.

VI. Nos. 68-73. I close with half a dozen 'Epigrams' from *Addit. MS.* 15,227.

And so I commend to the critic a selection which, while liable to the complaints of inclusion or omission customarily made of anthologies, is deprived by its very nature of the anthology's special attraction. It would have been far safer to decline the task, and that course would have saved me months of labour; but I believe the editor of a later day will thank me for having supplied him with some basis and information on which to work.

---

be made to fit stanzas 3-4. She pardoned him in October. Earlier in the year she had presented him with £7000 (*Dict. Nat. Biog.*).

[1] Cf. st. 9 'Patience (*var.* Patient) I am therefore I must be poore,' and st. 15 'ffiue yeares twise told wth promises p^{r}fume | my hope stuft head was cast into a slumber' (cf. marg reff.) with the language of Letter iii in Biog. App. vol. i. p. 393, 'as one of ye Queens patients, who have nothing applied thes ten yeres to my wantes but promises.'

I. Early Autobiographical: 1575–1580?

1. (From *Rawlinson MS. Poet.* 85, f. 22.)

<small>Victorye.
Lament-
inges
peace loue
refusall.
Deathe.
⟨*Euph.* ii.
75 ll. 33–6⟩</small>

When I behoulde the trees in the earthes fayre lyuerye clothed
Ease I do feele, suche ease as faulles to me wholy diseased
For that I fynde in them parte of my state represented
Lawrell showes what I seek, by y^e *Myrr* is showde how I seek it
Olyue poyntes me the pryce that I muste aspyre to by conquest   5
Myrtle makes me requeste, my requeste is vnsealde by a *Willowe*
Cipruss promisethe healpe, but healp y^t bringes me no comfort
Sweet Iuniper sayes thus, thoughe I burne, yet I burn in a sweet fyre
Ewe dothe make me thinke what kynd of bowe the boye houldethe,
Whiche shootes throughe wthout any noyse and deadlye wthout smarte. 10
Firr tree is great and greene fyxte one a hye hill but a barren.
Lyke to my noble thoughtes styll newe, well plaste, to me fruteless.

<small>⟨*Euph.* i.
223 l. 20⟩</small>

Figg that yealdes moste pleasaunt frute his shadow is hurtefull.
Thus be her guifts most sweet thus most dawnger to be neere her

<small>⟨*Euph.* i.
191 l. 9,
ii. 76 l. 35⟩</small>

But in Palme when I mark howe he dothe ryse vnder a burthen   15
And maye not I saye than get vp thoughe grefes be so wayghtye
Pyne is a maste to a shipp, to my shipp shall hope for a mast serue
Pyne is hyghe, hope is as hyghe, yet be my hopes budded.
Elme imbraste by a Vine, embracinge fancye reuiuethe.
Popler chaungethe his hewe, from a rysinge suñ to a settinge.   20
Thus to my sunn do I yealde, suche lookes her beames do afford me,
Ould aged oke cutt doune for new workes serues to the buildinge
So my desy^rs by feare cut downe for ye frames of her honor
Palmes do reioyse to be ioynde wth ye matche of a male to a femall
And shall sensiue things be so sensless as to resist sense   25
Ashe makes speare wch sheilds do resiste, hi^r force no repuls takes
Thus be my thoughts disperst thus thinkinge nowrsest a thought still
But to the Cædar queen of woodes when I lyft my betrayde eys
Than do I shape my selfe that forme wch raygnes so within me
And thinke ther she dothe dwell and here w^t pllaynts I do vtte^r   30

<small>⟨*Saph.* iv.
3, 4, 19⟩</small>

When that noble topp dothe nodd I beleiue she salutes me
Than kneelinge often thus I do speake to her image.
Onlye Iewell, all onlye Iewell, whiche onlye deserueste

23 for] by *MS.*

EARLY AUTOBIOGRAPHICAL

That mens heartes be my seat and endless fame be yⁱ seruante
O descend for a whill from this great hyghte to behoulde me
But nought else do beholude or it is not worthe the behouldinge
Se what a thought is wrought by thy selfe! and since I am alltred
Thus by thy werck disdayne not⟨e⟩ that wch is by thy selfe done. 5
In meane caues oft treasue^r abydes, to an hostry a kinge comes
—And so behind black cloudes full oft faye^r streams do ly hidden.

FINIS.

2. (From *Harl. MS.* 6910, f. 97.)

No PLACE commendes the man vnworthie praise.	⟨*Euph.* i.
No title of state doth stay vp vices fall: 10	270 l. 13,
No wicked wight to wo can make delayes,	317 l. 20⟩
No loftie lookes preserue the proude at all	
No brags or boast, no stature high and tall,	
No lusty yought, no swearing, stareing stout,	⟨No. 31.32;
No brauerie, banding, cogging, cutting out. 15	*Whip*, l. 119⟩

Then what availes to haue a Princly place,
A name of honour or an high degree,
To come by kindred of a noble race?
Except wee Princely, worthie, noble be.
The fruites declare the goodnes of the tree. 20
Doe br⟨a⟩gge no more, of birth or linage than,
ffor vertue, grace, and manners make the man.

3. (From *Harl. MS.* 6912, f. 101 v.)

How can he rule well in a common wealth,	⟨*Euph.* i.
Which knoweth not himselfe in rule to frame?	269, 276⟩
How should he rule himselfe in ghostly health 25	
Which neuer learn'd one lesson for the same?	
If such catch harme their parents are to blame:	
ffor needes must they be blinde, and blindly led,	
Where no good lesson can be taught or read.	

Some thinke their youth discreete and wisely taught, 30 ⟨*Ib.*⟩
That brag and boast, and weare their fether braue,
Can royst and rout, both lowre and looke aloft,
Can sweare and stare, and call their fellowes knaue,
Can pill and poll, and catch before they craue,
Can carde and dice, both cog and foyste at fare, 35
Play on vnthriftie, till their purse be bare.

Some teach their youth to pipe, to sing and daunce,
To hauke, to hunt, to choose and kill their game.

450 POEMS

⟨*Euph.* i. 277; ii. 50 ll. 15-25, 188 l. 5⟩

  To winde their horne, and with their horse to praunce,
  To play at tennis, set the lute in frame,
  Run at the ring, and vse such other game:
  Which feats although they be not all vnfit,
  Yet cannot they the marke of vertue hit.   5

  ffor Noble yought there is nothing so meete
  As learning is, to knowe the good from ill:
  To know the tongues, and perfectly endyte,
  And of the lawes to haue a perfect skill,
  Thinges to reforme as right and iustice will: 10
  ffor honnour is ordeyned for no cause
  But to see right maintayned by the lawes.

 4. (From *Harl. MS.* 6910, f. 110 v.)

⟨*Euph.* i. 265 l. 24⟩
⟨*Theob.*vol. i. p. 419 l. 7⟩

  What liquor first the earthen pot doth take,
  It keepeth still the sauour of the same.
  ffull hard it is a Camocke straight to make,   15
  Or wainscot fyne with crooked logges to frame.
  Tis hard to make the cruell Tiger tame.
  And so it fares with those haue vices caught:
  Naught once (they say) and euer after naught.

  I speake no⟨t⟩ this as though it past all cure   20
  ffrom vices vile to vertue to retire:
  But this I say, if vice be once in vre,
  The more you shall to quite your selfe require,
  The more you plunge yor selfe in fulsome mire,

⟨i.e. Syrtes, as *Euph.* i. 189 l. 8⟩

  As he that striues in soakte quicke sirts of sand,   25
  Still sinkes, scarce euer comes againe to land.

 5. (From *Harl. MS.* 6910, f. 164.)

⟨*Euph.* i. 246 sqq., 307 sqq.⟩
⟨*Euph.* i. 242 ll. 19-21, 189 l. 33, 251 ll. 7-8⟩

  O loath that Loue whose fynall ayme is Lust
  Moth of the mynde, Eclipse of Reasons light
  The graue of Grace, the mole of Natures Rust
  The wracke of witt, the wronge of euery wight.   30
   In Sũme an euill, whose harmes no tonge can tell
   In wch to Liue is death, to dye is Hell.

 6. (From *The Phœnix Nest*, 1593.)

⟨*Euph.* i. 188, ll. 9-15 &c.⟩

  The brainsicke race that wanton youth ensues,
  Without regard to grounded wisdomes lore,
  As often as I thinke thereon, renues   35
  The fresh remembrance of an ancient sore:

  15 Cramocke *MS.*   16 crooked logges with wainscot fyne *MS.*

Reuoking to my pensiue thoughts at last,
The worlds of wickednes that I haue past.

And though experience bids me bite on bit,
And champe the bridle of a bitter smacke,
Yet costly is the price of after wit, 5
Which brings so cold repentance at hir backe:
   And skill that's with so many losses bought,
   Men say is little better worth than nought.

(Euph. ii. 26 l. 22)

And yet this fruit, I must confesse, doth growe
Of follies scourge: that though I now complaine 10
Of error past, yet henceforth I may knowe
To shun the whip that threats the like againe:
   For wise men though they smart a while, had leuer
   To learne experience at the last, than neuer.

7. (From *Addit. MS.* 22,601, f. 55 v.)

I feare not death, feare is more paine
then death it selfe to courage true:
In youth who dies or else is slaine
paies nature but a debt y^ts due.
   Who yongest dies he doth ⟨but⟩ paye
   a debt (he owes) before the daye 20

(Euph. i, letter to Eubulus, and No. 10) 15

And such a debte longer to haue
doth nothinge profite men at all
Death is a debt nature doth craue
and must be pay'd by great & small.
   I loth not warres, nor longe for strife 25
   I feare not death, nor hate not life.

(No. 10 end)

8. (From *Addit. MS.* 22,601, f. 56 r.)

   I will not soare aloft the skye
   With Icarus so farr frō ground
   Least that ye Sunn my winges do ⟨fry⟩
   and fallinge downe wth him be dround 30
      The middle Region will I keepe
      when others wake secure to sleepe.

(Cf. No. 10)

And as high flights ile not attempt
So neither will I fly so lowe
to be a marke for base contempt 35
to shoote and hitt me with his Bowe.
   If y^t he striue to shoote so hie
   his Bowe about his eares shall flie.

POEMS

(Euph. ii.
39 l. 33: cf.
with this
stanza
No. 12)

Lowe shrubbs yᵉ silly beastes do cropp:
high trees great tempests do thē crack
The meane growe⟨n⟩ tree wᵗʰ slend⟨er⟩ topp
is free from beastes & tempests wrack

(Gall. v. 3.
187 sqq.;
Loves Met.
iii. 1.
121–6)

    Neither base nor treble will I singe   5
    the Meane is still yᵉ sweetest stringe.

9. (From *Addit. MS.* 22,601, f. 56 r.)
    Councell wᶜʰ afterward is soughte
    is like vntimely showres
  Distillinge from the duskie cloudes
    when heate hath parcht yᵉ flowres.   10

10. (From *Addit. MS.* 22,601, f. 60 r.)

⟨Cf. No. 8⟩

Soare I will not, in flighte the grounde ile see
The careless mind scornes fortunes angrie frowne,
Either life or death indifferent is to mee,
Preferr I do content before a crowne:
High thoughts I clipp, no stoutenes throwes me downe   15
Euen loftiest lookes in small regard I burie

(Euph. i.
225 l. 31,
ii. 94 ll.
23–4)

Not feare their force, nor force not of yᵉⁱʳ furie.

Riche in content, my Wealth is health & ease
A conscience cleare my chiefe & sure defence,
Disdaine I do by flatt'ringe meanes to please   20
For by deserts I will not giue offence.
Only a wronge reuenge shall recompence:
Rest Muse, I feare no foe, nor frowē on frend

⟨No. 7 end⟩

Dispise not life, nor yet I dreade not end.

11. (From *Addit. MS.* 22,601, f. 60 r.)
    If all the Earthe were paper white   25
    and all the sea were incke
    Twere not inough for me to write
    as my poore hart doᵗʰ thinke.

12. (From *Addit. MS.* 22,601, ff. 79 v.–80 r.)
The lofty trees whose brauches make sweete shades
Whose armes in springe are richely dighte wᵗʰ flowʳˢ   30
Without yᵉ roote their glory quickly fades
& all in vaine comes pleasant Aprill showʳˢ.
  No loue can be at all without yᵉ hart
  nor Musick made excep⟨t⟩ the Base beares parte.

The princely tow⁻ˢ whose pride exceedes in show
if ther foundations be not stronge & sownde
Are subiect to yᵉ smallest windes yᵗ blowe
& highest toppes are brought to lowest ground.
   No fielde is sweete whē all is scortchd wᵗʰ drowte   5
nor musick good when so yᵉ base is out.

⟨Cf. No. 8 st. 3⟩

13. (From A. Munday's *Banquet of Daintie Conceits*, 1588.)

   A Dittie, wherein is contained divers good and necessary documents, which beeing embraced and followed earnestly, may cause a man to shunne manie evilles and mischaunces, that may otherwise fall upon him, ere he can beware.   10

⟨*Quarr.* vol. i. p. 455 ll. 10-3⟩

This Ditty may be sung to the high 'Allemaigne Measure'; singing every last straine twise with the musicque.

   'Softe fire makes sweete mault,' they say;
Few words well plast the wise will way.
Time idle spent, in trifles vaine,   15
Returnes no guerdon for thy paine:
But time well spent, doth profite bring,
And of good works will honour spring.
Bestow thy time then in such sort,
That vertue may thy deedes support: 20
The greater profite thou shalt see,
And better fame will goe of thee.

   In talke be sober, wise, and sadde,
Faire to thy freend, kind to the badde;
And let thy words so placed bee   25
As no man may findé fault with thee.
Nor meddle not in any case
With matters which thy witte surpasse:
With things that not to thee pertaines,
It folly were to beate thy braines;   30
For sudden blame may hap to thee,
In medling unadvisedly.

⟨*Euph.* i. 195 l. 26⟩

   Take heede, in any wise, I say,
What things thou goest about to-day,
That thou to-morrow not repent,   35
And with thy selfe be discontent.
Speake not such words to others' blame,
As afterward may turne thee shame.

No. 13. *As reprinted in 'Harleian Miscellany,'* vol. ix. *p.* 234, *ed. Park*

454 POEMS

⟨Euph. ii.
31 ll. 3-5⟩

To-day thou speakest, and doost not care,
But of tomorrow still beware :
For then thou canst not call againe,
What lavishly did passe thy braine.

Keepe secrete closely in thy minde 5
Things that thy state and credite binde ;
Beware, if thou doo them disclose,
To whom and where, for feare of foes :

⟨Euph. i.
281 ll. 32
sqq.⟩

Especially of him take heede
Whose trueth thou doost not know in deede. 10
For hard it is thy freend to know
From him that is a flattering foe :
And many men in showe are kind,
Yet worse then serpents in their mind.

⟨Euph. ii.
31 l. 10⟩

Be not too hasty in thy deedes ; 15
Of too much haste oft harme proceedes.
Be sober, mute ; take good advise,
For things too much are full of vice.
With moderation rule thee so,
As thou aside no way maist go : 20
For 'haste makes waste,' as proofe dooth say,

⟨Euph. i.
279 ll. 6-7⟩

And little said, soone mend ye may.
Forecast what after may befall ;
So shalt thou not be rashe at all.

Have minde still of thine owne offence, 25
Regard thy faults with good pretence :
Seeke not a moate in one to spie,
First pull the beame out of thine eye.
And find no fault with any man,
Except amend thy selfe thou can : 30
And when thy faults amended be,
The good that others see in thee,
Will learne them so their deedes to frame,
As they may likewise scape from blame.

⟨Euph. ii.
31 ll. 22-4⟩

Of no man give thou bad report, 35
Backbite not any in thy sport :

⟨End. i. 3.
58⟩

For words doo wound as deepe as swords,
Which many use in jesting boordes ;
And slaunder is a hainous hate,
Which dooth nought els but stirre debate ; 40
And twixt good freendes makes deadly strife,
To hazard one another's life :

And all this may proceede of thee,
Except thou wilt advised bee.

Beare freendly with thy neighbours fault,
Remember thou thy selfe maist halt.
If he hath ought offended thee, 5
Forgive, as thou the like wouldest be:
And thinke, if thou hast gone awrie,
Thou for forgivenesse must apply:
So with thy neighbour's faults doo beare,
And of thine owne stand still in feare. 10
Pardon as thou wouldest pardoned be,
So God will pardon him and thee.

Be gentle unto every wight, ⟨*Euph.* ii.
Let courtesie be thy delight: 31 ll. 6–25⟩
Familiar be with few, I say; 15
For sure it is the wisest waie.
Too much familiaritie
May bring thy sorrowes suddainly:
Therefore, keepe gentlenesse in mind;
To rich and poore be alwaies kind: 20
So pride shall never conquer thee,
Which is man's cheefest enemie.

14. (From A. Munday's *Banquet of Daintie Conceits*, 1588.)

A Dittie, wherein the brevitie of man's life is described, how soone his pompe vanisheth away, and he brought to his latest home.

This Ditty may be sung to the 'Venetian Allemaigne.' 25 ⟨Cf. *Euph.*
  The statelie pine whose braunches spreade so faire, i. 252
    By winde or weather wasted is at length; ll. 2–10,
  The sturdie oake that clymeth in the ayre, 308–11⟩
    In time dooth lose his beautie and his strength;
      The fayrest flower that florisht as to daie, 30 ⟨No. 15 st.
      To-morrow seemeth like the withered haie. 5, 18 st.
        10⟩

So fares it with the present state of man,
  Whose showe of healthe dooth argue manie yeeres:
But as his life is likened to a span,
  So suddaine sicknes pulles him from his peeres; 35
    And where he seemde for longer time to-daie,
    To-morrow lies he as a lumpe of clay.

No. 14. *As reprinted in* '*Harl. Misc.*' *vol.* ix. *p.* 238, *ed. Park*

The infant yong, the milk-white aged head,
  The gallant youth that braveth with the best,
We see with earth are quickly over-spreade,
  And both alike brought to their latest rest:
    As soone to market commeth to be solde,   5
    The tender lambe's skin, as the weather's old.

Death is not partiall: as the proverbe saies,
  The prince and peasant both with him are one;
The sweetest face that's painted now a daies,
  And highest head, set forth with pearle and stone,   10
    When he hath brought them to the earthly grave,
    Beare no more reckoning then the poorest slave.

The wealthy chuffe, that makes his gold his god,
  And scrapes and scratches all the mucke he may;
And with the world dooth play at even and od;   15
  When Death thinks good to take him hence away,
    Hath no more ritches in his winding-sheete,
    Then the poore soule that sterved in the streete.

Unhappie man! that runneth on thy race,
  Not minding where thy crased bones must rest: 20
But woe to thee that doost forget thy place,
  Purchast for thee, to live amongst the blest.
    Spend then thy life in such a good regard,
    That Christe's blessing may be thy reward!   24

15. (From A. Munday's *Banquet of Daintie Conceits*, 1588.)

A Glasse for all Men to behold themselves in; especially such proude and prodigall-minded Men, and such delicate and daintie Women, who (Cf. *Euph.* building on the pride of their beautie and amiable complexion, thinke i, passim; scorne to become aged; and that their sweete faces should be wrinckled, Sybilla in or their youthfulnes brought into subjection by age.
Sapho; and
No. 18)

This Ditty may be sung to the 'Earle of Oxenford's Galliard.'   30

(*Euph.* i.
189 l. 20)
  You youthfull heads, whose climing mindes
    Doo seeke for worldly praise,
  Whose yong desires doo seeme to scorne
    Olde age's staied waies.
  Beare with the plaine-song of my note,   35
    Which is so plaine in deede,
  As daintie mindes will scant endure
    So harshe a tale to reade.

No. 15. As reprinted in '*Harl. Miscellany,*' vol. ix. *pp.* 246-8, ed. *Park*

As nature hath endued your shapes *⟨Euph.* i.
　With exquisite perfection; 202-3⟩
And gives you choyse of sweete delights,
　Wherein you have affection:
When time hath runne his course in you,　　　　5
　The selfe-same nature saies—
That all these daintie toyes must die,
　Whereof you made your praise.

Marke how the yeere in course doth passe:
　Note first the plesant spring;　　　　　　　10
The earth by nature then affoordes
　Full many a precious thing:
Of fruits, of flowres, of wholsome hearbes
　We gather as we please;
And all things els we lacke beside,　　　　　　15
　Our needfull wants to ease.

And likewise, in this pleasant time,
　We take delight to walke,
To run and play at barley-breake,
　And in our gardens talke;　　　　　　　　20
One freend an other dooth invite,
　They feast and make good cheere;
Both rich and poore doo make pastime,
　At this time of the yeere.

But wreakfull winter drawing on,　　　　　25 ⟨*Mar-*
　Withdraweth these delights, *Martine,*
And robbes us of them, one by one, st. 2⟩
　As toyes and trifling sights.
The scith cuttes downe the goodlie grasse,
　That grew so greene to day;　　　　　　　30
And all the sweete and pleasant flowers ⟨No. 14 st.
　Are changed then to hay. 1, 18 st.
　　　　　　　　　　　　　　　　　　　　　　　　10⟩
The trees, that bragged in their leaves,
　The bitter blasts doo bight;
And chaunge them from their goodly state　　35
　To olde and withered plight:
And they that flocked to the feeldes,
　When summer was so brave,
Nowe closelie creepe about the fire
　For winter warmth will have.　　　　　　40

Compare we now the yeerely chaunge,
　With man's appointed race,

(No. 28
l. 25, &c.)

Who in the Aprill of his age
   Greene humours dooth embrace:
And as Maie-flowers glad the eye,
   So in his youthfull time,
Man compasseth a world of joyes,   5
   Whereto his thoughts doo clime.

Behold, likewise, dame Beautie's gyrles,
   Whose daintie mindes are such,
As not the sun-shine, nor the wind,
   Must their faire faces touch: 10

(*Euph.*
i. 255
ll. 5 sqq.)

Theyr maskes, their fannes, and all the toyes,
   That wanton heads can crave,
To maintaine beautie in her pride,
   These prancking dames must have.

But elder yeeres approching on   15
   A little every daie,
Their daintie beautie dooth decline,
   And vanisheth away.
And as colde Winter chaseth hence
   The pleasant Summer daies,   20
So withered age encountreth youth,
   Amidst his wanton waies.

You that thinke scorne of auncient age,
   And hold him in contempt,
To make of beautie such a price,   25
   And to vaine thoughts are bent.
Remember Nature yeelds to course,
   And course his race will have,
From the first howre of your byrth
   Untill you come to grave.   30

Age is an honour unto them
   That live to see the same,
And none but vaine and foolish hands
   Will blot olde age with blame;
Who oftentimes are soone cut off,   35
   And not so happy blest,
To see the dayes their fathers did,
   Before they went to rest.

Thrise happy they that spend their youth
   In good and vertuous wise.   40
Forsaking all such vaine desires
   As wanton heads surmise,

And wholie doo direct themselves
Unto his will that made them,
Then Folly never can have power
From Vertue to disswade them.

II. EARLY LOVE-POEMS: BEFORE 1580?

16. (From *Addit. MS.* 22,601, ff. 56 v.–59 v.) ⟨Cf. *Euph.* and *Sapho*, passim⟩

Who loues and would his suite should proue
⟨To⟩ winn his Mistress to his will,
That she likes he must seeme to loue
And what she loues comend it still.
    Then at fitt time preferr yor sute
    Let not sharpe answers strike yo^u mute.   10

Their Castells on such ground are sett
as vndermyninge may them take
The walls so weake no strength can lett
shott soone therein a breache will make
    Their forces are so weake within   15
    small pow^r serues their forts to win.

If men haue tongues to craue & pray
aswell as women to deny
No stronger is their no or nay
then force of wise mens yes or I.   20
    For mens perswations stronger are
    then womens noes are much by farr.

Their no is weake & blunt also
such weapons weakely do defend
Mens yea so sharpe will pierce their no   25
and Conquer them if they contend.
    Then feare not force, where force is none
    least feare yor force do ouercome

There Sex withstands not place (if fitt⟨ ⟩)
no⟨r⟩ speache, for be she base or hie   30
A womans ey doth guide hir witt
hir witt doth neuer guide hir eye
    Then senceles is he y^t can speake
    feares to the best his loue to breake.

       The brauer mart the better matche
       and willinger of all is sought
       And willinge sute doth euer catche
       foule Vulcan so faire Venus cought
⟨*Euph.* ii. 53 l. 25⟩   Were she a Quene she would be wonne   5
          if cuñingly yor race you runne.

⟨*Sapho,* ii. 4. 76–7⟩ He that can rubb hir gamesome vaine
       and also temper toyes with art
       Makes Loue swim at hir eies amaine
       and so to diue into hir hart   10
          Their Sex are weake, weake forts cañott
          wthstand the force of Cañon shott.

       I argue not of hir estate
       but all my rest I sett on this
⟨*Euph.* ii. 53 ll. 15 sqq.; *Loves Met.* ii. 1. 111⟩ That oportunity will mate   15
       and winn the coyest she y^t is.
          for to be Courted they desire
          to further pleasure to aspire.

⟨*Euph.* ii. 105 ll. 17–8⟩ The towne wch will to parly come
       will yeld to peace (though hye in state)   20
       And those no doubt will soone be wonne
       y^t courtinge loue which none do hate.
          If bloody warres they ment to vse
          perswations milde they would refuse.

       Although they seeme to scorne loues beck   25
       and in all shew the same to hate
⟨*Euph.* i. 213 ll. 6–7⟩ And though at first they giue ye check
       at last they gladly take the mate.
          for pleasure they to play beginn
          in sport they lose in sport they winn.   30

⟨*Saph.* i. 4. 41–7⟩ In words & lookes theis Ladies braue
       haue coye disdaine voide of loues fire
       But in their mindes & harts they haue
       a feruent and a hote desire.
          Reiectinge words mens suits deny   35
          alluringe iestures do say yea.

⟨*Euph.* ii. 119 ll. 23–5⟩ Courtinge makes them stoope to lure
       and guiftes reclaimes them to the fist
       And with y^t bridle and saddle sure
       you well may ride them where yo^u list   40
          In such cariers they run on still
          y^t yo^u may breake yor Launce at will.

If bewtifull a Lady be   ⟨*Saph.* ii.
with praises great you must hir moue: 4. 66-9⟩
If witty then be wonn will she
wth fine conceites the art of loue.
    If coye she be wth prayers sue,   5
    if proude then guifts must pleade for youe.   ⟨*Ib.*⟩
If Couetous she be indeede
with promises you must assay:
If wayward then wth force proceede.
but all the fault cn bewtie lay: 10
    And in one instant also vse
    some rare delight wth a iust excuse.
Sayinge thus: yor bewty doth me drawe
and eke compell me this to doe
No faulte in me for as the strawe   15
drawne by pure Iett must leape thereto   ⟨*Euph.* i.
    So I beinge forc'd deserue no blame   228 l. 25⟩
    sith that yor bewty forc'd the same.
When you haue don no doubt but she
the better like and loue you will   20
faire Helen may example be
howe Menelaus she hated still
    His softnes made him woo in vaine
    she did his humblenes disdaine.
Enforcinge Paris she did loue   25 ⟨*Saph.* ii. 4.
and like for forcinge hir so well   93-5⟩
That greatest dangers she would proue
with him for to remaine & dwell.
    yet she confest as it was righte
    the Gretian was the better knighte.   30
But Menelaus takes hart, and soe   ⟨*Euph.* i.
by force recouers hir againe   234 ll. 28-
By force makes hir with him to goe   30⟩
by force enioyes hir not in vaine
    for when he manlike Deedes did vse   35
    to yeld to him she could not chuse.
And she y^t neuer like him coulde
for seruice and for reuerence
Did euer after deare him holde
and loue him eke for violence   40
    Tis modesty that they refraine
    what they refuse they would haue faine.

        41 that they] they not *MS.*

Though women striue & disagree
they meane not for to ouercome,
Though they full angrie seeme to be
well pleas'd they are when well tis done.
   They would not striue nor yet denye   5
   but y^t mens forces they would trye.

The modestie of Men I finde
they like not, yet it praises lend
They hate the fearefull dasterd minde
that offers not for feare t' offend   10
   Then feare not for to beard the best
   kindely they kindenes will digest.

If that she do dislike before
you do attempt hir for to win,
Then she can do at last no more   15
howe euer you hir vse therein.
   With lyinge still no forte is gott
   nor Castell battered wthout shott.

And women thinke there is no fire
where they no sparkes of furie see   20
for to be courted they desire
though they in shew displeased bee.
   In womens mouthes in case of loue
   no, no negatiue will proue.

A womãs hart and tongue by kinde   25
should not be Relatiues alwaye
Neither is y^t Prouerbe true I finde
What hart doth thinke, ye tongue doth say
   They like ye Lapwinge off do flye
   and farthest from their Nests do crye.   30

They vse denialls & sharpe quippes
not for because they do not loue
But partly for to shew their witts
and eke mens constancie to proue.
   Though they refuse it will appeare   35
   tis but th' obtayninge to endeare.

If women were not frendly foes
beinge hable for to ouercome
They would not softly strike wth noes
nor yet vnto a parley come.   40
   Or if mens suites they did disdaine
   to answer them they would refraine.

⟨*Euph.* ii.
92 ll. 4–5⟩
⟨*Euph.* ii.
4 ll. 18–9,
&c.⟩

EARLY LOVE-POEMS

Take heede do not at first shott yelde
their tongues will once the battell sounde
At last you sure shall winn the field
if that you well will keepe yor grounde
    If that ye forte she hold out longe   5
    the next assaults then make more stronge.

When as a fearfull Horsman backs
a ready horse the horse will bounde
And for to leape he neuer slacks
till he hath throwne him to the grounde   10
    But if a horsman good he finde
    will sitt him close he yeldes by kinde.

Vnworthy life y^t Hounde we deeme
wch giues ye chase of at first fault   ⟨*Euph.* ii.
So of such men they not esteeme   15 130 l. 28⟩
for one repulse wch leaues th' assault
    That loue is weakely built they knowe
    wch one denyall downe doth blowe.

If y^t in chase so ill you holde
as for one faulte to leaue the same   20
They will suppose yor suite is colde
and thinke you care not for ye game.
    for women this account do make
    they will say no and yet will take.

The Souldio^r faint wch standeth still   25 ⟨*Euph.* ii.
in battell fearing Enemies sight   106 l. 12⟩
Is sooner slaine then he y^t will
the brauest onsett giue in fighte
    Then if you loue be not afraide
    to beard the best as I haue saide.   30

17. (From *Rawlinson MS. Poet.* 148, ff. 2–3.)
            Of lingeringe Loue.   ⟨Cf. Nos.
                              18 and 48⟩
    1. In lingeringe Loue mislikinge growes,
      Wherby our fancies ebbs and flowes:
      We love to day, and hate to morne,
      And dayly wher we list to scorne.   35
          Take heede therfore,
      If she mislike, then love no more:
          Quicke speed makes waste,
      Loue is not gotten in such haste.

2. The sute is colde that soone is done,
   The forte is feeble easly wonne:
   The haulke that soone comes by her pray,
   may take a Toye and sore away.
      Marke what means this,
   Some thincke to hitt & yet they misse:
      ffirst creepe, then goe,
   Me thinke⟨s⟩ our loue is handled soe.

3. ffor lacke of Bellowes the fire goes out,
   Some say, the next way is about:
   ffew thinges are had without some sute,
   The tree at first will beare no fruite.
      Serue longe, Hope well,
   Loe heere is all that I can tell:
      Tyme tries out troth,
   And troth is likt' wher ere it goth.

4. Some thincke all theirs that they doe seeke,
   Some wantons wooe but for a weeke:
   Some wooe to shew their subtile witte,
   Such Palfreyes play vpon their bitte.
      ffine heads god knowes,
   That plucke a nettle for a rose:
      They meete their mach,
   And fare the woorsse because they snach.

5. We silly women can not rest,
   for Men that love to woe in iest:
   Some lay their baite in ev'ry nooke,
   And ev'ry fish doth spie their hooke.
      Ill ware, good cheape,
   Which makes vs looke before we leape;
      Craft, can cloke much,
   God saue all simple soules from such.

6. Though lingeringe Loue be lost some while,
   Yet lingeringe louers laugh and smile:
   Who will not linger for a day,
   May banish hope and happ away.
      Loue must be plide,
   Who thinckes to sayle must wayte ye tide:
      Thus ends this dance:
   God send all ling'rers happie chance.

          Finis.

36 May] To *Park*

Side notes:
⟨*Euph.* ii. 105 l. 17 and No. 18, passim⟩
⟨*Euph.* ii. 149 l. 30; No. 18 st. 6⟩
⟨*Euph.* ii. 81, 95, passim⟩

18. (From Clement Robinson's *A Handefull of Pleasant Delites*, 1584.)

A Warning for Wooers,

that they be not over hastie, nor deceived with
womens beautie.

To—'Salisburie Plaine.'

<pre>
Ye loving wormes, come learne of me,   5
The plagues to leave that linked be;
The grudge, the grief, the gret anoy,
The fickle faith, the fading ioy,
    In time take heed ;
In fruitlesse soile sow not thy seed :   10
    Buie not, with cost,
The thing that yeelds but labour lost.

If Cupids dart do chance to light,
So that affection dimmes thy sight ;
Then raise up reason, by and by,   15
With skill thy heart to fortifie ;
    Where is a breach,
Oft times too late doth come the Leach :
    Sparks are put out,
When furnace flames do rage about.   20

Thine owne delay must win the field,
When lust doth leade thy heart to yeeld :
When steed is stolne, who makes al fast,
May go on foot for al his haste :
    In time shut gate,   25
For had I wist, doth come too late :
    Fast bind, fast find ;
Repentance alwaies commeth behind.

The Syrens tunes oft time beguiles,
So doth the teares of Crocodiles ;   30
But who so learnes Ulysses lore,
May passe the seas, and win the shore.
    Stop eares, stand fast,
Through Cupids trips, thou shalt him cast ;
    Flie baits, shun hookes,   35
Be thou not snarde with lovely lookes.
</pre>

⟨*Camp.* v. 3. 30 note; *Euph.* ii. 13 l. 28 note⟩

⟨No. 41[2] l. 6⟩

⟨Cf. imagery, No. 25 stt. 2-3⟩

No. 18. *As reprinted in Park's 'Heliconia,' vol.* ii. *pp.* 53-7. *He also gave part of it in 'Censura Literaria,'* i. 143-6   6 leave] *qy.?* love

Where Venus hath the maisterie,
There love hath lost her libertie :
Where love doth win the victorie,
The fort is sackt with crueltie.
    First look, then leap,
In suretie so your skinnes you keepe ;
    The snake doth sting,
That lurking lieth with hissing.

Where Cupids fort hath made a waie,
There grave advise doth beare no swaie ;
Where love doth raigne, and rule the roste,
There reason is exilde the coast :
    Like all, love none,
Except ye use discretion :
    First try, then trust,
Be not deceived with sinful lust.

Marke Priams sonne, his fond devise,
When Venus did obtaine the prise ;
For Pallas skil, and Junoes strength,
He chose that bred his bane, at length.
    Choos wit, leave wil,
Let Helen be with Paris stil :
    Amis goeth al
Wher fancie forceth fooles to fall.

Where was there found a happier wight
Than Troylus was, til love did light ?
What was the end of Romeus ?
Did he not die, like Piramus ?
    Who baths in blis,
Let him be mindful of Iphis :
    Who seeks to plese,
May ridden be, like Hercules.

I lothe to tel the peevish brawles,
And fond delights, of Cupids thrawles ;
Like Momish mates of Midas mood,
They gape to get that doth no good :
    Now down, now up,
As tapsters use to tosse the cup :
    One breedeth ioy,
Another breeds as great anoy.

Some love for wealth, and some for hue,
And none of both these loves are true:
For when the mil hath lost her sailes,
Then must the miller lose his vailes:
    Of grasse commeth hay,
And flowers faire wil soon decay:
    Of ripe commeth rotten;
In age al beautie is forgotten.

Some loveth too hie, and some too lowe,
And of them both great griefs do grow;
And some do love the common sort,
And common folke use common sport.
    Looke not too hie,
Least that a chip fall in thine eie:
    But hie or lowe,
Ye may be sure she is a shrow.

But, Sirs, I use to tell no tales;
Ech fish that swims doth not beare scales;
In everie hedge I find not thornes;
Nor everie beast doth carrie hornes:
    I saie not so,
That everie woman causeth wo:
    That were too broad;
Who loveth not venom, must shun the tode.

Who useth still the truth to tel,
May blamed be, though he saie wel:
Say crowe is white, and snowe is blacke,
Lay not the fault on woman's backe;
    . Thousands were good,
But few scapte drowning in Noes flood:
    Most are wel bent;
I must say so, least I be shent.

FINIS.

19. (From Clement Robinson's *A Handefull of Pleasant Delites*, 1584.)

A Proper Sonet,
intituled, 'I smile to see how you devise.'
To anie pleasant Tune.

(Cf. Euph. to Lucilla, i. 239-40; *Woman*, iii, iv, v, pass.; and No. 47)

I smile to see how you devise
  New masking nets my eies to bleare;   5
Your self you cannot so disguise,
  But as you are, you must appeare.

Your privie winkes at boord I see,
  And how you set your raving mind:
Your self you cannot hide from me,   10
  Although I wincke, I am not blind.

The secret sighs, and fained cheare,
  That oft doth paine thy carefull brest,
To me right plainly doth appeare;
  I see in whom thy hart doth rest.   15

And though ⟨thou⟩ makest a fained vow,
  That love no more thy heart should nip;
Yet think I know, as well as thou,
  The fickle helm doth guide the ship.

The salamander in the fire,   20
  By course of kinde, doth bathe his limmes:
The floting fish taketh his desire
  In running streames, whereas he swimmes.

(No. 47 st. 3)

So thou in change doth take delight;
  Ful wel I know thy slipperie kinde: 25
In vaine thou seemst to dim my sight,
  Thy rowling eies bewraieth thy minde.

(*Ib.* st. 4)

I see him smile, that doth possesse
  Thy love, which once I honoured most:
If he be wise, he may well gesse,   30
  Thy love, soon won, wil soon be lost.

And sith thou canst no man intice,
  That he should stil love thee alone;
Thy beautie now hath lost her price,
  I see thy savorie sent is gone.   35

No. 19. As *reprinted in Park's 'Heliconia,' vol.* ii. *pp.* 65-7. *He also gave it in 'Cens. Lit.'* i. 143-6

FOUR SONGS

    Therefore, leave off thy wonted plaie ;
    But as thou art thou wilt appeare,
    Unlesse thou canst devise a waie
      To dark the sun, that shines so cleare.

    And keep thy friend, that thou hast won ;   5
    In trueth to him thy love supplie ;
    Least he at length, as I have done,
      Take off thy belles, and let thee flie.

20. (From *Addit. MS.* 15,232, f. 12 v.)

O happ moste harde where truthe doth most beguyle
O churlishe chaunce where love gives caus to loth   10
O face moste fals wch frowneth by a smyle
O fayned faithe wch loves and hateth both
My saftye stayes where dainger ever bydes
My settled truste standes faste one waveringe doutt
No steddfaste staye is that wch ever slydes   15
Displeased contente still neither in nor oute⟨.⟩
To maske my mynde where moste yt woulde be seen   ⟨Cf. No. 10⟩
To hyde my hurtes where healinge handes should helpe
To saye a naye where soothe doth beste beseeme
Shewes but a foole one Mother Cowardes whelpe   20
Wherefor I dare saye as I saide before
And faine woulde doe yf donne I live no more

III. FOUR SONGS
(TO REPLACE SOME MISSING FROM THE PLAYS)

21. (From Thomas Morley's *First Booke of Balletts*, 1600 : No. 4.)

    Sing wee and chaunt it,   ⟨Cf. *Camp.*
    While loue doth graunt it.   v. 3. 38 :
      Fa la la la.   25 the missing song
    Not long youth lasteth,   between
    And old age hasteth,   Milectus,
    Now is best leysure,   Phrygius,
    To take our pleasure.   and Lais⟩
      Fa la la la.   30

No. 20. *The MS., which includes some of the 'Astrophel and Stella' sonnets in a hand like Sidney's, has been associated, on no good authority, with his sister and Wilton. The last line of this sonnet suggests Donne's habit of punning on his name ; but I trace him nowhere else in the MS.*   No. 21. *Also in 'Cens. Lit.'* ii. 88, *and Bullen's 'Lyrics from Song-Books,' p.* 211

470   POEMS

    All things inuite vs,
    Now to delight vs.
        Fa la la la.
    Hence care be packing,
    No mirth bee lacking,   5
    Let spare no treasure,
    To liue in pleasure.
        Fa la la la.

⟨Cf. *Endim.* ii. 3. 40 'sing the inchantment for sleepe'⟩

22. (From *Harl. MS.* (c. 1596) 6910, f. 164.)

  Sleepe, Deathes alye, obliuion of teares,
   Silence of Passions, balme of angrie sore 10
  Suspence of loues, Securitie of feares
    Wraths Lenatiue, Hearts ease, stormes calmest shore,
    Senses and Soules repriuall from all Combers
    Benuming sense of ill with quiet slumbers

23. (From *The Phœnix Nest*, 1593.)

⟨Cf. Endimion's speeches ii. 1. 39–43, 3. 1–20, &c.⟩

  ⟨Possibly the missing song of Geron, in *Endim.* iii. 4. 1.⟩

  Like to a Hermite poore in place obscure, 15
   I meane to spend my daies of endles doubt,
  To waile such woes as time cannot recure,
   Where none but Loue shall euer finde me out.

  My foode shall be of care and sorow made,
   My drink nought else but teares falne from mine eies, 20
  And for my light in such obscured shade,

⟨No. 63 l. 28⟩

   The flames shall serue, which from my hart arise.

  A gowne of graie, my bodie shall attire,
   My staffe of broken hope whereon Ile staie,
  Of late repentance linckt with long desire, 25
   The couch is fram'de whereon my limbes Ile lay,

    And at my gate dispaire shall linger still,
    To let in death when Loue and Fortune will.

  No. 22. Also printed in Brydges' '*Excerpta Tudoriana*,' vol. i. *p.* 16.
  No. 23. Also in *Harl. MS.* 6910, *f.* 139. Park ('*Heliconia*,' vol. ii. *p.* 153) notes ' These are the original words of the celebrated song set by Alfonso Ferabosco and Nicholas Laniere, and referred to by Walton in his "Complete Angler," by North in his life of the Lord-Keeper Guildford, by Phineas Fletcher in his metaphrase of the 42d psalm, and by Butler in part i. canto 2, of "Hudibras."' Dr. Hannah printed it among '*Raleigh's Poems*' 1875, *p.* 12, with note '*Ascribed to Raleigh in " To day a Man, tomorrow none*" 1643–4; *King's Pamphlets* B. M. vol. 139. It is anonymous in "*Phœn. Nest*" *p.* 69; in "*Tixall Poetry*" *p.* 115; in *Rawl. MS.* 85, *f.* 21 *v.*; in *Harl. MS.* 6910, *f.* 139 *v.*, &c.'

24. (From John Dowland's *Second Booke of Songs or Ayres*, 1600 :
No. 1.)

⟨Cf. *Woman in the Moone*, i. 1. 224: the missing song of the Shepherds to calm Pandora.⟩

  I saw my Lady weepe,
And sorrow proud to bee aduanced so,
In those faire eies, where all perfections keepe :
  Hir face was full of woe,
But such a woe (beleeue me) as wins more hearts,   5
Then mirth can doe with hir intysing parts.

  Sorow was there made faire,
And passion wise, teares a delightfull thing,
Silence beyond all speech a wisdome rare,
  Shee made hir sighes to sing,   10
And all things with so sweet a sadnesse moue,
As made my heart at once both grieue and loue.

  O fayrer then ought ells,
The world can snew, leaue of in time to grieue,
Inough, inough, your ioyfull lookes excells,   15
  Teares kills the heart belieue,
O striue not to bee excellent in woe,
Which onely breeds your beauties ouerthrow.

IV. LATER LOVE-POEMS.

25. (From William Byrd's *Psalmes, Sonets, & songs*, 1588 : No. 25.)   ⟨Cf. No. 34⟩

Farewell false loue, the oracle of lyes,
A mortal foe, & enimie to rest :
An enuious boy, from whome all cares aryse,   20
A bastard vile, a beast with rage possest :
  A way of error, a temple ful of treason,
  In all effects contrarie vnto reason.

A poysoned serpent couered all with flowers,   25   ⟨Cf. imagery, No. 18⟩
Mother of sighes, and murtherer of repose,
A sea of sorows frō whēce are drawē such showers,
As moysture lend to euerie griefe that growes,
  A school of guile, a net of deepe deceit,
  A guilded hooke, that holds a poysoned bayte.   30

Nos. 24-5 *also in Bullen's* ' *Lyrics from Elizabethan Song-Books*,' *pp.* 13, 144 ; *and No.* 25 *in* ' *Censura Literaria,*' ii. 115. *No authors suggested*.

A fortress foyled, which reason did defend,
A Syren song, a feauer of the minde,
A maze wherein affection finds no ende,
A raging cloude that runnes before the winde,
 A substance like the shadow of the Sunne,   5
 A goale of griefe for which the wisest runne.

A quenchlesse fire, a nurse of trembling feare,
A path that leads to perill and mishap,
A true retreat of sorrow and dispayre,
An idle boy that sleepes in pleasures lap,   10
 A deepe mistrust of that which certaine seemes,
 A hope of that which reason doubtfull deemes.

FINIS.

26. (From William Byrd's *Songs of sundrie natures*, 1589: No. 10.)

When younglyngs first on Cupide fyxe their sight,
 And see him naked, blyndfold & a boy,   15
Though bow & shafts and fier-brand be his might,
 Yet weene they he can worke them none annoy.

⟨*LovesMet.* ii. 1.51–61⟩

And therefore with his purpill wings they play,
 For glorious semeth loue though light as fether,
And when they haue done they weene to skape away,   20
 For blynd men, say they, shoote they know not whether.

But when by proofe they finde that he did see,
 & that his wound did rather dym their sight,
They wonder more how such a lad as he,
 Should be of such surpassing powre and might: 25
  But Ants haue gals, so hath the Bee his styng,
  Then sheeld me heauens from such a subtyle thing.

⟨*Euph.* ii. 90 l. 23; and Nos. 41¹⁻²⟩

27. (From William Byrd's *Songs of sundrie natures*, 1589: No. 30.)

When I was otherwise then now I am,
I loued more but skilled not so much:
Fayre wordes and smyles could haue contented than,   30
My simple age & ignorance was such:
 But at the length experience made me wonder,
 That harts & tongues did lodge so farre asunder.

As watermen which on the Teames do row
Looke to the East, but West keepes on the way,   35

⟨*Gall.* iv. 2. 53–6; *Bisham,* p. 474 l. 5; *Sudeley,* p. 479 l. 14, &c.⟩
⟨*Endim.* iv. 2. 57⟩

No. 26. *Also in Bullen's ' Lyrics from Elizabethan Song-Books,' p. 72*

LATER LOVE-POEMS

My Soueraigne sweet, her countenance setled so,
To feede my hope while she her snares might laye.
And when she sawe that I was in her danger,
Good God, how soone she proued then a ranger.

I could not choose but laugh although to late,   5   ⟨*Euph.* i.
To see great craft diszifered in a toye,   228 l. 28;
I loue her still, but such conditions hate,   *Bee*, st. 11⟩
Which so prophanes my Paradice of ioy.
    Loue whetts the witts, whose paine is but a pleasure,
    A toy, by fitts, to play withall at leasure.   10

28. (From *Addit. MS.* 22,601, f. 26.)

    A Gentlewoman y^t married a yonge Gent who after
    forsooke ⟨hir,⟩ wherevppon she tooke hir Needle
      in wch she was excelēt & wo^{r}ked
         vpō hir Sampler thus

Come, giue me needle, stitch cloth, silke & chaire   15
    y^t I may sitt and sigh, and sow & singe
For perfect coollo^{r}s to discribe ye aire
    a subtile persinge changinge constant thinge   ⟨*Bisham*,
No false stitch will I make, my hart is true   p. 474 l.
    plaine stitche my Sampler is for to cōplaine   20   20⟩
How men haue tongues of hony, harts of rue.   ⟨No. 39
    true tongues & harts are one, men makes them twaine.   st. 3⟩
Giue me black silk y^t sable suites my hart   ⟨No. 27⟩
    & yet som white though white words do deceiue
No green at all for youth & I must part   25   ⟨P. 458
    Purple & blew, fast loue & faith to weaue.   ll. 1-2⟩
Mayden no more sleepeless ile goe to bedd
Take all away, ye work works in my hedd.

29. (From *The Phœnix Nest*, 1593.)

Feede still thy selfe, thou fondling with beliefe,
    Go hunt thy hope, that neuer tooke effect,   30
Accuse the wrongs that oft hath wrought thy griefe,
    And reckon sure where reason would suspect.

No. 28. *Printed with others from the same MS. in vol.* xv *of Early Eng. Poetry, Ballads,* &c., *Percy Society* ('*Poetical Miscellanies*' *No.* iv)   No. 29. *This and the next seven poems, as well as Nos.* 6 *and* 23, *are taken from Collier's reprint of* '*The Phœnix Nest*' *in* '*Seven English Poetical Miscellanies*,' 1867, *Pt.* iv

Dwell in the dreames of wish and vaine desire,
    Pursue the faith that flies and seekes to new,
Run after hopes that mocke thee with retire,
    And looke for loue where liking neuer grew.

Deuise conceits to ease thy carefull hart,   5
    Trust vpon times and daies of grace behinde,
Presume the rights of promise and desart,
    And measure loue by thy beleeuing minde.

Force thy affects that spite doth daily chace,
    Winke at thy wrongs with wilfull ouersight,   10
See not the soyle and staine of thy disgrace,
    Nor recke disdaine, to doate on thy delite.

And when thou seest the end of thy reward,
    And these effects ensue of thine assault,
When rashnes rues, that reason should regard,   15
    Yet still accuse thy fortune for the fault.

    And crie, O Loue, O death, O vaine desire,
    When thou complainst the heate, and feeds⟨t⟩ the fire.

30. (From *The Phœnix Nest*, 1593.)

⟨Cf. No. 31⟩

Those eies which set my fancie on a fire,
Those crisped haires, which hold my hart in chains,   20
Those daintie hands, which conquer'd my desire,
That wit, which of my thoughts doth hold the rains.

Those eies for cleerenes doe the starrs surpas,
Those haires obscure the brightnes of the Sunne,
Those hands more white, than euer Iuorie was,   25
That wit euen to the skies hath glorie woon.

O eies that pearce our harts without remorse,
O haires of right that weares a roiall crowne,
O hands that conquer more than Cæsars force,
O wit that turns huge kingdoms vpside downe.   30

    Then Loue be Judge, what hart can thee withstand:
    Such eies, such haire, such wit, and such a hand.

10 thy] the *Collier*   No. 30. *Also given in Mr. Bullen's 'Lyrics from Elizabethan Song-Books' from William Barley's 'New Book of Tabliture,' 1596, where the closing couplet is wrongly placed as ll. 5–6:* 'A free rendering of Desportes' sonnet, " Du bel œil de Diane est ma flamme empruntée," ' p. 221   23 doth *Bullen*   28 wear *Bullen*   31 can thee withstand] may therewith stand *Bullen*   32 haire] head *Bullen*

LATER LOVE-POEMS

31. (From *The Phœnix Nest*, 1593.) ⟨Cf. No. 30⟩

Those eies that holds the hand of euery hart,
  Those hands that holds the hart of euery eie,
That wit that goes beyond all natures art,
  That sence, too deepe, for wisdome to descrie,
    That eie, that hand, that wit, that heauenly sence,   5
    All these doth show my Mistres Excellence.

Oh eies that perce into the purest hart,
  Oh hands that hold, the highest harts in thrall,
Oh wit that weyes the deapth of all desart,
  Oh sence that showes the secret sweete of all,   10
    The heauen of heauens, with heuenly powrs preserue thee,
    Loue but thy selfe, and giue me leaue to serue thee.

To serue, to liue, to looke vpon those eies,
  To looke, to liue, to kisse that heauenlie hand,
To sound that wit, that doth amaze the wise,   15
  To knowe that sence, no sence can vnderstand,
    To vnderstande that all the world may know,
    Such wit, such sence, eies, hands, there are no moe.

32. (From *The Phœnix Nest*, 1593.)

By wracke late driuen on shore, from Cupids Crare,
  Whose sailes of error, sighes of hope and feare,   20
Conueied through seas of teares, and sands of care,
  Till rocks of high disdaine, hir sides did teare,
    I write a dirge, for dolefull doues to sing,
    With selfe same quill, I pluckt from Cupids wing.

Farewell vnkinde, by whom I fare so ill,   25
Whose looks bewitcht my thoughts with false surmise,
Till forced reason did vnbinde my will,
And shewed my hart, the follie of mine eies,
    And saide, attending where I should attaine,
    Twixt wish and want, was but a pleasing paine.   30

Farewell vnkinde, my floode is at an ebbe
My troubled thoughts, are turnd to quiet wars,
My fancies hope hath spun and spent hir webbe,
My former wounds are closed vp with skars,
    As ashes lie, long since consumde with fire,   35   ⟨Life, i. 26 (Letter)⟩
    So is my loue, so now is my desire.

31 floode] floate *Collier*

Farewell vnkinde, my first and finall loue,
Whose coie contempts, it bootes not heere to name,
But gods are iust, and euery star aboue,
Doth threat reuenge, where faiths reward is blame,   5
    And I may liue, though your despised thrall,
    By fond mischoyce, to see your fortunes fall.

Farewell vnkinde, most cruell of your kinde,
By whom my worth, is drowned in disdaines,
As was my loue, so is your iudgement blinde,
My fortune ill, and such hath beene my gaines,   10
    But this for all, I list no more to saie,
    Farewell faire proude, not lifes, but loues decaie.

33. (From *The Phœnix Nest*, 1593.)

A COUNTERLOUE.

⟨Cf. 'The Cooling Carde' *Euph*. i. 246–57⟩

Declare, O minde, from fond desires excluded,
That thou didst find erewhile, by Loue deluded.   15
An eie, the plot, whereon Loue sets his gin,
Beautie, the trap, wherein the heedles fall,
A smile, the traine, that drawes the simple in,
Sweete words, the wilie instrument of all,
    Intreaties posts, faire promises are charmes,   20
    Writing, the messenger, that wooes our harmes.

Mistresse, and seruant, titles of mischaunce:
Commaundments done, the act of slauerie,
Their coulors worne, a clownish cognisaunce,
And double dutie, pettie drudgerie,   25
    And when she twines and dallies with thy locks,
    Thy freedome then is brought into the stocks.

To touch hir hand, hir hand bindes thy desire,
To weare hir ring, hir ring is Nessus gift,
To feele hir brest, hir brest doth blowe the fire,   30
To see hir bare, her bare a baleful drift,
    To baite thine eies thereon, is losse of sight,
    To thinke of it, confounds thy senses quite.

⟨*Euph*. ii. 131 l. 24⟩

Kisses the keies, to sweete consuming sin,
Closings, Cleopatras adders at thy brest,   35
Fained resistance then she will begin,
And yet vnsatiable in all the rest,
    And when thou doost vnto the act proceede,
    The bed doth grone, and tremble at the deede.

Beautie, a siluer dew that falls in May,
Loue is an Egshell, with that humor fild,
Desire, a winged boy, comming that way,
Delights and dallies with it in the field,
   The firie Sun, drawes vp the shell on hie,   5
   Beautie decaies, Loue dies, desire doth flie.

     Vnharmd giue eare, that thing is hap'ly caught,
     That cost some deere, if thou maist ha't for naught.

(Euph. i. 189 l. 14)*

34. (From *The Phœnix Nest*, 1593.)

        The Description of Iealousie.

A seeing friend, yet enimie to rest,   10
   A wrangling passion, yet a gladsom thought,
A bad companion, yet a welcom guest,
   A knowledge wisht, yet found too soone vnsought,
From heauen supposde, yet sure condemn'd to hell,
Is Iealousie, and there forlorne doth dwell.   15

(Cf. *Euph.* ii. 226 l.10; and No.25)

And thence doth send fond feare and false suspect,
   To haunt our thoughts bewitched with mistrust,
Which breedes in vs the issue and effect,
   Both of conceits and actions far vniust,
The griefe, the shame, the smart wherof doth proue,   20
That Iealousie's both death and hell to Loue.

(Cf. No. 38 ll. 27–8)

For what but hell moues in the iealous hart,
   Where restles feare works out all wanton ioyes,
Which doth both quench and kill the louing part,
   And cloies the minde with worse than knowne annoyes,   25
Whose pressure far exceeds hells deepe extreemes,
Such life leads Loue entangled with misdeemes.

35. (From *The Phœnix Nest*, 1593.)

Short is my rest, whose toile is ouerlong,
   My ioyes are darke, but cleere I see my woe,
My safetie small: great wracks I bide by wrong,   30
   Whose time is swift, and yet my hap but sloe,
Each griefe and wound, in my poore hart appeeres,
That laugheth howres, and weepeth many yeeres.

Deedes of the day, are fables for the night,
   Sighes of desire, are smoakes of thoughtfull teares,   35

(*LovesMet.* iv. 1. 11–2)

No. 35. *Also in Harl. MS.* 6910, f. 148

My steps are false, although my paths be right,
   Disgrace is bolde, and fauor full of feares,
Disquiet sleepe, keepes audit of my life,
Where rare content, doth make displeasure rife.
The dolefull bell, that is the voice of time,   5
   Cals on my end, before my haps be seene,
Thus fals my hopes, whose harmes haue power to clime,
   Not come to haue that long in wish hath beene,
I seeke your loue, and feare not others hate,
Be you with me, and I haue Cæsars state.   10

⟨Cf. *End.* passim⟩

36. (From *The Phœnix Nest*, 1593.)

⟨*Ib.* i.2.30⟩
⟨*Ib.* and iii. 4. 175⟩

Praisd be Dianas faire and harmles light,
Praisd be the dewes, wherwith she moists the ground;
Praisd be hir beames, the glorie of the night,
Praisd be hir powre, by which all powres abound.

⟨*Ib.* i.1.38⟩

Praisd be hir Nimphs, with whom she decks the woods,   15
Praisd be hir knights, in whom true honor liues,
Praisd be that force, by which she moues the floods,
Let that Diana shine, which all these giues.

⟨*Ib.*⟩

In heauen Queene she is, among the spheares,
In ay⟨er⟩ she Mistres like makes all things pure,   20
Eternitie in hir oft chaunge she beares,
She beautie is, by hir the faire endure.

⟨*Ib.* i.1.57, ii. 1. 85⟩

Time weares hir not, she doth his chariot guide,
Mortalitie belowe hir orbe is plaste,
By hir the vertue of the starrs doune slide,   25
In hir is vertues perfect image cast:

⟨P. 429 l. 32, &c.⟩

   A knowledge pure it is hir worth to kno,
   With Circes let them dwell that thinke not so.

37. (From John Dowland's *First Booke of Songes or Ayres*, 1597: No. 3.)

⟨Cf. No. [1 ll. 12, 16, 18, 25, 30⟩

My thoughts are wingde with hop⟨e⟩s, my hop⟨e⟩s with loue,
   Moũt loue vnto the moone in cleerest night,   30

No. 36. *Also in* '*Englands Helicon*' 1600, 1614, *with title* The Sheepheards praise of his sacred Diana. *Said to be signed* S. W. R. (= *Sir Walter Raleigh*), *with* Ignoto *printed on a slip pasted over it in extant copies: in the Brit. Mus. copy there is neither slip nor signature, but signs of some erasure. Signed* Ignoto, *ed.* 1614. *It was printed, though without conviction, among* '*Raleigh's Poems*' 1875, *p.* 77, *by Dr. Hannah*   20 She Mistress-like makes all things to be pure: *Eng. Hel.* For ay qy.? earth   No. 37. *Also in* '*Eng. Hel.*' 1600, 1614 *with title* Another to

And say as she doth in the heauens mooue
In earth so wanes & waxeth my delight: ⟨Endim.
And whisper this but softly in her eares, ii. 1. 32⟩
Hope oft doth hang the head, and trust shed teares.

And you my thoughts that some mistrust do cary, 5
If for mistrust my mistrisse do you blame,
Say though you alter, yet you do not varry, ⟨Mid. ii.
As she doth change, and yet remaine the same: 1. 7–12⟩
Distrust doth enter harts, but not infect, ⟨Endim.
And loue is sweetest seasned with suspect. 10 i. 1. 30–9,
 iii. 4.
If she for this, with cloudes do maske her eies, 156–7⟩
And make the heauens darke with her disdaine,
With windie sighes disperse them in the skies,
Or with thy teares dissolue them into raine;
Thoughts, hopes, & loue returne to me no more, 15
Till *Cynthia* shine as she hath done before.

38. (From *Englands Helicon*, 1600.)

A Nimphs disdaine of Loue.

Hey downe a downe did *Dian* sing,
 amongst her Virgins sitting:
Ther. loue there is no vainer thing, 20
 for Maydens most vnfitting,
And so think I, with a downe downe derrie.

When women knew no woe,
 but liu'd them-selues to please:
Mens fayning guiles they did not know, 25 ⟨*Euph*. ii.
 the ground of their disease. 57 ll. 15
Vnborne was false suspect, sqq., 121
 no thought of iealousie: ll. 10 sqq.;
From wanton toyes and fond affect, *Loues Met.*
 The Virgins life was free. v. 2.14–32;
Hey downe a downe did *Dian* sing &c. 30 *End.* ii. 1.
 61,iv.1.27⟩

his Cinthia, *assigned in Fr. Davison's MS. list to* 'Earle of Cumberland.' *Collier wrongly reported Dowland as attributing it to Greville* ('Bibl. Cat'): *and Grosart included it in Greville's* 'Works' ii. 133 *as* 'much in the same vein.'   2 In] On E. H.   so] *Collier misprints* she *in* 'Seven Poetical Miscellanies'   16 *Followed in E. H. by this note* These three ditties were taken out of Maister Iohn Dowlands booke of tableture for the Lute, the Authours names not there set downe, & therefore left to their owners; *the two preceding ones being* 'Come away, come sweet Loue,' *and* 'Away with these self-louing Lads'   No. 38. *Dr. Hannah rejects it from his* 'Raleigh's Poems' 1875, *noting, p.* xxxi, *that it was* 'claimed for Raleigh by Brydges and the Oxford editors' *on the mere ground of the signature* Ignoto   25 Mens] *Collier misprints* Mars

At length men vsed charmes,
 to which what Maides gaue eare:
Embracing gladly endlesse harmes,
 anone enthralled were.
Thus women welcom'd woe,
 disguis'd in name of loue:
A iealous hell, a painted show,
 so shall they finde that proue.

Hey downe a downe did *Dian* sing,
 amongst her Virgins sitting:
Then loue there is no vainer thing,
 for Maydens most vnfitting.
And so thinke I, with a downe downe derrie.

Ignoto.

FINIS.

39. (From *Englands Helicon*, 1600.)

The Nimphs reply to the Sheepheard.

If all the world and loue were young,
And truth in euery Sheepheards tongue,
These pretty pleasures might me moue,
To liue with thee, and be thy loue.

Time driues the flocks from field to fold,
When Riuers rage, and Rocks grow cold,
And *Philomell* becommeth dombe,
The rest complaines of cares to come.

⟨No. 18 st. 10⟩

The flowers doe fade & wanton fieldes,
To wayward winter reckoning yeeldes,
A honny tongue, a hart of gall,
Is fancies spring, but sorrowes fall.

⟨*Wom.*ii.1. 133; No. 59 st. 5; No. 28 l. 21, &c.⟩

Thy gownes, thy shooes, thy beds of Roses,
Thy cap, thy kirtle, and thy poesies,
Soone breake, soone wither, soone forgotten:
In follie ripe, in reason rotten.

⟨No. 18 st. 10⟩

Thy belt of straw and Iuie buddes,
Thy Corall claspes and Amber studdes,
All these in mee no meanes can moue,
To come to thee, and be thy loue.

But could youth last, and loue still breede,
Had ioyes no date, nor age no neede,
Then these delights my minde might moue,
To liue with thee, and be thy loue.

Ignoto. 5

FINIS.

40. (From *Englands Helicon*, 1600.)

Another of the same nature, made since.

Come liue with mee, and be my deere,
And we will reuell all the yeere,
In plaines and groaues, on hills and dales: 10
Where fragrant ayre breedes sweetest gales.

There shall you haue the beauteous Pine,
The Cedar, and the spreading Vine,
And all the woods to be a Skreene:
Least Phœbus kisse my Sommers Queene. 15

The seate for your disport shall be
Ouer some Riuer in a tree,
Where siluer sands, and pebbles sing,
Eternall ditties with the spring.

There shall you see the Nimphs at play, 20
And how the Satires spend the day,
The fishes gliding on the sands: ⟨*Woman*,
Offering their bellies to your hands. v. 1. 30⟩

The birds with heauenly tuned throates, ⟨*Ib*. iii. 1.
Possesse woods Ecchoes with sweet noates, 25 79, 2.
Which to your sences will impart, 167-8⟩
A musique to enflame the hart.

Vpon the bare and leafe-lesse Oake,
The Ring-Doues wooings will prouoke
A colder blood then you possesse, 30
To play with me and doo no lesse.

In bowers of Laurell trimly dight, ⟨*Ib*. iii. 1.
We will out-weare the silent night, 81⟩
While *Flora* busie is to spread:
Her richest treasure on our bed. 35

---

5 Ignoto] *printed on the page itself in the Br. Mus. copy* 1600, *and not on a slip pasted over the initials* S.W.R., *as is said to be the case in other extant copies: also* Ignoto *ed.* 1614

482   POEMS

  Ten thousand Glow-wormes shall attend,
  And all their sparkling lights shall spend,
  All to adorne and beautifie:
  Your lodging with most maiestie.

  Then in mine armes will I enclose   5
  Lillies faire mixture with the Rose,
  Whose nice perfections in loues play:
  Shall tune me to the highest key.

  Thus as we passe the welcome night,
  In sportfull pleasures and delight,   10
  The nimble Fairies on the grounds,
  Shall daunce and sing mellodious sounds.

  If these may serue for to entice,
  Your presence to Loues Paradice,
  Then come with me, and be my Deare: 15
  And we will straite begin the yeare.

    FINIS.   *Ignoto.*

⟨*Euph.* ii.
9⟩ ll. 22–3;
No. 26 l. 26;
Camp. v. 4.
129–31⟩
⟨*Saph.*
Prol. 2 l. 10⟩

41¹. (From Davison's *Poetical Rapsody*, 1602.)

  Naturall comparisons with perfect loue

  The lowest Trees haue tops, the Ante her gall,   20
  The flie her splene, the little sparkes their heate:
  The slender haires cast shadowes, though but small,
  And Bees haue stings, although they be not great:
    Seas haue their sourse, & so haue shallow springs,
    And loue is loue, in Beggars, as in Kings.   25

⟨*Eu.* ii. 56 l.
17, 65 l. 23⟩
⟨*Ib.* ii. 176 l.
7, 219 l. 1⟩

  Where riuers smoothest run, deepe are the foords,
  The Diall stirres, yet none perceiues it mooue:
  The firmest faith is in the fewest wordes,
  The Turtles cannot sing, and yet they loue:
    True Harts haue eyes, & eares, no tongs to speake,   30
    They heare, & see, and sigh, and then they breake.

              Incerto

  11 grounds 1600, 1614: ground *Bullen*   16 straite] then *Collier*   17 Ignoto *printed on the page itself* 1600, 1614   No. 41¹. *The two stt. reversed in Harl. MS.* 6910, *f.* 140 *v.*   19 Naturall ... loue *this heading in* '*Poet. Raps.*' 1608 *and follg. eds. only*   20 smallest *Harl. MS.*   21 sparke his *Rawl. MS.* 148, *Harl.* 6910   22 And heares haue Shadowes though they be but smalle *Harl. MS.*   24 litle *Harl. MS.*   25 as] and *Rawl. MS.*   26 riuers] waters *Rawl. Harl. MSS.*   are deepest foords *Harl. MS.*: yᵉʳ deepest are yᵉ floodes *Rawl. MS.*   27 can see *Harl. MS.*   28 is fownd in fewest *Rawl. MS.*: should bee in fairest *Harl. MS.*   29 cannot] doe not *Rawl. MS.*   30 tongue *Harl. MS.* 32 *unsigned ed.* 1611: *signed* Sir ⟨Mʳ *erased*⟩ Edward Dier *Rawl. MS.* 148, *f.* 50

41[2]. *An Answere to the first Staffe, that Loue is vnlike in Beggers and in Kings.*

Compare the Bramble with the Cedar tree,
The Pismyres anger with the Lyons rage:
What is the Buzzing flie where Eagles bee?
A drop the sparke, no seas can Aetna swage.
    Small is the heat in Beggers brests that springs, 5
    But flaming fire consumes the hearts of Kings.

Who shrouds himself where slender hairs cast shade:
But mighty Oakes may scorne the Summer Sun:
Smal cure wil serue, wher Bees the woūd haue made 10
But Dragons poyson through each part doth run:
    Light is the loue that Beggers bosome stings,
    Deepe is the wound that *Cupid* makes in Kings.

Smal channels serue, where shallow springs do slide,
And little helpe will turne or stay their course: 15
The highest banks scarce holde the swelling tide,
Which ouer-throwes all stops with raging force:
    The baser sort scarce wett them in the springs,
    Which ouer-whelme the heads of mighty kings. 20

What though in both the hart bee set of Loue?
The self same ground both corne and cockle breeds
Fast by the Bryer, the Pine-tree mounts aboue,
One kinde of grasse, the Iade and Iennet feedes:
    So from the hart, by secret virtue springs, 25
    Vnlike desire in Beggers and in Kings.

                                            Anomos.

(P. 431 l. 140; Euph. ii. 219 l. 6; *Camp.* iv. 2. 8, v. 4. 129–31; *L. M.* iii. 1. 90) *(Endim.* v. 3. 107–8)

(Camp. ii. 2. 80 sqq.)

(Euph. i. 218 l. 22, ii. 138 ll. 19–20; No. 59 st. 5)

(Euph. ii. 22 l. 11)
(Euph. ii. 166 l. 14)

---

1 An Answere . . . Kings] in *Rawl. MS.* 148, *f.* 53 *the poem is headed* The aunswe to M^r: Diers ditie *and begins with the follg. additional stanza*
    Thoughe lowest trees haue topps, ye Ante some gall,
    The flie some spleene, ye sparke some little heat:
    Though slender heares cast shadowes, yet but small,
    Though Bees haue stinges, alas they are not great.
        Seas haue their sourse, vnlike to shallow springs:
        And loue vnlike, in Beggers and in Kinges.
4 with 1611, *Rawl. MS.* 148: which 1602   7 brest *Rawl. MS.* 148   10 mighty Oakes] curled lockes *Rawl. MS.* 148   11 cure] Antes *Rawl. MS.* 148   15 slide] glide *Rawl. MS.* 148   16 course] source *Rawl. MS.* 148   18 force] course *Rawl. MS.* 148   20 mighty] royall *Rawl. MS.* 148   21 set *i.e.* seat, *as Rawl. MS.* 148   24 grasse] meat *Rawl. MS.* 148   27 Anomos] *unsigned in later eds. of 'Poet. Raps.' and Rawl. MS.* 148

42. (From John Dowland's *Second Booke of Songs or Ayres*, 1600: No. 9.)

⟨*Sudeley*,
p.482 l.31⟩

Praise blindnesse eies, for seeing is deceit,
Bee dumbe vaine tongue, words are but flattering windes,
Breake hart & bleed for ther is no receit,
To purge inconstancy from most mens mindes.
  And so I wackt amazd and could not moue,   5
  I know my dreame was true, and yet I loue.

And if thine eares false Haralds to thy hart,
Conuey into thy head hopes to obtaine,
Then tell thy hearing thou art deafe by art,

⟨*Euph.* ii.
57 ll. 15
sqq.;
No.38 st.2⟩

Now loue is art that wonted to be plaine,   10
Now none is bald except they see his braines,   ⟨*Euph.* ii. 48 l. 28;
Affection is not knowne till one be dead,   cf. *M. Bom.* i. 1. 51⟩
Reward for loue are labours for his paines,
Loues quiuer made of gold his shafts of leade.
  And so I wackt amazd and could not moue,   15
  I know my dreame was true, and yet I loue.

43. (From John Dowland's *Second Booke of Songs or Ayres*, 1600: No. 11.)

⟨*LovesMet.*
iv. 1. 11–2;
No. 35 l.
35⟩

If fluds of teares could cleanse my follies past,
And smoakes of sighes might sacrifice for sinne,
If groning cries might salue my fault at last,
Or endles mone, for error pardon win,   20
Then would I cry, weepe, sigh, and euer mone,
Mine errors, fault, sins, follies past and gone.

I see my hopes must wither in their bud,
I see my fauours are no lasting flowers,
I see that woords will breede no better good,   25
Then losse of time and lightening but at houres,
Thus when I see then thus I say therefore,
That fauours hopes and words, can blinde no more.

No. 43. *Also in Harl. MS. 6910. f. 156, and printed last among the 'sundry other rare Sonnets of divers Noblemen and Gentlemen' at the close of Nash's surreptitious (?) ed. of Sidney's 'Astrophel and Stella' 1591. ('Pierce Pennilesse,' Sh. Soc. 1842, p. xxi.) In 'Sh. Soc. Papers' vol. i. 1844, art. xviii, these two stanzas were printed as 'attributed to Thomas Nash,' i.e. by Collier in op. cit., from a manuscript copy in one of Tanner's books in the Bodleian, followed by the first stanza of the poem last given 'Praise blindnesse,' &c., which the writer of the article, 'G. L.,' rightly suspected to belong to some other piece*   23 their] the *Harl. MS.*   24 no] not *Harl. MS.*   25 breede] breath *Harl. MS.*   28 can] shall *Harl. MS.*

44. (From John Dowland's *Third and Last Booke of Songs or Aires*, 1603: No. 1.)

Farewell too faire, too chaste but too too cruell,
Discretion neuer quenched fire with swords:
Why hast thou made my heart thine angers fuell,
And now would kill my passions with thy words.
    This is prowd beauties true anatamy,   5
    If that secure seuere in secresie,
        farewell, farewell.

Farewell too deare, and too too much desired,
Vnlesse compassion dwelt more neere thy heart:
Loue by neglect (though constant) oft is tired,   10
And forc't from blisse vnwillingly to part.
    This is prowd beauties true anatamy
    If that secure seuere in secresie,
        farewell, farewell.

⟨Sudeley, pp. 479–80⟩
⟨Euph. ii. 90 l. 16; *Saph.* ii. 4. 110; *Mia.* v. 3. 18⟩
⟨Euph. ii. 176 ll. 11–9⟩

45. (From Robert Jones' *First Booke of Songes & Ayres*, 1600: No. 1.)

    A Womans looks   15
    Are barbed hooks,
    That catch by art
    The strongest hart
When yet they spend no breath,
    But let them speake   20
    & sighing break,
    Forth into teares,
    Their words are speares
Y^t wound our souls to death.

    The rarest wit   25
    Is made forget,
    And like a child
    Is oft beguild,
With loues sweete seeming baite:
    Loue with his rod   30
    So like a God,
    Commands the mind,
    We cannot find
Faire shewes hide fowle deceit.

    Time that all thinges   35
    In order bringes,

486   POEMS

Hath taught me now
To be more slow,
In giuing faith to speech:
Since womens wordes
No truth affordes,   5
And when they kisse
They thinke by this,
Vs men to ouer-reach.

46. (From Robert Jones' *First Booke of Songes & Ayres*, 1600: No. 2.)

⟨*Euph.* i.
248 ll. 25
sqq.;
Endim. iii.
4. 123 sqq.⟩

Fond wanton youths make loue a God,
Which after proueth ages rod,   10
Their youth, their time, their wit, their arte,
They spend in seeking of their smarte
    And which of follies is the chiefe,
    They wooe their woe, they wedde their griefe.

All finde it so who wedded are,   15
Loues sweetes they find enfold sowre care:
His pleasures pleasingst in the eie,
Which tasted once, with lothing die:
    They find of follies tis the chiefe,
    Their woe to wooe to wedde their griefe.   20

⟨*Euph.* ii.
220 ll. 32
sqq.⟩

If for their owne content they choose,
Forthwith their kindreds loue they loose:
And if their kindred they content,
For euer after they repent.
    O tis of all our follies chiefe,   25
    Our woe to wooe to wedde our griefe.

In bed what strifes are bred by day,
Our puling wiues doe open lay:
None friendes none foes we must esteeme,
But whome they so vouchsafe to deeme: 30
    O tis of all our follies chiefe,
    Our woe to wooe to wedde our griefe.

⟨*Pappe*, p.
411 ll. 3-4⟩

Their smiles we want if ought they want,
And either we their wils must grant,
Or die they will or are with child,   35
Their longings must not be beguild:
    O tis of all our follies chiefe,
    Our woe to woo to wedde our griefe.

36 longings] laughings *Songbook*

Foule wiues are iealous, faire wiues false,   ⟨*Loves*
Mariage to either bindes vs thrall: *Met.* i. 2.
Wherefore being bound we must obey,   125-9⟩
And forced be perforce to say:
    Of all our blisse it is the chiefe,   5
Our woe to wooe to wed our griefe.

47. (From Robert Jones' *First Booke of Songes & Ayres*, 1600: No. 4.)   ⟨Cf. No. 19⟩
  Once did I loue and yet I liue,
    Though loue & truth be now forgotten.
  Then did I ioy nowe doe I grieue,
    That holy vows must needs be broken.   10

  Hers be the blame that caus'd it so,
    Mine be the griefe though it be little,
  Shee shall haue shame I cause to know:
    What tis to loue a dame so fickle.   ⟨*Euph.* i. 240 ll. 1

  Loue her that list I am content,   15 sqq.⟩
    For that Camelion like shee changeth,   ⟨*Endim.* iii. 4. 129⟩
  Yeelding such mistes as may preuent:
    My sight to view her when she rangeth.   ⟨No. 19 st. 6⟩

  Let him not vaunt that gaines my losse,   ⟨*Ib.* st. 7⟩
    For when that he and time hath prou'd her,   20 ⟨*Euph.* ii.
  Shee may him bring to weeping crosse: 28 l. 36⟩
    I say no more because I lou'd her.

48. (From Robert Jones' *First Booke of Songes & Ayres*, 1600: No. 7.)
  Where lingring feare doth once posses the hart,   ⟨Cf. No. 17
    There is the toong   Of linger-
    Forst to prolong,   25 inge Loue⟩
  & smother vp his suite, while that his smart,
  Like fire supprest, flames more in euery part.   ⟨*Euph.* i. 210 l. 21⟩

  Who dares not speake deserues not his desire,   ⟨Cf. No. 16⟩
    The Boldest face,
    Findeth most grace: 30
  Though women loue that men should thẽ admire,
  They slily laugh at him dares come no higher.

No. 47 ⎫ *Also given in Bullen's 'Lyrics from Elizabethan Song-Books,'* ⎧ *p.* 83
No. 48 ⎭   ⎩ *p.* 151

⟨*Saph.* i. 4.
37-40⟩

Some thinke a glaunce expressed by a sigh,
    Winning the field,
    Maketh them yeeld:
But while these glauncing fooles do rowle the eie,
They beate the bush, away the bird doth flie.   5

A gentle hart in vertuous breast doth stay,
    Pitty doth dwell,
    In beauties cell:

⟨*Ib.* ll. 41 sqq.⟩

A womans hart doth not thogh tong say nay
Repentance taught me this the other day.   10

Which had I wist I presently had got,
    The pleasing fruite,
    Of my long suite:
But time hath now beguild me of this lot,

⟨Letter, vol. i. p. 390 and passim⟩

For that by his foretop I tooke him not.   15

49. (From Robert Jones' *First Booke of Songes & Ayres*, 1600: No. 8.)

Hero care not though they prie,
I will loue thee till I die,
Ielousie is but a smart,
That tormentes a ielous hart:
    Crowes are blacke that were white,   20
    For betraying loues delight.

They that loue to finde a fault,
May repent what they haue sought,

⟨*Euph.* ii. 63 ll. 5-7⟩

What the fond eie hath not view'd,
Neuer wretched hart hath rew'd: 25
    Vulcan then, prou'd a scorne,
    When he saw he wore a horne.

Doth it then by might behoue,
To shut vp the gates of loue,

⟨*Euph.* ii. 226 ll. 12-4⟩

Women are not kept by force,   30
But by natures owne remorse.
    If they list, they will stray,
    Who can hold that will away.

⟨Often⟩

Ioue in golden shower obtain'd,
His loue in a towre restrain'd,   35
So perhaps if I could doe,
I might hold my sweete loue to:
    Gold keepe out at the doore,
    I haue loue that conquers more.

LATER LOVE-POEMS

Wherefore did they not suspect,
When it was to some effect,
Euery little glimmering sparke,
Is perceiued in the darke: ⟨*Euph.* ii.
    This is right, howlets kinde,   5   92 l. 7⟩
    See by night, by day be blinde.

50. (From Robert Jones' *First Booke of Songes & Ayres*, 1600: No. 9.)

When loue on time and measure makes his ground,
Time that must end though loue can neuer die,
Tis loue betwixt a shadow and a sound,
A loue not in the hart but in the eie,   10
  A loue that ebbes and flowes now vp now downe,
  A mornings fauor and an euenings frowne.

Sweete lookes shew loue, yet they are but as beames,
Faire wordes seeme true, yet they are but as wind,
Eies shed their teares yet are but outward streames: 15
Sighes paint a sadnes in the falsest minde.
  Lookes, wordes, teares, sighes, shew loue when loue they leaue,
  False harts can weepe, sigh, sweare, and yet deceiue.

51. (From Robert Jones' *First Booke of Songes & Ayres* 1600: No. 11.)

Women, what are they, changing weather-cocks,
That smallest puffes of lust haue power to turne,   20
Women what are they, vertues stumbling blockes,
Whereat weake fooles doe fall, the wiser spurne,
    Wee men, what are wee, fooles and idle boies,
    To spend our time in sporting with such toies.

⟨For the pun cf. *Euph.* i. 241 l. 12⟩

Women what are they? trees whose outward rinde,   25
Makes shew for faire when inward hart is hollow:
Women what are they? beasts of Hiænaes kinde, ⟨*Euph.* i.
That speak those fairst, whō most they meane to swallow: 250 ll. 8–10⟩
    We men what are wee? fooles and idle boies,
    To spend our time in sporting with such toies.   30

Women what are they? rocks vpon the coast,
Where on we suffer shipwracke at our landing:

No. 50. *The first stanza is given in Rawlinson MS. Poet.* 148, *f.* 59 *headed* Uni, soli, semper. J. L. (*not in John Lilliat's hand; see p.* 444) *with accompanying music, and* 'The residue of this Ditie in fol. 8 before' (*fol.* 8 *is wanting*). *Also given in Bullen's* 'Lyrics from Elizabethan Song-Books,' *p.* 95   No. 51. *Also given in Bullen's* 'Lyrics from Elizabethan Song-Books,' p. 136   26 hallow *Songbook*

Women what are they? patient creatures most,
That rather yeld thē striue gainst ought withstāding
We men what are wee? fooles and idle boies,
To spend our time in sporting with such toies.

52. (From Robert Jones' *First Booke of Songes & Ayres*, 1600: No. 14.)

⟨*Euph.* i.
185 ll. 11–
2, 268 l. 37⟩

If fathers knew but how to leaue 5
Their children wit as they do wealth,
& could constraine them to receiue
That physicke which brings perfect health,
    Y^e world would not admiring stand,
    A womans face and womans hand. 10

Women confesse they must obey,
We men will needes be seruants still:
We kisse their hands and what they say,
We must commend bee 't neuer so ill.
    Thus we like fooles admiring stand, 15
    Her pretty foote and pretty hand.

We blame their pride which we increase,
By making mountaines of a mouse:
We praise because we know we please:
Poore women are too credulous 20
    To thinke that we admiring stand,
    Or foote, or face, or foolish hand.

53. (From Robert Jones' *Muses Gardin for Delights*, 1610.)

⟨No. 54
l. 12⟩

⟨*Euph.* ii.
176 l. 7,
219 l. 1⟩
⟨Cf. *Euph.*
ii. 175–6
and No. 44⟩
⟨*Euph.* ii.
56 l. 17,
65 l. 23⟩

The fountaines smoake, and yet no flames they shewe,
  Starres shine all night, though undesern'd by day,
And trees doe spring, yet are not seene to growe, 25
  And shadowes moove, although they seeme to stay,
    In Winter's woe is buried Summer's blisse,
    And Love loves most, when Love most secret is.

The stillest streames descries the greatest deepe,
  The clearest skie is subject to a shower, 30
Conceit's most sweete, whenas it seemes to sleepe,
  And fairest dayes doe in the morning lower;
    The silent groves sweete nimphes they cannot misse,
    For Love loves most, where Love most secret is.

No. 52. *Also given in Bullen's 'Lyrics from Elizabethan Song-Books,' p.* 50
No. 53. *Reprinted in 'Ancient Ballads and Songs,' p.* 56

The rarest jewels hidden vertue yeeld,
  The sweete of traffique is a secret gaine,
The yeere once old doth shew a barren field,
And plants seeme dead, and yet they spring againe;
  Cupid is blind the reason why is this: 5
  Love loveth most, where Love most secret is.

V. Later Autobiographical: 1595–1600?

54. (From *Harl. MS.* 6910, ff. 126–7.)

Where wardes are weake, and foes encountering strong:
Wher mightier doe assault, then do defend:
The feebler part puts vp enforced wrong,
And silent sees, that speach could not amend.   10
Yet higher powers must thinke though they repine,
When Sunne is set: the litle starres will shine.

While Pike doth range, the silly Tench doth flye,
And crouch in priuie creekes, with smaler fish:
Yet Pikes are caught when litle fish goe bye: 15
These, fleete a flote; while those, doe fill the dish.
There is a tyme euen for the wormes to creepe:
And sucke the dew while all their foes doe sleepe.

The Marlyne cannot euer sore on high,
Nor greedie Grey-hound still pursue the chase: 20
The tender Larke will fynde a tyme to flie,
And fearfull Hare to runne a quiet race.
He that high growth on Ceders did bestow:
Gaue also lowly Musnrumpts leaue to grow.

  Wee trample grasse, and prize the flowers of May: 25
  Yet grasse is greene, when flowers do fade away.

⟨No. 53 l. 24⟩

No. 54. *Also in Addit. MS.* 22,601, *f.* 71 *v.*   7 wardes] words *Add. MS.* incoūter *Add. MS.*   8 doe ... then] doth ... and *Add. MS.*   14 secreat holes *Add. MS.*   19 alwaies *Add. MS.*   25 Wee ... away] *this closing couplet is replaced in Add. MS. by the foll. additional stanza*

           The Sea of fortune doth not euer flowe
           she drawes hir fauo^t to ye lowest ebb
           Hir Tides hath equall tyme to come & goe
           Hir Lome doth weaue ye course & finest webb
             No joy so great but runneth to an end
             No happ so hard but may in fine amende.

55. (From John Dowland's *First Booke of Songes or Ayres*, 1597 : No. 14.)

Al ye whŏ loue or fortune hath betraide,
All ye that dreame of blisse but liue in greif,
Al ye whose hopes are euermore delaid,
Al ye whose sighes or sicknes wants releife :
Lend eares and teares to me most haples man,   5
That sings my sorrowes like the dying Swanne.

Care that consumes the heart with inward paine,
Paine that presents sad care in outward vew,
Both tyrant like enforce me to complaine,
But still in vaine, for none my plaints will rue,   10
Teares, sighes, and ceaseles cries alone I spend,
My woe wants comfort, and my sorrow end.

56. (From John Dowland's *First Booke of Songes or Ayres*, 1597 : No. 20.)

Come heauy sleepe, ye Image of true death :
And close vp these my weary weeping eyes,
Whose spring of tears doth stop my vitall breath, 15
And tears my hart with sorrows sigh swoln crys :
⟨No. 66 ll. Com & posses' my tired thoghts, worne soule,
14-5⟩   That liuing dies, till thou on me be stoule.

Come shadow of my end : and shape of rest,
Alied to death, child to this black fast night,   20
Come thou and charme these rebels in my brest,
Whose waking fancies doth my mind affright.
O come sweet sleepe, come or I die for euer,
Come ere my last sleepe coms, or ⟨else⟩ come neuer.

57. (From *Addit. MS.* 22,601, f. 61 v.)

Concerninge his suit & attendaũce at ye Courte. 25

Moste miserable man, whome wretched fate
hath brought to Court, to sue for Had-I-wist :
that few haue found, & many one haue mist.
Full little knowest thou, that hast not tride
what Hell it is, in suinge longe to bide.   30
To loose good dayes, that mighte be better spent,
to waste longe nightes in pensiue discontent,

To speed to day, & be put back to morrowe,
Now fedd wth hope, now Crost wth wailfull sorrow
To haue thy Princes grace yet want hir Peeres,
to haue thy askinge, yet waite many yeres.
To frett thy soule with Crosses & wth cares,   5
to eat thy hart wth Comfortless dispaires:
To fawne, to crouche, to waite, to bide, to run:
To spend, to giue, to want, to be vndon.
    Vnhappy wighte, borne to disastrous end:
    That doth his life, in so longe tendance spend.   10

       Pereunt nil pariunt Anni,
                      verte

58. (From *Addit. MS.* 22,601, f. 62.)

The thundringe God whose all-embracinge powre
Circles ye modell of this spatious rounde
When first he fram'd old Adams earthly bowre   15
ordain'd all thinges th' Emperiall vaile doth bound
    Should lend their aide to others mutuallie
    but all combine serue man continuallie.

So heau'n wth heate, the dankish aire wth dew
this solid element of Earth reuiue   20
with gentle warm'th & robes of verdant hew
on wch ye horned Kyne & sheepe do liue
    And as those bodies ministred their good
    So they againe do turne to humane foode.

Man seru'd of all, seru'd none of all but God   25
but mighte his pleasures take wthout controule
Saue only what Jehouah had forbod
the carefull Soueraigne of his simple soule.
    This was ye age wise Poets term'd of gold
    for liberty in dearest prize they holde.   30

But theis succeedinge Seasons arm'd in steele,
Tramples hir downe & in tryumphant sorte
Not fearinge like contempts of fate to feele
Leades hir as Captiue, mate to poorest sorte
    Yet Patience promis'd Liberty distrest   35
    should reape for paine, a gayne, for vnrest, rest.

W^{ch} Prophesy of hirs indeede mighte serue
for a perswation that my seruice doñe

   12 verte] No. 58 *follows immediately in MS., f. 52 r.*

⟨Bee, st. 9⟩

would at yᵉ length enfranchisemᵗ deserue
wᵗʰ aunswʳ to mine expectation.
    But when I thinke twas Patience yᵗ spoke
the golden vessell of my hope is broke.

For she's a Sainte & scorninge vniust earth   5
is fledd to heau'n. All vertues are ingros't
In Gods owne hand, tis yᵗ wᶜʰ breedes yᵉ dearth
of due rewardes, & makes my labour lost
    Or at yᵉ moste repaies my louinge minde
wᵗʰ large delayes, vaine wordes & some vnkinde.   10

Since then yᵉ first worlde can not be recald
nor this our rusty Iron age refinde
Since Patience is in starry heau'n install
Let euery Seruitour beare this in minde
    That howsoeu'r he serue, obserue, deserue   15

⟨Bee, st. 12⟩
    if nought but Aire he purchase he may sterue.

    Sarrire quam seruire satius.

59. (From *Egerton MS.* 923, ff. 5–7.)

⟨THE BEE.⟩

It was a tyme when silly Bees could speake
and in that time I was a silly Bee
who suckt on time, vntill the hart gan breake   20
yet never founde that tyme would fauour me
    Of all the swarme I onely could not thriue
    yet brought I wax & honey to yᵉ hiue

⟨Euph. i. 309 ll. 21–4⟩
Then thus I busd when time no sap would giue
Why is this blessed tyme to me so dry   25
Sith in this tyme, yᵉ lazie Drone doth liue
yᵉ waspe, yᵉ worme, yᵉ Gnat, yᵉ butterfly
    Mated wᵗʰ greif I kneeled on my knees
    And thus complain'd vnto yᵉ King o⟨f⟩ Bees

My leige god grant thy time may haue no end   30
and yet vouchsafe to heare my plaint of tyme

No. 59. *For titles in various MSS. see Introd. pp.* 445–6   18 It] There *Rawl.*
112, *Sl., Add.*   silly] *om. Sl.*   20 on] no *Eg.*   the ... gan] my ... did
rest   23 I] both *Add.*   26 lazie ... liue] busy ... liue *Tann.*:
happy ... thryve *Rawl.* 112   27 worme] Ante *Sl.*   28 Mated] In
a tyme *Sl.*   28–9 I kneeled ... And] lowe bended ... I *Rawl.* 172   29
Quene *Rawl.* 112   30 haue no] neuer *rest*   31 yet ... of] eake not
fayle to heare my playneing *Ashm.*

LATER AUTOBIOGRAPHICAL

Synce every fruitlesse fly hath found a freind
& I cast downe while Attomies doe clyme
  The king replide but thus, peace peevish Bee
  Thou art borne to serve the time, ye time not thee

The time not thee, this word clipt short my wings   5
And made me worme-like creepe y^t once did fly
Awfull regard disputeth not wth kings
Receauethe a Repulse not asking why?
  Then from the tyme, I for a tyme wthdrew
  To feed on Henbane, Hemlock, Nettles, Rue,   10

But from those leaues no dram of sweete I drayne
their head strong furry did my head bewitch
The iuice disperst black bloud in every veine
for hony gall, for wax I gathered pitch
  My Combe a Rift, my hiue a leafe must bee   15
  so chang'd; that Bees scarce took me for a Bee

I work on weedes when Moone is in ye waine
whilst all ye swarme in sunnshine tast ye rose
onn black Roote ferne I sitt & sucke my baine
whilst on ye Eglentine the rest repose   20
  haueing too much they still repine for more
  & cloyd wth fullnes surfeit on y^{eir} store

Swolne fatt wth feasts full merrily they passe
In sweetned Clusters falling from ye tree
where finding me to nibble on ye grasse   25

⟨*Euph.* i.
218 l. 22⟩
⟨No. 39
st. 3, and
passim⟩

⟨*Euph.* ii.
172 l. 18⟩
⟨*Ib.* ii. 184
l. 16⟩
⟨*Tiltyard*,
p. 411 top;
Theob. p.
418⟩

---

1 Synce ... found] W^{ch} ... found *Tann.*: When every fayntest flye may fynd *Rawl.* 112: Whome euery feareless flye may fynd *Sl.*: In wch ech fruitlesse flye may fynd *Harl.* 6910   2 while ... clyme] in cheifest of my prime *Rawl.* 172   3 but] by *Eg.*   4 Th'art home *Ashm.*   5 cutt *Sl.*   6 stoope *Harl.* 6910, 2127, *Tann., Rawl.* 112, 172   7 kings] things *Eg.*   8 Receiueth the repulse yet neuer asketh whye *Sl.*: Receiues repulse dares aske no Reason why *Add.*: Receiues repulse & neuer asketh why *Harl.* 6910, 2127, *Ashm.*: Receiues rebukes but neuer asketh why *Rawl.* 112: But doth repulse & neuer asketh why *Tann.*   9 Then . . a tyme I me *Tann., Harl.* 2127, *Sl., Add.*: Then ... forthwth I me *Harl.* 6910, *Rawl.* 172: Then for y^t I mee frome tyme *Rawl.* 112   from] for *Eg.*   10 Nettles] yarrow *Rawl.* 112   11–6 But ... for a Bee] this st. only in *Eg., Rawl.* 148, *Sl., Collier's MS.*   11 drayne] draw *Eg.*   12 ffortune *Rawl.* 148, *Sl.*   13 arift *Rawl.* 148   17 I ... waine] *Ashm.* om., *inserting as* 4th l. To light on wormewoode leaues they me constrayne work ... is] workt on wood ... was *Tann.*: suckt the ... was *Rawl.* 112   18 swarme] rest *Rawl.* 112   tast y^e] suck the *Add.*: tasted *Rawl.* 112   19 onn] me *Harl.* 6910   Roote ... sitt] roote ... seeke *Rawl.* 148, *Harl.* 2127, *Add. Tann.*: ferne loe I seeke *Sl.*: ferne rootes I seek to suck *Rawl.* 112, 172   21 they ... repine] yet still they gape *Add.*   22 fullnes *Eg., Rawl.* 148: sweetnes rest on] in *Rawl.* 112, 148, *Add.*   24 In] On *Rawl.* 148   sweetned] swarming *Harl.* 6910, 2127, *Rawl.* 112, 172: swarmes and *Sl.*   falling] feedinge *Ashm.* from y^e] on a *Harl.* 6910, 2127, *Tann., Ashm., Add., Sl.*

496 POEMS

⟨*Euph*. i. 318 l. 1⟩
⟨*Ib*. ii. 148 l. 36, &c.⟩

⟨*Ib*. ii. 169 l. 25 and Biog. App. Letter iii. p. 393⟩
⟨*Saph*. ii. 4. 60–1⟩

⟨*Euph*. i. 228 l. 28. P. 473 l. 5⟩

    some scorne, some muse, & some doe pitty me
      And some envy & whisper to the king
        Some must be still & some must haue no sting
    Are Bees waxt waspes, or spiders to infect
    Doe hony bowells make ye sperit gall   5
    Is this ye iuce of flowers to stir suspect
    Ist not enought to tread on them that fall
      what sting hath patience but a sighing grief
      That sting⟨s⟩ nought but itselfe wthout Relief

    True patience ye prouender of fooles   10
    sad patience that waiteth at the doore
    Patience y^t learnes thus to conclude in schools
    Patience I am therefore I must be poore
      Great king of Bees y^t rightest euery wrong
      Listen to patience in her dying song   15
    I cannot feed on fennell like some flyes
    nor fly to euery flower to gather gaine
    myne appetite waites on my prince his eyes
    Contented with contempt, & pleased wth payne
      and yet expecting of an happy houre   20
      when he shall say this Bee shall suck a flower

    Of all the greifes y^t must my patience grate
    there's one that fretteth in ye high'st degree
    To see some Catterpillers bred vp of late
    cropping the fruit y^t should sustaine ye Bee   25
      yet smiled I, for y^t the wisest knowes
      that mothes doe frett ye Clothe Canker ye Rose

1 scorne] scornes *Harl.* 6910: scorned *Tann.*: storme *Rawl.* 112, *Ashm.* 2 envyed, & whispered *Harl.* 6910, *Rawl.* 172. *Add.*: me *bef.* envie *Harl.* 2127, *Sl.*, *Tann.*   3 still] kild *Rawl.* 148   4 infect *Eg.*, *Sl.*: aflicte *rest*   5 Doth Honny bowell & *Harl.* 6910   6 stir] sture *Harl.* 6910: moue *Rawl.* 112: flie *Tann.*   7 on] no *Eg.* . them] him *Harl.* 6910   8 sighing] sighe and *Sl.*: stinginge *Ashm.*: lingring *Harl.* 6910: single *Tann.*   9 nought but it] not but it *Harl.* 6910: none but my *Rawl.* 112   itselfe and yealded no selfe releefe *Ashm.*   10 True patience &c.] *ll.* 1–4 *are thus in Ashm.*
    Sad patience, that attendeth at the dore,
    And teacheth wise-men thus conclude in schooles:
    Patience I am, and therfore must be poore:
    Fortune bestowes her riches not on fooles.
y^e] is fitt *Sl.*   11 that . . . at] watcheth still, and keepes *Sl.*   13 Patient *Rawl.* 148, 172, *Harl.* 2127   14 Great king] Great Quene *Rawl.* 112 : Greatest *Rawl.* 172   rightest euery] onely rightest *Harl.* 6910, 2127, *Rawl.* 112, 172 15 Harken *Rawl.* 172   16 Hemlock *Sl.*   18 tendes *Ashm.*   20 expecting of] expectinge for *Tann.*, *Rawl.* 112: I still expect *Sl.*: expecting such *Add.* 21 he shall say] shee may say *Sl.*, *Tann.*: it shalbe sayde *Rawl.* 112   22 must *Eg.*: doe *Rawl.* 148, *Ashm.*: most *rest*   24 bred vp] vpstart *Rawl.* 112: hired *Rawl.* 172: birde bredd *Sl.*   26 smiled I] sighed I *Rawl.* 172 (*om.* for that): smile I maye *Rawl.* 112: did I smile *Rawl.* 148: singled I *Sl.*   27 doe frett] will eate *Sl.*, *Harl.*, *Add.*, *Rawl.* 112, 172   Mothes eate the cloth, cankers consume *Ashm.*

LATER AUTOBIOGRAPHICAL 497

Once did I see by flying in the feild   ⟨*Euph.* i.
fowle beasts to browse vpon ye Lilly fayre   185 l. 1,
Virtue & beauty could noe succour yeild   242 l. 17,
All's prouender for Asses, but the ayre   251 ll. 7-8⟩
    the partiall world of this takes litle heed   ⟨P. 498
        to giue them flowers y^t should on thistles feed   5 l. 1⟩

This onely I must draine Ægiptian flowers
haueing noe sauo^r, bitter sap they haue
& seeke out Rotten Tombes & dead mens bowers
and bite on nightshade growing by the graue   10   ⟨*Tiltyard*,
    If this I cannot haue, as hapless Bee   p. 415 ll.
        witching Tobacco I will fly to thee   14, 20⟩

what thoughe thou dy mens lungs in deepest black
A mourning habitt suites a sable hart
what if thy fumes sound memory doe crack   15
fforgettfullnes is fittest for my smart
    ô vertuous fame let it be graued in oke
        y^t wordes, hopes, witts & all ye worlds but smoke

ffiue yeares twise told wth promises p^{r}fume   ⟨Biog.
my hope stuft head was cast into a slumber   20   App. Letter
Sweete dreames of gold, on dreames I then p^{r}sume   iii. p. 393;
& mongst ye Bees thoughe I were in ye number   and, for the
    waking I founde, hiues hopes had made me vaine   language,
        Twas not Tobacco stupifyed ye braine   vol. ii. 372,
            and *Euph.*
Ingenium, studium, nummos, spem, tempus, amicos   25   i. 194 l. 17⟩
    Cum male perdiderim : perdere verba leue est.

    2 Lillyes *rest*   3 beauty] bountie *Rawl.* 112   5 of . . . litle] takes very carelesse *Ashm.*   7 This] Tis *Add., Sl., Harl.* 2127 : Thus *Tann.*   8 Findinge *Ashm.*   bitter sap *Harl.* 6910 *and all, except* better sap *Rawl.* 148, better say *Eg.*   9 out] of *Harl.* 6910 : the *Add.*   10 nightshade *Harl.* 6910, *Rawl.* 172 : Lotos *Rawl.* 148, *Harl.* 2127, *Tann.*: Pathos *Eg.*, *Sl.*: wormwood *Add.*: withered age growing to the graue *Rawl.* 112   graue] ground *Harl.* 6910   11 this . . . haue] these . . . finde *Sl.*   I *cm. Eg.*   as] ah *Harl.* 6910, *Rawl.* 112, 172, *Ashm., Sl.*   12 witching] Wishing *Harl. MSS.*: Wished *Tann., Add.*: Smokeing *Rawl.* 112   13 thoughe] if *Harl.* 6910 *&c.*   mens *Eg.*: my *rest*   14 A] To *Harl.* 6910 *&c.*: Tis *Rawl.* 112   15 sound] some *Harl.* 6910, *Add., Rawl.* 172: my *Rawl.* 112   17 fame] fame *Rawl.* 148 : flames *Rawl.* 172   graued *Eg.* : caru'd *rest*   18 hopes] healpe *Rawl.* 172   19 yeares] tymes *Sl.*   p^{r}fume] perfumed *rest, excpt.* vnperformed *Sl.*   20 hope stuft] hopes iust *Sl.*: stuft head *om. Rawl.* 172   21 dreames^1] draynes *Harl.* 6910   22 Amongst *rest* Bees] best *Rawl.* 112   I thought myself in number *Rawl.* 148   23 Waking *&c.*] *Tann. MS. gives the couplet* Late wakinge, hyues, hopes, had made me vayne, | Was but Tobacco stupyfied my brayne. *Ashm. gives this line* But wakinge found hyues, hopes, and all was vayne   tymes hopes *Harl.* 6910 *&c.*: hie hopes *Rawl.* 148 : hiue, but hopes *Sl.*   24 not] but *Tann., Ashm.*: Don *Rawl.* 172   stupifyed] had so stupifyed *Sl.*: had supplyed *Rawl.* 112   25-6 *Rawl. MS.* 148 *only (altered from Ov.* '*Her.*' vii. 5-6*), followed by translation (an English quatrain) signed* Eng^d. Ιω. λιλλιατ.

60. (From *Rawlinson MS. Poet.* 148, f. 32 v.)

⟨*Bee*, st. 12⟩

In Thesaly, ther Asses fine are kept,
fayre, smoth, plump, fat and full:
The mangers they are fild, ye stables clenly swept
And yet their pace is very slow and dull.
So sotes oft tymes haue vnto honour crept, 5
when wiser men haue hadd a coulder pull,
If Asses haue such luck what shall I say?

⟨No. 64 st. 2⟩

Let Scollers burne their bookes & goe to play.
finis.

61. (*Ibid.*)

As oft we see before a sudden showre, 10
The sunne shines hottest & hath greatest powre:
Euen so whom fortune meaneth to deride,
She liftes a loft, from whence he soone may slide.

62. (*Ibid.*)

⟨*Euph.* i. 277 l. 24, ii. 99 l. 35⟩

Princes be fortunes children, & with them
she deales as mothers vse their babes to still: 15
Vnto her darlings giues a diadem,
A pretie toy their humor to fulfill.
And when a little they haue had their will,
Looke what she gaue she taketh at her pleasure:
Vsinge the rod, when they are out of measure. 20

63. (From *Rawlinson MS. Poet.* 148, f. 46 v.)

⟨*End.*iii.4⟩

Ouer theis brookes, trustinge to ease myne eyes,
Mine eyes euen great, in laboure with their teares:
I layde my face, wherin (alas) ther lies,
Clusters of clowdes, wch no Sunne euer cleeres.
    In watrie glasse, my watrie eyes I see: 25
    Sorrowes ill easd, wher sorrowes paynted be.

⟨No. 23 l. 22⟩

My thoughtes imprisned in my secret woes,
With flamie breastes doe issue oft in sownde:
The sownde to this strange ayre no sooner goes,
But that it doth with Ecchôs force rebownde. 30
    And makes me heare, ye playntes I would refrayne:
    Thus outward helpes, my inward grifes mayntayne.

⟨*Mid.* Intr. p. 109 l. 14⟩

Now in this sand, I would discharge my mynde,
And cast from me, part of my burd'nous cares:

---

17 their] his *MS*. No. 63. *Also in Robert Jones' 'Second Booke of Songes and Ayres,'* 1601: *No.* 11 22 their] her *Songbook* 23 wherein (alas) *Rawl. MS.*: my face wherein *Songbook* 29 no *Songbook*: om. *Rawl. MS.* 31 make *Songbook*

LATER AUTOBIOGRAPHICAL

But in the sand, my Tales foretold I fynde,
And see therin, how well yᵉ writer fares.
   With streame, ayre, sand, myne eyes & ears conspire:
   What hope to quench, wher ech thinge blowes yᵉ fire.

64. (From *Harl. MS.* 6910, f. 140.)
Why ⟨*the rest of the line wanting in MS.*⟩   5
When life is my true happinesse disease?
My soule, my soule, thy saftie makes me flie
The fault is meanes, that might my payne appease.
   ⟨*a line wanting in MS.*⟩
   But in my hart her seuerall tormentes dwell.   10

Ah worthlesse witt to traine mee to this woe,   ⟨Cf. *The
Deceiptfull arts that nourish discontent :   Bee*⟩
Ill thriue the follie that bewitcht me so,
Vaine though⟨t⟩s adieu for now I will repent.
   And yet my wantes perswade me to proceed,   15 ⟨Lines to
   Since none takes pittie one a Scholers need.   Lok, vol. i.
                                                                    p. 67;
forgiue me God althought I curse my birth,   No. 60⟩
And ban the ayre wherin I breath a wreatch :
Since miserie hath daunted all my mirth,
And I am quite vndon through promis⟨e breach⟩   20
   Oh frendes, no frendes that then vn⟨kind⟩ly frowne,
   When changing fortune casts vs headlong downe.

Without redresse complains my carelesse Verse,
And *Mydas* eares relent not at my moane
In some farr land will I my griefe rehearse,   25
Mongst them that wilbee mooued when I groane,
   Ingland adieu the soyle that brought mee forth
   Adieu vnkinde where skill is no⟨t⟩hing worth.

65. (From *Rawlinson MS. Poet.* 85, fol. 47.)
Some mē will saye there is a kynde of muse
That healps the myrde of eache man to indyte   30
And some will saye (that oft these Muses vse)
There are but Nyne that euer vsed to wryte
   Now of these nyne if I haue hytt on one
   I muse what Muse 'tis I haue hytt vpon.

---

2 writer] waters *Songbook*   3 With streame] Since streames *Songbook*   4 ech thinge] all theis *alternative in MS.*   No. 65. *Also in Harl. MS.* 6910, ff. 147-8

Some poetes wryte there is a heauenly hyll
Wher Pallas keeps: and it Pernassus hyghte
There Muses sit for-sothe, and cut the quyll
That beinge framde doth hidden fancyes wryte
    But all these dames diuyne conceyts do synge   5
    And all theyr penns be of a phœnix winge.

Beleeue me now I neuer sawe the place
Vnless in sleepe I drem'de of suche a thynge
I neauer vewed fayre Pallas in the face
Nor neauer yet could heare the Muses synge   10
    Wherby to frame a fancye in her kynde
    Oh no! my muse is of an other mynde.

From Hellicon? no no from Hell she came
To wryte of woes and myseryes⟨:⟩ she hyghte
Not Pallas but Alass hir Ladyes name   15
Who neuer calles for dittyes of delyghte.
    Her pen̄ is Payne; and all her matter moane
    And pantynge harts she paynts her mynd vpon.

A harte not Harpe is all her instrumēt
Whose weakned strynges all out of tune she strayns   20
And than she strikes a dumpe of discontente
Tyll euery strynge be pluckt in two with paynes
    Than in a rage she clapps it vpp in Case:
    That you maye see her instruments disgrace.

Her musick is in sum̄ but sorrowes songe   25
Wher discorde yealds a sound of small delyghte
The dittye is: o lyfe that lastes so longe
To see desyre thus crossed wth despyte
No faythe on earth: alas I know no frende!
So with a syghe she makes a solem̄ ende.   30

Vnpleasant is the harmony godd knowes
When out of tune is allmost euery strynge
The sownde vnsweet, y^t all of sorrow growes
And sadd the muse, that so is fourced to synge
    Yet some do synge that else for woe would crye   35
    So dothe mye Muse: and so, I sweare, do I.

        Finis.

⟨*Loves Met.* iv. 1. 9–10⟩
⟨*Sud.* pp. 478 l. 32, 479 l. 17⟩
⟨*Loves Met.* iii. 1. 118–9⟩

13 came. *Rawl. MS.*   19 not *Harl. MS.*: and not a *Rawl. MS.*

66. (From Robert Jones' *First Booke of Songes & Ayres*, 1600: No. 6.)

Lie downe poore heart and die a while for griefe,
Thinke not this world will euer do thee good,
Fortune forewarnes ȳ looke to thy reliefe,
And sorrow sucks vpon thy liuing bloud,
    Then this is all can helpe thee of this hell,   5
    Lie downe and die, and then thou shalt doe well.

Day giues his light but to thy labours toyle,
And night her rest but to thy weary bones,
Thy fairest forture followes with a foyle:
And laughing endes but with thine after grones.   10
    And this is all can helpe thee of thy hell,
    Lie downe and die and then thou shalt doe well.

Patience doth pine and pitty ease no paine,
Time weares the thoughts but nothing helps ye mind,   ⟨No. 56
Dead and aliue aliue and dead againe: 15 ll. 17-8⟩
These are the fits that thou art like to finde.
    And this is all can helpe thee of thy hell,
    Lie downe and die and then thou shalt doe well.

67. (From Robert Jones' *First Booke of Songes & Ayres*, 1600: No. 15.)

    Life is a Poets fable,
    & al her daies are lies   20
    Stolne from deaths reckoning table,
For I die as I speake,
Death times the notes that I doe breake.

    Childhood doth die in youth,
    And youth in old age dies,   25
    I thought I liu'd in truth:
But I die, now I see,
Each age of death makes one degree.

    Farewell the doting score
    Of worlds arithmeticke,   30
    Life, Ile trust thee no more,
Till I die, for thy sake,
Ile go by deaths new almanacke.

    This instant of my song,
    A thousand men lie sicke,   35
    A thousand knels are rong:

No. 66. *The first two stt. also in Bullen's 'Lyrics from Elizabethan Song-Books,'*
p. 189   10 their *Songbook*

      And I die as I sing,
    They are but dead and I dying.

      Death is but lifes decay,
      Life time, time wastes away,
      Then reason bids me say,   5
    That I die, though my breath
  Prolongs this space of lingring death.

VI. Epigrams.

68–73. (From *Addit. MS.* 15,227.)

Venetia.

Vrbe tot in Veneta, scortorum millia cur sunt?
  In pmtu causa est, est Venus orta mari. (fol. 8.)   10

(Gall. v. 1. 44–9)

Cur diebus Veneris vescamur piscibus.

Quod mihi quoq̨ die Veneris màre præbeat escam
  Arbitror hinc fieri q^d Venus ortà mari. (fol. 79.)

(Ib.)

Luna.

The moone beeing clouded presently is mist,   15
But litle stars may hide them when they list.
Gnattes are vnnoted whereso ere they flie
But Eagles guarded are with every eye. (ib.)

(No. 41², Endim. v. 3. 107–8)

In fœminæ deformitates.

Though men can cover crime wth bold sterne lookes,   20
Poore womens faces are their owne faults bookes. (fol. 80.)

In Priamum.

Had doting Priam checkt his sonnes desire,
Troy had beene bright with fame, and not with fire. (ib.)

(Euph. i. 188 ll. 8 sqq.)

Lucretiæ querela ad Colatinum.   25

In thy weake hiue a wandering waspe hath crept,
And suckt the honey, wch thy chast bee kept. (ib.)

(Euph. ii. 45 l. 26)

    1 I²] they *Songbook*   24 Troy] They *MS.*

NOTES

ENDIMION.

Page 17. TITLE: *The Man in the Moone*: see Prologue. The phrase is used, as Fairholt says (vol. ii. p. 282) 'to signify any wild story out of the reach of ordinary rules of criticism,' alluding to the popular fable that the man supposed visible in the 'spotty globe' was either Isaac carrying sticks for his own sacrifice, Cain bearing the thorns used in his unworthy offering, or the man stoned for gathering sticks on the Sabbath in *Numbers* xv. 32-6. The only shadow of literal justification for the title would be found in the classical Endymion's sleep in the moonlight, or in his dramatic representative's choice, here, of a bank of lunary or moon-wort on which to slumber (Act ii. 3. 10). Cynthia is evidently holding her court, not in heaven, but on earth (iii. 1. 49-50, and Epiton's allusion to a Thames barge iv. 2. 57); and the fountain which Eumenides finds on his way to Thessaly (iii. 4. 17) is probably meant for that of Gargaphie in Bœotia, sacred to Diana (Ov. *Met.* iii. 156), where also Ben Jonson locates his *Cynthias Revels*, which owes something to our play.

5. *on Candlemas day at night*: I can find no authority for the reading 'on New Yeares Day at night' given in Lowndes' report of the title in his *Manual*, and substituted for the true reading in the title given by Fairholt and Baker in their editions of the play. Mr. Baker asserts it to be the reading of Blount's edition: but in the half-dozen copies of the *Sixe Covrt Comedies* examined by me there is no title-page for *Endimion* at all, a point wherein it differs from the other five plays. The text immediately follows Blount's address 'To the Reader.'

P. 19, 9. DRAM. PERS., SIR TOPHAS: later consideration confirms my suspicion, unindulged in the Introduction, that this figure, though not without some original in Plautus, *Roister Doister* and other work, is too much of a burlesque to escape suggestion by the Sir Thopas of Chaucer, to whom I have noted some points of Lyly's indebtedness (vol. i. p. 401), especially in *Gallathea*. Lyly adapts Chaucer's parody of the romancers to his own purpose of comic relief, and parody of the romantic Endimion and Eumenides (iv. 2. 18, 70 and Essay, vol. ii. 276). Sir Tophas' care for equipment and personal appearance, i. 3, iii. 3. 27-35, is reproduced from the 'ryme' wherein it forms the staple: his preoccupation with hunting, fishing, and shooting (i. 3) is developed from stanza 5, where the mention of a 'ram' may suggest 'the Monster Ouis' and the pun (ii. 2. 94): his insensibility to the lures of Scintilla and Favilla (ii. 2. 103-53) has its model in the coyness of Chaucer's hero (stanza 6); his dream, and passion for the witch Dipsas (iii. 3) in Sir Thopas' conversion by a dream to a passion for the elf-queen (stt. 13-4): while the pages' talk about his married diet (iii. 3. 92-103) may be suggested by st. 22. Even the burlesque verses (iv. 2. 26) are suggested by the disyllabic lines in stt. 14-7. Lyly did not mean the parallel to be obvious; but the lines followed are the same, with some exaggeration of tone and addition of detail.

11. DRAM. PERS., DARES, *Page to Endimion* } Preceding editors
SAMIAS, *Page to Eumenides* transpose the names of the masters here, misled by the reading of the quarto and Blount in i. 3. 43-4 'I am Samias, page to Endimion.' 'And I Dares, page to Eumenides,' a passage directly contradicted by three later passages (iii. 3. 71-5; iv. 2. 1, 73-5), and indirectly by two others (ii. 2. 1-2; v. 1. 1-2), in all five of which all editions ancient and modern agree, so that the transposition in i. 3. 43-4 is clearly a compositor's mistake.

17. FLOSCULA, *her attendant*, &c.: in i. 2 her attitude seems that of a confidential dependant. She need not accompany Tellus to prison.

P. 20, 7. *apply pastimes*: interpret our sport as of real persons or facts. The disclaimer was perhaps necessary in order to obtain the licence of the Revels Office, which would be refused to a play treating matters of State: but *qui s'excuse s'accuse*, and Lyly knew well that there was no danger of his flattery failing to reach its mark.

P. 21, 19. *peeuish*: foolish, as in *Euph*. i. 190 l. 23 'peeuishnesse,' *Moth. Bomb*. i. 3. 166. Fairholt cites *Com. of Errors*, iv. 1. 93.

23. *Cease of*: 'cease,' like 'leave,' is used either absolutely or transitively, and in the latter case sometimes with the preposition 'of' or 'off,' though Shakespeare has no instance of 'cease of.'

P. 22, 24. *melancholy blood*: melancholy was considered by Elizabethans as mainly physical, an excess of black bile.

54. *fayre face . . . Summers blase . . . Winters blast*, &c.: *Euphues*, i. 202 ll. 15-6.

P. 23, 64. *downe into thy swath clowtes*: i.e. back to thy infancy.

9. *had beene worth*: i.e. might have been thought worth.

10. *Gods . . . laughers at Louers deceipts*: cf. *Rom. and Jul*. ii. 2. 93 'at lovers' perjuries, | They say, Jove laughs,' from Tibull. iii. 6. 49 'periuria ridet amantum | Iupiter.'

P. 24, 20-2. *whose vaines are Vines . . . whose eares are Corne . . . whose heares are grasse*: Dilke notes the confusion resulting from the attempt to reconcile the attributes of Cynthia and Tellus as women, with their allegorical attributes as the Moon and the Earth respectively. But the analogy, natural to Lyly's quest of ingenuity, is not very seriously pursued; and was perhaps adopted chiefly as a blind, at the outset, to

ENDIMION

the more daring allegory. The passages are collected in the separate essay, above, p. 82.

P. 25, 70. *Affection . . . bred by enchauntment*: with Floscula's assertion of the vanity of love-philtres, confirmed by Dipsas i. 4. 22-5, compare the answer made by Psellus, the physician, to Philautus in *Euph. and his Eng.* ii. 114 ll. 7-9, 118 ll. 20-5.

76. *fish taken with medicines*: i.e. caught, as Tellus suggests below, with poisoned dough. Again, vol. i. 427 ll. 20-2, ii. 108 ll. 23-4.

P. 26, 4. *wyl you see the deuill?*: i.e. 'Talk of the devil,' &c. (Dilke).

8. *lyuer, from whence Loue-mongers in former age . . . proceede*: the liver in the classics is the seat of the passions, e.g. of Hercules' love for Hylas, *Theocr.* xiii. 71. Dilke quotes *Much Ado* [iv. 1. 233] 'If ever love had interest in his liver.' Again in this play ii. 2. 12-3.

11. *pursie*: cf. *Haml.* iii. 4. 153 'the fatness of these pursy times.'

12. *some deuise of the Poet*: i.e. love is such.

25. *imbroder my bolts*: 'embroider' fantastically. The bird-bolt was a flat-headed arrow for knocking down small birds; cf. iii. 3. 38 'my bowe and bolts' (Dilke).

31. *Annuals*: there is no need to emend it, as do Blount and the moderns, '*Annals*': the proverb might be found more readily in an almanack than a history.

P. 27, 32. *you shall see how vnequall you be to mee*: Baker, though he inserts no stage-direction, suggests that Sir Tophas here actually measures his height with the pages', before proceeding.

38. *quod supra vos*, &c.: as in *Euphues*, i. 195 l. 26, where see note.

46. *Occupation*: the Elizabethan use generally implies inferiority, as of manual labour, as in *Coriolanus*, iv. 1. 14; *Jul. Caes.* i. 2. 269. Cf. 'occupied' = wrought, carved (of beech-wood), *Euph.* i. 196 l. 12.

53. *the fine wooll of Seres*: I emend 'Ceres' of all previous eds. Ceres was not the goddess of flocks. Cf. *Euph.* ii. 152 l. 23 'Wooll, which the Seres sende,' and *Sapho*, iii. 1. 38. Lyly is probably thinking of Virg. *Georg.* ii. 121 'Velleraque ut foliis depectant tenuia Seres.'

60. *wound . . . confound*: Dilke notes that the repetition *confound . . . confound* of Q Bl. may be a mark of Tophas' poverty of language, like 'a Poet is as much as one shoulde say, a Poet' above, l. 17: but urges on behalf of his proposed solecism, 'contund,' that it is such as Tophas might well use. Is the first *confound* a misprint for *confound* ('sound with my words')?

P. 28, 72. *wilde Mallard*: wild drake. It seems a pity not to hand on Fairholt's note, however little to the point:—'There is an annual merry-making at All Souls' College, Oxford, thus described in the Rev. J. Pointer's *Oxoniensis Academia*, 1749: "Another custom is that of celebrating their Mailard-night every year on the 14th of January, in remembrance of a huge mallard or drake, found (as tradition goes) imprisoned in a gutter or drain under ground, and grown to a vast bigness, at the digging for the foundation of the college." '

80. *heerein*: in the shield, i. e. the fish-basket.

88. *Simiter*: Fairholt notes that the Asiatic curved weapon was first used in England *temp.* Henry VI.

94. *weapons . . . the weapon*: here at least the repetition should be considered as an instance of one of Lyly's recognized marks of style: see Introd. Essay to *Euphues*, p. 124.

102. *Latine . . . saued your lyues*: allusion to the neck-verse.

P. 29. S.D. DIPSAS: 'Dipsas, as Mr. Stevens informs us in a note to the *Malcontent*, is the fire-drake, a serpent of a directly opposite nature to the hydrus ; the one is supposed to kill by inflammation, the other by cold' (Dilke). It is found in Aelian, vi. 51.

2. *trauell*: travail.

21. *remooue the Moone out of her course*: Virg. *Ecl.* viii. 70 'Carmina vel coelo possunt deducere Lunam.'

P. 30, 24. *not able to rule harts*: so Psellus, in *Euphues*, ii. 114 ll. 7–9.

40. *aslaked*: 'abated. Chaucer's *Knight's Tale* [l. 902] "Till at the last aslaked was his mood"' (Dilke). Again *Euph.* i. 307 l. 5, note.

P. 31, 14. *my solitarie life, almost these seauen yeeres*: see Introduction—Date, p. 13 (note). Eumenides iii. 4. 53–4 speaks of seven years' silence in connexion with Semele, and iv. 2. 114 Dares speaks of waiting seven years for a wise word. In all three cases seven years is probably merely used for a long period. But cf. *Euph. and his England*, ii. 52 ll. 35–6, where picturing the hardships of courtship Fidus says 'Besides this thou art to be bounde as it were an Apprentice seruing seauen yeares,' &c. If any more special reference is intended here, we should count seven years, perhaps, from Leicester's marriage to Lady Essex in 1578.

31. *thy fish Cynthia in the floode Araris*, &c. : Baker quotes *Euph.* i. 232 l. 19 'the fish Scolopidus in the floud Araris at the waxinge of the Moone is as white as the driuen snow, and at the wayning as blacke as the burnt coale:' This wonder is borrowed from the *Pseudo-plutarchea—De Fluuiis* vi, the Arar being the Saône in Gaul. Aelian too (*De Nat. Animal.* xv. 4) mentions a fish called *luna* of dark colour, whose size varies with the moon.

P. 32, 43. *see euerie vaine, sinew . . . of my loue*: cf. *Euph.* i. 254 l. 22 'Searche euery vayne and sinew of their disposition.'

P. 33, 82. *No more was Vesta*: cf. *Loves Met.* v. 1. 18 'Diana hath felt some motions of loue, Vesta doth, Ceres shall.' Lyly is perhaps thinking of those instances of supposed frailty in Vestal virgins cited *Euph.* ii. 209.

89. *the Wrastler in Olimpia*, &c.: it was customary for a wrestler,

on his entrance into the arena, to lift a heavy weight, as an index, or preliminary bracing, of his powers. Cf. *Euph.* ii. 6 l. 4.

92. *recure*: as substantive again iii. 1. 26, 4. 21, and Lydgate's *Complaint of the Black Knight*

'that I may not attayne
Recure to finde of myn adversite'
(misquoted by Dilke and Fairholt).

The verb is frequent, and occurs l. 651 of the same poem.

7. *tipt on the side*: lightly touched or smeared on the side; opposed to being plunged bodily in, like the 'tongues dipt to the roote,' above.

P. 34, 9. *lurcher*: 'lurch' is a variant of 'lurk,' and carries the sense of dishonest or nefarious purpose. 'Tom Lurcher' is the name given to the robber in Fletcher's *Night-Walker*.

10. *spleene that they cannot laugh*: cf. *Measure for Measure*, ii. 2. 122 'who, with our spleens, Would all themselves laugh mortal,' and other instances in Schmidt's *Shakespeare Lexicon*.

14. *rodde... vnder thy girdle*: i. e. applied below that point. The antithetic form again casts a doubt on the meaning; but the expression is exactly repeated, of parental discipline, in *Euph.* i. 185 l. 15.

19. *but a sparke... bee not much more then a sparke*: the first alludes to Favilla's small size and few years (see below); the second, more commonly of a man, indicates showy superficiality unfit to inspire a genuine 'flame.'

28. *That! that!*: addressed to Scintilla, by way of egging her on (Bak.).

30. *babies*: i. e. children's dolls (Fairholt). Cf. *Macb.* iii. 4. 106.

32. *Pantables bee higher with corke ... feete ... higher in the insteppes*: 'pantables,' more usually 'pantofles' (Fr. *pantoufles*) are embroidered shoes, or slippers, not necessarily a woman's. Dilke quotes Massinger's *City-Madam* 'have ready His cap and pantables.' Fairholt quotes Stubbes' *Anatomy of Abuses* 'corked shoes, puisnets pantofles, and slippers; some of them of black velvet, some of white, some of green, and some of yellow; some of Spanish leather, and some of English; stitched with silk and embroidered with gold and silver, all over the foot, with other gew-gaws innumerable.' 'To stand on the pantuffles,' and 'to be high in the insteppe' occur, as proverbial expressions for pride, in *Euphues*, i. 196 l. 24, 255 l. 36, and i. 202 l. 24.

44. *short*: ill-humoured, curt, but of course with a Parthian shot at Favilla's stature, as above.

P. 35, 60. *vse his garbe*: 'show his demeanor, style, fashion' (Baker). Cf. *Haml.* ii. 2. 390 'let me comply with you in this garb.'

65. *be our enemies fatte?*: referring to trout [or birds] carried in a basket, on the shield, by Epiton, the result of 'fortifying for fish,' i. 3. end (Bak.).

78. *This passeth!*: 'exceeds belief,' again iii. 4. 78. Brewer's *Lingua* 'Your travellers so dote upon me as passes.'

P. 36, 84. *vntewed*: uncombed, undressed; AS. *teóhan*, pull, draw, whence to tow; or else ME. *tewen, tawen*, AS. *tawian*, dress leather.

P. 37, 125. *pelting*: paltry. *Meas. for Meas.* ii. 2. 112 'every pelting, petty officer.'

140. *made for money*: Baker suggests that Sir Tophas may be alluding to the use of 'squirrel' as a cant term for a prostitute. Such a sneer would hardly be in keeping with his character, though it would give point to Dares' next speech, with whom the allusion, if any, lies. Fairholt informs us that the Tapestry of Nancy, found lining the tent of Charles the Bold, after his death at the siege of that place in 1476, contains a lady of rank seated with a favourite squirrel secured to her wrist by a chain.

P. 38. SCENE III.—*A Grove*, &c.: see iv. 3. 160.

3. *iudged vnfaithfull*: Dipsas may perhaps be supposed to have fulfilled her promise at the end of Act i to inspire Cynthia with a distrust of him, a symptom to which he has also alluded in ii. 1. 5, 28.

6. *Ebone, which no fire ... sweet sauours*: hastily from Pliny xii. 9 '[Ebenum] accendi Fabianus negat: uritur tamen odore iucundo.'

10. *Lunary*: moonwort, says Johnson. *Euph.* ii. 172 l. 18 'Lunaris hearbe, as long as the Moone waxeth, bringeth forth leaues, and in the waining shaketh them of.' Baker quotes *Sapho and Phao*, iii. 3. 43 'an hearbe called Lunary, that being bound to the pulses of the sick, causeth nothinge but dreames of weddings and daunces.' Cf. Drayton's 'Man in the Moone' in *Poemes* (1604 or -5, 12mo)

'As my great brother, so haue I a flower
To me peculiar, that doth ope and close
When as I rise, and when I me repose.'

P. 39, 36. *The malice of Tellus*, &c.: since the end of ii. 2 Tellus has apparently wrought upon Dipsas to lay the spell of sleep upon him. He complains, above, of an inexplicable lethargy; and just below Dipsas goes out to 'finish' the necessary ceremonies. Dipsas' remark 'from her gather wee all our simples to maintaine our sorceries,' in addition to adding a touch to the physical allegory, may refer to the large allowance drawn by the Shrewsburies for the support of Mary of Scotland and her ladies.

40. *sing the inchantment for sleepe*: everyone will share Dilke's regret that the song on this beautiful theme, which should appear after the first words of Bagoa's following speech, has been lost. I suggest one p. 470, below.

A DUMBE SHEW: first given in Blount; its absence from the quarto being probably attributable to the fact that Lyly was his own stage-manager and did not embody in his original MS. what he could teach orally, stage-directions being rare. It is a representation of the dream Endimion narrates in v. 1. p. 66, and forms the complement of the Court history Lyly is allegorically relating. He never uses Dumb Show elsewhere: nor is there any instance of its separate employment in Greene's works, though both *James IV* and *The Looking Glass for London* have a large spectacular element. Kyd uses it in *Jeronimo*: Peele in *The Battle of Alcazar*. It is unused by Marlowe, Lodge, and Nash. It marks, in fact, an earlier date than that at which these dramatists wrote, and is characteristic rather of the pseudo-classic drama, where it atones in a measure to the spectators for the lack of action imposed by adherence to classical rules. Excellent examples of it occur in *Gorboduc*, 1561, and in Thos. Hughes' *The Misfortunes of Arthur*, where the authorship, in part, of the elaborate shows before the Acts is attributed to Francis Bacon. Shakespeare casts a slur upon it in Hamlet's advice to the Players, and introduces it in the puppet-play as part of the style and practice of a past age; reflecting, in the king's question about the argument immediately after, that neglect of it by the audience which, as the dramatists learnt to tell their tale directly by dialogue and action, must gradually have driven it from the stage.

P. 40, 9. *Endimion onely was*: was your one thought.

17. *malepart ouerthwarts*: impertinent wranglings (Fairholt). *Loves Met.* v. 4. 141; *Camp.* iii. 2. 38.

P. 41, 29. *compasse of the earth*: i. e. the circuit, the power of going or sending all round it. Another touch to the physical allegory.

37. *camock*: a word of Gaulish origin, represented in modern Welsh and Gaelic, meaning a crooked staff or crook. ME. *kambok*, LL. *cambuca*. Cf. *Euph.* ii. 23 l. 21 note; *M. Bombie*, i. 3. 108; and Glossary. Heywood's *Prouerbes*, 1546 has 'It pricketh betimes that will be a good thorne,' and 'Timely crooketh the tree, that will a good camok bee' (p. 159, Sharman's reprint).

43. *worke stories or poetries?*: Fairholt quotes from John Taylor's *Needles Excellencie*, 1640—

'poses rare and anagrams,
Signifique searching sentences from names,
True history, or various pleasant fiction
In sundry colours mixt, with art's commixion.'

46. *Enchaunters in Thessaly*: cf. 'Thessalicum venenum,' Ov. *Am.* iii. 7. 27; Hor. *Od.* i. 27. 21; *Ep.* 5. 45; 'Thessala philtra,' Juv. vi. 610; and Fotis, the Thessalian enchantress, in Apuleius' *De Asino*.

P. 42, 11. *no sweeter musicke . . . then dispayre*: this attitude is repeated in Geron, iii. 4. 6–9 and in Shakespeare's *Richard II*, &c.

20. *sound nothing but terror*, &c.: so *Mid.* ii. 1. 102 'soundest but bloud and terror.'

P. 43, 19. *cannot stand without another*: here, as elsewhere, e. g.

M. Bomb. iii. 2. 12-4, Lyly is reproducing the language of the Latin Grammar in exclusive use throughout the realm, being the original Grammar by W. Lilly and John Colet with an English Introduction. The earliest edition I have seen is that entitled *A Shorte Introduction of Grammar,* &c., 1577, 4°. On fol. C iij recto, which treats of Interjections, occurs 'Some are of myrth: as *Euax, vah.* Some are of sorrow: as *Heu, hei,*' &c. On A 5 recto 'A Noune is the name of a thing, that may be seene, felt, hearde, or vnderstande[d] : ... A Noune Substantiue is that standeth by himselfe ... A Noune Adiectiue is that can not stande by himselfe, but requireth to be ioyned with an other woorde.'

27. *discouer*: uncover.

29. *Cedant arma togæ*: Cic. *de Off.* i. 22. 76.

32. *bella gerant alii,* &c.: seems suggested by Ov. *Her.* xiii. 84 'Bella gerant alii! Protesilaus amet' (Baker). But in *Her.* xvii. 254 the line occurs in a nearer form—'Bella gerant fortes: tu, Pari, semper ama.' Repeated *Midas,* iv. 4. 28-9.

35. *the bodkin beard or the bush*: Fairholt in a long note on *Midas,* iii. 2. 39 about the varying cut of the beard, says the bodkin-beard was '"sharp, stiletto fashion, dagger like" to use the words of Taylor, the Water Poet, in his *Superbiæ Flagellum.*' 'The bush' would be effected by leaving it untrimmed (Bak.).

36. *dicere quæ puduit,* &c.: Ov. *Her.* iv. 10 (Bak.).

39. *Scalpellum,* &c.: these two lines seem to be of Lyly's composition.

41. *bable*: for 'bauble.' See Glossary. Nares quotes Harring. *Epig.* ii. 96 'To be my foole, and I to be thy bable.'

P. 44, 43, *Militat omnis,* &c.: Ov. *Amor.* i. 9. 1 (Bak.).

47. *Non formosus,* &c.: Ov. *Ars Amat.* ii. 123 (Bak.).

50. *Quicquid conabar,* &c.: Baker notes that the line occurs in Ov. *Trist.* iv. 10. 26 'Et, quod tentabam dicere, versus erat'; but that in Sidney's *Defence of Poesie* it is given as here. As a matter of fact the first edition of Sidney's *Apologie for Poetrie* (1595) reads 'conabor . . . erit,' 'conabor' being corrected in an *erratum* to the imperfect. The reading 'conabar' is only found in the Codex Bernensis of Ovid, the other MSS. having 'tentabam.'

56. *Bytter*: bittern. 'ME. *bitoure, bytoure,* Chaucer *C. T.* 6554—F. *butor,* "a bittor"; Cotg.' (Skeat).

59. *thrifty ... no waste*: Dilke notes the recurrence of the pun in 2 *Henry IV,* i. 2. 161 'I would my means were greater, and my waist slenderer.'

68. *woodcock*: simpleton (Bak.).

P. 45, 83. *vaile bonet*: lower cap. ME. *aualen,* to descend or lower, F. *avaler,* fr. *à val,* Lat. *ad vallem.* (Skeat's *Concise Dict. of Mid. Eng.*)

ENDIMION

89. *without fashion . . . without fauour* : the first of shape, the second of features (Dilke).

98. *lumpe*: the fish is so named from its heavy shape.

powting: 'Powt or eel-powt,' Minsheu (Skeat).

101. *fretters*: the only known instance of the word, which the N. E. D. conjectures from the context to be a species of apple.

P. 46, 117. *The Witch* must be Dipsas.

121. *Bandogs*: originally *band-dog*, a large dog held in a band, or tied up. *Prompt. Parv.* p. 43 'bondogge or bonde dogge, *Molosus.*'

124. *batten*: properly 'to grow fat,' here of being left at ease, in comfort. Dilke quotes Dryden

'The lazy glutton safe at home will keep,
Indulge his sloth and batten on his sleep.'

144. *vntrusse the poynts*: undo the fastenings, points being the strings or ribbons with metal tags by which the dress was fastened before the advent of buttons. 'To trusse' is to fasten as a package or 'trusse,' a word found as subst. *Prompt. Parv.* p. 504 (Skeat).

P. 47, 156. *I præ, sequar*: Ter. *And.* i. 1. 144. Again in *M. Bomb.* ii. 4. 20.

1. *your sad musique . . . your mouthes ende*: another song lost, of a pathetic character, which should have commenced the scene. See Essay, vol. ii. p. 265. That suggested above, p. 470, seems exactly appropriate.

5. *these fiftie Winters*: compare v. 3. 21, where we learn that Dipsas has practised witchcraft 'almost these fiftie yeeres,' so that her husband must have been her earliest subject. This old man, living alone and brooding on the past, reminds us of Fidus or Cassander or Euphues himself in *Euphues and his England.*

P. 48, 34. *Eum. (aside). Ah Eumenides!*: caused by the sudden thought that he may win Semele by sacrificing his friend.

53. *Howe secrete hast thou beene these seauen yeeres*: cf. Endimion's lament over his 'solitarie life, almost these seauen yeeres,' ii. 1. 14. But if, as I believe, Eumenides and Semele represent Sir Philip Sidney and Penelope Rich, the 'seauen yeeres' must not be pressed. Sir Philip's first sight of Penelope Devereux was in the autumn of 1575 ; and their engagement, made probably in 1576, seems to have been broken off after the death of her father the Earl of Essex in Sept. of that year. She married Lord Rich early in 1581, which seems to have given new life to Philip's flame.

P. 49, 75. *and dissolue*: and let me dissolve. This double construction of *let*, first as a separate and then as an auxiliary verb, is thoroughly Lylian. See Introd. Essay to *Euphues*, vol. i. p. 125.

79. *the beleefe*: i. e. in the magic properties of the fountain.

86. *not a faithfull louer*: this may allude to Shrewsbury's falling under the influence of his domestic Eleanor Britton, and would form an

additional argument for a late date for the play. (See *Dict. Nat. Biog.* Talbot, George, 6th Earl.)

P. 50, 116. *Semele* ... *I, but Endimion*, &c.: for this rhetorical see-saw cf. Lucilla, balancing between Euphues and Philautus, *Euph.* i. 205 ll. 17–22, and the opposition between love and friendship in Geron's following speech reminds us of Euphues' reflections, i. 210.

129. *Camelion ... lunges*: Pliny, xxix. 29, has only 'cum id animal nullo cibo vivat'; it is rather Bartholomaeus Anglicus on whom Lyly is drawing (xviii. 21) 'and what is in his body is but of lytell flesh & hath but lytell blood ... And it is sayde that the camelion lyueth only by ayre.' *Euph.* i. 194 l. 21 differs somewhat—'ye Camelion thoughe hee haue most guttes, draweth least breath.'

P. 51, 144. *common as Hares in Atho*: again with Hybla bees as an instance of plentifulness, *Euph.* i. 221 l. 24; suggested by Ov. *Art. Am.* iii. 150 'Nec quot apes Hyble, nec quot in Alpe ferae.'

146. *Phœnix ... but one*: Pliny, x. 2 'phoenicem ... unum in toto orbe, nec visum magnopere.'

the Philadelphi in Arays: Baker gives a suggestion of Prof. Peck of Columbia College, that the mock orange (*philadelphus hirsutus*) is meant, whose flowers as a rule grow only in pairs, though they have been (rarely) found in clusters; and that Arays is Lyly's form for the Spanish Aranjuez, whose beautiful flower-gardens were laid out by Philip II. This is not wholly satisfying; but I find nothing in Pliny, Aelian, or Bartholomaeus Anglicus.

155. *in the same Piller*: the former inscription was 'in white marble engrauen,' l. 81. Cf. the 'crouned Pillar' of vol. i. 411 top, 456 l. 26, 466 l. 4.

175. *that our bodies might the better bee gouerned*: Barth. Ang. viii. 30 quotes from 'Ptholomeus' some effects of the moon on the human eyesight, &c.

182. *tell her the successe*: i. e. the succession, sequel, issue, as in *Wint. Tale*, i. 2. 394 'our parents' noble names, In whose success we are gentle'; and William Bercher's MS. *The Nobylytye off Wymen* (1559), fol. 16 B verso, 'Emonge the Ebrewes Maria Delbora and Anna knewe the Successe of thynges by their Dyvynytie.' Also *Gall.* i. 1. 19, &c.; see Glossary.

P. 53, 23. *stoute*: cf. 'stoutnesse,' *Loves Metam.* v. 2. 4.

26. *practise that which is most customarie to our sex, to dissemble.* All eds. read *contrarie*, Blount and Fairholt omitting Q's comma at *sex*, thus giving the sense that Tellus will pretend what it goes against the grain with women to feign, viz. love, a statement hardly more natural than that it avoids, which latter is contradicted by her attitude on the subject, ii. 1. 59–68. As emendation either *not contrarie* or *most common* would also do, always retaining the comma at *sex*.

41. *He that gaue Cassandra*, &c.: i.e. the Thymbraean Apollo; the curse was added in consequence of her resistance to his desires (Hygin. *Fab.* 93).

P. 54, 67. *nothing pleaseth her but the fairenesse of virginitie*: compare the speech of Diana (= Elizabeth) on this subject, *Gallathea*, iii. 4. 16-53, which I have illustrated in the notes by a long passage quoted from Halpin.

79. *I will in, and laugh . . . at Corsites sweating*: see under Place and Time, p. 14.

5. *pelting chafe*: the modern editors explain as merely 'irritable humour'; but *pelting* has its usual sense of paltry, petty, referring to Epi's small stature, as though a fly should exhibit passion.

P. 55, 27. *fodge*: move suit, go suitably.

29. *from the thombe to the little finger*, &c.: the satire is aimed at that ever-recurring attempt to cover poverty of thought and feeling under eccentricity of form which Addison (*Spectator*, No. 58) notes in some minor Greek poets. George Herbert has a good deal of it—'Easter Wings,' an 'Altar,' &c. Much modern verse exhibits, and some reviewers consider, form only.

33. *blacke Saunce*: black Sanctus, or hymn to St. Satan, ridiculing the monks; an example appears in the prologue to Sir John Harington's *Ajax*, and was republished in the *Nugae Antiquae* (Nares). But the term is commonly used in Elizabethan literature for any noisy or profane ditty, e.g. Nash's *Have with you*, &c. (of Lyly himself), 'With a blacke sant he meanes shortly to bee att his chamber window, for calling him the Fiddlestick of Oxford.' Dilke quotes Beaumont and Fletcher's *Mad Lover*, 'Prithee let's sing him a black santis.'

P. 56, 40. *Artillarie . . . nailes*: perhaps alluding to the boys' trick of flipping small objects.

41. *Sic omnia*, &c.: 'Cic. *Paradoxa Stoicorum*, I. i. "Omnia mecum porto mea." Ascribed to Bias by Cicero. Cp. Phaedrus, *Fab.* iv. 21' (Baker).

44. *Cælo tegitur*, &c.: Lucan, vii. 819 (Bak.). But Lyly's range of quotation is probably assisted by some collection of *Sententiae*.

57. *Westerne barge*: i.e. on the Thames. *Pugge*, or *pug*, a variant of Puck, is a term of good fellowship. Dilke quotes Marston's *Anton. and Mellida*, ii. 1 'Good pug, give me some capon.'

67. *certaine fountaine hard by*: see under Place and Time, p. 14.

71. *wambleth in his stomacke*: rumbles. Beau. and Flet. *Mad Lover*, i. 1. 280 'cold sallads . . . lie wambling in your stomachs.'

S. D. *Enter the Watch*: set by Cynthia to guard the sleeping Endymion; see below, l. 84, and iv. 3 l. 8. Gyptes, l. 160, merely approves.

P. 57, 91. *take me with you*: don't leave me out of consideration; like the 'Shall I have audience?' of Holofernes, *L. L. L.* v. 1. 130.

101. '*children and fooles speake true*' : compare William Bercher's MS. *Nobylytye off Wymen*, fol. 28 verso 'accordinge to the pverbe / ffoolis and children / be best prophetes.'

103. *All say, True* : i.e. by speaking 'True' they bring themselves within the proverb. Cf. *M. Bomb.* ii. 1. 99 'moras.'

105. *prouided from* : the Constable's mistake for 'avoided of.'

P. 58, 114. *watch 7. yeres for a wise worde* : i.e. the whole length of an apprenticeship, or any long period. See note on ii. 1. 14.

131 sqq. Cf. the squaring of the Serjeant in *M. Bomb.* iv. 2. 241.

137. *browne Bils* : brown, either from rust, or because painted to keep them from it (Fairholt and Baker).

roare : revel. Cf. the cant term 'roaring boy' for a swaggerer.

P. 59, 16. *braunfallen* : cf. *Euph.* i. 307 l. 30 'Milo, that great wrastler beganne to weepe when he sawe his armes brawnefallen and weake.' *Braun* is originally muscle, though used for boar's flesh, *P. Plowman*, B. xiii. 63, 91.

18. *lythernesse* : languor, as in *Euph.* ii. 50 l. 31. AS. líðe = gentle, soft, and is used in that sense in Chaucer's *House of Fame*, 118. Also AS. lyðer = evil, gives us 'litherly' = ill, in *Milleres Tale*, 113, and 'lyther' = vicious, in *The Cuckoo and the Nightingale*, l. 14 (Skeat).

22. *rent* : rend, as in v. 3. 42 'my rented and ransackt thoughts,' and *Euph.* ii. 17 l. 29.

27. *Hags—out alas! Nymphes!* : he substitutes a more complimentary term. The punctuation of Dilke and Baker quite misses the point, which is clear enough in the quarto. *Hags*, witches, as *Euph.* i. 255 l. 3, &c.

29. *pinch him* : suggested by Scot's *Discouerie of Witchcraft*, ii. 4. The parallel in Act v of the *Merry Wives* has been pointed out by Steevens and Fairholt. In *Old Ballads, Historical and Narrative*, by Thos. Evans, Lon. 1810, vol. i. p. 145, is printed, 'from a very rare collection of Songs, called Hunting, Hawking, Dancing, &c.; set to music by Bennet, Piers, and Ravenscroft, 4to,' a poem entitled *The Elues Dance*, which precisely corresponds to the situation in Lyly's play, and may have been substituted for it at some revival of which the record is lost. It runs as follows—

'Dare you haunt our hallow'd green?
None but fairies here are seen.
   Down and sleep,
   Wake and weep,
Pinch him black, and pinch him blue,
That seeks to steal a lover true.
When you come to hear us sing,
Or to tread our fairy ring,
Pinch him black, and pinch him blue,
O thus our nails shall handle you.'

P. 60, 41. *Heidegyes*: cf. *Shep. Kal.* June, ' But frendly Faeries . . . can chace the lingring Night | With Heydeguyes, and trimly trodden traces,' and Drayton's *Polyolb. Song* v. *Argum.* 'Dance hy-day-gies.' The sole etymology suggested is the unsatisfactory 'hey-day guise.'

49. *in colours*: of what is feigned, described or imagined.

52. *let vs walke to Endimion*: from Gyptes' following remark, and Cynthia's to Floscula, it is evident that Endimion is not supposed to be present. At her entry above we are to imagine her in her palace or its grounds; and during the 20 ll. between her proposal to 'walke to Endimion' and her exclamation 'Behold Endimion!' they walk up and down the stage as if in transit to the lunary-bank. Cf. under Place and Time, p. 14.

P. 61, 80. *I haue seemed strange*: this coldness of Cynthia, whether intended as the result of Tellus' machinations or not, was twice alluded to by Endimion, ii. 1. 27 sqq., and ii. 3. 3. *But* in the preceding line is probably adverb.

84-7. *like a Leopard . . . looke on thy hands*: see the Fairies' Song 'Spots ore all his flesh shall runne.'

P. 62, 111. *from this Caban*: noted by Baker as an inconsistency; but it merely shows that the lunary-bank occupied that central, covered, and sometimes raised, portion of the stage which did duty in turn for a mountain, castle, cave, inner room, &c., and was separated from the main stage by doors or curtains that could be drawn back at pleasure.

P. 63, 153. *in a cluster*: indistinguishable.

P. 65, 50. *slept fortie yeeres*: the inconsistency between this numbering and the 'almost twentie yeeres' of iii. 4. 19 was noted by Dilke. See under Place and Time, p. 15.

61. *Iustes, turneys*: Dilke quotes from Strutt's *Sports and Pastimes* the distinction between a tournament where parties of knights are opposed, and a joust where single knights are opposed.

P. 66, 81. *Methought I sawe a Ladie passing faire*, &c.; this description of the dream of Endimion, which is epitomized in the Dumb Shew, p. 39, is obviously allegorical, but not perhaps of the same events as those symbolized in the play, or not in the same aspect. The lady with the knife who is diverted from her cruel purpose is probably Elizabeth, in whom mercy overcomes anger (ll. 96-100). The stern damsel who incites the lady with the knife *may* be the Countess of Shrewsbury, but is more probably meant for Leicester's second wife, Lady Douglas Sheffield, who on the revelation by Simier, the French ambassador for the Duke of Alençon, of Leicester's marriage to the Countess of Essex, claimed her own marital rights, but was persuaded by Leicester's threats and, says Dugdale, by the offer of £700 a year, to withdraw her claim. The interview took place 'in the close arbour of the Queen's garden, Greenwich,' which corresponds to the lunary-bank in the play on which Endimion is dreaming (see Halpin's *Oberon's Vision*, p. 39). The third lady, who sympathizes with him, is the gentle Floscula of the play, Leicester's third wife, Lettice, widow of Essex. The old man with the book of counsels, policies, and pictures, the last alone of which Endimion accepts (a fable obviously suggested by that of Tarquin and the Sibyl), is possibly meant for Burleigh, endeavouring to guide by wisdom one who owns no law but that of the affections. The wolves barking impotently at Cynthia represent the ineffectual plots of which the reign was full. Ingratitude, Treachery, and Envy need no special identification ; but the drones or beetles that creep into the Eagle's nest to suck its blood are probably the Jesuit priests of Douai and Rheims, the perpetual fomenters of disorders in England, against whom stringent measures were taken in 1583. A pamphlet entitled *The Execution of Justice in England* . . . Imprinted at London 1583 (*Harl. Miscellany*, vol. ii. pp. 137-155) defends the penal laws recently enacted against papists, and is at pains to show that they were aimed at them not as papists, but as rebels. It alludes to the Pope's bull of excommunication, 1570, and to his commission to the Jesuit Fathers, Parsons and Campion, on their departure for England, April 14, 1580.

111. *pitching*: properly of fixing or fastening a sharp peg into the ground, as in 'pitching camp.'

P. 67, 127. *totterd*: a variant of 'tattered,' as in Marlowe's *Edw. II*, v. 5 'my totterd robes.' 'Totters' is found in Ford's *Sun's Darling*, i. 1. 2nd Song.

130. *Beetles . . . creeping vnder the winges*, &c. : repeated, with variety, from *Euphues*, ii. 215 l. 21, where see note.

P. 68, 5. *Lorde of misrule . . . keepeth Christmas* : the election of a Lord of Misrule to preside over Christmas festivities needs no illustration to-day. Collier's *History of Dramatic Poetry*, i. 132, quotes a long passage from Holinshed describing the appointment of George Ferrers as Edward VI's Lord of Misrule for the twelve days of Christmas, 1551-2, which speaks of such appointment as ' of old ordinarie course.'

22. *quyller* : an unfledged bird ; no other instance known, but 'quils' are used for 'feathers' in *Sapho and Phao*, iv. 3. 17, and *Gallathea*, i. 1. 31.

P. 69, 25. *Agnosco veteris*, &c. : *Aen.* iv. 23.

30. *Rabbet sucker* : a sucking rabbit. Steevens compares 1 *Henry IV* [ii. 4. 480] 'Hang me up by the heels for a rabbit sucker,' i.e. a tender innocent. Dugdale's *Origines* twice mentions a dish of them as figuring in a feast in Inner Temple Hall (Dilke).

31. *chicken peeper*: to 'peep' is to chirp, or cry. Skeat quotes *Isaiah* viii. 19 ' wizards that peep and that mutter,' and Nicholas of Guildford's *Owl and Nightingale*, 503.

47. *est Venus in vinis*, &c.: Ov. *Ars Amat.* i. 244 with *et* for *est* (Pak.).

48. *O lepidum caput*: Ter. *Adelphi*, v. 9. 9.

52. *My solicitors*: i e. sent to solicit Dipsas.

P. 70, 67. *The Turtle true hath nere a tooth*: nothing in Pliny, nor Barth. Angl. It sounds like a fragment of an old ballad.

79. *to an Aspen*: in Gascoigne's *Princely Pleasures* (1576) Zabeta converts Inconstancy into a quivering poplar.

82. *turne me to some goodly Asse*: allusion to the *De Asino* of Apuleius, where Fotis the witch so transforms the hero Lucius.

92. *grissels*: gristle is cartilage that may harden into bone; so here of tender, immature young girls.

94. *Animus*, &c.; Cv. *Ars Amat.* ii. 535 (Bak.).

95. *orient*: Pliny mentions Arabia and India as the locale of the finest pearls; but the word here carries some sense of the opaline tints of dawn. Cf. *Woman*, iii. 2. 9.

95 sqq. Cf. Thisbe on Pyramus, *Mids. N. Dr.* v. 1. 337-45.

96. *watchet*: light blue colour. Nares says probably from *wad* or *woad*, and quotes Browne's *Brit. Past.* ii. 3 'watchet deepened with a blew'; and Skeat refers to *The Milleres Tale*, 3321 'Al in a kirtel of a light wachet.'

P. 71, 101. *curtoll*: Baker supposes a pun on 'curtal,' a bob-tailed horse; and the idea may find faint support in the following words, *walke ... cold*, of exercising a fiery horse.

107. *graue ... grauitie*: the dying Mercutio repeats the pun, *Rom. and Jul.* iii. 1. 103.

5. *If Bagoa had not bewraied it ... Golde and fayre words*: the motives which actuated Bagoa in the play would seem from ii. 3. p. 30 pity and admiration for Endimion. It is the more difficult, or perhaps needless, to find any original of Bagoa; inasmuch as what is represented in the play as a plot against Endimion, which required some one to reveal it, was in the actual events simply the publication of facts that damaged him, publication about which there was no concealment; so that Bagoa's function has no precise counterpart in the facts, though in the Essay, p. 100, I have suggested for her Lady Lennox.

12. *her deadliest foes ... iniuries of her trayne*: this distinction, which seems to militate against our identifying Tellus with the Queen of Scots, must be considered as intentional mystification on Lyly's part. Though Mary had been clearly proved to be a party to Norfolk's treason, and Parliament had petitioned for her death in 1572, she had been spared; and her confinement in 1573-4 seems to have been far from rigorous.

P. 72, 42. *rented*: torn, participle of 'rent' = rend; cf. iv. 3. 22, and *Euph.* ii. 17 l. 29 'renting his clothes and tearing his haire,' and Sir Th. Elyot's *Governour*, Proheme 'to rente and deface the renoume of wryters' (*Cent. Dict.*).

P. 73, 62. *vnacquainted*: unknown. So *Gall.* iii. 4. 58; *Loves Met.* i. 2. 145. Cf. 2 *Henry IV*, v. 2. 139 'things acquainted and familiar to us.'

80. *colour*: explain, excuse.

P. 74, 88. *breaketh . . . and neuer brooseth*, &c.: cf. *Euph.* ii. 76 l. 1, &c.

98. *a continuall burning*, &c.: besides the ordinary metaphor of the fires of love, I think we have here, as in Tellus' last speech but one, another contribution to the purely physical allegory of the Moon and the Earth.

110. *smooth shoe vppon a crooked foote*: refers to the story of the cripple Demonides, Plut. *De Aud. Poet.* iii, alluded to *Euph.* i. 179 l. 27; and cf. vol. ii. 7 l. 6.

P. 75, 120. *enioying*: experience.

122. *haue him in the obiect of mine eyes*: a rare use of 'object' for aspect, sight, appearance. 'He advancing close | Up to the lake, past all the rest, arose | In glorious object' (Chapman): and 'The object of our misery is as an inventory to particularise their abundance,' *Coriolanus*, i. 1. 21 (*Cent. Dict.*).

124. *fryed my selfe*: *Euph.* i. 205 l. 4. 'Lucilla, who now began to frie in the flames of loue,' &c.

126. *I founde him in most melancholie*, &c.: referring to Act ii. Sc. 1.

P. 76, 157. *but in that shee saide I . . . swore to honour her*: in i. 2. 7 on her first entrance Tellus spoke to Floscula of Endimion's 'oathes without number' and 'kisses without measure'; and Endimion's soliloquy ii. 3. 11 seems to imply amatory relations with her: but in ii. 1. 22 he tells us that he has used her but as a cloak for his love for Cynthia; and, whatever the historical facts, Lyly does not intend to represent his hero as strongly swayed by any other passion.

P. 77, 219. *Speakes the Parrat?*: a conventional expression of contempt for some previous remark. *Speke Parrot* is the title by which Skelton excuses his abusive attack on Wolsey (Fairholt). Cf. Mercury's indignant comment on Nature's gift of his eloquence to Pandora, 'Thou pretty Parrat speake a while' (*Woman in Moone*, i. 1. 116).

P. 78, 230. *wanting a tongue to blaze the beautie of Semele*: if my conjecture for the originals of Eumenides and Semele be correct, this may be an allusion to some of the *Astrophel and Stella* sonnets, first printed in 1591, but handed about in manuscript for some years before, and mainly, if not entirely, composed after Lady Penelope's marriage to Lord Rich early in 1581.

239. *with what sodaine mischiefe*, &c.: cf. Portia's words when Bassanio selects the right casket

'O love! be moderate; allay thy ecstasy;
In measure rein thy joy; scant this excess:

ENDIMION

> I feel too much thy blessing ; make it less,
> For fear I surfeit!' *Merchant of Ven.* iii. 2. 111.

243. *louely looke* : loving look. This union of Tellus with Corsites is apparently the sole ground Halpin has for regarding Sir Edward Stafford as the original for the latter. He was married to Lady Douglas Sheffield after the disturbance in 1579, by Leicester's persuasion; but seems not to have been a soldier, nor to have taken any such part in Lady Sheffield's previous history as might support the analogy with Tellus. See essay on the Allegory, above, pp. 91–2.

265. *will you admit her to your Wife?* : the quarrel between the Earl and Countess of Shrewsbury was actually composed by Elizabeth's means, but not before 1586 (*Calendar of State Papers*, Domestic, 1581–1590); and in 1589 we find the Queen again writing to the Earl to allow his wife access to him.

P. 79, 267. *leude* : wicked.

277. *this tree* : Baker notes that the tree seems to have been placed on the stage at some time subsequent to the beginning of the scene, where Panelion speaks of 'an Aspen tree,' not '*this* Aspen tree.'

284. *a bots vpon thee !* : 'a kind of worms troublesome to horses' (Halliwell). Petruchio's horse has them, *Taming*, iii. 2. 54.

P. 80, *Epilogue* : 'made from the third of the fables of Avienus, usually printed as Aesop's' (Baker). Lyly has employed it before in Euphues' letter of advice to Philautus on the management of his wife, *Euph. and his England*, ii. 224 ll. 7–15.

MIDAS.

P. 114, 8. DRAM. PERS. LICIO, *Page to Cælia*, &c. : Dilke and Fairholt simply bracket the three boys as 'Servants,' describing Pipenetta also as 'a Servant,' and including Cælia simply among the 'Ladies of the Court'; but from i. 2. 1 and 113–5 it seems clear that Licio, Petulus, and Pipenetta all belong to Mellacrites' household, while Minutius (iv. 3. 79) is distinct.

19. ERATO : see note on iv. 1. 34.

SCENE: *Phrygia and Delphi*. But see note on Act iv. Scene i. p. 139.

P. 115. THE PROLOGVE IN PAVLES: i. e. in the singing-room of the Paul's choir, where they rehearsed the plays subsequently to be given at Court. The higher price charged for admission to these 'exercises' (cf. the marginal note in *Pappe*, p. 408 'If it be shewed at Paules, it will cost you foure pence: at the Theater two pence: at Sainct Thomas a Watrings nothing'), and the more select character of the audience, alluded to at the end of the present prologue and in *Jack Drum's Enter-*

tainment, pub. 1601 (Collier, i. 273), indicates not only the smallness of the space available as auditorium, but also perhaps that such a use of the singing-room was connived at rather than officially recognized. Malone (ed. Boswell, ii. 194) tells us it was situate 'behind the Convocation House.'

3. *sacietie*: a recognized, though now obsolete, variant.

5. *the Tayler . . . gone to the Paynters*, &c.: Fairholt quotes in illustration Ben Jonson's *The Staple of Newes*—

> I pray thee tell me, Fashioner, what authors
> Thou read'st to help thy invention? Italian prints?
> Or Arras hangings? they are taylors' libraries. [i. 1.]

For the variety of English fashions, see *Euphues*, ii. 194 l. 15 note.

8. *notes beyonde Ela*: i.e. beyond E, the highest note in the Hexachord, indicated in Solmisation by the general name *E la mi*, because it would bear either of those names according as the hexachord began on G, F, or C. See note on 'scarce sing sol fa . . . straine aboue E la,' *Euphues*, ii. 3 l. 24, and on *M. Bomb.* ii. 1. 132 'his knauerie is beyond *Ela*, & yet he knowes not *Gam vt*.'

9. *picktooths for the Spaniard*: Whitney says that an umbelliferous plant, *Ammi Visnaga*, has received the name of 'picktooth' on account of the use made in Spain of the rays of its main umbel.

10. *porridge*: *Pottage*, the variant in Blount, occurs again for *porridge* in *Euphues*, i. 189 l. 33 E rest.

our exercises: the same term is applied to their performances in the Blackfriars' Prol. to *Sapho and Phao*.

14. *Arras, full of deuise*: the fancifulness of the products of the Arras loom is alluded to *Euphues*, ii. 8 l. 5.

23. *he is idle*: see Life, p. 47.

26. *Stirps rudis*, &c.: the opposition of rose and nettle (cf. *Sapho*, v. 2. 74, and often) and the bad jingle at the end perhaps indicate the motto as Lyly's own.

P. 116. ACT I. SCENE I.—*Gardens before Midas' Palace*: that this scene, which nothing compels us to change in the first three Acts, and a return to which may be supposed in v. 2, is laid in the open air is clear from the 'stick' and 'stone' which Midas picks up at ll. 100-3, and the proposal 'let vs in' near the end of scc. 1 and 2: that it is near the palace may be inferred from the presence of the princess and her ladies, and that of the pages, as well as from the words of Mellacrites at the end of iii. 3.

2. *receiue good turns*: the service, namely, rendered to Silenus; see l. 108, and under Sources.

18. *Magnis tamen excidit ausis*: of Phaethon, Ov. *Met.* ii. 328.

22. *Eristus. Were I a king*, &c.: 'This contest between Eristus, Martius, and Mellacrites seems to be an imitation of a passage in the third and fourth chapters of the first book of Esdras, on the comparative

MIDAS

strength of wine, the king, and women' (Dilke, *Old English Plays*, vol. i). The resemblance, however, is but slight. It seems more certain that the scene suggested to Bacon the six councillors of the Prince of Purpoole in *Gesta Grayorum*, 1594.

P. 117, 39. *gold: this is the sinewes of warre*, &c.: with this eulogy of gold compare the lines in *Timon of Athens*, iv. 3. 26-46, 381-392.

49. *Quantum quisque sua*, &c.: Juvenal, *Sat.* iii. 143.

50. *ballance are*: the uninflected form used again with a plural verb at l. 92. Dilke compares *Merchant of Ven.* iv. i. 254 'Are there balance here to weigh the flesh?' 'I have *them* ready.'

quærenda pecunia primum est, &c.: Hor. *Ep.* i. 1. 53.

53. *& genus & formam*, &c.: Hor. *Ep.* i. 6. 37.

57. *Aurea sunt verè*, &c.: Ov. *Art. Am.* ii. 277.

59. *taken vp on interest*: i. e. at command of him who has gold.

tempt . . . true Subiectes: allusion to Philip's intrigues in England.

62. *quid non mortalia*, &c.: Virg. *Aen.* iii. 56.

P. 118, 64. *bred in the barrennest ground*: Pliny, xxxiii. 21 'montes Hispaniae aridi sterilesque, et in quibus [nihil] aliud gignatur, huic bono [sc. auro] coguntur fertiles esse.' Cf. Act ii. 2. 6 and *Gall.* Prol.

66. *In the councel of the gods, was not Anubis' . . . preferred before Neptunes*, &c.: I retain *Neptunes*, the reading of the old eds., which may be right (sub. *counsel*), *Anubis* also being possessive. In Lucian's *Iupiter Tragoedus*, 7, Mercury, being ordered to seat the gods in council according to the value of the material of which their statues were fashioned, answers Neptune's complaint of priority given to Anubis by reminding him that in the absence of gold at Corinth Lysippus had made his statue of bronze. Ἀνέχεσθαι οὖν χρὴ παρεωσμένον καὶ μὴ ἀγανακτεῖν, εἴ τις ῥῖνα τηλικαύτην χρυσῆν ἔχων προτετίμηταί σου. A little lower Apollo is ranged amongst the ζευγῖται; and is opposed to Aesculapius at a similar scene in the *Deorum Concilium*.

78. *golden winges . . . Swannes winges*: the wonted references to Danae and Leda, so often found together in Lyly.

80. *Hippomanes*: i. e. Hippomenes, Ov. *Met.* x. 575.

83. *a wagtaile*: as a synonym for impudence in *King Lear*, ii. 2. 73. *Res est ingeniosa dare*: Ov. *Amor.* i. 8. 62. Cf. *Saph. and Ph.* i. 4. 27.

84. *gates of cities . . . opened . . . of late*: referring, perhaps, to the English surrender of Gertruydenberg to the Spaniards, after an attack on the town by Count Maurice of Nassau. The English garrison, whose pay was in arrear, received from Spain twelve months' pay and a gratuity of five months' in addition. The town was handed over April 10, 1589. (Motley's *United Netherlands*, ii. 545-6.)

86. *Sub Ioue nunc mundus*, &c.: still unfound.

88. *the Moones braines*: implying that only a lunatic would dream of doing without money.

NOTES

97. *blesse thy guest*: like ξένος or *hospes*, for 'host.' Ovid (*Met.* xi. 98) represents Midas, after entertaining Silenus in Phrygia, as repairing with him to Lydia and there restoring him to Bacchus: but from the opening of this scene it is obvious that Bacchus has been Midas' guest.

99-103. *Take vp this stone* ... *This stick*: Ov. *Met.* xi. 108-10
'Vixque sibi credens, non alta fronde virentem
Ilice detraxit virgam ; virga aurea facta est.
Tollit humo saxum; saxum quoque palluit auro.'

P. 119, 109. *Pœnam pro munere poscis*: Hense notes the anachronistic use of Latin quotations in the mouth of Phrygian lords or Greek gods— ' Dass auch Bacchus lateinische Citate braucht, ist an sich nicht zu verwundern ; es mag aber auffallen, dass er die angeführten Worte der Rede des Sonnengottes entlehnt, mit welcher dieser, bei Ovid *Metam.* ii. 99, den Phaëthon vor der Annahme des gefährlichen Geschenkes gewarnt hatte.' *Jahrbuch der Deutschen Shakespeare-Gesellschaft*, Bd. vii. 254. At l. 18 Midas has compared himself by anticipation to Phaethon and quoted l. 328 from the same book of Ovid.

111. *these petty ilands*, &c.: identified in iv. 1. 171 as Lesbos, i.e. England.

114. *chast Celia shall yeeld*: Midas' unsuccessful suit to Cælia (cf. ii. 1. 20 sqq.) may possibly allude to Philip's former proposal for the hand of Elizabeth. In 1584 there was talk of a marriage between him and Catherine de Medici (Motley's *United Netherlands*, i. 69).

1. *Mellacrites ... his daughter*: probably Caelia is meant. See note on *Dram. Pers.*

3. *The Masculin gender ... feminine*: taken verbally from Lilly and Colet's Latin Grammar, *A Shorte Introduction*, &c., sig. c iiij recto.

4. *backare*: a cant word meaning 'go back !', borrowed from the proverbial saying ' Backare, quoth Mortimer to his sow,' ridiculing unfounded pretension to a knowledge of Latin (Nares). Cf. *Taming of the Shrew*, ii. 73 ' Baccare ! you are marvellous forward.'

10. *my mistres is a proper woman*: Fairholt points out that Launce's catalogue of his mistress' virtues (*Two Gentlemen*, iii. 1) in talk with Speed is probably borrowed from this scene. Shakespeare's play was probably produced in 1592 or 1593. Licio, however, is Caelia's attendant, not her lover.

P. 120, 30. *hazard*: each of the winning openings in a tennis-court; viz. in modern tennis, the dedans, the grille and the last gallery. So *Henry V*, i. 2. 263 à propos of the Dauphin's present of tennis-balls Henry promises that he 'will in France ... play a set shall strike his father's crown into the hazard.'

37. *tire*: Fr. *tirer*, of a hawk pulling or worrying the quarry with its beak. Cf. *Euph.* i. 325 l. 10 'tyred at a dry breast.'

MIDAS

41. *leaden dagger in a veluette sheath*: a favourite proverb with Lyly; cf. *Euph.* i. 215 l. 9, 255 l. 30 'painted sheth ... leaden dagger.'

45. '*a rope for Parrat*': this and the preceding were phrases taught to parrots. Dilke quotes Butler's *Hudibras*
> '— could tell what subtlest parrots mean,
> That speak and think contrary clean;
> What member 'tis of whom they talk,
> When they cry *rope*, and *walk, knave, walk*.'

P. 121, 51. *sweet tooth of a calfe*: which would take a lump of sugar from the hand.

55. *a Want, a Mole*: so still in Somerset.

58. *aske her a question*: i.e. an improper one.

65. *Beetle browed*: with overhanging brows. Dilke quotes 'the dreadful summit of the cliff | That beetles o'er his base,' *Hamlet*, i. 4. 71.

66. *hast a beetle head*: i.e. a stupid head, a head like a heavy rammer. 2 *Henry IV*, i. 2. 255 'a three-man beetle.'

75. *The purtenances*: Fairholt quotes from the comedy of *Lingua*, 1607, a similar but even lengthier catalogue of articles of ladies' dress, not confined, as here, to the head.

77–80. *caules*: nets. *Knotstrings*, for fastening on a *knot* or bunch of ribbon. *Coifes*, caps tied under the chin. *Borders*, embroideries to trim the edge of a cap. *Crippins*, variant of *crepines* or *crespins* (Fr. *crépines*), nets for the hair, or else a part of the hood. *Shadowes*, broad-brimmed hats. *Spots*, patches, beauty-spots. Cf. Petulus to Motto v. 2. 110 'You were best weare a veluet patch on your temples too.'

P. 122, 90. *rigge*: 'The verb *rigge*, to be wanton, occurs in Levins, col. 119 l. 6. Cp. "running such a rig," i.e. frolic, prank, in Cowper's *John Gilpin*' (Skeat). Cf. *Ant. & Cl.* ii. 2. 245 'riggish.'

92. *cases*: Petulus' reply affects to understand it as 'skins.' Cf. Beau. and Flet.'s *King and No King*, iv. 3. 82 'nor no man else that bears | His soul in a skin-coat.'

95. *takings*: predicaments. 'My taking is as bad or worse than hers,' Ben Jonson's *The Case is Altered*, iii. 3 (Whitney).

101. *prettie mops*: again to Pipenetta, ii. 2. 53.

103. *Hares ... male one yere, and the next female*: Pliny, viii. 81, repeats a statement of Archelaus that the same individual in this species possesses the characteristics of the two sexes, and becomes pregnant just as well without the male. Fairholt says the superstition is reproduced in Topsell's *Historie of Four-footed Beasts*, 1607.

105. *Badgers ... legs*: the fore-legs are, or seem, longer than the hind.

113–4. *my master ... his page*: i.e. Petulus; Pipenetta belonging, like them, to the household of Mellacrites.

120. *it is her owne when shee paies for it*: Fairholt traces the joke to Martial, *Epigr.* vi. 12—

'Iurat capillos esse, quos emit, suos
Fabulla: numquid, Paulle, peierat? nego.'

and says the custom of wearing false hair dates from ancient Egypt, decayed in the Middle Ages, and was revived in the seventeenth century.

P. 123, 127. *angels are gold*: a small gold coin, value ten shillings.

141. *drinke of a drie cuppe*: alluding to the phrase 'a dry beating,' 'dry' being intensive.

P. 124, 17. *a new shadow*: probably, a new portrait of themselves.

25. *Quorum si singula*, &c.: Ov. *Met.* ix. 608

'quorum si singula duram
Flectere non poterant, potuissent omnia mentem.'

Quoted also in Lyly's second edition, Life, p. 71.

47. *his meat turneth to massie gold*, &c.: Ov. *Met.* xi. 123-6

'Sive dapes avido convellere dente parabat,
Lamina fulva dapes, admoto dente, nitebant.
Miscuerat puris auctorem muneris undis,
Fusile per rictus aurum fluitare videres.'

P. 125, 55. *crownes*: the gold crown-piece was first struck by Henry VIII, and bore the royal arms on one side and the crowned rose of England on the other (Fairholt); they were also coined by Edward VI and Elizabeth (Dilke).

60. *gyude*: gyves were properly leg-fetters. Ben Jonson uses 'golden gyves' figuratively (Dilke).

67. *to follow a Louer with a gloue in his hatte*: i.e. either to imitate him, or to play second fiddle to him. For the glove in hat see note on *Campaspe*, iv. 3. 22, which passage may be compared with this.

70. *so rich*: provided he is rich, *so* being parallel to *if* in the other clause.

75. *golden ruddocks*: *ruddock*, i.e. robin redbreast, is used metaphorically for coins of red gold (Fairholt).

82. *of his mistres fauour*: of the colours she favours.

P. 126, 88. *The loue hee hath followed—I feare vnnaturall*: these words, repeated by Midas himself v. 3. 61, were probably inserted by Lyly on the play's publication in 1592 in reference to the report, widely circulated at that time, that Philip actually contemplated a union with his own daughter by Isabella of France, the Infanta Clara Isabella, who, if the Salic law could be set aside, was heiress to the French crown. Sir Edward Stafford, the English ambassador to France, stated in a letter of 1592 that Henry IV had assured him that Philip had, through Olivarez the Spanish ambassador at Rome, importuned Sixtus V before the latter's death in 1590 to grant him a dispensation for the marriage (Motley's *United Netherlands*, iii. 193). But the reference might be to his proposal to marry Elizabeth, after his previous marriage to her sister Mary.

100. *as the Ægyptians did dogs*: a reference to the dog-faced Anubis: see note on p. 113 l. 66 above.

101. *vtmost partes of the West . . . gold*: alluding, as Dilke points out, to the American possessions of Spain.

111. *roses . . . stalke . . . still*: the same imagery is used *Sapho and Phao*, ii. 1. 109–10 and *Euphues*, i. 203 ll. 15–6.

P. 127, 126. *Cælia . . . my father think of no meat*: at the end of i. 1 Midas acknowledged a passion for Cælia. Sophronia's anxious care for her father in his famine is repeated in, or from, Protea and Erisichthon in *Loves Metamorphosis*.

3. *I see it, and feele it not*: i. e. she cannot get her hand on any of it.

6. *of barren ground*: see note on i. 1. 64.

12. *Blirt to you both!*: this exclamation of contempt has been abundantly illustrated (see Nares). Skeat considers the verb 'blurt,' to deride, to be formed from *blore* or *blare*, and to mean originally 'to blow,' i. e. to puff away in contempt.

it was layd by the Sunne: popular guess anticipating Laplace and Herschel's nebular theory.

18. *idle . . . addle*: as often elsewhere, e. g. *Pappe*, p. 396 ll. 29–30.

21. *crackt crowne*: uncurrent, if the crack extended within the circle round the sovereign's head : *Hamlet*, ii. 2. 448, and *Woman*, iii. 2. 266.

P. 128, 37. *golde boyld, for a consuming bodie*: the efficacy of *aurum potabile* was a subject of dispute among mediaeval physicians. 'Matthiolus in the same place approves of potable gold, ... and holds " no man can be an excellent physician that hath not some skill in chemisticall distillations, and that chronic diseases can hardly be cured without mineral medicines."' Burton's *Anatomy of Melancholy*, Part 2. Sec. 4. 1, 4. Cf. 'Argentum potabile,' *M. Bomb.* ii. 2. 18.

41. *a portague*: a Portuguese coin worth four pound ten shillings, as explained by Weber in a note on Beaumont and Fletcher's *Sea-Voyage* (Dilke).

45. *dowe-baked*: i. e. half-baked, insufficiently considered.

55. *He hath made a spoke*: i. e. put a spoke in your wheel.

56. *our masters*: spoken generally, 'our betters.' All three were of Mellacrites' household.

P. 129, 72. *If Mars should answere thee*, &c.: Dilke is probably right in detecting a reminiscence of the story of Naaman 2 Kings v. 13.

83. *Sir boies you wait wel!*: as Petulus' answer shows, this refers to their not having accompanied the councillors on their expedition to Bacchus' temple at the end of the preceding scene. It is one of those back-references which show that Lyly generally intended his scenes as continuous in time.

89. *neer my selfe . . . . neere you as your skin*: the first of relationship or connexion ; the second of one injured or ' nearly touched.'

3. *successe*: sequel, issue, as often, e. g. *M. Bomb.* iii. 1. 10 'yeld to the succes of fortune, who, though she hath framd vs miserable, cannot make vs monstrous.'

P. 130, 8. *my minde were also a myne*: i. e. as dark.

12-13. *What should I doo . . . seauen foote of earth?*: the same sentiment, originally from Plutarch (*de Educ.* 8), is repeated in *Euphues*, i. 314 l. 35, *Campaspe*, v. 4. 49-53 (where see note), and 1 *Henry IV*, v. 4. 89.

15. *tooke small vessells*, &c.: an allusion to the freebooting exploits of Drake and the other Elizabethan seamen.

20. *Diomedes did his horse with blood*: an allusion repeated from the Epilogue at Court to *Campaspe*, where see note.

21. *Two bookes haue I alwaies carried*, &c.: I cannot find that Motley reproduces the tale.

26. *Getulia*: south of Mauretania, but probably written hastily for Galatia, which, like Lycaonia, borders Phrygia. 'Sola' may be suggested by Soli on the Cilician coast.

31. *made the sea to groane*, &c.: unmistakable allusion to the Armada. The expedition against Lesbos must be supposed, in spite of i. 1. 111, to have occurred before the commencement of the play, and not between Acts i and iii.

34. *whom hauing made slaues*, &c.: Dilke in a concluding note, written in 1814 before Napoleon's escape from Elba, points out with fine moral indignation the close applicability of this speech to the Emperor's career, and cannot resist admonishing him to be content with the position the lenity of the Allies has left him.

36. *to destroy their natural Kings*: referring to the plots to assassinate Elizabeth and William of Orange. In regard to the former may be instanced that for which Dr. William Parry suffered death at the beginning of March, 1585. Motley, speaking of this year, says 'There was hardly a month in which intelligence was not sent by English agents out of the Netherlands and France, that assassins, hired by Philip, were making their way to England to attempt the life of the Queen' (*United Netherlands*, i. 305). Many attempts, instigated from Spain, were made on the Prince of Orange's life, e. g. one in 1582, one in 1583, and one in 1584 before that by which he fell on the tenth of July in the same year. See Motley's *Dutch Republic*, iii. 407, 457, 467.

38. *vipers that gnawe the bowels*, &c.: cf. *Euphues*, ii. 5 l. 5 'with the Viper, loose my bloud with mine own brood,' they were supposed to force their way through the bowels of their dam. Pliny, x. 82 and Browne's *Vulgar Errors*, iii. 16.

43. *traitours to me*: urging that excuse for attacking them.

P. 131, 44. *mens hearts would bee touched with gold*: i. e. tried as by a touchstone. *Timon of Athens*, iv. 3. 389 'O, thou touch of hearts!'

54. *Haue not all treasons . . . by miracle*, &c. : compare the language of *Euphues*, pp. 197, 203, 210. Dilke considers this, and the lines immediately following and preceding, as added at a later date in allusion to James I and the Gunpowder Plot: a supposition of course irreconcilable with the date of the quarto, 1592.

71. *of kingdome proofe*: i.e. of metal that is proof against another kingdom's attack. *Proof*, subst. as *Rich. III*, v. 3. 219 'armed in proof.'

P. 132, 82. *Martius, thy councell hath shed as much bloud*, &c. : there can be little doubt that Martius represents the Duke of Alva, the exponent of the tyrannical policy which drove the Netherlands into revolt. So identified by Halpin and Mézières.

8. *cunning mens charms*: Fairholt quotes from Reginald Scot's *Discouerie of Witchcraft* [1584, not 1585] with which, as we saw under *Gallathea*, Lyly was familiar, some charms repeated for toothache, e. g. '*Strigiles falseque dentata dentium delorem personate*; O horsecombs and sickles that have so many teeth, come heale me now of my tooth-ache.'

10. *ouer-hearing vs*: so Motto below, l. 75, apparently in the sense of 'overreach.'

P. 133, 23. *herbage*: i. e. 'harbourage; safe-keeping' (Fairholt). Usually 'harb-' or 'herbergage,' but from a Fr. *herberge* (N.E.D.).

26. *badge of haire*: the original sense of *badge* seems to have been flag or standard.

34. *the knacking of the hands*: Fairholt quotes a passage from Stubbes' *Anatomie of Abuses* to show that snapping both of fingers and scissors was affected by barbers, as giving a finish to their work; and also from Ben Jonson's *Silent Woman*, i. 1, where Morose approves his barber, Cutbeard, because 'the fellow trims him silently, and has not the knack with his sheers or his fingers.'

35. *tuning of a Cittern*: 'It was the custom to keep a cittern, a species of guitar or lute, in barbers' shops to amuse customers waiting their turn to be operated on. In Burton's *Winter Evening's Entertainments*, 1687, is a representation of a barber's shop, where a person waiting his turn is playing on a lute' (Fairholt). Dilke quotes from the Second Part of Dekker's *Honest Whore*, where Matheo calls his wife 'A barber's cittern for every serving-man to play upon.'

38. '*how sir will you be trimmed?*' &c.: Fairholt has a long note on this passage, of which I reproduce some details. The 'spade-beard' was long and cut straight across the bottom, though occasionally rounded at the corners. The 'bodkin-beard' or *pique-a-devant* beard was that usually worn by Charles I, 'sharp, stiletto fashion, dagger-like' as Taylor the Water-Poet says in his *Superbiae Flagellum*. The 'penthouse' is the bushy moustache hanging over the lip. The 'allie on the chin,' Chaucer's 'forked beard,' parted the beard in the centre of the chin to hang like a double pendant. The 'bull's curls' rose one upon another in close contiguity upon the forehead. The 'dangling locks' were curled and allowed to flow over the shoulders. The 'love-lock' was a single lock worn long on the left side, and sometimes twisted in a ribbon or tied with a silken bow at the end. Dilke quotes from Greene's *Qvip for an Vpstart Courtier*, 1592, 'Will you be Frenchefied with a love-lock down your shoulders wherein you may wear your mistress' favour?' In *Endim.* iii. 3. 35 Sir Tophas 'feels a contention whether he shall frame the bodkin-beard or the bush.' Cf. *Pappe*, p. 506 l. 6.

43. *Goates flakes*: perhaps explains the 'lady's dangling flake' of Marston's 1st *Satire.*

58. *is that worde come into the Barbers bason?*: from Licio's later remark v. 2. 107 it is *rewme* that must be regarded as the 'courtly tearme' which surprises him in Motto's mouth, rather than *euaporated*. Yet the former, like the latter, occurs much earlier than 1588. Whitney quotes the *Promptorium Paruulorum* (printed 1499), p. 432 'Rewme of the hed or of the breste.' Probably it is the frequent or special application of the term that was new in fashion, just as ten years since but few folk claimed to have had the influenza.

P. 134, 59. *a Barber and a Surgeon*: the two professions were not dissevered before 1745. They were incorporated as early as 1540, when all persons merely practising shaving were forbidden to meddle with surgery, except to draw teeth and let blood, unless properly qualified as barber-surgeons. A work entitled *Il Barbiero* by a Neapolitan barber, Tiberio Malfi, published in 1626, contains engravings of various surgical operations (Fairholt).

75. *ouerheare me*: cf. above, l. 10.

85. *a paire of virginals*: the virginal, or virginals, was a harpsichord or spinet, 'called so, says Blount in his " Glossographia," because maids and virgins do most commonly play on them' (Dilke). *Paire* probably refers to the double row, of keys, and of jacks, which Petulus a few lines on compares to the double row of his teeth ; the jacks being short pieces of wood with a slip of quill at the side which strikes the string as the jack ascends, while in its descent the vibration is stopped by two small pieces of cloth. Or *paire*=set, as in ' pair of stairs,' ' pair of cards ' (obs.).

P. 135, 118. *maugre his beard*: proverbial expression, ' spite of all he can do.'

128. *cushions are stuft with beards*: again v. 2. 170, where Fairholt notes it as a jesting satire on the huge beards sometimes worn, and compares *Coriolanus*, ii. 1. 91 'Your beards deserve not so honourable a grave as to stuff a botcher's cushion.'

P. 136, 141. *Pellitory fetcht from Spaine*: Whitney gives ' Pellitory-of-Spain, *Anacyclus Pyrethrum*, growing chiefly in Algeria.' Its root is a powerful irritant promoting salivation.

142. *Mastick's a patch*: i. e. gum-mastick (a gum for chewing on)

is a fool, of no use. Dilke supposes it would be used for stopping a bad tooth.

149. *checkerd-apron men*: 'A barber is always known by his checque party-coloured apron,' Randle Holme's book on Heraldry (*The Academy of Armory*, 1688 fol.), quoted by Fairholt.

153. *By trickes they shaue a Kingdome round*: probably referring to the enormous number of executions by the scaffold, the stake, or the gibbet, that had marked Alva's rule in the Netherlands, 1567-1573.

13. *Qui latus arguerit*, &c.: the quotation betrays the source of Suavia's scandalous perversion of Penelope's motive. It is from Ovid's *Amores*, i. 8. 48:

   Penelope iuvenum vires tentabat in arcu
    Qui latus argueret, corneus arcus erat

i. e. arcus qui indicaret vires lateris, erat corneus ; Hom. *Odys*. xxi gives no hint of the material, though the κορώνη, or tip, would naturally be of horn.

P. 137, 18. *what shal we do? Ame. Tel tales*, &c.: Fairholt compares the question and answer of the Queen and her Ladies in *Richard II*, iii. 4.

33. *Hie she was in the instep*, &c.: 'high instep' implies pride, 'short heele' feminine frailty, 'straitlaced' stiffness of demeanour, not strictness of morals. Cf. *Euph*. i. 202 l. 24 'they be so straight laced, and made so high in the insteppe, that they disdaine them most that most desyre them.' So Philautus, ii. 179 ll. 4-6, accuses Fraunces of 'shorte heeles' and 'high instep.' Dilke remarks that Sue Shortheels is the name of a strumpet in Rowley's *A Match at Midnight*.

37. *larkes... caught... with... a glasse*: this allusion to the birdcatchers is explained by a passage in Pettie's *Pallace of Pleasure* (1576) fol. 59 r. 'For as the Larketaker in his day Net hath a glasse whereon while the birdes sit and gaze, they are taken in the Net, so your face hath sutch a glistering glasse of goodlynesse in it,' &c. Fairholt refers to Hone's *Every-day Book*, ii. 94 for an account of another device made with glass as used near Abbeville in 1827, as now in 1902, where a flat piece of wood inlaid with small bits of looking-glass is twisted on a pin rapidly by a string, and the larks who hover over it, attracted by the flashing light, are easily shot.

40. *as one that knew her good*: so *Euph*. ii. 161 l. 29 ; of knowledge of courtly *convenances* rather than of a sense of one's own interest.

P. 138, 60. *would make the tune of a hart out of tune*: (1) would put her lover's heart, now out of tune, in tune again; or (2) would have a love-plaint for its burthen.

62. *plaine song*: the melody without the variations, the vocal part without the harmony.

73. *Amerula, ... bitter, your name*, &c.: Fr. *amère*, Lat. *amara*.

P. 139, 94. *standing cup*: goblet with a stand, distinguished from a horn or vessel that would require to be emptied before being set down.

P. 139. ACT IV. SCENE I. *Glade in a forest on Mount Tmolus*: the classical scene of the contest (Ov. *Met.* xi. 156). Cf. Midas' own account v. 3. 40-4. Mount Tmolus is properly in the neighbouring country of Lydia, but near the Pactolus. Perhaps Lyly chose to regard Phrygia as including Lydia, and conceived Midas, like Croesus, as having his capital at Sardis: cf. Ov. *Met.* xi. 137 'Vade, ait, ad magnis vicinum Sardibus amnem.' In his letter prefixed to the first edition of *Astrophel and Stella*, 1591, Nash alludes to 'Pan sitting in his bower of delights, & a number of Midasses to admire his miserable hornepipes.'

1. *Apollo, who tunes the heauens . . . harmony*: the allusion is to the music of the spheres (Dilke); and I cannot but think Shakespeare had this phrase and ll. 13-4 'Had thy lute been of lawrell, and the strings of Daphnes haire' in mind when, about this time, he wrote in *Love's Labour's Lost*, iv. 3. 339

'as sweet and musical
As bright Apollo's lute, strung with his hair;
And, when Love speaks, the voice of all the gods
Makes heaven drowsy with the harmony.'

Compare too the opening of the song in *Henry VIII*, iii. I 'Orpheus with his lute made trees,' &c.

4. *Arion, that brought Dolphins*: Hyg. *Fab.* 194.

5. *Amphion . . . Thebes*: Horace, *Ars Poet.* 394.

P. 140, 10. *This pipe . . . was once a Nymph*: the transformation of the Naiad Syrinx, pursued by Pan, into a group of marsh reeds is the invention of Ovid, *Met.* i. 690 sqq. But see Lucretius, iv. 588.

34. *My Temple is in Arcadie . . . Erato the Nymphe*, &c.: this passage is founded on that in the Ἀρκάδικα of Pausanias (viii. 37. 11) παρὰ τούτῳ τῷ Πανὶ πῦρ οὔποτε ἀποσβεννύμενον καίεται. Λέγεται δὲ ὡς τὰ ἔτι παλαιότερα καὶ μαντεύοιτο οὗτος ὁ θεός, προφῆτιν δὲ Ἐρατὼ νύμφην αὐτῷ γενέσθαι ταύτην ἣ Ἀρκάδι τῷ Καλλιστοῦς συνῴκησε. Properly this nymph Erato, who appears below and is false to her master, is to be distinguished from Erato, the Muse of lyric and erotic poetry; but it is doubtful if Lyly meant to do so. Cf. Ov. *Art. Am.* ii. 16 'Nunc mihi, si quando, Puer et Cytherea, favete: | Nunc Erato; nam tu nomen amoris habes.'

P. 141, 46. *Loue-leaues*: probably a Kentish name.

47. *Iupiter a goose, and Neptune a swine*: Pan is wilfully misrepresenting matters. Jupiter became a swan, Neptune a bullock, a river, a ram, a horse, and a dolphin, but not a swine.

56. *Pan is all*: i.e. πᾶν means 'all.'

68. *what is thy follie?*: i.e. since fortune cannot be blamed, the fault must lie with yourself. Midas is irritated and depressed; cf. his own statement, v. 3. 40-7. Mellacrites in iii. 3. 101 speaks as a courtier merely. The king's attitude is intended to illustrate Ovid's 'pingue sed ingenium mansit,' *Met.* xi. 148.

MIDAS

P. 142, 96. *consent*: harmony of voice and lute, properly *concent*.

97. *Tha.*: Dilke is probably right in correcting *Thia*, the prefix of the old editions, to *Tha.* for Thalia, the muse of Comedy.

107. *Gitterne*: the same as *cittern* above, iii. 2. 35, as is shown by Dilke's quotation from Lord Falkland's *Marriage Night*, 'As a barber's boy plays o' th' gittern.'

109. *Cross-gartred Swaines*: 'The custom of enswathing the leg with long garters was peculiarly indicative of the Italian peasantry, and is still customary with them. It was equally common in Normandy until the middle of the last century. It was an Anglo-Saxon fashion, but considered boorish in our author's days' (Fairholt)—but not now.

P. 143, 124. *his piping as farre out of tune*: it is the instrument and the playing of it that is criticized by both the Nymphs and Midas; nothing is said of the two songs as poetry, and there is little to choose between them, though Ward says, 'it is difficult not to sympathize with Mydas for preferring Pan's song, poor as it is, to Apollo's, which is still poorer' (*Eng. Dram. Lit.* i. 299, ed. 1899).

P. 144, 177. *are his goldē mynes turnd into water*: the transference of Midas' golden gift to the Pactolus is here made to represent the danger to which the Spanish treasure-ships, and even their possessions in America, were exposed since the Armada's defeat.

183. *Sisq miser semper*, &c.: Ov. *Ibis*, 117.

P. 145, SCENE II. *A reedy place*: it must be supposed on the way between the wood and the palace, and not far from the latter, for Sophronia and her ladies to visit it in Scene iv. The words of Driapon, l. 11 'in his cwne Courtrey they . . . call him Tyrant,' imply not the shepherds' own exemption from Midas' sway, for they dread his power and complain of his taxes, l. 55, but merely their detachment from affairs.

5. *great King . . . hands are longer*: *Euph.* i. 221 l. 34 'kinges haue long armes,' from Ov. *Her.* xvii. 166

'An nescis longas regibus esse manus?'

11. *in his owne Countrey*, &c.: suggestive of the opening of bk. iii. cap. 32 of *The Diall of Princes*—'*Mydas* the auncient kyng of *Phrigia*, was in his gouernment a cruell tyrant, and contented not himself to play the tiraunt in his own proper countrey, but also mainteined rouers on the sea, and theeues in the lād to robbe straũgers . . . a freend of his of *Thebes* sayd vnto him these woords. I let thee to weete King *Mydas* that all those of thy oune realm doo hate thee, and al the other realms of *Asia* doo feare thee.'

29. *dissembling of Hyena*: Dilke and Fairholt are wrong in prefixing 'the.' It is as if its cunning and its plaintive imitation of the human voice gave it a semi-human character in human eyes. Cf. Psellus' language, *Euph.* ii. 116 l. 6-9 'the Beast *Hiena* . . . they accompt *Hyena*

their God ... take seauen hayres of Hyenas lippes '; also i. 250 l. 8 '*Hiena*, when she speaketh lyke a man, deuiseth most mischiefe,' where see note.

34. *woodden net ... the cod .. the corks*: Fairholt explains *cod* of the bag at the bottom of the net which held a stone to sink it, while the *corks* were to keep the sides of the net on the surface. *Woodden* net means, of course, a navy; hence *trees* and *woods* in this connexion.

P. 146, 43. *plod*: all editions agree, and the word is more expressive of laborious effort than ' plot.' Cf. *M. Bomb.* ii. 4. 5–6.

61. *three flocks*: three locks of wool. OF. *floc de laine*, 'a lock or flock of wool.' Cotg. Lat. *floccus*. In v. 2. 179 ' flockes ' are spoken of as used for stuffing mattresses.

SCENE III. *The same*: the closing words of the preceding scene indicate the present as continuous with it.

2. *call a dog a dog*, &c.: i. e. you have to learn a whole new phraseology, of which, as Fairholt points out, another specimen is given by Diana's Nymphs in *Gall.* ii. 1. 38–58. ' To call a dog a dog' was a proverb for using plain speech. *Pappe with a Hatchett*, 1589, on its title-page professes to be ' written by one that dares call a dog a dog.'

P. 147, 6. *faire flewde*: with large hanging chaps. *Well hangd*: with long drooping ears. Dilke illustrates the Huntsman's sense of the hounds' music by the passage in *Mid. N. Dream*, iv. 1. 120

' So flew'd, so sanded; and their heads are hung
With ears that sweep away the morning dew;

. . . . . .

Slow in pursuit, but match'd in mouth like bells,
Each under each.'

12. *pibble*: pebble, as in *Gall.* i. 1. 13; *Woman in Moone*, v. 1. 10.

16. *leasht*: i. e. beaten with the leash or leathern thong for holding in the dogs, which might also be used for their chastisement. But *lash* is originally the same word, in the sea-sense of binding two pieces up together. Skeat compares Germ. *lasche*, a flap, scarf or groove to join timber, referring it to an original Teut. base *lak* (Lat. and Gk. *lag*) to droop (cf. Lat. *laxus, languere*), from which is formed a subst. *laksa* or *laska*, a flap. The *lash* of a whip is the flexible or drooping part.

20. *Calamance*: according to Halliwell and the N. E. D. figurative application to language of *calamanco*, ' a Flanders woollen stuff of glossy surface, woven with a satin twill and chequered in the warp so that the checks are seen on one side only '—the glossy surface and invisibility of the pattern no doubt suggest the comparison. *The characters in a nutmeg* are the intricate veinings visible in a section taken through one.

26. *the single*: Halliwell's *Dict. of Archaic Terms* s. v. *Hunting*, where he gives an immense number of terms applied to animals that were objects of sport drawn from Blome's *Gentleman's Recreations*, &c., enu-

merates among 'terms of the tail'—'The *wreath* of a boar, the *single* of a buck, the *scut* of a hare or rabbit, the *brush* of a fox,' &c.

27. *imbost*: so of the stag in Scott's *Lady of the Lake*, i. 7 'Emboss'd with foam, and dark with soil.'

tooke soyle: so in Browne's *Britannia's Pastorals*, p. 84, a hind is represented as 'taking soyle within a flood' (Halliwell). But the word is the same as soil = ground, or defilement; the idea being that muddy water afforded most concealment (Skeat).

32. *This is worse than fustian*: printed as part of the Huntsman's speech in the old eds. and by Dilke, though Fairholt allots it, separately, to Minutius. In the Huntsman's mouth it refers to the ordinary speech Petulus has just substituted for the technical. Cf. 'Calamance,' l. 20 note.

36. *champing*: quasi *champaign*.

P. 148, 41. *fæcundi calices*, &c.: Hor. *Ep.* i. 5. 19.

43. *dizardum*: a dizard was a dancing fool. The opening line of the Anti-Martinist lampoon *A Whip for an Ape* is 'A Dizard late skipt out vpon our Stage.'

46. *scull of Phesants*: i. e. school, or shoal; either word being applicable, of course, only to fish.

49. *swad*: clown, bumpkin. Whitney quotes 'Let country swains and silly *swads* be still' (Greene, *Madrigal*). Again pp. 420 l. 92, 426 l. 108.

54. *remember all this!*: i. e. I'll make you pay for it.

68. *shrowd*: a recognized variant of *shrewd*.

72. *flyblow*: cf. N. E. D. s. v.

74. *shaue the Barbars house*: see note on *an inuentorie of all*, &c., below, v. 2. 4.

P. 149, 81. *a choakpeare*: Fairholt explains as 'a sort of gag shaped like a pear, which opened from the centre by a spring and forced the mouth to its utmost width. It was of Italian invention, used for purposes of punishment.' Minutius dedicates every particle of himself to the opening, i. e. robbing, of Motto's purse.

12. *suffers the enemies to bid vs good morrowe at our owne doores*: alluding, not as Dilke suggests, to Essex's expedition to Cadiz in 1596, which is much too late, but to that under Drake and Norreys in 1589 to establish Don Antonio on the throne of Portugal. They sailed from Plymouth Apr. 18, 1589; landed at Corunna, and obtained some advantages over the Spaniards. They even got possession of the suburbs of Lisbon; but were compelled to re-embark. On their return they took and burned Vigo, and ravaged the country round. They reached Plymouth again by the middle of July (Motley's *Unit. Neth.* ii. 554-6).

18. *This will make Pisidia wanton*, &c.: perhaps recollecting the Greek discontent at Alexander's assumption of Eastern dress and manners, as related in Plutarch's *Life*, c. 45.

20. *coutcht*: lodged, comprised. Udall's *Erasm. Par.* Pref. 14 'Couched together in this one weorke' (N. E. D.).

28. *Bella gerant alij*, &c.: adapted from Helen's Epistle to Paris (Ov. *Her.* xvii. 254) 'Bella gerant fortes: tu, Pari, semper ama.' Again, *Endim.* iii. 3. 32.

P. 150, 31. *Vilius argentum*, &c.: Hor. *Ep.* i. 1. 52, quoted in Lilly and Colet's Latin Grammar, ed. 1577, sig. Ij recto.

47. *a methridat*: properly an electuary, used in the general sense of remedy in *Sapho and Phao*, iii. 3. 13.

48. *Uno namq modo*, &c.: still unfound.

P. 152, 28. *my doom was his*: my judgement was passed upon him.

3. *table-men*: the wooden discs used in the game 'tables,' or back-gammon, which still employs just thirty. Fairholt says the game was kept in barbers' shops.

4. *an inuentorie of all ... to redeeme the beard*: the course of the action between the Pages and the barber is not absolutely clear from the text, but may be summarized as follows. During the song at the end of iii. 2 Motto must be supposed to effect the cure of Petulus' toothache, on their promise to redeem the beard which they have pawned. When next we meet them (iv. 3 end) they plot to 'shaue the Barbars house,' i.e. they are going to pretend that they have only induced the pawnbroker to release the beard on a promise that he shall receive a lien on Motto's goods, out of which the Pages mean to make their own profit. At their visit to Motto's house, which is not represented, Motto, having vainly tried to bully them, has finally recovered the beard by giving them a sham document in which he pokes fun at them. The nature of this document has become apparent to them before their entry in this scene, and the reading of it before the audience must be excused by their wish to taste Motto's humour more fully.

P. 153, 8. *pike deuant*: the 'bodkin' of iii. 2. 39.

10. *poynado*: poniard, an Italian termination being tacked on to a French word. Fr. *poignard*, 'a poinadoe or poniard,' Cotgrave. Dilke excuses the poverty of Petulus' wit by taking his 'conceald beard' of the golden beard: but the latter is now in Motto's hands; and Licio's next speech (end) shows him to mean his own ungrown beard.

21. *What els?*: the expression had not yet acquired its modern sense of *dissent*.

33. *moueables*: probably 'of easy virtue.' So Katharine to Petruchio (ii. 1. 198) in sense of 'any man's tool.'

38. *Fælix quem faciunt*, &c.: the line is given on fol. 3 of *Prouerbes and Adagies, gathered out of the Chiliades of Erasmus ... by Rycharde Tavener ... An. M.D.LII.* B.L. 8º, but I know of no classical origin for it, however familiar. It is translated by Eubulus in *Euph.* i. 189 l. 14.

40. *one of the Cole-house*, &c.: possibly an allusion to Grim the

Collier, who is victimized by the barbering of the Court-pages in Richard Edwardes' *Damon and Pithias*, lic. 1567. See vol. ii. p. 238.

P. 154, 48. *cum recumbentibus*: this ought to mean 'with interest.' In the following from John Heywood's *Prouerbs*, ed. Sharman, p. 146, it seems to be used as a sort of dog-Latin for 'recompense'—

'Had you some husband, and snapt at him thus,
I wis he would give you a recumbentibus.'

P. 155, 78. *Mine armes are all armarie, gules*, &c.: i.e. discoloured with fighting, or beating.

79. *pur, post, pare*, &c.: terms in a game of cards called 'Post and Pair,' in which *pur* seems to mean the knave: cf. Whitney s.v. *pur*. Licio, humorously, rather than blunderingly as Dilke says, ekes out his scanty stock of heraldic terms with others more familiar. 'Post and pair (=pack)' or 'post' is mentioned by Sir John Harington—

'The second game was *post*, until with posting
They paid so fast, 'twas time to leave their bosting.'
(Fairholt). *Pair*=pack.

96. *tongue tawde*: 'to *taw* is still used in Somersetshire in the sense of to tie, or to fasten' (Fairholt): but perhaps 'subdued to silence,' from *taw* or *tew*, to dress (leather).

98. *ympt*: 'to imp' is to graft, or to repair by splicing or addition: here 'reinforced.'

raser: pun on *raze*, to destroy, of the *ne plus ultra* of mischief; or else for 'racer.'

99. *a mort*: i.e. *amort* dull, dejected, as in *Taming*, iv. 3. 36.

101. *marie gup*: i.e. 'by Mary, gee up! or get up!' a stable expression, says Fairholt. Again *M. Bombie*, i. 3. 14.

is melancholy ... for a barbars mouth?: the affectation of melancholy is illustrated by *King John*, iv. 1. 14—

'when I was in France,
Young gentlemen would be as sad as night
Only for wantonness.'

and by Jonson's *Every Man in his Humour*, iii. 3 'Your true melancholy breeds your perfect fine wit, sir.' As a recognized mental state, it occurs as early as the *Utopia*, 1516. Sidney's character exhibits it. Possibly Lyly's hero, Euphues, set the fashion.

104. *in his muble fubles*: depressed in spirits. Nares quotes Gayton's *Festiv. Notes*, p. 46 'Sol in his mubblefubbles, that is long clouded.'

107. *the rewme*: see iii. 2. 58 (note).

108. *mushrumpes*: a corruption. The word is from OF. *mouscheron* or *mousseron*, 'a mushrome,' Cotg.

109. *a pose*: again for a cold or running at the nose in *M. Bomb.* iv. 2. 218 'A little rume or pose.'

a v luet patch: i.e. a beauty-patch, or black spot to set off the complexion.

P. 156, 127. *the wennes*: apparently a distinct word from *weams* of *Euph.* ii. 216 l. 14.

148. *you haue made a faire hand*: i.e. you have got into a nice mess, metaphor from one taking fresh cards from the pack on the chance of bettering his hand. Beaum. and Flet.'s *King and No King*, v. 2. Lygones, finding Spaconia, whom he has abused for light behaviour, is to be Tigranes' queen, says, ' Then have I made a fair hand: I call'd her whore.'

P. 157, 159. *but durante placito*: only during pleasure.

163. *couin*: old law-term for fraudulent agreement.

165. *ball* of soap.

166. *tria seqüuntur triaes*: the phrase is quoted again *Pappe*, p. 406 l. 18. It looks like some formula in alchemy or magic.

170. *beards, to stuffe ... cushions*: see iii. 2. 128.

173. *and a nayle*: a nail is a unit of English cloth-measure—$2\frac{1}{4}$ in.; to be understood here as added to the half-yard of breadth.

175. *lynes that she dryes her cloathes on*: the use of hair for clothes-lines is illustrated by *Tempest*, iv. 1. 237 ' Mistress line, is not this my jerkin? ... now, jerkin, you are like to lose your hair and prove a bald jerkin.'

P. 158, 12. *at barly-breake with Daphne*: a game, resembling our Warner or Prisoners' Base, in which two players, occupying a marked space called ' Hell ' in the centre of the ground, tried to catch the others as they ran through it from the two opposite ends, those caught being obliged to replace or reinforce them in the centre. The same application of it occurs in Middleton's fine play *The Changeling*, v. 3 of De Flores and Beatrice,

' Yes, and the while I coupled with your mate
At barley-break; now we are left in hell.'

13. *assaying on some Shepheardes coate*, &c.: Dilke notes the allusion to Apollo's having served Admetus in that capacity, and that the *serpents skinne* refers to his being god of medicine, or to the serpent Python which Apollo slew and the skin of which formed a covering for the tripod on which his priestess sat.

18. *quench fire with a sword*: cf. *Sapho and Phao*, ii. 4. 110 ' fire to be quenched with dust, not with swordes '—see note. Here of Alva's attempt to put down the indignant discontent of the Netherlanders by ruthless cruelty and military force.

23. *in eternitie*: represented by the offering of ' tapers,' to be kept always burning before the shrine.

P. 159, 61. *my affection ... vnnaturall*: see note on ii. 1. 88.

P. 160, 72. *peeuishnes*: folly, as *Sapho*, i. 1. 42, 4. 33, and very often, though the following words in this passage seem to show that it indicates a lighter degree of folly.

P. 161, 135. *Iô Pæans*: Ov. *Art. Am.* ii. 1.
P. 162. 139. *A Daphnean Coronet*: one of laurel.
144. *Delian King*: as born in Delos. Hyg. *Fab.* 140.

MOTHER BOMBIE.

P. 172. DRAMATIS PERSONAE: I have corrected Fairholt's descriptions of Prisius (cf. note on ii. 5. 63) and Sperantus (cf. i. 3. 183-90), and abolished his distinction between the 'men,' Dromio and Riscio, and the 'boys,' Halfpenny and Lucio, for which there seems no sufficient reason. (See his note on the Song in iii. 4.) Granted that Dromio and Riscio are somewhat older, yet all four are of a piece, and their confidential relation with their respective masters is much the same: the Hackneyman speaks of Dromio as 'Memphios boye,' v. 3. 360, and Stellio speaks of Riscio as 'the boy,' ii. 2. 7. Rixula, too, is clearly of Prisius' household (cf. iii. 4. 1-4).

SCENE—*Rochester*: see iii. 4. 90, iv. 1. 19, iv. 2. 188. For his one play of contemporary life Lyly chooses a scene in his own county.

P. 173, 8. *tread out*: beget, a term used of the generation of birds.

9. *bite hot on*: border close on.

13. *they saie, if rauens . . . black*: popular superstition, not traceable in Pliny, book x.

17. *Carue him . . . capon*: cock-chickens were castrated to improve the flesh. Dromio suggests that the same process applied to Accius will prevent his breeding fools.

P. 174, 29-31. *Aethiopian . . . faire picture*, &c.: Mr. P. A. Daniel would read *babie* for *ladie*. In Heliodorus' *Aethiopica*, iv. 8, Persina, queen of Ethiopia, tells her white daughter, Chariclea, that when she was begotten a picture of Perseus leading away the naked Andromeda hung in her view. The preface to Underdowne's translation, 1587, 4°, alludes to an earlier and incorrect edition. Cf. *Camp.* i. 1. 71 note.

37. *beg him for a foole*: cf. iv. 2. 108 'begd for a concealde foole.' 'Natural fools having property were wards in Chancery, and it was customary with persons who had sufficient interest to beg the guardianship of them in the time of our author, to profit by their lodging with them. Douce has given a curious anecdote " how the Lord North begg'd old Bladwell for a foole," and what came of it' (Fairholt).

39. *haue in*: come in with.

40. *fadge*: suit, succeed.

eate till thou sweate, &c.: a comparison with *Euph.* i. 251 ll. 1-2, to which Mr. P. A. Daniel draws my attention, suggests that the reading should be 'till thou' for 'thou shalt': 'these Abbaie lubbers . . . which laboured till they were colde, eat til they sweate, and lay in bed till their boanes aked.'

P. 175, 64. *mewed vp*: metaphor from falconry, *mews* being places where hawks were kept when sick or moulting.

65. *roisting*: earlier form of roystering: cf. Udall's *Roister Doister*, Prol. 'the roysting sort.' Also *Tro. and Cress.* ii. 2. 208.

74. *keepe my house from smoake*: with possible allusion to the proverb cited *Wife of Bath's Prol.* ll. 278–80 about smoke, rain dripping, and a scold. Cf. Proverbs xxvii. 15, and Skeat's *Chaucer*, vol. iii. p. 447. Or *smoake* may be colloquial, like 'dust,' for disturbance. Memphio again alludes to his wife's shrewish temper, v. 3. 114.

88. *ducats*: the average value of the gold ducat was rather over nine shillings.

98. *Expellas furca licet*, &c.: Hor. *Ep.* i. 10. 24 'Naturam expellas furca, tamen usque recurret.'

P. 176, 8. *How likest thou this head?*: probably referring to what he has just said, in the sense of 'Have I good wits? was this cunningly done?' but the context makes it possible that he produces at this point a miniature of his daughter.

15. *Quod natura*, &c.: still unfound.

P. 177, 47. *come not about you*: i.e. 'do not overreach you,' ed. 1814.

6. *wring*: ed. 1814 quotes *Hamlet*, iii. 2. 240 'let the gall'd jade wince, our withers are unwrung.' Cf. Milton, *Def. of Humble Remonstr.* 'Wee know where the shoo wrings you.'

12. *another gate*: another kind of; conn. with 'gait,' manner of going. Ed. 1814 says 'Still used in the North of England.' Cf. *Twelfth Night*, v. 198 'othergates,' in different fashion.

14. *better bread than is made of wheat*, &c.: this proverb for fastidiousness, which Ray, p. 3 (1678), gives as of Italian origin, occurs again in the *Epistle Dedicatorie* to the First Part of *Euphues* (vol. i. 181 l. 18).

P. 178, 25. *in place where*: 'in a more fitting place' (Fairholt), i.e. a more private.

26. *cog*: used here in sense of 'lie,' and two lines further on in special sense of cheating at dice, which would require a steady hand (ed. 1814).

33. *princockes*: pert youth.

41. *winke not*: i.e. if she can see straight.

47. *for catching cold*: i.e. to prevent it, as often, e.g. *Woman*, i. l. 178 'no noyse for waking her.'

P. 179, 60. *prick on a clout*: sew cloth; *Campaspe*, v. 4. 136 'pricking in cloutes.'

74. *my conceit may stumble on his staiednes*: my imagination may chance to become as sober as his own.

81. *The care is taken*: i.e. I have provided against that.

85. *cough mee a foole for his labour*: 'his coughing shall only make me think him the more fool.'

87. *broad-stitch*: a kind only imagined to suit the occasion.

P. 180, 90. *pieuish*: foolish (ed. 1814). In ii. 3. 71 Candius, commenting on Silena's lack of wits, says that people that know not how to discourse 'by some newe coyned by-word bewraie theyr peeuishnesse.' But see note above, on p. 160 l. 72.

104. *pap with a hatchet*: proverbial expression for rough treatment of children. See note on the title of Lyly's pamphlet *Pappe with an Hatchet*, p. 573. There is shrewd sense in Livia's remarks here, with which we may suspect the author to be more than half in sympathy.

108. *cammocke*: a crooked staff or crook, a word of Gaulish origin, ME. *kambok*, LL. *cambuca*. Again in *Endimion*, iii. 1. 36, 'timely crookes that tree that wil be a camock,' and *Euph.* ii. 169 l. 23, 'serching for a wande, I gather a cammocke.'

120. *cowslops*: this variant better represents the original meaning of this plant-name, cow-slobber, cow-dung.

for our names: the yellow cowslip representing the stem *liv-*, the white lilies the stem *cand-*.

121. *Sparrowes ... desires*: the bird's voracity and fecundity are familiar. In *Campaspe*, ii. 2. 60, Hephæstion reproaches Alexander, infatuated with Campaspe, with changing his eagle for a sparrow.

123. *the cockle & the Tortuse, because of Venus*: so Sapho in her appeal to Venus, iii. 3. 88–90, speaks of 'thy Tortoys ... thy Cockleshels.' See note on that passage.

P. 181, 125. *Abeston*: asbestos. Pliny, *Nat. Hist.* xxxvii. 54, gives no explanation of the name; but Solinus, c. 7, says "Ἀσβεστος, cui nomen est quod accensus semel extingui nequit.'

128. *lerripoope*: properly the degree of knowledge that would qualify one to wear a liripoop (liripipium) or scarf as doctor (Nares). Cf. *Sapho and Phao*, i. 3. 6 'Thou maist be skilled in thy Logick but not in thy Lerypoop,' where see note: and *Pappe*, p. 407 l. 31, *Sudeley*, vol. i. 483 l. 7.

136–8. *Principio ... duret amor*: Ovid, *Art. Amat.* i. 35–38. Candius omits after the first line the pentameter, '*Qui nova nunc primum miles in arma venis.*'

140. *pace*: a corruption of parse, from the notion of going over step by step.

148. *Non caret effectu*, &c.: Ov. *Amor.* ii. 3. 16.

P. 182, 172: *collop*: properly a slice of meat; original word probably *clop*, Du. *klop*, a knock, stroke (*Skeat*). Ed. 1814 compares 1 *Henry VI*, v. 4. 18 'thou art a collop of my flesh.'

181. *coope ... capon*: alluding to the fatting of fowls by confinement.

186. *masters ... gaffers*: '*master* being the title applied to gentlemen—*gaffer* that given to plain old countrymen' (Fairholt).

rake . . . forke: as in *Euphues*, ii. 16 ll. 1–2, *Pappe*, p. 412 l. 40.

187. *purchase our children armes*: i.e. heraldic arms, make our children gentlefolk (ed. 1814).

193. *loue vpon sops*: i.e. love in its most luxurious form, sops being cakes dipped in wine (Fairholt).

P. 183, 3. *Obuiam dare Dromio*: *obvium dare se* occurs Livy, i. 16, but Lyly meant *obviam ire* or *fieri*, or intended a mistake.

12. *Lupus in fabula*: a proverb for one who comes up as we are speaking of him (Anglicè 'talk of the devil, &c.'). It occurs Terence, *Adelphi* iv. 1. 21.

18. *conuey a contract*: manage one with secrecy. So below 'conuey knauerie,' and *Macbeth*, iv. 3. 71 'you may convey your pleasures,' i.e. indulge them secretly.

P. 184, 30. *a close marriage*: i.e. clandestine, accompanied by some neglect of due legal forms.

34. *wil make the foole bestride our mistres backs*, &c.: we will patch up some sort of a match between Accius ('the foole') and Silena ('our mistres')—'backs' is a vulgarism—and then take full reward from our masters.

35. *the bagge with the dudgin hafte . . . tantonie pouch*: 'An allusion to the constant custom, from the 14th to the 17th cent., of carrying the purse at the girdle, and the dagger thrust between the straps or cords by which it hung' (Fairholt). A dudgeon haft is a dagger-handle graven with cross lines; a dudgeon-dagger is one with such a handle, and especially one borne by a civilian, not a military weapon. Fairholt explains 'tantonie pouch' as one filled with coins or crosses, St. Anthony being known by his cross; and compares the saying 'He follows him like a *tantonie* pig,' the saint being always pictured with one of these animals.

39. *snaphance*: a firelock, a sense derived from Old Dutch *snaphaen*, a robber that snaps upon one on the highway, from *haan*, a cock, or cock of a gun (Skeat).

40. *purse with a ring . . . knaues hande from it*: Fairholt says the ring-purse was drawn together by a silken or leathern thong, and afforded greater facilities to the hand of the dishonest; while 'course a knaues hand from it' refers to the moral sentence engraved round the metal frame or ring—*course* = 'curse,' not 'chase.'

48. *coystrels*: Malone's explanation of 'coystrel' as first a wine-vessel, and then a mean drunken fellow, on which Fairholt enlarges, seems contradicted by *Tw. Night*, i. 3. 43 'he's a coward and a coystril that will not drink to my niece till his brains turn,' &c., and receives no support from the lexicographers, Murray, Whitney, Skeat, Schmidt. It means properly one that carries a *coustille* (F.) or poniard in attendance, and then a paltry fellow.

52. *nailed vp for slips*: 'counterfeit pieces of money, being brasse, and covered over with silver, which the common people call slips' (Robert Greene's *Thieves Falling Out*, &c., Harl. Misc. viii. p. 399, quoted by Nares). The following from Gascoigne's *Hundreth sundrie Flowres* (1573) seems to indicate a transition in the application of the term from a genuine to a counterfeit coin,—'a piece of mony which then was fallen to three halfpence : and I remember they called the Slippes'. Silver halfpennies were coined by Henry viii, Ed. vi, and Elizabeth (1582).

54. *slipstring*: Halfpenny's rejoinder is opposed to Fairholt's explanation, 'one who has escaped the gallows.' It is rather 'truant.' Also in Beau. and Flet. *King and No King*, ii. 2. 75.

56. *now is my hand on my halfepenie*: proverb for preoccupation of mind. In Gascoigne's *Hundreth sundrie Flowres*, the hero delaying to answer, a lady asks him, ' how now, sir, is your hǎd on your halfpeny ? ' : in Greene's *Menaphon* (p. 49 Arber) of an inattentive auditor 'twere necessarie he tolde vs how his heart came thus on his halfepenie ' : and in Lodge's *Rosalynde*, p. 22, 'is your heart on your halfepeny ? ' is a question to an absent-minded person. Here it almost = I have an idea.

59. *hammers*: i. e. I am hammering out something (Fairholt). See Glossary.

P. 185, 82. *Senties qui vir sim*: Ter. *Eun.* i. 1. 21 '*sentiet qui vir siem*'; but Lyly is recalling his school-book *A Shorte Introduction of Grammar*, on sig. C 5 recto of which it occurs as he quotes it.

98. *Cum mala . . . moras*: Ov. *Rem. Am.* 92.

99. *the least asse is the more asse*: at the word *long-as* in the preceding quotation he points to the taller of his interlocutors; at *mor-as* to the shorter.

P. 186, 109. *bodkin*: ' sheath ' l. 108 suggests the customary association of sword and *dagger* on one belt; 'case '=pair, as *Maydes Met.* ii. 2. 19. But 'bodkin' l. 111=needle. I find nothing about Tonbridge knives or needles. The latter were usually Spanish (*Gall.* iii. 3. 12): no important English manufacture before 1650.

111. *eares . . . boare them*: from the allusion iv. 2. 195-6 it would seem that boring the ears was, like cropping them, one of the punishments attending the pillory.

118. *Gods good* (sometimes ' gos-good ') occurs again *Euph. and his Engl.* ii. 17 l. 10 ' cannot make two meales, vnlesse Galen be his Gods good,' i. e. make them light and wholesome, as yeast does bread.

122. *Foure makes a messe*: for ' mess ' as a set of four cf. *Love's Lab. Lost*, iv. 3. 207 ' You three fools lack'd me fool to make up the mess.'

127. *brinch you mas Sperantus*: ' do you pledge Master Sperantus.' *Brinch* or *brince* = pledge. This rare and obsolete verb is a contraction of the noun *brendice* (from Ital. *brindisi*), a drinking or health to one.

The N.E.D. quotes Abp. Parker, *Psalter*, lxxv. 211 'The good at brynke cleare doth drynke, God *brinche* them gently so' (1556).

132. *beyond Ela . . . Gam vt*: 'Ut' and 'La' were respectively the lowest and highest in the Hexachord or scale of six notes, whose names were derived from the initial syllables in the lines of a Latin hymn to St. John. Calculated at first to commence on C, the scale was later transferred to G (Gamma, Gam), which gives E for the top note (Dict. of Music, art. *Solmisation*). Cf. *Euph.* ii. 3 l. 25, and the Prologue to *Midas*.

P. 187, 136. *shake three trees*: probably alluding to the three beams of a gallows. Cf. 'Tria sequuntur tria,' *Pappe*, p. 406 l. 18.

139. *let vs close to the bush*: i. e. let us quietly to the ivy-bush, slip into the tavern. But 'close' may='hard by.'

140. *Inter pocula philosophandum*: 'An philosophandum sit inter pocula' forms the subject of Plut. *Quaest. Conviv.* i. 1.

144. *print deeper in thy hand*: alluding to the old punishment for felony by branding the hand (Fairholt).

152. *Skinckers*: 'to skink' is to draw or serve wine. Shaksp. has 'under-skinker' in 1 *Henry IV*, ii. 4. 26 (Skeat).

155. *Nowle*: (noule, nole) head, as in *Faerie Queene*, VII. vii. 39.

P. 188, 4. *loitersacke*: cf. 'haltersack' in Beau. and Flet. *King and No King*, ii. 2. The suffix may imply inertness, laziness, or 'meant for hanging.'

6. *casting beyond the Moone*: cf. *Euphues* (vol. i. 222 l. 31).

15. *louing worme*: Fairholt quotes *Campaspe*, v. 4. 127 'Two louing wormes, Hephestion.' Cf. *Euph.* ii. 182 l. 3 'these louing wormes,' and *Tempest*, iii. 1. 31 'Poor worm! thou art infected.'

16. *This green nosegaie*: i. e. the ivy-bush.

17. *smelt to*: *Euphues*, ii. 160 l. 9 'to smell to a perfect Uiolet.'

18. *Argentum potabile*: *aurum potabile*, or gold held in a state of minute subdivision in some volatile oil, being one of the favourite elixirs of the alchemists, mentioned in Ripley's *Compound of Alchymy*, trans. 1591. Silver pennies were coined by all the Tudors and Stuarts. Cf. *Midas*, ii. 2. 37 'golde boyld' (note).

21. *be as bee may is no banning*: i. e. not bad language; evidently a proverb with folk who think affairs are going well and call for no extraordinary effort. Ed. 1814 understands it, too literally, as 'I do not curse my son when I discard him.'

24. *pigsnie*: for 'pig's eye,' a common term of endearment.

26. *sance*: sans.

28. *dodkin*: a Dutch coin worth one-eighth of a stiver (Fairholt). Halliwell quotes Weelkes' *Ayres*, Lon. 1608 'The stiching cost me but a dodkin.'

miching: skulking, loitering. Cf. *micher*, i. 3. 191, and *Euph.* ii. 59 l. 18 'made the Gods to trewant from Heauen, and mych heere on earth.'

30. *banquetting*: the context seems to require 'gambling,' to which sense the derivation from Ital. *banchetto* (dim. of *banco*, a table), coupled with the expression 'gamehouses and tabling houses' in *Northbrook against Dicing*, 1577, lends itself; but perhaps 'taking a nip,' a 'banquet' being a *slight* refection or dessert. A halfpenny was equivalent to threepence or fourpence.

P. 189, 9. *slip at*: metaphor from coursing.

14. *coming*: forward, yielding, as in Jonson's *Silent Woman*, v. 1 'What humour is she? Is she coming, and open, free?' and *Volpone*, iii. 5 'If you were absent she would be more coming.' *Comming*, willingness, is used *Euphues*, ii. 141 l. 28.

24. *Loue and beautie disdaine a meane, not therefore because beautie is no vertue, but because it is happines*: Lyly is thinking of the Aristotelian doctrine of virtue as a mean between two vicious extremes, while happiness, the end of virtue, sought for itself, is not to be measured by the same standard of comparison (*Ethics*, I. 7. 4-5).

P. 190, 46. *are you there with your beares?*: i.e. is that what you're about? Colloquialism from the bear-garden (Fairholt).

54. *the line of life*, &c : the furrow passing from the root of the thumb to the centre of the palm, whose length was supposed to denote the duration of the owner's life. 'Venus' mount' is the fleshy base of the thumb (Fairholt).

56. *well seene in cranes durt*: cf. Skeat's suggestion s.v. *pedigree*, of the phrase *à pied de grue*, as of something with only one leg to stand on.

poulter: 'poulterer: a young turkey is still termed a *turkey poult*' (Fairholt). Cf. 'roister' for roisterer (note on i. 1. 65).

67. *You need . . . so crustie*, &c.: given in Ray's *Proverbs* (1678, p. 237). 'Half-baked' is still a popular term for one of weak wits.

P. 191, 75. *fulsome*: satiating, and so distasteful. *Euph.* i. 182 l. 14 'Cheries be fulsome when they be through rype, bicause they be pléty.'

76. *neuer lesse wit in a yeere*: again in *King Lear*, i. 4. 160. The apparently otiose 'in a year' must mean 'in any year.'

78. *out of all scotch and notch*: one of a number of expressions (like 'out of all cry') for 'excessively.' Cf. *Hay any Worke*, p. 8 'The pleasure you haue done vnto me is out of all scotche and notche.'

97. *farewell frost*, &c.: Ray (1678, p. 243) gives the proverb as 'Farewell frost. Nothing got nor nothing lost.'

P. 192, 2. *ouertaken*: i.e. drunk (1814).

18. *cast this matter*: i.e. the liquor has made him sick, hence the need for bowl and broom (1814). The same joke repeated v. 1. 3.

20. *I præ, sequar* : Ter. *Andr.* i. 1. 144, quoted *End.* iii. 3. 156.

21. *que*: *queue*, cue. The pun that follows seems to substitute 'Q's and K's' for our 'P's and Q's.'

P. 193, 11. *hoysted in the Queenes subsidie booke*: hoisted into the list of wealthy persons who might be called on for a royal loan. In Beaumont and Fletcher's *Scornful Lady*, ii. 3 end, Morecraft the usurer fears that, if he assume knighthood, he will be 'hoist into the subsidy.'

21. *Rufus . . . a paire of hose*: stockings of skins or cloth were worn in Anglo-Saxon or Norman times.

28. *wag-halter*: one who will swing in a halter, a rogue: 'wag,' suggests Wedgwood, is an abbreviation of the term.

29. *spigot . . faucet*: if any distinction is really traceable, the faucet is the horizontal pipe or tap into which fits the perpendicular spigot that controls the flow of the liquor.

30. *black boule*: of leather, like a jack.

32. *stand*: a cask corresponding to a hogshead of beer. *George a Greene*, Dyce's ed. p. 267 *a* 'a stand of ale.'

P. 194, 47. *leere*: learning. ME. *leren*, to teach, or sometimes to learn.

48. *learne heere . . . at Ashford*: 'learn' here has the sense of 'teach.' Cf. Psalm xxv. 4 'Lead me forth in thy truth, and learn me.' In i. 3. 4-5 Prisius says Candius will have to be a schoolmaster. Hasted's *History of Kent*, vol. iii. p. 262, mentions no grammar-school as founded at Ashford before the reign of Charles I. The 'college' founded by Sir John Fogge in the time of Edward IV was a clerical endowment for saying masses, and seems to have been dissolved soon after 1503.

51. *Sine Cerere & Baccho friget Venus*: a proverb. Ter. *Eun.* iv. 5. 6 ('Libero' for 'Baccho'), Cic. *De Nat. Deor.* ii. 23. 60: quoted again by Lyly *Loves Met.* v. 1. 46.

58. *shall cost mee the setting on*: the 'spread' shall be at my charge.

63. *tenters*: a tenter was a frame for stretching cloth by means of hooks. Prisius, whose father was a tailor i. 3. 17, is probably proprietor of some fulling-mills. See v. 3. 144, where he threatens to grind Lucio to powder in his mill.

P. 195, 5. *without modestie*: ed. 1814 corrects to 'with modesty,' but the word here means confusion, shamefacedness, as I think in *Hamlet* ii. 2. 289 'there is a kind of confession in your looks which your modesties have not craft enough to colour.'

9. *our fathers*: so 'our parents' are spoken of l. 7; but only their putative mother, Vicinia, is introduced v. 3.

10. *the succes of fortune*: i. e. succession, sequel, whatever fortune may ensue. Cf. *Midas*, iii. 1. 3 'in thy successe vnfortunat.' *Winter's Tale*, i. 2. 394 'parents, in whose success we are gentle,' and probably *Macbeth*, i. 7. 4 'catch, with his surcease, success.'

21. *kindred . . . kindnes*: probably alluding to a proverb that Hamlet actually cites.

P. 196, 57. *bewraie our passions*: if the text is right *bewraie* must mean 'abandon,' 'give up.'

1. *Ingenium . . . . At nunc . . . nihil*: Ov. *Amor.* iii. 8. 3, 4.

2. *crock vp golde*: 'the old money-pot for savings was made of coarse earthenware and broken when filled' (Fairholt).

6. *rong all*: i. e. wrung, rated, abused, a sense derived from the wringing or pinching of a tight shoe (cf. *Euph.* ii. 10 l. 17). But possibly of the clatter of a peal of bells: cf. Beau. and Flet. *Humourous Lieut.* v. 1 'I would ring him such a lesson.'

P. 197, 10. *a quarter long*: a quarter of an hour long.

14. *euax, vah, hui*: Lilly and Colet's *A Shorte Introduction of Grammar*, ed. 1577, 4°, the authorized school Latin Grammar of the day from which Lyly frequently quotes, has on sig. C ij recto, treating of Interjections—'Some are of myrth : as *Euax, vah*. Some are of sorrow: as *Heu, hei* . . . Colling : as *Eho, oh, io.*' Cf. *Endim.* iii. 3. 5.

23. *cast*: arranged, as in ii. 4. 18 'cast this matter.'

29. *hauing Accius apparell should court Silena*: this would have accord with the 'noting the apparel' at the fools' first interview; but when the occasion arrives (iv. 2. 8) the fools actually wear Candius' and Livia's dress, which accords with Halfpenny's announcement just below, l. 50. The scheme was more plausible without this unnecessary change, which must be due partly to Lyly's love of balance (for it *was* essential that Candius and Livia should wear the fools' dress), partly to his fear that, if the fools appeared in their own clothes, the audience would forget that the father of each was to suppose his son or daughter to be some one else.

38. *fodges*: so QQ here and again pp. 116, 123, and in *Endim.* iv. 2 p. 55 as rhyme to 'lodge.'

41. *rundlet*: older form of 'runlet,' a small barrel.

P. 198, 44. *whitled*: drunk. 'A whittle was a clasped knife, and a person in liquor is still sometimes said to be *cut*' (1814). *Lie by it*: are laid up for it. Cf. *Pappe*, p. 17 'make you blush and lie by it,' i. e. hide your head.

47. *sod*: sodden. Skeat quotes no instance of 'sod' as past participle of 'seethe,' though it occurs as past tense in Gen. xxv. 29 'Jacob sod pottage.'

48. *spit white broth* Nares compares 2 *Henry IV*, i. 2. 237— doubtfully.

50. *they wonder*: i. e. Candius and Livia, to whom also 'marrie them' in the next speech refers.

P. 199, 22. *Accius tongue . . . his fathers teeth*: Ray's *Proverbs* (ed. 1678, p. 255) gives as 'of marriage'—'He hath tied a knot with his tongue that he cannot untie with all his teeth.'

27. *lapwing-like*, &c.: cf. *Euph. and his Eng.* Ep. Ded. (vol. ii. p. 4 l. 18).

34. *cursie*: courtesy. ' To strain courtesy' is to be wanting in it, as in *Euph.* ii. 81 l. 13, where Euphues fears to strain courtesy by arriving late at night.

P. 200, 2. *packe* : plot.

laie downe the packe : i. e. the bundle of clothes she is carrying.

5. *Omne solum*, &c. : Ovid, *Fast.* i. 493.

christendome . . . *Kent*: Ray (*Proverbs*, p. 313, 2nd ed.) considers ' Neither in Kent nor Christendom ' a reminiscence of the time when the Christian Britons gave Kent to the Pagan Saxon invaders, while Fuller refers it rather to the first Christianizing of Kent by Augustine, as one might say ' the first cut and all the loaf beside.' Probably the opposition is merely between the part and the whole.

7. *Patria [est] ubicumque [est] bene*: a line, possibly of Pacuvius, quoted Cic. *Tusc.* 5. 37.

13. *goose so gray in the lake*, &c.: Chaucer's *Wife of Bath's Prol.* D. 269-70 has the proverb.

29. *beatedst hempe* : i. e. in a house of correction (1814).

30. *crabbs she stampt*, &c. : ' crab apples are stamped or pounded to make verjuice ' (1814), and their sourness naturally associates them with a hard or wrinkled face.

P. 201, 34. *hang in a halter* sounds like a proverb for being of one and the same kind, and here seems equivalent to *arcades ambo*.

45. *noyse*: company of musicians. Halliwell quotes Dekker's *Belman*, 1608 ' Those terrible noyses with thredbare cloakes.'

50. *The Pag.*: Blount ' 4 Pag.' misled no doubt by Rixula's 'foure together' in the next line but one; but Dromio and Riscio have not yet entered, and she speaks merely in anticipation of their arrival.

55. *Phip, phip*: an abbreviation of Philip, and supposed to sound like the bird's note. Fairholt quotes from Skelton's *Elegy of Philip Sparowe*—

' And when I sayd Phyp, Phyp,
Then he wold lepe and skyp.'

57. *holds tack* : ' is appropriate,' that is, the parrot is naturally associated with ' ropery ' or roguery ; or else—the mention of rope is in keeping with such a subject as yourselves. Cf. Beau. and Fl. *Wit at Several Weapons*, iii. 1

'If I knew where to borrow a contempt
Would hold thee tack,' &c.

S. D. [*carrying clothes*, &c.] : the addition is warranted by the mention of ' baggage ' just below, and by Riscio's remark at the end of the scene ' Heere is Silenas attire.'

63. *heres euery man his baggage*: possibly also with proverbial sense ' this is every one's concern,' ' we are all in the same boat.'

P. 202, 101. *Brewish* or ' brewis ' is ' bread soaked in the liquor in which salt meat has been boiled, sometimes used for the liquid only' (1814). Cf. Fletcher's *Mad Lover*, ii. 2. 8 'Beef . . . lined with brewis.'

102. *poudred*: salted.

P. 203, 115. *hoxe*: hamstring. Whitney quotes Wyclif, Josh. xi. 6 'Thou shalt hoxe the horsis of hem.'

123. *a wedding fresh a beating*: ed. 1814 explains it as 'afoot,' and mentions that in Yorkshire 'beating' is equivalent to 'breeding.' But the notion is rather that of fashioning in metal, transferred to the brain. But cf. v. 3. 290 'a match in hammering,' and *Tempest*, v. 246

'Do not infest your mind with beating on
The strangeness of this business.'

127. *prest*: glazed (Fairholt).

130. *raisons of the sunne* or 'sun-raisins' are raisins dried on the vine, the leaves being removed, and the cluster-stem sometimes half-severed (Whitney).

131. *the quest*: i. e. the jury.

P. 204, 162. *because he doth die*: i. e. by the trade of dyeing.

175. *What is all our fortunes?*: i. e. how shall we fare in our *joint* enterprise?

P. 205, 180. *if you were*: i. e. found cozener, or cozened.

5. *and hee wise*: Dilke's emendation *wise* for *wist* yields better sense than to take *and*, as often, for *an*—'if he knew.'

S. D. *Enter Dromio, Risio*: Dromio and Riscio, rather than Halfpenny and Lucio, attend the betrothal of Candius and Livia, because they are supporting the characters of Accius and Silena. Similarly in Sc. 2 Halfpenny and Lucio attend the supposed Candius and Livia.

P. 206, 20. *spurre scholers*: ask, ply them with questions or retorts: simply the term of horsemanship applied, by established metaphor, to scholastic disputation. *Spere*, Lowl. Sc. *speir*, AS. *spyrian*, inquire, investigate, are allied, not derivative; AS. *spor*, a foot-trace. Again, iv. 2. 23, 185; *Pappe*, pp. 395 l. 3, 396 l. 21 'which (wit) if he spurre with his copper replie'; and *Rom. & Jul.* ii. 4. 70 'My wit faints,' 'Switch and spurs.'

22. *ten grotes . . . to saie seruice*: this would equal about eight times as much of our money, i. e. about 27 shillings. A guinea a service is the supposed honorarium to-day.

24. *hence to Canterbury*: i. e. 26 or 27 miles.

27. *some poast to his master*: i. e. sleepy fool who let him run wild. *Serued*, l. 25, probably = 'played a trick on,' i. e. the Hackneyman.

32. *Molle eius leuibus*, &c.: Lyly adapts (perhaps from the *Shorte Introduction of Grammar*, fol. L 5 verso) Ov. *Her.* xv. 79 'Molle meum, levibusque cor est violabile telis'; but Q^1 printed by mistake 'inviolabile,

which led Q² (Bl. F.) to corrupt 'Molle' into 'Male' (Male inviolabile = violabile), and so bring the line into accord with what follows. Lyly quotes the line, *Loves Met.* v. 2. 10, with omission of *que*, which lengthens *cor*.

33. *a heart named Ceruus*: execrable pun on 'hart.'

37. *comming*: step. Dilke's change to *coughing* (cf. i. 3. 65) is quite unnecessary.

45. *Bauins*: 'faggots of furze-wood' (Fairholt): 'rash bavin wits, Soon kindled and soon burnt' (1 *Henry IV*, iii. 2. 61).

P. 207, 54. *dangers in the Church: we*, &c.: Dilke's emendation, which by putting a colon at 'dangers' constructs 'in the Church' with what follows, is not absolutely necessary and destroys the Lylian balance. The 'dangers in the Church' which Livia anticipates are the risks attendant on the asking of the banns. Dilke notes that the canon forbidding a minister to celebrate matrimony without licence or banns was not enacted till 1603; and quotes Greene's *Tu Quoque* and the wedding of Isabella and Francisco in Beau. and Flet. *Wit without Money* for instances of weddings celebrated about 5.0 a.m. without licence or banns.

80. *to Memphios house*: Candius speaks in his rôle of Memphio's son.

81. *this cottons*: succeeds, suits; derived by Wedgwood from the matting or clinging together of a lock of wool or hair. Cf. 'So, twill cotton,' p. 210 l, 84. See N.E.D., s. v.

P. 208, 4. *It was too good to be true*, &c.: Halfpenny fears that their idea (of matching Acc. and Sil.) was too funny to become fact, for they will betray the scheme by laughing.

9. *to as much purpose as a hem in the forehead*: the injury inflicted on the proverb here 'knockt in the head' is too great for its recovery. 'Hem' is possibly for 'horn,' but this is unsatisfactory.

23. *Spurre*: ask; see note on 'spurre schollers,' p. 206 l. 20.

P. 209, 28. *I crie you mercy . . . ioynd stoole*: this proverb for an unfortunate apology or a pert reply is enumerated in Ray's *Proverbs*, occurs in *Lear*, iii. 6. 53, and is alluded to *Taming of the Shrew*, ii. 1. 199, where Katharine further explains her term 'moveable' as applied to Petruchio by the word 'joint-stool' (Nares).

29. *conduit*: 'in the time of our poet, the lower classes of people fetched the water in pails and other vessels from the conduits, and consequently a considerable assemblage of both sexes was frequently to be seen at such places' (ed. 1814).

32. *giue me the boots*: this allusion to the torture of the boot, which crushed the leg by pressure, had passed into a phrase for making game of a person. Cf. *Two Gentlemen*, i. 1. 27.

33. *coblers cuts*: seems to mean 'odds and ends.'

39. *gascoins . . . round hose*: 'gascoynes [gaskins or galligaskins] were loose wide breeches; the round hose fitted the leg closely' (Fairholt). The latter would therefore indicate a closer degree of acquaintance or

favour. In Dekker's *Shoemaker's Holiday*, ii. i, Sybil says of Lacy, her mistress' suitor, who has declined to recognize her in public, 'Go thy ways, thought I; thou may'st be much in my gaskins, but nothing in my nether-stocks.'

50. *a fraile of figges*: Nares gives it as a rush or mat basket holding about 70 pounds, and quotes *Mirrour for Mag.* p. 482 'Two hundred frailes of figs and raisons fine.'

52. *Sauing a reuerence*: salvâ reverentiâ, sometimes contracted to 'surreverence,' an apology for using a strong expression. Beau. and Flet. *Humourous Lieut.* iv. 1 'Surreverence, Love!' of what Celia knows to be lust.

P. 210, 64. *Theres a glicke . . . girde*: 'glicks and girds,' i. e. jests and sarcasms, occur together in *Pappe*, p. 412 l. 23.

66. *kild your cushion*: Silena is probably garbling the expression 'missed the cushion' or mark in archery, which occurs *Euph.* i. 237 l. 22.

79–84. *Stel. (aside to Luc.) What is she?* &c.: my change of the prefixes is warranted by the speeches of Memphio and Stellio (ll. 115–20), and by Memphio's later question to Halfpenny, l. 133. Each parent expects to find, not his own child, but some one personating his child; and each, being behind his child's back, asks who the personator is, and 'does not recognize that only the clothes are changed, until the children speak or turn round. (Cf. 'I['ll] looke him in the face,' l. 93.)

P. 211, 96. *I perceiue an olde sawe*: I recognize the truth of it. Dilke rightly observes that this speech (down to 'old foole') is 'somewhat out of character for Accius, and might be given with good point to Halfpenny'; or, I would suggest, annexed to the previous speech of Stellio.

108. *begd for a concealde foole*: see note on Act i. sc. 1. p. 74.

112. *improued to the vttermost*: i. e. you make the best show you can with brains so deficient. 'Improving,' as Halfpenny's next remark shows, was a term for raising rents. Comp. Beau. and Flet. *King and No King*, i. 1, where Arbaces chaffingly asks Mardonius whether the wenches 'improve themselves' or whether he 'sits at an old rent with 'em.'

128. *this geare must be fetcht about*: i. e. I must go *round*, another way about my purpose.

P. 212, 134. *Sperantus sonne*: *Prisius' sonne* of all eds. is obviously wrong, as Prisius has no son. See my note on the prefixes just above (on p. 210 ll. 79–84).

137. *Lucio (to Stellio) And so, sir*, &c.: Lucio's 'by nature' insinuates the folly of parents, so that his answer is the equivalent of Halfpenny's just before, 'they' meaning both Accius and Silena. Stellio's question as to why he told him it was Prisius' daughter is supposed to have been put, and parried: but I have my doubts whether the complexity of the plot has not led to some corruption of the text here, as above.

139. *ioyntes are not yet tied*: equivalent to 'bones not yet set.'

162. *go for a que*: i.e. q., the arithmetical mark for a farthing (quadrans).

P. 213, 163. *currantly*: either 'fluently' or 'in ordinary fashion.'

171. *alecie*: Halfpenny coins a word to suggest that the Hackney-man is drunk.

180. *bottle*: truss. Bottom in *Mid. N. Dream*, iv. 1. 37 has 'a great desire to a bottle of hay.'

185. *spurd him*: pun on the use of *spur* in the sense of 'ask,' as above, notes on pp. 206 l. 20, 208 l. 23.

188. *stand vpon no ground*: in Peele's *Polyhymnia*, 1590, Nedham's 'lusty horse . . . Would snort, and stamp, and stand upon no ground.'

192. *gently*: 'as to a gentleman,' who would use him decently; or, but less probably, 'at an easy rate.'

193. *neither would cry wyhie, nor wag the taile*: Ray's *Proverbs*, 2nd ed. (1678), p. 157, gives 'It's an ill horse can neither whinny nor wag his tail.' In Marston's *The Fawne*, Act iv 'al that can wyhee or wag the taile' is used as a synonym for 'all of any spirit.'

195. *boare him thorough the eares*: probably done for purposes of identification, when a horse was grazing among others. A slit in the ear serves this purpose on the prairies to-day. The implication is that Dromio had earmarked with intent to steal him. Compare with this, or with Lucio's suggestion of the pillory, Halfpenny's remark, as bodkin, ii. 1. 111.

P. 214, 201. *tyre, and retire*: *tyre* possibly (in a sense derived from that of a hawk 'tiring on' (Fr. *tirer*), pulling at her prey) of pulling at the bridle, trying to get his head; or, with *seruice*, 'be busy about,' 'make a fuss'; or simply 'grow tired.' *Retire*, i. e. jib.

206. *So he shall when I make him a bargen*: i. e. I'll take good security when next I deal with him.

213. *maltmare*: i. e. brewer's horse, dray-horse.

214. *trotted before and ambled behinde*: i. e. with fore and hind legs respectively, to express the discomfort caused to the rider by his action.

218. *pose*: a cold or running at the nose: *Midas*, v. 2. 109 'a catarre, the pose, the water euill.' 'By the pose in thy nose,' Beau. and Flet. *The Chances*, v. 3 (Nares). Ed. 1814 quotes Chaucer—

> 'He speketh in his nose
> And sneseth fast and eke he hath the pose.'
> *Manciple's Prologue* [l. 62].

223. *towne borne children*: so of Philautus in *Euph*. i. 199 l. 21.

225. *statute Marchant*: obsolete form of bond, acknowledged before the chief magistrate of a trading-town, the forfeiture of which might be followed by an execution against body, lands and goods (*Cent. Dict.*).

P. 215, 245. *They will ride them* : i. e. ride our wits. Cf. *Pappe*, p. 395 l. 2 'If he ride me, let the foole sit fast, for my wit is verie kickish.'

246. *bleed their follyes* : i. e. give them vent, exhibit them.

3. *cast it vp* : Elizabethan stomachs were strong enough for a repetition of the joke of ii. 4. 23.

4. *pen out of the pot* : pun on pen in sense of beak or nose. *Henry V*, ii. 3. 17 'his nose was as sharp as a pen.'

7. '*Iost there vp, bay Richard!*' : as he would cry to a horse.

8. *horsebread* : made after special recipes, of which Nares s. v. quotes two from books on hunting. In Fletcher's *Night-Walker*, v. 1, Toby, the coachman, cries

'Oh that I were in my oat-tub with a horse-loaf,
Something to hearten me!'

P. 216, 13. *in these same yeeres* : i. e. in your long experience.

P. 217, 11. *spittle for his pinne* : i. e. to make the pegs which tightened the strings hold fast. The Century Dict. quotes 'ye'll make a pin to your fiddle' *The Bonny Bows o' London* (*Child's Ballads*, ii. 362).

14. *into the leads for a hobler* : 'into the gutter for a mark to throw at' (Fairholt). 'Hobler' seems to be identical with 'hob,' which Halliwell gives as a piece of wood set up on end with a halfpenny on the top to be pitched at. So, by association, 'hob nob' for 'hab nab' (*habban* and *ne habban*—'not to have'), which Skeat gives as 'hit or miss,' 'at random,' and which occurs in *Euphues*, ii. 123 l. 11.

19. *brabble* : brawl, quarrel, used as verb in Massinger and Middleton's *Love's Cure*, ii. 2 'I did never brabble,' and as a noun, *Twelfth Night*, v. 68 'In private brabble did we apprehend him.'

to morrow is a new daie : a common phrase in deferring the settlement or pursuit of a subject. In Fletcher's *Night-Walker*, ii. 3 Lurcher replies to his mistress' wish to examine the chest at once with 'To morrow's a new day, sweet'; also *Custom of the Country*, iv. 4.

20. *I am sorrie I speake in your cast* : Bedunenus apologizes. The phrase means to interrupt or put another speaker out, 'cast' being the part allotted to an actor. Cf *Euphues*, ii. 172 l. 24, and 55 l. 6 'If I may speak in your cast, quoth Iffida,' the preceding speaker having paused to drink. The N. E. D. quotes Roger's *Naaman* (1642), 46 'As when the minde is filled with businesse, all that is spoken is, as it were, spoken in a man's cast.'

S. D. *Sing* : The song is not given, perhaps, as Fairholt suggests, because it was not by Lyly, but a popular song in common use on such occasions ; but Blount omits many others (see below, pp. 592–3, and Essay, vol. ii. p. 265). 'The Loue Knot' would not be inappropriate as a title for the 'catch' given some twenty lines further on ; but Synis' words there seem to imply choice of a different song to suit a patron of higher rank.

P. 218, 32. *fairely hanged. Nas. So he is, sir*: the pun may be to take 'hanged' in the sense of 'hooked,' or 'hung up,' 'settled in life.'

38. *I thinke it was Memphios sonne*: Synis adopts the attitude Candius requires of him, for the benefit of Sperantus (listening above), who in iv. 1 witnessed, as he thought, the troth-plight of Memphio's n and Stellio's daughter.

44. *ten shillings is money in master Maiors purse*: the angel was worth about 10*s*., i. e. eight times as much now, and Bedunenus' remark seems to be a proverb, with the sense 'ten shillings is a sum a rich man might look twice at.' Fairholt wrongly supposes an allusion to Memphio, who on the next page 'stands to be Maior.'

48. *cry at the Sizes, a marke in issues*: what the cry really represents escapes me, as it has escaped previous editors; but I am afraid there is no doubt that Lyly intends the execrable pun 'a mark (i. e. 13*s*. 4*d*.) in [h]is shoes.'

52. *handsell*: instalment. Bedunenus is open to further offers.

P. 219, 66. *Tick-tacke*: or tric-trac. Nares quotes *The Compleat Gamester*, p. 113 'This is the plain game of tick-tack, which is so called from *touch and take*, for if you touch a man you must play him, though to your loss,' and the present passage seems to show that the derivation, if erroneous, was that popularly accepted.

77. *a huddle*: 'an embrace,' says Fairholt: but the word is usually applied to old men, from their multitudinous wraps; and was possibly occasionally used, for the same reason, of a baby.

78. *crouding*: fiddling. 'Crowd,' a fiddle, from Welsh *crwth*, anything swelling out, a bulge or belly (Skeat).

87. *the roodes bodie*: the figure of the crucified Saviour on the rood-screen.

100. *the foure waites*: i. e. the town waits, or musicians (Fairholt). *Wring*, 'bear the brunt of it.'

P. 220, 111-3. *a wise man is melancholy*, &c.: Lyly anticipates Rosalind's 'I had rather have a fool to make me merry than experience to make me sad.' *A. Y. L. I.* iv. 1. 30. For 'mooneshine in the water' cf. *End.* ii. 2. 2.

114. *dames chafing*: for Memphio's shrewish wife cf. i. 1. 2, 73-80.

116. *I would her tongue were in thy belly*: explained by the allusion to 'pinching' l. 122. Memphio humorously wishes that his wife's economical preachments could be embodied in Dromio's appetite: or means simply, that so much of a tongue as hers would be enough to stay even Dromio's stomach.

119. *that makes*: *clapper* is antecedent to *that*.

133. *rustle into*: come with whispered gossip into.

P. 221, 141. *imbesell*: 'embezzle,' showing the derivation of the word from a verb corresponding to O. French 'imbécill' or 'imbécel,' meaning to weaken, diminish, or enfeeble (Skeat).

MOTHER BOMBIE

144. *grinde thee to pouder in my mill*: Prisius is probably a fuller by trade. See note on ii. 5. 63.

155. *the clocke cryed*, &c.: i.e. the wedding was concluded within legal hours, before twelve struck.

P. 222, 173. *giglot*: wanton girl.

189. *oatemeale groate*: no particular coin alluded to, 'oatmeal' being a cant term for a swaggerer or profligate. In Ford and Dekker's *The Suns Darling*, i. 1, Folly has a song in which he says he will 'Do mad prank with | Roaring boys and Oatmeals.'

198. *conuey*: polite term for stealing. *Merry Wives*, i. 3. *Rich. II*, iv. ad fin.

P. 223, 208. *schritch owle*: cf. *Euphues*, ii. 78 l. 13, 79 l. 32.

219. *beeing trust*: i.e trussed, with my trousers up, as the context shows, hose and breeches being one garment. Dilke wrongly interprets 'As good confess here, whilst I am trusted, as at home when I am trussed up for whipping.'

229–31. *met ... no mountaines; ... tauern ... mortall*: with the first cf. *As You Like It*, iii. 2. 186 ''tis a hard matter for friends to meet; but mountains may be removed with earthquakes and so encounter': and 'Though mountains meet not, Louers may,' in the last stanza of a poem in Davison's *Poet. Rapsody*, 1602 'It chanct of late a shepherds swain,' from which the signature 'Anomos' (=A.W.) is withdrawn after the first edition, and which might be Lyly's: cf. above, p. 443. The second seems to allude to the comparison of human life to an inn, of which we have an instance in *Quarrendon*, vol. i. p. 468 ll. 1–4.

233. *trouble the water before they dronke*: Lyly is alluding to this fact recorded of camels by Pliny, *Nat. Hist.* viii. 26 as before *Euphues*, ii. 143 l. 14 note, and after in *Pappe*, p. 396 l. 16.

P. 224, 268. *the humble-bees kisse*: 'sting' is frequent in the dramatists of sexual action.

269. *banes*: banns, as in *Euph.* i. 199 l. 36.

P. 225, 308. *mandrage*: mandragora. Nares quotes 'Dioscorides doth particularly set downe many faculties hereof, of which notwithstanding there be none proper unto it, save those that depend upon the drowsie and sleeping power thereof' (Gerard's *Herbal*, in *Mandragoras*).

313. *as I haue pittied them*: i.e. Memphio and Stellio's children, in not killing them, as she had intended to do with her own offspring.

P. 226, 325. *be cosned by cosners*: this part of the prophecy must be supposed to have been fulfilled by the revelation of Vicinia's cozening, which has frustrated the servants' plot to match Accius and Silena.

330. *neuer doing harme, but still practising good*: Memphio here endorses a public repute that has found expression twice before, from Serena, iii. 1. 27, and from Riscio, iii. 4. 89: with which we may compare the respect shown by Vicinia, v. 2, and the mingled kindness and

dignity of her reception of the five servants in iii. 4, especially her refusal of money and insistence on civility, iii. 4. 183. Lyly, in fact, seems to have intended a protest against the prejudice often entertained against these 'wise women' as witches in league with Satan, a distrust indicated in Mæstius and Serena, iii. 1 and partly in the Pages in iii. 4.

342. *thy fact* : common of some bad or monstrous act.

P. 227, 352. *balde* : i. e. barren, useless, poor.

eate . . . pie : potato-pie, a supposed provocative, common at wedding-feasts.

370. *Ile crie quittance* : a threat, not an overture : ' I'll be even with you.'

373. *such a Nouerint as Cheapside,* &c. : the exordium of Latin deeds, equivalent to 'Know, all men.' Cf. the oft-quoted passage about 'leaue the trade of *Noverint,* whereto they were borne' in Nash's Epistle prefixed to Greene's *Menaphon,* p. 9 (Arber). Legal summonses are associated with Cheapside because the Court of Arches was held in the church of St. Mary le Bow (*de Arcubus*) in that street. Cf. Nash's *Haue with you* ' into the Arches we might step, and heare him plead,' quoted vol. i. p. 61, note.

P. 228, 392. *tosse it* : toss pots, drink.

396. *a cast of your office* : specimen, example.

402. *vpseekings* : I know of no other instance. Possibly a confusion is intended with the prefix ' upsee ' or ' upsey ' (q.v. Nares) associated with phrases for intoxication. What Silena means is 'we are not responsible for that.'

THE WOMAN IN THE MOONE.

P. 240, 4-10. DRAM. PERS.—SATURN, &c. . . . *Seven Planets* : the Ptolemaic system of the universe, which, in spite of Copernicus, still and for a century later dominated popular conceptions, conceived the Earth as the centre round which revolved the Planets in seven successive spheres, of which the Moon was nearest, Saturn the farthest, and the Sun ('the glorious Planet Sol,' *Troil. & Cress.* i. 3. 89) the fourth.

12. GANYMEDE, &c. : a stage-direction in the quarto (ii. 1. 175) mentions Jove's 'Exit with Ganimede,' though his presence has not been indicated before, and no part is written for him. He is mentioned by Juno, ii. 1. 54, and twice by Pandora, iii. 2. 81, 148, who should therefore have seen him. He must be supposed to have been conferring with Jupiter in the space behind the balcony, from the time of the latter's disappearance ii. 1. 81 till his re-entry ib. l. 168.

15. PANDORA : to what is said under Sources, pp. 234-6, I add that Turbervile, dedicating to Anne Countess of Warwick his *Epitaphes, Epigrams, Songs, and Sonets,* 1567, in an introductory poem describes the gods and goddesses uniting to make the Countess perfect in mind

and person; and that Elizabeth had been called Pandora in the earlier eds. of Warner's *Albion*, 1586, 1589.

P. **241**, 3. PROL.—*A point beyond the auncient Theorique*: i.e. not mentioned in the received system of astronomy.

5. *Vtopia*: distinguished from known countries by an Arcadian simplicity, but imagined as somewhere on the earth's surface: cf. i. 1. 11 '*this* Massiue earth,' and v. 263 'conuey her from the earth.'

17. *Remember all is but a Poets dreame*: this apology for faults is borrowed, as Fairholt points out, by Shakespeare in the Epilogue to *Mids. N. Dream*, which bears other resemblances to Lyly's play—

<blockquote>
If we shadows have offended,
Think but this and all is mended,
That you have but slumber'd here
While these visions did appear.
</blockquote>

P. **242**, 5-6. { *Heere I suruey the pictured firmament,*
{ *With hurtlesse flames in concaue of the Moone*, &c.:
this rather vague description, suggested I think by Pliny, bk. ii. ch. 4, is intended to represent Utopia as a storehouse of Nature's materials. The four elements are enumerated as in Pliny—Fire in these two lines, Air in the two following, Water in the next two, and then Earth. Ll. 5-6 imply that Nature has in her workshop a model of the starry universe; not the reality, because the flames are *hurtlesse*. *Concaue* I take to mean no more than 'sphere,' 'orb t.' Cf. '1651 H. More in *Enthus. Triumph* (1656) 191 "All to the very concave [i.e. sphere] of the Moon"' (N. E. D.).

9. *mutuall Ioynter*: mutual embrace or joining. It is probably suggested by 'huius (aeris) vi suspensam, cum quarto aquarum elemento, librari medio spatio tellurem. Ita *mutuo complexu* diversitatis effici nexum' in the passage of Pliny, ii. 4.

11. *rundle*: ball or globe : ' imam atque mediam in toto esse terram, eandemque universi cardine stare pendentem, librantem per quae pendeat,' Pliny, ii. 4.

P. **243**, 29. *Nature workes her will from contraries*: probably from Arist. *De Mundo*, cap. v Ἴσως δὲ καὶ τῶν ἐναντίων ἡ φύσις γλίχεται, καὶ ἐκ τούτων ἀποτελεῖ τὸ σύμφωνον, οὐκ ἐκ τῶν ὁμοίων κ. τ. λ.

S.D. *roundelay*: Skeat, who quotes no instance earlier than the *Sheph. Kal.* June l. 49 (1579), gives it as from Fr. *rondelet*, dimin. of *rondel*, by confusion with *lay*. *Rundelayes* again, l. 222.

P. **244**, 60. *A merror of the earth*: a glass for humanity or a combination of all that is best in humanity, or perhaps referring simply to its being compounded of all the four elements.

dispight: envy (Fairholt).

82. *vntyed*: error for 'tyed' or 'not yet vntyed' (with ellipse of 'are').

P. 245, 95. *Saturn's deepe conceit*: 'conceit' = thoughts, as above, p. 179 l. 75. Saturn, the oldest, is reputed the wisest of the gods.

103. *Iunoes armes, Auroraes hands, and louely Thetis foote*: recalling the Homeric epithets λευκώλενος, ῥοδοδάκτυλος, and ἀργυρόπεζα, applied respectively to these deities.

113. *the Saint*: frequently used for the object of a lover's devotion ; e. g. *Euph.* i. 215 l. 1.

116. *Parrat speake a while*: 'Speaks the Parrot?' was a stock phrase (*Endim.* v. 3. 219) for suggesting that a person's talk was empty or foolish.

117. *faire Cynthia*: Luna addresses Pandora in mockery, not herself.

P. 246, 135. *signorize*: lord it.

138. S. D. *He ascends*: i. e. takes his place in the balcony at the back above the stage, which played so conspicuous a part in the Elizabethan drama, and in which each of the Planets takes up position in turn. Of course the term is also used in the astrological sense of 'being in the ascendant.'

152. *For honors due*, &c.: for the due obedience that belongs to her will.

163. *Questionest*: The *Cent. Dict.* quotes 'Duns, with all the rable of barbarous *questionistes*'—Ascham's *Scholemaster*, ed. Arber, p. 136.

P. 247, 169. *Marchants eares, To beare*, &c.: i. e. to hear the wind blow, and betray no anxiety for his vessels. I know no parallel for this very poetical expression for patience and self-control.

174. *grudge*: murmur, repine. ME. *grochen, grucchen*. Again iii. 1. 47.

178. *for waking her*: 'for fear of waking her,' a use of 'for' tolerably common in the Elizabethan poets, e. g. Beaumont and Fletcher, though Schmidt quotes only five instances of it in Shakespeare, e. g. Sonnet 52. 4 'the which (treasure) he will not every hour survey, For blunting the fine point of seldom pleasure.' Cf. *M. Bomb.* i. 3. 47 'lies with his mother for catching cold.'

P. 248, 205. *sollemne daunce*: in the classical sense of festival, or annual, dance.

217. *sounds*: i. e. swounds, swoons. Cf. 'almost sounded,' *Euph.* i. 218 l. 5.

222. *Rundelayes*: roundelays. See note on p. 243, S. D.

P. 249, 1. *A Ioue principium*, &c.: I believe this line is Lyly's founded on the following opening of a Latin translation of Aratus' *Phoenomena* bound in the often-mentioned edition of Hyginus, 1578, p. 204

' A Ioue principium: quem nunquam mittimus ipsi
   Infatum: plena verò Iouis omnia quidem compita,
   Omnes verò hominum coetus: plenum verò mare,
   Et portus. vbique autem Ioue indigemus omnes.'

THE WOMAN IN THE MOONE

5. *regiment*: government.

14. *Calisto*: the hunting-companion of Artemis, who became pregnant by Zeus, and incurred Artemis' displeasure. Hyg. *Poet. Astr.* ii. 2 (p. 58 ed. 1578).

21. *discusse*: shake apart, dissolve. Cp. Skeat, s. v.

23. S. D. [*Discovers himself*]: probably by throwing aside wrappings.

P. 251, 87. *lay thy hands vnder my precious foote*: a token of submission, as in *Taming of Shrew*, v. 2. 178.

96. *Did sinke*: either this is intrans. 'there did sink,' and the preceding line parenthetic (nom. abs.), or else *eyes* in the preceding line must be taken as subj. of *did sinke* as a causative verb.

101. *cursies*: 'curtsies,' as often.

P. 254, 173. *weep curst hart away*: cure her shrewishness by weeping (Fairholt).

183. *And why not Iphicles*, &c.: here for the first time others besides Pandora are affected by the Planet in the ascendant. This improvement is maintained more or less in the case of the remaining Planets, e.g. Sol influences Stesias to a ludicrous solemnity over Pandora's verses, iii. 1. 105 sqq.; Venus, iii. 2. 33 sqq. converts the hitherto respectful Gunophilus into a lover; and Mercury in iv. 1 makes all the shepherds intriguers.

192. *fayre and far off, for feare of hurt*: apparently a proverb of one who maintains a cautious and civil distance.

P. 255, 197. *is my mistresse mankinde*: i. e. become masculine. A coarse female was termed 'a mankind creature.' Cf. *Wint. Tale*, ii. 3. 66, Leontes calls Paulina 'A mankind witch' (Fairholt).

204. *of an ingratefull minde*: *of* in the sense of 'from.'

210. *Wilt thou incounter*, &c.: i.e. oppose it.

P. 256. S. D. *Enter Sol and take his seate*: i. e. the entry is made, as in all the other cases, below; and he ascends to the balcony from the stage.

P. 257, 21. *recure* for 'cure' occurs several times in *Endimion*.

24. *misdid thee*: did amiss to thee (Fairholt).

48. *our country gods*: i. e. our country's gods.

50. *Ceres and her sacred Nymphes*: the mention of these nymphs, who do not figure in the myth of Ceres, is doubtless a reference to Lyly's play *Loves Metamorphosis*, and as such is important as tending to establish a later date for this. Cf. also *Bisham*, 1592, vol. i. 476 l. 2.

53. *demeane*: demeanour. Lyly probably saw the word in *Faerie Queene*, ii. 9. 40 'modest of demayne' (pub. 1590), though the N. E. D. quotes instances in 1450 and 1534.

P. 258, 55. *his libertie*: the possessive 'its' is not found before 1598.

63. *depart*: departure. Except in the romance *Arthur and Merlin*, c. 1330, the word is not found before 1590 (*Fa. Queene*, iii. 7. 20).

earne: i.e. yearn, in its second sense of 'grieve,' the only one that Shakespeare uses, e.g. *Jul. Caes.* ii. 2. 129 (Skeat). The earliest use is in the *Sheph. Kalender* (1579), March, l. 76; also *Faerie Queene*, i. 1. 3, to which instance the N. E. D. prefixes the date of the *second* ed., 1596.

67. *our holly hearbe Nicotian*: 'the tobacco plant; so named from Jean Nicot, Lord of Villemaine, the French Ambassador to Portugal, who first brought it into notice at the French Court about 1561. His name was given to the herb (its essential oil is still termed *nicotine*), which was entirely valued by him for its curative virtues; indeed, he and others thought, with Captain Bobadil, that it was "the most sovereign and precious weed that ever the earth tendered to the use of man." The "tabaco of Trinidada" is termed *Sana Sancta Indorum*, in Gerard's *Herball*, 1597' (Fairholt). Chambers' *Encyc.* attributes its introduction into England to Sir John Hawkins in 1565, though Sir Walter Raleigh encouraged its growth in 1586.

79. *recorde our happines*: i.e. celebrate it, but with a distinct allusion to the musical instrument the 'recorder.' Lyly uses it, *Euph.* ii. 58 l. 7 'recording theyr sweete notes.' The *Cent. Dict.* quotes 1590, *Arcadia*, bk. iii, 'he recorded to her music ... and with the conclusion of his song,' &c. Cf. Ben Jonson's *Penates*, 'Sweet robin, linnet, thrush, | Record from every bush.' Darwin quotes it as a bird-catcher's phrase, *Descent of Man*, i. 53.

90. *vnacquainted*: unfamiliar. *Endim.* v. 3. 62 'this vnacquainted and most vnnaturall practise.'

P. 259, 101. *Vtopiæ Stesias*, &c.: 'Soluere amorem' seems to be a phrase of Lyly's coinage (cf. l. 106): it is not given by Forcellini. The sense of the couplet will be 'So long as the holy powers of heaven ordain, Stesias spends his love on the Phoenix of Utopia.' He makes the *e* in *Stesias* doubtful.

P. 260. ACT III. SCENE II: this is the only Act in which more than one scene is marked, but even here the scene is really unbroken, Sol still occupying the balcony as in the preceding scene.

S. D. [*with Cupid and Joculus*]: obviously summoned from Hor. *Carm.* i. 2. 33

'Sive tu mavis, Erycina ridens,
Quam Iocus circum volat et Cupido.'

(Hense, *Shakespeare-Jahrbuch*, vii. 246.)

[*Sol descends*]: I insert this stage-direction in conformity with the procedure in the case of the other Planets.

9. *in her orient robe*: this seems a reminiscence of Homer's epithet, κροκόπεπλος, applied to Eos (not Thetis), *Il.* viii. 1, &c. There seems no classical warrant for these two latter loves of Sol. Lyly is thinking of the natural connexion between the sun and water (through evaporation), and the sun and the dawn. In the ed. of Hyginus' *Fables*, &c., 1578, Fulgentius (*Mythologicon*, ii. p. 143) explains Thetis 'vt aqua, id est humor.'

17. *Quo mihi fortuna*, &c.: Hor. *Ep.* i. 5. 12. The 4º reads *fortuna* (abl. with *uti*), following a gloss found in many MSS. of Horace, due (it suggested) to the omission of the contraction-mark over the *a* (=*am*).

21. *Tis not the touching of a womans hand*, &c.: this speech is a reminiscence of the discussion in *Euph. and his Eng.* ii. 160 ll. 19 sqq.

P. 261, 54. *Hospitis*, &c.: the kind assistance of Professor Ellis renders my puzzled footnote superfluous. The line which has so constantly escaped me occurs after all in Lyly's favourite source, Ov. *Art. Am.* ii. 360 'Hospitis est tepido nocte recepta *sinu*.' It was too late to emend the text.

P. 262, 76. *wondrous*: scanned as trisyllable.

94. *of that condition*: on that condition.

P. 263, 109. *Tantalus that feasted*, &c.: 'Iupiter Tantalo concredere sua consilia solitus erat, & ad epulum deorum admittere,' Hyg. *Fab.* 82.

P. 264, 163. *Maremaydes glasse*: Fairholt refers to *Loves Met.* iv. 2. p. 322, where the Syren has 'a glasse in her hand and a combe.'

167–8. *Wilt thou for my sake goe into yon groue,*
And we will sing vnto the wilde birdes notes, &c.

It is impossible not to recall the song in *As You Like It* 'Under the greenwood tree,' with the lines 'And turn his merry note Unto the sweet bird's throat.'

P. 265, 186. *the Theban Lord . . . Hippodamia*: the reference is to the battle of Centaurs and Lapithae begun by Eurytus at the marriage-feast of Pirithous and Hippodamia, as described Ov. *Met.* xii. 210–244, though I find no authority for calling Eurytus 'Theban.'

190. *in this caue, for ouer this theyle sitte*: evidently the cave is supposed to be underneath the stage. Five lines farther on Stesias talks of 'rising out of this hollow vault.'

P. 266, 208. *wonder not at it, good people!*: addressed to the audience. So Cupid in soliloquy addresses the audience with 'Ladies,' *Gallathea*, ii. 2. 13, where see note. Cf. S. D. in *Maydes Met.* ii. 1. p. 354.

209. *hire romes to lay in wine*: i. e. in the vaults Pandora's nails have digged in his face. I see no cause for reading, as Fairholt suggests, 'hire them as rooms.'

213. *cornute*: give him horns.

216. *beware of kissing, bretheren!*: Gunophilus parodies the Puritan preachers; and the words cause Stesias in alarm to raise the trap-door a little.

P. 267, 254. *Sic vos non vobis*: from the lines attributed to Virgil in Donatus' *Life*, 17, which run as follows

'Hos ego versiculos feci; tulit alter honores:
  Sic vos non vobis nidificatis, aves;
  Sic vos non vobis vellera fertis, oves;
  Sic vos non vobis mellificatis, apes;
  Sic vos non vobis fertis aratra, boves.'

266. *clipt within the ringe*: the coin was not current 'if the clipping took away the outer inscription, or encroached within the ring which formed the boundary of the letters' (Fairholt). Cf. *Ham.* ii. 2. 448, and *Mid.* ii. 2. 21 note.

P. 268, 287. *busky*: i.e. 'bosky,' woody. It occurs in the old eds. of 1 *Henry IV*, v. 1. 2.

P. 269, 301. *made a stale*: properly a decoy, an imitated or a real bird by which another bird is caught, from AS. *stalu*, theft: then of any one deceived or made a joke of.

320. *Hollow! hollow!*: i.e. hallo! hallo!

P. 271, 28. *Cætera quis nescit?*: Ov. *Am.* i. 5. 25. Cf. *Euph.* ii. 83 l. 12.

38. *Apolloes tree*: i.e. Daphne.

P. 272, 67. *Which may be venom*: 'may which be,' 'and may they be,' &c.—a wish.

73. *falsor*: cheat. 'The falsers fraude,' *Sheph. Kal. Epil.*

74. *infestious*: injurious, dangerous. Cp. N. E. D., s.v.

80. *when he comes*, &c.: i.e. Stesias on his recovery will inquire about the kid missing from his flocks.

89. *Gun.* (*aside*) *Looke how she winkes*: addressed to the audience, as above 'good people,' iii. 2. 208 (where see note).

P. 274, 135. *Oscula*, &c.: Ov. *Her. Ep.* xvii. 27, 28.

145. *leefest*: dearest.

157. *mate*: checkmate, confound. 'My mind she has mated, and amazed my sight,' *Macb.* v. 1. 86. Skeat derives it from Arabic root *máta*, 'he died.' OF. *mat*.

165. *Enipeus*: Lyly transfers to his Utopia the Thessalian river mentioned in Ovid, Hyginus, &c.

P. 277, 248. *When will the sun*, &c.: this and the following six lines remind one strongly of Juliet's 'Gallop apace,' &c.—iii. 2. 1 sqq., the first four lines of which passage are found in the first Quarto of *Rom. & Jul.* 1597. I incline to think Shakespeare the borrower.

267. *So will not I*: i.e. deceive you.

P. 278, 268. *Iewels and his pearles*: thieving being one of the effects of Mercury's predominance.

282. *Comes facetus*, &c.: Publ. Syrus, *Sententiae*, 85 'Comes facundus in via pro vehiculo est' (Harbottle).

290-1. *heauen . . . fall . . . haue Larkes*: 'When the skie falth we shall have Larkes' is in Heywood's *Proverbes*, i. ch. 4. Compare Rabelais' *Gargantua*, ch. 11 'Si les nues tumboyent, esperoyt prendre les alouettes toutes rousties' (Bartlett).

292. *This is Enipeus banke, here she should be*: i.e. 'here Iphicles expects her to be.' Stesias alludes to the appointment Pandora made with Iphicles, iv. 1. 165, Lyly attributing to Stesias a knowledge possessed in reality only by the audience. See under Place and Time, p. 237.

293. *What, is it midnight?*: i.e. really, he is before his time.

P. **279**, 306. *Away from my groue* ... *warning*: alluding to his previous cudgelling and words, iv. 1. 237-43.

S. D. *Enter Luna*: Mercury's descent and exit is supposed to have occurred in the interval between the Acts.

2. *erring starres*: wandering stars, planets. Cynthia is 'lowest' because her sphere immediately adjoins the Earth.

10. *almost at the sea side*: evidently this elopement with Gunophilus is one with that begun in Act iv. ll. 268-92, though they have made some progress towards the coast: i.e. strictly, in spite of the balcony, the scene is changed, though this is not the abrupt transfer of iv. 1. 292 and elsewhere. See pp. 237-8.

P. **280**, 21. *Ouer the chayne, Iacke!* &c.: cf. *Pappe*, p. 412 l. 12 'like an olde Ape hugges the Vrchin so in his conceipt, as though it should shew vs some new tricks ouer the chaine.' Fairholt quotes Jonson's *Bartholomew Faire* 'a juggler with a well-educated ape to come over the chaine for the King of England, and back again for the Prince, and sit still on his haunches for the Pope and the King of Spain.' Marston's *Scourge of Villanie*, sat. ix, addresses an 'apish' person as 'Old Jack of Parisgarden.'

23. *sweares by his ten bones*: i.e. the fingers. Fairholt cites it as an oath used by Peter in 2 *Henry VI*, i. 3. From this passage it appears to have been associated with apes, as again in *Pappe*, p. 406 l. 6 'Martin sweares by his ten bones : nay, I will make him mumpe, mow, and chatter like old Iohn of Paris garden before I leaue him.'

24. *Did I not tell you I should haue Larkes*: addressed to the audience, and referring to his words on his exit in the preceding Act, l. 291.

40. *Nocte latent mendæ*: Ov. *Ars Am.* i. 249, but Lyly remembered it as quoted in his namesake's Grammar under the head of Ablative of Time—*A Shorte Introduction*, &c., I. vii. 5.

45. *Lucretia toto Sis*, &c.: Martial, *Epigr.* xi. 104:
'Si te delectat gravitas, Lucretia toto
Sis licet usque die; Laida nocte volo.'
But the old editions of Martial read, as Lyly, 'Thaida.'

P. **281**, 56. *Belike I was a spirit all this while*: Gunophilus' suggested explanation of her not seeing him 'till now,' l. 54.

80. *Shall I make their cracke?* &c.: Fairholt suggests this as lovers' play, a mode of divination by the cracking or not cracking of the joints, like Margaret's pulling of the flower-petals in *Faust*.

89. *a whiting moppe*: a young whiting. Again in Fletcher and Rowley's *Maid in the Mill*, ii. 1.

P. **282**, 101. *a pible stone*: i.e. a pebble. So *Gall*. i. 1. 13 'a heape of small pyble.'

104-9. *Ile giue thee streames*, &c.: it has been suggested to me that these imaginative lines are imitative of Marlowe; but Lyly has always been a coiner of picturesque marvels.

106. *Musk flyes*: a purely imaginary kind.

115. *absolute*: faultless, perfect; 'an absolute courtier,' *Merry Wives*, iii. 3. 66.

119. *O Marce fili*, &c.: these words, untranslatable as they stand, form the opening of Cic. *De Offic.* i. 1 'Quanquam te, Marce fili, annum iam audientem Cratippum, idque Athenis, abundare oportet praeceptis institutisque philosophiae,' &c.

120. *a breaching boies*: Fairholt explains as a boy of age for breeching, i. e. of 12 or 14 years. Schmidt, *Shaks. Lex.* explains 'no breeching scholar,' *Taming*, iii. 1. 18, as 'no schoolboy liable to a flogging.' The verb 'to breech' is used in both senses.

P. 283, 145. *Yours, as his owne, G.*: parodying letter-signatures, e. g. 'thine to vse more then his owne, Philautus,' ii. 144, and 152, 154, 222.

152. *That she hath made her to obscure her selfe*: that she hath darkened her own beauty by creating Pandora.

P. 284, 164. *vald*: bent, lowered. 'To vale' or 'vail' is from Fr. *avaler*, fr. Lat. *ad vallem*. Cf. *Merch. of Ven.* i. 1. 28 'Vailing her high top lower than her ribbes.' Again *End.* iii. 3. 83, *Euph.* i. 255 l. 37.

168. *alone*: either 'only,' or 'more than all.'

193. *hediockes*: (i = j) given in the N. E. D. as a 16th cent. form of 'hedgehogs' (though no instance is quoted); *hedgehock* is a 17th cent. form. In *Euph. and his Eng.* ii. 139 l. 12, we get 'Hedgehogge.'

194. *let me see thy hand*, &c.: allusion to palmistry, whereby the influence of planets was traced in the hand. Fairholt refers to *M. Bomb.* ii. 3 p. 97, where Candius professes to read Silena's hand.

P. 285, 219. *Willing me to deny the wordes I spoke*: 'persuading me to tell you that I lied in accusing her of falseness to yourself.' So below, Iphicles l. 231—'promised to deny my wordes.'

P. 287, 272. *Vanish into a Haythorne*: i. e. a hawthorn. Accordingly at the stage-direction '*Exit Gunophilus*,' just below, a bush is thrust forth upon the stage behind which Gunophilus retires: the bush remains, for Stesias below, l. 317, threatens to 'rend' it. Compare the restoration of Bagoa from an aspen-tree in *Endimion*, v. 3. 277 (note).

274-81. *place Pandora in my sphere*, &c.: cf. *Funeral Oration*, vol. i. p. 512 l. 1 'Petrarch knew not in what Sphere of Planets to lodge his Lawra.'

280. *forsake Aglauros loue*: Lyly is thinking of Ov. *Met.* ii. 710 sqq. (spelt 'Agraulos' in Apollodorus and Pausanias) where, however, Herse is the real object of Hermes' passion, which her sister Aglauros opposes.

283. *stay in the woods, Or keepe with Pluto*: as Diana, or Hecate.

290. *two Parramours, ... Thetis ... morne*: as above, iii. 2. 9, where see note.

P. 288, 318. *beare this bush*: 'This transformation of Stesias to the Man in the Moon, and Gunophilus to the thornbush on his back, is an ingenious variation of a popular fable, which, says Grimm, declared this man either to be Isaac carrying sticks for his own sacrifice; Cain, bearing the bundle of thorns unworthily sacrificed by him to the Deity ; or the unfortunate man who gathered sticks on the Sabbath-day, and was stoned by the Jews, as related in the Book of Numbers, chap. xv. 32-36. Ritson, in his *Ancient Songs of England*, has printed a curious song upon this popular personage, composed in the early part of the fourteenth century. Shakespeare has introduced the character in the clowns' masque at the end of his *Mids. Night's Dream*: and Halliwell, in his folio edition of the poet's works, has brought together a large mass of curious information on this fable ' (Fairholt).

320. *steede*: stead, place.

329. *aspects ... coniunction*: 'aspects' of planets are their relative position (astrologically) as seen from the Earth: 'coniunction' is their proximity from the same point of view.

LOVES METAMORPHOSIS.

P. 300. DRAM. PERS.: the name Montanus is borrowed by Lodge in *Rosalynde*, and Celia by Shakespeare in *As You Like It*, where also Silvestris becomes Silvius, and Erisichthon suggests Corin's 'master ... of churlish disposition,' ii. 4. 80. Ceres is introduced with nymphs again in the *Bisham Ent.* 1592, vol. i. 476 l. 2.

P. 301, 1. *fain'd ... that Loue sat vpon the Chaos*, &c.; Lyly is probably recalling Arist. *Metaphys.* i. 4, where this opinion is attributed to Parmenides and Hesiod ; and from the former is quoted

πρώτιστον μὲν ἔρωτα θεῶν μητίσατο πάντων

and from the latter

πάντων μὲν πρώτιστα χάος γένετ', αὐτὰρ ἔπειτα
γαῖ' εὐρύστερνος,
ἠδ' ἔρος, ὃς πάντεσσι μεταπρέπει ἀθανάτοισιν,

an imperfect version of *Theog.* 116 sqq.

10. *begot by the fraile fires of the eye*: Fairholt quotes the song in *The Merchant of Ven.* iii. 2 'It is engender'd in the eyes, With gazing fed.' The sentiment occurs in *Euphues*, e.g. ii. 59 l. 13 ' Loue commeth in at the eye, not at the eare,' &c.

P. 302, 31. *Penelopen ipsam*, &c.: Ov. *Art. Am.* i. 477.

33. *Fructus abest*, &c.: Ov. *Art. Am.* iii. 398.

38. *Riualem patienter habe*: Ov. *Art. Am.* ii. 539.

4. *Salamints*, &c.: no such name in Whitney, nor in Cotgrave, nor Halliwell; probably Lyly's invention, founded on what Pliny says, xxi. 21,

of the 'polion herbam . . . folia eius mane candida, meridie purpurea, Sole occidente caerulea aspiciuntur.' Cf. 'Polyon,' *Saph.* ii. 1. 90, note.

10. *Cypres leaues* . . . *beareth the least fruit*: Pliny, xvi. 60 'Cupressus . . . natu morosa, fructu supervacua,' &c. Cf. *Euph.* i. 202 l. 12 'Cypresse . . . beareth no fruite.'

P. 303, 19. *wake-Robin*: 'The old English name for the *Arum maculatum*, or cuckoo-pint' (Fairholt).

21. *telling* . . . *tale of hunting* . . . *passion of loue*: compare the Neapolitan prince (*Merchant*, i. 2. 38), who, as Portia's suitor, 'doth nothing but talk of his horse.'

24. *hearts* . . . *Harts*: the pun occurs again *Moth. Bomb.* iv. 1. 33.

30. *fond Hobbie*: foolish hawk.

31. *Buntings*: popular name for several kinds of little birds of the *Emberiza* genus, of which the corn-bunting (*Emberiza miliaria*) is one, and the yellow bunting or yellow-hammer (*Emberiza citrinella*) another. Nisa means that foresters think all birds alike, or all fair game. Schmidt quotes *All's Well*, ii. 5. 7 'I took this lark for a bunting.'

40. *throwe one off* . . . *whole hand* . . . *pull him againe* . . . *little finger*: cf. *Euph.* ii. 75 l. 23.

42. *if they censure* . . . *froward*: cf. *Euph.* i. 249 l. 12 'Peruersly do they alwayes thinck of their louers,' &c., and 253 ll. 36 sqq.

44. *Cedit amor rebus*, &c.: Ov. *Rem. Am.* 144.

46. *Sat mihi si facies*, &c.: probably an adaptation of Ov. *Her.* xvii. 38 'Aut mea sit facies non bene nota mihi.' I cannot find the exact line in *Heroides, Amores*, or *Ars Amatoria*.

50. *Victoria tecum stabit*: Ov. *Art. Am.* ii. 539 'Rivalem patienter habe: victoria tecum | Stabit.' Niobe replies to her lover by completing the line, the first part of which he had written for her, i. 1. 38.

P. 304, 56. *Præcibus* . . . *addet*: Ov. *Met.* ii. 397, where the true reading is '*addit*.'

57. *Cantant et saltant*: the song is lost.

61. *giglots*: wantons. Skeat suggests 'a base *gig* applied to rapid motion, and thence to light behaviour.'

63. *drew yron like Adamants*: Pliny, xx. 1 'ferrum ad se trahente *magnete* lapide,' and *Euph.* i. 321 l. 2, ii. 111 l. 35.

65. *Thessalides*: no such name in *Dict. Class. Biog.* The point of Erisichthon's invective being, not oratory, but wanton arts, I suggest that this is one of the numerous instances of mistakes arising from setting up type from an ignorant oral reading of Lyly's MS., and that what he really wrote was 'Messalina's' or 'Messalina's.'

67. *vnkembd*: uncombed, unkempt. Cp. Skeat s. v.

75. *addicted to Ceres*: vowed to, given up to—a Latinism; of. Hor. *Ep.* i. 1. 14 'Nullius addictus iurare in verba magistri.' Skeat quotes an instance from Grafton's Chronicles, Henry VII. an. 4 (R), and Whitney from Ben Jonson's *Cynthias Revels*, iv. 3 'Yours entirely addicted, Madam.'

79. *pieuish*: foolish, as *M. Bomb.* i. 3. 90, and repeatedly.

86. *the tree powreth out bloud, and I heare a voice*: see under Sources, p. 293.

P. 305, 101. *Cinyras ... Mirrha*, &c.: Ov. *Met.* x. 300–500. '*Miretia*' in 4° is merely the compositor's misreading of Lyly's MS. In regard to Daphne and Myrrha see Sources, pp. 293-4.

P. 306, 145. *vnacquainted*: unheard of, as in *Gall.* iii. 4. 58; *Endim.* v. 3. 62; *Saph.* ii. 4. 1.

10. *on yonder hill ... lyeth famine*, &c.: for this powerful allegorical description Lyly is entirely indebted to Ovid, *Met.* viii. 784-810. Spenser has no specific description of Famine. It is perhaps worth while to quote the preceding English verses on the subject from Sackville's *Induction*, pub. in the second ed. (1563) of *The Mirrour for Magistrates*, stt. 50-52—indebted, doubtless, to Ovid's description of Erisichthon:

'A grisly shape of *Famine* might we see,
 With greedy looks, and gaping mouth, that cried
 And roar'd for meat, as she should there have died;
   Her body thin, and bare as any bone,
   Whereto was left nought but the case alone.
 And that, alas, was gnawn-on every where,
 All full of holes, that I ne might refrain
 From tears, to see how she her arms could tear,
 And with her teeth gnash on the bones in vain,
 When, all for nought, she fain would so sustain
   Her starven corpse, that rather seem'd a shade,
   Than any substance of a creature made.
 Great was her force, whom stone wall could not stay,
 Her tearing nails snatching at all she saw;
 With gaping jaws, that by no means ymay
 Be satisfied from hunger of her maw,
 But eats herself as she that hath no law:
   Gnawing, alas, her carcass all in vain,
   Where you may count each sinew, bone, and vein.'
           (*Library of Old Authors—Sackville* (1859), pp. 113-4.)

P. 307, 24. *as liuely*: as like life, as exactly.

38. *they that thinke it straunge ... virginitie*: this remark, and the tone of Ceres towards Cupid generally, is in marked contrast to the fierce virginity of Diana in *Gallathea* (iii. 4. 16 sqq.), where the attitude of Ceres and her nymphs, respectively, is exactly reversed. The change is considered by Mézères (*Prédecesseurs et Contemporains de Shakespeare* (1863), ch. 3 p. 71) as significant of an increased tenderness in Elizabeth

for Leicester. He places the play as probably one of Lyly's latest works, but perhaps forgets that Leicester died Sept. 4, 1588.

50 sqq. Nisa's exposé of poetic fictions is suggested by Watson's *Hecatompathia*, 19.

P. 308, 76. *Dianas Nymphes*, &c. : a reference, as Fleay has pointed out, to *Gallathea*, ii. 2 and iii. 1.

79. *This is the temple* : some five lines back Ceres said, 'Well, let vs to Cupid.' That we have here one of the imaginary transfers of scene common upon the early stage is clear from a comparison of l. 5 of this scene—' heere lyeth the tree '—with iv. 1. 130, where the foresters, being before Cupid's temple and deciding to seek the nymphs, say, ' certainely wee shall find them about Ceres tree, singing or sacrifizing,' which they would not say if tree and temple were supposed as occupying the stage at once. See Essay, vol. ii. p. 269.

P. 309, 109. *idlenesse* : cf. Ov. *Rem. Amor.* 139 ' Otia si tollas, periere Cupidinis arcus.'

P. 312, 80. *Polypus*, &c. : Pliny, ix. 46 ' Colorem mutat ad similitudinem loci.' Cf. *Euph.* i. 219 l. 8.

P. 313, 116. *consent* : (or concent), Lat. *concentus*, harmony.

122. *no base string*, &c. : this series of musical puns, ' base,' ' meane,' ' treble,' are repeated from *Gall.* v. 3. 187-93, as Fairholt points out.

128. *Salamich* : salamander.

S. D. *Cantant* : the song is lost.

P. 314, 140. *met withall* : a current phrase for ' finding your match,' or being ' made to pay for it.' Cf. Beaumont and Fletcher's *King and No King*, ii. 2, where the Citizen's Wife answers the impudent shopman with ' Well, stripling, I shall meet with you ' ; and *Night-Walker*, i. 1, Lurcher, of Algripe who has injured him, ' I may meet with him | Yet, ere I die.'

152. *whether all those that loue Niobe do like* : i. e. hang themselves. There is no need to alter the text, as Fairholt suggests, though ' do the like ' would have been clearer.

164. —*scilicet* : this word is not part of the quotation from Ov. *Art. Am.* ii. 539, but Silvestris' comment thereon.

165. *posies* : mottoes. Fairholt refers to *Camp.* iv. 3. 14 ' posies of loue in their ringes.'

P. 315, 12. *race* : erase.

P. 316, 41. *Gentleman?* : Lyly here turns to excellent characteristic account Ovid's three words ' Dominum generosa recusat.' See on Sources, p. 292.

44. *Your conditions brought in your obligations* : ' A satirical allusion to the wording of old bonds, which began with " The condition of this obligation," &c.' (Fairholt).

P. 317, 70. *know their good as well as Gentlemen* : ' to know one's good ' appears to be a phrase for courteous behaviour. In *Euphues*,

ii. 161 l. 29, the hero's gentle answer to Camilla's reproach is prefaced by
'Euphues as one that knewe his good, aunswered hir in this wise.'

16. *and so did Iphis*: not the Iphis of Ovid, *Met.* ix. 665-795, but
he of *Met.* xiv. 698-738, who hung himself in despair of Anaxarete's love.
Cf. *Euph.* ii. 112 l. 37, and *Poems*, p. 466 ll. 30-2, in both of which the
instances of Hercules and Iphis are found, as here, together.

21. *Swans and Turtles . . . truth and iealousie*: the turtle-dove has
several times been adduced as an instance of truth, e. g. *M. Bomb.* i. 3.
121. The 'iealousie' of swans seems a derivative from their well-known
ferocity. They are said to pair for life.

P. 318, 52. *sauours are not found of louers*: i. e. not noticed by. The
allusion, which apparently did not offend Elizabethan taste, becomes clear
by a reference to Shakespeare's 130th Sonnet, line 8. Fairholt stupidly
corrupts 'found of' to 'fond of.'

P. 319, 89. *Bird that liueth only by ayre*, &c.: this feeding on air and
living only in the air was in accord with the current belief about birds of
Paradise, which had been recently discovered by the Dutch in their
voyages to New Guinea—the fact being that the natives who sold the skins
used to deprive them of feet and wings (*Encyclop. Brit.* iii. 778).

99. *to blast*: used intransitively also *Two Gent.* i. 1 'blasting in the
bud, | Losing his verdure,' &c. (Whitney).

P. 320, 103. *in the morning weare . . . at night . . . heeles*: repeated
from *Euph.* Add. to Gent. Readers, i. 182 ll. 12-3.

109. *a thicke mist which Proserpine shall send*: Proserpine is chosen
as the goddess of the world below whence the mist is to rise; and also
perhaps as the carrier into effect of human curses (Hom. *Od.* x. 494, xi. 226,
Il. ix. 457, &c.), also because she and Ceres are brought into Hyginus (*Fable*
cxli dealing with the Sirens). The mist is of course the suggested stage-
contrivance by which the transformation is to be effected (cf. the appeal
to Venus, v. 4. 34, to send down a shower, when the nymphs are to be
re-transformed); and, since we are nowhere made witnesses of the transformation, the mention of it may point to the subsequent excision of a
later scene in the same Act, in which, originally, it occurred.

117. *let your othes be without number*: some of these precepts are
repeated from Sybilla's advice to Phao in *Sapho*, ii. 4. 76 sqq.

130. *wee shall find them about Ceres tree*: since, however, the rock,
rose, and bird to which they are transformed are obviously present in the
last scene, v. 4 (and cf. v. 2. 24-5), which is laid before Cupid's Temple,
we have to suppose the transformation as taking place near the latter,
on some visit of the nymphs to the shrine.

134. *let all Ladies beware*, &c.: this warning, including the words
about the crow's-foot and the black ox, is repeated from *Euph.* i. 203
ll. 6-7. Fairholt notes these same two expressions for advancing age in
Saph. iv. 2. 20-1.

P. 321, 18. *vnfortunate shore*: because rocky. See below, l. 75 and p. 295.

27. *remoued*: softened. In reply to 'hates' of the Syren's preceding speech.

29. *by whose subtilties I am halfe fish, halfe flesh*, &c.: a previous deception by man forms no part of the classical myth of the Sirens, who were made like birds and condemned to their alluring part by Ceres for not assisting Proserpine (Hyg. *Fab.* 141). Lyly unites with the classical myth of the Sirens the Teutonic and Northern superstition of the mermaid, with her fish-tail (found also in later representations of the Sirens), long hair, and the glass and comb in her hand; and, further, her statement that she has been reduced to her present position by mens' 'subtilties' shows that she is intended as allegorical of a courtesan. Cf. *Euph.* i. 189 l. 28, 255 ll. 8-13. In the *Woman*, ii. 2. 163, Iphicles alludes to 'Maremaydes glasse.'

P. 322, S. D. [*Exit into structure at back*]. I supply the stage-directions here and below, l. 96, some cover being required for the assumption and the laying aside of her disguise as Ulysses.

P. 323, 66. *dottrell*: the bird called by this name was a proverb for foolishness, because it was supposed to invite capture. The name, like 'dotard,' is der. of 'dote.'

72. *measureth the hot assault*, &c.: Euphues, i. 192 l. 36, uses precisely the same words to the aged Eubulus.

74. *Apes, who kill by culling*: *Euph.* ii. 5 l. 4. To 'cull,' or 'embrace,' is obsol. variant of *coll*, prob. from Fr. *coler = accoler*, to put the arms round the neck (*col*).

P. 324, S. D. TIRTENA: announced in the list of characters who take part in the scene, yet with no speech allotted her. Perhaps it points to more excision.

6. *Sic volo, sic iubeo*: this proverbial form of authoritative assent is from Juvenal, vi. 222 '*Hoc* volo, sic iubeo, sit pro ratione voluntas,' in allusion to the question '*Velitis Ivbeatis*' at the head of a bill proposed to the Roman *comitia tributa*.

Quæ venit ex merito, &c.: reversing Ov. *Her.* (Oenone Paridi) v. 7 'Leniter ex merito quicquid patiare, ferendum est, Quae venit indignae poena, dolenda venit.'

13. *and to bee more terrified*, &c.: i. e. and maketh Jove to be more terrified, &c.

18. *Diana hath felt . . . loue, Vesta doth*: the allusion to Diana can only be supported by Cynthia's kiss of Endimion. Cf. *Endim.* ii. 1. 82, where Vesta is also urged as an instance that virgins may be conquered. Lyly is probably adapting those supposed instances of frailty in the Vestal virgins, cited *Euph.* ii. 209, to the goddess herself. But cf. *Euph.* ii. 150 l. 13.

LOVES METAMORPHOSIS

P. 325, 46. *Sine Cerere*, &c.: this Latin proverb is quoted by Terence *Eun.* iv. 5. 6, Cic. *Nat. De.* ii. 23. 60, and by Lyly before in *M. Bomb.* ii. 5. 51.

48. *Otia si tollas*, &c.: Ov. *Rem. Am.* 139.

P. 326, 4. *stoutnesse*: stubbornness. *End.* iv. 1. 23.

10. *Molle meum*, &c.: Ov. *Her.* xv. 79 with omission of *que*, thus lengthening *cor*. Lyly has made use of it before, *M. Bomb.* iv. 1. 32.

13. *Omnia vincit amor*, &c.: Virg. *Ecl.* x. 69.

22. *I did this*, &c.: Petulius is perhaps excusing his affair with the Syren, while Protea's answer refers to hers with Neptune.

24. *deserts*: deserters, defaulters.

29. *A faire warning*, &c.: this banter of two assured lovers possibly suggested that of Lorenzo and Jessica, *Merchant of Ven.* iii. 5. 80 sqq.

P. 327, 5. *ready at receipt*: Ceres uses a hunting-term appropriate to the Foresters. 'To stand at receipt' was to await game driven towards the hunter by beaters. Cf. *Euph.* ii. 178 l. 32 note.

P. 328, 34. *send downe that showre*: some stage-device, the drawing of a semi-transparent curtain, or perhaps a thick shower of torn paper, to conceal the substitution of the nymphs for the rock, rose-bush, and bird. Cf. the 'thicke mist' spoken of by Cupid (iv. 1. 109) as accompanying their first transformation.

P. 331, 141. *ouerthwarts*: vexing speeches. *End.* iii. 1. 17 'malepart ouerthwarts.'

153. *Non custodiri*, &c.: Ov. *Amor.* iii. 4. 6 'Nec custodiri, ni velit, illa potest.'

156. *Sit modo, non feci*, &c.: Ov. *Amor.* iii. 14. 48.

P. 332, 166. *Hippomanes . . . Venus . . . vowes*: the version is that related by Venus herself, Ov. *Met.* x. 680-95. Lyly spells 'Hippomanes' for 'Hippomenes' in two or three other places.

THE MAYDES METAMORPHOSIS.

P. 346, 132. *desires*: trisyllable. So *houre* l. 139 is a dissyllable.

133. The trick of repetition noticeable in this song is seen also in the first and last songs of the Fairies (ii. 2), and in that of the Muses (v. 2).

P. 348, 200. *neate*: more common as a plural than a singular. Spenser *F. Q.* VI. ix. 4 'Whereas the Heardes were keeping of their neat.'

229. *record*: recollect, bethink thee of. *Euph.* i. 303 l. 31, and Glossary.

P. 349, 238. *vncoth*: unknown, wild. Bullen quotes *As You Like It*, ii. 6 'this uncouth forest.' Also, of forest paths, *Quarr.* vol. i. 465 l. 18.

P. 350, 277. *wreake*: reck, as in v. 1-31.

297. *safetie*: a trisyllable.

314. *A hunts vp*: hunting-song, réveillée for the hunters—Bullen;

who mentions one, with music by J. Bennet, in a collection of Ravenscroft, 1614.

P. 351, 324. *the good Athenian knight*: Theseus.

340. *rascalls*: 'the regular name for a lean deer: *As You Like It*, iii. 3, &c.' (Bullen).

P. 353, 16. This speech and the remaining speeches of Joculo are printed, like the rest of the scene, as verse by the Q. Bullen distinguished the prose here and in later scenes; but I have not invariably followed him.

26. *such a dearth at this time*: Fleay (*Biog. Chron.* ii. 42).

39. *legeritie*: (Fr. *légèreté*) *Henry V*, iv. 1. 23 'With casted slough and fresh legerity'—rare.

41. *Coate*: cote, cottage.

P. 354, 50. *drawe drie foote*: follow by the scent, *Com. of Errors*, iv. 2 (Bullen).

P. 355, 113. *A duskie Caue*, &c.: Bullen notes the imitation of the cave of Morpheus in the *Faerie Queene*, I. i.

123. *whisht*: silent. *Tempest*, i. 2. 378
'Curtsied when you have, and kiss'd
The wild waves whist.'

125. *plancher*: (Fr. *planche*) a plank. *Arden of Feversham*, i. 1 'Whilst on the planchers pants his weary body': *Meas. for Meas.* iv. 1 'a planched gate' (Bullen).

P. 356, 139. *incontinent*: immediately. So *Euph.* i. 227 l. 8 'content incontinently to procure the meanes.'

147. *Swifter then thought*, &c.: here the audience are to suppose one of the imaginary transferences of scene found in the pre-Shakespearean drama. See Essay on 'Lyly as a Playwright,' vol. ii. p. 269. It is quite irreconcilable with ll. 170–1 below, where they are still at Ascanio's sleeping-place.

P. 357, 175. *Three sonnes I haue* . . *Morpheus*, &c.: founded on Ov. *Met.* xi. 633–43

'At pater e populo natorum mille suorum
Excitat artificem, simulatoremque figurae,
Morphea. Non illo iussos solertius alter
Exprimit incessus, vultumque sonumque loquendi.
Adiicit et vestes, et consuetissima cuique
Verba. Sed hic solos homines imitatur. At alter
Fit fera, fit volucris, fit longo corpore serpens.
Hunc Icelon Superi, mortale Phobetora vulgus
Nominat. Est etiam diversae tertius artis
Phantasos. Ille in humum, saxumque, undamque, trabemque,
Quaeque vacant anima, feliciter omnia transit.'

202. *slake*: slacken, abate.

THE MAYDES METAMORPHOSIS 571

P. 358, 1. Sc. II. *Terlitelo*, &c.: Mopso's and Frisco's songs are, says Bullen, evidently fragments of old ballads.

11. *Fortune my foe*, &c.: these four lines are from the old ballad of *Fortune my foe*, printed in the Bagford Ballads (ed. Ebsworth, pt. iv. 962-3): the music in Chappell's *Popular Music of the Olden Time*, i. 162.

P. 359, 19. *cace of rope-ripes*: set or pair of rogues ripe for the gallows. 'Rope-ripe terms' for low abuse, Chapman's *May-day*, Act iii (Nares).

23. *Apple-squier*: pimp.

24. *bale of false dice*: set of dice, usually three. 1577 Holin. *Chron.* iii. 848 'Diuerse bales of dice' (N. E. D.).

40. *Buske poynt*: the end of the strip of whalebone that stiffens the front of the corset.

53. *By the moone*, &c.: this song, and that on p. 361, l. 105, were reprinted in Thos. Ravenscroft's *Brief Discourse*, &c. 1614, and by Mr. Bullen in his *Lyrics from Elizab. Song-Books*, p. 205.

P. 360, 60. *Mawmets*: mammets, puppets.

77. *Cricket*: Bullen quotes Drayton's *Fairy Wedding*

'Besides he's deft and wondrous airy,
And of the noblest of the fairy!
Chiefe of the Crickets of much fame
In fairy a most ancient name.'

and *Merry Wives*, v. 5. 47.

P. 362, 24. *growne*: dissyllable, probably for *growen*.

37. *Phebus*: the last syllable elided, as also at ll. 71, 78, 85, but not at ll. 43, 87. In spite of Masson (*Milton's Poet. Works*, i. 122), l. 66 of *Comus*—'To quench the drouth of Phœbus, which as they taste'—is probably to be scanned in the same way.

56. *Amyclas' sonne*: Hyacinth is called 'Amyclides' in Ov. *Met*. x. 162. The author substitutes the sledge-hammer for Ovid's discus.

P. 363, 75. *Eurania*: as if one of the Graces. But from the description of the 'Graces' seat in v. 1. 100 and the consequent introduction of 'Muses' in v. 2 it is clear the author recognized no distinction.

81. *My grief's of course*: i. e. natural and inevitable. See *Euphues*, i. 201 l. 22, note, ii. 141 l. 3.

P. 364, 128. *a standing*: *Cymbeline*, ii. 3. 75 'yield up their deer to the stand of the stealer.'

P. 366, 193. *And feele it too*: the 4° prints Apollo's speech as a complete line, of which this is the last portion.

222. *euer*: pronounced here and at l. 233 as monosyllable *e'er*. So *whether* l. 229, and l. 218.

P. 367. [Scene II] rightly printed as prose by the 4° except in one or two short speeches.

1. *iettest*: struttest. Whitney quotes J. Udall's *Flowres*, fol. 97 'jettyng like a lord.'

21. *Whattin a God*: Whitney gives '*Whaten, whatten,* what kind of—prov. Eng. and Scotch. "Whatan a face!" *Noct. Ambros.* Oct. 1828.'

P. 368, 53. *Bullaze*: '*Bullace,* a wild plum larger than the sloe' (N. E. D.). *Wildings,* crab-apples.

60. *the mare, the man rode on to Midleton*: evidently an old English parallel to the 'House that Jack built.'

62. *burne our caps*: apparently a proverb for novel and reckless action in some utterly unexpected event, such as Frisco's speaking anything wise; or else for extravagant hilarity, cf. *M. Bomb.* ii. 1. 166.

P. 369, 89. *Assoyle*; clear up, resolve. The N. E. D. quotes instances from Chaucer, Caxton, and Whiston (1696), and one from Puttenham's *Arte of Poesie* of *assoil* as a substantive.

94. *murlemewes*: perhaps allied to *merligoes* or *mirligoes,* a Scotch word given by Whitney for dizziness, for which a doubtful derivation from 'merrily goes' is suggested.

P. 370, 13. *Record*: of singing, or musical sound, as in *The Woman,* iii. 1. 79, *Euphues,* ii. 58 l. 7, and below sc. 2 l. 42.

118. *right his wrong*: must mean 'correct his error.'

P. 371, 35. *Ile make you . . . for . . . prating more*: a use evidently parallel to the ironical 'fit,' meaning 'disable from,' assisted by the preventive use of 'for' as noted on p. 178 l. 47. The N. E. D. quotes under *fit* '1605-8 Roxb. Ballads, vii. 470 "His Lass . . . devised To fit him for his whoring."' Cf. Beau. and Flet. *Hum. Lieut.* iv. 1.

50-1. The quarto prints these two lines as prose. If verse, we should have five blank lines in succession, which occurs nowhere else in the play.

P. 373, 117. *Lost or forlorn*: the latter, properly a past partcp. of *forlese,* to lose, must be distinguished as meaning 'doomed to destruction,' 'ruined,' though she may know her whereabouts well enough.

133. *stands on ioynts*: probably means 'consists in piecing together,' 'is merely inferential,' alluding to Aramanthus' questions. But no such use is quoted; and it may refer to his movements or astrological figures.

P. 374, 145. *Antick*: as adjective. Drayton's *Heroic. Ep.* xi. 13 'A Satyres Anticke parts he play'd.'

155. *defie*: OF. *defier,* renounce faith or allegiance to.

157. *this is leape yeare*: this conflicts with a production before 1600, or more probably compels us to suppose it first produced in 1596.

P. 375, 188. *Heres old transforming*: the intensive *old,* which Bullen rightly renders by 'fine,' 'rare,' rather than 'frequent,' 'abundant,' hardly needs illustration; but cf. *Euph.* ii. 7 l. 11 'his feet shold haue ben olde Helena,' i. e. absolutely beautiful.

14. *taketh keepe*: takes care (of the sheep), *in loue* being merely 'for love.' Chaucer's *Prol. to Wif. of B.* 231 'We loue no man that taketh kepe or charge Wher that we goon.'

18. *Albe*: albeit, as below, l. 82.

21. *Erynnis stop thy throte*: merely = 'A Fury on thy bawling!'

P. 376, 31. *Instruct*: only with personal object in modern speech.

P. 377, 70. *Sib*: kin; used as subst. or adj. Still in Scotch: cf. R. L. Stevenson, *Catriona*, p. 56 'Sib to the Advocate.'

82. *set no sale But truth vpon thy tale*: put no value or estimate but truth on it, i. e. give an air of truth to.

86. *wonning*: dwelling (Ger. *wohnen*), as repeatedly in Spenser, &c.

P. 378, 21. *What though thy habit differ from thy kind*: Ascanio of course recognizes only a change of dress (*habit*): her change of sex or nature (*kind*) is only acknowledged below, ll. 40 sqq. How Eurymine has got rid of Silvio and Gemulo is not explained.

P. 381, 113. *base*: i. e. bass.

135. *well ouertaken*: Joculo's distinction merely means that he is the surprised party, or the one followed. Cf. 'well ouertane,' v. 1. 51.

P. 382, S.D. *Muses*: In v. 1. 109 and in iii. 1 they were 'Graces' or 'Charites,' but in the earlier scene l. 75 Apollo addressed one of them as 'Eurania': so that evidently the distinction is not to be pressed.

P. 383, 14. *Or that*: *or* possibly as temporal conjunction, = before that (takes place), as often in the phrase 'or ever'; but more probably the simple disjunctive, 'that' being constructed with 'see' l. 12.

23. *Hide not, oh hide not*, &c.: the same trick of repetition was noticeable in Eurymine's song in Act i.

25. *Illustrate*: again *Love's Labour's Lost*, v. 1. 118 'this most gallant, illustrate, and learned gentleman.'

P. 386, 142. *mistresse*: no need to insert *is*: *mistresse* is probably intended as a trisyllable. Cf. the pun on 'mysteries,' *Gall*. iv. 4. 21.

148. *Iunos balme*: balm was sprinkled at nuptial solemnities, e. g. at the marriage of Cupid and Psyche, Apuleius' *Met.* vi. 24 'Gratiae spargebant balsama.'

152. *Caull*: a little net for the head, often in *Euphues*.

PAPPE WITH AN HATCHET.

(In the following Notes the letters J. P. refer to John Petheram's reprint of the pamphlet, 1844, 12ᵐᵒ, as No. 3 of 'Puritan Discipline Tracts.')

P. 393. TITLE—*Pappe with an hatchet*: the proverbial nature of this phrase, which occurs in the text at p. 404 l. 33 'The babie comes in with *Nunka, Neame*, and *Dad*: (Pappe with an hatchet for such a puppie)', is indicated by the alternative titles, and by its use in *Mother Bombie*, i. 3. 104 'they giue vs pap with a spoon before we can speak, and when wee speake for that wee loue, pap with a hatchet': and in the *Discourse of Marriage*—'He that so old seeks for a nurse so young, shall have pap with a hatchet for his comfort' (*Harl. Misc.* ii. 171, quoted by J. P.).

Mr. Saintsbury parallels it with 'giving him his gruel.' The evident sense is that of unkind treatment where kindness might be looked for. 'Hatchet' bore its present meaning as early as *Piers Plowman*, B. iii. 304 ' Axe other [or] hatchet' (Skeat); and in the absence of more definite information as to the origin of the phrase, we may perhaps imagine an irate housewife catching up the first implement that came handy in order to silence her squalling infant.

9. *patch*: properly an allusion to the motley of the Fool: cf. *Tempest*, iii. 2. 71 'What a pied ninny's this! thou scurvy patch!'

11. *call a dog, a dog*: proverb for plain speech, as *Mid.* iv. 3. 2.

13. *Iohn Anoke*: Noakes or Nokes, which Halliwell gives as 'ninny,' 'simpleton,' is a typical rustic name (cf. 'A Countrie cuffe' above), allusive here (with 'John Astile') to the manner adopted in the pamphlet.

14. *Bayliue of Withernam*: *Withernam* is a law term signifying *reprisal*, or 'taking of other goods or cattle in lieu of those unjustly taken and effoined, or otherwise witholden' (Rees' *Cyclopædia*, 1819), AS. *wiðre*, against, and *nehmen*, to take. On April 2, 1583, the Lord Mayor writes to the Council of a disturbance in London about the exaction of 'the Custom of Withernam' upon London vessels within the liberties of the Cinque Ports, suggesting that London might retaliate.

18. *sentence*: proverb or motto.

P. 394, 1. *To the Father and the two Sonnes*, &c.: i.e. Martin Marprelate, Martin Senior, and Martin Junior. Mr. Saintsbury reminds us that Huffe, Ruffe, and Snuffe are characters in Preston's play *Cambyses* [acted c. 1561, printed 1579-1585]. The pseudonym Martin Marprelate first appears on the title-page of *The Epistle* issued between Nov. 1-14, 1588. The first mention of Martin Senior is in the second Marprelate tract, *The Epitome*, issued about Feb. 2, 1589—' my sonne Martin senyor, that worthy wight' (Puritan Discipline Tracts, No. 2, p. 47). *Theses Martinianæ*, issued about July 22, 1589, profess to be 'set foorth as an after-birth of the noble Gentleman himselfe, by a prety stripling of his, Martin Jvnior'; and these are followed about July 29 by *The iust censure and reproofe of Martin Junior*, wherein 'the boy hath his lesson taught him ... by his reuerend and elder brother, Martin Senior, ... where also hee is not bereaued of his due commendations.'

3. *take pepper in the nose*: i.e. take offence; a common phrase, proper to the sternutatory names above.

6. *grating*: intentional perversion of 'greeting.'

7. *royster*: earlier form of 'roysterer.' Cf. 'roisting,' *Moth. Bomb.* p. 175 l. 65.

9. *more worke ... wood enough to cleaue*: alluding to the Marprelate tract *Hay any work for Cooper*, issued about March 23, 1589, in answer to the *Admonition to the people of England* by Thomas Cooper, bishop of Winchester.

12. *shoot bookes like fooles bolts*: referring to the proverb 'a fool's bolt is soon shot.' Six Marprelate tracts appeared in 1589 before *Pappe*.

18-9. *mist . . . mist*: same pun *M. Bomb.* iii. 4. 160.

23. *list*: the border or edge of a piece of cloth.

28. *cutters*: swashbucklers, swaggerers, bullies.

ale dagger: compare Nash's *A Countercuffe*, sig. A iij recto 'a swapping Ale-dagger at his back, containing by estimation some two or three poundes of yron in the hyltes and chape.' The term is witness to the frequency of tavern-brawls like that in which Marlowe was killed, June 1, 1593.

P. 395, 3. *copper replie*: suggests the use of cheap spurs of this metal. Cf. 'spurre schollers,' *M. Bomb.* iv. 1. 20. *All to*, quite, as p. 404 l. 34.

5. *play at chestes, as well as his nephewe the ape*: 'chestes' for 'chess,' a corrupt pl. of *checks*, OF. *eschecs*, 'kings,' occurs *Euph.* ii. 162 l. 36, and Halliwell quotes '*Jouer aux eschets*, to play at chests or tables,' *Nomenclator*, 1585, p. 294. 'Nephew' in the general sense of 'relation' or 'descendant.' 'Martin' seems to be a common name for an ape, like 'Ned' for a donkey, 'Wat' for a hare, &c. Cf. *Whip for an Ape*, st. 2 'Who knoweth not that Apes men Martins call.' Lyly must have in mind some monkey trained to play, or seem to play, the game.

6. *scaddle*: 'Thievish, generally in a petty way only; used in contempt. *Kent*' (Halliwell). Mr. Saintsbury explains it, on Skeat's authority, as AS. *scadol* (from *scathe*), 'mischievous,' with secondary sense 'thievish,' and tertiary 'timid' or 'skulking.' Here probably a combination of all three.

7. *dydoppers*: Skeat quotes '*Doppar*, or *dydoppar*, watyr-byrde, mergulus,' *Prompt. Parv.* p. 127. Lyly compares the anonymity of Martin to the dabchick's habit of hiding its head in the water. The same notion of secrecy is implied in its use by Fenton, *Tragicall Discourses*, fol. 64 'make theym seme maydenlike (althought they haue alreadie playd the dydopper).'

12. *your dads dictionarie*: Martin Marprelate's 'grammar and lexicon' are twice mentioned in *The iuste reproofe*, C 4 and D 1.

14. *at an houres warning*: in *An Almond for a Parrat*, p. 12 (J. P.), Nash alludes to 'the extemporall endeuour of the pleasant author of Pap with a hatchet.'

15. *Double V*: = W, i. e. a match for two of you.

P. 396, 13. *answered by the grauitie of learned Prelates*: as in the Bishop of Winchester's *Admonition*.

16. *camels neuer drinke, til*, &c.: Pliny, *Nat. Hist.* viii. 26 'implentur, cum bibendi occasio est, et in praeteritum, et in futurum, obturbata proculcatione prius aqua: aliter potu non gaudent.' An allusion to the same circumstance occurs in *Euphues*, ii. 143 l. 14, and *Mother Bombie*, v. 3. 233.

22. *The Scithian slaues . . . tamde with whippes,* &c.: Herodotus, iv. 3, as before *Euphues,* ii. 147 l. 26.

29. *addle egges . . . idle heads*: same annomination in *Euph.* i. 299 l. 32, 325 l. 13, *Midas,* ii. 2. 18.

31. *the theeues, that had an yron bed,* &c. : i.e. Sciron and Procrustes (Hyg. *Fab.* 38), whom Lyly incorrectly represented as partners before, in *Euphues,* ii. 97 l. 30.

P. 397, 3. *cast in Martins mould, his religion must needes mould*: same pun occurs elsewhere.

4. *He saith he is a Courtier*: in *The Epitome,* p. 2, 'I haue bene entertayned at the Court,' and p. 4, ' It will be but follie for you to prosecute the Courtier Martin,' cf. *ib.* p. 59 and *Hay any Worke,* p. 59.

P. 398, 1. *anie musique this morning*: the custom of morning serenading is illustrated by the song ' Hark, hark! the lark,' &c. in *Cymbeline,* by *Rom. and Jul.* iv. 4. 21, by *Mother Bomb.* v. 3, and alluded to in Nash's *Haue with you to Saffron Waldron* (1596) ' With a blacke sant he meanes shortly to bee at his chamber window, for calling him the Fiddlesticke of Oxford.'

7. *Bastard Iunior . . . Bastard Senior,* &c.: see note on p. 394 l. 1.

13. *Bishops bobbs* : blows from the bishops. *As You Like It,* ii. 7. 55.

15. *restie*: angry, out of temper: the word soon lost its original sense of a stubbornness that will *not* move for whipping.

16. *Maukin*: Malkin, diminutive of Mary, i. e. *Mal* and *kin* (Nares). Marg. *mazer* : a large drinking-bowl.

17. *Elderton*: ' Elderton's company of players is mentioned, under the year 1572, in Collier's Annals of the Stage, i. 205 [199] ' (J. P.). He is mentioned in *An Almond,* &c. p. 22, and in Harvey's *Pierce's Supererogation* (1593) (*Archaica,* ii. p. 86) ' it goeth hard, when Scoggin, the Iouiall foole, or Skelton the Malancholy foole, or Elderton the bibbling foole, or Will Sommer the chollericke foole, must play the feate.' He is recorded as playing fourth Son to the Lord of Misrule in 1552, and as ending his career as a popular ballad-maker famous for his red nose. Died before 1606. Several of his ballads are printed in the *Somers Tracts,* vols. i, ii.

18. *hacker . . . cut it*: the context suggests that ' hacker ' is a synonym for ' cutter,' i. e. swaggerer, rowdy. Nares gives only ' hackster,' a hacknied person. Perhaps it is a misprint for *hawker,* pedlars being the usual ballad-vendors.

20. *those of Bonner, or the ierkes for a Iesuit* : ballads against Bishop Bonner, of Mary's reign. In the *Harleian Miscellany,* i. 612-17, is printed ' An Epitaph . . . vpon the Life and Death of Dr. Bonner, who dyed the Fifth of Sept. in the Marshalsie . . . 1569 Sept. 14.' A note on the above adds ' Some verses of more merit, and little less causticity, were addressed to Bonner, by the father of the celebrated Sir John Harington, and are printed in *Nugae Antiquae,* ii. ed. 1804. Other verses, made upon Bonner's picture, appeared in the *Mirrour of Martyrs*, 1615; but the most virulent piece of personal invective against this hated man was intitled 'A Commemoration, or Dirige of Bastarde Edmonde Boner, alias Savage, usurped Bisshoppe of London,' and printed in 1569. It closes with a lineal pedigree, in which the descent of Bonner is pretended to be traced from a juggler, a cutpurse, and a Tom o' Bedlam.' On p. 407 l. 14 naughty children 'ought to be ierkt.' Cupid in *Sapho and Phao*, i. 1. 41, is afraid Sapho 'wil ye-ke me, if I hit her.'

23. *a little wag in Cambridge . . . Saint Seaton . . . Sillogismes*: Nash is referred to. In *Almond*, p. 42, Nash speaks of Penry 'whiles hee was yet a fresh man in Peterhouse, and had scarce tasted, as we say, of *Seton's modalibus*'—evidently a treatise on logic. The *Epistle*, pp. 44-7, contains a string of formal arguments.

P. 399, 1. *cast a figure . . . conclusion*: i. e. a horoscope conducting to the gallows.

11. *play three a vies wits . . . drop vie stabbes*: 'to vie' is to wager. Skeat quotes Cotgrave, OF. '*envier (au jeu)*, to vie'; and Florio, '*inuitare (al giuoco)*, to v e or to reuie at any game, to drop vie'; and Wedgwood, 'From the verb was formed the adverbial expression *à l'envi*, E. a-vie, as if for a wager: "They that write of these toads strive *a-vie* who shal write most wonders of them," Holland, tr. of Pliny, xxxii. 5.' 'Play three a vies wits,' therefore, means 'match or wager three wits against thine'—the three being Lyly, Nash, and Greene (cf. Life, i. 54 note 2, 58 note 2, but see also note on p. 407 l. 2); and 'drop vie stabbes' means similarly 'match thee at stabbing.'

14. *an Hospitall*: the Savoy is alluded to; see Life, vol. i. pp. 17-8. 'The circuite of Westchester' is the diocese of Chester. Lyly is replying to *Hay any Worke*, p. 11, 'Our brother Westchester, had as liue playe twentie nobles in a night, at Priemero on the cards, as trouble him selfe with any pulpit labor . . . What a bishop such a cardplaier?'

15. *an old stabber at passage*: ' " Passage" from the French "passedix." "Passage is a game at dice to be played at but by two, and it is performed with three dice. The caster throws continually till he hath thrown dubblets under ten, and then he is out and loseth, or dubblets above ten, and then he *passeth* and wins."—*Compleat Gamester*, 1680, p. 119. From the same, excellent authority we learn that "stabbing the dice" was one of the tricks practised by the cheats of old times, p. 12' (Petheram's Reprint, p. 45). *Cater tray*, the throw of four and three at dice. *Cater caps*, four-cornered college caps: see note on p. 401 l. 31.

20. *foyne*: push or thrust.

22. *dicker*: ten, of any commodity; e. g. 'a dicker of cow-hides,' Heywood, first part *King Ed. IV*, 1600 (Nares).

23. *spleene*: impulse, mood; *stroakt*, soothed.

25. *a warming, as shall make . . . like wood*, &c.: cf. *Euph*. i. 296

l. 10, note: 'You shall conceyue heate and bringe foorth woode, your owne consciences shall consume you lyke fire.'

26. *woodsere*: the Cent. Dict. quotes 'The froth which they call woodseare, being like a kind of spittle, is found but upon certain herbs . . . as lavender . . . sage, &c. Bacon, *Nat. Hist.* § 497.' Cf. *Gallathea*, v. 1. 32.

28. *colde stomacke*: synonym for indigestion, as the context shows. 'Cinnamom-water' is water percolated through cotton moistened with oil of cinnamon.

29. *an Estritch a two penie naile*: *Euphues*, i. 260 l. 29 'the estridge disgesteth harde yron to preserue his healthe,' where see note.

30. *did your Father die at the Groyne?*: in the Epilogue to *Theses Martinianæ*, Martin Junior, speculating on the whereabouts of Martin Marprelate, says, 'Others giue out, that in the seruice of his countrey, and her Maiesties, he died, or was in gret däger at the Groine.' In April, 1589, an expedition of 14,000 men sailed, under Sir John Norris and Sir Francis Drake, in aid of the Portuguese prince Don Antonio against Philip of Spain; and on their way to Lisbon landed at the Groyne (La Coruña, Corunna), defeated a Spanish force, and captured the lower part of the town. Alluded to, *Midas*, iv. 4. 12, where see note (p. 533).

36. *rochet*: bishop's surplice.

39. *biggin*: night-cap.

41. *Sudburie*: on the borders of Suffolk and Essex. The story was probably supplied by Nash.

P. 400, 7. *Wye*: in Kent near Ashford. Nash in *The Return of Pasquill* (C ii r.) recounts a meeting of Puritans at the latter place at which he and Lyly were present: see Life, vol. i. p. 52 note.

hostesse of the Swanne in Warwicke: probably a sympathizer or confederate with Job Throckmorton, supposed to be joint author with Penry of *Martin Junior*, *Martin Senior* (i. e. *Theses Mart.* and *The iust censure*, &c.), and of the arrested pamphlet *More Worke for Cooper*, at whose house at Haseley, 3½ miles NW. of Warwick, the *Protestatyon* was printed. See Arber's *Introductory Sketch* to the Controversy, pp. 78, 175-84, 193-6; and Life, vol. i. pp. 54-5.

10. *shewe the Queene*: metaphor from cards, meaning here 'protest loyalty,' as is done in *The Epistle*, pp. 13-4 (ed. Arb.), *Hay any Worke* (Pur. Discip. Tracts), pp. 45-7.

18. *a hundred merrie tales, and the petigree of Martin*: alluding probably here, and again pp. 401 l. 37, 405 l. 12, under the title of the well-known Jest-book, to Nash's projected *Lives of the Saints*, i. e. scandal about the Martinists, announced in *Countercuffe*, A i v.

21. *secundum vsum Sarum*: Ray's *Proverbs* gives it as a proverb for 'things done with exactness, according to rule and precedent.' The office was drawn up by Bishop Osmund of Sarum, c. 1090, and came into general use.

22. *can tell twentie*: either (1) to be able to count up to twenty was an early proverb for a forward child or a person with his wits about him, or (2) it had some reference to beads, and the repetition of prayers. Cf. Beaum. and Flet. *Scornful Ladie*, ii. 1, where Martha snubs the chaplain's offer to say grace with 'pray tell your twenty to yourself.' The allusion is to the *Defence of the Government established in the Church of England*, by Dr. John Bridges, dean of Salisbury, which started the Marprelate controversy.

24. *so translate you out of French into English . . . lie by it*: i. e. expose you so plainly that you will have to hide your head. In *M. Bomb.* iii. 2. 46 'lie by it' is used of the old men laid up after their drinking bout. The person referred to may possibly be Lyly's friend Thomas Watson, author of the *Hecatompathia*, 1582, who imitated Ronsard and other French poets: but the allusion that immediately follows makes it far more probable that Lyly is thinking of Harvey's friend Spenser, whose *Shepheardes Kalender*, 1579, contained so much paraphrase or adaptation of Marot, and ten sonnets by whom, translated from Du Bellay, had previously appeared in Vandernoodt's *Theatre for Worldlings*, 1569.

25-42. *And one will we coniure vp . . . Epistle about . . . Earthquake . . . tiburn-wright*: this long passage refers to Gabriel Harvey, and to his publication of *Three Proper and Wittie familiar Letters lately passed betweene two Vniuersitie men: touching the Earthquake in Aprill last, and our English refourmed Versifying . . .* 1580. The first of these letters (reprinted in Grosart's ed. of Harvey's Works, vol. i) is from Spenser to Harvey about versifying. The second is Harvey's 'Pleasant and Pithy and Familiar Discourse of the Earthquake in Aprill last,' addressed to his 'loouing friende M. Immerito,' i. e. Spenser; and this letter, written after his disappointment about the Public Oratorship, contained reflections on the University and Dr. Perne, Master of Peterhouse, which brought him into trouble. From Harvey's *Four Letters and certaine Sonnets*, pub. 1592, we learn that 'The sharpest part of those unlucky letters was overread at the Council Table' (Brydges' *Archaica*, ii. p. 15), but that he escaped imprisonment. The third letter (of 1580) was about versifying, and contained a satire on travellers in hexameters entitled 'Speculum Tuscanismi,' in regard to which Harvey in the *Four Letters*, &c., writes as follows with allusion to the present passage in *Pappe*—'another company of special good fellows (whereof he was none of the meanest that brauely threatened to conjure up one which should massacre Martin's wit or should be lambacked himself with ten years provision) would needs forsooth very courtly persuade the Earle of Oxforde that something in those letters, and namely the Mirrour of Tuscanismo, was palpably intended against him: whose noble Lordship I protest I neuer meante to dishonour,' &c. The origin of Lyly's ten years' grudge against Harvey, of which this slander of him to Oxford is the first sign, remains obscure. See Life, vol. i. pp. 30–1.

30. *full of latin endes* : Harvey was lecturer on rhetoric. The first of his course in 1577 was published as *Ciceronianus*, and the two first of the course in 1578 under the name of *Rhetor* (Morley's *Eng. Writers*, ix. 17).

32. *bable*: fool's bauble.

35. *lambacke* : beat or bastinado, also spelt ' lambeake,' which contradicts the obvious etymology. Halliwell quotes Greene's *Discovery of Coosnage*, 1591, 'gave unto him halfe a score of sound lambeakes with their cudgels.'

38. *Shoomakers hall in Sainct Martins* : a burlesque locality. The real Shoemakers Hall is given by Stow, iii. 9 (end), as in Bread St. Ward, opposite G^t. Distar St. I believe this and other similar allusions in *Pappe* are to *Hay any Worke*, p. 64, where ' Cliffe an honest and a godly cobler, dwelling at Battell bridg' is brought forward as having refuted, and ready again to refute, some statement of Archbishop Whitgift. Cf. *Mar-Martine*, p. 426 l. 98 (note).

39. *nor the footcloth, nor the beast that wears it, be he horse or asse* : this seems to be a recurrence to a ribald quatrain in *Mar-Martine*, p. 424, for which quatrain Lyly was possibly responsible :

' Many would know the holy Asse,
And who mought Martin been,
Plucke but the footecloth from his backe,
The Asse will soone be seene.'

41. *Martins, sonne, Iohns, sonne, or Richards, sonne . . . tiburn-wright* : alluding to Gabriel Harvey's younger brothers John and Richard ; while ' tiburn-wright ' alludes, as Fleay points out, to his father's occupation as a rope-maker. There is no reason to suppose that Gabriel or any of the Harveys had as yet taken any part in the controversy ; though Lyly was possibly led to suspect Gabriel's hand in the abuse of Dr. Perne as 'Andrew turnecoat,' &c., which some of the Martinist tracts contained. Now, however, Gabriel wrote the *Advertisement to Papp-Hatchett*, which is dated Nov. 5, 1589, though only published as the Second Book of *Pierces Supererogation* in 1593; and in 1590 Richard Harvey, the second brother, issued his *Plaine Perciuall* and *The Lamb of God*, in the latter of which an epistle to the reader, composed perhaps by Gabriel, perhaps by the brothers in collaboration, vilified by name Lyly, Nash, and the ' make plaies and make bates ' of London in general.

42. *cart-wright*: alluding to Thomas Cartwright, the champion of Puritan views against Whitgift, 1572–1577.

P. 401, 9. *the Heraldes*: Stow's *Survey* mentions that Derby House in Castle Baynard Ward (now Queen Victoria St.), transferred to the Crown 1553 in exchange for lands in Lancs, was given by Queen Mary

PAPPE WITH AN HATCHET 581

to the Heralds' Office in 1555, but says nothing of its use as a Puritan conventicle.

13. *shoomaker*: see about Cobler Cliffe, p. 426 l. 96 note.

14. *caught by the stile*: having just dropped into euphuistic punning and alliteration.

16. *leuell . . . roue at thee*: aim true . . . shoot wide. 'Rovers' were marks on the target wide of the bull's eye. 'To run at rovers,' run wild.

Marginal note. *Martin Iunior . . . vnder a bush*: referring to *Theses Mart*. C iii 'If you demaund of mee, where I founde this, the trueth is, it was taken vp (together with certain other papers) besides a bush, where it had dropped from some body passing by that way.'

18. *crochet on thy head*: a punning allusion to his music: *on* for 'in.'

19. *Bull*: evidently from the allusions here and on pp. 404 l. 28, 406 l. 15, and *Almond*, p. 14 'Bul's slicing,' he is the executioner.

23. *him that walkes on his neats-feete*: i. e. on shoe-leather = 'any man.'

31. *foure cornerd cap*: 'The horned cappe' is enumerated among the 'grosse pointes of popery' in Antony Gilby's *Pleasaunte Dialogue*, 1581, which summarized the Puritan objections. 'Catercaps' is a frequent Martinist term of abuse for Prelatists, e. g. p. 399 l. 18.

P. 402, 2. *coyne words, as Cankerburie, Canterburines*: the first occurs on the title-page of *Theses Martinianæ*, the second is to be found in *The Epistle*, pp. 19, 22 of Petheram's Reprint.

a foole that shall so inkhornize you with straunge phrases . . . For Similes, theres another, &c.: the first is obviously Nash; the second as obviously himself, and intended to conceal his identity in the present pamphlet.

4. *bodges*: same as 'botches.' It occurs again in a marginal note at the end of *Mar-Martine*, p. 426.

P. 403, 2. *casting of figures . . . figures a flinging*: 'figure flinger, an astrologer' (Halliwell).

7. *dudgin*: 'grave matter,' the same as *dudgeon*, which Skeat derives from Welsh *dygen*, malice cf. *dueg*, melancholy, spleen.

13. *gnawe the bowels*, &c.: like the viper, as *Euph*. ii. 5 l. 5, &c.

19. *Bastard Iunior complaines of brothells . . long Megg of Westminster*: *Theses Mart*. D ii r. 'Concerning Mar-martin . . . that rime of his sheweth that hee had no other bringing vppe, then in a brothel house . . . I cannot be induced to thinke, that hee hath had his bringing vp at any other trade, then in carryeng long Meg of Westminsters hand-basket,' &c. The rhyme *Mar-Martine*, probably shared between Lyly and Nash, issued May–June 1589, was answered a month later by the rhyme *Marre Mar-Martin*, attacking both sides. The virago alluded to has been adequately embalmed in contemporary literature and its comment. *Suspect you*, l. 21, i. e. of like fault.

35. *Martin will not sweare, but with indeede*, &c.: Lyly is thinking

of Martin's reflections in *The Epistle*, pp. 5, 6, on Bishop Aylmer's bad language—'Sweare as commonly you do like a lewd swag.'

38. *the wit ant*: in or of it.

P. 404, 4. *wēt but a paire of sheres betweene*, &c.: common phrase—'you were both cut out of the same piece.'

6. *Aesops crab*: givèn as the 245th ('Cancri') in *Fabulæ Æsopicæ plures quingentis ... Lugdvni, M.D.LXXI.* p. 275.

11. *no such chāge*: as the abolition of the order of Bishops and the substitution of government by elders, the chief demand of *The Epistle*.

20. *Thou ... preachest Aesops fables*: anticipating a supposed objection against his own method.

22. *Pueriles and Stans puer ad mensam*: school-books mentioned in *An Almond*, &c., at pp. 40 and 29 respectively. The Farmer in Peele's *Edward I*, sc. xii, says, 'I remember I read it in Cato's *Pueriles*, that *Cantabit vacuus*,' &c., and Mr. Bullen notes 'Dionysius Cato's *Disticha Moralia* was a famous old school-book; and there was another school-book, *Pueriles Confabiatiunculae*. But Cato's *Disticha* was also known as *Sententiae Pueriles*.' It was edited by Erasmus 1514, 4°, and by Taverner 1553, 8°, and in the Stationers' Register, i. 418 (between Nov. 1569 and July 1570), occurs·'Recevyd of henry bynyman for his lycense for pryntinge of a boke intituled sententia[e] pueriles in laten ... iiij^d.' Halliwell-Phillipps, *Life of Shakespeare*, i. 53, says 'The Sententiæ Pueriles was, in all probability, the little manual by the aid of which he (Shakespeare) first learned to construe Latin, for in one place, at least, he all but literally translates a brief passage, and there are in his plays several adaptations of its sentiments. It was then sold for a penny, equivalent to about our present shilling, and contains a large collection of brief sentences collected from a variety of authors, with a distinct selection of moral and religious paragraphs, the latter intended for the use of boys on Saints' Days.' The *Stans Puer* was a poem on manners at table, by John Lydgate. It was printed by Pynson, and repub. 1588 (Halliwell in *Sh. Soc. Papers* (1849), iv. 31, with quotations from it).

27. *Aptots*: i.e. indeclinable, like the numerals 3-100 above.

28. *Bulls voider*: properly a basket or tray for carrying out the relics of a meal; here from the context the cloth ('apron') in which the executioner took away the head. Bull is mentioned pp. 401 l. 19, 406 l. 15.

33. *Nunka, Neame, and Dad*: Theses *M.* is 'dedicated to his good neame and nuncka Maister Iohn Kankerbury.' 'Neme,' or 'neam' is the same as 'eam,' uncle; the *n* properly belonging, as in 'nunka,' to the possessive 'mine.'

34. *all to*: quite, as p. 395 l. 3.

36. *Hui ?*: perhaps in parody of 'I cannot but laugh, py hy hy hy' in *Hay any worke*, p. 10.

38. *Que*: queue, cue, as in *Moth. Bomb.* ii. 4. 21.

P. 405, 4. *moyst conceit, and drie counsell*: 'moyst' and 'drie' as of plants which are flourishing or the reverse. The 'dry brain' is an Elizabethan term for mental slowness or confusion, e. g. *As You Like It*, ii. 7. 39 of Touchstone. But cf. *Sapho*, iii. 4. 50 note.

8. *seeke to fish for the Crown*: the same argument as on pp. 395 l. 7, 407 ll. 22–6, 412 ll. 1–2, and *Whip for an Ape*, st. 14.

11. *abate of an hundred [tales] in the next booke*: i. e. the 'hundred merrie tales' promised pp. 400 l. 18, 401 l. 37.

13. *a cloake hauing sleeues*: among the 'Grosse pointes of poperie' enumerated in Gilby's *Pleasaunte Dialogue*, 1581, is 'The great wide sleeued gowne, commaunded to the Ministers, and the charge to weare those sleeues vpon the armes, be the weather neuer so hote.' Cf. *Almond*, p. 46 'The blinde, the halt, or the lame, or any serues the turn with them, so he hath not on a cloak with sleues, or a cap of the vniuersity cut.'

17. *a sleeuelesse conscience*: cf. *Euph.* i. 253 l. 17 'fayne any sleeueless excuse,' i. e. vain, bootless. Since printing that note I have found the true explanation in a custom noted in the following passage from Lady Charlotte Guest's trs. of the *Mabinogion* (Dream of Maxen Wledig): 'Now this was the guise in which the messengers journeyed; one sleeve was on the cap of each of them in front, as a sign that they were messengers, in order that through what hostile land soever they might pass no harm might be done them.' Without the sleeve they might never be able to perform their errand. The Welsh princess on their arrival recognizes 'the badge of envoys.' Cf. *Tro. and Cr.* v. 4. 9 'a sleeveless errand.'

18. *rippier*: or 'ripier,' one who brings fish from the coast to sell in the interior, from Lat. *ripa*, or from Eng. *ripp*, the basket in which the fish were carried, to avoid contact with which the cape of the cloak, as the man rode, would be cast back over the shoulder.

25. *kixes*: or kexes, hollow stems of hemlock. Beau. and Flet., *King and No King*, v. 2 'make these wither'd kexes bear my body.'

31. *Mas*: for 'Master': 'Mas Sperantus,' *Moth. Bomb.* ii. 1. 127.

33. *like Primero, foure religions*, &c.: the hand in Primero called 'prime' had four cards of different suits (inferior to a flush) (Nares).

40. *sod*: past of *seethe*, boil: Genesis xxv. 29 'Jacob sod pottage.'

42. *Elderberrines*: parodying 'Canterburines,' *Epistle*, pp. 19, 22.

P. 406, 6. *a pikede vaunt*: the Charles I beard. Cf. p. 133 l. 38 note.

sweares by his ten bones: i. e. the fingers. So *Whip*, l. 22, *Woman*, v. 1. 23, of apes.

8. *old Iohn of Paris garden*: a monkey. Collier (*Annals*, iii. 279) quotes from an account of Paris Garden written 1544, 'At the same place a poney is baited, with a monkey on its back, defending itself against the dogs by kicking them; and the shrieks of the monkey, when he sees the dogs hanging from the ears and neck of the pony, render the scene very laughable' (J. P.). Cf. note on p. 280 l. 21.

9. *fight Citie fight* : as in a street brawl, with any weapon to hand.

16. *three times motion of Bull*: i.e. 'this is my third allusion to B.,' the other two being at pp. 401 l. 19, 404 l. 28. In '*tria sequuntur tria*' the first 'tria' refers to the three beams of which the gallows was built, called 'three trees' in *Mother Bombie*, ii. 1. 136. The phrase is quoted again *Midas*, v. 2. 167 (note).

17. *olde Rosses motion of Bridewell* : Ross is presumably a turnkey, or a pursuivant.

28. *Tobacco*: 'this is the earliest notice of tobacco, in the form of snuff with which I am acquainted' (J. P. who refers to Rymer's *Fœdera*).

31. *with the Archbishop and a Counsellor* : only one person intended. Cf. *The Epitome*, p. 2 'I speake not against him, as he is a Councellor, but as he is an Archbishop, and so Pope of Lambeth.'

37. *Discite iustitiam*, &c. : Virg. *Aen*. vi. 620.

38. *more sower than wig*: Halliwell gives '*Wig*. A small cake. "Eschaudé, a kind of wigg or symnell," Cotgrave. *Var. dial.*"' : and the *Century Dict.* quotes 'Home to the only Lenten supper I have had of *wiggs* and ale,' *Pepys' Diary*, ii. 117.

P. 407, 1. *three honest men* : i.e. Lyly, Nash, and Greene, see p. 399 l. 11 note. W. Maskell, however, suggests that Dr. Bancroft, by whose advice the Bishops employed the wits to vindicate them, may himself have shared in the production of Anti-martinist tracts, his own *Dangerous Positions and Proceedings*, 1593, being something in the same style (*Martin Marprelate Controversy*, ch. vii. p. 167).

3. *xxiiij Bishops* : including the two Archbishops. They are enumerated, as they sat in the Parliament of 1563, in Harrison's 'Description of Britain' prefixed to Holinshed, bk. ii. ch. 5 p. 165.

7. *poore Iohns* : a name given to a coarse kind of fish.

11. *fretteth in time like quicksiluer into the bones*: Bartholomaeus Anglicus, xvi. 8 '[Quicksilver] perseth, boreth and fretith other matters . . . the fome therof healeth wounds . . . and freteth away superfluitie of dede fleshe, and letteth it not growe,' &c.

14. *ierkt* : hit ; for the sense of punishment cf. 'ierkes for a Iesuit,' above p. 398 l. 20.

19. *beame . . . milstone*: causes of offence or of sinking, alluding to speeches of our Lord.

31. *but my Liripoope*: properly the degree of knowledge that entitled a person to wear the *liripipium* or scarf as doctor ; then of common knowledge, or matter of common sense, opposed to more formal or deeper learning: so in *Saph. and Phao*, i. 3. 6, *Moth. Bomb*. i. 3. 128.

36. *chiuerell* : cheveril, cheverel ; Fr. *chevreuil*, doe-skin.

P. 408, 13. *boulted* : winnowed, sifted. *Wint. Tale*, iv. 4. 375 'the fanned snow That's bolted by the northern blasts.'

17. *Sed heus tu, dic sodes* : 'Heus puer dic sodes,' Ter. *And*. i. 1. 58.

18-24. *Would those Comedies might be allowed to be plaid that are pend . . . He shall not bee brought in as whilom he was . . . with a cocks combe, an apes face,* &c.: cf. *An Almond,* p. 22 'as he was attired like an Ape on ye stage.' Further details about this presentation of Martin on the stage are found in Nash's *Returne of Pasquill* (C iii verso) issued after *The Protestatyon* and probably just after *Pappe*: it is dated near the end ' 20 Octobris.' ' Methought *Vetus Comœdia* began to pricke him at London in the right vaine, when shee brought forth *Diuinitie* wyth a scratcht face, holding of her hart as if she were sicke, because *Martin* would have forced her; but myssing of his purpose, he left the print of his nayles vppon her cheekes, and poysoned her with a vomit, which he ministred vnto her to make her cast vppe her dignities and promotions.' This passage shows that the form chosen was the allegorical form of the Morality, as J. P. points out; and a date for this performance is roughly indicated by another passage in *Martin's Months Minde* (Aug.) E 3 verso, which recounts as successive sufferings of Martin that he was 'drie beaten,' then 'whipt that made him winse,' then 'made a *Maygame* vpon the stage, and at length cleane Marde,' four allusions which are made perfectly clear by the printed marginal notes (1) 'T. C.' (2) 'A whip for an Ape,' (3) 'The Theater,' (4) 'Marre-martin.' See for these Anti-Martinist plays, *Life*, vol. i. pp. 52-4.

28. *stage plaier . . . cobler by occupation* : here 'stage plaier' is obviously used of one who performed for the nonce in a Miracle-play presented on a movable stage, not of a professional actor.

30. *qui tantum constans,* &c.: parody of Ovid, *Trist.* v. 8. 18 'Et tantum constans in levitate sua est.'

32. *Mardocheus*: Mordecai—'play' meaning ' stand for,' ' represent.'

36. *stride from Aldgate to Ludgate, and looke ouer all the Citie at London Bridge*: i.e. be taken in a cart from prison to place of execution, and finally have his head stuck on a pole as a traitor at the south end of the Bridge.

Marginal note: the point of the allusion is that St. Thomas a Waterings, a place for watering horses at a brook beside the second milestone on the Canterbury road, was also the Tyburn of Surrey, and a real hanging of Martin would be free to the public. John Penry, the chief author of the Marprelate tracts, was actually hanged there on May 29, 1593. ' J. P.' quotes the Prol to the *Canterbury Tales*, l. 826.

Marginal note: this reference to *The iust reproofe* does not seem to be particular. Gracchus is chosen as an extreme example of sedition.

42. *Aue Cæsar*: Machyn's Diary states that a 'play' called *Julius Cæsar* was represented at Court in 1561 (Collier's *Annals*, i. 90).

P. 409, 5. *thus gouerne*: i.e. by bishops.

37. *Bedlam and Bridewell*: the two are mentioned together again, p. 412 l. 30, and in connexion with Martin's language; and Jack Straw (as here) in *A Whip for an Ape*, stt. 7, 15.

39. *the Black-smith*: probably Wat Tyler.

P. 410, 1. *the glasse*: i.e. the skylight.

8. *Prosper broke his horses*, &c.: in Michael Baret's *Hipponomie or the Vineyard of Horsemanship* (1618), bk. ii. ch. 20 ('Of the Headstraine'), p. 71 occurs—'For when Signior Prospero, first came into England, he flourished in fame for a time, (through that affectionated blindnes we are vailed withall, in exalting strangers for their strange fashions) and so, though he vsed such tormenting Cauezans [Fr. *caveçon*, It. *cavezzone*, nose-band of iron, leather or wood, fixed to the nostril] as were more fit for a massacring butcher then a Horseman, yet for all that well was he that could goe neerest him in such Turkish tortures: And besides those, hee would haue a thicke truncheon to beat those Cauezans into his nose, the further to torment him, as if Art had consisted in cruell torturing poore horses.'

9. *muzroule*: Halliwell gives 'Musroll. The nose-band of a horse's bridle. (*Fr.*) Still in use.'

portmouth: 'I presume, a kind of twitch' (Saintsbury).

14. *cuckingstoole*: or ducking-stool, a chair on the end of a plank for immersing scolds or disorderly women.

15. *Bishops English*: *The iust censure*, &c. devotes a paragraph on C 4 to this subject, e. g. 'the bishops English is to wrest our language in such sorte, as they will drawe a meaning out of our English wordes, which the nature of the tongue can by no meanes beare,' &c.

17. *his powting croscloath*: Halliwell (in Nares) gives 'Cross-cloth. A kerchief, or cloth to wrap round the head or bosom. "A crosse-cloath, as they tearme it, a powting-cloth, plagula." *Withal's Dictionarie*, ed. 1680, p. 275 "Thy crossecloth is not pinned right before." *Cranley's Amanda*, p. 33.' In *Euphues*, ii. 63 l. 26 Iffida is described as walking in a gallery 'w^t hir frowning cloth, as sick lately of the solens.'

19. *mubble fubbles*: a cant term for causeless depression. Nares quotes Lyly's *Midas*, v. 2. 104 'now euerie base companion, beeing in his mublefubles, sayes he is melancholy'; and Gayton's *Festivous Notes*, p. 46 'Whether Jupiter was not joviall, nor Sol in his mubblefubbles, that is long clouded,' &c.

20. *Here . . . appeared olde Martin*: i.e. at this point in Lyly's composition of the tract was issued *The Protestatyon*, which he proceeds to criticize.

25. *hauncing*: tilting. Halliwell gives '*Haunce*. To raise, to exalt. A.-N.' and quotes in his ed. of Nares, s.v. 'hanced,' an instance from 'Taylors Workes' of its use in the sense of 'intoxicated.' Cf. our 'elevated.'

29. *in two sheetes*: *The Protestatyon* does actually contain 16 leaves small 8°.

35. *abi in malam crucem*: 'go and be hanged,' frequent in Plautus, also Ter. *Phorm.* ii. 3. 21.

PAPPE WITH AN HATCHET 587

39. *the holie maid of Kent*: Elizabeth Barton, who settled in 1527 in a cell of the Priory of St. Sepulchre at Canterbury. She was credited with prophetic gifts, and was instigated to prophesy against the divorce of Catharine of Arragon. When Cranmer became archbishop he obtained confession of her frauds, and she was executed at Tyburn, Ap. 20, 1534.

P. 411, 13. *as though hee should bee a martir*: see *Protestatyon*, pp. 5, 14.

14. *burnt seauen yeares agoe*: referring perhaps to Whitgift's persecution of the Puritans on his accession to the archiepiscopate in 1583.

16. *surgeans caliuer*: explained by the context as a syringe.

18. *the curtall wrinches*: a curtall was a docked horse, and the context shows 'wrinch' to be the same as 'winch' or 'wince.'

22. *bea*: i.e. baa! as in *Sudeley*, vol. i. 481 l. 11.

flockes: an inferior kind of wool, used to stuff mattresses. Lyly puns on the word in *Midas*, iv. 2. 61.

26. *Shepheards tarre-box*: must mean the Bishops' prisons.

29. *they bee all in celarent . . . ferio*: no distinction meant between these two perfect moods of the syllogism: merely a pun on the ordinary sense of the Latin words.

33. *Ora whine meg*: *Protestatyon*, p. 26. Laneham's letter on the Kenilworth Festivities quotes 'Over a whinny Meg' as the first words of an old ballad (Dyce's *Skelton*, ii. 340, quoted by J. P.).

34. *shaking of the sheetes*: 'the name of an old dance, often mentioned with a double entendre by our early dramatists,' J. P.

39. *best subiects . . . Martinists*: *Protestatyon*, p. 25.

41. *abiects . . . subiects*: as *Euph.* ii. 208 l. 36.

P. 412, 1. *wet . . . feete . . . not care how deepe they wade*: *Euph.* ii. 6 l. 11; *Sudeley*, i. 483, &c.

3. *racked*: Halliwell gives it as a pace between trot and amble.

5. *souterlie*: cobbler's. The allusion is to the few lines on the last page of the *Protestatyon*, which profess to be a list of 'faults escaped,' in which allusion is made to Dean Bullen's dog 'Spring.' George Boleyn was dean of Lichfield from 1576 to his death in Jan. 1602-3: his opposition in 1582 and 1583 to the exactions of his bishop (Overton) is recorded in Strype's *Life of Whitgift*, i. 208.

10. *sliues*: cuts, slices. ME. *sylvyn*, 'cleave' (*Prompt. Parv.*): from it *slive*, sb., with diminutive *sliver*. Cf. *Protestatyon*, p. 31 'I so sliued Dick Bancroft ouer the shoulders.'

talboothe . . . vulnerall sermon . . . the Epistle: the *Protestatyon*, pp. 24-31 professes to give an account of the contents of the Martinist tract *More worke for Cooper*, which was seized during the printing of it at Newton Lane near Manchester in Aug. 1589. The funeral sermon alluded to was preached by 'olde Lockwood of Sarum' on the sudden death of Dr. Perne. *Talboothe* is probably the Edinburgh prison.

12. *olde Ape . . . new tricks ouer the chaine*: i.e. to leap over it at one name, or sign, and to refuse at another, &c. In *Woman in the Moone*, v. 1. 21 (note), Pandora addresses Gunophilus as an ape 'Ouer the chayne, Jacke!'

15. *roage*: cf. l. 33 'a roaging foole.' *The Century Dict.* gives it as 'to wander,' 'to tramp,' and quotes 'Yf he be but once taken so idlye roging, he may punnish him more lightlye, as with stockes or such like,' Spenser's *State of Ireland*.

19. *writes merely*, &c.: writes merrily, &c. This defence of Martin's ribald style occurs in *Hay any Worke*, p. 33 'perceiuing the humors of men in these times (especially of those that are in any place) to be given to mirth,' &c.

23. *glicks and girds*: 'jests and sarcasms,' J. P.

24. *another Scogen*: not Henry Scogan, Lord Haviles, and tutor of Henry IV's sons, to whom Chaucer about 1393 addressed the *Lenvoy a Scogan*; but John Scogan, fool to Edward IV, fl. 1480. His 'jests' profess to be compiled by the physician Dr. Andrew Boorde, who died 1549. 'The geystes of Skoggon gathered together in this volume' were licensed to Thomas Colwell 1565-6, but the earliest surviving ed. is of 1626. Cf. *Whip for an Ape*, l. 56 'Whose cause must be by *Scoggins* iests maintainde.'

39. *tedd abroad . . . forke . . . rake*: 'to tedd' is to spread hay. Cf. *Euph.* ii. 16 l. 1 'tedding that with a forke in one yeare, which was not gathered together with a rake in twentie,' and *Mother Bombie*, i. 3. 186-7.

41. *foure & twentie orders of knaues*: the *Liber Vagatorum*, edited by Martin Luther in 1528 and translated by J. C. Hotten 1860, devotes 28 chapters to 28 several orders of mendicant rogues, 'for there are xx ways, *et ultra*, whereby men are cheated and fooled,' p. 8.

P. 413, 1. *saist thou art vnmarried*: cf. *Protestatyon* (?).

3. *cannot abide, Good Lord deliver vs*: alluding to the Puritan dislike of the Litany.

9. *Moldwarpe*: a mole, alluding to Martin's anonymity.

14. *Pasquil . . . liues of the Saints: Countercuffe* (A i verso) 'Pasquill hath posted very dilligently ouer all the Realme, to gather some fruitfull Volume of THE LIVES OF THE SAINTS,' i.e. scandal about the Martinists.

21. *old cutter at the locke*: Halliwell gives a phrase 'to be at his old lock = to follow his old practices,' and perhaps this is the same use, meaning 'old hand at cutting.'

Nam mihi sunt vires, &c.: Ov. *Her*. xvi. 352.

28. *first venew*: 'venue' is an assault or attack in fencing, &c. The phrase, like the exordium 'Room,' &c., may be taken as evidence that *Pappe* is Lyly's first contribution.

30. *fleech*: 'turn or bout,' J. P.

PAPPE WITH AN HATCHET

32. *Matachine*: 'It was well known in France and Italy, by the name of the dance of fools or *matachins*, who were habited in short jackets, with gilt paper helmets, long streamers tied to their shoulders, and bells to their legs. They carried in their hands a sword and buckler, with which they made a clashing noise, and performed various quick and sprightly evolutions,' Douce, *Illustrations of Shakespeare*, ii. 435 (J. P.).

A WHIP FOR AN APE.

P. 418, 1. *Dizard*: actor, dancer, 'fool.' The N. E. D. regards it as a modification of earlier *disour*, a professional story-teller.

11. *Martin Marr-als face*: the earliest instance of the name. Dryden's comedy, *Sir Martin Marrall*, 1667, was an adaptation of an earlier play called *Sir Martin Marplot*.

13. *moppes and mowes* grimaces and wry faces. Generally together, as of Prospero's sprites, *Tempest*, iv. 47 'with mop and mow.' Also as verbs, variant of or allied to *mock*, and of Dutch origin (Skeat).

16. *States*: higher orders of men, as in lines 47, 103.

20. *a Woodcocke tries*: proves himself a woodcock; often as emblem of stupidity, e. g. *L. L. L.* iv. 3. 82 'four woodcocks in a dish,' of the four anchorites in love.

23. *passe*: care (always with negative); only once in Shakespeare (2 *Henry VI*, iv. 2. 136). It may result from a confusion of *pass* as (1) disregard, (2) sanction (cf. the opposed intr. uses (1) scrape through, (2) excel), i.e. the appearance of later favourable senses led to the addition of a negative to express the disfavour properly inherent in the word; but a more simple explanation is 'budge,' 'stir,' 'be altered or affected by.'

25. *Such fleering, leering, iarring*, &c. : cf. Marprelate's *Epistle*, p. 12 (ed. Arber), 'Fleering | iering | leering: there is at all no sence in this period.'

26. *weehees*: the accepted representation of a horse's neigh. *Moth. Bomb.* iv. 2. 194, of the hired hack ' hee neither would cry *wyhie*, nor wag the taile.'

28. *roysters ray*: Halliwell gives *ray* (1) a kind of dance, (4) array, order; either of which will do here.

29. *catch* : breath.

33. *Dame Lawsens lustie lay*: alluding to an encounter between Aylmer, Bishop of London, and the famous shrew and virago Meg Lawson, in which his lordship came off worst, as related in Marprelate's *Epistle*, pp. 10-11 (ed. Arber).

34. *Sir Ieffries ale tub* : alluding to the story told in Marprelate's *Epistle*, p. 38, that Sir Geoffrey Jones, a clergyman in Warwickshire, having sworn an oath not to go to the alehouse again, evaded it by getting his man to carry him thither on his back.

NOTES

49. *Noddie*: 'a fool, *Minsheu*' (Halliwell). Cf. Nash's *Almond*, p. 56 (Petheram), 'bon nute to your Noddishippe.'

51. *patters*: for the grammar, cp. 'staies,' l. 64.

53. *Now Tarleton's dead*: the famous jester died in the previous year, 1588. 'Consort,' company.

56. *Scoggins iests*: cf. *Pappe*, p. 412 l. 24 'deuise some iestes, & become another *Scogen*,' where see note.

67. *rent*: a variant of *rend*, used several times by Shakespeare. Cf. 'Renting his clothes,' *Euphues and his England*, ii. 17 l. 29.

68. *Cappes, Tippets, Gownes, blacke Chiuers, Rotchets white*: among the 'Grosse pointes of poperie' enumerated in Antony Gilby's *Pleasaunte Dialogue*, 1581, are '20 The popish apparaile of the Archebishop and Bishop, the blacke Chimere or sleeueless coate, put vppon the fine white rotchet [surplice]. 21 The great wide sleeued gowne 22 The horned cappe 23 The Tippet.' (Arber's *Introd. Sketch*, p. 32.)

P. 420, 78. *gaine of learning*: university endowments.

85. *The Germaine Boores*, &c.: this allusion is probably one with that which follows, to *Iacke Leydon*. John Becock of Leyden, born at The Hague c. 1490, and brought up as a tailor (butcher, *Harl. Misc.* viii. 258) at Leyden, travelled, and imbibed Anabaptist opinions at Münster in Westphalia. By his preaching there he overthrew in 1534 the authority of the prince-bishop, and was himself named king; but after he had endured a six months' siege, the bishop's troops were admitted by treachery in June, 1535, and John of Leyden was put to death with tortures in January, 1536.

89. *Iacke Strawe*: one of the leaders in Wat Tyler's rebellion, 1381.

ring: i. e. wring, squeeze, press, inveigh against. Cf. *M. Bomb.* iii. 2. 7.

91. *chwere*: ich were, I were. So, often, 'chill,' I will.

92. *swads*: clowns. Whitney quotes 'Let country swains and silly swads be still!'—Greene, *Madrigal*.

94. *raught*: obsolete past participle of 'reach.'

97. *in euery towne*, &c.: cf. *Epitome* (Petheram), p. 36. The *Epistle, Epitome*, and *Hay any Worke* are all devoted to urging the authority of 'pastors, doctors, elders, and deacons, without any bishops.'

101. *Scotland ... whose King so long they crost*, &c.: alluding to the contest of the Presbyterians against episcopacy, from 1575 onwards. They successfully resisted James VI's nomination of Montgomery as archbishop of Glasgow in 1581, and by the Raid of Ruthven in 1582 secured the person of the king and held him prisoner for two months. See Buckle's *Hist. of Civilization*, iii. 94-114, &c.

106. *gegge*: gag.

P. 421, 122. *do without*: effect from outside.

136. *old Lanam ... his rimes*: the only contemporary instances of the name known to me are Robert Laneham, the author of the *Letter* about the Kenilworth festivities (1575), and John Lanham, one of the five

of his players for whom Leicester procured the first royal patent, in May, 1574 (Morley's *English Writers*, viii. 385). The latter is more likely to be alluded to here. In *Martin's Months Minde*, F 2 recto, Martin on his deathbed speaks of jests and 'twittle twattles learned in Alehouses, and at the Theater of Lanam and his fellowes'; and G verso 'All my foolerie I bequeath to my good friend Lanam; and his consort, of whom I first had it.' Collier, *Bibl. Cat.* ii. 513 supposes him author of the *Whip*.

146. *thy worke, and more worke*: More work was promised at end of *Hay any worke* c. March 23, just before *Whip* (vol. i. 50, 55).

P. 422, 153. *a rimer of the Irish race*, &c.: cf. Rosalind in *As You Like It*, iii. 2, where Steevens quotes Ben Jonson's *Poetaster* 'Rhime them to death, as they do Irish rats,' and Malone Sidney's *Defence of Poesie* 'rimed to death, as is said to be done in Ireland.'

MAR-MARTIN.

P. 423, 19. *Let neighbour-nations learne*, &c.: let the religious quarrels of France and Flanders teach, &c. Cf. *Bisham*, vol. i. 475 ll. 12-3.

P. 426, 92. *bumfeges*: cf. *Hay any worke*, p. 24 l. 1 'For ise so bumfeg the Cooper, as he had bin better to haue hooped halfe the tubbes in Winchester, then write against my worships pistles.'

93. *steale counters*: cf. *Hay any worke* (Petheram's Reprint, p. 24, l. 17), 'that old steale counter masse priest, John o Glosseter.'

96. *Cobler Cliffe*: cf. *Hay any worke*, p. 64. 'His grace denieth that euer he hard of any such matter, as that the Iesuit should say, he would becom a braue Cardinal, if popery should come againe. I knowe T. C. that long since he is past shame, and a notorious lyer, otherwise how durst he deny this, seeing Cliffe an honest and a godly cobler, dwelling at Battell bridg, did iustifie this before his grace his teethe, yea and will iustifie the same againe if he be called. So will Atkinson too. Send for them if he dare.'

THE TRIUMPHS OF TROPHIES.

P. 428, 23. *one neck*: recalling Caligula in Suetonius, c. xxx.

P. 429, 42. *bring Palladium in*, &c.: probably Paus. i. 23 § 9, where Demophon protects Attica from Diomede's ravages by capturing the Palladium.

66. *Aser shoes*: Deuteronomy xxxiii. 24-5.

P. 430, 73. *Phætonissa*: name not in Jos. *Ant. Iud.* vi. 14. Probably 'deducere lunam,' Virg. *Ecl.* viii. 70, suggests parallel with Phaeton.

86. *vnseene . . . Giges ring*: confusion of Gyges with Polycrates.

P. 431, 123. *Crowes in Athens*: Plin. x. 15 'omnes e Peloponneso et Attica regione volaverunt,' from Arist. *Hist. Animal.* ix. 40.

137. *Romulus staffe*: a hasty reading of Plut. *Life*, xx. 12.

INDEX OF FIRST LINES OF SONGS AND POEMS.

PLAYS.

		vol. page
Arme, arme, the Foe comes on apace	(*Saph. & Ph.* iii. 2)	ii. 395
Cvpid and my Campaspe playd	(*Camp.* iii. 5)	ii. 343
Fvll hard I did sweate	(*Moth. Bomb.* iii. 4)	iii. 201
Here snores Tophas	(*Endim.* iii. 3)	iii. 45
In Pactolus goe bathe thy wish, and thee	(Oracle, *Mid.* ii. 2)	iii. 128
Iô Bacchus! To thy Table	(*Moth. Bomb.* ii. 1)	iii. 187
'Las! how long shall I	(*Mid.* v. 2)	iii. 154
Merry Knaues are we three-a	(*Saph. & Ph.* ii. 3)	ii. 388
My Daphne's Haire is twisted Gold	(*Mid.* iv. 1)	iii. 142
My shag-haire Cyclops, come, lets ply	(*Saph. & Ph.* iv. 4)	ii. 409
O cruell Loue! on thee I lay	(*Saph. & Ph.* iii. 3)	ii. 399
O Cupid! Monarch ouer Kings	(*Moth. Bomb.* iii. 3)	iii. 198
O for a Bowle of fatt Canary	(*Camp.* i. 2)	ii. 322
O my Teeth! deare Barber ease me	(*Mid.* iii. 2)	iii. 136
O yes, O yes, if any Maid	(*Gall.* iv. 2)	ii. 458
Pan's Syrinx was a Girle indeed	(*Mid.* iv. 1)	iii. 142
Pinch him, pinch him, blacke and blue	(*Endim.* iv. 3)	iii. 59
Rockes, shelues, and sands, and Seas, farewell	(*Gall.* i. 4)	ii. 438
Sing to Apollo, God of Day	(*Mid.* v. 3)	iii. 161
Stand: Who goes there?	(*Endim.* iv. 2)	iii. 58
Stesias hath a white hand	(*Woman,* v. 1)	iii. 281
The Bride this Night can catch no cold	(*Moth. Bomb.* v. 3)	iii. 218
Weigh not in one ballance gold and iustice	(Oracle—*Mid.* v. 3)	iii. 160
Were I a man I could loue thee	(*Woman,* iii. 2)	iii. 261
What Bird so sings, yet so dos wayle	(*Camp.* v. 1)	ii. 351
When Pan Apollo in musick shall excell	(Oracle—*Mid.* v. 3)	iii. 158

SONGS MISSING FROM PLAYS, THOUGH NOTED IN TEXT.

Campaspe, v. 3. 38 by Milectus, Phrygius and Lais (cf. vol. iii. p. 469) ii. 353
Endimion, ii. 3. 40 'the inchantment for sleepe' (cf. vol. iii. p. 470) iii. 39
    „   iii. 4. 1 by Geron . . . . (cf. vol. iii. p. 470) iii. 47

INDEX OF FIRST LINES

	vol. page
Mother Bombie, v. 3. 21 ' The Loue Knot '	iii. 217
Woman in Moone, i. 1. 54 'a roundelay in praise of Nature'	iii. 243
,, i. 1. 224 by the Shepherds to calm Pandora (cf. vol. iii. p. 471)	iii. 248
Loves Metamorphosis, i. 2. 57 by the Nymphs	iii. 304
,, iii. 1. 135 by Niobe and Silvestris	iii. 313
,, iv. 2. 44, 48 by the Syren	iii. 322

ENTERTAINMENTS.

Aoniis prior, & Diuis es pulchrior alti (*Elvetham*)	i. 445
Beauties rose, and Vertues booke (*Harefield*)	i. 495
Behold her lockes like wiers of beaten gold (*Cowdray*)	i. 423
Cynthia Queene of Seas and lands (*Harefield*)	i. 499
Elisa is the fairest Queene (*Elvetham*)	i. 450
Faire Cinthia the wide Oceans Empresse (*Elvetham*)	i. 442
Faire Daphne staye, too chaste because too faire (*Sudeley*)	i. 479
Fortune must now noe more in tryumphe ride (The Lots—*Harefield*)	i. 500
Happie houre, happie daie (*Quarrendon*)	i. 463
Hearbes, wordes, and stones, all maladies haue cured (*Sudeley*)	i. 482
His Golden lockes Time hath to Siluer turn'd (*Tiltyard*)	i. 411
How haps that now, when prime is don (*Elvetham*)	i. 443
I Loricus, Bodie sicke (*Quarrendon*)	i. 467
I that abide in places vnder ground (Aureola in *Elvetham*)	i. 449
I was a giants daughter of this isle (legend on the box, *Theobalds*)	i. 418
If euerie Ioy now had a tongue (*King's Welcome*)	i. 505
In the merrie moneth of May (*Elvetham*)	i. 447
Let fame describe your rare perfection (*Sudeley*)	i. 480
My hart and tongue were twinnes, at once conceaued (*Sudeley*)	i. 479
Now drowsie sleepe, death's image, ease's prolonger (*Quarrendon*)	i. 455
Nuper ad Aonium flexo dum poplite fontem (*Elvetham*)	i. 435
O come againe faire Natures treasure (*Elvetham*)	i. 451
O see sweet Cynthia, how the watry gods (*Elvetham*)	i. 451
Sing you, plaie you, but sing and play my truth (*Sudeley*)	i. 479
Sweet Ioe vouchsafe once to impart (*King's Welcome*)	i. 507
Swel Ceres now, for other Gods are shrinking (*Bisham*)	i. 476
Sylvanus comes from out the leauy groaues (*Elvetham*)	i. 444
Tell me, O Nymphes, why do you (*Harefield*)	i. 497
Th' ancient Readers of Heauens Booke (*Tiltyard*)	i. 414
The fish that seeks for food in siluer streame (*Cowdray*)	i. 429
There is a bird that builds her neast with spice (*Cowdray*)	i. 426
To that Grace that sett us free (*Quarrendon*)	i. 458

594   INDEX OF FIRST LINES

	vol. page
When Neptune late bestowed on me this barke (*Elvetham*)	i. 446
While at the fountaine of the sacred hill (*Elvetham*)	i. 437
With fragrant flowers we strew the way (*Elvetham*)	i. 439

Missing.

'Another song sung of farewell' (*King's Welcome*)	i. 507
'Two Sonnets' (*Rycote*)	i. 489

POEMS (DOUBTFUL).

A seeing friend, yet enemie to rest	iii. 477
A Womans looks	iii. 485
Al ye whom loue or fortune hath betraide	iii. 492
As oft we see before a sudden showre	iii. 498
By wracke late driuen on shore, from Cupids Crare	iii. 475
Come, giue me needle, stitch cloth, silke & chaire	iii. 473
Come heauy sleepe, ye Image of true death	iii. 492
Come liue with mee, and be my deere	iii. 481
Compare the Bramble with the Cedar tree	iii. 483
Councell wch afterward is soughte	iii. 452
Declare, O minde, from fond desires excluded (A Counterloue)	iii. 476
Farewell false loue, the oracle of lyes	iii. 471
Farewell too faire, too chaste but too too cruell	iii. 485
Feede still thy selfe, thou fondling with beliefe	iii. 473
Fond wanton youths make loue a God	iii. 486
Had doting Priam checkt his sonnes desire	iii. 502
Hero care not though they prie	iii. 488
Hey downe a downe did Dian sing	iii. 479
How can he rule well in a common wealth	iii. 449
I feare not death, feare is more paine	iii. 451
I saw my Lady weepe	iii. 471
I smile to see how you devise	iii. 468
I will not soare aloft the skye	iii. 451
If all the Earthe were paper white	iii. 452
If all the world and loue were young	iii. 480
If fathers knew but how to leaue	iii. 490
If fluds of teares could cleanse my follies past	iii. 484
In lingeringe Loue mislikinge growes	iii. 463
In Thesaly, ther Asses fine are kept	iii. 498
In thy weake hiue a wandering waspe hath crept	iii. 502
It was a tyme when silly Bees could speake (*The Bee*)	iii. 494
Lie downe poore heart and die a while for griefe	iii. 501
Life is a Poets fable	iii. 501
Like to a Hermite poore in place obscure	iii. 470

INDEX OF FIRST LINES 595

	vol. page
Moste miserable man, whome wretched fate	iii. 492
My thoughts are wingde with hopes, my hopes with loue	iii. 478
No place commendes the man vnworthie praise	iii. 449
O happ moste harde where truthe doth most beguyle	iii. 469
O loath that Loue whose fynall ayme is Lust	iii. 450
Once did I loue and yet I liue	iii. 487
Ouer theise brookes, trustinge to ease myne eyes	iii. 498
Praisd be Dianas faire and harmles light	iii. 478
Praise blindnesse eies, for seeing is deceit	iii. 484
Princes be fortunes children, & with them	iii. 498
Quod mihi quoque die Veneris mare præbeat escam	iii. 502
Short is my rest, whose to le is ouerlong	iii. 477
Sing wee and chaunt it	iii. 469
Sleepe, Deathes alye, obliuion of teares	iii. 470
Soare I will not, in flighte the grounde ile see	iii. 452
'Softe fire makes sweete mault,' they say	iii. 453
Some men will saye there is a kynde of muse	iii. 499
The brainsicke race that wanton youth ensues	iii. 450
The fountaines smoake, and yet no flames they shewe	iii. 490
The lofty trees whose braunches make sweete shades	iii. 452
The lowest Trees haue tops, the Ante her gall	iii. 482
The moone beeing clouded presently is mist	iii. 502
The statelie pine whose braunches spreade so faire	iii. 455
The thundringe God whose all-embracinge powre	iii. 493
Those eies that holds the hand of euery hart	iii. 475
Those eies which set my fancie on a fire	iii. 474
Though men can cover crime with bold sterne lookes	iii. 502
Vrbe tot in Veneta, scortorum millia cur sunt	iii. 502
What liquor first the earthen pot doth take	iii. 450
When I behoulde the trees in the earthes fayre lyuerye clothed	iii. 448
When I was otherwise then now I am	iii. 472
When loue on time and measure makes his ground	iii. 489
When younglyngs first on Cupide fyxe their sight	iii. 472
Where lingring feare doth once posses the hart	iii. 487
Where wardes are weake, and foes encountering strong	iii. 491
Who loues and would his suite should proue	iii. 459
Why . . . (words wanting)	iii. 499
Women, what are they, charging weather-cocks	iii. 489
Ye loving wormes, come learne of me	iii. 465
You youthfull heads, whose climing mindes	iii. 456

GLOSSARY

Reference is to volume, page, and line. Where no interpretation is given, it is to be found in the Notes by the reference first given, or by that to which 'note' *is appended; or it is unneeded. A few words, e.g.* Anatomy, Controwle, Dissemble, Mislyke, Peevish, Personage, Quesie, Successe, *are used by Lyly in the modern sense, as well as in that here given.*

Abate, blunt, ii. 454. 30, 468. 47.
Abiect, outcast, i. 300. 30, ii. 208. 36, iii. 411. 41.
Aboade, prophesy, i. 435. 7.
Absolute, perfect, ii. 336. 7, 372. 13.
Accustomable, i. 217. 31, ii. 129. 9, 144. 15. *Customable*, grounded on custom, ii. 195. 7.
Adamant, magnet, i. 321. 2, ii. 111. 35.
Adde to, incline to, ii. 457. 25.
Aduentures, at all, chance how it might, ii. 136. 20.
Aegyptian, gipsy, ii. 98. 25.
Affects, affections, disposition, ii. 22. 34, 140. 26, 333. 12.
All to (adv.), all over, iii. 395. 3, 404. 34.
Allude to (tr.), ii. 334. 24.
Alter, change, refresh, ii. 54. 24. Contrast Fr. *altérer*, to make thirsty.
Alteration, distemper, i. 204. 35.
Amiable (of beauty), i. 214. 14, ii. 59. 8, 65. 5, 82. 4, 135. 1, &c.
Amisse (sb.), ill, iii. 274. 151.
Amort, iii. 155. 99.
Anatomy, diagram, descriptive plan, i. 180. 6, iii. 307. 25.
Another gate, another kind of, iii. 177. 12.
Apple-squier, iii. 359. 23.
Argent, money, i. 265. 16.
Argue from a place, ii. 387. 62.
Argue of, accuse of, i. 236. 22.
Armoury, arms (heraldic), ii. 99. 25, 340. 92.
Arrant, arrande, errand, ii. 110. 13, 221. 9, 374. 41.
Aslake, i. 307. 5, iii. 30. 40.
Assayes, at all, ii. 58. 15.
Assoyle, iii. 369. 89.
Assure, affiance, betroth, i. 228. 29, ii. 220. 32, 223. 22, iii. 222. 196. So *assurance*, ii. 218. 31.

Astrologian, astronomer, i. 272. 25.
Astronomer in *mod.* sense, ii. 86. 20; = astrologer, 452. 28.
Attach, take prisoner, i. 213. 9.
Attonement, reconciliation, ii. 146. 5.
Auoide, empty, quit, ii. 398. 80, iii. 56. 71.

Bable, bauble, iii. 43. 41, 154. 61, 400. 32.
Baby, doll, iii. 34. 30; fairy, iii. 63. 166.
Backare, iii. 119. 4.
Bale, pair (of dice), iii. 359. 26.
Ballance (pl.), iii. 117. 50, 118. 92.
Bandora, i. 450. 11 note.
Banket (banquet), dessert, light refection with wine, i. 448. 32; (vb.) i. 199. 15, iii. 188, 30 (to drink nips).
Bare (sb.), naked flesh, iii. 476. 31 (Cf. *King and no King*, ii. 1. 192).
Barly-breake, iii. 158. 12, 457. 19.
Batfowling, ii. 452. 43.
Bauin, i. 218. 32, &c.
Bayte, refreshment, rest, i. 323. 9, ii. 35. 9.
Bear a white mouth, i. 181. 16 note, ii. 21. 14, 82. 10, 224. 36.
Beetle, hammer, iii. 394. 11; (adj.) 121. 66, 403. 10; (adj.) overhanging, iii. 410. 18.
Biggin, nightcap, iii. 399. 39.
Bill, a hedger's tool, i. 180. 28; a weapon, ii. 106. 13, iii. 58. 3.
Bite hot on, border on, iii. 173. 9.
Blacke Oxe treade on their foote, i. 203. 7, ii. 404. 21, iii. 320. 136.
Blanch, head back, ii. 440. 39.
Blancke (scholastic), failure to reply in argument, i. 299. 22.
Blast, withered or fruitless sprout, i. 317. 5, 322. 9, 325. 13, 30, iii. 126. 109. So *to blast* (intr.), ii. 22. 12.

GLOSSARY

Bleere, ii. 460. 5
Blirt! iii. 127. 12.
Bob (sb.), ii. 335. 40, iii. 398. 13;
  (vb.) iii. 186. 100.
Bodkin, dagger, i. 256. 12, 503. 22,
  ii. 28. 12, 385. 5, iii. 186. 29; *bodkin
  beard*, iii. 43. 35, 133. 39.
Boordes, jests, iii. 454. 38 ; cf. ii. 103.
  32 (?), but also iii. 189. 30, ii. 34. 25,
  105. 6.
Bord and cord, i. 448. 16.
Bottle (of hay), truss, iii. 212. 180.
Boult, winnow, ii. 408. 13.
Bouse, booze, iii. 426. 92.
Brabble, brawl, iii. 217. 19.
Bracke, break, flaw (in velvet), i. 179.
  20, 184. 17, 271. 35.
Brawnefallen, i. 263. 27, 307. 30, iii.
  59. 16.
Breaching (adj.), iii. 282. 120.
Breast, voice, ii. 251. 18.
Brewys, brewish, i. 256. 32, iii. 202.
  101.
Brinch, iii. 186. 127.
Broad-stitch, iii. 179. 87.
Broken, torn, i. 182. 6.
Broomy, stubbly (of a beard), i. 480. 5.
Bullaze (pl.), iii. 368. 53.
Bumfege (vb.), iii. 426. 92.
Burbolt, birdbolt, iii. 28. 68, 26. 5 note.
Burn ones cap, iii. 368. 62.
Bushell of salt with, to eate a, i. 197.
  18, 247. 9.
Buske poynt, iii. 259. 40.
Busky, bosky, iii. 268. 287.
Buy, the, the bye, side-issue, i. 245. 16,
  ii. 188. 7.
Bytter, bittern, i. 449. 8, iii. 44. 56
  note, 45. 96.

Caddys, i. 224. 4, ii. 9. 21.
Calamance, iii. 147. 20.
Caliuer, syringe, iii. 411. 16.
Cammocke, i. 196. 1, ii. 23 21, 391.
  108, iii. 41. 37, 450. 15, &c.
Canckred, infected i. 193. 13.
Caper, privateer, ii. 439. 97.
Carbonado, ii. 385. 21.
Carp (tr.), ii. 4. 21 ; cf. i. 428. 27.
Carren, carrion, ii. 157. 24.
Carsie, ii. 199. 33.
Carte, to the, to the gallows, i. 275. 7.
Carterly, i. 190. 28.
Case, pair, iii. 186. 108, 359. 19.
Cast, specimen, iii. 228. 396.
Cast, consider, iii. 123. 3, ii. 25. 85,
  192. 18. *Cast beyonde the Moone*, i.
  222. 31, ii. 152. 27, iii. 188. 6.
Catch, breath, iii. 418. 29.
Cater cap, college-cap, iii. 399. 18.

Cater-tray (dice), iii. 399. 17.
Caule, i. 210. 7 (cf. ii. 155. 23), iii. 121.
  77, 386. 152.
Cease of, iii. 21. 23.
Censer, censure, opinion, ii. 94. 6.
Chamber, small cannon, i. 440. 4, 448.
  23.
Chatting (of birds), i. 491. 19, ii. 315. 3.
Chaundrie, i. 432. 28.
Chaunge ones coppie, i. 224. 31, 236.
  18, ii. 432. 20.
Chestes, chess, ii. 162. 36, i. 484. 27, iii.
  395. 5.
Chicken peeper, iii. 69. 31.
Chirk, chirp, i. 491. 18.
Chiuer, iii. 419. 68.
Chiuerell, doeskin, iii. 407. 36.
Choakpeare, gag, iii. 149. 81.
Chrysocolla, ii. 138. 10, 195. 31, 410.
  21.
Chuffe, miserly churl, iii. 456. 13.
Citterne, gitterne, guitar, i. 450. 11, iii.
  133. 35, 142. 107.
Clap hands, conclude a bargain, ii. 218.
  23.
Claw, sooth, ii. 60. 15, 135. 25, 142. 32.
Cloase, response (fig. from music), i.
  214. 7.
Closing, embrace, iii. 476. 35.
Cloth of estate, ii. 342. 32.
Cockeringe, i. 187. 13, 243. 14, 250. 35,
  iii. 176. 27. *Cockney*, spoiled child,
  i. 244. 17.
Cog, cheat, ii. 378. 29, iii. 178. 26, 449.
  15.
Colde as a clock, i. 247. 2.
Coleworte, cabbage, ii. 154. 17.
Collop, slice, offspring, iii. 182. 172.
Comming (sb.), complaisance, ii. 141.
  28. So *coming* (adj.), iii. 189. 14.
Compasse, calculation, i. 235. 7.
Compasse, to sleepe, ii. 58. 2. *To lyue
  compasse*, ii. 96. 12.
Concaue, sphere (Ptol.), iii. 242. 6.
Conduct, conduit, iii. 116. 8.
Confer, compare, ii. 105. 31, &c.
Consent, harmony, ii. 328. 50, &c.
Consort, company, iii. 419. 53.
Conster, construe, ii. 456. 15, &c. So
  construction, ii. 129. 27.
Contemplature, ii. 51. 3.
Contrary (vb.), ii. 341. 120.
Controwle, rebuke, i. 190. 16, 306. 22,
  ii. 178. 6, iii. 410. 5.
Conuey, contrive, iii. 183. 18. So *con-
  ueiaunce*, ii. 410. 15.
Cony-gat, i. 418. 16.
Cookemate, cockmate, i. 208. 2, 278. 22,
  280. 1.
Copheigth, on, i. 425. 32.

Corasiues, i. 241. 17, 253. 23, 285. 32, ii. 444. 94, &c.
Cornute, iii. 266. 213.
Cosinne of, to make a, to cozen, ii. 21. 22.
Cote, comment, ii. 51. 28 ; quote, ii. 93. 33.
Cotton (vb.), ii. 340. 117, iii. 207. 81, 210. 84.
Couin, iii. 157. 163.
Counterfaite, portrait, i. 179. 20, 181. 8, ii. 3. 13, &c. So *counterfeiting*, ii. 321. 57.
Counteruaile, i. 207. 5.
Course accompt of, to make, i. 202. 22, 261. 6. *Of course*, conventional, i. 235. 32 (cf. 254. 11), ii. 141. 3.
Coystrel, iii. 184. 48 (see note).
Crabbs, to stamp, iii. 200. 30.
Crake of, i. 235. 22, ii. 67. 8.
Crare, bark, iii. 475. 19.
Craze, crack slightly, i. 189. 22, 205. 28, 466. 7.
Crick-crack, iii. 359. 33 ; cf. iii. 367. 11.
Crippin, hair-net, iii. 121. 80.
Crock vp, pot, iii. 196. 3.
Croslet, crucible, ii. 442. 10.
Crosscloth, i. 502. 26, iii. 410. 17 ; cf. ii. 63. 26.
Crowde, fiddle, ii. 328. 50. So *crouding*, iii. 219. 78.
Crye creeke or *creake*, i. 247. 4.
Cucurbit, ii. 143. 28, 442. 18.
Cull, embrace, ii. 5. 4, 139. 9.
Cullis, i. 212. 16, ii. 342. 51.
Cure, patient, i. 214. 2.
Curtoll, iii. 71. 101. *Curtall* (sb.), iii. 411. 18.
Cutter at the locke, iii. 413. 21.

Dandle, indulge, spoil, iii. 179. 60.
Decensore, ii. 442. 19.
Defie, renounce, iii. 374. 155.
Dehort, dissuade, i. 246. 28.
Delicatest, i. 185. 36.
Dent at, aim or pierce at, ii. 139. 22.
Depriue, destroy, i. 233. 21.
Descry, declare, iii. 490. 29.
Deskant, harmony, as opposed to melody, i. 236. 3, 254. 23, 272. 11.
Dicker, set of ten, iii. 399. 22.
Discusse, shake asunder, iii. 249. 21.
Disordinate, ii. 181. 14.
Dispence with, tolerate, ii. 414. 8.
Dissemble, conceal, ii. 3. 17, 130. 2.
Dissolute, untidy, i. 256. 23.
Diuision, musical variation, i. 443. 20.
Dizard, iii. 418. 1, 148. 43.
Dodkin, Dutch coin, iii. 188. 28.
Dogbolt, ii. 320. 8.

Dragges, ii. 56. 23 note.
Drib, ii. 453. 5.
Drie cuppe, beating, iii. 123. 141.
Dudgin, dudgen, marked with cross-lines, iii. 184. 36. *Dugeon, dudgin* (sb.), gravity, displeasure, iii. 207. 74, 403. 7.
Dyaper, variegation, iii. 354. 56.
Dydopper, dabchick, iii. 395. 7.
Dysease (as general negative of *ease*), i. 230. 27, 236. 16, 245. 12, iii. 136. 139.

Earn, yearn, iii. 225. 297 ; grieve, 258. 63.
Eftsoones, soon after, ii. 25. 28.
Eiesse, i. 249. 8.
Elemente, the, the atmosphere, i. 293. 23, 31, ii. 34. 23.
Eleuation, latitude, ii. 86. 20.
Epact, ii. 453. 68.
Escape, escapade, fault, i. 280. 24, 282. 35, ii. 213. 6.
Espial, spy, ii. 26. 12, 31. 5.
Euet, eft, ii. 89. 29.
Ewery, i. 432. 28.
Excantation, ii. 118. 33.
Expire (tr.), i. 222. 17, 457. 21.
Extended, be, pass on, operate on (legal), i. 457. 17.
Eye full, to drink but ones (of abstinence), ii. 56. 8. Cf. *Eare ful*, ii. 200. 29.

Faburthen, ii. 83. 32. [342.
Fact, deed, ii. 207. 34, 336. 14, iii. 226.
Fadge, fodge, iii. 55. 27, 174. 40, &c.
Falling bande, i. 503. 4.
False, break (a vow), ii. 447. 23. So *falsor*, iii. 272. 73.
False fire, blank cartridge, ii. 98. 31. (Cf. *Ham.* iii. 2. 277).
Fangle, i. 255. 6.
Fardle, bundle, iii. 398. 26.
Fare, prob. faro, iii. 449. 25.
Fauour, colours, iii. 125. 82 ; features, look, ii. 15. 5, 321. 67, &c.
Feate, apt, i. 195. 33.
Feather, cut a, make a foam at the bows, ii. 439. 97 ; split a hair (ib.).
Fetch a windlesse, ii. 51. 20.
Fleech, flitch, slice, iii. 413. 30.
Fleete, skim, scrape, ii. 107. 23.
Fleeting, fickleness, i. 197. 15, 205. 33, 239. 11.
Fletcher, arrow maker, i. 180. 29, ii. 409. 53.
Flewde, iii. 147. 7.
Flock, lock of wool, iii. 146. 61, 157. 149, 411. 22.
Foote cloth, ii. 347. 9, i. 507. 30, &c.
Force, make of force, care for, i. 225.

GLOSSARY 599

31, ii. 94. 24. *No force*, no matter, ii. 48. 14.
Forslow, neglect, i. 266. 31.
Foyne (sb.), thrust, iii. 399. 20.
Foyste, cheat, iii. 449. 35.
Fraile (*of figges*), iii. 209. 50.
Fretter, kind of apple, iii. 45 101.
Friskett, small sparrow, i. 491. 19.
Frowning cloth, ii. 63. 26. *Powting cros-cloath*, iii. 410. 17, i. 502. 26.
Frumpe, taunt, i. 237. 35, 249 6, &c.
Furious, mad, ii. 326. 134.

Gally mafrey, hodge podge, ii. 322. 80, iii. 115. 18.
Garde, trimming, ii. 10. 21.
Gascoins, iii. 209. 39.
Gawde, toy, iii. 245. 109.
Gawlded, i. 257. 7 (*gauled*, i. 285. 15).
Gall, a sore, ii. 129. 20.
Gaze, treasure, iii. 432. 182.
Geason (adj.), rare, i. 195. 19.
Gegge, gag, iii. 420. 106.
Gestures, *want*, lack social readiness, i. 200. 12.
Giglot, iii. 222. 173, 304. 61.
Girde (tr.), taunt, ii. 183. 10; (sb.) ii. 68. 34. So *girders*, ii. 334. 30.
Girdle, *a rod under the*, iii. 34. 14, i. 185. 15.
Glazeworme, glasseworme, i. 274. 14.
Glead, ii. 224. 26.
Glorious, boastful, ii. 82. 13.
Glyeke, *gleek*, *glicke*, i. 237. 21, ii. 68. 35.
Go by, get one gone, ii. 395. 61.
Gods blessing . . . warme sunne, i. 322. 4, ii. 93. 36 (opposition, originally, of those who entered the cool cathedral for service, and those who sat on the alebench outside?).
Gods good, yeast, iii. 186. 117; digestive, ii. 17. 10.
Good cheape, i. 195. 2.
Gore bloud, *in a*, ii. 406. 28.
Grauelled, ii. 153. 25.
Greate horse, i. 287. 10, ii. 452. 35.
Grisping, twilight, ii. 20. 7.
Gryphe, griffin, ii. 445. 111.
Guest, host, iii. 118. 97.
Gup, iii. 155. 101, 177. 14.

Hab, *nab*, ii. 123. 11. Cf. *Hobier*.
Hacker, swaggerer, iii. 398. 18.
Hag, witch, i. 255. 3, ii. 442. 5, iii. 59. 27, 140. 21.
Haggard, wild hawk, i. 219. 35. So *haggarde* (adj.), i. 253. 23, ii. 391. 1; *haggardnes*, i. 191. 12.
Haire, *against the*, ii. 359. 10.

Hammers, *head full of*, iii. 184. 59; cf. iii. 203. 123, 225. 291, 409. 19.
Handsel, earnest-money, iii. 218. 52.
Hangby, hanger on, iii. 426. 99, 125.
Haue no shew, i. 191. 13, 209. 32, 321. 8, ii. 461. 16.
Haunce, tilt up, iii. 410. 24.
Heaue at, be nauseated with, ii. 317. 18.
Heavers at, i. 419. 28.
Hediock, iii. 284. 193.
Heedie, ii. 170. 22.
Heele, *short in the*, of frailty, iii. 137. 33, ii. 179. 5, i. 504 note.
Heidegyes, dances, iii. 60. 41.
Herbor, arbour (=harbour, Skeat), ii. 129. 10. Cf. *herbage*, iii. 133. 23.
Highte (ptcp.), iii. 357. 175, 377. 87.
Hobby, falcon, ii. 219. 9, &c.
Hobler, mark for tossing at, iii. 217. 14.
Hold tack, iii. 201. 57.
Honnie Moone (as a time of careless youth), ii. 49. 29.
Hose (sing.), stocking or breech, ii. 7. 5.
Hoxe, hamstring, iii. 203. 115.
Huddle (sb.), what is huddled in wraps, what is coddled and petted; of a baby, iii. 219. 77; of old men, i. 194. 9, iii. 184. 38; of a girl's lover, i. 247. 4; of luxurious livers, ii. 345. 76.
Hungerly, i. 206. 13, ii. 20. 22; cf. *angerlie*, i. 466. 31.
Husband, husbandman, i. 253. 4.
Hymen, nuptial hymn, ii. 472. 194.

Iack, coat of leather sewn over iron, ii. 193. 24.
Ieniting, early apple, i. 492. 24.
Iennet, i. 282. 37, 313. 1, ii. 166. 14, iii. 483. 24.
Iel (vb.), strut, iii. 367. 1, 375. 8.
Illustrate, illustrious, iii. 383. 25.
Imbost, beaded with sweat, iii. 147. 27.
Impe (sb.), i. 185. 23, 192. 4, 248. 8, 260. 22, 267. 4; (vb.) ii. 34. 4.
Improue, raise rent, iii. 211. 12.
Incontinently, immediately, i. 227. 8.
Induction, reasoning, plan, ii. 44. 17 (cf. *Rich. III*, i. 1. 32).
Infer, allege, instance, ii. 145. 16.
Infestious, dangerous, iii. 272. 74.
Ingramnesse, ignorance, iii. 426. 95 (tr. *ingram*, corruption of law-term *ignoramus*, Cent. Dict.).
Iniurie, injure, ii. 337. 43.
Iniurious, insulting, iii. 22. 31.
Insteppe, *high in the*, of pride, i. 202. 24, 504 note, ii. 179. 5, iii. 34. 34, 137. 33.
Intend, attend to, i. 418. 6.
Intention, tightening, ii. 147. 23.
Iost there vp (to a horse), iii. 215. 7.

GLOSSARY

Ioynd stoole (folding), iii. 209. 28.
Ioynter, joining, iii. 242. 9.
Iump with, to be, ii. 326. 130.

Key colde, iii. 206. 43.
Kinde (sb.), nature, iii. 374. 142, 379. 44, 463. 12. *Kynde* (adj.), true bred, natural, i. 206. 11, 31, 247. 7, 459. 23, ii. 130. 28.
Kixes, iii. 405. 25.
Knacking (of the hands), iii. 133. 34.
Knottes, garden-beds, i. 187. 30, 37, ii. 82. 1, 205. 7.
Know ones good (generally), ii. 23. 36; (specially, of polite or proper behaviour), ii. 161. 29, iii. 137. 41, 178. 38, 317. 70.

Lady longings, kind of fruit, iii. 45. 101.
Lambacke (vb.), cudgel, iii. 400. 35.
Larkes, to haue, iii. 278. 291 note.
Lauish, reckless, abusive, iii. 394. 29, 396. 28, 426. 111. So *lauishnes*, ii. 148. 21; *lavishly*, iii. 454. 4.
Laund, lawn, i. 424. 9.
Lay cushions vnder the elbowe of, i. 195. 31, 282. 4. Cf. ii. 348. 31.
Leach, jelly, i. 449. 19.
Leade Apes in hell, i. 220. 32, 230. 26, ii. 61. 14.
Leads, gutter, iii. 217. 14.
Leash (vb.), iii. 147. 16.
Leaue (intr.), cease, ii. 194. 25.
Leefekye, lyfkie, i. 255. 7.
Leere, tape, i. 224. 4; learning, iii. 194. 47.
Legeritie, nimbleness, iii. 353. 39.
Legge, to make a, ii. 440. 24.
Leies, leas, ii. 453. 6.
Leripoope, elementary knowledge, common sense, *savoir faire*, i. 483. 7, ii. 377. 6 (see note), iii. 181. 128, 407. 31.
Leuell, aim, ii. 468. 80, iii. 401. 16.
List, edge, iii. 394. 23.
Local, medical term for remedies of external application, ii. 396. 20.
Loitersacke, idle rogue, iii. 188. 4.
Longis, i. 254. 2, ii. 97. 35.
Look, look for, i. 194. 32.
Louely, loving, iii. 78. 243, 137. 51, 465. 36.
Louing wormes, ii. 182. 3, 357. 127, iii. 188. 15.
Lump, lump-fish, i. 429. 20, iii. 45. 98.
Lurcher, robber, iii. 34. 9.
Lynces, lynxes, ii. 316. 15.
Lyste (sb.), desire, i. 201. 17, ii. 44. 3. 103. 12.
Lysteth, it (impers.), i. 315. 27.
Lythernesse, ii. 50. 31, iii. 59. 18.

Make, mate, i. 239. 20, &c.
Make (one) for, disable, iii. 371. 35.
Makebate, libeller, iii. 421. 130.
Malice (tr.), i. 439. 6, ii. 41. 23, 139. 18.
Maltmare, iii. 214. 213.
Mammering, i. 253. 14, 488. 31, ii. 75. 25, 148. 22.
Manchet, i. 256. 33.
Manne (vb.), escort, ii. 68. 25, 439. 90; tame (a hawk), ii. 139. 1.
Manuary (adj.), i. 289. 21.
Mase, frighten, ii. 195. 27.
Masticke, iii. 136. 142.
Matachine, iii. 413. 32.
Mate, confound, iii. 274. 157, 494. 28.
Mawmet, iii. 360. 60 (i. 54, note 2).
Meane, moderate, ii. 83. 5, 108. 26, 324. 43, &c.
Mecocke, i. 249. 2.
Medicines, drugs, poisons, i. 427. 21, ii. 108. 23, iii. 25. 76.
Meetly, moderately (fr. vb. *mete*), i. 256. 37.
Mermaid, a fish, i. 449. 12; cf. 428. 5.
Messe, set of four, iii. 186. 122.
Methridate, a medicine, ii. 126. 34, 396. 12; sovereign remedy, ii. 116. 5, 396. 13, iii. 150. 47.
Mingle-mangle, iii. 115. 19.
Misdeeme (sb.), iii. 477. 27.
Mislyke, displease, i. 180. 16.
Miss the cushion, i. 237. 22.
Mockage, ii. 114. 14.
Moneths minde, ii. 217. 26.
Moppe, grimace (with *mowe*), iii. 418. 13.
Moulwarpe, moldwarpe, mole, ii. 119. 31, iii. 413. 9; also *molde*, i. 478. 16, *moole*, 489. 15, *moold* (ib.), and *mowle*, ii. 383. 131.
Mouse (of beef), ii. 377. 11.
Mowe (vb.), grimace, iii. 280. 20, 406. 7; (sb.) iii. 418. 13, 421. 133.
Moysture, moisten, ii. 396. 18.
Muble fubles, iii. 155. 104, 410. 19.
Mue, mew, prison, properly the place where hawks are kept, i. 425. 5; (vb.), iii. 186. 113.
Mump, whine, iii. 214. 213, 406. 7.
Murlemewes, riddles, iii. 369. 94.
Murrian, Moor, ii. 89. 13.
Muses, in hir, i. 237. 11.
Mushrumpe, mushroom, iii. 155. 108.
Muzroule, noseband, iii. 410. 9.
Mych, ii. 59. 18, iii. 188. 28. *Micher*, iii. 182. 191, 221. 162.
Mysell, to rain fine drops, ii. 406. 59.

Nayle (cloth measure), iii. 157. 173.

GLOSSARY

Neate (pl.), cattle, iii. 348. 200.
Neats-feete, walk on ones, iii. 401. 23.
Neere, come (fig. of a home-thrust), ii. 448. 76, iii. 129. 90.
Nethermore (adv.), ii. 32. 7.
Nippe, biting saying, i. 200 31, &c. *To nippe in the head* (of a sudden, disconcerting speech or incident), i. 237. 26, ii. 127. 5.
Nowle, iii. 187. 155.

Occupy, use, i. 196. 3, 12, ii. 32. 2.
Occupation, mechanical trade, iii. 27. 46.
Oft (adj.), iii. 478. 21. Cf. *seldome*.
Olde (intensive adj.), absolute, excessive, ii. 7. 11, iii. 375. 188.
Onely (adj.), mere, bare, i. 216. 29, iii. 252. 126; cf. ii. 464. 61.
Oppugne, attack, iii. 425. 74.
Orient (colour), iii. 70. 95, 260. 9.
Ouerhear, overreach, iii. 132. 10, 134. 75.
Ouerlashinge, i. 209. 5, 246. 9, 280. 35, 309. 20.
Ouertaken, drunk, iii. 192. 2.
Ouerthwart (vb.), ii. 104. 32, 143. 13; (sb.) i. 65. 1, ii. 335. 38, iii. 40. 17, 331. 141; *ouerthwartnesse*, i. 203. 23.
Owches, gems, ornaments, i. 224. 3.

Pace, parse, iii. 181. 140.
Painted sheth with leaden dagger, i. 215. 9, 255. 30, iii. 120. 41.
Pantuffles, pantophles, pantables, iii. 34. 32 note, &c.
Pap with a hatchet, iii. 180. 105, 404. 33.
Partlet, ii. 68. 8.
Pass (abs.), excel, exceed, ii. 320. 27; care, iii. 418. 23 note.
Passage, game at dice, iii. 399. 15.
Pastery, bakehouse, i. 433. 7.
Pax, sacred tablet, i. 488. 7.
Payre, pack, ii. 437. 32, iii. 155. 79.
Pease (sing.), ii. 5. 10, i. 481. 33, 492. 15.
Peece, a (implying beauty), ii. 88. 1, 457. 48.
Peeuishnes, folly, iii. 160. 73 note, and often. So *pieuish*, ii. 42. 1, &c.
Pellitory, iii. 136. 141.
Pelting, paltry, ii. 352. 12, &c.
Pendant, pennon, i. 433. 31.
Penthouse, moustache, iii. 133. 39.
Pepper in the nose, to take, i. 257. 5, ii. 141. 21, iii. 394. 3.
Perish (tr.), ii. 383. 125.
Personage, personal beauty, ii. 73 note, and often.
Petegree, pedigree, ii. 153. 29, iii. 400. 19.

Petitoes, iii. 138. 54.
Pheere, i. 197. 25, 230. 23, 235. 6, 256. 9.
Picke (vb.), pitch, i. 428. 30.
Pigges nye, pigsnie, i. 253. 14, iii. 188. 24.
Pike deuant (beard), iii. 153. 8, 406. 6.
Pike of pleasure, a firework, i. 448. 30.
Pin, pen up, ii. 376. 27, 437. 20.
Pinch of, ii. 8. 29.
Pinch courtesie (two senses), i. 215. 32 note; cf. *strain courtesie*.
Pinch on the parsons side, i. 230. 33.
Pingler, i. 249. 15.
Pink, small Dutch vessel, i. 486. 33.
Pink, stab, flicker, iii. 410. 21.
Pismyre, ant, iii. 483. 4.
Pitch, fix, iii. 66. 111, 160. 102.
Pitty at, i. 186. 31.
Plancher, pallet, iii. 355. 125.
Platforme, picture-scheme, ii. 355. 78.
Playne, open, i. 277. 32, ii. 432. 1.
Plight, pleat, ii. 10. 20.
Point, a tagged lace, ii. 438. 1, i. 501. 10.
Politian, politician, ii. 378. 25.
Polt foote, i. 179. 10, 239. 22.
Portague, iii. 128. 41.
Portmouth, twitch, iii. 410. 9.
Pose, cold, iii. 155. 109, 214. 218.
Pottle-pot, ii. 444. 82.
Poudred, salted, iii. 202. 102.
Powting, eel-powt, iii. 45. 98.
Prefer, plead, urge, ii. 39. 19.
Pretence, proposition, contention, i. 191. 5; mental attitude, iii. 454. 26.
Prick in cloutes, sew, ii. 357. 136, iii. 179. 60.
Prick song, ii. 351. 36.
Priest, be ones, perform one's funeral, ii. 102. 4.
Princockes, pert youth, iii. 178. 33.
Print, in (of immaculate appearance), ii. 168. 33.
Proofe, armour, iii. 131. 71.
Proyne, i. 263. 25.
Pugge, good fellow, iii. 56. 58.
Pur, post, pare (cards), iii. 155. 79.
Pursnet, iii. 453. 67.
Put to ones trump, ii. 339. 60.
Puttocke, i. 235. 26.
Pyble, ii. 432. 13, iii. 282. 101.
Pykes, rocks, i. 189. 7, 253. 25.

Quatted (Lat. *coactare*), i. 194. 7.
Que, cue, iii. 192. 21, 404. 38.
Quesie, nauseating, i. 194. 8.
Quest, jury, iii. 203. 131.
Questionest, disputant, iii. 246. 163.
Quiddity, i. 272. 23.

GLOSSARY

Quils, feathers, ii. 405. 17, 433. 31.
Quyller, half-fledged bird, iii. 68. 22.
Quippe (vb.), i. 183. 5, 184. 14, ii. 334. 28.
Quirk, i. 272. 22, ii. 8. 15 note, &c.
Quod, i. 179. 13.
Quoyings, ii. 57. 17.

Rabbit sucker, iii. 69. 30.
Rack, stretch, strain (of raising rents), i. 427. 18, iii. 211. 114; (of laborious composition), iii. 412. 3.
Racke (of mutton), iii. 203. 112.
Raisons of the sunne, iii. 203. 130.
Rampe, jade, romp, ii. 395. 80.
Rascall, lean deer, iii. 351. 340.
Rase, scraping, remnant, ii. 28. 25 (but ph. = *race*).
Rate from (of a dog), ii. 353. 27.
Raught, reached, iii. 420. 94.
Raughter, raft, ii. 436. 6.
Ray, array, iii. 418. 28, 430. 80.
Reap vp, rip up (found i. 511. 22, &c.), ii. 143. 30.
Receite, position taken to await driven game, ii. 178. 32, iii. 327. 5.
Record, remember, i. 303. 31, ii. 25. 14, 35. 19, 185. 8, iii. 348. 228; flute or sing (of birds), i. 439. 32, ii. 58. 7, iii. 258. 79, 376. 42.
Recumbentibus, cum, iii. 154. 48.
Recure (vb.), i. 208. 21, 36, &c., probably originally identical with *recover*, M.E. *recoeuren*, though distinguished from it by Lyly, i. 320. 25-6; (sb.) iii. 33. 92, &c.
Reduce, bring back, i. 234. 30, ii. 19. 12.
Refell, ii. 109. 28, &c.
Rent, rend, ii. 17. 29, iii. 59. 22, 72. 42, 409. 40, 419. 67, 423. 9; also as past tense of 'rend,' iii. 66. 109.
Resiluation, ii. 90. 8.
Resorte, society, i. 192. 23 (cf. *Two Gent.* i. 2. 4).
Rest (tr.), desist from, ii. 129. 1.
Rest, set vp ones, iii. 398. 14.
Restoritie, restorative, ii. 129. 23 (also in Ab. Fleming's Pref. to his transl. of Dr. Caius's treatise on *English Dogs*, 1576).
Retchles, i. 185. 18.
Rid, remove, ii. 404. 31, iii. 175. 86.
Rigge (vb.), iii. 122. 90.
Ring, wring, abuse, iii. 196. 7, 420. 89; (intr.) bear the blame, iii. 219. 101.
Rippier, fish-carrier, iii. 405. 18.
Rising, yeast, iii. 186. 117.
Roage, tramp, iii. 412. 15, 33.

Rochet, iii. 399. 36, 419. 68.
Rod under the girdle, put a, i. 185. 15, iii. 34. 14.
Roist (vb.), iii. 175. 65, 449. 32. *Royster* (sb.), iii. 394. 7.
Rope-ripe, rascal, iii. 359. 19.
Rore, roare, to, to revel, riot, ii. 388. 108, 395. 76, 438. 88.
Roue at (of a bad aim), iii. 401. 16.
Round (vb.), whisper, i. 217. 23.
Round hose, iii. 209. 39.
Rowle (of hair), i. 254. 37, iii. 121. 78.
Ruddock, robin, iii. 125. 75.
Rundle, globe, iii. 242. 11.
Rundlet, runlet, iii. 198. 41.
Russet (sb. or adj.), ii. 199. 31, i. 424 footnote.
Ryfe (adv.), frequently, i. 189. 25.

Salamich, iii. 313. 129.
Salfe, ii. 142. 8. *Salfely*, ii. 144. 6.
Sallet, salad, iii. 115. 9.
Saunce, Sanctus, a hymn, iii. 54. 33.
Scaddle, thievish, iii. 395. 6.
Scamble, scramble, ii. 393. 3, 405. 6.
Score (sc. yards), i. 432. 19, 448. 34.
Sealed (fig. of a bird whose eyes are sewn up to make it fly high), ii. 344. 41.
Searcloth (cerecloth), ii. 33. 35.
Seek to, resort to, ii. 110. 2.
Seldome (adj.), ii. 31. 20.
Sensiue, reasoning, iii. 448. 25.
Sentence, maxim, ii. 94. 5, 158. 17, 322. 77.
Sequel, subordinate, ii. 45. 35.
Set a sale on, give an air to, iii. 377. 82.
Setting on, entertainment, iii. 194. 59.
Sew, drain, exhaust, ii. 174. 13.
Shadow, bonnet-border, i. 255. 7, iii. 121. 80.
Shadow, represent in painting, i. 180. 2, ii. 3. 8, &c. *Shadowes*, paintings, ii. 42. 20, 153. 20, iii. 124. 18 (?).
Shake ones eares, ii. 35. 12.
Shark, play pirate, i. 499. 27.
Sheeres to goe betweene, i. 195. 30, iii. 404. 4.
Shent, scolded, iii. 37. 143, 467. 32.
Shiuers, fragments, iii. 66. 110.
Shoar vp, ii. 20. 32.
Shrinke, quit, iii. 214. 224.
Shrowd, shrewd, iii. 148. 68.
Sib, related, iii. 377. 70.
Single, buck's tail, iii. 147. 26.
Sirts, quicksands, iii. 450. 25.
Sise, regulate, measure, ii. 31. 36.
Sithence, since, ii. 328. 46, &c.
Sizing, yeast, iii. 186. 117.

GLOSSARY

Skilleth, matters, ii. 30. 12, 151. 18, 355. 56.
Skin, become skinned over, i. 309. 12.
Skincker, iii. 187. 152.
Slake (intr.), iii. 357. 202.
Sleeke stone, i. 219. 6, ii. 9. 19. *Sleek* (vb.), i. 254. 33.
Sleeuelesse, bootless, i. 253. 17 note, iii. 405. 17 note.
Slibber, i. 254. 34.
Slights, sleights, i. 221. 24, &c.
Slip, counterfeit coin, iii. 184. 53.
Slipstring, truant, iii. 184. 54.
Sliue (vb.), slice, iii. 412. 10.
Smacke, taste, ii. 12. 22; smattering, i. 287. 11, 316. 29, ii. 13. 30.
Smell to, ii. 160. 9, iii. 188. 17, 307. 31.
Smother, smoulder, i. 190. 36.
Snaphance, firelock, iii. 184. 39.
Snort, snore, ii. 213. 12, 401. 57.
Snuffkin, snuftkin, muff, i. 520. 25.
Soake, exhaust, i. 186. 5.
Sod, past tense of *seethe* (intr.), iii. 405. 40; (tr.) iii. 198. 47.
Soile oneself, take refuge, ii. 127. 12 (?). So *take soyle*, iii. 147. 27 note.
Soiourn, sojourner, ii. 192. 12 (but cf. ii. 221. 7).
Sooth, flatter, i. 186. 5, &c.; affirm to be sooth, i. 262. 15.
Sound (vb.), swoon, i. 218. 5, 483. 1, ii. 86. 3, 107. 5, iii. 248. 216. *A sowne*, a swoon, ii. 392. 22.
Souterlie, iii. 412. 5.
Speak in your cast, ii. 55. 6, 172. 24, iii. 217. 20.
Spill, destroy, mar, ii. 440. 32
Spotte (for the face), i. 255. 7, iii. 121. 80.
Springall, youngster, iii. 409. 22.
Spurblinde, short-sighted, ii. 384. 20.
Spurne (sb.), kick, iii. 399. 23.
Spurre (vb., of disputation), ii. 206. 20, 208. 23, 213. 185, 395. 3, 396. 21.
Squat, at the, low-couched, ii. 180. 11.
Squirrell (vb.), iii. 188. 13, 399. 9.
Squirrilitie, scurrility, iii. 399. 8.
Stain, dim, outshine, i. 199. 29, ii. 22. 36, 317. 12.
Stale, pretext, i. 226. 20, 238. 23; decoy, iii. 269. 301.
Stand, cask, iii. 193. 32.
Stand on ioynts, iii. 373. 133.
Stand vpon, consist in, ii. 194. 36; be arrested by, ii. 323. 28; take one's stand on, ii. 386. 30.
Stand vpon no ground, iii. 213. 188.
Standes mee vppon, it, i. 190. 14, ii. 52. 16.
Standing (hunter's), iii. 364. 228.

Standing cup, ii. 96. 35, iii. 139. 94.
Starter, runaway, truant, i. 205. 17, 222. 10. So *start*, shirk, ii. 72. 3.
States, people of rank and position, i. 312. 9, 428. 27, ii. 378. 29, iii. 418. 16, 420. 103, 426. 102.
Statute Marchant, iii. 214. 225.
Sterne, to rule the, i. 310. 28.
Sterue, die, i. 218. 31.
Stocke, capital, ii. 226. 27.
Stomacher, front of bodice, i. 503. 71, ii. 10. 20.
Straine curtesie, or *cursie*, be unceremonious, ii. 81. 13, iii. 199. 34; be ceremonious, ii. 220. 9.
Straunger, foreigner, ii. 84. 6, 90. 12, 102. 12, &c.
Strike the stroke, ii. 194. 34.
String, in a, ii. 92. 26, 374. 39. Cf. *in a chaine*, iii. 37. 138.
Striued, ii. 53. 11, iii. 430. 82.
Stroken, i. 292. 20, 293. 20, ii. 17. 27.
Stroute, strowte, strut, iii. 28. 86.
Successe, issue, sequel, i. 225. 12, ii. 129. 8, iii. 51. 182, 129. 3, 195. 10.
Succorie, chicory, i. 470. 2.
Suckat, a sweetmeat, i. 449. 19.
Sulloume, i. 189. 37, 254. 20, ii. 85. 2.
Solens, the, ii. 63. 26, 392. 26.
Supersticious, scrupulous, i. 210. 15. So *supersticiously*, i. 207. 15.
Surbated, wearied, i. 478. 22.
Suspition, implication, ii. 178. 20.
Swad, iii. 148. 49, 420. 92, 426. 108.
Swallow a gudgen, i. 214. 33, 240. 1.
Swelt, broil, iii. 425. 65.

Table, picture, i. 271. 36, ii. 6. 32, 204. 18. *Tablet*, miniature, ii. 86. 28.
Table-men (backgammon), iii. 152. 3.
Taint (vb.), tent (medical), i. 212. 11, ii. 88. 20. *A tent*, ii. 132. 24.
Take hart at grasse, i. 212. 12, ii. 54. 31.
Take keepe, iii. 375. 14.
Taken tardie (of truants caught), ii. 328. 37, iii. 192. 1.
Takings, in your, iii. 122. 95.
Tantonie, St. Anthony, iii. 184. 37.
Tedd, ii. 16. 1, iii. 412. 39.
Teen, keen, i. 184. 30, ii. 34. 3.
Teene, injury, vexation (AS. *teóna*), i. 457. 13.
Tenter, stretching-frame, iii. 194. 63.
Tetars, ii. 128. 1.
Thoughts cannot hang together (of inconstancy), ii. 379. 30, 459. 37.
Tickle, unstable, ii. 212. 18.
Timpany, dropsy, ii. 24. 3.
Tosse (books), i. 241. 23.
Totterd, tattered, iii. 67. 127.

GLOSSARY

Touch, touchstone, i. 207. 11, 219. 15, ii. 122. 5; also *touchstone*, ii. 102. 11.
Tourne my tippet, i. 246. 32.
Toy, take a, i. e. fancy, iii. 464. 4.
Trayn by the bloud, ii. 104. 20.
Trayne (intr.), i. 186. 1; (tr.) ii. 435. 1, &c.
Treacle, a medicine or healing plant, i. 236. 26, 242. 5, ii. 99. 30, 126. 28, &c.
Trudge (sb.), rebuke or blow, i. 272. 14; but cf. *Cent. Dict.* s. v.
Turkie, turquoise, ii. 317. 12, 404. 14.
Tuske, beat (woods), ii. 440. 56.
Tyre, pull, i. 325. 10, iii. 214. 201 (?).

Vailes, fees, iii. 467. 4.
Vaine, blood, relative, i. 456. 5; or 'spirit,' 'temper.'
Vamp, ii. 388. 109.
Vary, quarrel, iii. 223. 209.
Vayle, lower (Fr. *avaler*), i. 255. 37, iii. 45. 83, 284. 164.
Venew, thrust, bout, iii. 413. 28.
Vies, a, iii. 399. 11; *drop vie*, ib.
Virginals, iii. 134. 85.
Visarde, i. 189. 1, 200. 20, ii. 92. 19, 105. 28.
Vnacquainted, unknown, ii. 388. 1, &c.
Vncoth, i. 465. 18, iii. 349. 238.
Vnhappily (of mischief or naughtiness), ii. 356. 112; so *vnhappy*, ii. 413. 55, 440. 37.
Vnkembd, iii. 304. 67; *vnkempt*, i. 473. 25.
Vntewed, iii. 36. 84.
Vntruss, iii. 46. 144, 223. 218, 284. 199, 412. 15.
Voider, iii. 404. 28.
Vre, use, iii. 450. 22.

Wag-halter, rascal, iii. 193. 28.
Wakenesse, ii. 447. 48.
Wamble, rumble, iii. 56. 71.
Wand, riding switch, i. 282. 37, ii. 100. 7, 138. 31, iii. 173. 6, 215. 6, 396. 20.
Want, mole, iii. 121. 55.
Watch (sb.), guard, i. 455. 10, iii. 63. 161.
Watchet, light blue, iii. 70. 96.

Water bough, ii. 5. 33, 376. 41.
Water euill, cold, iii. 155. 109.
Water thy plantes (i. e. plaints?), i. 253. 13.
Weam, ii. 216. 14.
Weeping crosse, ii. 28. 35, iii. 487. 21.
Wennes, the, iii. 156. 127.
Whattin, iii. 367. 21.
Whist, silent, ii. 62. 15, 215. 30, iii. 278. 294, 355. 123.
Whiting moppe, iii. 281. 89.
Whitled, drunk, iii. 198. 44.
Wilde, bold, ii. 20. 27. So *wildnes*, ii. 43. 23.
Wimple (vb.), iii. 118. 90; (sb.) iii. 419. 70.
Winch, wrinch, i. 257. 7, ii. 151. 26, iii. 177. 7, 411. 18.
Wiredrawer, iii. 405. 29; (fig.) precisian, i. 246. 33, 487. 34.
Wist (wrongly as) know, ii. 173. 10, 181. 11; knew, iii. 488. 11, &c.
With, willow, ii. 113. 15, 151. 25.
Withernam, reprisal, iii. 393. 14.
Wonne, dwell, iii. 377. 86.
Wood Culuer, ii. 111. 30.
Wood the ship was made of, tell what, ii. 32. 37.
Woodcock, simpleton, iii. 44. 68, 418. 20.
Woodden (fig.), i. 484. 29, iii. 370. 121.
Woodquist, ii. 405. 3.
Woodsere, froth, iii. 399. 26.
Wreake, reck, iii. 378. 31.
Wreakefull, destructive, iii. 422. 12, 457. 25.
Wreath twist, bend, ii. 114. 28.
Wrinckle, trick, i. 202. 29, ii. 153. 13, 453. 74.
Wronge, wrung, ii. 10. 17, 129. 21, 151. 27, 390. 79, 410. 26.
Wyhie (neigh), iii. 213. 194, 418. 26.

Yerke, ii. 227. 30 (?), 374. 41, iii. 407. 14; *Ierkes* (sb.), strokes, iii. 398. 20.
Ynche, at an, i. 251. 24.
Youthly, i. 192. 22, &c.
Yrke, be uneasy, iii. 345. 92.

INDEX

Reference is to volume and page only ; where the line is added '1.' is prefixed.

Abuses, play at Greenwich, July 30, 1606, possibly by Lyly, i. 352.
Aelian, *Varia Historia* used in *Sapho*, ii. 364-5 ; some reff. to *De Nat. Animalium* or *V. H.* in *Euph.*, i. 158, 344, 348, ii. 501, 511, 513, 518, 520, 531, 534, 535, 545.
Aesop, frequent allusions to, i. 157, 373, 480 l. 3; ii. 43 (named), 495 ; ii. 497 (Satyr and Fire), 341 ; ii. 535, iii. 67 (Eagle and Beetle) ; ii. 533, iii. 80 (Sun and Wind).
Alchemy, introd. in *Gallathea* from Scot and Chaucer, ii. 423-4, 567-8 ; in England, ii. 477 note.
Alençon, Duc d', his suit to Elizabeth, ii. 366-7, 562, 564.
Allegory : allegorical personification of the Moral-Plays, ii. 232, the step to right characterization, 235, rejected by Lyly except in framework of *The Woman*, 250, 255 ; his view of, iii. 83-4 ; his methods for imparting concreteness, ii. 255-6, iii. 84 ; limiting conditions of his political allegory, iii. 85-6 ; story of his plays independent of it, ii. 257-8 ; moral allegory in *Endim.*, iii. 83, 103 ; physical allegory in *Endim.*, iii. 82-3, ii. 255, in *The Woman, ib.*, in *Love's Met.*, ii. 256 ; political allegory in *Endim.*, ii. 9-10, 86-102, Endimior's dream, 102 note, 515-6 ; Sapho's dream, ii. 552 ; political allegory of *Midas*, iii. 129-10, ii. 257, 260. See also under 'Lyly as a Playwright.'
Anachronism, in Edwardes, ii. 240; in Lyly, 270-1, 491.
Andrewes, Lancelot, sermons attended by Lyly and Nash, i. 60-1 ; member of Society of Antiquaries, 396 ; M.A. Camb. incorporated M.A. Oxon, 16.
Anthologies, Elizabethan, iii. 439-43 ; mediocrity of much of their verse, 434-6.
Antiochus Epiphanes and the sacred books, i. 367.
Arber, Prof. E., his Reprint of *Euphues* 1868, i. 104-5, 112, 118 ; list of editions, 84 ; on the Morley copy of Part I, 87-8 ; his review of opinion on *Euphues*, 81, 115 ; *Introd. Sketch to Marprelate Controversy*, 49 note, &c. ; *Transcript of Stationers' Register*, cited passim.
Ariosto, founder of modern written drama, ii. 473 ; asserted debt of Lyly's Alchemist and Peter to *Il Negromante*, 476-7, 479 ; his *Suppositi*, 473, 478-9, iii. 167; Spenser's Fradubio and Fraelissa borrowed from, iii. 293 ; alluded to *Euph.*, ii. 199.
Armada, the, allusions to, i. 408 ; in *Midas*, iii. 109, 119, 131, i. 47 ; Theobalds, i. 418 ; Cowdray, 425 ; Elvetham, 442, 408 ; ' octogesimus octauus' in *Gall.* antecedent, ii. 422, 425, 452, 462.
Ascham, Roger, loose style alluded to by Harvey, i. 80 note ; *Toxophilus* cited, 129-30 ; *Scholemaster* suggests Lyly's title, 327 ; the 'Englese Italionato,' ii. 509.
Assurance, the formal ceremony of betrothal, ii. 536 (note on ii. 218, l. 30).
Astrology, introd. in *Gallathea*, ii. 421-2, 573; in *The Woman*, iii. 235-6, ii. 278.
'Atheos, Euphues and,' text of, i. 291-305, notes on, 364-9, analysis of, 364-5.
Aulus Gellius, allusion from, ii. 354 note, iii. 430.

Bacon, Francis, his essay on Marprelate Controversy, i. 51 note ; Lyly's apophthegms sometimes like, i. 163-4 ; his speeches of Prince of Purpoole's Counsellors suggested by *Midas*, i. 380 note, 385 ; Solicitor-General, June 25, 1607, 396.
Baker, Mr. G. P., his Biographical Introduction to *Endimion*, i. 2, iii. 8 ; theory of early connexion between Leicester and Lyly, and date for *Endimion* 1579, i. 21-2, 47 note, iii. 12-3, 95 note ; suggested emendations of Halpin's view of the allegory, iii. 87-8 ; remark on Scene in *Endimion*, 14 ; connects delay of *Gallathea* with writ to Thos. Giles, i. 32 ; cited, i. 43, 48,

INDEX

&c.; argument for date of *M. Bomb.*, iii. 168; bearing of ref. in 'Advt. for Pap-Hatchett' on date of *Midas*, iii. 111; date for *Loves Met.*, 296.

Bartholomaeus Anglicus, his *De Proprietatibus Rerum*, i. 131, 156–7 note; source of some of Lyly's similes, 132, 332, 333, 338, 339, 340.

Bartholomew's, St., the hospital, Lyly's residence in or near, i. 44, 42, Watson's, 386; entries in the register of church (St. Barth. the Less), 43–4, 66, 386; Lyly assessed as living in that parish, 72; burials, 76, 398 note.

Basse, William, and Rycote, i. 386; imitates Lyly's *Woman*, iii. 237; cited, ii. 496, 510, 519, 555, i. 334, 345.

Bees, ii. 391 l. 122, i. 194 l. 17; Fidus's description, origin of pass. in *Henry V*, ii. 44–6, 498–9; poem, *The Bee*, discussed, iii. 445–7, text, 494–7.

Beeston, Sir Hugh, i. 391, 395–7.

Bellum Grammaticale, play given Ch. Ch. Oxon (Sp. 24, 1592), Lyly's possible authorship of, i. 379–80; Sir J. Harington's allusion to, 380 note 1.

Bestiaries, not a probable source for Lyly's similes, i. 336, ii. 514.

Bisham, Speeches at, i. 471–7, 405, 529–30.

Bishop of London, with Archbishop of Canterbury, Censors of Press, i. 44, 49–50; number of bishops, ii. 527.

Blackfriars, Prologues or Epilogues at, ii. 315, 359, 371, 416; Revels' properties moved to, i. 38, 25 note; acting here before Burbage's theatre of 1596–7, i. 24–5 note; Burbage's theatre leased by Nath. Gyles in 1600, i. 43; wedding at, June 16, 1600, 380–1.

Blount, Edw., *Sixe Covrt Comedies* by Lyly, ent. Sta. Reg. 1627–8, pub. 1632, i. 64; title of, iii. 1; introductory matter of, 2–3; cited, i. 76, 81, ii. 299; followed latest quartos, and added to their corruptions, ii. 305, and for details see under ' Text and Bibliog.' in introduction to each play; he first gave the Songs, i.e. 21 out of 32, ii. 264–5: prints *Endimion* first, iii. 11.

Bloxam, Dr., on Magd. Coll. Register, i. 1 note, 10 note; on the College records, 15; references to Lyly, 32.

Boccaccio, his *Filocopo*, i. 135, 161; his *Ameto*, suggestions for *Loves Met.* in story of Acrimonia, ii. 481–2; his *Filostrato*, i. 401.

Boxley, near Maidstone, probably Lyly's birthplace, i. 5; fuller's earth at, *ib.*; no trace of name Lyly on tombstone or monument, 384 note; family of Wyatts at, 384–5.

Breton, Nicholas, probable author of song in *Elvetham*, i. 447–8, 385, 408, 524–5, and of *An Olde Mans Lesson*, 399–400; style like Lyly's, 404–5.

Brydges, Giles, Lord Chandos, i. 530.

Bullen, Mr. A. H., his edition of Peele, i. 519; of the *Poet. Rhapsody*, 534; on the Elizabethan lyrics, iii. 435–6, 442–3; ed. of Marlowe, 442; on *Maydes Met.*, iii. 334, 338.

Burleigh, Lord, Lyly's early connexion with, i. 4; perhaps assists Lyly at college, 6, 12; Lyly's Latin letter to 1574, 12–5; probably introduces Lyly at Court, 12, 385, ii. 198; complaint to by Cambridge authorities, i. 14–5; house near Savoy, 17; authority over Savoy, 17–8; Lyly's eulogy of, ii. 198, i. 21, 22, 417 l. 9, 419 l. 3; recommends Lyly to his son-in-law Oxford, i. 24, 29 note 4; Lyly's letter to, about Oxford's displeasure 1582, 27–9; anxiety about the navy 1583–4, 32; as Earl Marshal, order for procession 1588, 40; correspondence with Lord Mayor, &c. about Anti-Martinist plays, 53; attitude to the Martinists, 55; visited at Theobalds by Eliz. 1591, i. 379, 520; house at Pymms, 519–20; failing health, 69, 391; action in regard to petition of Revels' creditors 1597–8, 69–70; earlier complaint to him by a costumier 1571, 71; his death, 71. Lyly's letter of condolence with Cecil on, 391–3; Latin epitaphs on, 393; opposition between, and Leicester, 22, 77; alluded to? ii. 23 l. 7 (i. 130).

Byrd, William, 'doubtful' poems from, iii. 440.

Caesar, Jul., borrowed from in *Euph.*, ii. 31–2, i. 157; notes on the passage, ii. 495; and Dover Castle, 496.

Calendar, the, Gregory XIII's rectification of, ii. 490.

Cambridge in 16th century, Lyly probably at, i. 16, 51–2, ii. 193; incorporation between, and Oxford, i. 16 note; protest by Vice-Chancellor and Heads against abuse of royal appointment to Fellowships, 14; Elizabeth's visits to, ii. 213; Harvey and the Public Oratorship, i. 30.

Campaspe, text, ii. 313–60; introduction, 301–12; notes, 540–54; editions, 302–5; dates of composition and performance, i. 23, 25, ii. 309–11; sources, 244, 306–9; criticism of, 244, 246, 248,

INDEX

249; our first historical play, 251–2; not allegorical, 256, 550; structure, 272, 274; abrupt transfer in the course of a scene, 269; marks of style, 289; other marks, 246, 250, 261, 264–5, 271–2, 280, 282, 283, 284, 238, 296–8; its effect, i. 31–2; adaptation of, ii. 311.

'Carde, A Cooling,' warning letter of Euphues to Philautus against love and women and court life, i. 246–57; alluded to, ii. 14, 86, 93.

Cato, Dionysius, his *Disticha de Moribus*, iii. 582.

Cecil, Sir Robert, letters to from Lyly, (1) Jan. 17, 1594–5, i. 289–90, (2) Dec. 22, 1597, 68–9, (3) Jan. 23, 1597–8, 391, (4) Sept. 9, 1598, 391–3, (5) Feb. 27, 1600–1, 393–5, (6) Feb. 4, 1602–3, 75; Lok a petitioner of, 67; Secretary of State 1596, 67, 520; rivalry with Essex, 69, 74; house protected 1600, 18; jealous of Greville, 75, 77; figures in Gardener's speech, 417–8; embassy to Paris, 391 notes; correspondence about Deanery of Christ Church, 393 note.

Cervantes' *Galatea*, Lyly unindebted to, ii. 479, 483.

Chalmers's payment-lists from Council Registers, ii. 310, 425; gap in, June 26, 1505—Feb. 19, 1586, iii. 11 note; iii. 111, 296.

Chaucer, Geoffrey, summary of Lyly's debt to, i. 400–1; Alchemist partly taken from, ii. 423–4; Sir Tophas and Sir Thopas, iii. 503–4; Aureola in *Elvetham* and Chaucer's Proserpine, i. 401, 525.

Child, Mr. C. G., essay on *John Lyly and Euphuism*, i. 119, freely borrowed from here, 120, 123, 126, 128, 135, &c.; table of Euphuism in the Plays, ii. 289, 290, cf. iii. 12.

Choir-boys employed as actors, i. 34–7; effects of on the drama, 36; petition against the practice 1600, 35, ii. 426; forbidden 1626, i. 37.

Chronological summary of facts in Lyly's life, i. 398–9.

Colet's School, relation of the Paul's choir-boys to, i. 34 note.

Collier, J. P., *Hist. Dram. Poetry* cited, ii. 232–3, 473, and passim; *Bibliograph. Catalogue*, i. 390, 525, &c.

Cooper, Thos., Bishop of Winchester, his *Admonition*, i. 50, iii. 574; master of Magd. Coll. School 1566–7, i. 10; alluded to by Nash, 60 note.

Cotton, Sir Robert, i. 396; letter from Lyly to, 389, 395–7.

Cowdray, Entertainment at, i. 422–30, 405, 409, 520–2.

Cranes, ii. 488, 176, 514.

Cumberland, George Clifford, 6th Earl of, i. 381, 519, 524; succeeds Lee as Champion, 384, 410–1; Ode at his Shew on Horseback, 414–5; complaining speech, 415–6; probably secures Lyly his seat for Appleby, 384.

Dante, perhaps recalled, ii. 88 (cf. note).

Date of Philautus's last letter wrong, why, i. 22 note 5, ii. 537 (note on ii. 222).

Davies, Sir John, supposed author of the 'Lottery.' at Harefield, i. 385, 535; presents a copy of *Euphues*, i. 385 note 5; i. 519.

Diet, ii. 528, 200 l. 28, 201 l. 27, 411 l. 9.

Dilke, C. W., his *Old Eng. Plays*, *Endimion* edited in, iii. 8; fails to perceive the allegory of *End.*, ii. 257 note; *Midas* edited, iii. 108, allegory first noted by, ii. 257; *Mother Bombie* edited, iii. 166; a friend of Keats, iii. 103.

Diogenes Laertius, *Vitae Philosophorum* used in *Campaspe*, ii. 309; many quotations, 543–51.

Doddridge, Sir John, Solicitor-General, interested in Lyly, i. 396–7.

Domenichi, Lodov., his *Nobiltà delle Donne*, recalled in several passages, i. 175 note, ii. 503, 535.

Dover, described briefly, ii. 35; pier, ii. 496; Euphues' landing at, i. 375.

Dowland, John, 'doubtful' poems from, iii. 435, 444.

Drayton, Michael, i. 539; his *Man in the Moone*, iii. 103.

Dreams, utterances on, ii. 405–7, iii. 202–4; Lyly's dramatic use of, ii. 247, 264; Sapho's, 562; her ladies', 292; Endimion's, iii. 10, 102, 515–6, represented, 39, recounted, 66–7; Sir Tophas's, a parody, ii. 276; Lucio's and Halfpenny's, iii. 202–3.

Dress, *Euph.*, i. 319 l. 27, ii. 9 (ll. 18–22, 34–6), 10 (ll. 3–6, 14, 19–21), 194 ll. 15–26, 199.

Dumb Shew, ii. 263, iii. 508–9; in *Endim.* iii. 39.

Education, treatise on, paraphrased from Plutarch, i. 260–86; Lyly's additions to Plutarch, 352–3; sir John Elyot's transl. of Plutarch's treatise, i. 352 sqq.

Edwardes, Richard, Puttenham's mention of, i. 24; connexion with the

INDEX

Chapel, 35; *Damon and Pithias*, comic servants, 36, ii. 238; a model for Lyly, i. 159 note, ii. 238, 274; criticism of, 239–41, 252, 253; Prologue, our first critical utterance, 239; Unities in, 267.

Egerton, Sir Thos., i. 533; the Egerton Papers, 383, 534.

Elizabeth, Queen, abuse of royal recommendation to Fellowships, i. 14–5; flattery of in Lyly's work (see 'Flattery,' &c.); shot fired on the Thames, i. 22, ii. 207, 532; confines Oxford, i. 27; not offended with *Sapho*, i. 31; doubtful if with *Woman*, 63, 390, ii. 256–7, iii. 236; removes inhibition, i. 32; countenances use of choir-boys as actors, 35–6, iii. 295; Lyly's wife attendant on her? i. 43, 75; her varying attitude about love perhaps reflected in the plays, 45; suitors to, ii. 533; age, 532, i. 381 note; her love for Leicester and rivalry with Mary allegorized in *Endim.*, i. 46, ii. 259, iii. 87–91, 101–2; her jealousy of marriages, ii. 553, 570–1, iii. 88, 98, 297; Alençon's courtship of, allegorized in *Sapho*, ii. 366–7, alluded to, 534; represented by Diana and Ceres in *Gall., Loves Met.*, ii. 259, possibly by Pandora or Luna, 256, i. 390 note; supposed satire of in *The Woman, ib.*, i. 63–4; allusions to in *Midas*, i. 47; Lyly's petitions to, i. 64–6, 70–1, 75, 378, 392; her appointment of him to Revels' Office and vague promise of the Mastership 1588, 394; her complaint about Tentes and Toyles, 66, 71, 383, 390; lines to, in Lok's *Ecclesiastes*, 67; relations with Essex alluded to *L. M.* 74, iii. 297; death, i. 76; Lyly's *Funeral Oration* on, 388–9, 509–16; at Oxford, ii. 534, i. 379–80; at Anne Russell's wedding, 381 note; pastoral shows offered to her, 407; speeches to, on Ascension-day, 410–6; at Theobalds, 417–9; at Cowdray, 421–9; at Elvetham, 431–52; at Quarrendon, 453–70; at Bisham, 472–7; at Sudeley, 477–84; at Rycote, 485–90; at Harefield, 491–504.

Elvetham, entertainment at, i. 431–52, 405, 408, 522–6.

Elyot, Sir John, translation of Plut.'s *De Educatione*, i. 352 sqq.

Endimion, text, iii. 17–80; introduction, 5–15; notes, 503–19; editions, 6, 8; sources, ii. 245, iii. 9, 503; the allegory in, 9–10, i. 46, separate Essay on, iii. 81–103, physical side of, 82–3, ii. 255, Court side of, Halpin's view, iii. 81, 86–7. Mr. Baker's changes rejected, 87–8, widened scope suggested, 88, 101, ii. 258–9, &c.; the characters discussed, iii. 89–101; date, 10–3, i. 46–7, Baker's date, 1579, untenable, *ib.*, Mr. Spingarn's, iii. 13 note; criticism, ii. 246, 247, 249, 254, 258–9, 261–2, 268, 269, 271, 273, 275–6 (structure), 284 (Tellus, Sir Tophas); marks of style, 289–90; poetry in, 246, 292; gave suggestions for Falstaff, Dogberry, *M. N. D.*, &c., 297, iii. 81, 98–9 (Oberon's speech).

England, William Harrison's description of, used in the 'Glasse,' ii. 191–6, see notes 526–30.

Englands Helicon, poems in, from Lyly's *Ents.*, i. 409, 524, 530–1; 'doubtful' poems taken from, iii. 435, 441.

Entertainments by Lyly, list of, i. 404; remarks on his authorship, 379–86, 404–5; introduction to, 404–9; text of, 410–507; notes on, with detailed discussion of his authorship of each, 517–38; importance of marginal reff., i. 405–6.

'Ephœbus, Euphues and his,' text of, i. 260–90; its relation to Plutarch's *De Educatione*, 352–3; Lyly's additions, *ib.*; notes on, 352–64.

Erasmus, his *Adagia* cited, i. 331, 334, ii. 487, 501, 508, 543, 560, and often.

Essays in this Edition:
Life of John Lyly, i. 1–82.
Biographical Appendix, i. 377–402.
Text and Bibliography of *Euphues*, i. 83–118.
Euphues and Euphuism, i. 119–75, 539–41.
Entertainments, introduction, i. 404–9.
Lyly as a Playwright, ii. 231–99.
Italian Influence on Lyly's Plays, ii. 473–85.
On the Allegory in *Endimion*, iii. 81–103.
Poems, Introduction, iii. 433–47.

Essex, Robert, Earl of, sent to Ireland, i. 72; his revolt, 74; represented by Erisichthon, *ib.*, ii. 257, 259, iii. 297; poem on the Bee attributed to, 446–7; his fall alluded to in Lyly's Second Petition and in a letter, i. 70, 393–5.

Essex, Walter Devereux, Earl of, Leicester suspected as causing his death, iii. 96.

EUPHUES: composition, publication, and success of, i. 19–24: revision of, 20, 43, 45, 107–12; sources of its matter, 154–9; North's *Diall*, 154–6; Plutarch, 156; Pliny, *ib.*; Ovid, Hy-

INDEX

ginus, Aesop, Cicero, Caesar, Aelian, &c., 157-8; Harrison, Heywood, Tylney, Gascoigne, &c., 158-9; Italian suggestions, ii. 477, 479-80; its originality—the first English Novel, 159-61; feminine and modern interest, 160-1; the tale, 161-2; deficient in action, 162; Part II the best, 162-3; mixture of priggishness, humour, good sense, and philosophy, 163-4; Shakespeare's intimate knowledge of, 164-75; close parallels in *Hamlet*, 164-5, *Rom. and Jul.* 165-7, *As You Like It* (Jaques), 167-8, many others, 168-75; titles suggested by, 327.
Bibliography of, 83-118.
List of Editions, 100-105 : five previous lists, 84.
Earliest editions distinguished, Part I, 85-95, Part II, 95-7.
Text and method followed, 98-9.
Textual Footnotes, explanation of, 178, ii. 2, iii. 4.
Quartos of, Titles, Colophons, Results of Collation of, 106-18.
Augmentations in second edition, 107-8.
Adaptation of 1716, 113-4.
Arber's Reprint, 114, 118, 85-7.
Landmann's (partial) Reprint of Part I, 104, 115, 138, 143, 149, 154-6.
Text of, Part I, i. 177-326.
— Part II, ii. 1-228.
Notes on, Part I, i. 327-75.
— Part II, ii. 486-540.
EUPHUISM : first use of term i. 119 note; modern writers on, i. 119-20, 143; Professor Arber's review of opinion on, 81, 115; contemporary opinion on, 79-80; contemporary disapproval or parody, 132-3, 385 note 5, 150 note 3; imitation of, 79, by Greene and Lodge, 148-9, by Shakespeare, 152-4 and notes, ii. 287-8; 18th cent. depreciation, 81 ; Blount's testimony about, iii. 3.
STRUCTURAL MARKS OF, i. 120-30 :
A. (i) Antithetic balance or parisonity, 120-2, 539-41 ; (ii) Rhetorical questions, 122 ; (iii) Repetition, *ib.*
B. (i) Alliteration, simple or transverse, 123-4 ; (ii) Word-likeness—
1. complete (consonance, and repetition), 124; 2. partial (assonance, annomination, rhyme, puns, and wordplay), 125-6.
Logical continuity somewhat neglected, 126; occasional loose syntax, due to preoccupation with words, 126-8; vocabulary, little obsolete, 128-30.
Sentence-structure in *Euphues*, 539-41.

ORNAMENTAL DEVICES OF, 130-4 :
1. Allusions and anecdotes—historical, or invented, 130; 2. Mythological allusions, 131 ; 3. Natural History— the Similes, 131-4; 4. Proverbs, 134.
ORIGINS OF, 134-42 : classical study, 135, Italian influence on contemporary life, 135-6: (1) North's *Diall of Princes* 1557, 136-8; Guevara's title, editions, translations from, other works, *ib.*; Lyly's debt in matter and treatment, 154-6. (2) Pettie's *Pallace of Pleasure* furnished exact model of Lyly's euphuism, 138-41, and largely of handling, 141-2; Lyly's additions to style insignificant, 143.
Earlier English Prose, 144; Lyly authoritatively asserts the need of precision, elegance, and design, 145-7; relation of thought and language, 145 ; Nash's incoherence, 146 ; Lyly's defects, 148.

Fairholt, F. W., edition of Lyly's eight plays, 1858, ii. 305; details of his text (see under ' Text,' &c., in introd. to each play).
Fairies in Chaucer, in Lyly (*Elvetham*, &c.), in Greene, i. 525-6.
Ferrers, George, i. 518, 526, iii. 516.
Feuillerat, Mons. Albert G., discovers Lyly's letter to Cotton, &c., i. 389, 395.
Flattery of Elizabeth, *Euphues* i. 323, ii. 37-44, 85, 204-17 (Glasse) ; *Campaspe* Prol. and Epil. at Court ii. 316, 360, 331 ll. 80 sqq. (cf. note on 356 l. 97); *Sapho* i. 31, ii. 366; *Gallathea* ii. 454-5, 465; *Endimion* ii. 258-9, iii. 9, and essay 82-3, &c.; *Midas* (Sophronia) i. 47, iii. 125-6, &c. ; *Loves Met.* i. 74, ii. 258-9; *Entertainments* i. 408, &c.; *Poems*, iii. 448-9, 474?; *Funeral Oration*, i. 389, 510-6.
Fleay, Rev. F. G., his *Biog. Chron. of the English Stage*, reasons suggested for delay of Part II, i. 21-2 ; dates for the plays, *Sapho* ii. 367, *Gall.* 425, 427, *End.* iii. 11 note, *M. Bomb.* 167, *Loves Met.* 296 ; sees polit. allegory in *Camp.* ii. 550, 553 ; detects allegory of Eliz. and Alençon in *Sapho*, ii. 257, 367; on *Abuses*, i. 382; on *The Maydes Metamorphosis* iii. 337-8.
Friendship, as a subject, i. 159 note, 197-8, 233-4, 281-2, ii. 95-100, 143, 145, 147-9, 329, iii. 26, 31; compared with love by Geron iii. 50 ; Harvey's with Lyly, i. 7, 17 note, 77 ; reff. to *De Amicitia*, 334.
Funeral Oration on Elizabeth, i. 388-9; text, 509-16; notes, 538-9.

Gallathea, text, ii. 429–72; introduction, 417–28; notes, 564–74; editions, 418; sources, 245, 420–4, 475, 476–7, 481–2; date, 424–7, i. 32; criticism, ii. 245, 246, 247, 249, 254, 256, 259, 261, 263–4, 266, 267, 268, 271, 272 and 275 (structure), 281, 285, 297; rustic comedy in, mixed with ideal pastoral, 281, 475; marks of style, 289; poetry, 292; present form probably a revision, i. 32, ii. 426–7; Petrarcan love-conceits, 292.

Gascoigne, George, no, contributor to Lyly's style, i. 144; his *Aduentures of F. I.* partly anticipates *Euphues*, 159; *Supposes*, 1566, ii. 252, 287, 473, 479; *Princely Pleasures*, 1576, suggested by Italian work, ii. 474, gave slight suggestions for *Gallathea*, 475, and for transformation into trees, 477 note, ii. 266; learned Italian in London, 479 note 3.

Gesta Grayorum, 1594–5, Lyly's possible hand in, i. 380 and note, 383.

—— 1617–8, song in *Antimasque of Mountebanks*, ii. 572.

Glasse for Europe, Euphues', i.e. an account of England and flattery of Elizabeth, ii. 191–216.

Gongora, Luis de, i. 151.

Gosson, Stephen, his *Ephemerides of Phialo* alluded to *Euphues* ii. 99; his description of the lost *Straunge Newes out of Affrick*, and Lyly's possible authorship of the latter, i. 22 note.

Greene, Robert, M.A. of Cambridge incorporated at Oxford, 1588, i. 16 note 5; refutes the Harveys' attack in his *Qvip*, 58; relations with Nash, 58–9, 60 note 2; his end, 58, 79; Harvey's revenge on, 59; his *Menaphon*, Nash's epistle to, i. 51, 80 note, 133 note, 146–7, allusion to *Euph*. in, 385 note 5; in which works Euphuistic, 148–9; his *Planetomachia* and *The Woman*, ii. 245, iii. 234–6; *Bacon and Bungay* compared with *Campaspe*, ii. 252, 254; fairies in *James IV*, 254, i. 526; abrupt transfer in course of a scene, ii. 269; 'Delphos' in *Pandosto*, 271; tenderness of his women, 283; dialogue, 291; use of Dumb Show, iii. 509.

Greville, Fu'ke, interested on Lyly's behalf, i. 74–5, 77, 400; iii. 439, 441.

Guevara, Antonio de, historiographer to Charles V, i. 136–8; his *Libro del emperador*, &c., titles, colophons, &c. of earliest eds. *ib.*, Berner's translation of, and North's, *ib.*; other works transl. into English, 137 note; Landmann on, 138, 154–5; action subordinate, 141; misogynist tirades, 142, 155; form, tone, and subjects of his work reproduced in *Euphues* Part I, 154–6; Part II unindebted to, 156; country and court opposed by, 155, ii. 484, followed in ' A Cooling Carde,' i. 246 l. 13 note.

Gunton, Mr. R. G., and Lyly's letters at Hatfield, i. 75, 389.

Halpin's essay *Oberon's Vision*, its theory of the allegory in *Endimion*, i. 46, iii. 9–10, 86–8, 90 note, 91, 94, 96 note, 97, 98; his note on Elizabeth's jealousy of marriages, ii. 570–1; view of allegory in *Midas*, ii. 260, iii. 109–10.

Harefield, Entertainment at, i. 491–504, 381, 405, 533–7; Lottery at, i. 499–504.

Harefield Place, history of, i. 533.

Harvey, Gabriel, his attack on Lyly in *Advt. for Papp-Hatchett*, writt. 1589, pub. as part of *Pierce's Supererogation*, i. 57, 59: referred to, 7 notes, 8, 17 note, 24 note, 29 note, 33, 37, 43, 44, 51, 54 (note 2), 57, 59, 77 note, 80 note, 131, 388; degrees at Cambridge and Oxford, 7, 16 notes; says nothing of Lyly at Cambridge, 16; acquaintance with Lyly in the Savoy, 17–8 note; possible satire on Lord Oxford in the *Three Letters* 1580, 30–1; his own account of the matter in *Foure Letters* 1592, *ib.*; impartial attitude in Marprelate Controversy, 57; attack on the London playwrights, 57–8, answered by Greene, 58; revenge on Greene, 59; consequent controversy with Nash, 59–60; pleads in the Court of Arches, 61 note; parade of friendship with Spenser, 63; his opinion of *Euphues*, 80 note; of *Pappe*, 56; perhaps saw Lyly in the part of Midas, 37; the original of Sir Tophas, iii. 100–1.

Harvey, John, the third brother, i. 58.

Harvey, Richard, his *Astrological Discourse* used for *Gallathea*, i. 32, quoted from, ii. 421–2; *Plaine Percevall*, i. 57; *The Lamb of God*, its attack on Lyly, Greene, and Nash, 57–8 and note; Greene's reply, *ib.*; reply by Lyly threatened, 59–60.

Hazlitt, Mr. W. C., his *Handbook* 1867, editions of *Euphues* here rejected, i. 84–5, 86; on ed. 1630, 105.

Hazlitt, William, his remark on Accius and Silena, ii. 246, 277; misinterprets allegory in *Endim.*, ii. 257 note.

Hense, on Euphuism, i. 119, 148 note, on Lyly's Anachronisms, ii. 271.

INDEX 611

Hertford, Earl of, i. 523.
Hesiod, quoted, i. 363; among sources for *The Woman*, passage quoted, iii. 234.
Heywood, John, his *Proverbes*, i. 158 and Notes to *Euphues*, vols. i and ii passim; his Interludes, ii. 232; influenced by Chaucer, i. 401.
Homer, alluded to by Lyly, i. 158, 179, 230 l. 13 (343), 261 l. 8, 268 l. 4, 272 l. 14, ii. 5 (ll. 21, 29), 28 l. 19, 25 (ll. 27, 33), 78 l. 5, 94 l. 11 (? see note), 96 l. 16, 131 l. 31, 143 l. 19, 183 l. 33, 197 (ll. 19, 32), 316, 431 l. 2, 454 l. 24, 563, &c.
Hospitals, ii. 527; see also 'Savoy' and 'Bartholomew's, St.'
Howard, Frances, i. 523, iii. 99.
Humber, bore on 1571, ii. 422–3, 565; Danes invade England by, *ib.*
Hyginus, C. Julius, his *Fabularum Liber*, used by Lyly, i. 157, 344, ii. 421 (*Gall.*), iii. 235 (*Woman*).

Iffida, her name, whence, ii. 501; a real flame of Lyly's? *ib.* i. 3–4, 385; pathos of, 163.
Incident on the Thames, i. 22, ii. 207, 532.
Incorporation between the two Universities, i. 16.
Inhibition of Paul's, and Chapel, Children, 1583, i. 32; inhibition removed from Paul's Boys, Ap. 26, 1585, i. 32 (acc. to Fleay 1587, i. 425), from Chapel Boys 1597, iii. 295; fresh inhibition of Paul's Boys, temporary, 1589, i. 53, iii. 295, permanent bef. Oct. 1591, i. 60, removed 1598 or 1599, i. 72–3, iii. 296.
Italian influence on Lyly, Oxford's tour, i. 31, ii. 479; Petrarch, i. 135, ii. 88, 129, 199, 292; Castiglione, i. 135, 161; fashions in *Euph. ib.*; 'the Italionate pen,' 146 (cf. 130); Ariosto, Sannazarro, Tasso, see under; plays how far indebted to Italy, ii. 473–85; Italian actors, 473; 'Italionated,' ii. 88 l. 27.

James I, King, perhaps relieves Lyly, i. 397–8; compliments and shows offered to on King of Denmark's visit, 381–2, 505–7.
Jaques, Shakespeare's, a reproduction of Lyly's character, Euphues, i. 167–8.
Jones, Robert, his Song-Books, iii. 434, 'doubtful' poems from, 444.
Jonson, Ben, supposed satire on Lyly in Fastidious Brisk, i. 61, 74; allusion by Brisk and Fallace to, *Euphues*,

149; does not ridicule Lyly's style in *Every Man out of his Humour* or *Cynthia's Revels*, 151; influenced by Lyly, ii. 243; *Catiline* and *Sejanus* extend Lyly's example of transcript from the classics, 252; sacrifice of plot to 'humours' avoided by *Moth. Bombie*, 253; *Cynthia's Revels* and Masques indebted to *Endimion*, &c. 254, 292; allusion to revival of *Loves Met.* i. 73; Subtle resembles Ariosto's Negromante, ii. 477; allusion to Lyly in First Folio verses, i. 79; with Lyly at Theobalds?, 381, 385, 537, at Cotton's house?, 396.
Jusserand, Mons. J. J., his *The Eng. Novel in the Time of Shakespeare*, i. 82, 120, 160, 369.
Juvenal, iii. 208; alluded to, ii. 76 l. 30 (note).

King of Denmark's Welcome, i. 505–7, 381–2, 537–8.

Landmann, Dr. Friedrich, his (incomplete) edition of *Euphues*, Part I, i. 104, 115, 119, &c.; list of editions, 84; discussion of Euphuism, 119, 138; underrates effect of contents of *Euphues*, 143; Lodge, 149; discovery of editio princeps of *Euph.* anticipated by Dr. Sinker, 85; the first to exhibit Lyly's debt to Guevara, 154–5.
Latin Grammar of Lilly and Colet, jokes on in the plays, i. 34, 380, ii. 261, 328 l. 42, 463, iii. 42–3, 197, 204, 206; in Sudeley, i. 483.
Laws of England, ii. 529.
Lee, Sir Henry, rents chambers in the Savoy, i. 17 note; cousin of George Wyatt of Boxley, 384; employs Lyly to write speeches, Tilt-yard, 518, and entertainment of Queen at Quarrendon, 526–7, text, 454–70; probably secures his Parliamentary seat for Aylesbury, 384; resigns Championship to Cumberland, 410–1; poem on this occasion, *ib.*; sons of, 518.
Leicester, Robert Dudley, Earl of, chancellor of Oxford University, i. 8, 21; connexion of with Lyly in 1579 supposed by Mr. Baker, 21, 47 note, iii. 12–3, 95 note; probably known to Lyly, 18; in general opposition to Burleigh, 22, 47, 77; goes to Netherlands Dec. 10, 1585, 46; original of Lyly's Endimion, i. 46–7, ii. 259, iii. 9, 81, 87–9, 102, not necessarily with his connivance, i. 47; project for his marriage with Mary Queen of Scots, iii. 9, 90, 102; marriages with Lady

Sheffield and Lady Essex, 87, 90-91 note, Elizabeth's displeasure at, 87-8, 90 note, 99, 101 ; visit to Chatsworth, 94 ; Sussex his enemy, *ib.*; defended by Sidney against *Leicester's Commonwealth*, 95 ; suspected of Essex' murder, 96 and note 2 ; opposes the French match, 95, 101 ; represented by the stock-dove in Sapho's dream, ii. 562 death, i. 47.
'Letters of Euphues,' i. 306-23, notes on, 163, 369-74 ; epistolary form borrowed from Guevara, 369, used by Gascoigne, 159, by Richardson, 369.
Letters of Lyly, (1) to Burleigh 1574 (Latin), i. 13-4, (2) to Watson 1582 (printed), 26-7, (3) to Burleigh 1582, 28-9, (4) to Cecil 1594-5, 389-90, (5) to Cecil 1597, 68-9, (6) to Cecil 1597-8, 391, (7) to Cecil 1598, 391-3, (8) to Cecil 1600-1, 393-5, (9) to Cecil 1602-3, 75, (10) to Cotton 1605, 395-6. (Nos. 3-10 are given from Lyly's autograph.)
Littledale, Professor H., of Cardiff, suggestions from, i. 401, ii. 574, iii. 174 l. 29 note.
Lodge, Thos., his imitation of Lyly's style, i. 79, 149, errata ; his *Rosalynde*, *ib.*, suggests to Shakespeare to revive Euphues in Jaques, 167-8 (and perhaps the girls' disguise from *Gallathea* ii. 254), Phœbe's sonnet in, probably suggested by Lyly's 'Hey downe a downe' in *Englands Helicon*, iii. 442.
Lok, Henry, his *Ecclesiastes*, 67 ; a petitioner of Cecil, *ib.*
Loves Metamorphosis, text, iii. 299-332 ; introduction, 289-98 ; notes, 563-9 ; editions, 289-91 ; sources, 291-5, ii. 246, 477, 481-2 ; date, iii. 295-6, ii. 45-6 ; present form probably a revision, iii. 297-8 ; treats Unities as in *Gall.* or *Endim.* 298 ; farcical element absent, perhaps expunged, ii. 249, 258, allegory in, 258-60, iii. 297 ; criticism, ii. 249, 256, 260, 263, 264, 269, 272, 273, 279 (structure), 281, 283, 285 ; marks of style, 289, 291, 293.
Lucan, *Pharsalia* quoted, i. 308 l. 10.
LYLY, JOHN :
HIS LIFE ; born 1553-1554, prob. Oct. 9, 1553—March 24, 1553-4, i. 1-2 ; autobiographical element in *Euphues*, 2-4 ; probably son of William Lyllye, yeoman of Boxley near Maidstone, 4-5, 29 ; no Will of father or son in Somerset House, 5-6 ; enters Magd. Coll. Oxford, spring 1569; reputation there as wit and madcap, 7-8, 15 ; his studies there, 8-12 ; three years' absence from the University, perhaps due to plague, perhaps to some tutorial employment, 10-11 ; his later attack on Oxford, 12, 20, 273-6 (the attack), 324-6 (disclaimer), 359, ii. 344-5 (repetition); takes B.A. and M.A., 6, 12 ; acquaintance with Burleigh, 12-15, 385, 391-3, ii. 198; candidature for Magd. Fellowship, i. 13-5 ; Latin letter to Burleigh on this subject, *ib.*; unpaid battells-bill, 15 ; status in college uncertain, *ib.*: degree at Cambridge, and probable residence there, 16 ; comparison of it with Oxford, ii. 193 ; residence in the Savoy Hospital, 1577, or earlier, i. 17-8 ; acquaintance there with Harvey, *ib.*, probably with Spenser, 18-9, Greville, 75 and Dyer, *ib.*, iii. 443, and possibly Sidney and Leicester, 18, 21-2, 77, iii. 88, 95, 439 ; *Euphues*, Part I, finished summer 1578, i. 19, pub. Dec. 1578, *ib.*; relation with Sir William West, the dedicatee, 4, 11-2, 19-20, 48 ; success of *Euphues*, 20; delay in writing Part II, 21-3 ; probable intervention of *Campaspe*, 23, ii. 311 ; *Euphues*, Part II, pub. spring 1580, i. 24 ; secretary to Earl of Oxford, 24, 28-9, 31, 44 ; begins writing for the stage (*Campaspe, Sapho and Phao*), 24-5, 31 ; letter prefixed to Watson's *Hecatompathia*, 25-7 ; some love-poetry, 26 ; falls under Oxford's displeasure, 27-8 ; autograph letter to Burleigh on the subject, 28-9 ; charge against, of dealing in magic, 29-30 ; prejudices Oxford against Harvey, 30-1 ; vicemaster of the Paul's Boys, 1585, 33-4, 394 ; his duties in this connexion, 34-7 ; perhaps composed music for songs in the plays, 36, ii. 265 ; post in the Revels Office (Clerk-Controller) with Tentes and Toyles, 37-41 ; probably appointed, not 1585, but 1588, 394 (correcting pp. 41, 44, 46) ; duties, status and receipts at the Office, 41-2 ; receipts from other sources, 42-3 ; marriage, 43 ; resident in St. Bartholomew's Hospital, probably from 1588, 44, 66-7, 72 ; possibly acts as deputy to the Press-Censors, 44, 392 ; produces *Gallathea*, *Endimion*, 1585-6?, *Loves Metamorphosis*, 1586-9?, *Midas*, 1589-90?, 44-7 ; bad verses on suppression of Babington's plot, 401-2 ; sits

INDEX 613

in Parliament (1588–9, 1592–3, 1597–8, 1601), 47–9 (and *see* 384); enlisted with Nash to defend the Bishops against Martin Marprelate, 50–1; incident described in Nash's *Returne*, 52 note; Lyly's contribution limited to *Pappe*, and perhaps *Whip for an Ape*, some of *Mar-Martine*, and share in one or both of two Anti-Martinist plays, 52–4, 55–7, 388; perfunctory performance, 56, 59; passages from Nash throwing light on the matter and on Lyly, notes on 52–4, 58–60; small of stature, 60; a smoker, 60–1; attends Andrewes' sermons, *ib*; Jonson's caricature in Fastidious Brisk, 61, 74; probable vanity of dress, 61; produces *Mother Bombie* 1590, 61; Paul's Boys suppressed, 1591, 62; probable tribute by Spenser, 62–3; share in producing royal Entertainments from 1589 onwards, 379–84, 404–9; *Sonet* 1590, 410–2; at Theobalds, *Cowdray*, *Elvetham* 1591, 417–52; *Quarrendon*, *Bisham*, *Sudeley*, *Rycote* 1592, 453–90; *Woman in the Moone* 1593, 63; intended satire on Elizabeth very doubtful, 63, 390, ii. 256–7 note (Mézières); possible share in *Gesta Grayorum* 1594, i. 380, 383; these shows perhaps caused the Queen's displeasure 1594, 383, 390, 66, 71; letter to Cecil, 1594–5, 389–90; his children, 66 note; lines in Lok's *Ecclesiastes*, 67; letter to Cecil, Dec. 22, 1597, 68–9, 394; another, Jan. 23, 1597–8, 391; quarrel among the Revels officials, 69: the First Petition 1598, 64–5, 394 (date corrected); poem on the Bee, iii. 445–7; letter of condolence to Cecil, Sept. 9, 1598, i. 591–3; Lyly's brother, *ib*.; assessments made on, 72; Paul's Boys recommence 1599?, 72; *Loves Met.* revised with additions and excisions, *Maydes Met.* produced, 73; Essex' revolt, 74–5; letter to Cecil, Feb. 27, 1600–1, 393–5; the Second Petition 1601, 70–1, 377, 394 (date corrected); *Harefield Entertainment* 1602, 491–504; letter to Cecil, Feb. 4, 1602–3; referring to a lost Third Petition, 75; *Funeral Oration* on Elizabeth, 509–16; letter to Sir Robert Cotton, Ap. 30, 1605, pointing to a grant of land, 395–8; probable share in King of Denmark's *Welcome* 1606, 381–2, 505–7; *An Old Mans Lesson* 1606, not his, 399; burial, Nov. 30, 1606,

76; character, 3, 7–8, 11 note, 353, 76–80; contemporary repute, 79–80; later neglect and partial recovery, 81–2; no surviving portrait, 23 note; his *Poems*, here first collected, of varying degree of authenticity and merit, iii. 434–9; his distrust of himself herein, 439.
his knowledge of Greek, i. 400, 352, 355 (note on 266, l. 13).
his knowledge of Medicine, i. 157, 208, 212, 213, 241, 251, ii. 55, 65, 94, 125, 126 ll. 6–35, 132, 396, 543, iii. 128 l. 37, 134; Italian physicians, ii. 73, 109; Galen's *Aphorisms*, i. 241, 345.
his knowledge of Music, i. 7 note 4, 8, 15, 34, 36, ii. 3, 328 l. 50, 407 l. 77, 451 l. 18, 472, 508, 551, iii. 37 l. 129.
his knowledge of Painting, i. 23 note 4, 187, ii. 1–7 and notes, 339–40 and *Camp.* passim.
his knowledge of Sport, i. 38, 383, ii. 484, 173–4, 178–9, 440, iii. 146–8.
his imagination works better in general conception than in detail, ii. 247.
his invention, alluded to by himself, i. 71 l. 3, 65, 68–9, 390, ii. 246, 484.
Education, views on, *see* 'Euph. and his Ephœbus,' and notes on, i. 352–3 sqq.; experience in, i. 11, 34.
Theology, youthful essay in, i. 364; allusions to, 8, 10, 252, 286–90; Nash's remark, 52 note.
lost works perhaps by—*Straunge Newes out of Affrick*, i. 22 note; *Lyllies light*, 60 note, 66; two or more Anti-Martinist plays, 53–4 and notes, 388; *Bellum Grammaticale*, a (Latin?) play, 379–80; *Abuses*, a play, 382; *The Hunting of Cupid*, 517.
his Plays, Chronological Table of, ii. 230, Essay on, 231–99. Text of, with Introductions and Notes, vols. ii and iii.
his Protestantism, i. 74 note, 124, iii. 110, 407 l. 16, 428 l. 30.
his reading, desultory but wide, i. 12; classics, 156–8, 400, ii. 112–8, 244–5, 306–9, 420–1, iii. 234–5; English authors, 154, 158–9, see also under 'Sources' in introductions to the several plays; Chaucer, 400–1; Italian authors, 161, 175 note, iii. 479–83, 199 (see also under *Petrarch* and *Ariosto*).
as a Poet, i. 386–7, 408–9, iii. 434–9; some marks, iii. 436–7; qualified

nature of his impulse, 439; anonymity, 434, 439; satirizes irregular metre, 55; verses on Elizabeth's death, i. 389, 514–6; see also under 'Songs.'
LYLY AS A PLAYWRIGHT, ii. 231–99; Chronological Table, 230.
I. *Drama before Lyly*, 231–43. Moralities, 231–2. Mixed kinds before 1580, 232–4. Moralities secularized the drama, 234–6, introducing character, 235, and asserting rights of the imagination, 235–6. But drama in 1580 still undecided in methods, 237, in stage-custom, *ib.*, in vehicle and literary form, 238. Illustrations: Edwardes' *Damon and Pithias*, 238–41, critical Prologue, 239, grasp of connexion, 239–40, metrical irregularity, 241; Whetstone's *Promos and Cassandra* some improvement, 242–3.
II. *Lyly's Dramatic Work*, 243–99. Lasting influence on Shakespeare, 243, i. 152–4.
1. *Invention and handling of materials*, 244–7 (see also under 'Sources' in Introd. to each play): his subjects classical, with recombinations, additions, and suggestions from contemporary work and life, 244–6; artistic sense, 246; monotony due to dialogue, 246; popular elements, 247.
2. *Use and fusion of different species*, 247–62. Artistic sense of form, 248, and of distinction of styles, 248–51; introduces refined ideal Comedy, 248, 251. Classification of the Plays, 249. Treatment of *History* in *Campaspe*, 246, 249, 251–2, 288; *Farce* in *Moth. Bomb.* 252–3, farcical element in all but *Loves Met.* 249—Shakespeare imitates his farcical scenes, and refined comic style, 253; *Masque and Pastoral* in *Sapho, Gallathea, Endimion, Midas, The Woman*, 253–4; his models in this kind, *ib.*, 473–5, 481–4; *Allegory*, 250, pure abstractions in *The Woman*, 255—Lyly infuses concreteness (1) by identifying qualities with the classical deities, 255, (2) by interweaving physics, 255–6, (3) by introducing real personages under a mask, 256–60; the plays intelligible without the allegory, 257–8; *Sapho, Gall., Endim., Loves Met.*; varying degree of fusion of allegory with plot, 259–60; *Satire* in *The Woman*, 256 note, other cases, 261; *Tragic element* inconspicuous, 261–2.

3. *Construction and Technique*, 262–79. Through him the idea of form and art passes from the pseudo-classics to the romantic playwrights, 263, 248, 244. Sparing use of classical devices, 263; uses disguises, 263–4; dreams, ballet (cf. Aureola, i. 449), 264; Songs, 264–5, 293, iii. 434, 437, 439, their omission from the quartos, ii. 265; stage-furniture, 265–6. Treatment of the Unities, 266–70 (cf. 'Time and Place' in Introd. to each play); their Greek derivation, 266, gradual modification, 267; Lyly observes Time in two plays, 267, Place in all save two (in three very closely), 268, and partial continuity of scenes, *ib.*; seven cases of abrupt transfer during a scene, 269; disregards scenic propriety at first, 270; his practice a balance between rule and freedom. Anachronisms, 252, 270–1. In Plot he understands need of action, and of working to an issue, 271–2, exceptions, 272; fixed character-scheme, balanced groups, 273; steady advance in plot-weaving, in fullness and complexity, and in the connexion of the comic matter—in *Endimion* it parodies the main action—the plots discussed, 274–9.
4. *Characterization*, 279–86: description of one character by another, 280; grasp of class-characteristics, 280–1; servants, 281–2; excellence of his women on lighter side, 282–3; single figures not so good, 284; but attempt to individualize members of a group is clear, 284–5.
5. *Dialogue, diction, and poetry*, 286–96. Effect of care for style on matter not always the same, 286. Lyly makes prose the vehicle for Comedy, 286–7; perceives need of heightening with wit and point—his work in Comedy parallels Marlowe's in tragedy, 287: distinguishes dramatic dialogue from ordinary prose, 287–8; appropriateness of his dialogue, 246–7, 250–1, 280–1, 288–9, 291; diminishing Euphuism, 289–90; retains Latin quotations and gnomic utterances, 290; seldom coarse, 291; long speeches and soliloquies continue, *ib.*; poetic tincture of his prose, instances, 292–3; the best songs, 293–4; blank verse of *The Woman*, 294–5, iii. 233–4; transition to prose for comic matter, ii. 296.
6. *Shakespeare's debt to Lyly's plays*, 296–9; detailed reminiscences, *ib.*

INDEX 615

his dramatic influence on successors, ii. 243, 252, 254, 261, 263, 276, 279, 280, 282, 295, 296–9.
gave form, and refinement, to the stage, 248, 250–1, 255, 263, 279, 286–7, 291. See also under ' Imitations ' or ' Stage-History ' in introductions to the several plays.
his plays written for children, effect on his art and on the drama, i. 36–7.
Lyly, Lylie, Lillie, Lilly, Lilley, Lyllye, &c.,
relatives of author—William Lylly the elder, of Maidstone (his great grandfather?), 1500, i. 385 note.
John Lylly of Maidstone, 1507, i. 385 note.
William Lyllye of Boxley or Maidstone, 1571-2 (his father?), i. 5–6, 385–6, 399.
Mr. Lyllye, chaplain of the Savoy, 1598 (his brother), i. 392–3.
Elizabeth Lilley, married Ed. Shakerly, (his sister?), i. 5.
the author's children, i. 66 note.
? Mary Lillie of Bromley 1604, i. 6 note (Appeal, Som¹. Ho.).
? Geoffrey Lyllie, draper of London, cousin of the preceding, i. 6 note (Will, Som¹ Ho.).
? Edward Lyllie, husbandman of Gilden Morden, Camb., with brothers John, Richard, Henry, Thomas, and a mother living in 1599, i. 6 note (Will, Som¹. Ho.).
others—' Thomas Lillye, gent,' has son buried at St. Bart. the Less, 1607, i. 66 note.
John Lyllie, yeoman of Bramford, Suffolk, 1590, i. 6 note.
Richard Lylly, yeoman of Gloucestershire, 1583-99, his Will, Som¹. Ho., i. 48.
Emmanuel Lillye, died in the Counter, prob. son of the preceding, i. 66 note (Will, Som¹. Ho.).
William Lilly, the grammarian, i. 6; jokes on his grammar, ii. 261.
George Lyllye, prebendary of Canterbury, son of preceding, i. 6 (Will, S. H.).
Edmund Lilly, Dr., Fellow of Magd. Coll., Oxford, and Vice-Chancellor, i. 6, 15, 48, 393.
Peter Lyllie, delegate of Press-Censors, 1597, &c., i. 44 note, 392.
William Lilly, the astrologer, not born before 1602, i. 60 note.
John Lilly, assists a Jesuit to escape, 1599, i. 74.

Mr. Lilly, atheist, opponent of Joseph Hall, 1601, i. 400.
Lyrics, unsigned Elizabethan, remarks on, iii. 434–6.

Magdalen College, Oxford, William Lylly, grammarian, at, i. 6; George Lyllye, preb. of Canterbury, at, i. 6; William Camden, chorister at, i. 9; Edmund Lilly, Fellow of, i. 6, 15; Dr. Humphrey, President of, i. 15; John Lyly, at, 1569, i. 6–16; the College grammar-school, i. 9, 10; migration to Brackley, 1571 or earlier, i. 11; Lyly seeks a Fellowship at, i. 12–15; the Rev. H. A. Wilson, present librarian of, information supplied by, i. 11, 15; communarii, semi-communarii, socii, &c., in, i. 15.
Magic, Lyly accused of, i. 29; his ridicule of in *Euph.* ii. 114–8, 480; introduced in *Endim.* ii. 247.
Malone, Edmund, favourable notice of Lyly in his *Shakespeare*, 1790, i. 81; list of editions of *Euphues*, 84; regards Lyly as subject of Spenser's lines in *Teares of the Muses*, 62–3; quotation from *Jack Drum's Ent.*, 73.
Marlowe, Christopher, his *Tamburlaine* establishes blank verse, i. 63; his repute and Lyly's, 78, 79, and note 4; his influence on Shakespeare less than Lyly's, ii. 243; glanced at in Pistol, i. 151; his effect on Tragedy (vehicle, and manner), paralleled by Lyly's on Comedy, ii. 287; his blank verse and Lyly's, 294, iii. 233–4; his comic transition to prose, 296; imitated by Lyly?, iii. 442, 562.
Mar-Martine, portions of, iii. 423–6; notes, 591; authorship, i. 387–8.
Marriage, discussion of, i. 228-30, 283 ll. 5–11, ii. 58–63, 158–9; from Plut. *Coniug. Præcepta* and Tylney's *Flower of Friendship*, ii. 223–7; Diana's sermon reflects Elizabeth's jealousy of, ii. 570–1; the Queen's changing attitude towards, i. 45.
Martin Marprelate Controversy, i. 49–60; Prof. Arber's *Introductory Sketch*, 49–51 notes, &c.; the Martinist writers, 49–50; the Bishops enlist secular pens in their defence, 50–1; methods adopted by Lyly and Nash, 51–2; Anti-Martinist plays, 52–4 and notes, ii. 257–8, action of the authorities against, i. 53; pamphlets and lampoons on either side, 49–52, 54–9, 387–8; *Pappe with an Hatchet*, 55–7, text of, iii. 393–413, introduction to,

388-92, notes, 573-89; *Almond for a Parrat* not Lyly's, i. 56 note; the Harveys' share in, 57, resultant paper-war between Greene, Harvey, and Nash, 58-60; *Whip for an Ape* possibly Lyly's, i. 52, 57, iii. 415-6, text of, iii. 417-22; *Mar-Martine* perhaps partly Lyly's, i. 387-8, text, iii. 423-6.

Mary, Queen of Scots, the original of Tellus, iii. 89-91; plan for her marriage with Leicester, 90, 102; her captivity under Shrewsbury, 93-4, under Paulet, 92; procures marriage of Lord Chas. Stuart with Eliz. Cavendish, 94, 98, 100; 'Romish Iesabell,' 429.

Maydes Metamorphosis, The, text of, iii. 341-87; introduction, 333-9; notes, 569-73; editions, 333; argument, 335; date, 336; arguments for and against Lyly's authorship, 335-7, probably retouched by Lyly, 337, i. 73.

Metre, progress followed by in early drama, ii. 238; of Edwardes, 240-1; of Whetstone, 242; vehicles regularized by Lyly and Marlowe, 286-8; lyrical element admitted, 294-5; blank verse of Lyly and Marlowe *ib.*, iii. 233-4.

Mézières, his *Prédécesseurs et Contemporains de Shakespeare*, i. 119, 135; on the influence of euphuism upon Shakespeare, 152-3 note; his suggestion of a satire on Elizabeth in Pandora, ii. 256-7 note, i. 63-4.

Midas, text, iii. 113-62; introduction, 106-12; notes, 519-37; editions, 106-8; source, 108-9, ii. 245; allegory in, iii. 109-10, i. 47, ii. 257, criticized, 260; date, iii. 110-11; imitations, 112; criticism, ii. 248-9, 250, 254, 257, 263, 264, 268-9, 270, 271, 272, 273, 276-7 (structure), 283, 284; marks of style, 289; poetic phraseology, 293.

Mizauld, Antoine, French physicist, ii. 537.

Money, purchasing power of in Lyly's time, i. 5, 42, 533.

Montacute, Lord, i. 521.

Moral-Plays, Moralities, stages in, ii. 231-3; their function in the drama's development, 234-6; their use of allegorical abstractions, 232, 250, 253, 255, 258, iii. 82.

Morley, Prof. H., his opinion of *Euphues*, i. 78; rejects political allegory in *Endimion*, iii. 83; his copy of *Euphues*, i. 83, 85, 87-93, 95-8, 108-9, 115; *Quarterly* essay on Euphuism, 119; *English Writers ib.* (quoted passim).

Mother Bombie, text, iii. 171-228; introduction, 164-9; notes, 537-54; editions, 164, 166; no special source, 167, ii. 245, 478; date, iii. 167-8; time occupied, 168; scene unchanged, 169; criticism, ii. 246, 250, 252-3, 264, 268-9, 271, 273, 277 (structure), 284; Nash's allusion, i. 61 note.

Mountebanks, Antimasque of, ii. 572.

MSS. examined for Lyly's Poems, iii. 438, 444-5.

Munday's *Banquet*, 'doubtful' poems from, iii. 439-40.

Musa, Antonius, Augustus' physician, ii. 543.

Nash, Thomas, allusions to Lyly in *Haue with you*, i. 8, 59-61; his *Anatomie of Absurditie*, 51; epistle to Greene's *Menaphon*, 51, 80 note, 133 note, 146-7, reflections aimed at Lyly's style in, 146-7; style of his earlier prose, 56 note, 146, 147; *Martin's Months Minde*, 51-5 and notes; *An Almond for a Parrat*, 51, 56 note, iii. 111; *Returne of Pasquill*, anecdote of Lyly in, i. 52 note, description of Anti-Martinist plays in, 53-4 notes, date, 55; *Pierce Penilesse* 1592, 59; *Strange Newes* 1593, 59, quotations from, 59-60 notes; *Jacke Wilton*, dedication of, 56 note, picture of the Court-page in, ii. 282; his opinion of *Euphues*, i. 60 note 2, 80, 146-7; relations with Greene, 54 note 2, 58-9, 60 note 2; alluded to (by Harvey?) in *Marre Mar-Martin*, 387-8; question of his authorship of the *Whip*, iii. 415-6; possibly wrote some of *Mar-Martine*, 416.

Navarre, Queen Margaret of, ii. 535.

Norris, Lord, his wife and sons, i. 532.

North, Sir Thomas, his *Diall of Princes* 1557, i. 20, Lyly's model for treatment and subject matter, 136-8, 154-6; quotations from, 343, 347, ii. 531; his transl. of Plutarch used for *Campaspe*, ii. 307-9, 252.

Novel, *Euphues*, the first English, i. 20, 159-61; Part II deserves that title best, *ib.*, ii. 486; immature methods of, i. 141-2, 162-3, ii. 502.

Olde Mans Lesson, &c., An, Lyly's authorship suggested and disallowed, i. 399-400.

Ovid, Lyly's chief source for mythology, i. 157, ii. 244-6, *Sapho*, ii. 364, *Gall.*

INDEX 617

420, *End.* iii. 9, *Mid.* 109, *Loves Met.* 291-2.
Oxford in 16th century, curriculum indeterminate, i. 8-9, details supplied by Mr. Andrew Clarke, i. 9 note; degrees at, i. 9-10; 'dispensations,' i. 8, 10, 11; 'graces,' i. 3; students often engaged in teaching, i. 11; visitations of the Plague, i. 8, 10, 11; Lyly's attack on the morals and discipline of in 'Euphues and his Ephœbus' under name of Athens, i. 273-6; comments on this attack, i. 12, 359; Lyly's disclaimer in address to the Gentlemen Scholers, i. 324-6; attack repeated in *Campaspe*, ii. 344-5, 550; compared with Cambridge in the 'Glasse,' 193; the Queen's visits to, 213, 534, i. 379-80, 531; Carfax, ii. 494.
Oxford, Edward de Vere, Earl of, rents tenements in the Savoy, i. 17; dedicatee of *Euphues* Part II, 24; Lyly's master, *ib.*, 28-9, 31, 44; his lost comedies, 24; his company of 'boyes,' *ib.*, 32; dedicatee of Watson's *Hecatompathia*, 25; his suspicious and quarrelsome temper, 27; his displeasure with Lyly, 28; possibly originating in Lyly's tale-bearing in 1580, 30-1.

Pappe with an Hatchet, text, iii. 393-413; editions, 388-90; introduction, 389-92; notes, 573-89; place in the controversy, i.55-7; Harvey's reply, *ib.*
Parliaments in which Lyly sat, i. 47-9 and note, 384.
Pasquin et Marforio, i. 55.
Pastoral, Dramatic, in England, i. 406-8, 383, ii. 253-4; pastoral in *Gall.*, *Loves Met.*, *Midas*, precedes Lyly's *Entertainments*, ii. 250, 474; Mr. Thorndike's remarks on, i. 407-8, ii. 474; comic rusticity in, *ib.*; Lyly's examples more English than Italian, 474, 477-9; owes something to Sannazarro and Tasso, 479-84; see also ii. 248, 256, 266, 277-8, 285; *Endim.* hardly a pastoral, i. 40; Lyly eliminates pessimism. ii. 484 (but contrast *Cowdray*, i. 426); idyllic grace in *Gall.* and *The Woman*, ii. 254, 294-5, 297-8.
Pausanias, i. 35; alluded to, ii. 97 l. 3 (note), iii. 429 l. 42 (note)
Peele, George, i. 26; *Old Wives Tale*, ii. 253, oracular fountain in borrowed from *Endimion*, 254, 292; *Arraignment of Paris*, poetry in, 294; Hermit's speech at Theobalds 1591, i.

385, 519; not the author of the Tiltyard 'Sonet,' 517, nor of Gardener's or Molecatcher's Speeches, 519-20.
Penry, John, the Martinist, i. 16 note, 49-50, 55, 60.
Petitions to the Queen, Lyly's, (1) 1598, text, ii. 64-5, date, 392, 394 (correcting Life, 33, 64), unfavourable reception of recorded in *Bee* poem, i. 386, 392, iii. 446; (2) 1601, text, i. 70-1, 378, date, 394, allusion to Tentes and Toyles, 40, 71, 383, 390; (3) (lost) 1602-3, i. 75, 389, 397; copies of (1) and (2) i. 64, 75, 377.
Petrarch, influence at Florence and on Elizabethan poetry, i. 135, iii. 436; studied by Camilla, ii. 129, cf. 199; recalled, i. 512, ii. 88, cf. note; Petrarcan love-conceits in scenes with Cupid of *Gall.* and *Loves Met.*, 292.
Pettie, George, his *Pallace of Pleasure* 1576, i. 20, Lyly's model for style, 136; his language sometimes borrowed by Lyly, 138 note; examples from Pettie of all the marks of style discussed under Euphuism, 139-42; bad use of metrical rhythm, 143; preface to, 160.
Phœnix Nest, The, dialogue from *Quarrendon*, i. 458-63; Mr. Bullen on, iii. 436; 'doubtful' poems from, 440-1.
Place and Time, see 'Unities, the.'
Pliny, Lyly's large use of, i. 156, 146, 23, ii. 306; quoted in Notes passim.
Plutarch, Lyly's large drafts on, i. 156, 146, ii. 307-8; quoted in Notes passim; chief works laid under contribution, i. 156.
Poems, Doubtful, by Lyly, iii. 448-502, i. 386-7; whence taken, iii. 443; introduction to, 434-47; verses on Babington's plot, 427-32, i. 401-2; Anti-Martinist verse, iii. 415-26, i. 387-8; on death of Elizabeth, i. 514-6, 389; in the *Entertainments*, 408-9: see also under 'Songs.'
Poetical Rapsody, Davison's, i. 519, 534-5, iii. 435; poem from, 442-3.
Popular types and elements in the plays, ii. 247.
Powle, Sir Stephen, his dated copy of Lyly's second Petition, i. 377-8, 394.
Progresses of Elizabeth, 1591, 1592, 1602, i. 519, 521, 523, 526, 529, 535-6.
Prologues and Epilogues, ii. 263 note 2; in *Campaspe*, 304; acknowledgement of allegorical intention, ii. 258, iii. 85 (*Endim.*).
Proverbs, a feature of Euphuism, i. 134,

141, 401, ii. 290, of Elizabethan verse, iii. 436.
Pymms, Burleigh's house, i. 520.

Quarrendon, Speeches at, i. 453–70, 405, 526–9.

Register of Oxford University, entries about Lyly, i. 1, 6 notes, about Harvey, 7 note; edited by Mr. Andrew Clark, 9; details of University work bearing on the period of Lyly's residence, 9 note; entries of Cambridge M.A.'s incorporated M.A.'s of Oxford, 16 note.
Registers of some London churches, i. 44 note; of St. Bartholomew the Less, 43–4, 66 note, 67, 76, 386.
Revels Accounts, cited i. 24, 34 note, 38 note, 41, 42, 335, 407, ii. 266, 310, 425–6, 500, 502, 542, 552; gap in (Nov. 1585—Nov. 1587), iii. 11 note, 12; Paul's and Chapel Children not mentioned at Christmas 1583–4, i. 32; Lyly's name not found in, i. 41, 398.
Revels, Office of the, Lyly not a candidate for the Mastership in 1579, i. 21–2; no veto of on *Sapho*, 31; Lyly's appointment in, 37–41, 394; advised to aim at the Mastership of, 65, 33; the reversion promised to Buck 1597, granted 1603, 68, 391; properties moved from Warwick Inn to Blackfriars, 38, 25 note; office moved to the Priory of St. John of Jerusalem in Clerkenwell before 1571, 34, 38; gift of the Priory to Lord d'Aubigny 1610, 38; amalgamation of properties with those of Tentes and Toyles already at St. John's, 38–9; connexion of with Tentes and Toyles, 37, illustrated from a MS. of 1573, 39–41; duties and receipts of the officers, 41–2, 70; lending out of the costumes, 41 note 2, 71; properties employed at Harefield 1602, 381, 383; Queen's complaint, 66, 71, 383, 390; appeal of workmen for pay in arrear, 69; Masters of, Sir Th. Cawarden, 38, 40, Sir Th. Benger, 39, Edmund Tylney, 21, 69, Sir Geo. Buck, 68; other officers, Phelipps, Blagrave, Kirkham, Buggyn, Honings, Pagenham, 38, 40–1; informal connexion between, and the choirs, 35, 34; two annual periods of active service in, 42; rehearsals at, 34; John Dauncey, porter of, 38; *Gall.* and *Loves Met.* possibly censured by Master, ii. 426–7, iii. 297.

Robinson, Clement, his *Handefull*, &c., 'doubtful' poems from, iii. 440.
Russell, Lady, of Bisham, and her daughters, i. 381, 529–30.
Rycote, Speeches at, i. 485–90, 532.

Sannazarro, his *Arcadia*, ii. 474; suggestions for *Euphues* and plays, ii. 479–81; his *Eclogæ Piscatoriæ*, and *Loves Met.*, ii. 481.
Sapho and Phao, text, ii. 369–416; introduction, 362–8; notes, 554–64; editions, 362–4; sources, 364–6, 244, 254, 482–3; allegory, 366–7, 244, 258–60; delay in printing, i. 31–2, ii. 368; date, 367–8, i. 25; criticism of, ii. 246, 248, 254, 261, 263, 264, 270, 271, 273, 280, 282, 288, 291–2; continuity of scene or Act, 268; structure, 272, 274–5; portraiture of women, 282–3; marks of style, 289.
Savoy Hospital, the history of, i. 17–8; masters of, *ib.*; chaplains of, 392; Lyly's brother a chaplain of, *ib.*; Lyly resident there 1577 or before to 1585 or 1588, 18, 44; makes Harvey's acquaintance there, 18; other residents, 17 note 3; gambling in, 18; Loftie's *Memorials of*, 17–8.
'Scarborows warning,' i. 527.
Scene, abrupt transfer of, ii. 269–70, 242, 548; continuity of, ii. 268; how far the Unity of Place observed, *ib.*
Schücking, Herr L. L., work on connexion of English with Italian stage, ii. 475–9.
Scot, Reginald, his *Discouerie of Witchcraft* used for *Gallathea*, i. 32, 401, ii. 423–4.
Sententiæ Pueriles, see 'Cato, Dionysius.'
Sentence-Structure in *Euphues*, Note on, i. 539–41.
Shakespeare, William, obscure in 1591, i. 62; remark about child-actors, 36; his early clowns, adumbrated in Manes (*Camp.*), ii. 547, perhaps influenced Lyly in Gunophilus, 63, iii. 233; *Mids. Night's Dream*, &c. influenced by *The Woman*, iii. 232–3, or by *Endimion*, ii. 297–8; his rise unfortunate for Lyly, i. 78; the cause of revived study of Lyly, 81; parody of euphuism 1 *Hen. IV*, 133, 150 notes; his prose influenced by Lyly's euphuism, 150, 152–4, list of passages, 153 note; *Loves Lab. Lost* ridicules courtiers and empty talk rather than euphuism, 151, ii. 262; other instances of his ridicule, i. 151–2; his debt,

INDEX 619

in direct reminiscence, to *Euphues* in *Hamlet*, 164-5, *Rom. and Jul.* 165-7, in Jaques, 167-8, in many other plays, 168-9, comparative table of passages, 169-75; Lyly his chief dramatic model, ii. 243; variety in repetition, 246, 285-6; Hymen in *As You Like It*, the scroll in *Cymbeline*, 250; draws on Plutarch, after Lyly, 252; 2 *Hen. VI* and *Camp.*, 252; imitates Lyly's farcical scenes, and refined comic style, 253; fairies of *M. N. D.* and *Merry Wives*, cf. *Endim.* iii. 59-60, and Aureola i. 449; superior truth and humanity over Lyly's, ii. 262, 296; *L. L. L.* structural likeness to Lyly, 262, scene of love confessions, 297, other points, 276, iii. 13; advancing skill in connecting comic matter with main action, 270; parody of main action, suggested by *Endimion*, 276; learnt dramatic architecture from Lyly, 279; extends Lyly's trick of describing one character by mouth of another, 280; debt to Lyly's women, 282; succeeds to improvements in form made by Lyly and Marlowe, 287, and to Lyly's dialogue, 287-8, long speeches, 291, and fusion of lyric feeling with dramatic work, 294-5; summary of his debt to Lyly's plays, 296; disguised girls in, 297; detailed reminiscences of Lyly's plays, 296-9, and Notes passim; rustic comedy in *L. L. L.* and *As You Like It* probably suggested by Lyly's *Entertainments*, 474-5; perhaps at Cotton's house, i. 396; *Othello* first produced Harefield, Aug. 1602, 381.

Ship-building, alluded to in *Gallathea*, ii. 425, 438 l. 71, i. 32.

Shrewsbury, Earl and Countess of, originals of Geron and Dipsas, iii. 97-8; custody of Mary, 93-4; protest of the Earl before Privy Council, 97.

Sidney, Sir Philip, Thomas Cooper his tutor c. 1567, i. 10 note; probably known to Lyly, 18; Leicester's nephew, goes with him to Netherlands end of 1585, 46; death, *ib.*; original of Lyly's Eumenides, 467, ii. 259, iii. 9, 95; shares Leicester's opposition to the French match, iii. 95; his flame for Penelope Devereux, represented in Eumenides and Semele, iii. 96; *Astrophel and Stella*, iii. 96, i. 80 (allusion to Lyly's style); Drayton's allusion to, i. 80, 133; Harvey's, *il.*; his *Apologie for Poetrie*, its reflections on euphuism, 132-3, not the first dramatic criticism, ii. 239, its distinction between farce and comedy, ii. 251, upholds Unities, 267; his *Arcadia*, its carelessness of construction, i. 146-47, its stilted metaphor, 149-50; Arcadianism supersedes Euphuism, *ib.*

Silixsedra, Mount, ii. 540, i. 167-8.

Similes from Natural History, from Pliny, i. 131-2, &c., from Bartholomaeus Anglicus, i. 132, 332-3, &c., from Aelian, 158, ii. 513, from Bestiaries (?), 336, ii. 514; the toad, i. 335; from Pettie, 332, 334, 336; ridicule of them, 132-4, 150-1 note, 386 note; probably borrowed by Shakespeare, 169 and note.

Sinker, Dr. Robert, first identifies ed. princ. of *Euphues*, i. 85.

Social customs as shown in *Euphues*, i. 135, 162, 198 ll. 9-11, 199 ll. 13-21, 33-4 (cf. 213 l. 19), 200 ll. 14-24, 203 ll. 28-9, 215 ll. 14-6, 217 ll. 30-3; ii. 9 ll. 1-2, 35 ll. 18-20, 54 ll. 22-31, 55 ll. 12-4, 58 ll. 11-2 (cf. 70 l. 11), 69 ll. 24-6, 77 ll. 34-7, 78 ll. 24, 30 (proxy wooing), 84 ll. 15-20, 103 ll. 19-20, 33-6 (cf. 104 l. 8, 105 l. 25), 133 ll. 31-3, •136-7 ll. 4-6, 27, 3-4, 17, 161 ll. 16-7, 162 ll. 26-9, 33 sqq. (522 notes), 186 ll. 1 sqq., 194-5, 198-9, 201 l. 27; 218 ll. 25-35, 220 l. 35, 226 ll. 21-6.

Songs, 21 out of 32 preserved by Blount, ii. 264; why not in quartos, ii. 265, i. 36, Add.; compared, 293-4; the missing nine, 265, suggestions for, iii. 440; unequal merit, i. 387; Lyly's title to corroborated by *Entertainments* and *Poems*, i. 386-7, iii. 434, 439.

Spenser, Edmund, probably knew Lyly in 1578-9, i. 18-9, iii. 439; tribute to Lyly in *Teares of the Muses*, 62-3; Lyly alludes to his death, i. 516, 539; the example of his allegory in *The Shepheardes Kalender*, ii. 256; his *Faerie Queene* influences *Loves Met.* i. 74; iii. 293; *Three Letters* 1580 between him and Harvey, 30; Harvey's parade of friendship with, 63.

Stage-furniture, ii. 265-6, 270, iii. 14, 519, 559, 562, 567; Diogenes' tub, ii. 547.

Steinhäuser, his essay *John Lyly als Dramatiker*, ii. 244; on Lyly's use of Allegory, 255-6, 258 note; his objection to plots of *Camp.*, *Sapho*, and *Gall.*, 272; Sir Tophas as parody of main action in *Endimion*, 276; Venus protagonist of *Sapho*, 272, Tellus of *Endimion*, iii. 89.

Stow, John, i. 396 note; his *Survey*, i. 17, 38, 67 note.

Sudeley, Speeches at, i. 477–84, 405, 409, 530–1.
Symonds, J. A., his *Shakspere's Predecessors* recognizes Lyly's importance, i. 119, ii. 243, 485.

Tasso's *Aminta*, suggestions for *Sapho* and *Gallathea*, ii. 482–4.
Tentes and Toyles, Office of, i. 38–40; Lyly Clerk-Controller of, with Revels, 40, 70, 378, 383.
Text, treatment of, in *Euphues*, i. 98–9, 178, ii. 2; in the Plays, ii. 301, 305; iii. 4; see also list of 'Editions' and 'Text and Bibliography' in introductions to the several plays.
Theobalds, Speeches at, i. 417–9; song at, 505–6, 385, 537.
Thorndike, Mr. A. H., Essay on Pastoral in *Mod. Lang. Notes* Ap. 1899, i. 379, ii. 473–4.
Tilt-yard, the, Whitehall, celebration of anniversary of the Accession, i. 410–1; speeches at, text of, 411–6; notes on, 517–9.
Time and Place, see 'Unities, the.'
Toad, jewel in head, i. 335.
Travel, ii. 25–8, 30, 31, i. 164–5, 167; Lyly probably no traveller, ii. 34 ll. 21–33, 479 ll. 21–2, i. 399 (note i).
Triumphs of Trophes, The, verses by Lyly on suppression of Babington's conspiracy, i. 401–2, text of, iii. 427–32.
Tylney, Edmund, appointed Master of the Revels July 24, 1579, i. 21; censorship of plays vested in, 25, 42, 53; 34 note; 40 note; signs the Accounts, 41; pay double that of the other officers, 42; difference with them, 69; profits by new arrangement, 70; his *Flower of Friendship* 1568, used by Lyly, 158, 248 l. 13 note, ii. 522, 525, 537–40.

Unities, the, their origin, ii. 266, decadence, 267; Lyly's inconsistencies herein, 267–8; more careful of Place than of Time, 268; most careful in his two last plays, 267–8, iii. 298; most irregular in *Endim.*, iii. 15; Baker's remark on Scene in *Endim.*, iii. 14; abrupt transfer—seven or eight instances, ii. 269, one in Whetstone, 242, several in Greene, 269; Lyly's advance in propriety, 269–70. See also under 'Time and Place' in the introductions to the several plays.

Viper, ii. 177, 488, 500, 517, 518, iii. 130 l. 38.
Virgil, alluded to by Lyly, i. 158, 232 l. 13, ii. 79 l. 23, 86 l. 35, 113 l. 22, 130 l. 15, 152 l. 22, 565, &c.; Hense's remark, i. 148 note 2; Cyclops in *Sapho* from, ii. 365, 554; Eurota in *Gall.* ii. 421; pastoral names, ii. 481.

Warner, William, his *Albion*, i. 390 note.
Watson, Thos., his friendship with Lyly, i. 25; Wood's account of, *ib.*; Lyly's letter to 1582, 26–7, 387; probable collaboration in *Elvetham Ent.*, 386, 522–4; burial at St. Bartholomew the Less 1592, 386.
West, Sir Thos., M.P. with Lyly for Aylesbury, 48.
West, Sir William, Lord de la Warre, i. 19–20 note 7, 4, 11–2, genealogy, 48.
Whip for an Ape, A, text, iii. 417–22; editions, 415; date and authorship, 415–6; notes, 589–91.
Woman in the Moone, The, text, iii. 239–88; introduction, 229–38; notes, 554–63; editions, 229, 231; sources, 234–6, ii. 245, 484; date, iii. 231–3; Unities strictly observed, 237–8; verse of, 233–4, ii. 294–5; criticism, ii. 246, 247, 249, 250, 254, 256, 263, 264, 268–9, 271, 272, 273, 277–8 (structure); suggested satire on the Queen, i. 63–4, ii. 256 note, iii. 236; delay in printing, i. 63–4, 390 note; stage-directions in, iii. 236; imitated in Basse's *Vrania*, 237.
Women, their importance in Lyly's view, i. 160–1; his admirable representation of their lighter side, ii. 282–3; Euphues' misogynist tirades, i. 142, 202, 241, 249, 253–6; amends to, 257–9, especially to English; ii. 86, 91, 100, 198–202; satire on in Pandora, ii. 63–4 note, i. 63–4.
Wood, Anth., account of Lyly, i. 7; mention of Plague at Oxford, 8, 10; of William Camden, 9; account of Watson, 25 note.
Wyatt family, at Allington and Boxley, i. 384–5; rebellion 1554, *ib.*, 5.

THE END.

WITHDRAWN from the Alma College Library